HANDBOOK OF CULTURAL HEALTH PSYCHOLOGY

HANDBOOK OF CULTURAL HEALTH PSYCHOLOGY

Edited by

SHAHÉ S. KAZARIAN
Departments of Psychology and Psychiatry
The University of Western Ontario
London, Ontario, Canada

DAVID R. EVANS
Department of Psychology
The University of Western Ontario
London, Ontario, Canada

ACADEMIC PRESS

A Harcourt Science and Technology Company

San Diego   San Francisco   New York   Boston   London   Sydney   Tokyo

Academic Press
A Harcourt Science and Technology Company
525 B Street, Suite 1900, San Diego, California 92101-4495, USA
http://www.academicpress.com

Academic Press
Harcourt Place, 32 Jamestown Road, London NW1 7BY, UK
http://www.academicpress.com

Library of Congress Catalog Card Number: 2001086987

International Standard Book Number: 0-12-402771-7

PRINTED IN THE UNITED STATES OF AMERICA
01 02 03 04 05 06 SB 9 8 7 6 5 4 3 2 1

To our fathers, Sarkis Kazarian and
Stanley R. Evans, who were professionals and who,
like us, experienced the health systems of diverse cultures.

CONTENTS

PART I

HEALTH PSYCHOLOGY FROM A CULTURAL PERSPECTIVE: THEORETICAL CONSIDERATIONS

1

HEALTH PSYCHOLOGY AND CULTURE: EMBRACING THE 21ST CENTURY

SHAHÉ S. KAZARIAN AND DAVID R. EVANS

2

HEALTH CARE PRACTICE IN A MULTICULTURAL CONTEXT: WESTERN AND NON-WESTERN ASSUMPTIONS

MESFIN SAMUEL MULATU AND JOHN W. BERRY

3

CROSS-CULTURAL DIFFERENCES IN ILLNESS MODELS AND EXPECTATIONS FOR THE HEALTH CARE PROVIDER–CLIENT/PATIENT INTERACTION

TAMARA L. ARMSTRONG AND LEORA C. SWARTZMAN

4

HEALTH PROMOTION, DISEASE PREVENTION, AND QUALITY OF LIFE

DAVID R. EVANS AND SHAHÉ S. KAZARIAN

5

ADHERENCE TO HEALTH CARE

HEATHER M. SHEARER AND DAVID R. EVANS

PART II

HEALTH PSYCHOLOGY AND CULTURE: SPECIFIC HEALTH CONCERNS

6

FROM THE HEARTLAND: CULTURE, PSYCHOLOGICAL FACTORS, AND CORONARY HEART DISEASE

BRIAN BAKER, ALAN RICHTER, AND SONIA S. ANAND

7

CULTURAL ASPECTS OF CANCER PREVENTION AND CONTROL

CAROLYN COOK GOTAY, MILES MURAOKA, AND JOAN HOLUP

8

CULTURALLY TAILORING HIV/AIDS PREVENTION PROGRAMS: WHY, WHEN, AND HOW

ANITA RAJ, HORTENSIA AMARO, AND ELIZABETH REED

9

PAIN FROM THE PERSPECTIVES OF HEALTH PSYCHOLOGY AND CULTURE

CHRISTINE T. KOROL AND KENNETH D. CRAIG

10

CULTURAL ISSUES IN SUICIDAL BEHAVIOR

SHAHÉ S. KAZARIAN AND EMMANUEL PERSAD

PART III

HEALTH PSYCHOLOGY: ISSUES WITH SPECIFIC CULTURAL GROUPS

11

CULTURE AND LATINO ISSUES IN HEALTH PSYCHOLOGY

HECTOR BETANCOURT AND JOSÉ L. FUENTES

12

HEALTH ISSUES IN NORTH AMERICAN
PEOPLE OF AFRICAN HERITAGE

SHAHÉ S. KAZARIAN

13

HEALTH PSYCHOLOGY AND THE NATIVE
NORTH AMERICAN CLIENT

GEORGE S. RENFREY AND RENDA R. DIONNE

14

HEALTH BELIEFS AND EXPERIENCES
IN ASIAN CULTURES

XINYIN CHEN AND LEORA C. SWARTZMAN

15

HEALTH PSYCHOLOGY: SOUTH ASIAN PERSPECTIVES

PRAFUL CHANDARANA AND JOSEPH R. PELLIZZARI

16

WOMEN'S HEALTH: A CULTURAL PERSPECTIVE

EMILY A. WISE, STACY KOSER CARMICHAEL, CYNTHIA D. BELAR, CAREN B. JORDAN, AND NICOLE E. BERLANT

CONTRIBUTORS

Numbers in parentheses indicate the pages on which the authors' contributions begin.

Hortensia Amaro (195) School of Public Health, Boston University, Boston, Massachusetts 02118

Sonia S. Anand (141) Divisions of Cardiology and General Medicine, McMaster University, Hamilton, Ontario L8L 2X2, Canada

Tamara Armstrong (63) Department of Psychology, The University of Western Ontario, London, Ontario N6A 5C2, Canada

Brian Baker (141) Department of Psychiatry, University Health Network, and University of Toronto, Toronto, Ontario M5T 2S8, Canada

Cynthia D. Belar (445) University of Florida Health Science Center, Gainesville, Florida 32610

Nicole E. Berlant (445) University of Florida Health Science Center, Gainesville, Florida 32610

John W. Berry (45) Department of Psychology, Queen's University, Kingston, Ontario K7L 3N6, Canada

Hector Betancourt (305) Department of Psychology, Loma Linda University, Loma Linda, California 92350

Stacy Koser Carmichael (445) University of Florida Health Science Center, Gainesville, Florida 32610

Praful Chandarana (411) Department of Psychiatry, The University of Western Ontario, London, Ontario N6A 5C2, Canada

Xinyin Chen (389) Department of Psychology, The University of Western Ontario, London, Ontario N6A 5C2, Canada

Kenneth D. Craig (241) Department of Psychology, University of British Columbia, Vancouver, British Columbia V6T 1Z2, Canada

Renda R. Dionne (343) Indian Child and Family Services, Temecula, California 92590

David R. Evans (3, 85, 113) Department of Psychology, The University of Western Ontario, London, Ontario N6A 5C2, Canada

José L. Fuentes (305) Department of Psychology, Loma Linda University, Loma Linda, California 92350

Carolyn Cook Gotay (163) Cancer Research Center of Hawaii, University of Hawaii, Honolulu, Hawaii 96813

Joan Holup (163) Cancer Research Center of Hawaii, University of Hawaii, Honolulu, Hawaii 96813

Caren B. Jordan (445) University of Florida Health Science Center, Gainesville, Florida 32610

Shahé S. Kazarian (3, 85, 267, 323) Departments of Psychology and Psychiatry, The University of Western Ontario, London, Ontario N6A 5C2, Canada

Christine T. Korol (241) Department of Psychology, University of British Columbia, Vancouver, British Columbia V6T 1Z2, Canada

Mesfin Samuel Mulatu (45) Section on Socio-Environmental Studies, National Institute of Mental Health, National Institutes of Health, Bethesda, Maryland 20892

Miles Muraoka (163) Cancer Research Center of Hawaii, University of Hawaii, Honolulu, Hawaii 96813

Joseph R. Pellizzari (411) Mental Health Care Program, London Health Sciences Center, London, Ontario N6A 4G5, Canada

Emmanuel Persad (267) Department of Psychiatry, The University of Western Ontario, London, Ontario N6A 5C2, Canada

Anita Raj (195) School of Public Health, Boston University, Boston, Massachusetts 02118

Elizabeth Reed (195) Department of Endocrinology, Brigham and Women's Hospital, Boston, Massachusetts 02115

George S. Renfrey (343) Phoenix C & D, Barrie, Ontario L4N 8N4, Canada

Alan Richter (141) QED Consulting, New York, New York 10025

Heather M. Shearer (113) Department of Psychology, The University of Western Ontario, London, Ontario N6A 5C2, Canada

Leora C. Swartzman (63, 389) Department of Psychology, The University of Western Ontario, London, Ontario N6A 5C2, Canada

Emily A. Wise (445) University of Florida Health Science Center, Gainesville, Florida 32610

PREFACE

The field of health psychology encompasses approaches to health promotion and maintenance; the treatment, rehabilitation and prevention of ill health; the identification of etiologic and diagnostic correlates of ill health, disability, and handicap; and the analysis and reform of health care systems and policies.

Culture, however, has received marginal consideration in health psychology even though the value of culture in human behavior in general, and health in particular, has had historical and contemporary recognition. Several indicators have supported the assertion of cultural neglect in the science and practice of health psychology. Most textbooks on health psychology have failed to treat culture as a critical consideration in the understanding of behavior and behavior change, in the development of effective strategies to treat and prevent ill health, in the promotion of health, in the enhancement of quality of life, and in the development of health care policy in a pluralistic society. Further, publications in health psychology journals have rarely focused on cultural issues. Finally, culture as a substantive domain has not been incorporated in the formal education and training of the majority of health professionals.

Over the past 5 years, there has been increased recognition of the value of culture in health psychology, in both research and practice, as well as an increase in systematic efforts to integrate the fields of health psychology and the psychology of culture. Nevertheless, resources to familiarize researchers, practitioners, and students in the field of health with the role of culture in the science, practice, and training of health care have been absent. The availability of a conceptual framework that considers the interface between health behavior and cultural psychology is essential for the advancement of a more culturally competent and ethically sound approach to health.

The purpose of this book is to approach the various domains of health psychology from a cultural perspective by providing a meaningful integration of the knowledge from the fields of health psychology and cultural psychology that will influence future research, practice, and training in health psychology. The proposed new approach allows the cultural domain to assume an integral consideration in the promotion and maintenance of health, in the prevention and treatment of ill health, in the understanding of the etiologic and diagnostic correlates of health, and in the advancement of culturally appropriate health care systems. The equal emphasis of cultural considerations on the science and practice of health psychology is vital to and consistent with the scientist–practitioner model of training adapted by many academic programs in health and public health.

One can debate the merits of a single-authored versus a multiauthored textbook. In the case of this book, we feel that the multiauthored approach is important. First, it provides readers with different perspectives on the many topics in cultural health psychology because each author has a different worldview. The second advantage is that each chapter is written by authorities in the subject area of that chapter. Given the range of topics covered, it would be difficult for one or two authors to master the material. A third advantage is that some authors approach their topics from an intracultural perspective, while other authors approach their topics from an intercultural view. This permits the reader to understand the complexity of health psychology when it is viewed from a cultural perspective.

As we sought authors to write the various chapters, it became evident that the topic of health psychology from a cultural perspective was indeed an underdiscussed and poorly researched area. Some authors refused our request because of the lack of material on which to base their chapters. Other authors commented on the lack of literature in their topic area relative to the cultural perspective, but persisted regardless. The amount of culturally relevant material available has affected the range of discussion and research on culture presented in each chapter. In some chapters, the material is abundant and in others, it is sparse. This variation in cultural content serves to highlight those areas in which there is an urgent need to research health psychology from a cultural perspective.

This book will be of benefit to health practitioners and researchers interested in the cultural aspects of health, health research, and health care policy. It can be used by students in medicine, nursing, health administration, public health, and health psychology. The ultimate aim is the pursuit of scientific knowledge, the development of sound and ethical professional practice, and the advancement of culturally relevant health care systems and policies. It is our hope that this book will contribute to this cause.

Shahé S. Kazarian
David R. Evans

ACKNOWLEDGMENTS

We thank our contributors for their exemplary collaborative spirit and professional response to our editorial comments. We also express gratitude to our wives, Levonty (Aroutian) Kazarian and Margaret Hearn, for their invaluable assistance in reading drafts of chapters and their capacity to endure our preoccupation with this book.

Next, we thank Nikki Levy, Academic Press Publisher, for her foresight and invaluable support in the development of this book. Thanks to the Academic Press staff for their warmth and competent guidance and for their contagious drive in piloting the *Handbook* to its final form. In particular, thanks to Barbara Makinster, Editorial Coordinator; Jocelyn Lofstrom, Production Manager; Trevor Daul, Promotions Manager; and Bonnie Baranoff, Marketing Manager.

HEALTH PSYCHOLOGY FROM A CULTURAL PERSPECTIVE

THEORETICAL CONSIDERATIONS

1

HEALTH PSYCHOLOGY AND CULTURE: EMBRACING THE 21ST CENTURY

SHAHÉ S. KAZARIAN* AND DAVID R. EVANS†

*Departments of Psychology and Psychiatry
†Department of Psychology
The University of Western Ontario
London, Ontario, Canada

Psychology has a long history of kinship with health. The initial link with one aspect of health, mental health, was formalized in North America in 1896 with the establishment of the first child clinic in the world in Pennsylvania. Toward the end of World War I, psychologists in Canada and the United States were involved in the rehabilitation of service personnel who had been wounded or had psychological problems as a result of the war. Psychology's formal link with health assumed completeness eight decades later with the emergence of the field of health psychology in 1978 in the United States and in the 1980s in Canada and in Europe. At present, health psychology is holistic in that its science and practice embrace both the "mind and body" aspects of health.

The focus of the present chapter is on the evolving concept of health and its relation to culture, the historical underpinnings of the field of health psychology, and the interface between health psychology and cultural psychology. In addition, cultural health psychology is proposed as a viable integration of these two domains. The value of incorporating culture into the science and practice of modern health psychology is highlighted.

CULTURE AND HEALTH

In Western societies, health care policies, perspectives, and practices have received both positive and negative reviews. On the negative side, it has been suggested that health beliefs and practices in culturally pluralistic Western societies are embedded in the Western tradition. The consequences of the Western bias in health are (1) neglect of cultural and linguistic demographics; (2) lack of consideration of cultural diversity in health service planning, implementation, and evaluation; (3) creation of discriminatory health service practices and disparities in health care access, utilization, and outcome; and (4) marginalization of the indigenous health structures, beliefs, and practices of diverse cultures (Airhihenbuwa, 1995; Dana, 1998; Denboba, Bragdon, Epstein, Garthright, & Goldman, 1998; Landrine, 1996; Ontario Ministry of Health, 1993; Teo & Febbraro, 1997). For example, Landrine has argued that the knowledge base of illness treatment and health promotion practices "remain saturated in Eurocentric assumptions and values while simultaneously lauding the virtues and benefits of multiculturalism" (Landrine, 1996, p. 143). More recently, Dana (1998) has indicated that the Euro-American power structure has contributed to the development of "a technology of parsimony in managed care." A significant negative consequence of the technology of parsimony is homogenization of health service recipients, i.e, minimization of distinctions and differences among patients and failure to consider treatment assumptions and practices within a cultural pluralistic context.

On the positive side, there has been an increasing recognition of the value of multiculturalizing health care systems that are monoculturalistic in derivation but are nevertheless embedded within a culturally pluralistic context (Dana, 1998; Gil & Bob, 1999; Masi, Mensah, & McLeod, 1993; Ontario Ministry of Health, 1991; The Writing Group for the Consortium for Health and Human Rights, 1998; Yoe, 1993). An essential requirement for the multiculturalization of health has been cultural competence in health research, practice, training, and ethics within a human rights framework.

THE CONCEPT OF HEALTH

Health is an evolving rather than a static concept. A meaningful understanding of the concept of health in a cultural context requires consideration of several factors: beliefs with respect to anatomy and physiology; components of health; health cognitions and classification of disease; and health interventions. Lack of knowledge among health professionals about cultural health concepts and practices, in addition to intercultural communication difficulties, has been a major issue in health care provision in multicultural countries.

Beliefs about Anatomy and Physiology

Views about anatomy and physiology are culturally determined and crucial to perceptions of health and disease. Helman (1984, 1995) has discussed the cultural definitions and the social and psychological significance of three aspects of body image on health and disease: beliefs relating to body shape, size, and adornments (e.g., clothing and body piercing); beliefs with respect to the structure of the body; and beliefs about body functioning. Beliefs about body shape, size, and adornments vary across cultures and serve as sources of social communication and social functioning (e.g., group membership and social rank). The right of Canadian women to walk topless on the beach or in the streets has drawn considerable attention across the country. Beliefs about the inner structure of the body also vary across cultures and influence perceptions and presentations of bodily complaints and responses to interventions. Finally, beliefs about the inner workings of the body show differences among cultures and have significant effects on human behavior. Helman (1984) describes at least three different lay models of the inner functioning of the body: the Balance Model, the "Plumbing" Model, and the Machine Model.

The Balance Model

Theories associated with the Balance Model describe the healthy functioning of the body as a harmonious balance between two or more elements or forces within the body. Harmonious balance is also viewed as a function of both external (e.g., diet, environment, supernatural agents) and internal factors (e.g., hereditary weakness). The humoral theory represents the most widespread view of the Balance Model. The roots of humoral theory date back to China and India, and its elaboration into a system of medicine to Hippocrates (Helman, 1984). According to humoral medical beliefs, the basic functions of the body are regulated by the four bodily fluids or humors of blood, phlegm, black bile, and yellow bile. Excess of yellow bile is associated with chronic anger and irritability; excess of black bile with chronic sadness and melancholy; excess of blood with sanguinity or optimism; and excess of phlegm with calmness and listlessness. Each of the fluids or humors is also characterized by a combination of hot/cold and wet/dry: hot and wet for blood, cold and wet for phlegm, cold and dry for black bile, and hot and dry for yellow bile. The wet and dry conditions are believed to be less important than the hot and cold conditions. In fact, the hot–cold balance is considered to be the secret for good health. The Greek theory of humoral pathology was elaborated in the Arab world, imported to Spain as scientific medicine during the Muslim domination, and transmitted to the Americas at the time of the Spanish Conquest (Henderson & Springer-Littles, 1996). Needless to say, harmonious balance is a contemporary lay belief about health and illness in a variety of cultures, including those of Latin America, the Islamic world, and the Caribbean.

The "Plumbing" Model

The "Plumbing" Model of the body represents the Western conceptualization of body structure and functioning. In this model, the body is conceived of as a "series of hollow cavities or chambers connected with one another, and with the body's orifices, by a series of 'pipes' and 'tubes.' The major cavities are usually 'the chest' and 'the stomach,' which almost completely fill the thoracic and abdominal spaces respectively"(Helman, 1984, p.15). Central to the Plumbing Model is the view that "health is maintained by the uninterrupted flow of various substances—including blood, air, food, faeces, urine and menstrual blood—between cavities, or between a cavity and the exterior of the body via one of the orifices. Disease, therefore, is the result of 'blockage' of an internal tube or pipe" (Helman, 1984, p.15).

The Machine Model

The Machine Model characterizes "the body as an internal combustion engine, or as a battery-driven machine" (Helman, 1984, p.16). According to Helman, indicators for the operation of the Machine Model in Western medicine include the use of such metaphors as "Your heart isn't pumping so well," or "I need a rest, doctor—my batteries need recharging." To these can be added the "I need a tune-up" metaphor. The view of the body as a machine-like entity that operates according to principles of physics and chemistry and requires the doctor to repair the machine is embraced by both Western religion and medical science (Engel, 1977).

Beliefs about the Components of Health

Health as a total state may also be viewed as encompassing two separate states—physical health and psychological well-being. In combination, the physical and psychological states result in different health outcomes: poor physical health or debilitating disease with or without concomitant poor psychological well-being; and poor physical or psychological well-being in the absence of identifiable physical disease (Downie, Fyfe, & Tannahill, 1990). Kleinman (1980) has made the distinction between disease and illness. Illness entails a subjective experience and represents a personal response to discomfort. Disease, on the other hand, refers to observable and measurable deviations in body structure and function.

Beliefs about Health and Classification

In addition to the cultural determination of beliefs about anatomy and physiology, culture dictates disease classification, beliefs about etiology, and help-seeking behavior. In relation to disease classification, Western systems include the DSM-IV *(Diagnostic and Statistical Manual–4th Edition)* and the ICD-10 *(International Classification of Diseases–10th Edition)*. Classification systems have also been developed in non-Western cultures with significance for Western cultures. Read (1966) has described a threefold classification system from the African cultural perspective: (1) trivial or everyday complaints that can be treated by home remedies; (2) European diseases that require Western scientific interventions; and (3) African diseases which are not responsive to modern medical treatments.

Beliefs about Health Interventions

Health may be equated with curative medicine or seen as a "field concept," i.e., the product of human biology, lifestyle, environment, and the health care system (Lalonde, 1974). The curative medicine perspective views "health as just a matter of hospitals, doctors and patients" (Premier's Council on Health, Well-being and Social Justice, 1994). In contrast, the "field concept" of health allows a health promotion framework in which health-related inequities are reduced, focus on prevention is increased, and individual coping is enhanced (Health and Welfare Canada, 1986). In the health promotion framework, self-care, mutual aid, and healthy environments are emphasized. Implementation strategies that foster public participation, strengthen community health services, and coordinate healthy public policy are also supported.

DEFINITION OF HEALTH

The most widely quoted quantitative definition of health is "the absence of disease." The most widely quoted qualitative definition of health is "a state of complete physical, mental and social well-being, and not merely the absence of disease or infirmity" (WHO; World Health Organization, 1948). The WHO definition of health was developed at the International Health Conference in New York on July 22, 1946, at which 61 nations were represented. Three significant aspects to the WHO definition are worthy of consideration. The first is insistence on health being not simply the absence of illness. The second is inclusion of psychological and social dimensions of health. The third is recognition of the importance of the application of psychology to health care.

The WHO definition of health was expanded in Canada in 1986. The expansion was in terms of broadening the concept from the individual to the family, to the community, and to public policy (Yoe, 1993). In a discussion document released by Health and Welfare Canada, health was defined as "a resource which gives people the ability to manage and even change their surroundings . . . a basic and dynamic force in our lives, influenced by our circumstances, our beliefs, our culture and our social, economic and physical environments" (Health and Welfare Canada, 1986, p. 3). The Canadian definition of health involves an active concept. It allows psychological and social determinants greater prominence. It also impels both an individualistic and a collectivistic view of health. Finally, it places greater emphasis on individual–environment interactions than on individual traits (Health and Welfare Canada, 1988). In the Canadian definition of health, environment is "interpreted in its broadest sense, and includes not only our physical surroundings, both natural and artificial, but also the social, cultural, regulatory and economic conditions and influences that impinge on our everyday lives" (p. 4).

MODELS OF HEALTH CARE

Three conceptual models of health care have dominated Western thinking (Dubos, 1960; Evans, 1997; McKeown, 1979): the biomedical model, the prevention model, and the health promotion model.

The Biomedical Approach

The biomedical approach has been symbolized by the Greek hero Asclepius, the god of healing and medicine. It represents the approach to curing disease or correcting accidental imperfections or birth defects (Garman, 1996). This biomedical view of health gained favor for three centuries beginning in the 17th century. The second view has been symbolized by Hygieia, the daughter of Asclepius, and represents the approach to discovery of healthy living for the purpose of achieving longevity and quality of life. This social view of health has regained favor since the mid-1970s with its emphasis on prevention rather than cure (Garman, 1996). Differences between the biomedical and social views of health are summarized in Table 1.1.

The germ theory of disease that emerged in the 1800s provided an impetus to the biomedical model of health care and its continued application in the 20th century. The major premises of the germ theory are that every disease has a specific pathogenic cause and that treatment is best achieved by removal or control of the offender. The germ theory contributed significantly to efforts to discover "magic bullets," i.e., drugs to kill or control the cause of the disease and to restore the body to a state of health. The biomedical model has had enormous influence on medical research and practice, but it also has deemphasized the role of psychological, lifestyle, and personality factors in the precipitation, exacerbation, outcome, and prevention of illness (Steptoe & Wardle, 1994). On the other hand, the biomedical model has enabled the development of effective medical treatments for diseases and has minimized blame and responsibility on those "victimized" by disease.

The biopsychosocial approach to health care, as an alternative to the biomedical model, was formally advanced two decades ago (Engel, 1977). While the role of pathogens in ill health was acknowledged in the biopsychosocial model, the interplay of biological and psychological factors in disease was asserted. The biopsychosocial model assumes that individual susceptibility to disease and pat-

TABLE 1.1   Differences between the Biomedical and Social Models of Health

	Biomedical model	Social model
Definition of health	Absence of disease	Holism
Health care provider	Physician, specialist	Multidisciplinary team or professional
Focus of care	Body	Whole person
Knowledge base	Biomedical	Social sciences, traditional wisdom
Locus of care	Hospital with walls	Hospital without walls, clinic
Nature of illness	Acute	Chronic
Goal of intervention	Cure	Well-being
Role of consumer	Passive	Active

terns of subjective experiences of illness and recovery are affected interactively by psychosocial factors, the immune system, stress and social support, and quality of helper–helpee relationship (Reynolds, 1996). Psychosocial factors include personality, coping skills, and lifestyle.

Numerous empirical studies, both human and animal, have supported the biopsychosocial perspective by demonstrating the somatic effects of social and psychological factors. The personality and psychosocial attributes that have been examined include Type A behavior, stress, social isolation, hostility, and perceived locus of control (Carmody & Matarazzo, 1991). The biopsychosocial approach, however, has been criticized on three major grounds (Sadler & Hulgus, 1990; Reynolds, 1996). First, it is more relevant to the science of health than to the practice of health. Second, it overestimates the influence of social and psychological factors in disease. Third, it stigmatizes sick people for the chronicity of their condition or for their presumed engagement in health-jeopardizing lifestyles.

The Prevention Approach

An alternative to the biomedical approach to health care is the prevention or public health model. Several factors provided the impetus to the prevention approach. The first relates to the recognition of the link between lifestyle and health. The second is the increased awareness that disease could be caused by unhealthy conduct. The third relates to the success in reducing the onset and spread of communicable diseases (e.g., typhus, tuberculosis, cholera) by systematic implementation of public health measures, i.e., improvements in diet, housing, quality of air and water, public sanitation, and personal hygiene.

According to the 1994 Statistical Abstract of the United States, the health profile of the United States is such that the top 10 killers or causes that lead to death are heart disease, cancer, cerebrovascular disease, pulmonary diseases, accidents, pneumonia, diabetes, suicide, AIDS, and homicide. Similarly, malignant neoplasm, diseases of the heart, cerebrovascular diseases, chronic obstructive lung disease and allied conditions, accidents and adverse effects, pneumonia and influenza, diabetes mellitus, suicide, and HIV infection are among the 11 highest mortality rates in Canada (Statistics Canada, 1994). An understanding of "behavioral pathogens" (e.g., smoking, high-fat diet, and physical inactivity) that produce these diseases, with a view to devising strategies to tackle them before they affect individuals adversely, is within the purview of preventive health (Carmody & Matarazzo, 1991).

Western societies are increasingly recognizing the critical role that socioculturally based belief systems play in health behavior, including initiatives dedicated to "keeping healthy people healthy" (Engel, 1977; Kleinman, Eisenberg, & Good, 1978). Culturally based belief systems or explanatory models (Kleinman, 1980) exist among lay individuals and health care providers for a variety of illnesses (e.g., cancer). Kleinman (1980) has described five basic elements associated with explanatory models: cause of illness, circumstances surrounding the onset of sickness, how sickness produces its effects, the course of illness, and possible illness treatments (Kleinman, 1980). Landrine and Klonoff (1992) have identified five major etiological agents of illness that are universal across a variety of cultures: (1) violations of interpersonal norms; (2) social role violations; (3) emotions associated with social norms and role violations; (4) moral and religious transgressions; and (5) quasi-natural agents (e.g., hot–cold foods or weather) and blood "states" (e.g., weak, thin, bad). Lack of understanding of cultural explanatory models in pluralistic cultures precludes culturally competent health care, disease prevention, and health promotion. Cultural explanatory models are likely to be reflected in a variety of forms. These include communication patterns and routines, and expressions, phrases, and metaphors with respect to health and illness. The role of cultural explanatory models in response to illness and coping is illustrated by two case reports (Eisunbruch, 1990; Saykao, 1990; both cited in Pauwels, 1995). In the first case, the parents of a Turkish boy who were desperate about their son's worsening condition decided to give him back blood—and, so they hoped, life. Their son had been admitted to the hematology ward of a hospital and diagnosed as having lymphatic leukemia. Despite being placed on powerful cytotoxic medications, his health was gradually deteriorating. His condition was requiring constant withdrawal of blood, leaving him in a state of physical weakness. The parents arrived at the hospital on a wintry day with bulging overcoats. In their son's room, they opened up the coats to reveal two live squawking roosters. They cut off the heads of the roosters and sprinkled the blood over him.

In the second case, a Hmong woman arrived at a hospital for an operation for a ruptured ectopic pregnancy. The woman's condition was so severe that failure to receive the operation would result in her bleeding to death. Doctors informed her that the operation would mean "tying" one of her fallopian tubes. When she heard this, she and her family flatly refused the operation. For this woman, it was important which fallopian tube would be tied, as one tube is involved in producing boys and another in producing girls. The woman had only one son, and she wanted to have more. She believed that tying the "boy tube" in the operation might leave her unable to have any more boys.

The Health Promotion Approach

An important extension of the prevention approach, which can be argued to include prevention approaches, is the health promotion model (Evans, 1994, 1997). The focus of the health promotion model is on those factors and behaviors that enhance an individual's health and quality of life. As such, the focus is on positive behaviors (e.g., exercise, a healthy diet, and good interpersonal relations). On the other hand, the focus of many prevention programs is on the management of negative behaviors (e.g., smoking cessation, control of diet, reducing alcohol consumption). Many companies are working to develop wellness programs for their employees (Evans, 1997). While the emphasis in health promotion programs to date has been on physical factors, there is a growing belief that psychological and social factors are equally important. The health promotion approach is discussed in more detail in Chapter 4.

HEALTH CARE SYSTEMS

Health care systems are designed to provide quality care for the purpose of improving the health status of consumers. The health care systems in Canada and the United States are dissimilar with respect to health care funding. In the United States, persons age 65 and over are covered by Medicare, those considered poor are covered by Medicaid, and the remainder of the population is covered by private insurance paid for by the individual, an employer, or some individual–employer combination. According to the U.S. Bureau of Census 1990 and 1992, 13.4% of Americans have no health insurance coverage, the rates being lower for non-Hispanic Whites (10.2%) but higher for Puerto Ricans (15.5%), non-Hispanic African Americans (19.7%), Cuban Americans (20.3%), and Mexican Americans (36.9%).

Unlike the system in the United States, most health care in Canada is supported by a publicly funded universal insurance program and is considered the most sacred social program of the country (Marmor, 1994; Mueller, 1993). Some health care, including, for example, dentistry, psychology, and physiotherapy, is still funded for the most part by a private system. Canada's version of socialized medicine was introduced by the passage of the Hospital Insurance and Diagnostic Services Act in 1957 by the Canadian Parliament. This act stipulated public financing for hospital services for all citizens and allowed the sharing of costs for such services equally with the provincial governments. The Medical Care Act was passed in 1968, stipulating the extension of universal access to physician services and articulating the five principles of "Medicare" (see Table 1.2). The Canada Health Act was passed in 1984. This act replaced the previous two acts,

TABLE 1.2   Five Principles of the Health Insurance Program in Canada

Principle 1: Public Administration
Administration and operation of the provincial health care insurance plan by a public authority on a nonprofit basis.

Principle 2: Comprehensiveness
Provincial coverage of all necessary medical and hospital services; hospital-based surgical dental procedures; and selected other services on the basis of a single payer.

Principle 3: Universality
Total (100%) entitlement of insuree to the insured health services on uniform terms and conditions basis.

Principle 4: Portability
Medical and hospital insurance of citizens in other jurisdictions or countries equal to their home province.

Principle 5: Accessibility
Absence of financial barriers (e.g., user fees, extra billing) to insured health services, citizen choice of service provider or hospital, and provincial legislative power for the establishment of provincial systems of payment for health services.

affirmed the five principles of Medicare, and specified sanctions for provinces that attempted to undermine the Medicare principles.

The American health care delivery system is the most expensive in the world. According to the Organization for Economic Cooperation and Development Health Data for 1994, the U.S. spends 14.3% of its Gross Domestic Product on health care (http://www.oecd.org). Canada spends 9.8% of its Gross Domestic Product on health care. The U.S. health care system still scores poorly, by international standards, on a variety of indicators: health outcomes, overall costs, efficiency, coverage, consumer satisfaction, and equity of access. For example, the life expectancy figures for 1989 in Canada were 73.7 years for males and 80.6 years for females, whereas the comparable rates in the United States for the sexes were 71.8 and 78.9 years, respectively (Federal, Provincial, and Territorial Advisory Committee on Population Health, 1996; U.S. National Center for Health Statistics, 1993).

While Canadians are concerned about the future of health care and its overburdening with aging baby boomers, the health insurance program in Canada is a source of pride for them and an essential aspect of their identity and separateness from their neighbors to the south. Resistance, outrage, or rational objections to proposed changes to the health system in Canada are not uncommon. Proposals such as user fees are a source of threat to Canadian identity and to the principle of equity in Canadian society. In response to a question on user fees, a noted Canadian expert in health care and its funding has responded in the following manner: "It's partly because user fees sound like a good idea. It's only when you look at them carefully that you see they are not like Robin Hood, taking from the rich to give to the poor. They are more like the Sheriff of Nottingham, punishing the sick or the poor for being sick" (The Atkinson Letter, 1996, p. F6).

Two key assumptions with respect to health care systems require clarification. The first is that health care organizations in culturally pluralistic societies can operate on a culturally monolithic desert island. This assumption is no longer tenable and is under increasing challenge. Several social, political, and economic contexts are sources of pressure for reform in Western health care systems. The first factor is the soaring costs of health care without concomitant and substantial improvements in health status. A second factor is the exclusive focus on the sick person at the expense of sociocultural and ecological determinants (social and physical environments, employment, housing, and social support) of illness behavior and well-being (Federal, Provincial, and Territorial Advisory Committee on Population Health, 1996; Vingilis, 1996). A third factor is the perceived superiority of Western medicine and continued marginalization of alternative but complementary approaches to Western health practices. A fourth factor is the growing dissatisfaction of consumers from diverse cultures with the system's failure to meet their health care needs. In one case, a health professional refused to see a patient because of the patient's limited competence in the English language. In another case, a health professional agreed to see a patient provided the patient made her own arrangements for a cultural interpreter. In a third case, a health professional conducted a gynecological interview with a patient using the patient's preadolescent children as interpreters.

Several contemporary health reform initiatives have been introduced in North America and elsewhere for the purpose of increasing system effectiveness and efficiency. These initiatives include decentralization, restructuring or reengineering (Health and Welfare Canada, 1993; Joint Task Force, 1993), client/patient-centered or consumer-driven care (Lathrop, 1991; Mang, 1995), continuous quality improvement and benchmarking (Helyar, Flett, Hundert, Fallon, Mosher, & Crawford, 1998), holistic care (including alternative medicine) and community-focused rather than bed-based care (Health & Welfare Canada, 1993; Kazarian, McCabe, & Joseph, 1997), and multiculturalization of health care (Masi et al., 1993).

The second assumption with respect to health care systems is their insulation from the reality of health care pluralism. Health care systems do not just consist of physicians and hospitals with walls. Individuals suffering from physical discomfort have a multiplicity of treatment options at their disposal in the pluralistic health care theatre: self, family, friends, priests, folk healers, doctors, and psychologists, among others. The various actors on the health care pluralism stage play different roles, portray different world views, and eschew the virtues of their own "indecent proposals" for healing. Kleinman et al. (1978) have identified three overlapping sectors of health care in complex societies: the popular, the folk, and the professional. Similarly, in culturally pluralistic societies, formal and informal sectors within the health care system have been identified, each with its own cultural and social attributes. The formal system is identified as the scientific Western medical system, is considered the superior system, and is upheld by law. The informal system is identified as the alternative smaller system comprising faith healers and folk healers such as African American folk healers, folk healers of indigenous people, Muslim Hakims, Hindu vaids, and Mexican American *curanderas* (female) and *curanderos* (male) or herbalistas. An individual with a specific health problem is likely to seek help from both the informal health care system and the formal health care system.

An understanding of health care pluralism in a culturally diverse community and the cultural and social aspects of the formal and informal systems and their interrelationships is essential for culturally competent and ethically sound health care service delivery. The Western formal health care system dichotomizes the mind and the body. The informal health care system, on the other hand, assumes a holistic perspective and considers the balance among individuals, their society (including relatives and friends), and their physical environment. The cross-cultural application of interventions continues to be subject of debate and opposing views. Patterson (1985) and Toukmanian and Brouwers (1998) maintain that Western methods of therapy are appropriate in other cultures, whereas Saeki and Borow (1985) consider the opposite view. These authors highlight fundamental incompatibility in cultural values and orientations. For example, a health care practitioner with a Western view of self (i.e., a self that is unique and independent) will consider an *individualistic* approach to healing. On the other hand, a health care professional with an Eastern view of self (i.e., a self that is interdependent and that relies on the in-group for decision making and conformity) will consider a *collectivistic* approach to healing. In the individualistic approach, a diagnosis may be offered only to the patient, whereas in the collectivistic approach, the diagnosis may be conveyed to the whole family and even withheld from the patient. The view of self as an extension of family and kin may also affect the process of hospitalization, the patient role, and the outcome of care. There is likely much more tolerance of the intense involvement of family and community in the collectivist approach to inpatient care than in the individualist approach to hospitalization.

It is important to recognize that health practices, whether Western or non-Western, are derived from basic needs and fears rather than from ignorance. Practitioners from both sectors also share common characteristics, i.e., fostering hope in patients, inspiring confidence in their competence and healing power, showing an empathic attitude, having an authoritative approach, and promoting a participatory role in the healing process. Nevertheless, the relationship between the formal system and the informal may be marked by mutual distrust and suspicion rather than by collaboration. Western professionals in health may view shamans and other folk healers as "quacks" and "charlatans" who do harm to their patients' health rather than as allies with a shared objective, namely, the welfare of patients. Although health care practices of indigenous curers may be perceived and defined as primitive or marginal by "dominant" cultures, they are functional for the persons within their own culture. Health care providers need to start from where the helpee is in terms of their cultural values and health care beliefs and practices. Western-based practices may not always be the best intervention or health promotion approaches. Whichever method is used, the helpee's beliefs should be respected. In fact, in all situations, respect for the individual and the culture, trust, and a positive regard are needed for a competent healing process (Henderson & Springer-Littles, 1996).

HEALTH PSYCHOLOGY

HISTORICAL OVERVIEW

The theory and practice of holistic health, i.e., the view that there are delicate interrelationships between the mind and the body, are found in ancient literary documents from Babylonia and Greece. On the theoretical level, for example, Hippocrates proposed a relationship between bodily fluids or humors and personality temperaments. On the practice level, physicians embraced the holistic approach to health by virtue of having multiple roles: philosophers–teachers, priests, and healers.

The 17th century, however, marked the demise of holistic health. The traditional view of the reciprocal relationship between the psyche and the soma was considered unscientific. It culminated in the relegation of the study of the mind to religion and philosophy and the study of the body to physical medicine. For example, the dualistic view of health espoused by the French philosopher Rene Descartes was further entrenched in medical research and practice by the discovery in the 19th century of microorganisms as causal agents in certain diseases. Mechanical laws or physiological principles assumed acceptable approaches to the science and practice of medicine.

The strict dualistic approach to health mellowed in the mid-19th century, and holistic health reemerged in the 20th century. Renewed interest in holistic health was due primarily to the inherent limitations of the biomedical approach. The biomedical model presented difficulties in the diagnostic classification of diseases. It did not provide complete understanding of the etiology and maintenance of a variety of diseases, nor the comprehensive treatment of physical disorders. For example, the dualistic orientation of medicine was a source of puzzlement for those dealing with disorders in which the influence of the "emotions of the mind" seemed apparent (McMahon & Halstrup, 1980). An individual with an unexplained pain in the back baffled practitioners with a strictly biomedical model. An important consequence of the inherent limitations of the biomedical approach to health was the gradual emergence of "an ambiguously defined diagnostic category . . . called 'nervous' . . . to accommodate what we know today as 'psychosomatic' disorders" (McMahon & Halstrup, 1980).

A second important historical consequence of the limitation of the biomedical approach to health was the emergence of the psychoanalytic and psychodynamic theories (Alexander, 1950), in particular that of Sigmund Freud. The psychoanalytic/psychodynamic theories postulated unconscious mechanisms in physiological processes and contributed to the growth of the field of psychophysiological medicine (e.g., Wolff, 1953). Social and psychological factors were investigated in physical health and well-being and contributed to the development of effective psychological approaches to the treatment of physical disorders (Feuerstein, Labbe, & Kuczmierczyk, 1986; Gatchel & Baum, 1983; Lipowski, 1977). Health psychology contributed significantly to the mental health and developmental disabilities components of health in the aftermath of World War II. Since the 1960s, the contribution of health psychology to the integration of the behavioral sciences with the science and practice of medicine has been noteworthy (Carmody & Matarazzo, 1991; Matarazzo, 1980; Schofield, 1969). The development of health psychology as the 38th division of the American Psychological Association (APA) in 1978 and the establishment of several health psychology journals since 1982 are testimony to the significant role that psychology played in the field of behavioral medicine.

The history of health psychology in Canada is not well documented (Hearn & Evans, 1993). While Canadian psychology entered into the field of health through medicine early in the 20th century, there was difficulty defining its role both in medical schools and within the health care system. The two major operative reasons were the dominance of the biomedical model in medicine and the experimental orientation of psychology (Hearn & Evans, 1993; Matheson, 1983). Nevertheless, the Section of Health Psychology was established as Section 8 of the Canadian Psychological Association in 1980. The factors that provided the impetus for the eventual birth of health psychology in Canada were manifold. Psychologists became involved in the physical rehabilitation of World War I veterans. Psychologists also established psychology departments as autonomous entities in general hospitals. Needless to say, the numbers of psychologists working with physicians and their clientele continue to grow. A brief sketch of the short but explosive history of health psychology in North America and Europe is presented in Table 1.3.

The field of health psychology in North America and Europe has evolved considerably and is in a state of maturity, with continued potential for growth and development. For example, four years after the foundation of Division 38, a membership of 2400 for the field of health psychology was reported (Belar, Wilson, & Hughes, 1982). Surveys of education and training in health psychology at the predoctoral, internship, and postdoctoral levels have shown considerable opportunities and growth in these programs (Belar & Siegel, 1983; Belar et al.,

TABLE 1.3　Historical Landmarks in Health Psychology

1975	National Register of Health Service Providers in Psychology
1978	Foundation of Division 38, Health Psychology, American Psychological Association
1980	Foundation of Section 8, Health Psychology, Canadian Psychological Association
1982	Publication of first issue of *Health Psychology*
1983	Arden House Training Conference
1984	Foundation of Council of Directors of Health Psychology Training Programs
1985	Publication of first issue of *Psychology and Health*
1986	European Health Psychology Society
1987	Canadian Register of Health Service Providers in Psychology
1992	European Federation of Professional Psychologists' Associations Task Force on Health Psychology
1993	Full affiliation status of American Board of Health Psychology with American Board of Professional Psychology
1993	Publication of the first issue of the *Canadian Health Psychologist*
1994	Emergence of cross-cultural health psychology
1996	Publication of the first issue of *Journal of Health Psychology*
1996	Publication of the first issue of *British Journal of Health Psychology*
1997	Formal APA recognition of Health Psychology as a Specialty

1982; Gentry, Street, Masur, & Askin, 1981). Whereas a survey of graduate training programs in psychology in 1980 identified 6 of 42 programs offering pre-doctoral training in health psychology within another area of psychology (Belar et al, 1982), about a decade later, 46 doctoral programs with a primary focus on health psychology were listed in the 1991 Division of Health Psychology. At present, health psychologists play a vital scientist–practitioner role on a variety of health care teams, including anesthesiology, cardiology, dentistry, family practice, oncology, pediatrics, and rehabilitation.

Several factors, summarized in Table 1.4, have contributed to the maturity of the field and its potential for continued growth (Bishop, 1994; Carmody & Matarazzo, 1991; Marks, 1996; Sarafino, 1998; Taylor, 1999). The prevailing biomedical model of health has been incomplete in explaining health behavior. The model has also been limited in its focus on infectious disease, oblivious to behavioral sciences contributions to health behavior, and invariant with respect to issues pertaining to chronic care and illness prevention. The fields of behavioral medicine, behavioral health, and health psychology have made significant scientific and practical advancements in chronic pain, cardiovascular disease, neurological disorders, behavioral oncology, and the psychology of treatment adherence (Carmody & Matarazzo, 1991). Issues relating to quality of life, health care costs, and alternate approaches to traditional health care, however, have been of concern from both the biomedical and biopsychosocial perspectives on health.

DEFINITION AND SCOPE OF PRACTICE

Behavioral medicine, medical psychology, psychosomatic medicine, and health psychology are not synonymous terms. Medical psychology has a narrow focus and refers to traditional psychiatry in Great Britain, the practice of psychology in medical schools, or the study of psychological factors associated with

TABLE 1.4   Factors Associated with Growth of Health Psychology

Evolving concept of health

Limitations of the Western biomedical model

Increased focus on chronic disease

Emergence of Behavioral Medicine and Behavioral Health

Increased concern with health determinants and illness prevention

Increased concern with quality of life issues in health and illness

Recognition of role of life styles in health and illness

Health care costs

Alternative medicine

physical health, in addition to illness treatment at the individual, group, and systemic levels (Belar & Deardroff, 1995). Historically, psychosomatic medicine referred to the unity of psyche–body relationships with the implication of psychological causation of disease. There is an important distinction between the fields of behavioral medicine and health psychology, namely, the interdisciplinary approach of behavioral medicine and the discipline-specific approach of health psychology to health. As pointed out by Belar and Deardroff (1995), psychology cannot "practice" behavioral medicine nor psychosomatic medicine. Health psychology, however, is one of several health care and basic science fields that contribute to the understanding of health and the consequent treatment, rehabilitation, and prevention strategies that evolve from such an understanding (Feuerstein et al., 1986). Other health care and basic science fields that contribute to behavioral medicine include service professionals (nursing, dentistry, physical therapy, and dietetics), the behavioral sciences (sociology, anthropology, and epidemiology), biomedical sciences (physiology, biochemistry, immunology, and biostatistics), and medicine (psychiatry, cardiology, neurology, family medicine, physical medicine, and occupational medicine).

In addition to its endorsement by the APA Division of Health Psychology, Matarazzo's (1980) broad definition of health psychology has not been subject to much controversy even though a narrower definition (Pomerleau & Brady, 1979) for the field has been proposed. The broad definition of health psychology explicates the application of the diverse discipline of psychology to understanding of and intervening in health system issues: sensation and perception, emotion and motivation, learning, developmental, social, neuropsychology, experimental, industrial and organizational, individual differences, personality, and clinical (Feuerstein et al., 1986). An important focus of health psychologists is the prevention of disease and health promotion (Evans, 1994, 1997; Weiss, 1982).

The broad definition of health psychology also allows varied scientific (e.g., basic research, research on new interventions, and program evaluation) and practice activities (e.g., diagnosis, treatment, rehabilitation, and health promotion) within health care systems. Stone (1982, 1984) proposed a conceptual model of a health system in which the "Person Whose Health Is at Issue" is centered, and which delineates the activities of health psychologists. He identified four descriptive dimensions of relevance to the activities of health psychologists. The first dimension pertained to "the site in the health system that is the focus of work." This dimension entailed the interaction of the person whose health is at issue (PHAI) with environmental components (e.g., hazards, stressors, protective factors, sociocultural influences, and political systems), in addition to intrasystem transactions of elements. The second dimension pertained to the "health axis." This dimension entailed risk factors and coping, illness behavior, sick role, choice of health care, treatment, and rehabilitation. The third dimension pertained to "the level of address within the individual at which the phenomenon of concern is approached by the psychologists." The levels of address included the physiological, the complex culturally determined behavioral patterns, and the social/interactional. The fourth dimension pertained to the type of activity, and included basic research for problem identification and solution, design and implementation of interventions, and effectiveness evaluation.

EDUCATION AND TRAINING IN HEALTH PSYCHOLOGY

A number of education and training issues confronted health psychology in North America and Europe as it evolved as an independent field in psychology (Belar, 1998; Marks et al., 1998; Wallston, 1993). These included education and training standards, availability and adequacy of applied training settings, degree offered, core curricula, and entry-level credential, i.e., predoctoral versus postdoctoral, and model of training, i.e., training of health psychologists as clinicians versus as both researchers and clinicians (Belar, 1998; Belar & Siegel, 1983; Belar et al., 1982; Taylor, 1987). In addition to advocating involvement of health psychologists in the four primary areas of teaching, research, professional service, and management, Matarazzo (1983) identified four imperatives for education and training in health psychology: advancement of scientific knowledge, development of high-quality training resources in academic settings, establishment and maintenance of professional standards with respect to competence, and a socially responsive code of ethics.

Detailed recommendations for graduate education and training in health psychology were developed in a 1983 national conference in New York, the Arden House National Working Conference (Olbrisch, Weiss, Stone, & Schwartz, 1985; Stone, 1983). At this conference, the delegates identified a three-step system of education for health psychology, namely, predoctoral, internship, and postdoctoral. They also endorsed both the doctoral level of education and the scientist–practitioner model at every level of training (Stone, 1983). The delegates to the conference recommended substantive areas for training and education: biological, social, and psychological bases of health and disease; health consultation, assessment, intervention, and evaluation; health policy and organization; interdisciplinary collaboration; health research methodology and statistics; and ethical, legal, and professional considerations. In addition to the core curriculum, the delegates endorsed the need for experience in multidisciplinary health care settings with professional health psychologists on staff and adherence to APA accreditation criteria.

Sheridan et al. (1988) have recommended that a mandatory 2-year residency for entry into the independent practice of health psychology be required at the postdoctoral level. In addition to recommendations with respect to salary and benefits and funding, Sheridan et al. (1988) recommended that postdoctoral candidates possess "a Ph.D. or PsyD degree from an APA-approved program of training in professional psychology, either identified as or with a track in health psychology," and completion of a formal 1-year predoctoral internship. Sheridan et al. (1988) recommended residencies in health psychology, postdoctoral faculty, and rotations as ideal components of postdoctoral training programs. Finally, they recommended at least 6 of 14 techniques and skills for acquisition during the 2-year clinical postdoctoral residency. The list included such techniques and skills as relaxation therapies, psychotherapy (individual, group, family), assessments (neuropsychological, specific client populations such as pain patients), biofeedback, behavior therapy, health promotion, and compliance motivation. The availability of the Internet and the telehealth technology are important training challenges in the science and practice of health psychology.

CULTURE AND HEALTH PSYCHOLOGY

In this section, the interface between cultural psychology and health psychology is examined in a culturally pluralistic context.

CULTURAL PLURALISM

Except for the indigenous populace, all North Americans can trace their origins back to immigrants who were foreign to the prevailing cultures of their countries of settlement. While early settlers in North America were primarily European, the majority of more recent immigrants are non-European or of globally diverse origins. The globalization of immigrants in North America and other countries is seen in settlement patterns from South Asia, Southeast Asia, Central and South America, Africa, and China.

Currently, Canada, the United States, and Australia are the three countries with the highest rates of immigration, Canada being the lead country. According to the 1994 U.S. Bureau Census, in 1990 (April), the population of the United States was 248,710,000, 7.9% of whom (19,767,000) were foreign-born. For the same period, immigration in the United States was at 1,536,483. In 1991, the population of Canada was slightly over 27 million, 16% of whom (4.3 million) were born outside the country. For the same period, immigration in Canada was at 219,250 and emigration at 43,692.

Cultural pluralism in North America is not a recent reality. The phenomenon of the cultural mosaic or "tossed salad" is as old as North American history. For example, the estimated 200,000 indigenous people who inhabited the vast territories of modern Canada when the Europeans first landed on the continent comprised several distinctive cultural and linguistic groups (Tepper, 1994). As asserted by Dickason (1992), "Canada has fifty-five founding nations rather than the two that have been officially acknowledged." The first census following the Canadian Confederation was in 1871. This census showed the cultural and ethnic heterogeneity of the Canadian population at the time: French (1,082,940 people), Irish (846,000), English (706,000), Scots (549,946), German (202,000),

Dutch (29,000), Africans (21,000), and other cultural groups (Welsh, Swiss, Italians, Spanish, and Portuguese). In the 1870s, Canada received settlers from the Scandinavian countries (Denmark, Sweden), while in the 1880s it became a haven to thousands of destitute Jews who escaped persecution and pogroms in such European countries as Russia, Lithuania, Russian Poland, Ukraine, and Romania.

According to the 1991 Census Canada, 29% of the population is British only, 23% French only, 4% British and French only, 3% Canadian only, and 42% of other ethnic origin. The 1996 Canada Census data indicate that 17.1% of the Canadian population is British Isles only; 9.5% French only; 18.7% Canadian; 10.2% British Isles and/or French and/or Canadian; 16.1% other and British Isles, French, or Canadian; and 28.6% of other single and multiple origins. These data indicate that Canada is currently a community of minorities with no majority population. In fact, Tepper (1994) has pointed out that the numerical predominance of a single group in Canada ended over half a century ago.

The United States is also a community of diverse cultures even though the "melting pot" ideology dominated its policy up until the middle of the 20th century (Bourhis, Moise, Perreault, & Senecal, 1997; Kazarian, 1998). The "demographic face" of the United States continues to evolve. According to the 1990 U.S. Census, the leading ancestral groups in the country include German (57,947,000), Irish (38,736,000), English (32,652,000), African American (23,777,000), Italian (14,665,000), Mexican American (11,587,000), and French (10,321,000). At present, roughly 30% of the U.S. population is composed of individuals from so called "minority" racial and ethnic groups. It is projected that within 40 or 50 years, the "minority" group will constitute the country's majority (U.S. Bureau of Census, 1995). The changes in population demographics, values, and practices in North America and other Western countries are challenges that psychology must confront in order to prevent irrelevance, stagnation, and obsolescence (Hall, 1997).

Finally, it is important to consider the policies of different multicultural host countries respecting their citizenry. The two most common multicultural host culture ideologies are the assimilation (melting-pot) ideology and the multiculturalism ideology. The assimilation ideology dictates a citizenry that sacrifices its own cultural and linguistic distinctiveness for the sake of the host culture and the values of the dominant group. Of course, assimilation may be forced on a cultural group. A historical prototype of forced assimilation was the establishment of 80 residential schools in Canada for the purpose of stamping out "the Indian in the child," and stamping in (European) culture supreme. In contrast to the assimilation ideology, the premise of the multiculturalism ideology is that "it is considered of value to the host community" that citizens "maintain key features of their cultural and linguistic distinctiveness while adopting the public values of the host culture" (Bourhis et al., 1997, p. 373).

Two issues concerning host-culture policies are the moral sources of the policies and their intended outcomes. In addressing the first issue, Fowers and

Richardson (1996) indicated that "multiculturalism is, at its core, a moral movement that is intended to enhance the dignity, rights, and recognized worth of *marginalized* [our emphasis] groups" (p. 609). The view of multiculturalism as an ideology for the marginalized segment of a culturally pluralistic community is distorted. In reality, the moral source of multiculturalism is enhancement of the dignity, rights, and recognized worth of *all* people. For example, two core objectives of the Canadian Multiculturalism Policy are "to ensure that *all* [our emphasis] individuals receive equal treatment and equal protection under the law, while respecting and valuing their diversity" and "to promote the full and equitable participation of individuals and communities of *all* [our emphasis] origins in the continuing evolution and shaping of all aspects of Canadian society and assist them in the elimination of any barriers to that participation" (Canadian Multiculturalism Act, 1988). In integrating into Canadian society, the multiculturalism policy affords a person with an Irish heritage the same rights and opportunities as those afforded a person with an African heritage.

The second issue concerning host-culture policy is intended outcome. A major contributory factor to host-culture adoption of a melting-pot ideology is perceived threat to national unity. There is no foundation to this fear. Berry and Sam (1998) have pointed out that multiculturalism is not antithetic to nationalism; i.e., "retaining one's cultural identity does not diminish one's commitment to the larger national unity."

THE INTERFACE BETWEEN CULTURAL PSYCHOLOGY AND HEALTH PSYCHOLOGY

Three sources of information are used to explore the courtship between the psychology of culture and health psychology.

PsychLit Search

Article, chapter, and book citations on the PsychLit using *culture* and *health psychology* as key words are limited. For example, a search on chapters and books for the period of 1987 to 1996 produced 13 citations, only 2 of which (i.e., Keitel, Kopala, & Georgiades, 1995; Schroder, Rescheke, Johnston, & Maes, 1993) were specifically related to culture and health psychology. The PsychLit citation for books, however, was not inclusive of the volume edited by Dasen, Berry, and Sartorius (1988): *Health and Cross-Cultural Psychology: Toward Applications.*

Health Psychology Curriculum Resources

A survey of available volumes on health psychology in the home-university library of the authors found two volumes that focused on culture or diversity issues (Kato & Mann, 1996; MacLachlan, 1997). Culture in the majority of the remaining volumes was either not indexed or received limited coverage, such coverage usually being in the context of pain. An exception was the inclusion of a chapter on culture and essential hypertension (Anderson & Jackson, 1987) in the edited volume on health psychology by Stone et al. (1987).

An examination of the content and subject index of two health psychology textbooks (Sarafino, 1998; Taylor, 1999) showed that the subject index of Taylor's book listed a total of nine citations in the text for culture, cross-cultural view, and ethnic factors. On the other hand, Sarafino (1998) included, as appropriate, a gender and sociocultural section in the various chapters of his book on health psychology. Nevertheless, coverage of culture in Sarafino's book related primarily to ethnicity.

Health Psychology Journal

As a journal, *Health Psychology* publishes articles relating to the relationship between psychological and behavioral variables and physical health. The journal has been described as a primary publication outlet for the field of health psychology and as one of the most widely read APA publications in the area, with over 9000 subscribers (Krantz, 1995; Marks et al., 1998). In the editorial section of the first issue of *Health Psychology,* the editor indicated that "original studies, concise and authoritative reviews, well-documented descriptions of clinical, organizational, and educational interventions in the health system, and psychological analyses of issues of health policy" would be published in the journal (Stone, 1982, pp. 3–4). While Stone (1982, 1984) incorporated sociocultural influences and culturally determined patterns of behavior in the context of a health system model, he failed to mention absence of cultural studies in the journal during the first three years. Rather, he identified significant gaps in studies on "the psychology of legislators, policy makers, administrators, community members, and consumers who tolerate the presence and promotion of known hazards."

Landrine and Klonoff (1992) reviewed the titles of 326 articles published in *Health Psychology* for the period of 1982 to 1990 and found 11 articles (3.3%) on culture (i.e., ethnicity and race) and health. The current authors conducted similar reviews on the journal *Health Psychology* and the *Journal of Behavioral Medicine* for comparison purposes for the period from 1991 to 1995. Of the 337 articles published in *Health Psychology,* 25 (7.4%) were on culture and health. Surprisingly, the rate for the *Journal of Behavioral Medicine* was lower (4.1%). Of the 194 articles published in that journal, only 8 were on culture and health. While the rate of publication on culture and health in the journal *Health Psychology* commends a higher grade than the *Journal of Behavioral Medicine,* and the results indicate increased consideration of culture as a factor in health in its publications, the findings also suggest continued lack of substantial attention to culture in health psychology publications. Of the 25 articles published after 1990, one was by Landrine and Klonoff (1992) in which the authors provided convincing evidence for the importance of integrating cultural health beliefs in health. The December 1995 issue of the journal was a special issue providing a publication forum for the recommendations of the eight task groups of the National Conference on Behavioral and Sociocultural Perspectives on Ethnicity and

Health for "future research, research funding and research training relevant to so-ciocultural and behavioral perspectives on ethnicity and health" (Anderson, 1995, p. 649).

It is important to underscore that Krantz (1995) expressed a clear editorial support for cultural publications in *Health Psychology*. In the editorial titled "Health Psychology: 1995–1999," Krantz (1995) outlined "the editorial philoso-phy and procedures that will characterize the journal in the upcoming years." These included commitment to the publication of more behavioral intervention studies, prioritization of submissions with direct relevance to issues of physical rather than mental health, and, of most significance in this context, strong en-couragement to "the inclusion of women and ethnic minorities when possible in research studies" in health psychology.

THE LIMITED INTERFACE BETWEEN CULTURE AND HEALTH PSYCHOLOGY

The limited coverage of culture in health psychology is paradoxical because health psychology has prided itself, since its inception, on drawing its talents and skills from a variety of fields of psychology. The reasons for the relative neglect of culture in health psychology are varied (Marks, 1996) and overlap with those in other fields in psychology, e.g., clinical psychology (Kazarian & Evans, 1998).

A likely factor for the limited consideration of culture in health psychology is the historical theoretical and practice context of health psychology. The major theories adopted by health psychologists were developed primarily within main-stream psychology (Marks, 1996). The culture-blindness of mainstream psy-chology has been asserted frequently over time even though the founders of psy-chology had regarded culture with affection (Kazarian & Evans, 1998). On the other hand, it is likely that the founders of health psychology initially sought depth rather than breadth. This may have been arguably necessary for the field to establish itself within both the mainstream psychology culture and the health psychology culture and to receive acceptance and credibility before the health psychology field felt secure to venture into wider areas of theoretical, research, and professional training and practice horizons. In addressing public policy is-sues about two decades after the official founding of health psychology, Car-mody and Matarazzo (1991) advocated the application of the health psychology knowledge base to health issues of most relevance to society, including efforts to better understand the health needs of cultural groups, women, and specific client populations.

The theoretical embeddedness of health psychology in mainstream psychol-ogy is also reflected in its individualistic bias (Marks, 1996). As asserted by Marks, the individualism value entrenched deeply in North American and West-ern European cultures has allowed health psychology activities on "contextless or detached" individuals, precluding meaningful consideration of theoretical, re-search, and practice developments that are inclusive of the "context" and the "collective" (e.g., family, community, ecology, and culture) of the individual.

In relation to the historical practice context of health psychology, the Western biomedical model and the medical setting it provided for health psychologists dictated an "illness psychology" approach to practice and precluded meaningful consideration of culture as an important determinant of health (Marks, 1996). Needless to say, the individualism bias of health psychology was compatible with the prevailing biomedical model of disease in the health care system.

Even though there was early recognition of the basic link between health and culture (Berry, 1994), it was only in the late 1980s and early 1990s that the importance of culture as an important determinant of health worthy of the consideration of health psychologists reemerged (Dahlgren & Whitehead, 1991; Dasen et al., 1988; Ilola, 1990; Williams, 1995). The foresight of the founders of psychology has been demonstrated by the prolific research on the relevance of culture in health, its mediating role in a variety of disease conditions, including coronary heart disease, cancer, and AIDS, and its significance in health prevention and promotion initiatives in culturally pluralistic contexts.

CULTURAL HEALTH PSYCHOLOGY

Health psychologists and other health professionals are not receiving the necessary training for culturally competent health science and health practice. Few academics and clinical supervisors in the different health professions have developed cultural competence in the science and practice of health. Consequently, students in the health professions are not acquiring the knowledge, attitude, and skills for effective cultural health research and practice. For example, Henderson and Springer-Littles (1996) indicate that therapists who graduate from their respective training programs are ill-prepared for their role within a culturally pluralistic society and "intrude in the lives of 'foreigners' and do great harm."

The lack of cultural competence in health is of legal and ethical concern and a violation of the social responsibility principles of the health professions. The state of cultural incompetence is also a violation of the human rights provisions of the United Nations as they pertain to health (Dana, 1998; Gil & Bob, 1999; Hall, 1997; The Writing Group for the Consortium for Health and Human Rights, 1998). As music without music grammar is not music, so is cultural health psychology without cultural grammar not cultural health psychology. While the discourse on multiculturalism and psychology has begun (Ekstrom, 1997; Fowers & Richardson, 1996, 1997; Gaubatz, 1997; Teo & Febbraro, 1997; Yanchar & Slife, 1997), the firm entrenchment of culture in the fabric of modern health psychology requires integration of the two solitudes in psychology: cultural psychology and health psychology.

Berry (1994) has recognized the value of integrating the two perspectives in psychology, health psychology and cross-cultural psychology. He has proposed a new field, cross-cultural health psychology, as a valid approach to such integration. We prefer the term cultural health psychology. In this section, cultural health psychology is described, with a major focus on both the cultural domain in health and the imperative of cultural competence.

CULTURE IN CULTURAL HEALTH PSYCHOLOGY

Two approaches to the use of culture in health research have been described: the packaged approach and the unpackaged approach. Examples of both approaches are described throughout this book.

Packaged Approach

The cross-cultural comparative approach (Van de Vijver & Leung, 1998) inherent in cross-cultural psychology has dominated research on the link between health and culture. Ethnicity and race have been the two most common cultural indicators used in cross-cultural comparative studies. Typically, two or more racial or ethnic groups are selected and compared cross-racially or cross-culturally for quantitative differences on such dependent variables as disease prevalence and patterns of service utilization.

Three major issues, however, are associated with the application of the ethnicity and race constructs to the science and practice of cultural health psychology. The first issue pertains to the relevance of "minority" health research to the multitude of cultural groups in multicultural societies. The perception of racial and ethnic groups in multicultural contexts respecting race and ethnicity research is that of irrelevance, skepticism, and mistrust. For example, Donovan (1984) reviewed research on ethnicity and health and concluded that "there are differences between the perceptions of the professionals and of the [cultural] people over which health problems are of particular importance" (p. 668). Individuals from diverse cultures want culturally sound health science and culturally relevant health practice.

The second issue relates to conceptual ambiguities surrounding the use of race and ethnicity as independent variables in health research (Ahdieh & Hahn, 1996; Anderson, 1995; Bhopal, 1997; Bhopal & Donaldson, 1998; Ellison & de Wet, 1997; Phinney, 1996; Shiang, Kjellander, Huang, & Bogumill, 1998; Williams, 1995). Williams (1995) analyzed U.S.-based empirical research published in the journal *Health Services Research* from 1966 to 1990. Williams (1995) identified 10 different terms used to refer to the concept of race and ethnicity. These included color, race or origin, racial and ethnic minority groups, and minority status. Williams (1995) also found that 121 of 192 publications (63%) used race/ethnicity primarily to distinguish "blacks" from "whites" and that the term race/ethnicity was defined or justified in only 13% of the studies, with not a single article providing an explicit definition of race. Williams (1995) reported that the terms race and ethnicity were frequently used interchangeably, and no efforts were made to distinguish nationality and ancestry clearly from race. In one of the studies reviewed, ethnicity was operationalized as a broad category of the following racial, ethnic, and nationality groupings: U.S. White, Canadian, British, Scandinavian, Italian, Russian, Polish, Mexican, and Negro. On the basis of these findings, Williams (1995) underscored the importance of conceptual and measurement clarity in the use of race and ethnicity as cultural indices in health research.

Bhopal and Donaldson (1998) widened the debate on the race/ethnicity nomenclature in health research. The authors observed that the "White" label and other descriptive terms (Caucasian, European, Europoid, Western, Occidental, majority, native, and indigenous) were largely bypassed. Ahdieh and Hahn (1996) called for clarity, explicitness, consistency, and validity in the use of the categories of race, ethnicity, and national origin. Bhopal and Donaldson (1998) discussed the need to explore the possibility of a shared understanding of terms among the international research community. Phinney (1996) argued that ethnic categories and labels are problematic in that they are not reliable indicators of group membership and mask within-group differences. Phinney (1996) suggested focus on three meanings associated with ethnicity; namely, cultural values and practices (e.g., collectivism), ethnic identity, and status within the larger society.

The third issue pertains to inferences drawn from the use of race and ethnicity as independent variables in quasi-experimental health research. Greenfield (1998) indicated that rival explanatory hypotheses are not easily ruled out in the "packaged or indexical" use of race and ethnicity as antecedent variables. Thus, findings of differences between ethnic groups on access to medical care may be due to factors other than ethnicity. Alternate explanations include poverty, the relative absence of health care providers in rural areas and inner cities, inadequate numbers of culturally diverse service providers, distrust of the health care system, and racial discrimination. Even in studies in which cultural differences on the dependent variable are attributed to race and ethnicity as independent variables, "it is almost impossible to pin down which aspect of culture is responsible for the observed differences, in the absence of additional data" (Van de Vijver & Leung, 1998, p. 260). The interchangeable and indiscriminate use of such labels as immigrant, white, ethnic minority, race, and nonwhite in health research or their inadvertent consideration as proxy for socioeconomic status or surrogates for poverty confounds biological, social, and cultural components of health. Such use also contributes to drawing erroneous inferences with respect to genetic and behavioral traits.

Bhopal (1997) has characterized much of historical research on race, intelligence, and health as "unethical, invalid, racist, inhumane and ineffective." Bhopal (1997) has also pointed out that such research has emphasized the negative aspects of the health of immigrants and "ethnic minority" groups, in addition to both damaging their social standing within the larger community and deflecting attention from their health priorities. Bhopal (1997) has warned that failure to recognize the difficulties associated with research into ethnicity and health and inaction to rectify the conceptual and methodological weaknesses will allow the

20th-century health and ethnicity research to "suffer the same ignominious fate as that of race science in the 19th century" (p. 1751).

The status of "minority" studies, like an aching tooth in the jaw of cultural health research, needs replacement with a healthy, if not golden, tooth. An important call-for-action strategy is international consensus on the definition of cultural labels used in health research (e.g., race, ethnicity). Conceptual clarification of cultural variables is paramount to elucidating the culture–genetic–environment interplay in health. A second call-for-action strategy is promotion of cultural competence in health research. A third strategy is participation of diverse cultural groups in both theory-driven research in health and health policy development, implementation, and evaluation (see also Bhopal, 1997).

Unpackaged Approach

Bhopal (1997, p. 1752) argued that most research in health in which race and ethnicity are used for finding the cause of disease is "black box epidemiology," i.e., "epidemiology where the causal mechanism behind an association remains unknown and hidden ('black') but the inference is that the causal mechanism is within the association ('box')." Greenfield (1998) recommended the "unpackaged or decomposed" use of culture in health research. Cultural syndromes and acculturation processes and outcomes represent the unpackaged use of culture in health research. A study examining the relationship between individualism and cardiovascular heart disease in diverse cultural groups in Canada (e.g., Armenian Canadians versus English Canadians) is an example of an "unpackaged" intracultural health research. A study that compares the rate of cancer in two countries (Armenia, a collectivist culture, and the United States, an individualist culture) varying in degree of individualism represents an example of an "unpackaged" cross-cultural health research.

Cultural Syndromes

Triandis (1996) reviewed various definitions of culture and concluded that almost all researchers agree that culture consists of shared elements "that provide the standards for perceiving, believing, evaluating, communicating, and acting among those who share a language, a historic period, and a geographic location" (p. 408). Triandis (1996) also described two methodological approaches to the study of cultural differences: the cultural regions approach and the cultural syndromes approach. In the cultural regions approach, cultures are discriminated on a regional basis (e.g., geography, social structure). Methodologically, the cultural regions approach is similar to the medical geography approach (Ilola, 1990) in which the relationships between disease and the geographic features of environments, including latitude, rainfall, and temperature, are examined. In the medical geographic approach, such health status indicators as morbidity, mortality, and debility are mapped at various levels of scale using ethnographic field methods, household surveys, and clinic records in a particular region to infer relationships and causal links between cultural, political, economic, and institutional factors and health status (Ilola, 1990).

Cultural syndromes represent individual-level and culture-level dimensions or world views. In the cultural syndrome approach, psychological constructs are used to identify dimensions of cultural variation (Hofstede, 1980; Kim, Triandis, Kagitcibasi, Choi, & Yoon, 1994; Smith & Schwartz, 1998; Triandis, 1990, 1996). According to Triandis (1996), "cultural syndromes consist of shared attitudes, beliefs, norms, role and self definitions, and values of members of each culture that are organized around a theme" (p. 407). The dimension of cultural variation that has received considerable research attention and is of relevance to cultural health psychology is individualism and collectivism. The two terms "allocentrism" and idiocentrism" are also used to refer to the individual-level characteristics of collectivism and individualism, respectively.

Kagitcibasi (1998) has reviewed the literature on individualism/collectivism and has concluded that there have been numerous conceptualizations of the construct. Nevertheless, Triandis (1995) has identified four major attributes that define individualism/collectivism. The first attribute pertains to the meaning of the self (autonomous and independent in individualistic cultures and interdependent in collectivistic cultures). The second attribute pertains to the structure of goals (priority to in-group goals in collectivistic cultures and priority to personal goals in individualistic cultures). The third attribute pertains to behavior as a function of norms and attitudes (higher weighting of norms in collectivistic cultures and higher weighting on attitudes in individualistic cultures). The fourth attribute pertains to the focus on in-group needs or social exchanges (increased focus on communal relationships in collectivistic cultures and exchange relationships in individualistic cultures). Triandis (1995, 1996) has also suggested variations in collectivistic and individualistic cultures on the vertical (hierarchical) and horizontal (egalitarian) cultural dimension and has proposed a fourfold cultural pattern: Collectivistic–Vertical, Collectivistic–Horizontal, Individualistic–Vertical, and Individualistic–Horizontal (see Armstrong and Swartzman chapter for details). Finally, Triandis (1996) has described a variety of approaches to the measurement of cultural syndromes and their inferences with respect to cultural adaptation or acculturation. The methods described include the use of sentence-completion (e.g., I am . . .) and attitudinal items (e.g., I am a unique person, separate from others. Self-sacrifice is a virtue). More recently, Triandis, Chen, and Chan (1998) described a method that uses scenarios for the measurement of horizontal and vertical individualism and collectivism across cultures.

Individualism/collectivism has been studied in relation to a variety of psychological processes and behavioral outcomes. These include social perception and cognition, emotions, attributions, social interaction, self-serving bias, communication, and pace of life (Draguns, 1995; Kagitcibasi, 1998; Levine & Norenzayan, 1999; Segal, Lonner, & Berry, 1998). In addition to continued conceptual and methodological refinements (Niles, 1998; Singelis, Bond, Sharkey & Lai, 1999), the implications of the individualism/collectivism construct for health behavior and outcome is gaining increasing consideration. For example, there is evidence to suggest that smoking and cardiovascular heart disease are associated with economic vitality (productivity) and individualism, both factors influencing and being by-products of pace of life (Levine and Norenzayan, 1999). There is also evidence for a similar paradox of higher suicide and higher psychological well-being rates in individualistic cultures than in collectivistic cultures (cited in Levine and Norenzayan, 1999).

Acculturation

Culturally pluralistic societies consist of a variety of individuals or groups adapting to the host culture. People adapting to host cultures include those from ethnocultural groups, indigenous peoples, newcomers, and refugees (Berry & Sam, 1998). Two main factors influence the culture change strategies available to individuals or groups in a multicultural host society. The first factor is the acculturation orientation of the culturally diverse individual or group in the host culture. Berry (1990a) has defined individual or psychological acculturation as "the process by which individuals change, both by being influenced by contact with another culture and by being participants in the acculturative changes under way in their own culture" (p. 235). Berry and Sam (1998) have also defined acculturation strategy in terms of both attitudes toward four acculturation alternatives and actual behavioral manifestations of the four acculturation alternatives. The acculturation options are assimilation, integration, separation, and marginalization (Berry, 1990a, 1994, 1998, 1999). The acculturation strategies are derived on the basis of the simultaneous consideration (yes, no) of two fundamental questions: (1) Is it considered of value to maintain cultural identity and characteristics? (2) Is it considered of value to maintain relationships with the dominant society?

In assimilation, individuals relinquish their cultural heritage and identity and embrace the cultural identity of the country of settlement. Weizmann (1949) described the typical assimilationist Jewish physicians in Pinsk. The assimilationist physicians distinguished themselves by refusing to talk anything but Russian to their Jewish patients. The assimilationist physicians knew Yiddish as well as their patients, but considered "Russian bon ton—one could charge higher fees in Russian" (p. 28). Separation represents the opposite of assimilation by virtue of individuals maintaining their culture of origin and rejecting the culture of settlement. An individual who lives in England but feels Chinese, speaks only Chinese, and interacts only with Chinese represents the separation acculturation strategy. In integration, individuals embrace the cultural identity of the country of settlement without relinquishing the values, beliefs, and practices of the culture of origin. A person with an integration orientation is an individual who speaks the host culture language in addition to the language learned in the formative years, who participates in the economic, social, and political domains of the host culture, and who develops friendships with people from the host culture and the culture of origin. Finally, Marginalization represents loss and alienation experiences in which individuals reject both their own traditional culture and the culture of settlement. Misfit, psychological limbo, and anomie are additional descriptors for people who are marginalized.

The fourfold acculturation model has assumed a universalist perspective, i.e., acculturation processes are common to *host* and *culturally diverse* individuals or groups in multicultural societies (Berry, 1998; Berry & Sam, 1998), even though research thus far has focused primarily on "minority" cultures (Berry & Kim, 1987; Berry, Kim, Power, Young, & Bujaki, 1989; Dona & Berry, 1994; Sands & Berry, 1993). These studies have shown integration to be the preferred approach to adaptation in the host country and marginalization the least preferred. Berry and Sam (1998) have also concluded that research "strongly supports a positive correlation between the use of this strategy [integration] and good psychological adaptation during acculturation" (p. 298).

The value of the acculturation construct as conceptualized by Berry in health behavior has received considerable support. Berry (1998) reviewed a number of health studies in which the effects of psychological acculturation on disease patterns were investigated. Berry (1998) concluded that the health outcome of psychological acculturation was highly *variable,* ranging from personal growth to acculturative stress and ill health. Acculturative stress refers to "a reduction in health status (including psychological, somatic and social aspects) of individuals who are undergoing acculturation, and for which there is evidence that these health phenomena are related systematically to acculturation phenomena" (Berry, Kim, Minde & Mok, 1987, p. 491). Berry et al. (1987) and Berry (1990b) have reported that those with the integration mode of acculturation show lower levels of acculturative stress than those with the marginalization and separation strategies; those with the assimilation strategy show intermediate levels of acculturative stress.

The second factor that influences individual or group adaptation to host culture is the acculturation orientation of the *host culture* with respect to individuals or groups from the diverse cultures (Berry, 1998; Bourhis et al., 1997; Kazarian, 1997a). Bourhis et al. (1997) proposed that the acculturation orientation of the host culture can take the form of integration, assimilation, segregation, and exclusion. A host culture with an assimilation orientation is a melting-pot culture. Melting-pot dictates a "uniculturalization" adaptation process in which the dominant host community expects all citizens to relinquish their heritage culture and adopt the culture of the mainstream group. A host culture with an integration orientation allows a "biculturalization" process in which a person is encouraged to identify with the mainstream host culture without having to relinquish heritage culture and language. A host culture with a segregation orientation dictates an adaptation process in which the host culture distances itself from individuals or groups from diverse cultures and disallows influence from those individuals or groups on host culture. The forced creation of Indian reserves or cultural ghettos represents a segregationist orientation of host culture. Finally, a host culture with an exclusion orientation refuses to allow individuals or groups from diverse cultures to adopt mainstream culture and values. Such a culture also denies individuals or groups from diverse cultures the freedom to maintain their cultural heritage.

When host-society acculturation orientations and individual or group acculturation orientations are considered together, two orientation profiles (concordant and discordant) and three relational outcomes (consensual, problematic, and conflictual) emerge (Bourhis et al., 1997). A concordant profile represents a match between the acculturation orientation of the host culture and that of the individual or group. A discordant profile, on the other hand, represents a mismatch (very little or no match at all). Concordant profiles yield positive (consensual) relational outcomes whereas discordant profiles yield negative (problematic or conflictual) relational outcomes. For example, a host culture with an integration orientation and a newcomer with an integration orientation represent a concordant acculturation profile and a positive (consensual) relational outcome. On the other hand, a newcomer with an integration adaptation orientation and a host culture with an assimilation orientation represent a discordant profile and yield a negative (conflictual) relational outcome.

Bourhis et al. (1997) describe several relational outcome indicators at the social psychological level. These include patterns of intercultural interaction between members of the host culture and those from diverse cultures, intercultural attitudes (stereotypes, racism, and discriminatory behavior), and acculturative stress.

To date, the interactive effects of the individual acculturation orientation and the host culture acculturation orientation on health behavior have not been the subject of intense investigation. Most, if not all, research on adaptation and health (acculturative stress) has focused on the acculturation orientation of the individual rather than the individual acculturation orientation in the host culture acculturation orientation context. Berry (1994) has speculated that *the cultural orientation of the host society* may account for the high variability in individual acculturative experiences and health outcomes. Berry (1992, 1998) reported that acculturative stress is lower in those with functional social support systems (i.e., those receiving assistance from an ethnic community during the settlement process) and "when tolerance for diversity and ethnic attitudes in the larger society are positive."

The psychological acculturation model of Berry (1998) and the host community acculturation orientation model of Bourhis et al. (1997) have important implications for understanding health care systems generally and identifying psychological processes and outcomes associated with health care system restructuring. Kazarian (1996) has described the combined acculturation orientation profiles of two culturally distinct institutions (achievement-oriented institutional culture versus affiliation-oriented institutional culture) facing the challenge of an organizational merger and their relational outcome (successful merger versus interhospital rivalry and resistance).

The acculturation models also have important implications for the health behavior of health consumers and health professionals. A health acculturation model considers the health acculturation orientation of health *consumers* and the health acculturation orientation of health *professionals*. In relation to the health acculturation orientation of health consumers, it can be assumed consumers of health confront two central health-related issues: maintenance of the cultural health beliefs and practices of their heritage culture (i.e., is it considered of value to maintain cultural health beliefs and practices?) and adoption of the health beliefs and practices of the host society (i.e., is it considered of value to adopt the health beliefs and practices of the host society?). As in psychological acculturation (Berry, 1998), simultaneous consideration of the two health-related issues in the host society allows four individual strategies or options for health consumers: health assimilation, health integration, health separation, and health individualism. The health assimilation strategy dictates adoption of host culture (e.g., Western) health beliefs and practices and abandonment of culture-of-origin health beliefs and practices. The health integration option allows maintenance of heritage culture health beliefs and practices and adoption of host-culture health beliefs and practices. The health separation strategy dictates maintenance of culture-of-origin health beliefs and practices and rejection of host-culture health beliefs and practices. Finally, the health individualism option represents idiosyncratic health beliefs and practices, i.e., those that are reflective of neither culture-of-origin beliefs and practices nor host culture beliefs and practices.

In a similar vein, health professionals confront two central health-related issues. The first relates to decisions whether beliefs and practices associated with the culture of origin of consumers are of value and should be supported by health professionals (is it considered of value that the health beliefs and practices of the culture of origin are maintained?). The second central health-related issue pertains to decisions respecting the value of supporting adoption of host-culture beliefs and practices by cultural groups and their individual members (is it considered of value that the health beliefs and practices of the host-society are adopted by cultural groups and their members?). Simultaneous consideration of the two health-related issues in a multicultural host society allows four individual strategies or options for health professionals: health assimilation, health integration, health segregation, and health exclusion. In health assimilation, health professionals expect individuals to relinquish their culture-of-origin health beliefs and practices and adopt those of the host culture. In health integration, health professionals accept and value the maintenance of culture-of-origin health beliefs and practices and adoption of the host-culture health beliefs and practices. In health segregation, health professionals distance themselves from individuals from diverse cultures but accept their efforts to maintain their heritage culture health beliefs and practices. In health exclusion, health professionals reject the health beliefs and practices of cultural groups and their members and disallow adoption of host-culture health beliefs and practices. Exclusionist health professionals deny diverse cultures their right to cultural heritage health beliefs and practices. They believe that "foreigners" lack the capacity to integrate to host culture and consider deportation a viable solution to the problem.

It is not difficult to surmise from the proposed health acculturation model that the health acculturation orientation profiles of health consumers (service recipients) and those of health professionals (service providers) are either concordant or discordant and that the relational outcomes between the two parties are either positive (consensual) or negative (problematic or conflictual). As depicted in Table 1.5, a concordant health acculturation profile entails a health consumer and a health professional with integrative health acculturation orientations. The resultant health relational outcome is consensual in that both parties have an understanding and acceptance of the value of host culture and heritage culture beliefs and practices in disease intervention or prevention. A discordant health acculturation profile, on the other hand, is seen in a health professional with an assimilationist health acculturation orientation and a health consumer with an integrational health acculturation orientation. More specifically, a health professional who discounts the value of "alternative medicine" is likely to be infuriated and rejecting of a patient who is adhering to the prescribed treatment but also undergoing various "alternative" therapies that in the opinion of the health professional have no scientific basis or are nothing more than quackery.

Needless to say, the proposed health acculturation model is an extension of Berry's (1998) and Bourhis et al.'s (1997) models to the field of multicultural health. The model's benefit to health science and health practice needs to be evaluated and its premises empirically scrutinized. At the very basic level, the model suggests consideration of the development of assessment strategies and tools specific to health acculturation orientations. Profiling the health acculturation orientations of health consumers and health professionals may be highly useful for positive relational outcomes in health.

Cultural Competence Imperative

The cultural competence imperative entails academic and professional preparation in cultural health psychology inclusive of the professional standards and code of ethics. Failure to provide the academic knowledge base to health scientists and practitioners and negligence in supporting their continuing education

TABLE 1.5   Health Acculturation Model: Relational Outcomes of Health Consumer and Health Professional Acculturation Orientations

	Health Consumer			
Health Professional	*Integration*	*Assimilation*	*Separation*	*Individualism*
Integration	Consensual	Problematic	Conflictual	Problematic
Assimilation	Problematic	Consensual	Conflictual	Problematic
Segregation	Conflictual	Conflictual	Conflictual	Conflictual
Exclusion	Conflictual	Conflictual	Conflictual	Conflictual

endeavors toward cultural competence have negative professional, ethical, and legal consequences to individual professionals and their profession.

Competence in cultural health psychology requires consideration of culture in health promotion and maintenance; prevention, treatment, and rehabilitation; advancement of etiological theories of illness; and health care system analysis and formulation. Both the American Psychological Association (APA) and the Canadian Psychological Association (CPA) standards, guidelines of practice, and accreditation standards support the principle of cultural sensitivity and competence (APA, 1985, 1992, 1993; CPA, 1991, 1994, 1996; Kazarian, 1997b; Kazarian & Evans, 1998). For example, the APA standards require psychologists to ensure cultural competence in service provision (e.g., training, experience, supervision). They also require psychologists to respect the rights of those who hold values, attitudes, and opinions different from their own and to refrain from "unfair discrimination." Similarly, APA and CPA accreditation standards stipulate consideration of cultural issues in the training of students (APA Committee on Accreditation, 1991; CPA, 1994).

Nevertheless, the 1992 APA standards have been subjected to trenchant criticism (Dana, 1998) from the perspectives of cultural research and cultural malpractice (Bersoff, 1994; Payton, 1994; Gil & Bob, 1999). A major criticism is APA's shift from a "social responsibility" value orientation to a "scientific knowledge base" value system. Dana (1998) expressed that the 1992 APA Ethics Code is "a device protecting providers by limiting professional accountability, eschewing external monitoring, and forsaking an historic humanity" (p. 291). Social responsibility as an overriding value in health is consistent with the recent call for action of The Writing Group for the Consortium for Health and Human Rights (1998). The Writing Group has asked all health professionals to "explore the connections between health and human rights by examining the Universal Declaration of Human Rights and declarations, conventions, and laws that it helped generate" (p. 462).

Even though cultural competence from the perspectives of practice, research, and ethics is a prerequisite to a socially responsive health care in a culturally pluralistic context, the concept has entered into the vocabulary of health professionals, generally, and health psychologists, particularly, only recently. On the other hand, discussion on cultural competence in mental health has progressed to the point that general and domain-specific (provider, agency, policy, and consumers) definitions have been proposed (Abe-Kim & Takeuchi, 1996; Hall, 1997; Dana, 1998; Gil & Bob, 1999). It is understood that cultural competence represents a level above and beyond cultural sensitivity. Needless to say, definitional activities within mental health would be of considerable value to definitional consensus-building in health, generally, and the psychology of health, particularly.

At the basic level, cultural competence in health psychology requires recognition of the core role culture assumes in shaping the attitudes (cognition, affect, and behavior) of health professionals and the science and practice of health. Cultural competence can be enhanced by the knowledge base provided by cultural health psychology and cross-cultural training (Brislin & Yoshida, 1994; Singelis, 1998; Brislin & Horvath, 1998; Evans, Hearn, Uhlemann, & Ivey, 1998). Brislin and Horvath (1998) have conceptualized cross-cultural training in terms of four components: awareness of culture, knowledge of other culture, coping with the other culture, and culturally appropriate behavior. Consistent with the several psychology codes of ethics and practice, awareness of culture entails in-depth understanding of one's own culture and its influence on one's thinking, feelings, and actions. Whereas knowledge of one's own culture is a prerequisite to understanding other cultures, the second component of cross-cultural training, knowledge of other cultures, entails awareness of the values, beliefs, norms, and behaviors of individuals from cultures other than one's own. Awareness of other cultures provides for culturally accurate and appropriate cognitions, attributions, and emotional reactions with respect to the cultural practices and cultural interpretations of individuals within a single culturally pluralistic context. Coping with other cultures entails development of an awareness of negative feelings toward people from different cultures and approaches to their adaptive resolution, as well as assumption of tolerance and nonjudgmental attitudes toward the culturally different. The fourth and final component of cross-cultural training, culturally appropriate behaviors, entails supplementing cultural knowledge and understanding with engagement in culturally meaningful behaviors. Culturally appropriate behaviors relate to verbal and written communications, nonverbal communications, and cultural protocol at the individual and health care system levels.

SUMMARY

Western health care systems and institutions have been monoculturalistic or culture-blind in their approach to health practice. They have also fostered a health science that is ethnic and racial in its focus. While health psychologists in Europe and North America have made significant contributions to a holistic approach to understanding the etiology of disease, identifying the determinants of health, and promoting health initiatives, they have lagged in integrating culture in their approach to the psychology of health. The integration of the cultural perspective into health psychology is an imperative. Nourishment of cultural models of health and a culturally sound structure and process in the science and practice of health psychology allows a socially responsible and ethically sound vision for the alleviation of suffering and the promotion of psychological well-being.

CASE STUDY

Heraldo is a 12-year-old Hispanic boy. He was hospitalized because of the acute onset of psychotic symptoms, including auditory hallucinations.

Dr. White sought permission from Mrs. Lopez, Heraldo's grandmother and legal guardian, to treat his psychotic symptoms with psychotropic medication. However, Mrs. Lopez refused to give Dr. White permission to medicate Heraldo. Mrs. Lopez believed that her grandson was possessed by the devil and, as a respected *bruja* in her community, she insisted that she perform exorcism on him (which she was well qualified to do) to expel the devil out of him. The health care staff and Mrs. Lopez resolved their impasse by reaching a "multicultural" agreement: Mrs. Lopez would perform the exorcism in the hospital and then sign a consent form for medication treatment for her grandson. When Heraldo himself showed reluctance to take medication, Mrs. Lopez assisted the health care professionals by offering to bless the medication tray in a ritual Heraldo could witness. Heraldo's condition improved to the satisfaction of Mrs. Lopez and the health professionals involved in his care. This description is based on Chachkes and Christ (1996).

1. What were the relational outcomes of the health acculturation orientations of the health care staff, Mrs. Lopez, and Heraldo?
2. Would the American solution of a court order to override Mrs. Lopez's objections have ensured a positive outcome (i.e., medication compliance)?
3. Is liability for health care professionals increased when "multicultural" solutions are implemented, as in Heraldo's case?

SUGGESTED READINGS

Dana, R. H. (1998). *Understanding cultural identity in intervention and assessment.* Thousand Oaks, CA: Sage.

Kato, P. M., & Mann, T. (Eds.). (1996). *Handbook of diversity issues in health psychology.* New York: Plenum.

Kazarian, S. S., & Evans, D. R. (1998). *Cultural clinical psychology: Theory, research and practice.* New York: Oxford University Press.

MacLachlan, M. (1997). *Culture and health.* Chichester, UK: Wiley.

Pederson, P. B., Draguns, J. G., Lonner, W. J., & Trimble, J. E. (Eds.). (1996). *Counselling across cultures* (4th ed.). Thousand Oaks, CA: Sage.

Ponterotto, J. G., & Casas, J. M. (1999). *Handbook of racial/ethnic minority counseling research.* Springfield, IL: Charles C. Thomas.

Singelis, T. M. (Ed.). (1998). *Teaching about culture, ethnicity and diversity: Exercises and planned activities.* Thousand Oaks, CA: Sage.

REFERENCES

Abe-Kim, J., & Takeuchi, D. T. (1996). Cultural competence and quality of care: Issues for mental health service delivery in managed care. *Clinical Psychology: Science and Practice, 3,* 273–295.

Ahdieh, L., & Hahn, R. A. (1996). Use of the terms 'race', 'ethnicity', and 'national origins': A review of articles in the American Journal of Public Health, 1980–1989. *Ethnicity and Health, 1,* 95–98.

Airhihenbuwa, C. O. (1995). *Health and culture: Beyond the Western paradigm.* Thousand Oaks, CA: Sage.

Alexander, F. (1950). *Psychosomatic medicine.* New York: Norton.

American Psychological Association (1985). *Standards for educational and psychological testing.* Washington, DC: Author.

American Psychological Association (1992). Ethical principles of psychologists and code of conduct. *American Psychologist, 47,* 1597–1611.

American Psychological Association (1993). Guidelines for providers of psychological services to ethnic, linguistic, and culturally diverse populations. *American Psychologist, 48,* 45–48.

American Psychological Association Committee on Accreditation (Summer, 1991). The nature, scope and implementation of Criterion II: Cultural and individual differences. *Capsule* (pp. 1–5).

Anderson, N. B. (1995). Summary of task group research recommendations. *Health Psychology, 14,* 649–635.

Anderson, N. B., & Jackson, J. S. (1987). Race, ethnicity, and health: The example of essential hypertension. In G. C. Stone, S. M. Weiss, J. D. Matarazzo, N. E. Miller, J. Rodin, C. D. Belar, M. J. Follick, & J. E. Singer (Eds.), *Health psychology: A discipline and a profession* (pp. 265–284). Chicago: University of Chicago Press.

Belar, C. D. (1998). Clinical health psychology: A specialty for the 21st century. *Health Psychology, 18,* 411–416.

Belar, C. D., & Deardoff, W. W. (1995). *Clinical health psychology in medical settings: A practitioner's guidebook.* Hyattsville, MD: American Psychological Association.

Belar, C. D., & Siegel, L. J. (1983). A survey of postdoctoral training programs in health psychology. *Health Psychology, 2,* 413–425.

Belar, C. D., Wilson, E., & Hughes, H. (1982). Health psychology training in doctoral psychology programs. *Health Psychology, 1,* 289–299.

Berry, J. W. (1990a). Psychology of acculturation: Understanding individuals moving between cultures. In R. W. Brislin (Ed.), *Applied cross-cultural psychology* (pp. 232–252). Newbury Park, CA: Sage.

Berry, J. W. (1990b). The role of psychology in ethnic studies. *Canadian Ethnic Studies, 23,* 7–21.

Berry, J. W. (1992). Acculturation and adaptation in a new society. *International Migration, 30,* 69–85.

Berry, J. W. (1994). Cross-cultural health psychology. *Canadian Journal of Health Psychology, 2,* 37–41.

Berry, J. W. (1998). Acculturation and health: Theory and research. In S. S. Kazarian & D. R. Evans (Eds.). *Cultural clinical psychology: Theory, research and practice* (pp. 39–57). New York: Oxford University Press.

Berry, J. W. (1999). Intercultural relations in plural societies. *Canadian Psychology, 40,* 12–21.

Berry, J. W., & Kim, U. (1987). Comparative studies of acculturative stress. *International Migration Review, 21,* 491–511.

Berry, J. W., & Sam, D. (1998). Acculturation and adaptation. In J. W. Berry, M. H. Segall, & C. Kagitcibasi (Eds.), *Handbook of cross-cultural psychology: Vol. 3* (pp. 291–326). Needham Heights, MA: Allyn & Bacon.

Berry, J. W., Kim, U., Minde, T., & Mok, D. (1987). Comparative studies of acculturative stress. *International Migration Review, 21,* 491–511.

Berry, J. W., Kim, U., Power, S., Young, M., & Bujaki, M. (1989). Acculturation attitudes in plural societies. *Applied Psychology: An International Review, 38,* 185–206.

Bersoff, D. N. (1994). Explicit ambiguity: The 1992 ethics code as an oxymoron. *Professional Psychology: Research and Practice, 25,* 382–387.

Bhopal, R. (1997). Is research into ethnicity and health racist, unsound, or important science? *British Medical Journal, 31,* 1751–1756.

Bhopal, R., & Donaldson, L. (1998). White, European, western, Caucasian, or what? Inappropriate labelling in research on race, ethnicity, and health. *American Journal of Public Health, 88,* 1303–1307.

Bishop, G. D. (1994). *Health psychology: Integrating mind and body.* Needham Heights, MA: Allyn & Bacon.

Bourhis, R. Y., Moise, L. C., Perreault, S., & Senecal, S. (1997). Towards an interactive acculturation model: A social psychological approach. *International Journal of Psychology, 32,* 369–386.

Brislin, R. W., & Yoshida, J. (Eds.) (1994). *Improving intercultural interactions: Modules for cross-cultural training programs.* Thousand Oaks, CA: Sage.

Brislin, R., & Horvath, A. M. (1998). Cross-cultural training and multicultural education. In J. W. Berry, M. H. Segall, & C. Kagitcibasi (Eds.), *Handbook of cross-cultural psychology, Vol. 3* (pp. 327–370). Needham Heights, MA: Allyn & Bacon.

Canadian Multiculturalism Act (1988). SC 1988, c.31; RSC 1985, c. 24 (4th Supp.).

Canadian Psychological Association (1991). *Canadian code of ethics for psychologists, 1991.* Ottawa: Author.

Canadian Psychological Association (1994). *Accreditation criteria for professional psychology programs and internships and accreditation procedures.* Ottawa: Author.

Canadian Psychological Association (1996). *Guidelines for non-discriminatory practice.* Ottawa: Author.

Carmody, T. P., & Matarazzo, J. D. (1991). Health psychology. In M. Hersen, A. E. Kazdin, & A. S. Bellack (Eds.), *The clinical psychology handbook* (2nd ed., pp. 695–723). New York: Pergamon.

Chachkes, E., & Christ, G. (1996). Cross cultural issues in patient education. *Patient Education and Counselling, 27,* 13–21.

Dahlgren, G., & Whitehead, M. (1991). *Policies and strategies to promote equity in health.* Stockholm: Institute of Future Studies.

Dana, R. H. (1998). Problems with managed care mental health care for multicultural populations. *Psychological Reports, 83,* 283–294.

Dasen, P. R., Berry, J. W., & Sartorius, N. (Eds.). (1988). *Health and cross-cultural psychology: Toward applications.* Newberry, CA: Sage.

Denboba, D. L., Bragdon, J. L., Epstein, L. G., Garthright, K., & Goldman, T. M. (1998). Reducing health disparities through cultural competence. *Journal of Health Education, 29,* S47–S53.

Dickason, O. P. (1992). *Canada's first nations: A history of founding peoples from earliest times.* Toronto: McClelland & Stewart.

Dona, G., & Berry, J. W. (1994). Acculturation attitudes and acculturative stress of Central American refugees. *International Journal of Psychology, 29,* 57–70.

Donovan, J. L. (1984). Ethnicity and health: A research review. *Social Science and Medicine, 19,* 663–670.

Downie, R., Fyfe, C., & Tannahill, A. (1990). *Health promotion: Models and values.* New York: Oxford Univ. Press.

Draguns, J. G. (1995). Cultural influences upon psychopathology: Clinical and practical implications. *Journal of Social Distress and the Homeless, 4,* 79–103.

Dubos, R. (1960). *Mirage of health.* London, UK: George Allen & Irwin.

Ekstrom, R. D. (1997). Compliments to Fowers and Richardson. *American Psychologist, 52,* 658.

Ellison, G. T., & de Wet, T. (1997). The use of "racial" categories in contemporary South African health research: A survey of articles published in the South African medical journal between 1992 and 1996. *South African Medical Journal, 87,* 1671–1679.

Engel, G. L. (1977). The need for a new medical model: A challenge for biomedicine. *Science, 196,* 129–136.

Evans, D. R. (1994). Enhancing quality of life in the population at large. *Social Indicators Research, 33,* 47–88.

Evans, D. R. (1997). Health promotion, wellness programs and quality of life. *Canadian Psychology, 38,* 1–12.

Evans, D. R., Hearn, M. T., Uhlemann, M. R., & Ivey, A. E. (1998). *Essential interviewing: A programmed approach to effective communication.* Pacific Grove, CA: Brooks/Cole.

Federal, Provincial, and Territorial Advisory Committee on Population Health (1996). *Report on the health of Canadians.* Ottawa: Minister of Supply and Services.

Feuerstein, M., Labbe, E. E., & Kuczmierczyk, A. R. (1986). *Health psychology: A psychobiological perspective*. New York: Plenum.

Fowers, B. J., & Richardson, F. C. (1996). Why is multiculturalism good? *American Psychologist, 51*, 609–621.

Fowers, B. J., & Richardson, F. C. (1997). A second invitation to dialogue: Multiculturalism and psychology. *American Psychologist, 52,* 659–661.

Garman, S. (1996). Social models of health and illness. In V. Aitken & H. Jellicoe (Eds.), *Behavioral sciences for health professionals* (pp. 71–79). London, UK: W.B. Saunders.

Gatchel, R. J., & Baum, A. (1983). *An introduction to health psychology*. Reading, MA: Addison-Wesley.

Gaubatz, M. (1997). Subtle ethnocentrism in the hermeneutic circle. *American Psychologist, 52,* 657–658.

Gentry, W. D., Street, W. J., Masur, F. T., & Askin, M. J. (1981). Training in medical psychology: A survey of graduate and internship training programs. *Professional Psychology, 12,* 224–228.

Gil, E. F., & Bob, S. (1999). Culturally competent research: An ethical perspective. *Clinical Psychology Review, 19,* 45–55.

Greenfield, P. M. (1998). Culture as process: Empirical methods for cultural psychology. In J. W. Berry, Y. H. Poortinga, & J. Pandey (Eds.), *Handbook of cross-cultural psychology, Vol. 1* (pp. 301–346). Needham Heights, MA: Allyn & Bacon.

Hall, C. C. I. (1997). Cultural malpractice: The growing obsolescence of psychology with the changing U.S. population. *American Psychologist, 52,* 642–651.

Health and Welfare Canada (1986). *Achieving health for all*. Ottawa: Government of Canada.

Health and Welfare Canada (1988). *Mental health for Canadians*. Ottawa: Government of Canada.

Health and Welfare Canada (1993). *Planning for health: Toward informed decision-making*. Ottawa: Government of Canada.

Hearn, M. T., & Evans, D. R. (1993). Applications of psychology to health care. In K. Dobson & D. Dobson (Eds.), *Professional psychology in Canada* (pp. 247–284). Toronto: Hogrefe & Huber.

Helman, C. (1984). *Culture, health and illness*. Bristol: John Wright PSG Inc.

Helman, C. G. (1995). *Culture, health and illness: An introduction for health professionals* (3rd ed.). Oxford, UK: Butterworth-Heinemann.

Helyar, C., Flett, J., Hundert, M., Fallon, G., & Crawford, R. (1998). Benchmarking comparisons of the efficiency and quality of care of Canadian teaching hospitals. *Hospital Quarterly, 1,* 14–25.

Henderson, G., & Springer-Littles, D. (1996). *A practitioner's guide to understanding indigenous and foreign cultures: An analysis of relationships between ethnicity, social class, and therapeutic intervention strategies*. Springfield, IL: Charles Thomas.

Hofstede, G. (1980). *Culture's consequences*. Beverly Hills, CA: Sage.

IIola, L. M. (1990). Culture and health. In R. W. Brislin (Ed.), *Applied cross-cultural psychology* (pp. 278–301). Newbury Park, CA: Sage.

Joint Task Force. (1993). *Moving forward: Strengthening health planning in Ontario*. Toronto: Association of District Health Councils and Ministry of Health.

Kagitcibasi, C. (1998). Individualism and collectivism. In J. W. Berry, M. H. Segall, & C. Kagitcibasi (Eds.), *Handbook of cross-cultural psychology, Vol. 3* (pp. 2–49). Needham Heights, MA: Allyn & Bacon.

Kato, P. M., & Mann, T. (Eds.). (1996). *Handbook of diversity issues in health psychology*. New York: Plenum Press.

Kazarian, S. S. (1996). Cultural encounters of the third kind. *Prism, 1,* 17.

Kazarian, S. S. (1997a). The Armenian psyche: Genocide and acculturation. *Mentalities, 12,* 74–87.

Kazarian, S. S. (1997b). Assessment and treatment of adults and children. In D. R. Evans (Ed.) *Law, standards of professional conduct and ethics in the practice of psychology* (pp. 173–200). Toronto, Canada: Emond Montgomery.

Kazarian, S. S. (1998). *Diversity issues in policing*. Toronto: Emond and Montgomery.

Kazarian, S. S., & Evans, D. R. (Eds.) (1998). *Cultural clinical psychology: Theory, research and practice*. New York: Oxford University Press.

Kazarian, S. S., McCabe, S. B., & Joseph, L. W. (1997). Assessment of service needs of adult psychiatric inpatients: A systematic approach. *Psychiatric Quarterly, 68,* 5–23.

Keitel, M. A., Kopala, M., & Georgiades, I. (1995). *Multicultural health counselling.* Thousand Oaks, CA: Sage.

Kim, U., Triandis, H. C., Kagitcibasi, G., Choi, S. G., & Yoon, G. (Eds.). (1994). *Individualism and collectivism: Theory, methods and application.* Thousand Oaks, CA: Sage.

Kleinman, A. (1980). *Patients and healers in the context of culture.* Berkeley, CA: University of California Press.

Kleinman, A., Eisenberg, L., & Good, B. (1978). Culture, illness and care: Clinical lessons from anthropological and cross-cultural research. *Annals of Internal Medicine, 88,* 251–258.

Krantz, D. S. (1995). Editorial: Health psychology: 1995–1999. *Health Psychology, 14,* 3.

Lalonde, M. (1974). *A new perspective on the health of Canadians.* Ottawa: Government of Canada.

Landrine, H. (1996). Culture and the lathe of failure. *Health Psychology, 1,* 143–144.

Landrine, H., & Klonoff, E. A. (1992). Culture and health-related schemes: a review and proposal for interdisciplinary integration. *Health Psychology, 11,* 267–276.

Lathrop, J. P. (1991, July/August). The patient-focussed hospital. *Health Care Forum Journal,* 17–20.

Levine, R. B., & Norenzayan, A. (1999). The pace of life in 31 countries. *Journal of Cross-Cultural Psychology, 30,* 178–205.

Lipowski, Z. J. (1977). Psychosomatic medicine in the seventies: An overview. *American Journal of Psychiatry, 134,* 233–243.

MacLachlan, M. (1997). *Culture and health.* Chichester, UK: Wiley.

Mang, A. L. (1995). Implementation strategies of patient-focussed care. *Hospital and Health Services Administration, 40,* 427–435.

Marks, D. F. (1996). Health psychology in context. *Journal of Health Psychology, 1,* 7–21.

Marks, D. F., Brucher-Albers, C., Donker, F. J. S., Jepsen, Z., Rodriguez-Marin, J., Sidot, S., & Backman, B. W. (1998). Health psychology 2000: Development of professional health psychology–European Federation of Professional Psychologists' Association (EFPPA) Task Force on Health Psychology Final Report. *Journal of Health Psychology, 3,* 149–160.

Marmor, T. R. (1994). *Understanding health care reform.* New Haven, CT: Yale Univ. Press.

Masi, R., Mensah, L., & McLeod, K. A. (1993) (Eds.). *Health and cultures: Exploring the relationships, Vol. I & II* Oakville, ON: Mosaic Press.

Matarazzo, J. D. (1980). Behavioral health and behavioral medicine: Frontiers for a new health psychology. *American Psychologist, 35,* 807–817.

Matarazzo, J. D. (1983). Education and training in health psychology: Boulder or bolder. *Health Psychology, 2,* 73–113.

Matheson, G. (1983). Health psychology: An opportunity, a responsibility. *The Ontario Psychologist, 15,* 4–10.

McKeown, T. (1979). *The role of medicine: Dream, mirage or nemesis.* Oxford, UK: Basil Blackwell.

McMahon, C. E., & Halstrup, J. L. (1980). The role of imagination in the disease process: Post-Cartesian history. *Journal of Behavioral Medicine, 3,* 205–217.

Mueller, K. J. (1993). *Health care policy in the United States.* Lincoln, NE: University of Nebraska Press.

Niles, F. S. (1998). Individualism–Collectivism revisited. *Cross-Cultural Research, 32,* 315–341.

Olbrisch, M. E., Weiss, S. M., Stone, G. C., & Schwartz, G. E. (1985). Report of the National Working Conference on Education and Training in Health Psychology. *American Psychologist, 40,* 1038–1041.

Ontario Ministry of Health (1991). *Guidelines to promote cultural/racial sensitivity and awareness in health care programs and services.* Toronto: Author.

Ontario Ministry of Health (1993). *Time for change: Immigrant, refugee and racial/minority women and health care needs.* Toronto: Queens Printer for Ontario.

Patterson, C. H. (1985). *The therapeutic relationship: Foundations for an eclectic psychotherapy.* Monterey, CA: Brooks/Cole.

Pauwels, A. (1995). *Cross-cultural communication in health sciences: Communicating with migrant patients.* South Melbourne, Australia: MacMillan Education Australia Pty Ltd.

Payton, C. R. (1994). Implications of the 1992 ethics code for diverse groups. *Professional Psychology: Research and Practice, 25,* 317–320.

Phinney, J. S. (1996). When we talk about American ethnic groups, what do we mean? *American Psychologist, 51,* 918–927.

Pitts, M. (1996). *The psychology of preventive health.* London, UK: Routledge.

Pomerleau, O. F., & Brady, J. P. (Eds.). (1979). *Behavioral medicine: Theory and practice.* Baltimore, MD: Williams & Wilkins.

Premier's Council on Health, Well-being and Social Justice (1994). *Health for all Ontarians.* Toronto: Queens Printer for Ontario.

Read, M. (1966). *Culture, health and disease.* London, UK: J. B. Lippincott Company.

Reynolds, F. (1996). Models of health and illness. In V. Aitken & H. Jellicoe (Eds.), *Behavioral sciences for health professionals* (pp. 3–21). London, UK: W. B. Saunders Company.

Sadler, J. Z., & Hulgus, Y. F. (1990). Knowing, valuing, acting: Clues to revising the biopsychosocial model. *Comprehensive Psychiatry, 31,* 185–195.

Saeki, C., & Borow, H. (1985). Counselling and psychotherapy: East and West. In P. Pederson (Ed.), *Handbook of cross-cultural counselling and therapy* (pp. 301–327). Westport, CT: Greenwood Press.

Sands, E. A., & Berry, J. W. (1993). Acculturation and mental health among Greek-Canadians in Toronto. *Canadian Journal of Community Mental Health, 12,* 117–124.

Sarafino, E. P. (1998). *Health psychology: Biopsychosocial interactions.* New York: John Wiley & Sons.

Schofield, W. (1969). The role of psychology in the delivery of health service. *American Psychologist, 24,* 565–584.

Schroder, H., Rescheke, K., Johnston, M., & Maes, S. (1993). *Health psychology: Potential in diversity.* Regensburg, Germany: S. Roderer Verlag.

Segal, M. H., Lonner, W. J., & Berry, J. W. (1998). Cross-cultural psychology as a scholarly discipline: On the flowering of culture in behavioral research. *American Psychologist, 53,* 1101–1110.

Sheridan, E. P., Matarazzo, J. D., Boll, T. J ., Perry, N. W., Weiss, S. M., & Belar, C. D. (1988). Postdoctoral education and training for clinical service providers in health psychology. *Health Psychology, 7,* 1–17.

Shiang, J., Kjellander, C., Huang, K., & Bogumill, S. (1998). Developing cultural competency in clinical practice: Treatment considerations for Chinese cultural groups in the United States. *Clinical Psychology: Science and Practice, 5,* 182–210.

Singelis, T. M. (1998). *Teaching about culture, ethnicity, and diversity: Exercises and planned activities.* Thousand Oaks, CA: Sage.

Singelis, T. M., Bond, M. H., Sharkey, W. F., & Lai, C. S. Y. (1999). Unpackaging culture's influence on self-esteem and embarrassability: The role of self-construals. *Journal of Cross-Cultural Psychology, 30,* 315–341.

Smith, P. B., & Schwartz, S. H. (1998). Values. In J. W. Berry, M. H. Segall, & C. Kagitcibasi (Eds.), *Handbook of cross-cultural psychology, Vol. 3* (pp. 77–118). Needham Heights, MA: Allyn & Bacon.

Statistics Canada (1994). http://www.statcan.ca/

Steptoe, A., & Wardle, J. (Eds.) (1994). *Psychosocial processes and health: A reader.* Cambridge, UK: Cambridge University Press.

Stone, G. C. (1982). Health psychology, a new journal for a new field. *Health Psychology, 1,* 1–6.

Stone, G. C. (Ed.) (1983). National training conference on education and training in health psychology: Proceedings. *Health Psychology, 2,* whole #5 (Supplement).

Stone, G. C. (1984). A final word–Editorial. *Health Psychology, 3,* 585–589.

Stone, G. C., Weiss, S. M., Matarazzo, J. D., Miller, N. E., Rodin, J., Belar, C. D., Follick, M. J., & Singer, J. E. (Eds.) (1987). *Health psychology: A discipline and a profession.* Chicago: University of Chicago Press.

Taylor, S. E. (1987). The progress and prospects of health psychology: Tasks of a maturing discipline. *Health Psychology, 6,* 73–87.

Taylor, S. E. (1999). *Health psychology.* New York: McGraw-Hill.

Teo, T., & Febbraro, A. R. (1997). Norm, factuality, and power in multiculturalism. *American Psychologist, 52,* 656–657.

Tepper, E. L. (1994). Immigration policy and multiculturalism. In J. W. Berry & J. A. Laponce (Eds.), *Ethnicity and culture in Canada (pp. 95–123).* Toronto: University of Toronto Press.

The Atkinson Letter (December 1, 1996). Can Medicare be "saved"? *The Toronto Star,* F6.

The Writing Group for the Consortium for Health and Human Rights (1998). Health and human rights: A call to action on the 50th anniversary of the Universal declaration of human rights. *Journal of the Medical Association, 280,* 462–464.

Toukmanian, S., & Brouwers, M. (1998). Cultural aspects of self-disclosure and psychotherapy. In S. S. Kazarian & D. R. Evans (Eds.), *Cultural clinical psychology: Theory, research and practice* (pp. 106–126). New York: Oxford University Press.

Triandis, H. C. (1990). Theoretical concepts that are applicable to the analysis of ethnocentrism. In R. W. Brislin (Ed.), *Applied cross-cultural psychology* (pp. 24–55). Newbury Park, CA: Sage.

Triandis, H. C. (1995). *Individualism and collectivism.* Boulder, CO: Westview Press.

Triandis, H. C. (1996). The psychological measurement of cultural syndromes. *American Psychologist, 51,* 407–415.

Triandis, H. C., Chen, X. P., & Chan, D. K. S. (1998). Scenarios for the measurement of collectivism and individualism. *Journal of Cross-Cultural Psychology, 29,* 275–289.

U.S. Bureau of the Census. (1995). *Statistical abstracts of the U.S.* (115th ed.). Washington, DC: Author.

U. S. National Center for Health Statistics (1993). *Health, United States, 1992.* Washington, DC: U.S. Government Printing Office.

Van de Vijver, F., & Leung, K. (1998). Methods and data analysis of comparative research. In J. W. Berry, Y. H. Poortinga, & J. Pandey (Eds.), *Handbook of cross-cultural psychology: Vol. 1* (pp. 257–300). Needham Heights, CA: Allyn & Bacon.

Vingilis, E. (1996). Introduction. In R. Alder, E. Vingilis, & V. Mai (Eds.), *Community health and well-being in Southwestern Ontario* (pp. 1–10). London, Canada: Middlesex Health Unit and Faculty of Medicine.

Wallston, K. E. (1993). Health psychology in the USA. In S. Maes, H. Leventhal, & M. Johnston (Eds.), *International review of health psychology: Vol. 2* (pp. 215–228). Chichester, UK: Wiley.

Weiss, S. M. (1982). Health psychology: The time is now. *Health Psychology, 1,* 81–91.

Weizmann, C. (1949). *Trial and error: The autobiography of Chaim Weizmann.* New York: Harper & Brothers.

Williams, D. R. (1995). The concept of race in health services research: 1966–1990. *Hospital Services Research, 30,* 261–274.

Wolff, H. G. (1953). *Stress and disease.* Springfield, IL: Charles C. Thomas.

World Health Organization (1948). *Constitution of the World Health Organization.* Geneva: Author.

Yanchar, S. C., & Slife, B. D. (1997). Parallels between multiculturalism and disunity in psychology. *American Psychologist, 52,* 658–659.

Yoe, M. (1993). Toward an ethic of empowerment for health promotion. *Health Promotion International, 8,* 225–235.

2

HEALTH CARE PRACTICE IN A MULTICULTURAL CONTEXT: WESTERN AND NON-WESTERN ASSUMPTIONS

MESFIN SAMUEL MULATU

National Institute of Mental Health
National Institutes of Health
Bethesda, Maryland

JOHN W. BERRY

Department of Psychology
Queen's University
Kingston, Ontario, Canada

Much of the work on the relationship between health and culture has focused on the international dimension (Aboud, 1998; Dasen, Berry, & Sartorius, 1988). This material has dealt with a broad sweep of issues across societies, including the conceptions of health in different cultures, the promotion of health globally, and attempts to render programs of treatment more culturally sensitive and relevant across cultures (Basch, 1990; Huff, 1999; MacLachlan, 1997). However, cultural variation is just as important to understand *within* societies that are culturally diverse. In these multicultural settings, conception, promotion, and treatment should also be relevant to the needs of all the peoples that live in, and contribute to, the society and its institutions. The health needs of diverse groups should not be assumed to be exactly the same as those of the dominant cultural groups; hence, health services need to be as diverse as the populations they serve. Moreover, such immigrant and ethnocultural groups not only bring their cultures with them, but there are likely to be health needs that arise during the process of their acculturation to their new society (Berry, 1998). In this chapter, we address these two sets of needs among diverse peoples living in multicultural societies: those that are rooted in their heritage cultures and those that arise during their adaptation to their new society.

APPROACHES TO MULTICULTURALISM

We begin by contrasting views about cultural diversity in general, both across and within nation states. Then we pose two questions related to health. First, how fundamental are cultural factors to understanding the domain of health and illness: are they superficial, allowing us to largely ignore their potential contribution, or conversely, is culture so much part of the meaning of health and illness that no understanding is possible without first taking the cultural context into account? Second, depending on one's orientation to the first question, how are we to approach health care practice among ethnocultural groups living together in culturally plural (multicultural) societies? Should such groups be treated as minor variants (minorities) to a mainstream and, hence, as side issues in a standard health system, or should they be treated as complete cultural communities, with their own cultures largely intact, and therefore with their own health conceptions, values, and behaviors? The first question is primarily a theoretical one, while the second is more a practical one.

In studying relationships between culture and behavior, three orientations can be discerned: *absolutism, relativism,* and *universalism* (Berry, Poortinga, Segall, & Dasen, 1992). The absolutist position is one that assumes that human phenomena are basically the same (qualitatively) in all cultures: honesty is honesty and depression is depression, no matter where one observes it. From the absolutist perspective, culture is thought to play little or no role in either the meaning or display of human characteristics. Assessments of such characteristics are made using standard instruments (perhaps with linguistic translation) and interpretations are made easily, without alternative culturally based views being taken into account.

In sharp contrast, the relativist approach is rooted in anthropology and assumes that all human behavior is culturally patterned. It seeks to avoid ethnocentrism by trying to understand people "in their own terms." Explanations of human diversity are sought in the cultural context in which people have developed. Assessments are typically carried out employing the values and meanings that a cultural group gives to a phenomenon. Comparisons are judged to be problematic and ethnocentric and are thus virtually never made.

A third perspective, one that lies somewhere between the first two positions, is that of universalism. Here, it is assumed that basic human characteristics are common to all members of the species (i.e., constituting a set of biological givens), and that culture influences the development and display of them (i.e., culture plays different variations on these underlying themes). Assessments are based on the presumed underlying process, but measures are developed in culturally meaningful versions. Comparisons are made cautiously, employing a wide variety of methodological principles and safeguards, and interpretations of similarities and differences are attempted that take alternative culturally based meanings into account.

Related to these three orientations (about how seriously to take culture generally) is the issue of how to deal with cultural diversity within plural societies. Diversity is a fact of life; whether it is the "spice of life" or a significant irritant to people is probably the fundamental psychological, social, cultural, and political issue of our times. As such, it affects how we think about health and how we deliver health services to diverse populations.

All contemporary societies are now culturally plural. There are no longer any societies that can claim to be homogeneous with respect to objective cultural markers (such as ethnic origin, language, religion) or subjective indicators (such as one's ethnic identity or personal expressions of one's culture). Such diversity elicits a variety of responses at a number of levels: national societies, institutions, and individuals can celebrate or deny it; they can share it or isolate it; they can accommodate it or attempt to squash it. Regardless of the attitude or course of action toward diversity, however, both history and contemporary experience provide compelling evidence that cultural pluralism is durable, even if its forms and expression evolve over time. Such continuing diversity challenges the conceptualization and functioning of all societies. It is likely that a long-established consensus about how to live together may no longer be widely shared, because so much of human behavior is demonstrably rooted in culture (Berry, Poortinga, & Pandey, 1997; Berry, Dasen, & Saraswathi, 1997; Berry, Segall, & Kagitcibasi, 1997).

For many reasons (colonization, migration, enslavement), all contemporary societies have become culturally plural. That is, people of many cultural backgrounds have come to live together in a diverse society. In many cases, they form cultural groups which are not equal in power (numerical, economic, or political). These power differences have given rise to popular and social science terms such as "mainstream," "minority," "ethnic group," etc. In this chapter, while recognizing these unequal influences, we employ the term *cultural group* to refer to all groups in plural society and preface it with the terms *dominant* and *nondominant* to refer to their relative power where such a difference exists and is relevant to the discussion. This is an attempt to avoid a host of political and social assumptions that have distorted much of the work on variations in human behavior and intercultural relations, in particular, the assumption that minorities are inevitably (or should be in the process of) becoming part of the mainstream culture (Berry, 1990). While this does occur in many plural societies, it does not always occur, and, in some cases, it is resisted by either or both the dominant and nondominant cultural groups, resulting in continuing cultural diversity (UNESCO, 1985).

There are two contrasting, usually implicit, models of cultural group relations in plural societies (see Fig. 2.1). In one (the *mainstream–minority*), the view is that there is (or should be) one dominant society, on the margins of which are various minority groups; these groups typically remain there, unless they are "gently polished and reclaimed for humanity" (as Montaigne phrased French colonial policy) and incorporated as indistinguishable components into the mainstream. In the other (the *multicultural*) view, there is a national social framework of institutions (the *larger society*) which accommodates the interests and needs of the numerous cultural groups, which are fully incorporated as *cultural groups* into this national framework. Both implicit models refer to possible arrangements in plural societies: the mainstream–minority view is that cultural pluralism is a problem and should be reduced or even eliminated. The multicultural view is that cultural pluralism is a resource, and inclusiveness should be nurtured with supportive policies and programs.

Our answers to these two questions are explicitly pluralist. We consider that an understanding of culture is fundamental to understanding all behavior, including health and illness. With respect to the three orientations, we adopt a universalist perspective, viewing many aspects of health as pan-human in their roots and in their scope, while accepting that their definition, their recognition, their treatment, and their care are all culturally rooted phenomena. With respect to the implicit models, we adopt the multicultural view, accepting that no program of prevention or care is likely to be helpful if the ethnocultural circumstances of the people are ignored. In both cases, we assert that cultural ignorance is simply "bad medicine."

RELATIONSHIP BETWEEN CULTURE AND HEALTH

If these answers are valid, how can we proceed to engage in culturally sensitive health care across and within societies? One scheme (Berry, 1997) is to rec-

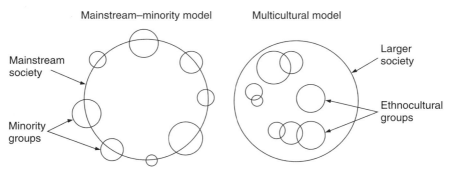

FIGURE 2.1   Models of cultural groups relations in plural societies. From Mulatu & Berry, 2001. © John Wiley & Sons Limited. Reproduced with permission.

ognize both the distinction (and the intimate relationships) between the cultural (community) and psychological (individual) levels of understanding. In Table 2.1 are four categories of health phenomena and two levels of analyses (community and individual). Crossing the two dimensions produces eight areas in which information can be sought during the study of links between culture and individual health. The community level of work typically involves ethnographic methods and yields a general characterization of shared health conceptions, values, practices, and institutions in a society. The individual level of work involves the psychological study of a sample of individuals from the society and yields information about individual differences (and similarities), which can lead to inferences about the psychological underpinnings of individual health beliefs, attitudes, behaviors, and relationships.

The reason for taking cultural-level health phenomena into account is so that the broad context for the development and display of individual health phenomena can be established. Without an understanding of this background context, attempts to deal with individuals and their health problems may well be useless, even harmful. The reason for considering individual-level health phenomena is that not all persons in a cultural group hold the same beliefs or attitudes nor do they engage in the same behaviors and relationships. Without an understanding of their individual variations from the general community situation, again harm may well be inflicted.

Examples of work in the eight areas of interest are numerous in the research and professional literature. At the cultural level, the way in which a cultural group defines what is and is not health can vary substantially from group to group. These collective *cognitive* phenomena include shared conceptions and categories, as well as definitions of health and disease (Huff, 1999). At the individual level, health beliefs and knowledge, while influenced by the cultural conceptions, can also vary from person to person (Dasen et al., 1988). Beliefs about what causes an illness or disability, or about how much control one has over it (both getting it and curing it), show variation across individuals and cultures (Berry, Dalal, & Pande, 1994). For example, in one community the general be-

TABLE 2.1   Aspects of Health Phenomena Considered under Different Levels of Analyses[a]

| Levels of analyses | Categories of health phenomena | | | |
	Cognitive	Affective	Behavioral	Social
Community (cultural)	Health conceptions and definitions	Health norms and values	Health practices	Health roles and institutions
Individual (psychological)	Health knowledge and beliefs	Health attitudes	Health behaviors	Interpersonal relationships

[a]From Mulatu & Berry, 2001. © John Wiley & Sons Limited. Reproduced by permission.

lief is that if pregnant women eat too much (or even "normally"), there will be insufficient room for the fetus to develop; hence, undereating is common, and prenatal malnutrition results with an associated increase in infant disability. However, there are variations across individuals in this belief, with education, status, and participation in public health programs making a difference.

With respect to *affective* phenomena, the value placed on health is known to vary from culture to culture and within cultures across subgroups. Within Jewish cultures, for example, Judaic Law prescribes that health is given by God, and it is the responsibility of the individual to sustain it. The value placed on good health is thus a shared belief among practicing Jews. However, there is significant variation in the acceptance of this value across three Jewish subgroups. Orthodox Jews accord it the highest value, Reformed Jews a lower value, and Secular Jews an even lower value (Dayan, 1993). And, within the three groups there are further variations according to a number of personal and demographic factors.

Health practices and *behaviors* also vary across cultures and individuals. For example, with respect to nutrition (Dasen & Super, 1988), what is classified as suitable food and who can eat it are matters of cultural practice. Many high protein "foods" are not placed in the food category in Western cultures (e.g., grubs, brains) and are avoided, while in other cultures they are an important part of the diet. Within these general cultural practices, however, individuals vary in what they can eat, depending on age, status, or factors related to clan membership. The *social* organization of health activities into instructions and the allocation of roles (e.g., healer, patient) are also known to vary across cultures. Religious or gender issues may affect the role of healer (e.g., only those with certain spiritual qualities or only males may become healers), while in other cultures, the high cost of medical or other health professional training limits the roles to the wealthy. In some cultures, health services are widely available and fully integrated into the fabric of community life (e.g., Averasturi, 1988) while in others, doctors and hospitals are remote, mysterious, and alien to most of the population. In the former case, individual patient–healer relationships may be collegial, in which a partnership is established to regain health, while in the latter, the relationship is likely to be hierarchical, involving the use of authority and compliance.

VARIATIONS IN HEALTH CONCEPTS IN MULTICULTURAL SOCIETIES

Given the importance of culture in understanding health, it is not surprising that researchers and health care workers have made various attempts to come up with an acceptable definition of health. However, the concept of health has eluded a clear and comprehensive definition that captures variations within or across cultures. Nor has it been possible to establish a consensus on the meaning of health among the different scientific disciplines whose subject is the study of one or more aspects of well-being. More importantly, the conceptions of health by lay and professional people are divergent in almost every society (Furnham, 1988; Helman, 1994). In fact, it appears that with increasing Western health education, one finds a parallel increase in abstraction of the meanings of health away from everyday understanding of it. To a lesser extent, this asymmetry of health conception between lay and professional people is also true in other cultures. Given this as a background, we will look at the various ways health has been conceived within and across nations.

As noted in the previous section, with the increasing possibility of constant migration and relocation of people globally, it has become almost impossible to find a society composed of people of a single cultural heritage. In effect, societies have become more and more multicultural as this century begins. This increasing cultural pluralism is particularly evident among the industrial nations of the Western Hemisphere, where immigrant groups are attracted by economic opportunities away from sociopolitical violence in their society of origin.

Variations in health concepts within and across nations can be seen from two perspectives. One approach is by examining the variations among the three overlapping health sectors (i.e., the popular, the folk, and the professional) found in almost all societies (Kleinman, 1980; Helman, 1994). The popular sector includes lay or everyday theories and practices of health. The folk sector consists of loosely systematized health concepts held and practices carried out by indigenous specialists or healers. The professional sector consists of well-systematized, organized, and officially sanctioned health concepts and practices, such as Western biomedicine or Indian Ayurvedic medicine (Helman, 1994).

Given that highly systematized health systems, such as Western biomedicine, show less variation across cultural contexts, another approach taken by anthropologists is to examine lay or folk theories of well-being or illness across nations. The locus of popular or folk explanations of ill health and other misfortunes has been classified into four sites: the individual, the natural world, the social world, and the supernatural world (Helman, 1994). Individual-centered explanations of illness make the patient responsible for his or her own illness. For instance, a patient with heart disease may blame or be blamed for his or her condition because of failure to exercise or regulate diet. Ill health may also be attributed to social factors, including social conflicts, social stress, and witchcraft (Helman, 1994). Murdock (1980) further expanded the natural explanations to include infection, stress, deterioration, or accidents, and the supernatural explanations to include mystical (e.g., fate, magical contagion), animistic (e.g., soul loss, spirit aggression), and magical causes (e.g., witchcraft, sorcery). Although generalizations across regions or groups of cultures are less informative and often less accurate, it has been suggested that supernatural and social theories of ill health predominate in less developed and non-Western societies whereas natural and individual-centered illness theories predominate in more developed and Western cultures (Helman, 1994).

Within any pluralistic society, conceptions about health and illness can be seen from at least three perspectives. First, health may be looked at from the perspective of the predominant Western health paradigm, i.e., biomedicine. In most cases, the biomedical view of health stresses the absence of identifiable pathophysiology (e.g., viral infection, broken legs, abnormal levels of blood sugar) as primary markers of health and its focus has been largely on pathologic processes and the cure of diseases. Although health has been broadly understood along the lines of the World Health Organization's (WHO) conceptualization as "a state of complete physical, mental, and social well being and not merely the absence of disease or infirmity" (cited in Basch, 1990, p. 29), Western biomedicine has historically ignored mental and social well-being and their promotion. Disagreements among different professional disciplines and subcultures as to what "complete well being" means also abound. Nonetheless, the WHO definition of health appears to capture the views of most health care professionals. While disregarding the health conceptualization of other non-Western cultures, this conceptualization of health is also currently the most accepted definition of health among international organizations and national governments (Basch, 1990).

Second, health in pluralistic societies may be conceived from the perspective of the dominant or mainstream cultural frame of reference. In North America, for example, traditional conceptions of health among European Americans or Canadians may be held as the only acceptable or standard conception. For instance, health among European Americans is equated with specific personal lifestyles and choices. A healthy person is popularly believed to be someone who eats right, avoids consumption of addictive substances, exercises regularly, and/or lives by Protestant moral codes. To some extent, these health conceptions of the dominant social groups in the Western world overlap with biomedical conceptions insofar as the latter is, at least in part, the product of Western culture and philosophy (Airhihenbuwa, 1995; MacLachlan, 1997).

Third, health may be conceived from the standpoint of the nondominant social and ethnocultural groups. Here, one may include not only native minority groups that have lived with the dominant group for a lengthy period of time, but also those recent immigrants to the society. In many plural societies, for example, concepts of health that differ from the dominant culture or that are uniquely held by minority cultures are found. Among Native Americans, for example, health is believed to reflect living in harmony with oneself and the surrounding environment (Hollow, 1999; Spector, 1996). Traditional health systems of Native Americans are strongly linked to their religious beliefs and are generally holistic in approach. Ill health is believed to occur because of disruptions in the harmonious relationships between the mind, the spirit, the body, and the natural environment. Negative activities, such as displeasing the holy people of the past or the present, disturbing animal and plant life, misuse of sacred religious ceremonies, strong and uncontrolled emotions, and breaking social rules and taboos, are believed to lead to ill health (Hollow, 1999; Spector, 1996). According to Spector (1996), many traditional health systems of Native Americans do not subscribe to the germ theory of illnesses. Like Native Americans, African Americans and recent immigrants have health conceptions that differ from and, in some cases, contradict the Western biomedical model or health concepts of the dominant society (Huff, 1999).

Among recent immigrants to the Western world, the Chinese come from a unique and well-developed system of health and medical tradition. As a result, Chinese immigrants to North America or Europe may have a different way of looking at health and well-being. Indigenous Chinese and similar other Asian cultures conceive health as "a state of spiritual and physical harmony with nature" (Spector, 1996, p. 243). Indigenous Chinese medicine is based on a system of the theories of *yin* and *yang,* with the five elements (i.e., wood, fire, earth, metal, and water), and other principles grounded on Chinese philosophy and religion. The theory of *yin* and *yang* provides a framework for the understanding of health and illness. According to this theory, the human body is an organic whole composed of elements with opposing aspects in a mutually complementary and interacting system (Huff, 1999; Yanchi, 1988). Some of these elements are classified as yin, which is a negative energy representing the forces of darkness, cold, and emptiness (Spector, 1996; Yanchi, 1988). Examples of yin elements of the body include the interior of the body, the feet, and organ systems that control storage of vital substances (heart, liver, spleen, lung, and kidneys). The yang is considered as a positive energy that transforms substances and produces light, warmth, and fullness (Spector, 1996; Yanchi, 1988). The exterior of the body, the head, and organ systems that transport and digest food (gallbladder, stomach, small and large intestines, urinary bladder) are examples of the yang elements. Similarly, elements of the natural and social environment are also classified as yin and yang. Whereas the moon, earth, poverty, sadness, and some foods (e.g., pork, fish, fresh fruits) are considered yin, the sun, heaven, fire, goodness, wealth, and such foods as chicken, beef, eggs, and spicy foods are regarded as yang.

The yin and yang are believed to engage in a constantly changing relationship of support and opposition to each other. This dynamic balancing relationship is referred to as mutual restraint. Whereas balance between the forces of the yin and yang leads to health, a preponderance of one over the other leads to ill health (Spector, 1996; Yanchi, 1988). Yanchi (1988) notes that such an imbalance in yin and yang can be caused by external pathogenic factors the body encounters or by changes in the body's own resistance (e.g., internal weakness or injury). It is to be noted that the indigenous Chinese health concepts and theories are much more complicated than the above simplistic presentation of the yin and yang theory. Readers are referred to Yanchi (1988) and Chapter 14 of this book for detailed and interesting analysis of Chinese health concepts, theories, and practices. In general, what may be different in both Native American and Chinese health systems, compared to Western biomedicine, is the emphasis on maintaining balance among the dynamic elements of the body, the mind, the spirit, and the natural environment.

Like Western pluralistic societies, non-Western pluralistic societies also have multiple health belief and care systems. Variations in health conceptions and practices in such societies arise because of the existence of multiple ethnocultural groups within their national boundaries and because of incorporation of new cultures as a result of colonialism, immigration, and cultural hegemony. One especially important source of variation in health concepts of non-Western societies is the pervasive penetration of Western biomedical concepts and practices into the health care systems of these cultures. This penetration encroaches over the boundaries of indigenous health systems, directly threatening their existence or limiting their functioning in some countries and leading to their near extinction in others. With the exception of few countries (e.g., China, India), Western biomedicine is the only official health system in many developing nations in Africa, Asia, and Latin America, despite the fact that a significant majority of the populace has limited or no access to it. Although there appears to be a movement toward greater involvement of indigenous health systems in these countries, the efforts of national and international health agencies are limited and, hence, achievements appear to be minimal. In contrast, efforts to expand Western biomedicine have been relatively intensive and successful.

In sum, health concepts in pluralistic societies tend to reflect the sociohistorical contexts in which they occur. Western biomedical health concepts focus on disease as marked by pathophysiologic processes while discounting spirituality as part of well-being. Non-Western conceptions tend to be holistic in approach and to view health as a balance between the facets of the body, the mind, the spirit, and the natural environment. Moreover, religion and spiritualism are integral parts of non-Western health conceptions.

VARIATIONS IN HEALTH PRACTICES IN MULTICULTURAL SOCIETIES

In the preceding discussion, we have argued that health conceptions vary from one cultural context to another. It has also been argued that health conceptions, by and large, determine the nature of health practices in which people engage to protect or promote their health and cure their illnesses (as portrayed in Table 2.1). It should, however, be noted that there is not always a direct correspondence between beliefs about health or illness and the health practices adopted. Also, people may hold different health conceptions at one time without apparent difficulty or cognitive dissonance. This is exemplified in various sub-Sahara African contexts, where both Western biomedical and indigenous health beliefs and practices are accepted as the basis for understanding and managing ill health. This phenomenon, also found in other developing and developed regions of the world, has been referred to as "cognitive tolerance" (MacLachlan, 1997).

We use the term *health practices* to refer to the various methods employed to maintain, protect, and restore health (Spector, 1996). Medical anthropologists and cross-cultural health psychologists underline the fact that every culture has its own health system with theories and practical guides that determine its health care delivery (e.g., Helman, 1994; MacLachlan, 1997). In every culture, there are indigenous health practices that are applied to manage issues related to physical, mental, social, or spiritual facets of health. As noted earlier, Western biomedicine has also penetrated the health care system of every country in the world. Thus, pluralism in health care practices is as common as pluralism in the conceptualization of health.

Cultural examination of differences in health care practices within or across nations is possible using the same approach we employed when exploring cultural variations in health concepts. That is, health practices may be looked at from the perspective of popular, folk, and professional health sectors. Within each of these layers, the targets of the health practices (e.g., correcting pathophysiology, negotiating person–spirit relationship) may also be examined.

Popular health practices are those everyday health behaviors that nonprofessional people engage in to maintain, protect, or restore the health of themselves, their family members, and, in some cases, their communities. Popular health practices include various home-based activities ranging from the preparation of special foods to the performance of religious rituals. Patient and healer relationships are informal and nonmonetary (Helman, 1994). Family members, religious leaders, the elderly, or people with similar experiences in the past may be consulted regarding the health problem. The patients themselves or their close family members then apply therapeutic information and/or *materia medica* gathered by such consultative means. In Western societies, the use of megavitamins, over-the-counter medications, massages, and herbal preparations has gained increasing popularity (Eisenberg et al., 1998). Other popular health practices in the West tend to be adoptions of non-Western practices, including meditation, yoga, and other relaxation techniques.

In non-Western societies, health practices in the popular sector often blend both natural and spiritual remedies. As in the West, special foods and home herbal concoctions are prepared, but unlike the West, these preparations are taken with appropriate spiritual blessing or rituals. In a study of illness treatment choice sequences in a rural Cameroonian village, for instance, Ryan (1998) identified that about 82% of all treatment episodes reported involved home-based remedies, including herbal medicines, special bathing, hot compresses, and special foods, as well as Western pharmaceuticals. He also noted that people are very likely to combine home-based remedies with treatments from traditional healers.

Folk health practices are those health-protective, -maintenance, or -restorative actions taken by indigenous specialists or healers. Folk health practices tend to reflect the health concepts and worldviews of the culture from which they originate. It has been estimated that as much as 80% of the population in developing countries relies on indigenous health services, including consulting folk health practitioners, as its primary source of health, even though such services are not usually part of the official health care system (Bodeker, 1995; DeJong, 1991; Helman, 1994). Despite the often-cited characterization of folk health practices as spiritual or supernatural in orientation, these practices often have both empirical and magico–religious components. In northwestern and central Ethiopia, for example, both empirical and magico–religious healers are found (Bishaw, 1991; Young, 1976). Empirical folk healers include the *medhanit awaqi* (herbalist), *wogessha* (surgeon, bonesetter), and *yelimid awalj* (midwife); magico–religious healers include *atmaqi* (baptizer, priest healer), *bala-zar* (*zar* spirit medium), and *tenquay* (shaman, seer). Despite these distinctions, the holistic view of health requires that almost all healing take place in social contexts with appropriate religious or spiritual rituals. For example, the herbalist prepares and administers his or her herbal medicines according to appropriate spiritual guidelines. Medicinal plants may only be cut at certain times (e.g., early morning) or by certain individuals (e.g., virgin boys) to maintain their potency. Similarly, indigenous healing by Native Americans includes both empirical and natural approaches in combination with spiritual ceremonies (Hollow, 1999). Among the natural healing techniques used by native people are surgery, massage, fracture setting, wound dressing, and herbal medicines. These therapies are often accompanied by spiritual and bodily cleansing ceremonies, such as sweat lodges, prayer, chanting, dancing, and divination (Hollow, 1999; Huff, 1999; Spector, 1996).

In Western societies, although one may argue that Western biomedicine is also one form of folk medicine, most therapies included under the rubric of "complementary and alternative medicine" (CAM) are considered folk health practices. While some CAM therapies have their roots in Western culture, others are brought from non-Western societies by immigrants. In North America and Western Europe, for instance, CAM therapies, including acupuncture, homeopathy, chiropractic, therapeutic massage, biofeedback, herbal medicines, various relaxation techniques, and spiritual healing, are used by between 10 and 35% of the population at a given time period (Eisenberg et al., 1998; Paramore, 1997; Vincent & Furnham, 1997). Despite their increasing popularity, only some of these techniques (e.g., chiropractic) are slowly being acknowledged as legitimate health services by governmental and health insurance agencies.

Regardless of the cultural differences, a common thread that runs across folk health practices is their holistic approach toward health or the absence of it. Quite often, folk health care systems embody the healing of the body, the mind, and the spirit. Dissimilar to Western biomedicine, the focus in folk health practices is not only curing disease but also restoring balance among the elements of the body, the mind, and the spirit. Patients are not seen as helpless victims but as active participants in their recovery. In most cases, therapy takes place in a social context where close family members and other patients can be counted on to provide social support.

Professional health practices include those health-related actions carried out by well-trained, officially sanctioned health care workers. This, in Western societies, means exclusively biomedical care involving biomedical health care professionals. As noted earlier, Western biomedicine is also the only official health care system in almost all non-Western societies. Despite the growing tendency to organize and professionalize indigenous health care systems in many non-Western cultures, the contributions of indigenous healers still remain unrecognized by national governments. Western cultural hegemony has been blamed for the underdevelopment and neglect of indigenous health care practices (Airhihenbuwa, 1995; Alderete, 1996).

Although the Western biomedical system may differ across nations in terms of resources, organization of programs, financing, management methods, and delivery of services (Roemer, 1991), very little variation is found in the basic components of the practice of health, which primarily focuses on curing diseases by heavy reliance on surgical alterations and use of drugs. By its very nature, Western biomedicine is a highly systematized, hierarchical, and bureaucratic health care delivery system. Health services are provided at different levels and varieties of care facilities (e.g., hospitals, clinics, pharmacies). Various trained health care professionals (e.g., physicians, nurses, pharmacists) are involved, each specializing in some aspects of care. As a result of cross-national standardization of training and practice, actual services provided for patients (e.g., removal of a tumor or alleviation of postsurgical pain) in the United States or Germany are very likely to be similar, if not identical, although financial and service-delivery arrangements are different.

Other well-developed and officially recognized professional health care systems include Chinese indigenous medicine and Indian Ayuverdic medicine. Although not as expansive as Western biomedicine, indigenous Chinese and Indian health care traditions have similar patterns of systematization and organization. In both countries, national governments have officially recognized the value of indigenous health care systems and have supported the development of formal degree-granting training programs and institutions. Moreover, in both China and India, there are hospitals where the services of both indigenous and Western biomedical systems are integrated (Basch, 1990; Huff, 1999; Spector, 1996).

As discussed earlier, the indigenous Chinese health system approaches health care from the holistic perspective and employs both empirical and spiritual or religious means to correct the imbalance responsible for the suffering of the patient. For instance, ill health conditions that are caused by the preponderance of yin forces (e.g., pregnancy-related problems) are treated with application of yang foods or yang treatment modalities (e.g., moxibustion) in order to restore balance between the two forces (Huff, 1999; Spector, 1996). Overall, a variety of health practitioners employ various healing strategies including, among others, herbal remedies, acupuncture, acupressure, meditation, acumassage, cupping, coining, moxibustion, as well as shamanistic rituals (Huff, 1999; Spector, 1996). Indigenous Chinese healers are also known to use amulets consisting of jade charms to ward off evil spirits, to maintain and protect health and to gain wisdom, wealth, and immortality (Spector, 1996).

SUMMARY

Health practices in multicultural societies are complex, made up of a myriad of indigenous and foreign activities aimed at maintaining, promoting, and restoring health. Within such societies, differences tend to reflect health practices in the popular, folk, and professional sectors. Cross-national differences are greatly determined by the presence or absence of well developed, systematized, and recognized indigenous health systems. Western biomedicine has penetrated and influenced almost every health care delivery system in the world, usually at the expense of indigenous health care systems. There is a greater variability in health care practices in the popular or folk sectors than in the professional sector, both within and across nations. When compared to Western biomedicine, indigenous health care systems tend to be more holistic in their therapeutic approaches, where the goal of therapy is not only correcting pathophysiologic processes, but also promoting a harmonious relationship between the elements of the body, the mind, the spirit, and the social and natural environments.

CASE STUDY

Several thousands of Ethiopian Jews migrated to Israel within the past 20 years. Along with them, they took their traditions, customs, and beliefs, including explanatory models for health, illnesses, and other misfortunes that are deeply rooted in northwestern Ethiopian culture. Reports indicate that, like other immigrant communities, the Ethiopian Jews' adaptation to their new Western-oriented society of settlement has not been straightforward (e.g., Arieli & Ayche, 1993). Conflicts of culturally patterned expectations, standards, and practices with those of the dominant society are observed in every aspect of their lives, including the health care setting. The health beliefs and practices of Ethiopian Jews continue to reflect their Ethiopian roots and require considerable attention from Western health care providers (Reiff, Zakut, & Weingarten, 1999). In this brief case study, we would like to present one instance where health care-related conflicts are the product of parallel health beliefs and practices between the patient and her health care providers.

The case study is about the phenomenon of *zar* spirit possession. The belief in *zar* spirits is commonly found in several northeastern African societies, including Ethiopia, Sudan, and Egypt. These spirits are not malicious in nature, tend to possess more women than men, and often pass from mother to daughter. In general, *zar* spirits are considered as guardians of the individuals they possess and their families against illnesses and misfortunes. Among Ethiopians, *zar* possession per se is not considered a health problem. Health problems are believed to be the results of punishment by *zar* spirits that are angry because of neglect of the necessary rituals. Discontented *zar* spirits are believed to lead to various physical and psychological symptoms, including apathy, convulsive seizures, proneness to accidents, hysteria, catatonic states, and self-mutilating behaviors. In some extreme cases, angry *zar* spirits are also believed to lead to serious physical illness, such as tuberculosis, smallpox, or typhoid. Management of health problems associated with this spirit possession usually entails performance of the appropriate rituals and negotiation with the spirit in a supportive environment (Kahana, 1985).

A 45-year-old Jewish Ethiopian woman presenting with symptoms of dysphoria and somatization was seen in a mental health center in Israel (see Grisaru, Budowski, & Witztum, 1997, for details of this case). Initially, like other patients who present with these symptoms, the woman was treated with antidepressants, apparently because of the suspicion of a depressive disorder. Antidepressant medication was reported to be unsuccessful. Six months later, the woman was seen at the center again, presenting with depressive symptoms as well as severe headache and stomach pains for which no organic cause was found. After clinical interview and observation of the woman, pharmacological treatment for obsessive–compulsive disorder was also tried because of repetitive movements, ritualistic ceremonies, and severe anxiety associated with not being able to carry out the ceremonies. Once again, the woman was not responsive to drug treatment. With the help of a translator, assessment of the woman's views about her problem, and open-minded observation of her behavior at the center and at home, the health care workers realized the problem was *zar* possession. For the woman, her problems were spiritual punishment for being unable to perform rituals and ceremonies at her apartment because of restrictions by resettlement authorities. The most successful treatment was to transfer the woman from her smaller apartment to a larger one and to allow her to perform the required rituals and ceremonies that satisfy the demands of her *zar* spirit. In sum, this case demonstrates that different cultures do not necessarily share the same health concepts and health care approaches. Cultural awareness and competencies are essential for providing equitable, sensitive, and appropriate health care services in pluralistic societies.

1. What are the cross-cultural conflicts in the conception and treatment of the condition described in this case?
2. How might such conflicts be avoided in health care settings in plural societies?

ACKNOWLEDGMENTS

We are grateful to Rahel Adamu, M. P. H. and Sara Haile, M. P. H. for their very helpful comments on an earlier version of this chapter.

SUGGESTED READINGS

Aboud, F. E. (1998). *Health psychology in global perspective.* Thousand Oaks, CA: Sage.
Airhihenbuwa, C. O. (1995). *Health and culture: Beyond the Western paradigm.* Thousand Oaks, CA: Sage.

Helman, C. G. (1994). *Culture, health, and illness: An introduction for health professionals* (3rd ed.). Oxford, UK: Butterworth-Heinemann.
Huff, R. M., & Kline, M. V. (Eds.) (1999). *Promoting health in multicultural populations: A handbook for practitioners.* Thousand Oaks, CA: Sage.
Spector, R. E. (1996). *Cultural diversity in health and illness* (4th ed.). Stamford, CT: Appleton and Lange.

REFERENCES

Aboud, F. E. (1998). *Health psychology in global perspective.* Thousand Oaks, CA: Sage.
Airhihenbuwa, C. O. (1995). *Health and culture: Beyond the Western paradigm.* Thousand Oaks, CA: Sage.
Alderete, E. (1996). The formulation of a health research agenda by and for indigenous peoples: Contesting the Western scientific paradigm. *Journal of Alternative Medicine, 2,* 365–372.
Arieli, A., & Ayche, S. (1993). Psychopathological aspects of the Ethiopian immigration to Israel. *Israeli Journal of Medical Sciences, 29,* 411–418.
Averasturi, L. (1988). Psychosocial factors in health: The Cuban model. In P. Dasen, J. W. Berry, & N. Sartorius (Eds.), *Health and cross-cultural psychology: Towards applications.* London, UK: Sage.
Basch, P. F. (1990). *Textbook of international health.* New York: Oxford University Press.
Berry, J. W. (1990). Psychology of acculturation. In R. Brislin (Ed.), *Applied cross-cultural psychology* (pp. 232–253). London, UK: Sage.
Berry, J. W. (1997). Cultural and ethnic factors in health. In A. Baum et al. (Eds.), *Cambridge handbook of psychology, health and medicine* (pp. 98–103). Cambridge, UK: Cambridge University Press.
Berry, J. W. (1998). Acculturation and health. In S. S. Kazarian & D. R. Evans (Eds.), *Cultural clinical psychology: Theory, research and practice* (pp. 39–57). New York: Oxford University Press.
Berry, J. W., Dalal, A., & Pande, N. (1994). *Disability beliefs attitudes and behaviors across cultures.* Report from the International Center for the Advancement of Community Based Rehabilitation. Kingston, Canada: Queen's University.
Berry, J. W., Dasen, P. R., & Saraswathi, T. S. (Eds.). (1997). *Handbook of cross-cultural psychology: Vol. 2. Basic processes and human development.* Boston, MA: Allyn & Bacon.
Berry, J. W., Poortinga, Y. H., & Pandey, J. (Eds.). (1997). *Handbook of cross-cultural psychology: Vol. 1. Theory and methods.* Boston, MA: Allyn & Bacon.
Berry, J. W., Poortinga, Y. H., Segall, M. H., & Dasen, P. R. (1992). *Cross-cultural psychology: Research and applications.* New York: Cambridge University Press.
Berry, J. W., Segall, M. H., & Kagitcibasi, C. (Eds.). (1997). *Handbook of cross-cultural psychology: (Vol. 3) Social behavior and application.* Boston, MA: Allyn & Bacon.
Bishaw, M. (1991). Promoting traditional medicine in Ethiopia: A brief historical review of government policy. *Social Science and Medicine, 33,* 193–200.
Bodeker, G. (1995). Traditional health systems: Policy, biodiversity, and global interdependence. *Journal of Alternative Medicine, 1,* 231–243.
Dasen, P., & Super, C. (1988). The usefulness of a cross-cultural approach in studies of malnutrition and psychological development. In P. Dasen, J. W. Berry, & N. Sartorius (Eds.), *Health and cross-cultural psychology: Towards applications.* London, UK: Sage.
Dasen, P., Berry, J. W., & Sartorius, N. (Eds.). (1988). *Health and cross-cultural psychology: Towards applications.* London, UK: Sage.
Dayan, J. (1993). *Health values, beliefs and behaviors of Orthodox, Reformed and Secular Jews.* Unpublished master's thesis, Queen's University, Kingston, Ontario, Canada.

DeJong, J. (1991). *Traditional medicine in sub-Saharan Africa: Its importance and potential policy options*. Washington, DC: World Bank.

Eisenberg, D. M., Davis, R. B., Ettner, S. L., Appel, S., Wilkey, S., Van Rompay, M., & Kessler, R. C. (1998). Trends in alternative medicine use in the United States, 1990–1997: Results of a follow-up national survey. *Journal of the American Medical Association, 280,* 1569–1575.

Furnham, A. (1988). *Lay theories: Everyday understanding of problems in social sciences*. Oxford, UK: Pergamon.

Grisaru, N., Budowski, D., & Witztum, E. (1997). Possession by the "Zar" among Ethiopian immigrants to Israel: Psychopathology or culture-bound syndrome? *Psychopathology, 30,* 223–233.

Helman, C. G. (1994). *Culture, health, and illness: An introduction for health professionals* (3rd ed.). Oxford, UK: Butterworth-Heinemann.

Hollow, W. B. (1999). Traditional Indian medicine. In J. M. Galloway, B. W. Goldberg, & J. S. Alpert (Eds.), *Primary care of Native American patients: Diagnosis, therapy, and epidemiology* (pp. 31–38). Boston, MA: Butterworth-Heinemann.

Huff, R. M. (1999). Cross-cultural concepts of health and disease. In R. M. Huff & M. V. Kline (Eds.), *Promoting health in multicultural populations: A handbook for practitioners* (pp. 23–39). Thousand Oaks, CA: Sage.

Kahana, Y. (1985). The Zar spirit, a category of magic in the system of mental health care in Ethiopia. *International Journal of Social Psychiatry, 31,* 125–143.

Kleinman, A. (1980). *Patients and healers in the context of culture*. Berkeley, CA: University of California Press.

MacLachlan, M. (1997). *Culture and health*. Chichester, UK: Wiley.

Mulatu, M. S., & Berry, J. W. (2001). Cultivating health through multiculturalism. In M. MacLachlan, Cultivating health: Cultural perspectives on promoting health (pp. 15–35). Chichester, UK: Wiley.

Murdock, G. P. (1980). *Theories of illness: A world survey*. Pittsburgh, PA: University of Pittsburgh Press.

Paramore, L. C. (1997). Use of alternative therapies: Estimates from the 1994 Robert Wood Johnson Foundation National Access to Care Survey. *Journal of Pain and Symptom Management, 13,* 83–89.

Reiff, M., Zakut, H., & Weingarten, M. A. (1999). Illness and treatment perceptions of Ethiopian immigrants and their doctors in Israel. *American Journal of Public Health, 89,* 1814–1818.

Roemer, M. I. (1991). *National health systems of the world: Vol. 1*. New York: Oxford Univ. Press.

Ryan, G. W. (1998), What do sequential behavioral patterns suggest about medical decision-making process?: Modeling home case management of acute illnesses in rural Cameroonian village. *Social Science and Medicine, 46,* 209–225.

Spector, R. E. (1996). *Cultural diversity in health and illness* (4th ed.). Stamford, CT: Appleton and Lange.

UNESCO (1985). *Cultural pluralism and cultural identity*. Paris: Author.

Vincent, C., & Furnham, A. (1997). *Complementary Medicine: A Research Perspective*. Chichester, UK: Wiley.

Yanchi, L. (1988). *The essential book of traditional Chinese medicine: Vol. I. Theory*. New York: Columbia University Press.

Young, A. (1976). Internalizing and externalizing medical belief systems: An Ethiopian example. *Social Science and Medicine, 10,* 147–156.

3

CROSS-CULTURAL DIFFERENCES IN ILLNESS MODELS AND EXPECTATIONS FOR THE HEALTH CARE PROVIDER–CLIENT/ PATIENT INTERACTION

TAMARA L. ARMSTRONG AND
LEORA C. SWARTZMAN

Department of Psychology
The University of Western Ontario
London, Ontario, Canada

Patients and health care providers do not necessarily share the same explicit or implicit assumptions/expectations about the nature of health and illness nor about how the patient–health care provider interaction should proceed. These expectations may be culturally shaped. To the extent that the health care provider and patient come from different cultural backgrounds (as is often the case for immigrant/minority populations), hold diverse views about illness, and have different expectations about how the health care provider–patient interaction should proceed, there is a potential for miscommunication (Johnson & Snow, 1982) with subsequent adverse impact on health outcomes. The premise is that mismatches in models (i.e., expectations about illness and health interactions) between the patient and the health care provider may render medical care "psychologically" inaccessible to ethnic minorities, resulting in poorer health outcomes for these populations (possibly via noncompliance). In this chapter, we will first define what we mean by the term "culture" and will discuss the individualism/collectivism distinction, a key dimension along which cultures vary (Triandis, 1972), and one which, we argue, might also drive cultural differences in expectations about the nature of health and illness and the health care provider–patient interaction.

CULTURAL DIVERSITY AND ACCESSIBILITY OF HEALTH CARE

There are data to suggest that, in Western culture, health care is inaccessible or ineffective for many cultural groups. Health services research has repeatedly shown the comparatively poor health status of culturally diverse groups. Moreover, these disparities remain even when controlling for variables such as accessibility, premorbid health, and socioeconomic status (Flack et al., 1995; see National Center for Health Statistics, 1991, for a review).

Not only do culturally diverse populations demonstrate poorer health status, they display different patterns of utilization. For example, although African Americans suffer from poorer health than do Euro Americans (and, thus, would be expected to have *more* physician visits than Euro Americans), African Americans obtain needed physician care *less* readily than do European Americans, even after controlling for health insurance coverage (Penn, Kar, Kramer, Skinner, & Zambrana, 1995). Similarly, Leclere, Jensen, and Biddlecom (1994) found that after controlling for socioeconomic status, access to health insurance, and differences in morbidity, recent immigrants were still much less likely than native-born Americans to receive timely health care.

If individuals who have adequate health insurance coverage are not getting care, could it be that the utilization differences can be accounted for by differences in health care decision-making? Some research that has specifically addressed this issue has focused on Asian immigrants' use of mental health services. Lin, Tardiff, Donetz, and Goresky (1978) found that recent Chinese immigrants to Vancouver in need of psychiatric care were much slower to seek medical help than were Western patients and there were prolonged efforts by the family to intervene in the presenting problem before formal health care was sought. Tracey, Leong, and Glidden (1986) also found that the help-seeking process for Asian Americans in Manoa is different from that of Euro Americans in an Illinois university student population. The problems these two groups perceived as appropriate for counseling, and the variables related to these problems, differed substantially.

These studies indicate that individuals' cultural backgrounds, in some way, may influence their pattern of help-seeking. It is difficult to know, however, what specifically about their cultural background is influencing their use of the health care system. Are they dissatisfied with the system? Are they distrustful of the care they might receive? Are they not knowledgeable about available care? These are just a few possible explanations for the differential use patterns of minority patients. A study by Anderson (1986) was aimed at determining the specific reasons for the relative underuse of health care services by culturally diverse patients.

In an ethnographic study of immigrant Chinese families caring for a chronically ill child at home, Anderson (1986) examined reasons for the relative underuse of health care services by Chinese immigrants to Canada. One of the prescribed ways for working with children with long-term disabilities stressed in the North American literature is the use of rehabilitative procedures aimed at enabling the child to live a life as close to normal as possible. Anderson (1986) found that the imperative of treating the child as *normal* structured the ways in which "white" parents managed their child's treatment. In contrast, for the Chinese families, "looking after" the child and fostering the "*happiness*" and "*contentment*" of the child took precedence over normalization. Thus, it seems to be the Chinese families' values of "happiness" and "contentment" rather than "normalization" that resulted in the differing utilization of the health care system (Anderson, 1986).

The Anderson (1986) study suggests that patients' expectations and values are not necessarily consistent with the type of care typically delivered by our Western health care system, and these patients may choose to conduct their health care in accordance with their particular expectations or beliefs. Before any further discussion of how culture may influence expectations of health care, our approach to defining "culture," namely, that of Triandis (1972), will be put forth.

A DEFINITION OF CULTURE

The general trend of scientific research has been to define cultural groups based largely on *objective* traits such as geographical region, race, language, and religion. Triandis (1972), however, recommended that definitions of culture focus on *subjective* features such as shared beliefs, values, and ideas rather than on these objective aspects of culture. He argues that by switching the focus to these subjective aspects of culture, thereby breaking free from geographical or racial ties, the definition of culture becomes more pliable and adaptable to many different groups.

According to Triandis (1972), to meet the criteria of a cultural group, a group of individuals must share some of these *subjective* aspects of culture. This is only likely to happen when that group shares experiences and passes these experiences along to other members of the group. Although having geography or race in common certainly facilitates the sharing of subjective culture, these commonalties are not the only routes through which cultural groups can form. For example, under this definition *women* can be considered a cultural group to the extent to which they may share common experiences, goals, and values. Using the same logic, the elderly can be considered a cultural group, as can *physicians*. It is this definition, namely, one that emphasizes *subjective aspects of culture*, that is being adopted here.

Many scholars have searched for meaningful *subjective* dimensions of culture. By far, most cultural research and theorizing has focused on the dimension of individualism–collectivism. Triandis (1996) suggests that, of all the subjective dimensions of culture that have been examined, the individualism–collectivism dimension emerges most reliably and accounts for the most variance among cultures.

INDIVIDUALISM VERSUS COLLECTIVISM

The major difference between individualistic and collectivistic world views lies in the relative importance of the "other." How collectivists and individualists define the self, what drives their behavior, and how they prioritize their goals differ in the extent to which the focus falls on the self versus another individual or a group. Generally speaking, those from collectivistic cultures define the self as an aspect of a collective (e.g., the family) whereas those from individualistic cultures tend to define the self as independent and autonomous from collectives. The individualistic view of the self is sometimes referred to as an "independent" self construal whereas the collectivistic view of the self is referred to as an "interdependent" construal of the self.

This attention to the "other" can manifest itself in many ways. Maintaining this connection with others means constantly being aware of others and focusing on their needs, desires, and goals. Collectivists have individual goals that are compatible with the goals of their in-groups. If there is a discrepancy between the two sets of goals, collectivists give priority to the in-group goals rather than to their own personal goals. This constant engagement with the in-group involves the willingness and ability to feel and think what others are feeling and thinking and to absorb this information without being told. For collectivists, the requirement is to "read" the "other's" mind and thus to know what the other is thinking or feeling. In return, one expects the other to be aware of one's own feelings and needs without the need to explicitly express them (Nilchaikovit, Hill, & Holland, 1993). To accomplish this, collectivists attend closely to *context* (emotional expressions, touching, distance between bodies, body orientation, level of voice, eye contact) when they communicate. *Accordingly, collectivists are not often explicit or verbally direct because they rely on a substantial amount of paralinguistic communication to fully understand the other, which helps to maintain valued harmonious relationships.* In contrast, for individualists, it is one's responsibility to "say what's on one's mind" if one expects to be attended to or understood. Likewise, one is not expected to implicitly know what someone needs or wishes without its being explicitly stated. *Accordingly, in individualis-*

tic cultures, people distrust what is not said clearly. Emphasis is placed on what is said and on specificity; the unspoken is deemed unimportant and largely ignored.

One further distinction made by Triandis (1996) completes the individual-ism–collectivism picture. He proposes two types of individualism and collec-tivism, each defined by their relationship with another cultural dimension—ver-tical and horizontal relationships. In vertical cultures, hierarchy is very important, and in-group authorities determine most social behavior. In contrast, in horizontal cultures, social behavior is more egalitarian. Vertical collectivism includes perceiving the self as a part (or an aspect) of a collective and accept-ing inequalities within the collective. Horizontal collectivism includes perceiv-ing the self as a part of the collective, but seeing all members of the collective as the same. Thus, equality is stressed. Vertical individualism is a cultural pat-tern in which an autonomous self is postulated, but individuals see each other as different, and inequality is expected. Horizontal individualism is a cultural pattern where an autonomous self is postulated, but the individual is more or less equal in status with others (Singelis, Triandis, Bhawuk, & Gelfand, 1995). For instance, an Israeli kibbutz would be an example of a society that is very collective and yet considers all members of the community equal, thus demon-strating a form of horizontal collectivism. In contrast, the People's Republic of China operates from the same collective principles as a kibbutz, yet emphasizes subordination to superiors, and is thus quite hierarchical in nature. Thus, kib-butz society is a good illustration of horizontal collectivism whereas the Peo-ple's Republic of China is an example of vertical collectivism. The United States is known for its citizens' independent drive and belief that they can achieve any of its many social levels with hard work and perseverance. These ideas of independence and social elitism exemplify a vertical individualistic so-ciety. Sweden, on the other hand, also has citizens who hold strong beliefs in the independence of individuals, but has a government that strives to ensure the equality of each of its citizens. It is, thus, a good example of a vertical individ-ualistic society.

THE REFERENTIAL–INDEXICAL SELF

Landrine (1992) refers to cultural differences in the construal of the self as the "referential" versus the "indexical" self, somewhat analogous to the individ-ualistic–collectivistic distinction. For Landrine (1992), the referential self is the separated, encapsulated self of Western culture and is conceptualized as a "god," in that it is presumed to be the originator, creator, and controller of behavior. In-herent in this conceptualization is the view that regarding one's behavior as con-trolled by someone/something other than oneself is a sign of psychopathology. The nonself realm (e.g., others, spirits, objects) is assumed to function on its own with its own principles and processes and largely independently of the self. Thus, to believe that events within the encapsulated self (e.g., thoughts, feelings) are responsible for events in the nonself realm is also seen as a sign of psychopathology in the Western world. In contrast, the indexical self is defined in relation to specific contexts. For those holding an indexical view of the self, believing that one's behavior is controlled by someone/something other than the self is quite rational. That is, given that the self is seen to exist only in relation to someone/something, it would be quite reasonable to believe that the self can both influence and be influenced by the nonself realm.

Another important aspect of the indexical/referential distinction, according to Landrine (1992), is the fact that for the referential (individualistic) self, relationships are derivative. That is, they are secondary to the self. Community, nation, family, roles, and relationships are all secondary to the self and are conceptualized as being "instrumental" to the self. Each of these larger social units is thought to exist in order to meet the self's needs and will be rejected if it fails to do so. In contrast, the indexical (collectivistic) self is not an entity existing independently of the relationships and contexts in which it is presented (Landrine, 1992). The indexical self is constituted by social interactions and exists only in and through these interactions. Thus, this self has no enduring, trans-situational characteristics, no needs or desires of its own apart from its relationships and contexts (Landrine, 1992). In addition, the lines between the indexical self, others, the supernatural, and the natural world are blurred. These lines are semipermeable, in that the self includes other people and portions of the natural and supernatural worlds. Table 3.1 summarizes these individualistic–collectivistic and indexical–referential systems of self-construal.

TABLE 3.1   Distinctions between Individualistic and Collectivistic Cultures Relevant to Health Communications

	Individualistic	Collectivistic

1. View of the self	Separate from others
	Self is largely defined by
	  stable, internal traits
		Connected to others
		Self is largely defined by one's social
		  relationships

2. View of illness	Materialistic Reductionistic Cause resides within the individual	Holistic Multiple determinants Cause can reside outside the individual Focus can be on the "other"

3. Treatment goals	Self-focused
	Valued outcomes are health
	  or the reduction of symptoms
		Valued outcomes may be to return to
		  role functions
		Nonverbal, subtle, and indirect

4. Style of communication	Verbal, open, and direct Emphasis is on what is explicitly stated	Emphasis is on what is left unsaid

INTRACULTURAL VARIATION: IDIOCENTRISM VERSUS ALLOCENTRISM AND AGENCY VERSUS COMMUNION

Triandis, Chan, Bhawuk, Iwao, and Sinha (1995) propose individual-level constructs, labeled "allocentrism" and "idiocentrism," which correspond to the cultural-level concepts of collectivism and individualism, respectively. Triandis et al. (1995) administered measures originally designed to assess individualism–collectivism and found that they could also differentiate among individuals within the same culture, thereby providing evidence that the individual-level constructs of idiocentrism and allocentrism were similar to their cultural-level counterparts. These individual-level constructs provide one with the opportunity to look within cultures for variations in individualism and collectivism.

Within an U.S. sample (a decidedly individualistic society), Triandis et al. (1995) found support for the hypothesis that women are more allocentric than are men. This was also observed within their Japanese sample. That is, Japanese women's mean allocentric values were higher than that of the men, whereas the Japanese men were higher than the women on idiocentric values. Furthermore, Triandis, McCusker, and Hui (1990) found that Chinese-American subjects who scored low on allocentrism had profiles that looked more like the non-Chinese Americans than those who scored relatively high on allocentrism. The latter had profiles that looked very much like the typical People's Republic of China profiles. That is, the idiocentrism–allocentrism measure distinguished *among* the Chinese American sample. These results lend credence to these individual-level measures' abilities to distinguish *intra*cultural differences.

These intracultural differences are not at all surprising if one considers the "agency versus communion" literature. Agency and communion are terms developed by Bakan (1966) to reflect two fundamental modalities of human existence. Agency reflects one's existence as an individual, and communion reflects the individual as but a part of a larger social context. Agency involves the motives of self-protection, self-assertion, self-expansion, self-control, and self-direction and emphasizes the forming of separation (i.e., autonomy) from others. In contrast, communion emphasizes group participation, cooperation, attachment, connections between people, and emphasizes the creation of unions (Helgeson, 1994). Thus, the parallels between agency and communion and individualism (idiocentrism) and collectivism (allocentrism) are striking. Bakan (1966) stated that agency and communion are present in both men and women but that agency is more characteristic of men and communion is more characteristic of women. The elements of agency and communion that are most often emphasized are the focus on the self versus the focus on the other. Notably, this is the same key differentiating characteristic of individualism versus collectivism.

Thus, the relative importance of the self versus other seems to be an important differentiating characteristic both between different cultural groups and within cultural groups. This pervasive difference in focus between (and within) groups is likely to be reflected in many aspects of an individual's life and, arguably, could be an important influence on how people think about illness and organize illness experiences. Specifically, one might expect the extent to which the "other" plays a role in beliefs about the cause of illness, the goals for treatment, and appropriate treatment choices to be influenced by this culturally influenced characteristic. Moreover, between- and within-culture variations in the horizontal/vertical dimension may be likely to manifest themselves in the extent to which the health care provider is viewed as the expert. That is, expectations about patient and health care provider status differences and power differentials in the context of the relationship are likely to be influenced by the extent to which one is horizontally versus vertically oriented.

CULTURAL DIFFERENCES IN ILLNESS MODELS

The question to be addressed in this section is how might what individuals think about health and illness differ cross-culturally and to what extent might this be driven by cross-cultural differences in collectivism (i.e., allocentrism, communion) and individualism (i.e., idiocentrism, agency)? One would also expect an individual's mental representation of illness to be highly influenced by the dominant medical model of their particular culture. Thus, we begin with a brief review of three of the world's major medical models: biomedical, Traditional Chinese, and Ayurvedic.

THE BIOMEDICAL MODEL

Historically, the dominant paradigm of Western medical science has been the biomedical model. The biomedical model is based on two fundamental assumptions: reductionism and materialism. Reductionism is the view that an individual can be understood by studying his or her smallest constituent parts. From this perspective, illness can be understood by examining biochemical processes (Engel, 1977a). Materialism is the view that individuals are physical beings whose existence and functions can be explained solely by the principles of physiology, anatomy, and biochemistry. Inherent in this model is the view that psychological processes are unimportant in determining health. Thus, from the perspective of the biomedical model, disease is a disruption in biological structures (or physiological processes) caused by some physical or chemical factor. Intervention, thus, would involve the introduction of a corrective physical or chemical agent. One might typify this model as a "one cause, one cure" paradigm. Accordingly, interventions that do not involve a biological or chemical manipulation are not considered "medicine." This model leaves no room for the social, cultural, psychological, or behavioral dimensions of disease.

It is important to note, however, that the biomedical model has not been the only influence on Western medical thought. The biopsychosocial model, wherein health and illness are seen to be determined by an interplay of biological, psychological, and social factors, was formally articulated by Engel in 1977. Although the article by Engel (1977b) has been labeled as the marker of the beginning of a new *zeitgeist,* the biopsychosocial model has tended to remain in the realm of ideology and has not become a general guide to daily practice (Sadler & Hulgus, 1992).

For example, in the Mersey Region of England, the Royal College of General Practitioners found that the majority of those polled believed that physicians should work within a biomedical rather than a biopsychosocial model of health care (Dorwick, May, Richardson, & Bundred, 1996). Moreover, a study designed to examine physicians' decision-making processes showed that biomedical variables alone predicted the preferred treatment correctly in 53% of the cases (Denig, Haaijer-Ruskamp, Wesseling, & Versluis, 1993). Although the authors note that prediction was improved by adding "social environment" variables, these variables—opinions of consulted colleagues, pharmacists, and family physicians—arguably are biomedical rather than social variables.

The biomedical model also dominates psychiatric clinical practice and research (Cohen, 1993), as illustrated by the fact that 86% of the papers presented at the 1992 annual meeting of the American Psychiatric Association were biomedically oriented, and nearly all departments of psychiatry are now chaired by persons committed to biomedical research (Cohen, 1993).

These data suggest that most Western physicians are still trained in, and subscribe to, the biomedical rather than the biopsychosocial model. It would not be unreasonable to conclude that the biomedical model drives most Western physicians' medical communications to the patient.

THE TRADITIONAL CHINESE MEDICAL MODEL

The dominant medical model that has been practiced for centuries in many Asian countries (e.g., China, Japan, Vietnam, Hong Kong, Taiwan) is the traditional Chinese medical model. This traditional form of medicine is based on a theory of internal and external balances (Topley, 1976). According to the theory, an individual's physical well-being is determined by the movement of certain elements. When someone is in a state of good health, the relationship between the elements is one of balance or harmony. When imbalances occur, ill health is presumed to follow (Harwood, 1981). Some imbalances are seen as inevitable, given that human society is always in flux. People are being born, marrying, and dying, and these transitions cause instability. These instabilities, in turn, are seen to affect the internal balance in the human body. The traditional Chinese society also considers supernatural forces as potential disturbances of internal balance (Gould-Martin, 1978). These health and illness beliefs reflect the collectivistic belief of the importance of the other.

Thus, from the perspective of the traditional Chinese medical model, disease is a disruption in the balance of internal elements caused by some physical, social, emotional, or supernatural factor. Interventions are aimed at restoring the natural balance of the individual (Hoang & Erickson, 1985). One might typify this model as holistic because it attends to all elements that affect the individual whether they are biological or more social in nature. This model encompasses the social, psychological, and even the supernatural dimensions of disease and the notion of balance permeates ideas of health and illness similarly. It clearly reflects the Asian collectivistic philosophy of the self in harmonious relation to others (see also Chapter 14).

THE SANSKRIT THEORY OF AYURVEDIC MEDICINE

The classical Sanskrit theory of Indian medicine, known as Ayurveda, dominates the medical traditions of all of South Asia and, to a lesser extent, Southeast Asia. Ayurveda has a developed theory of physiological function and dysfunction which includes a physiological theory of the three humors consisting of elements found in nature (Obeyesekere, 1976). Physical health is maintained when the three humors are in harmonic balance. When the balance is upset, they become "troubles" for the organism. Illness thus arises when the homeostasis of the three humors is disrupted, and treatment is aimed at restoring balance (Weiss et al., 1988).

Given that these humors are believed to consist of elements which are all found in nature, their balance may be influenced by natural elements such as the weather, the seasons, and food. It is also believed that these humors can be affected by emotion, which can raise one humor relative to another (Obeyesekere, 1976). Thus, as with the traditional Chinese medical model, the notion of *balance* permeates the Ayurvedic tradition. Moreover, the social realm plays an important role in health and illness, because those close to us are the most likely to stir emotions that may disturb the harmonic balance of our humors.

Similarly, the supernatural world, including dead ancestors and spirits, is likely to stir emotions that disturb the individual's natural balance. Again, the importance of the other in Southeast Asian cultures, which tend to be collectivistic, is reflected in their dominant medical model (see also the Chandarana and Pellizzari chapter).

To summarize, compared to the mechanistic biomedical (i.e., individualistic) model, the traditional medical models of the East (e.g., traditional Chinese and Ayurveda) are much more holistic in that they consider the natural, social, and supernatural influences of health and illness. The notion of internal balance or harmony, which permeates both the traditional Chinese and Ayurvedic (i.e., collectivistic) medical models, also differentiates these traditional medical models from the biomedical model of the Western world.

CONGRUENCE BETWEEN LAY MODELS AND MEDICAL MODELS OF DISEASE

Medical models, and particularly the biomedical model, are often devised by medical scientists for the study of disease. Models, however, are not necessarily veridical. Indeed, broadly defined, a model is nothing more than a system of beliefs used to explain natural phenomena. Such efforts at explanation are arguably socially adaptive (Engel, 1977b). Socially and culturally derived belief systems about disease could be termed "popular" or "lay" models of illness. Thus, one could argue that individuals raised in Western cultures may develop mental representations of illness that represent a subset of the dominant biomedical model. Likewise, individuals raised in non-Western cultures likely develop illness cognitions congruent with a subset of the dominant medical model of their country of origin.

The existing literature abounds with case reports of Western lay familiarity with biomedical symptom sets indicative of both minor illness and major disease (e.g., Bishop, 1984, 1987; Pennebaker, 1984). For example, Bishop and Converse (1986) tested lay diagnostic skills by presenting Western (i.e., American) participants with symptom sets previously judged to be representative of both serious (epilepsy, heart attack, stomach cancer, ulcer, stroke, and pneumonia) and nonserious (measles, hay fever, strep throat, flu, mumps, and chicken pox) diseases. Subjects exhibited excellent diagnostic skills by providing accurate disease labels when given consistent symptom descriptions. Their diagnostic skill deteriorated when inconsistent symptoms replaced some of the diagnostically congruent symptoms, suggesting that there was an illness model "template" from which they were operating. Lay familiarity with biomedical taxonomies has been demonstrated by other investigators as well (Lau & Hartman, 1983; Leventhal, Meyer, & Nerenz, 1980).

Lay diagnostic abilities indicate that biomedical taxonomies of disease serve as meaningful representations of symptom sets in lay medical thought. Familiarity with medical taxonomies, however, does not presuppose a firm grasp on the entire biomedical model. There is evidence that, within Western culture, mismatches between lay models and physician models of disease can lead to poor health outcomes (presumably through miscommunication).

INCONGRUENCE BETWEEN PATIENT AND HEALTH CARE PROVIDER MODELS WITHIN WESTERN CULTURE

Mismatches between illness models can occur (and affect patient outcome variables) even when the patient and health care provider are presumed to be operating from the *same* biomedical model. The belief that one can detect symptoms of high blood pressure, and thus recognize when one's blood pressure is elevated, was contradictory to the biomedical view that hypertension is asymptomatic and, thus, there are no detectable symptoms. Meyer, Leventhal, and Gutmann (1985) found Western hypertensive patients who believed that they could detect when their blood pressure was elevated were three times as likely to drop out of treatment than those who didn't believe they could tell when their blood pressure was elevated. The mismatch in belief systems between patients and physicians was presumed, by the authors, to be what led to the increased dropout rate.

Similarly, Meyer et al. (1985) found that Western patients who believed that their hypertension was a variable condition were less adherent to prescribed regimens than patients who held the biomedically correct notion that their hypertension was a chronic, stable condition. Swartzman and McDermid (1993), using a vignette approach, further found that subjects who incorrectly attributed symptoms of heart attack to stress cues were less likely to recommend seeking medical care than subjects who did not attribute the symptoms to stress. Furthermore, Johnson and Snow (1982) have shown that misinformation and/or lack of information about the menstrual cycle contributes to unwanted fertility, particularly among black women attending an inner-city Detroit medical clinic. For example, women who believed they were most likely to conceive during menstruation (a time when the uterus is "open"), and consequently were "safe" at midcycle (when their uterus was "closed"), were prime candidates for unwanted pregnancy (Johnson & Snow, 1982). Therefore, "incorrect" information, that is, information that does not match the physician's biomedical explanation, has repeatedly been shown to lead to undesirable health outcomes.

INCONGRUENCIES BETWEEN THE BIOMEDICAL
MODEL AND NON-WESTERN ILLNESS MODELS
IN WESTERN SOCIETY

Most research in the area of cultural differences in illness cognitions has focused on causal attributions for health and illness. Landrine and Klonoff (Landrine & Klonoff, 1992, 1994; Klonoff & Landrine, 1994) have attempted to empirically determine cultural differences in beliefs about the causes of illness among those living in the United States. Their focus has been almost exclusively limited to the supernatural/natural distinction and has not focused on the notion of balance nor on the influence of the social relationships, the latter of which is presumed to more strongly differentiate cross-culturally. Landrine and Klonoff (1994) had their subjects judge the importance of 38 potential causes of illness. They found that "minority" (that is, Blacks, Latinos, and Asian/Pacific Islanders) subjects rated supernatural forces as more important causes of illness than did whites. However, in a replication and expansion of their previous work, Klonoff and Landrine (1994) failed to detect differences between minority (that is, African, Mexican, and Asian Americans) and "White" endorsement of causal explanations of illness. In this second study, subjects were asked to rate the importance of 41 possible causes of illness, with reference to six specific diseases.

One of the major differences in the methodology of these two studies lies in how they elicited the health beliefs of their subjects. In the first study, Landrine and Klonoff (1994) asked their subjects to rate the importance of possible causes of illness in general, whereas in the study that failed to show cultural differences (Klonoff & Landrine, 1994), subjects were asked to rate the importance of possible causes of illness with reference to six specific illnesses (headache, hypertension, AIDS, the common cold, diabetes, and lung cancer). This second methodology may have concretized the task by forcing a diagnostically paired cognitive set, such that group differences were not likely to emerge. Moreover, neither study sufficiently measured "culture" to adequately determine the model that might be driving the content of illness representations. That is, the "minority" and "white" groups in both studies were quite heterogeneous in that they encompassed many different cultural groups. Moreover, while the authors assumed that participants' cultural beliefs were driving their thoughts about illness, these beliefs were never measured.

Quah and Bishop (1996) examined this issue in a more homogeneous group of Chinese Americans. They believed that participants high in Chinese cultural orientation would be more likely to describe diseases using Chinese health concepts and less likely to describe diseases in terms of physical causality or chronicity (thought to represent biomedical thinking). These researchers went to great lengths to obtain adequate measures of cultural identity, including endorsement of traditional Chinese values, language spoken, religious affiliation, and generational information. These measures were then combined to form a measure of Chinese cultural orientation. Participants high in Chinese cultural orientation were more likely to describe diseases in terms of "internal imbalance," "blocked qi," "excess cold," or "excess heat." Conversely, participants with lower levels of Chinese orientation emphasized the physical causation of disease (Quah & Bishop, 1996). The authors found that participants who described diseases in terms of traditional Chinese medical concepts were more likely to seek help from a practitioner of Traditional Chinese medicine. They did not, however, include a truly "Western" comparison group and only included the one item ("caused by a virus") to tap endorsement of the biomedical model.

Armstrong and Swartzman (1999), in a study that improved upon some of the limitations of the aforementioned work, examined the effects of Western and Asian culture on causal attributions of illness and their implications for satisfaction with Western medical care. These researchers not only used multiple measures to assess cultural identity (including language, place of birth, time spent in Canada, and generational history), they also included a measure of acculturation—the Suinn–Lew Asian Self-Identity Acculturation scale (S–L ASIA; Suinn, Rickard-Figueroa, Lew, & Vigil, 1987). Furthermore, they improved upon the measures used by Landrine and Klonoff (1994), Klonoff and Landrine (1994), and Quah and Bishop (1996) to assess causal attributions, by ensuring an adequate number of items representing the biomedical and the traditional Chinese medical models in their list of causal attributions.

Armstrong and Swartzman (1999) hypothesized that Asian participants (predominantly first-generation Chinese, Vietnamese, and Taiwanese; all freshmen at a Canadian university) would endorse causes that were in line with the traditional Chinese medical model, whereas Western first-year undergraduates would endorse causal explanations more in keeping with the biomedical model. As predicted, Asian participants were less satisfied with the care they got from Western doctors than were the Canadian participants. Moreover, Asian participants more strongly endorsed items indicative of traditional Chinese medical beliefs (e.g., balance of yin/yang, supernatural forces, influence of family) than did the Western participants, and the Western participants more strongly endorsed biomedical causes (e.g., bacteria, viruses, hormones) than did the Asian participants. Moreover, these traditional beliefs were found to mediate the cultural differences in satisfaction with medical care. That is, the extent to which a participant endorsed items indicative of traditional Chinese beliefs explained the difference in satisfaction with Western medical care between the Western and the Asian groups and also accounted for satisfaction differences between more or less acculturated (based on the S–L ASIA scores) members within the Asian group. Thus, the stronger a participant's traditional Chinese views, the less satisfied they were with Western medical care (Armstrong & Swartzman, 1999).

The findings on cultural differences in causal attributions for illness are consistent with what one would expect, given the Western Biomedical versus traditional Chinese medical models. Asian cultures do seem to place more emphasis on the supernatural (e.g., dead ancestors, mystic forces) and the social realms as influences over health and illness. The notion of balance is also important in the illness representations of Asian participants. Moreover, these differences in illness representations seem to be affecting certain health outcomes, such as help-seeking patterns, and satisfaction with medical care. Although the research reported has focused on the Asian culture, findings arguably could be extended to include other cultures that share some of the values of the Asian culture. That is, members from other collectivistic/interdependent cultural groups could be expected to act in similar ways with respect to their thinking about health and illness.

A reexamination of cross-cultural differences in the definition of self and the relative importance that the other plays in an individual's self-concept leads to predictions regarding the content of illness cognitions that are borne out by these data. The extensive focus on the other in the collectivist self-concept may suggest a more significant contribution of the other in the content of illness cognitions. The findings from Armstrong and Swartzman (1999) suggest that the social realm (influence of family) plays a more important role in collectivists' attributions of illness than in individualists' attributions. The importance of the other could also potentially manifest itself in beliefs about the potential cure of illnesses (e.g., "if my relationship with my brother improves, so will my health"), consequences of illnesses (e.g., "I won't be able to help my family if I were to have this condition"), or any other domain of health and illness.

CULTURAL DIFFERENCES IN
TREATMENT GOALS

Cultural differences in *goals* may also conceivably affect the content of illness cognitions. For example, given that individualists are more self-focused, their treatment goals may be to feel better, alleviate symptoms, and maximize their own health outcome. This goal is consistent with the goal of the typical biomedical encounter, that is, to cure the patient. With the self as priority, there is only one person to please—oneself. However, for the collectivist, in-group goals will be weighed more heavily. Therefore, the goal for health care may not be the self-oriented goal of better health, but, rather, it may be return to work or to the family, thereby fulfilling social obligations, roles, and commitments. The priority of in-group goals may increase the range of desirable health outcomes. The focus of conversation during the physician–patient interaction, thus, may be influenced not only by the congruence of the medical models held by both, but also by the extent to which they value the same outcomes.

Given the Western individualistic bias, the focus on the other when making health decisions may mistakenly be interpreted as dependence, passivity, and helplessness (Banyard & Graham-Bermann, 1993) on the part of the health care provider. Consider Fine's (1985) case study cited by Banyard & Graham-Bermann (1993) of a woman who was brought into a U.S. hospital emergency room after being gang-raped. This woman decided not to press charges or make use of any of the counseling services offered to her. She was concerned only with getting out of the hospital as soon as possible so she could return to her child. Fine (1985) was struck by the ways in which some medical staff labeled her as someone who was making a bad health decision. Such an analysis disregarded the adaptive strategy, what Fine termed "relational coping," that the woman was actively employing. For her, the decision was not based on solely her needs. Rather, she was focused on how to keep her children safe. Thus, for collectivistic/interdependent individuals, health decisions may be based more on their potential impact on many other individuals than are those decisions made by individualists. Thus, what appears to be a bad decision from the point of view of the self-oriented individualist may actually be an adaptive decision for the collectivist in that it meets these more other-oriented goals.

Some have posited, however, that when taken to extremes, this focus on the other can indeed have deleterious effects on one's health (at least for those from Western culture). Helgeson (1994) uses the term *unmitigated communion* to describe the focus on others to the exclusion of the self. She postulates that an exaggerated focus on connection and concern with the preservation of relationships can be harmful if it undermines physical and psychological caring for oneself. Helgeson and Fritz (1996) found that American adolescent female diabetics scoring high on unmitigated communion were more strongly affected by events that involved social network members and that these sources of stress increased their own distress and detracted from their own health care. Therefore, when taken to the extreme, a focus on the other can interfere with the adoption of healthy (self-oriented) practices.

To summarize, illness cognitions have been postulated to be influenced by dominant medical models. Lay persons, or patients, have demonstrated familiarity with biomedical models. However, patient information is necessarily less complete than physician information and is occasionally inaccurate. Mismatches between and within cultures may result in poor health outcomes. In addition to mismatches with respect to medical models, mismatches regarding the focus of the other and the priority of in-group goals have been postulated.

LANGUAGE AS A REFLECTION AND SHAPER OF ILLNESS MODELS

What is said during the physician–patient interaction (that is, the content of the interaction) will be influenced by what individuals *think* about health and illness. That is, what is said depends largely on what is thought. The notion that thought and speech are linked is not a new one (Whorf, 1956). There is a widely held view that language is the vehicle of cognitive processes. An extensive discussion on whether thought influences language or language influences thought is beyond the scope of this chapter. The consensus seems to be that language and thought have reciprocal influences (Pederson, 1994). Therefore, what an individual thinks about health and illness is likely to be reflected in the "illness stories" they convey during their interactions with the health care provider.

Price (1991) studied illness stories of Ecuadorian individuals in natural discourse. Ecuadorian society is collectivistic in nature and tends to be organized vertically. The traditional medical model practiced in Ecuador is similar to other traditional medical models described in this chapter in that it is holistic in nature, in that natural, supernatural, and social realms are each important aspects of the Ecuadorian illness experience. During her year in the field, Price (1991) came to realize that these illness stories contained numerous "traces" of cognitive models that bear on interpretation of illness. Because tacit knowledge shapes natural discourse to such a large degree, important traces are found not only in what is said, but also in what is left unsaid. In telling these stories, narrators took for granted that the listeners shared many of their assumptions about how the world works. Price (1991) noted that the missing "shared knowledge" must be filled in if outsiders are to understand the logical connections among utterances and the cultural models that underlie them. It was also interesting to Price (1991) that some facets of a story were presented with what seems (to her) to be over-elaborate detail. She took these elaborations to indicate a deviation from the standard expectations for role behavior. Thus, these speech patterns (including what is said in the story) provide insight into the content of the illness cognitions of the speakers.

Using these speech patterns as indications of knowledge structures, Price (1991) uncovered some interesting trends in Ecuadorian illness stories. Responsibilities and activities of individuals other than the sick person involved in the illness episode occupied a distinct and central place in the Ecuadorian model of illness. Assumptions about mothers' roles were especially prominent and there appeared to be a special place for what Price (1991) calls the "physics" of health behavior. That is, the process of initiating health behaviors (e.g., going to see the physician) was very detailed and rule-governed. Ideas about the appropriateness of extrafamilial help and the hierarchy surrounding different health practitioners were also elucidated through these illness stories.

Price's (1991) analysis seems to support earlier hypotheses about the importance of social influences in different cultures. That is, the collectivistic illness stories studied had high social content. Others figured prominently in Ecuadorian illness stories. In fact, the roles of family members were central to these stories, with the patient seemingly absent from the ordeal. One would expect individualistic illness stories, on the other hand, to focus on the patient with little information regarding how the illness impacted upon others and more energy directed toward biomedical information such as the believed cause, the symptoms, and the implemented treatment.

Price's (1991) research has implications for understanding the physician–patient interaction. For example, the Ecuadorian illness stories reflected the focal position others take in that society. The content of illness schemata was thus reflected in speech. The implication here is that health care providers can glean how and what a patient thinks simply by attending to what the patient says (and does not say). Furthermore, one can assume that if health thoughts are reflected in health-relevant speech, health-relevant speech may serve to influence health thoughts. Thus, the physician may be in a position to influence a patient's thoughts about health and illness simply by providing them with the vocabulary and experience of biomedically congruent illness stories.

CROSS-CULTURAL DIFFERENCES IN DISCOURSE: THE PATIENT–HEALTH CARE PROVIDER RELATIONSHIP

There are also cultural trends with respect to what content is valued in conversation in general. The content of communication that is most valued in one culture may not be valued in another. For example, Western individuals tend to use small talk ("Beautiful weather today"), but other cultures do not engage in such talk to the same extent (Triandis, 1996). In some cultures, exaggeration is appropriate, whereas, in others, moderation is the rule. Although these tendencies may be very culture-specific, there are more general trends that follow the individualistic–collectivistic distinction proposed in the current framework.

Collectivists tend to be circumspect. That is, they tend to communicate all but the most important piece of information, which the listener is supposed to supply in order to make the whole message comprehensible (Triandis, 1996). This strategy has the advantage of permitting people to keep track of the other's feelings and thereby avoid tensions that might disturb the harmony. Conversely, individualists, who are not overly concerned with maintaining social harmony, get to the point so quickly that a collectivist may find it shocking. Thus, one can imagine a Western physician's frustration with a patient who is not "getting to the point," and a collectivistic patient's shock at a physician who delves right into personal information without the appropriate conversation that allows the patient to discover the nature of the interaction before any real information is exchanged.

SUMMARY

To summarize, we have made the argument that cross- (and within-) cultural variations in collectivism and individualism can have an impact on the physician–patient interaction. Societies that practice holistic medicine (e.g., traditional Chinese medicine) tend to be collectivistic in nature. Interdependent individuals in these societies are defined with respect to specific contexts; they do not exist in isolation. It follows, then, that treating the self would involve consideration of many domains outside of the physical entity of the individual, such as important others and spiritual entities. In contrast, mechanistic medical models (e.g., the Biomedical model) tend to be practiced by individualistic societies. The individual in these societies has an encapsulated self, that is, other individuals do not enter into the self-concept. Accordingly, in individualistic (e.g., Western culture) societies, the treatment of an illness focuses on the physical state of the afflicted individual.

These differing perspectives (treating the self-contained being versus treating the social being) have implications for exactly who is considered the patient. Operating from the individualistic, biomedical model, one would tend to consider only the afflicted individual as the identified patient. In contrast, a holistic medical model (e.g., traditional Chinese medicine) may lead one to consider others in one's range of desirable outcomes (Nilchaicovit et al., 1993). For example, Kleinman (1980) observed that Western-style physician–patient interactions were exclusively dyads (i.e., only the patient and the physician were present), whereas Chinese-style interactions often included several family members. This suggests that the Chinese-style physicians had a more inclusive definition of "patient" than did the Western-style physicians. There are also cultural differences with respect to expectations about *what* information is exchanged during the physician–patient interaction. Again, these differences can be explained by the extent to which the other factors into an individual's world-view. If the other is important in one's world-view, as it is in collectivistic cultures, maintaining good relationships is necessarily an important aspect of this focus. Maintaining relationships is often accomplished with careful and indirect (i.e., nonverbal) communication. This way, an individual can gauge the other's response to ideas by carefully skirting issues until the other's position is gleaned and then proceeding according to the other's reaction. A collectivistic patient, with the goal of maintaining harmonious relationships, is likely to give information to the health care provider cautiously and gauge the reaction of the provider before proceeding. This individual would expect the health care provider to move with equal caution and may be offended by a direct questioning manner. In contrast, an individualistic patient is more apt to be direct and to the point, relatively unconcerned with maintaining harmony in the health care provider–patient relationship, and easily frustrated by health communications that are vague or circumspect.

Thus, the individualistic–collectivistic distinction, and its concomitant degree of focus on the self versus the other, has been shown to have implications for beliefs about health and illness, expectations for the health care provider–patient relationship, and health communication preferences. The health care provider who is cognizant of these dimensions could arguably shape health communications (with respect to both content and process) in such a way as to improve health outcomes for culturally diverse patients. For example, when dealing with a patient from a collectivistic culture, a health care provider may pay special attention to the role of the other in the patient's health beliefs, goals for treatment, participants involved in the treatment (e.g., who is the identified patient), and patterns of communicating health information (e.g., paying attention to what is left unsaid) in order to facilitate positive health outcomes.

CASE STUDY

The following is a description of a program that was a joint attempt by Native leaders in southern Ontario and a nurse anthropologist to adjust the system of Native beliefs with respect to diabetes, in order to induce what were considered to be responses less detrimental to the individuals themselves and their families. The main vehicle for this adjustment was a narrative entitled *Nanabush and the Stranger* (McLeod, 1982). The story tells of Nanabush, the legendary figure who represents the teacher in Ojibway culture, and his encounter with the personified character of Diabetes. No one can lie to Nanabush, so what Diabetes tells Nanabush is taken to be the truth about himself.

The diabetes workshop is a day-long meeting of interested diabetic Natives with the Native Diabetes Program members (which include professional health care providers, Native diabetics, a Native storyteller, and the Spiritual Leader). An important feature of the workshop is that everyone is seated in a circle. Explanations are given as to how the circle represents the Native community in harmony with nature. The hosting elder may open the event with a prayer, followed by the Spiritual Leader bringing everyone to the circle in equal status—open to learn and share with each other—by making explicit pronouncements about "not being there to change anybody's ways" or "tell them what to do." This "teaching circle" then becomes the context in which to discuss beliefs about diabetes, personal difficulties with the disease, and hints to improve control of the disease.

This Native Diabetes Program, conducted in Toronto, has by no means reversed the "noncompliance" pattern with this population but with the described attention to cultural content and process, changes in attitude and behavior are reportedly beginning to take place (Hagey, 1984).

1. How were cultural beliefs about illness and the process of information exchange reflected in this intervention?
2. How could this approach be adapted for a different cultural group or medical condition?

SUGGESTED READINGS

Markus, H. R., & Kitayama, S. (1991). Culture and the self: Implications of cognition, emotion, and motivation. *Psychological Review, 98,* 223–253.
Nilchaikovit, T., Hill, J. M., & Holland, J. C. (1993). The effects of culture on illness behavior and medical care: Asian and American differences. *General Hospital Psychiatry, 15,* 41–50.

REFERENCES

Anderson, J. M. (1986). Ethnicity and illness experience: Ideological structures and the health care delivery system. *Social Science and Medicine, 22,* 1277–1283.
Armstrong, T. L., & Swartzman, L. C. (1999). Asian versus Western differences in satisfaction with Western medical care: The mediational effects of illness attributions. *Psychology and Health, 14,* 403–416.
Bakan, D. (1966). *The duality of human existence.* Chicago: Rand McNally.
Banyard, V. L., & Graham-Bermann, S. A. (1993). Can women cope? A gender analysis of theories of coping with stress. *Psychology of Women Quarterly, 17,* 308–318.
Bishop, G. D. (1984). Gender, role and illness behavior in a military population. *Health Psychology, 3,* 519–534.
Bishop, G. D. (1987). Lay conceptions of physical symptoms. *Journal of Applied Social Psychology, 17,* 127–146.
Bishop, G. D., & Converse, S. A. (1986). Illness representations: A prototype approach. *Health Psychology, 5,* 96–114.
Cohen, C. I. (1993). The biomedicalization of psychiatry: A critical overview. *Community Mental Health Journal, 29,* 509–521.
Denig, P., Haaijer-Ruskamp, F. M., Wesseling, H., & Versluis, A. (1993). Towards understanding treatment preferences of hospital physicians. *Social Science and Medicine, 36,* 915–924.
Dorwick, C., May, C., Richardson, M., & Bundred, P. (1996). The biopsychosocial model of general practice: Rhetoric or reality? *British Journal of General Practice, 46,* 105–107.
Engel, G. L. (1977a). The care of the patient: Art or science? *The John's Hopkins Medical Journal, 140,* 222–232.
Engel, G. L. (1977b). The need for a new medical model: A challenge of biomedicine. *Science, 196,* 129–136.
Fine, M. (1985). Coping with rape: Critical perspectives on consciousness. *Imagination, Cognition, and Personality, 3,* 249–267.
Flack, J. M., Amaro, H., Jenkins, W., Kunitz, S., Levy, J., Mixon, M., & Yu, E. (1995). Panel 1: Epidemiology of minority health. *Health Psychology, 14,* 592–600.

Gould-Martin, K. (1978). Hot, cold, clean, poison, and dirt: Chinese folk medical categories. *Social Science and Medicine, 12,* 39–46.

Hagey, R. (1984). The phenomenon, the explanations and the responses: Metaphors surrounding diabetes in urban Canadian Indians. *Social Science and Medicine, 18,* 265–272.

Harwood, A. (Ed.) (1981). *Ethnicity and medical care.* Cambridge, MA: Harvard University Press.

Helgeson, V. S. (1994). Relation of agency and communion to well-being: Evidence and potential explanations. *Psychological Bulletin, 116,* 412–428.

Helgeson, V. S., & Fritz, H. L. (1996). Implications of communion and unmitigated communion for adolescent adjustment to type 1 diabetes. *Women's Health: Research on Gender, Behavior, and Policy, 2,* 169–194.

Hoang, G. N., & Erickson, R. V. (1985). Cultural barriers to effective medical care among Indochinese patients. *Annual Review of Medicine, 36,* 229–239.

Johnson, S. M., & Snow, L. F. (1982). Assessment of reproductive knowledge in an inner-city clinic. *Social Science and Medicine, 16,* 1652–1657.

Kleinman, A. (1980). *Patients and healers in the context of cultures.* Berkeley, CA: University of California Press.

Klonoff, E. A., & Landrine, H. (1994). Culture and gender diversity in commonsense beliefs about the causes of six illnesses. *Journal of Behavioral Medicine, 17,* 407–418.

Landrine, H. (1992). Clinical implications of cultural differences: The referential versus the indexical self. *Clinical Psychology Review, 12,* 401–415.

Landrine, H., & Klonoff, E. A. (1992). Culture and health-related schemas: A review and proposal for interdisciplinary integration. *Health Psychology, 11,* 267–276.

Landrine, H., & Klonoff, E. A. (1994). Cultural diversity in causal attribution for illness: The role of the supernatural. *Journal of Behavioral Medicine, 17,* 181–193.

Lau, R. R., & Hartman, K. A. (1983). Common sense representations of common illnesses. *Health Psychology, 2,* 167–185.

Leclere, F. B., Jensen, L., & Biddlecom, A. E. (1994). Health care utilization, family context, and adaptation among immigrants to the United States. *Journal of Health and Social Behavior, 35,* 370–384.

Leventhal, H., Meyer, D., & Nerenz, D. (1980). The commonsense representation of illness danger. In S. Rachman (Ed.), *Contributions to medical psychology: Vol 2* (pp. 3–26). Oxford, UK: Pergamon Press.

Lin, T., Tardiff, K., Donetz, G., & Goresky, W. (1978). Ethnicity and patterns of health seeking. *Culture, Medicine, & Psychiatry, 2,* 3–13.

McLeod, J. (1982). *Nanabush and the Stranger, Illustrated pamphlet.* Unpublished, University of Toronto.

Meyer, D., Leventhal, H., & Gutmann, M. (1985). Common-sense models of illness: The example of hypertension. *Health Psychology, 4,* 115–135.

National Center for Health Statistics (1991). *Healthy people 2000 review.* Hyattsville, MD: Public Health Service.

Nilchaikovit,T., Hill, J. M., & Holland, J. C. (1993). The effects of culture on illness behavior and medical care: Asian and American differences. *General Hospital Psychiatry, 15,* 41–50.

Obeyesekere, G. (1976). The theory and practice of psychological medicine in the Ayurvedic tradition. *Culture, Medicine and Psychiatry, 1,* 155–181.

Pederson, E. (1994). *Language as context, language as means: Spatial cognition and habitual language use.* Nijmegen, The Netherlands: Max Planck Institute for Psycholinguistics.

Penn, N. E., Kar, S., Kramer, J., Skinner, J., & Zambrana, R. E. (1995). Panel VI: Ethnic minorities, health care systems, and behavior. *Health Psychology, 14,* 641–646.

Pennebaker, J. W. (1984). Accuracy of symptom perception. In A. Baum, S. E. Taylor, & J. E. Singer (Eds.), *Handbook of psychology and health: Vol. IV, Social psychological aspects of health* (pp. 189–212). Hillsdale, NJ: Erlbaum.

Price, L. (1991). Ecuadorian illness stories: Cultural knowledge in natural discourse. In D. Holland

& N. Quinn (Eds.), *Cultural models in language and thought* (pp. 313–342). Cambridge, UK: Cambridge University Press.

Quah, S., & Bishop, G. D. (1996). Seeking help for illness: The roles of cultural orientation and illness cognition. *Journal of Health Psychology, 1,* 209–222.

Sadler, J. Z., & Hulgus, Y. F. (1992). Clinical problem solving and the biopsychosocial model. *American Journal of Psychiatry, 149,* 1315–1323.

Singelis, T. M., Triandis, H. C., Bhawuk, D. P. S., & Gelfand, M. J. (1995). Horizontal and vertical dimensions of individualism and collectivism: A theoretical and measurement refinement. *Cross-Cultural Research, 29,* 240–275.

Suinn, R. M., Rickard-Figueroa, K., Lew, S., & Vigil, P. (1987). The Suinn-Lew Asian Self-Identity Acculturation Scale: An initial report. *Educational and Psychological Measurement, 47,* 401–407.

Swartzman, L. C., & McDermid, A. J. (1993). The impact of contextual cues on the interpretation of and response to physical symptoms: A vignette approach. *Journal of Behavioral Medicine, 16,* 183–198.

Topley, M. (1976). Chinese traditional etiology and methods of cure in Hong Kong. In C. Leslie (Ed.), *Asian medical systems: A comparative study* (pp. 243–265). Berkeley, CA: University of California Press.

Tracey, T. J., Leong, F. T. L., & Glidden, C. (1986). Help seeking and problem perception among Asian Americans. *Journal of Counselling Psychology, 33,* 331–336.

Triandis, H. C. (1972). *The analysis of subjective culture.* New York: Wiley.

Triandis, H. C. (1996). The psychological measurement of cultural syndromes. *American Psychologist, 51,* 407–415.

Triandis, H. C., Chan, D. K. S., Bhawuk, D. P. S., Iwao, S., & Sinha, J. B. P. (1995). Multimethod probes of allocentrism and idiocentrism. *International Journal of Psychology, 30,* 461–480.

Triandis, H. C., McCusker, C., & Hui, C. H. (1990). Multimethod probes of individualism and collectivism. *Journal of Personality and Social Psychology, 59,* 1006–1020.

Weiss, M. G., Desai, A., Jadhar, S., Gupta, L., Channabasavanna, S. M., Doongaji, D. R., & Behere, P. B. (1988). Humoral concepts of mental illness in India. *Social Science and Medicine, 27,* 417–477.

Whorf, B. L. (1956). *Language, thought and reality.* Cambridge, MA: MIT Press.

4

HEALTH PROMOTION, DISEASE PREVENTION, AND QUALITY OF LIFE

DAVID R. EVANS* AND SHAHÉ S. KAZARIAN†

*Department of Psychology
†Departments of Psychology and Psychiatry
The University of Western Ontario
London, Ontario, Canada

Health promotion and disease prevention have become important activities in the range of health care options available to individuals and groups (Bennett & Murphy, 1997; Davies & MacDonald, 1998; Naidoo & Wills, 1998). Most books and chapters on health promotion and disease prevention do not provide any consideration of culture at all. There exists, however, a limited literature describing health promotion and disease prevention programs with specific cultures. Sarafino (1998), in one of the leading books on health psychology, makes passing mention of culture in his chapter dealing with health promotion. Aboud (1998), in her chapter on health education and promotion, focuses on health education and provides some excellent examples of programs in a number of countries including Ethiopia, Tanzania, Bolivia, and Gambia. Huff and Kline (1999b) in their edited book, *Promoting Health in Multicultural Populations: A Handbook for Practitioners,* provide a number of introductory chapters on health promotion and disease prevention with multicultural populations, followed by chapters on programs with the major cultural groups in the United States. Despite the work of Aboud (1998) and Huff and Kline (1999b), there remains a need to provide a discussion of health promotion and disease prevention in which culture plays a more central role. The aim of the present chapter is to fulfill this need.

The first section of this chapter provides a brief review of the history of health promotion and disease prevention. This is followed by definitions of health promotion, disease prevention, and their related components. Next, a model of health that is synonymous with quality of life is presented, which allows for a range of both health promotion and disease prevention activities and cultural variation. In the latter part of the chapter, a broad array of health promotion and disease prevention programs are described that exemplify the many approaches used. The programs are grouped according to whether they employ a personal, group, organization, community, or media approach. The chapter concludes with a brief overview of resources that discuss program development and evaluation in health promotion.

A BRIEF HISTORY OF HEALTH PROMOTION AND DISEASE PREVENTION

The beginnings of health promotion lie principally in the public health movement which gained momentum in the 19th century (de Viggiani, 1997; Naidoo & Wills, 1994). In his discussion of the public health movement from the 1840s through the 1980s, de Viggiani (1997) argues that as a result of industrialization and urbanization, the state became more and more involved in the lives of people. One area of involvement was in improving living conditions, hygiene, and sanitation in the emerging urban centers created by industrialization. In 1848, the Public Health Act was passed in England and the responsibility for public health measures was vested in local authorities. The Public Health Act of 1875 in England provided for control of the water supply, sewage treatment, and animal slaughter (Naidoo & Wills, 1994). During the First World War, shock techniques were first used to dissuade soldiers from having sex and exposing themselves to venereal disease (Naidoo & Wills, 1994). A major goal of the public health movement was disease prevention.

Another important precursor of health promotion, which was a natural outgrowth of the public health movement, was health education (Baric, 1996; de Viggiani, 1997; MacDonald & Davies, 1998). Naidoo and Wills (1994) suggest that Medical Officers of Health appointed under the 1848 legislation provided health advice concerning the avoidance of contagion. Subsequently, a number of voluntary groups evolved whose goal was to educate the public. In England, these groups included the Health of Towns Association, the Sanitary Institute, and the National Association for the Prevention of Tuberculosis (Naidoo & Wills, 1994). In 1927, the Central Council for Health Education in the United Kingdom was established (Jones, 1997a). The goal of early health education programs was to provide information that would convince targeted groups to adopt more healthy behaviors (Jones, 1997a). Baric (1996) notes that since its inception, health education has undergone a number of changes centered on the increasing complexity of the models on which it is based. Several authors view health education as a tool of preventive medicine, based on a biomedical risk model targeted at high-risk groups for specific diseases (MacDonald & Davies, 1998; Naidoo & Wills, 1994). In more recent thinking, health education is considered an important component of health promotion (Baric, 1996; de Viggiani, 1997; Naidoo & Wills, 1994).

The origin of the term "health promotion" is generally ascribed to Marc Lalonde (1974) in his brief but important speech, titled "A New Perspective on the Health of Canadians" (de Viggiani, 1997; Naidoo & Wills, 1994). At the time, Lalonde was Minister of Health and Welfare, Canada. In the next quarter century, developments in health promotion were global and rapid (see Table 4.1). The "Health for All by 2000" template, agreed upon at the 30th World Health Assembly in 1977, had a major impact on the health and health promotion agendas in most countries throughout the world (de Viggiani, 1997). As the year 2000 approached, the World Health Organization (1998) began to extend "Health for All by 2000" by introducing its "Health Agenda for the 21st Century." The focus of the Alma Ata Conference in 1978 was on primary health care. It resulted in the declaration that health is a fundamental human right, and its attainment requires the action of many social and economic sectors in addition to the health sector (World Health Organization, 1978). Given that the central theme of the conference was primary health care, it is no wonder that primary health care was identified as the means to health promotion throughout the world.

TABLE 4.1   A Brief History of Health Promotion

Date	Event
1974	Lalonde (1974) introduced the term "health promotion" in his *A New Perspective on the Health of Canadians*.
1977	The 30th World Health Assembly passed a resolution that initiated the goal of "Health for All by 2000" (World Health Organization, 1993).
1978	At the Alma Ata Conference, health was endorsed as a fundamental human right, and primary health care was defined as the means to health promotion internationally (World Health Organization, 1978).
1986	The First International Conference on Health Promotion was held in Ottawa and resulted in the *Ottawa Charter on Health Promotion* (World Health Organization, 1986).
1988	The Second International Conference on Health Promotion was held in Adelaide with the theme of Healthy Public Policy (World Health Organization, 1988).
1990	The landmark report *Healthy People 2000: National Health Promotion and Disease Prevention Objectives* was released in the United States.
1991	The Third International Conference on Health Promotion was held at Sundsvall with a focus on Supportive Environments for Health (World Health Organization, 1991).
1993	The Joint Commission on Accreditation of Health Care Organizations (JCAHO) required consideration of cultural factors in the provision of patient education.
1997	The Fourth International Conference on Health Promotion was held in Jakarta, and was entitled "New Players for a New Era—Leading Health Promotion into the 21st Century" (World Health Organization, 1997).

In 1986, the First International Conference on Health Promotion was held in Ottawa, Canada. At this conference, Jake Epp (1986), in his capacity as Minister of National Health and Welfare, Canada, made a presentation titled "Achieving Health for All: A Framework for Health Promotion." His ideas were influential in the formation of the Ottawa Charter on Health Promotion, which was developed at the conference (World Health Organization, 1986). The Ottawa Charter identified three key methods of health promotion: advocacy, enablement, and mediation. It also established a number of health promotion objectives, including the development of healthy public policy, the creation of supportive environments, the strengthening of community action, the development of personal skills, and the reorientation of health services. The Second International Conference on Health Promotion, held in Adelaide, Australia, in 1988, was devoted to the topic of Healthy Public Policy (World Health Organization, 1988). A key recommendation of this conference was that, when making policy, all levels and sectors of government should consider its impact on health. The focus of the Third International Conference on Health Promotion held in Sundsvall, Sweden, was the creation of supportive environments for health (World Health Organization, 1991). A major issue considered at this conference was global accountability for the maintenance of supportive environments for health. In the years following this conference, a number of working groups were established to consider the implementation of health promotion in major settings, such as schools, the workplace, and hospitals (de Viggiani, 1997; Kelleher, 1998). The Fourth International Conference on Health Promotion was held in Jakarta, Indonesia, in 1997 and was concerned with leading health promotion into the 21st century. Priorities for health promotion in the 21st century developed at the conference were as follows: (1) promoting social responsibility for health; (2) increasing investment for health; (3) consolidating and expanding partnerships for health; (4) increasing community capacity and empowering individuals; and (5) securing an infrastructure for health promotion (World Health Organization, 1997).

THE DEFINITION OF HEALTH PROMOTION AND ITS COMPONENTS

From this brief history of health promotion and disease prevention, it is evident that these terms are frequently taken together, and both are related to health education (Aboud, 1998; Huff & Kline, 1999a; Naidoo & Wills, 1994). From another perspective, Yee and Lee (1977) have suggested that in the Eastern tradition, disease prevention and health promotion are one entity. Many authors view health promotion as an umbrella term, which includes such activities as disease prevention, health education, public health, and community development (Baric, 1996; Jones, 1997a; Naidoo & Wills, 1998). Nordenfelt (1995) adds health protection to the list. In sum, most authors agree that health promotion is a global concept that includes disease prevention, health education, and health protection.

In the sections that follow, health promotion and its several components will be defined.

HEALTH PROMOTION

Perhaps one of the earliest definitions of health promotion is that of the World Health Organization (1984). This definition suggested that a change in living styles and conditions is required in order to promote health.

> Health promotion represents a mediating strategy between people and their environments, synthesizing personal choice and social responsibility in health to create a healthier future.

More recently, Aboud (1998) has argued that health promotion involves a variety of activities that result in public awareness of health, healthy lifestyles and community action supporting health, and empowerment of people such that they influence their environment, systems, and policies to facilitate health and well-being. She observes that the methods by which these ends can be met include political action, social behavior, and educational activities conducive to health promotion.

Naidoo and Wills (1994) have concluded that the term "health promotion" is an "essentially contested concept," that is, it is used differently by different people depending on their values and goals (Caplan, 1993). After an extensive review of the definitions of health promotion, de Viggiani (1997) comes to a similar conclusion. He proposes that health promotion should be used as an organizing concept under which to subsume health education, disease prevention, and health protection. Huff and Kline (1999a) also use a definition of health promotion that views it as an aggregate of those activities designed to enhance individual and public health. Perhaps at this point, a variation of the simple definition provided by Jones (1997a) is best. Health promotion is a global term referring to those actions and interventions designed to support and enhance the health of people, understanding that the actions and interventions would include but not be limited to health education, disease prevention, and health protection activities.

HEALTH EDUCATION

As de Viggiani (1997) has observed, health education has a lengthy history and is carried out by a range of professionals, including teachers, public health personnel, physicians, nurses, and other health practitioners. Time and the personnel involved have influenced the definition of health education. Early definitions focused on the provision of information to individuals through a variety of media on the assumption that change would follow (Baric, 1996). Contemporary definitions are more complex, in that they include more steps in the educative and behavior-change process. Huff and Kline (1999a) rely on a two-step definition of health education as any intervention activity that facilitates "the voluntary acquisition of specific health-related knowledge, attitudes, and practices associated with achieving specific health-related behavior changes. (p. 4–5)." Bennett and Murphy (1997) adopt a similar definition. Aboud (1998) provides a three-step process to capture the meaning of health education, under which individuals perform engaging educational activities, make informed decisions, and then work toward the goal of acting on their decisions. Naidoo and Wills (1994) stress two aspects of health education that are distinguishing features: the focus on the individual and the voluntary nature of the individual's participation. Taking from the definitions discussed, health education can be defined as the provision of educational activities designed to engage individuals in the acquisition of knowledge, attitudes, and/or skills, that will assist them in making informed decisions, such that health-related behavior change will occur. This definition would suggest that the educational program must be designed to focus on all three components in the definition, i.e., knowledge acquisition, decision making, and behavior change.

DISEASE PREVENTION

Before proceeding with a definition of disease prevention, it is important to determine whether the correct term should be disease or illness prevention. "Illness" is generally taken to describe the perception patients have of their disorder and, as such, may or may not be an accurate representation of the symptoms and/or the syndrome that defines their disease (Naidoo & Wills, 1994). In contrast, "disease" refers to some pathology or abnormality of the body that is identifiable and verifiable. Hence, the term "disease prevention" is to be preferred. Unlike health promotion and health education, which may be positively (health) or negatively (disease) oriented, disease prevention is always disease centered. Furthermore, three categories of disease prevention have been defined, primary, secondary, and tertiary, the main defining characteristic of each being its relationship to the time course of the disease.

Primary Prevention

Refers to interventions designed to prevent the onset of a disease or injury (Alonzo, 1993; de Viggiani, 1997; Sarafino, 1998). For example, immunization is employed to prevent the onset of measles. Stretching exercises before jogging are engaged in to prevent injury.

Secondary Prevention

Refers to interventions designed to identify and treat a disease or injury early in its time course in order to lessen the impact of the disease (Alonzo, 1993; de Viggiani, 1997; Sarafino, 1998). Programs designed to identify potential alcoholics and provide them with an intervention, designed to offset the development of the disease, are representative of secondary prevention programs (Evans, Nesbitt, Pilgrim, Potts, & Albert, 1985). Implicit in the definition of secondary prevention is the proposition that early identification of a disease will make treatment easier and, hence, more effective (de Viggiani, 1997).

Tertiary Prevention

Refers to interventions designed to eliminate or reduce residual disability after a disease or injury (de Vigianni, 1997; Hussain, 1984; Sarafino, 1998). Tertiary prevention for persons suffering from arthritis would involve physical therapy and anti-inflammatory medication to permit the patient a more active life than if these interventions were not provided. With a depressed client, tertiary prevention could involve interventions to assist the client in developing new skills to decrease the probability of future depressive episodes.

HEALTH PROTECTION

Health protection involves activities of government to control behavior through either legislation or fiscal policies for disease prevention and/or health enhancement purposes (Naidoo & Wills, 1994; Nordenfelt, 1995). The health of others in the individual's sphere of influence may also be maintained or improved. Legislation designed to control the number of outlets selling alcohol and the hours of their service are aimed at reducing the consumption of alcohol and, hence, the occurrence of the diseases and injuries that are the result of excessive alcohol consumption. This, in turn, could reduce child and spousal abuse. In a similar sense, increasing taxes on alcohol and tobacco products may control the use of these products, having a similar effect to legislation to control consumption, with an added financial bonus for government. Other legislation directed at health protection involves a range of health and safety measures, banning smoking in government and other public facilities, and the use of seatbelts, to name just a few examples.

MEANS AND ENDS IN HEALTH PROMOTION

Returning to the definition of health promotion as a global term referring to actions and interventions to support and enhance the health of people, it is possible to further define the relationship between the various activities included in this section. Health promotion defines more the end goal of the enterprise, while health education, disease prevention, and health protection define more the means to that end. The means range from individual-oriented programs (health education) to community-wide programs (health protection). These approaches also vary in the degree to which the individual is free to participate or is required to participate under some form of state regulation (Bennett & Murphy, 1997). Disease prevention may involve, then, either voluntary or coercive programs involving individuals, groups, or whole communities (Naidoo and Wills, 1994). Nordenfelt (1995) argues against what he calls paternalistic or coercive interventions when possible. This would agree with the observation that health promotion programs are most successful when their participants are empowered and motivated to participate (Bennett & Murphy, 1997; Epp, 1986; Frankish, Lovato, & Shannon, 1999).

THE MEANING OF HEALTH

Several authors have argued that in order to understand the meaning of health promotion, it is important to identify what is meant by the end goal of health promotion, that is, health itself (Jones, 1997b; Naidoo & Wills, 1994; Seedhouse, 1997). What follows is a review of the definitions of health that have emerged in the health promotion field. Readers should contrast these definitions to those described in Chapter 1. As Jones (1997b) points out, each individual has a public and a private definition of health, both of which are shaped by the media, culture, and societal factors. She cites studies by Blaxter (1990) and Williams (1983) that show that older persons define health in terms of resilience and ability to cope, while younger persons equate health with fitness, strength, and vitality. In addition to the individual difference in the meaning of health, there are a range of meanings ascribed to health by both health practitioners and theorists. Authors have identified a number of major categories of meaning that define health (de Viggiani, 1997; Jones, 1997b; Naidoo & Wills, 1994; Seedhouse, 1997).

LAY DEFINITIONS OF HEALTH

Lay definitions of health differ across a number of factors, including age, gender, social class, and culture (de Viggiani, 1997; Jones, 1997b; Naidoo & Wills, 1994). Lay definitions of health have been identified by both quantitative and qualitative research. This research has suggested the following lay definitions, among others: (1) Health involves physical fitness and peak condition; (2) Health represents psychological fitness and happiness; (3) Health reflects a balance among natural forces within the body; (4) Health is related to one's spiritual activity or lack of it; (5) Health represents an absence of illness; and (6) Health is a reserve that provides resistance against illness. These definitions may vary among people and, frequently, a given individual may hold several definitions at the same time.

It is important that health practitioners understand the values and beliefs of the individuals they are to work with before developing health promotion programs for them (Huff, 1999; Jones 1997b). Several authors have stressed that failure on the part of health practitioners to understand that their clients' definitions of health can influence communication with them and their degree of compliance with programs (Huff, 1999; Naidoo & Wills, 1994). An important construct in the understanding of an individual's definition of health is health locus of control (Huff, 1999). Huff observes that in Western cultures, the locus of control for health is usually from within the person. In contrast, in Eastern cultures and other cultures within the developing world, locus of control for health is derived from forces outside the individual over which he or she has no control.

PROFESSIONAL DEFINITIONS OF HEALTH

Health as Disease or Illness

Jones (1997b) and Naidoo and Wills (1994), among others, state that within the Western scientific medical model, health is defined as the absence of disease or illness. They argue that this is the view of health held by most health practitioners in modern Western societies. Further, they observe that this view is transmitted to society at large through the media, particularly via dramas and documentaries seen on television. Naidoo and Wills (1994) characterize the Western medical model as biomedical, reductionist, mechanistic, and allopathic. Frequently, this definition is at odds with the lay definitions of health encountered in other cultures (Huff, 1999). Jones (1997b) has observed that a number of health practitioners are becoming reactive to the narrowness and negative orientation of this definition of health.

Health as an Ideal State

The World Health Organization (1946) has for many years defined health as "a state of complete physical, mental and social well-being, not merely the absence of disease or infirmity." This definition holds health to be an ideal state, which a number of authors have argued is unattainable (de Viggiani, 1997; Seedhouse, 1997). Despite concerns with the utopian nature of this definition, Bowling (1997) argues that it has focused attention toward a broader, more positive definition of health.

Health as Social/Psychological Construct

A number of sociologists and psychologists have proposed alternative definitions of health (Arnold & Breen, 1998; Bowling, 1997; de Viggiani, 1997). Health has been viewed as an optimal capacity that fits individuals to assume the responsibilities for which they have been socialized, as a commodity, as a state of self-actualization, as a narrative, and as a metaphor (de Viggiani, 1997; Naidoo & Wills, 1994). It has been argued that each of these definitions, due to its specificity, is limited as a meaningful and functional definition of health (Seedhouse, 1986, 1997). However, these definitions of health stress that health is influenced by politics, economics, culture, and environment in addition to biological factors (Jones, 1997b). Proponents of these models of health recognize the importance of social/psychological factors in the maintenance of good health.

Health as Quality of Life

Developing out of the World Health Organization (1946) definition of health as including physical, psychological, and social components, and as a synthesis of many of the social/psychological conceptions of health, the equation of health and quality of life has emerged over the last quarter century (Bowling, 1997; Evans, 1997; Naidoo & Wills, 1994). There are both global and health-related measures of quality of life, which implicitly define what is meant by quality of life as representative of health (Bowling, 1997; Evans, 1994, 1997; Rosenberg, 1995). The global measures, which include life satisfaction, well-being, and both positive and negative affect measures, represent the quality of life of the population at large, and as such are normative and represent a gold standard of quality of life (Evans, 1994, 1997).

In contrast, the majority of the health-related measures are specific to disease entities, such as coronary heart disease, cancer, epilepsy, and irritable bowel syndrome, and as such they tend to be more representative of physical functioning than of social and psychological functioning (Bowling, 1997; Evans, 1997; Farquhar, 1995). Quality of life measures can also be divided into those that are subjective and those that are objective (Evans, 1994). A number of authors have observed that there is little agreement on how quality of life should be measured, as evidenced by the vast array of measures available and the absence of theory behind the measures (Day & Jankey, 1996; Farquhar, 1995; Rosenberg, 1995). Evans (1997) has demonstrated that factor analysis of scores of a community sample ($N = 780$) on five of the principal global measures of quality of life results in a single factor on which all measures have high loadings. This result suggests that all these measures of quality of life, well-being, and affect are measuring essentially the same thing.

An Integrated Definition of Health

Seedhouse (1997) has argued that none of the above professional definitions of health is adequate to describe the end goal of health promotion. He also argues that all health promotion is driven by values and, hence, all health promotion activities are prejudiced. Thus, the health promoter is obliged to try to understand the political basis for his or her prejudices and for the prejudices of others. Both Buchanan (1995) and Seedhouse (1997) conclude that the definition of health adopted in health promotion must be theoretically grounded. Seedhouse (1997) suggests that the definition of health must go beyond the notions of health as disease and illness, an ideal state, a social/psychological construct, and well-being. He goes on to propose a definition of health that is theoretically based, which he freely admits, is prejudiced. His theory, he argues, can accommodate not only his values or prejudices but also, within limits, the prejudices of others. Gorin (1998) has argued that those working in health promotion must become more aware of the values behind what they do. This definition of health is integrating in that it incorporates most aspects of the several other definitions of health.

Seedhouse (1997) has proposed what he calls the Foundations Theory of Health. The essential components are summed up in the following quote:

A person's (optimum) state of health is equivalent to the state of the set of conditions which fulfil or enable a person to work to fulfil his or her realistic chosen and biological potentials (Seedhouse, 1997, p. 136).

He observes that some conditions are common to all people, while others are specific to an individual. The four broad conditions that are common to all individuals are (1) basic needs; (2) information management; (3) information-based decision making; and (4) responsible community participation. Seedhouse (1997) includes a fifth condition that is specific to an individual and is defined by the individual's abilities and circumstances.

Seedhouse (1997) suggests more specific content for each of the five conditions that constitute an individual's health. Basic needs are seen to include a home, security, adequate food, help to define goals, and rewarding employment. Information management includes access to information, help to understand it, and encouragement to use and discuss information. Information-based decision making encompasses literacy and numeracy, the ability to interpret information, and motivation for self and continuing education. Responsible community participation involves the understanding that one belongs to a community and that citizenship in that community involves support of others and commitment to the civic good. The fifth condition varies with the circumstances of the individual, and Seedhouse (1997) suggests that provision for medical and special needs that an individual might encounter are key components of this condition.

THE FOUNDATIONS THEORY OF HEALTH AND HEALTH PROMOTION

As Seedhouse (1997) points out, the five conditions that he has proposed to constitute health have defined limits. He states that these limits place ethical constraints on what is to be provided and maintained by health practitioners. Individuals are not precluded from extending their goals beyond these basic limits on their own. This, then, leads to a definition of health promotion as being restricted to providing those interventions necessary to close the gaps between the current status of the individual and his or her possession of the five basic conditions for health. The Jones (1997b) conceptualization of health promotion as the actions and interventions to support and enhance the health of people obtains further definition if the integrated definition of health is adopted.

THE FOUNDATIONS THEORY OF HEALTH AND QUALITY OF LIFE

Seedhouse (1997) argues against the position that a number of definitions of quality of life are, in fact, definitions of health in the sense that he defines it. His major argument is that most definitions of quality of life are subjective, as in the measures of subjective well-being (Diener, Emmons, Larsen, & Griffin, 1985; Diener, Suh, Lucas, & Smith, 1999) and affect (Watson, Clark, & Tellegen, 1988). He suggests that these measures vary in their meaning, both within and between individuals. He also argues against the use of the Quality of Life Adjusted Year, until such time as the basic conditions for health are in place for all persons (Seedhouse, 1997). What Seedhouse (1997) indicates is that the foundations theory of health provides a justified basis for developing measures of the health components proposed under this theory. This is in contrast to the largely atheoretical approach to measuring health and quality of life that has been pursued to date. He also notes that the foundations and their constituent elements, which are based on his values, are open to change based on an alternative set of values.

Evans, Burns, Robinson, and Garrett (1985) argued against measuring quality of life using either social indicators or subjective measures. They argued for measures based on an individual's behavior in response to the environment(s) in which the behavior occurred. The Quality of Life Questionnaire (Evans & Cope, 1989) was developed using the rational–empirical approach advocated by Jackson (1970). As Evans et al. (1985) have indicated, values associated with previous research on quality of life determine the constructs that are proposed for the questionnaire, and values of validation samples define the scales and items in the final version of the questionnaire. Thus, the makeup and norms associated with the Quality of Life Questionnaire are relative to the North American majority culture.

Some scales on the Quality of Life Questionnaire (Evans & Cope, 1985) compare with the four common foundations of health proposed by Seedhouse (1987). For example, the Material well-being scale represents the Basic needs foundation proposed by Seedhouse (1997) as a component of health. Similarly, the Personal growth scale on the Quality of Life Questionnaire represents the Information-based decision making component proposed by Seedhouse (1997). Many of the scales on the Quality of Life Questionnaire are representative of Seedhouse's (1997) fourth common component, Responsible community participation. The comparability between the theoretical foundations of health suggested by Seedhouse (1997) and the scales on the Quality of Life Questionnaire (Evans & Cope, 1989) are shown in Table 4.2. Indication that there are other potential combinations of foundations for health is suggested by the work of Cummins (1996) in his efforts to group 173 domain names used in quality of life research. He found that 65% of these domains could be captured under the following: material well-being; health; productivity; intimacy; safety; community; and emotional well-being.

It can be argued that the scales and dimensions on the Quality of Life Questionnaire represent the common foundations of health in the majority culture in North America. In contrast, psychometrically sound measures of health-related quality of life can be argued to measure the fifth and person-specific foundation of health defined by Seedhouse (1997). Examples of potential measures to represent this fifth foundation are the Sickness Impact Profile and the SF-36 (An-

TABLE 4.2   Foundations of Health and Quality of Life Questionnaire Scales

Foundations of Health (after Seedhouse, 1997)	Quality of Life Questionnaire (after Evans & Cope, 1989)
Basic needs	Material well-being
	Job characteristics
	Occupational relations
	Job satisfiers
Information management	**Not represented**
Information-based decision-making	Personal growth
Responsible community participation	Marital relations
	Parent–child relations
	Extended family relations
	Extrafamilial relations
	Altruistic behavior
	Political behavior
Not represented	Physical well-being
	Creative/aesthetic behavior
	Sports activity
	Vacation behavior

derson, Aaronson, Leplège, & Wilkins, 1996). Another approach to this fifth foundation when very specific health concerns are represented by it may be the modular approach, as developed in the cancer area (Cull, 1997).

Implicit in the development of the foundations theory of health (Seedhouse, 1997) and the Quality of Life Questionnaire is the need to accommodate inter- and intra-individual variance. Naidoo and Wills (1994) are critical of this flexibility in the theory. However, this flexibility becomes very important when endeavoring to provide for the tremendous variability across cultures. The scope of cultural variation runs from that within a given country (Charles et al., 1994; Huff & Kline, 1999b; Suh, Diener, Oishi, & Triandis, 1998) to the cultural variation among countries, which range from countries with developed market economies to those that are least developed (World Health Organization, 1998).

CULTURE, THE FOUNDATIONS THEORY OF HEALTH, AND HEALTH PROMOTION

Huff and Kline (1999b) include in their book chapters on the major cultures in the United States. These are the Hispanic/Latino, African American, American Indian, Alaska Native, Asian American, and Pacific Islander populations. Add to this other cultural groups, such as the deaf, men, and women, and the cultural complexity within just one country is illustrated. The diversity among countries is accentuated by the range of economic differences highlighted by the United Nations' classification of countries (World Health Organization, 1998). The classifications are Least developed (e.g., Afghanistan, Lesotho, Zambia), Developing (e.g., Algeria, Saint Lucia, Zimbabwe), Economies in transition (e.g., Albania, Latvia, Uzbekistan), and Developed market economies (e.g., Andorra, Japan, United States of America). To contemplate health and health promotion at a level that can incorporate both the within- and between-country cultural diversity is almost beyond comprehension. However, the foundations theory of health and health promotion does give a theoretical perspective that can incorporate such a range of cultural diversity.

Recall that the theory incorporates five foundations, four that are common and one that is health/disability-oriented and person-specific. The four common foundations are Basic needs, Information management, Information-based decision making, and Responsible community participation. Remember also that the characteristics falling within each of the five foundations represent a common level to which all should be assisted rather than an optimal level. Health promotion involves interventions to eradicate the gap between where individuals are and where they should be with respect to the key characteristics representing each of the five foundations. The characteristics within each foundation are organized hierarchically. For example, within the Information-based decision making foundation, they run from literacy and numeracy to the encouragement of lifelong learning. The gaps, if any, on each dimension will vary for individuals, cultures within countries, and between countries. In the spirit of "Health for All by 2000" or the more recent "Health Agenda for the 21st Century" (World Health Organization, 1993, 1998), the common levels established for each health foundation can be retained as the goals for all individuals worldwide. However, the gaps between current levels on each foundation and the status of any particular person, culture, or country would differ, as would the requisite health promotion program or programs. Another possibility would be to have the four common foundations across all countries, with an additional foundation which would be country-specific and then the person-specific foundation. This is the approach being employed by the World Health Organization Quality of Life Group (1993,1998), who are developing a quality of life measure for use throughout the world.

OBSERVATIONS ABOUT HEALTH PROMOTION PROGRAMS FROM A CULTURAL PERSPECTIVE

Werna (1996) has identified some of the historical trends that have affected the design of health programs in developing countries. Similar trends can be traced for diverse cultural groups within countries. From the 1940s through to the mid-1970s, the approach to developing countries was based on the belief that they would follow the same developmental course as that of the industrialized countries. It was eventually recognized that this approach was not appropriate and that it was not working. In the period between the mid-1970s and the mid-1980s, the focus was on local methods of programming with local community participation and programs that were culturally appropriate. Two views of culture emerged during this period, one that saw it as an obstacle and the other in which it was a potential resource for health development. Since the mid-1980s, the approach has been one of long-term planning with an emphasis on local capacity-building and the strengthening of local institutions (Werna, 1996). These stances on the part of such organizations as the United Nations, the World Bank, the World Health Organization, and the United Nations Children's Fund, have and will continue to affect the nature of health promotion in the transitional and developing countries in the world. The tenor of the programs within countries will also be moderated by the nature of government politics and policies, and the activities of nongovernment organizations in the country (Stone, 1992).

International and national political forces will impact the nature of health promotion programs. However, as Airhihenbuwa (1994) points out, failing to involve people at the community level can doom an otherwise well-conceived health promotion program. Perhaps because of the complex forces that must be considered in implementing health promotion programs in developing countries, there are more hypothesized programs than actually implemented and evaluated programs (Holtzman, Evans, Kennedy, & Iscoe, 1987). A review of the literature on health promotion programs across the cultures and countries of the world indicates numerous programs in the developed countries, particularly for the majority cultures in each, and far fewer programs in the developing and least developed countries. In the next section of this chapter, the rich variety and promise of health promotion programs will be sampled.

EXAMPLES OF HEALTH
PROMOTION PROGRAMS

There are a number of dimensions across which health promotion programs can be organized and considered. For example, interventions can be categorized as health education, primary, secondary, or tertiary prevention, and health protection programs. Another dimension for categorization is whether they impact the foundations of health proposed by Seedhouse (1997), i.e., basic needs, information management, information-based decision making, responsible community participation, and health/disability support. Programs can also be categorized according to the theory or model on which they are based, such as Social Learning Theory, Coping Theory, the Health Belief Model, the Health Action Model, the Stages of Change Model, or Theories of Organizational Change, to name but a few (Baric, 1996; de Viggiani, 1997; Frankish et al., 1999; Naidoo & Wills, 1994). Finally, programs can be considered in terms of their approach, that is, whether they are personal, group, organization, community, or mass media-oriented (Baric, 1996; Bennett & Murphy, 1997; Evans, 1997; Winett, 1995). The examples that follow will be organized under the latter categories, but examples will be included that highlight the other dimensions on which programs can be classified.

PERSONAL PROGRAMS

Health promotion programs that are personal or directed toward an individual are most frequently carried out by health care practitioners or through self-help media, such as pamphlets or books (Bennett & Murphy, 1997). For example, a physician or dietician may develop an appropriate diet for a person at risk for coronary heart disease (Winett, 1995). Baric (1996) has suggested that the most important processes involved in personal approaches to health promotion are learning, communicating, socialization, interviewing, and counseling. Bennett and Murphy (1997) would add behavioral and cognitive behavioral individual change approaches to this list.

Calfas (1998) has described a protocol for health care practitioners to instruct their clients about physical activity which is based on the Stages of Change Model developed by Prochaska and DiClemente (1984). The method is called the Physician-based Assessment and Counseling for Exercise (PACE) approach. On arrival at the health care practitioner's office, clients complete a one-page PACE assessment tool to assess their interest and level of physical activity, along with the Physical Activity Readiness Questionnaire (see Calfas, 1998, p. 194–195). This material is returned to the receptionist, who identifies the stage (precontemplator, contemplator, or active) clients are at and gives them a stage-relevant questionnaire to complete. On the back of the questionnaire is printed stage-relevant information for the client's future use. The questionnaires are placed in the client's file for the health practitioner's review before seeing the client. The health practitioner provides the client with brief stage-relevant counseling (see Calfas, 1998, p. 197–198) and, where appropriate, a physical activity goal is agreed during the client's routine visit.

Calfas (1998) reports the results of two multisite studies designed to evaluate the acceptability of the PACE program and its efficacy (Calfas et al., 1996; Long et al., 1996). In the first study, practitioners reported that the counseling was easy to do and that 80% of their clients were receptive or very receptive to it (Long et al., 1996). As for the clients, 80% indicated that the questionnaires and forms were easy or very easy to understand, and 72% reported the counseling helpful. In the second study, the PACE program was found to impact the stage of change of clients and their level of physical activity (Calfas et al., 1996). In a quasi-experimental study, 212 healthy sedentary adults were assigned to receive or not receive the PACE program as part of their routine visit. All were at the contemplation stage at the pre-visit assessment. They were assessed again 6 weeks after their visit. Clients who received the program were reported to be walking more than those not exposed to the program (75 versus 42 minutes per week).

More of those exposed to the program were reported to have moved into the action stage of change (52% versus 12%). The response to this program suggests that it is effective and easy to use.

G. M. Guthrie, H. M. Guthrie, Fernandez, Ruiz-Lambo, and Barba (1987) reported a program to offset malnutrition in young children in rural villages in the Philippines. Three rural centers around Cebu City participated in the study. Each one-room center was staffed by a midwife under the supervision of a government physician. For the purposes of the study, a field worker was assigned to each center. In all centers, the field worker offered mothers health education concerning how to offset malnutrition. In two centers, a reinforcement system was established (lottery/token system or picture of the child/family member). The field worker kept records on children and administered an education program and reinforcement system with each mother.

Compared to children in the control center, the programs of reinforcement had little impact. Weight loss in babies of mothers who joined the program in the first year of their child's life were comparable across groups. The reinforcement programs had some effect on the weight of children who were more than 1 year old when the program was instituted. The authors identified a number of cultural factors that could account for the relative failure of the program. For example, the mothers believed that anyone who paid attention to their baby was a witch who had designs on the baby; hence, social reinforcement was difficult. Further, mothers' cultural beliefs held that poor growth and illness were the result of factors other than diet. In fact, the authors did a side study that demonstrated that babies under 1 year old whose diet was supplemented had more days of sickness than did babies whose diet was not supplemented. The relative failure of this program can be attributed to its paternalistic nature and failure to take into account cultural beliefs that worked against the program.

There are a number of studies that provide comment on the education or continuing education of physicians and other health care workers in their health promotion role. Fidler and Costello (1995) demonstrated the major influence of physicians on infant feeding practices in South India. They concluded that physicians needed continuing education on appropriate feeding practices and the inappropriate promotional practices of companies. Hamilton (1995) outlines components of a medical curriculum that is designed to train physicians in the skills required for good practice, including health promotion. One thrust of this training is the development of the role for the medical staff as expert consultants to community organizations setting up health promotion programs. Hays (1995) has provided some discussion of the ways in which those health care workers using cognitive behavioral approaches can modify their practice to be more culturally sensitive.

Bastien (1990) describes a program used to train community health workers in Bolivia. At the time, there were 64 community health workers elected by their respective communities working on an unpaid basis. Bastien (1990) notes that an important aspect of the program is that the community health workers are actively involved with the members of their community in health development. A key element in training the community health workers is in the integration of Western and traditional medicine, rather than setting them apart from their communities as advocates of Western medicine. Bastien (1994) has also described a training program in Bolivia designed to facilitate cooperative practices between biomedical and ethnomedical health care practitioners. The training of health practitioners in appropriate methods of establishing health promotion programs for individuals is in itself an important health promotion activity.

GROUP PROGRAMS

As Baric (1996) observes, health promotion programs can utilize group dynamics and process in effecting the goals of programs. He notes that groups may exist (e.g., families, school classes) or be created for the purpose of the program. He suggests that group cohesiveness, pressures, goals, and structure can facilitate the success of group-based health promotion programs. Frequently, cardiac patients are offered brief group sessions about risk factors, nutrition, and lifestyle change as a form of tertiary prevention (Winett, 1995). Few members of these groups know each other; therefore, the only advantage of such groups is their efficiency. They do not capitalize on the group-process variables outlined by Baric (1996).

A similar program for groups of Hispanic mothers and their children using a culture-specific dietary intervention designed to reduce the risk of cancer was evaluated by Fitzgibbon, Stolley, Avellone, Sugerman, and Chavez (1996). They exposed one set of mothers and their children to an active intervention and another set to a literature-only intervention. The families exposed to the active intervention met in groups for 11 sessions during which mothers and children were encouraged to discuss a number of concepts, including such topics as cancer and diet, holiday meal planning, and the importance of exercise. The curriculum was designed to be activity-based, to accommodate both English and Spanish speakers, to accommodate culturally appropriate foods, and to focus on children's resistance to eating healthy foods. Unfortunately, the authors did not do any follow-up assessment of their groups. Pre- to posttreatment evaluation demonstrated that both sets of groups of mothers and children changed their behaviors. The authors discussed a number of design problems that may have produced comparable effects for treated and control groups.

Yee et al. (1995) describe the Positive Adolescent Choices Training (PACT) program designed for African American youth in the United States of America. The program involves the use of videotapes in small groups led by facilitators. The focus of the program is on skills that are essential to cope with anger and frustration without engaging in expressive violence. Didactic material on the skills is followed by the opportunity to practice the skills with feedback. Hammond and Yung (1991) have demonstrated that, in comparison to untrained youth, those that receive training demonstrate reduced violence-related school suspensions and increases in prosocial skills. This program capitalizes on group process, instructional technology, and cultural relevance. In contrast, many of the group programs reviewed were didactic in nature and few capitalized on the research on group process and dynamics to enhance their effectiveness.

ORGANIZATIONAL PROGRAMS

Organizational programs take advantage of already constituted organizations from which to launch health promotion programs. These programs include, for the most part, worksites, such as health care facilities, industrial sites, and the military (Bennett & Murphy, 1997; Winett, 1995). Religious organizations and schools have also been the location for health promotion programs (Holtzman, 1997; Yee & Lee, 1977). Holtzman (1997) describes the School of the Future project that was started in 1990 in culturally different neighborhoods in four cities in Texas. These schools were developed to provide a range of education, health, and social services to children, youth, and families in a single location. They were also designed to involve parents, teachers, local service providers, and local government personnel in the planning and delivery of a wide range of services, including education at the preschool, elementary, and middle school levels. Holtzman (1997) suggests that this model can be introduced, with appropriate modifications, in developing countries.

Vidaurre (1994) describes an interesting project in his article "Conscripts for Health." In Bolivia, basic education in health care and disease prevention is provided for all conscripts into the armed services. The program was begun in 1992 with the support of a number of international agencies, such as UNICEF and the Pan American Health Organization. The program of instruction and the content are military in nature. Participants learn such skills as the preparation of oral rehydration salts for the treatment of diarrhea, how to deliver a baby, and responsible parenthood. Vidaurre (1994) concludes that the military instructors have become skillful, and that the conscripts have become agents of change for the benefit of the health of their families and communities.

Worksite health promotion programs have increased phenomenally in the United States, Canada, Australia, Japan, and Europe over the past 15 to 20 years (Terborg, 1998). Terborg (1998) has provided an excellent overview of the research on worksite health promotion programs. He reports that, in these programs, physical fitness and smoking control were the most frequent, and programs on sexually transmitted diseases and prenatal education were the least frequent. Other programs offered dealt with such topics as nutrition, weight control, and stress management. Terborg (1998) concluded that the first-generation studies, which were poorly designed, tended to provide strong support for the effectiveness of worksite programs. The larger second-generation studies, which are better designed, have proved more conservative in the effectiveness of the programs studied.

COMMUNITY PROGRAMS

Community approaches to health promotion are many and varied and range from simply providing a specific intervention program in a community to modifying the community structure as the health promotion intervention. Baric (1996) has provided an extensive tabulation of the varied types of community approaches to health promotion. Space in this chapter permits only an overview of a few different types of community-based health promotion programs. Communities involve some form of government function; hence, health protection methods of health promotion become possible. Other community action may involve providing programs for individuals with disabilities, such as access to facilities, auditory cues at intersections, and braille in elevators (Winett, 1995). Bennett and Murphy (1997) have suggested that community- or population-based programs are likely to be the most cost-effective forms of health promotion.

There are a number of reports of community-based programs in rural communities in various cultures around the world (Aikins et al. 1998; Chen, 1989; Thapa, 1996). Thapa (1996) describes a program begun by CARE in 1990 in conjunction with the Ministry of Local Development centered in the Bajura district of Nepal. Program staff were placed in the villages of the area and their mandate was to mobilize the villagers' participation by forming mothers' groups, community development committees, and users' groups for such activities as providing drinking water, nonformal education, and bridge construction. Thapa (1996) reports a number of changes as a result of this program, including the building of at least one toilet in each village, the cultivation and consumption of vegetables, and a change in attitude to child immunization. Chen (1989) reports on a similar program in the Baram District of Sarawak, Malaysia. In this program, each longhouse of Penans selected a man or a woman to be trained as village health promoter. The health promoters were trained in their own language in the areas of health promotion, disease prevention, food production, proper nutrition, sanitation, care of mothers and children, and the treatment of common ailments. Chen (1989) has indicated positive effects of the program on birthing patterns and immunization. Yet another program is the insecticide-impregnated mosquito net program in Gambia, which has proved to be one of the most effective methods of reducing deaths in children under 10 years of age in that country (Aikins et al., 1998). A number of government-based health protection programs are reviewed in the article by Elder (1987), the results of which are mixed.

Douglas (1996) describes the Smethwick Heart Action Research Project (SHARP) in England. SHARP was developed to provide research-based information to influence policies that would improve the health of communities, such as Smethwick in general and diverse cultures within them in particular. The program was of 3 years' duration and members of all cultures in Smethwick were involved in the development and management of the project. The program was started with a needs assessment involving 300 participants from the African Caribbean, Bangladeshi, Indian, Pakistani, and White communities in Smethwick. The results of the needs assessment revealed differences among cultural groups and led to the development of some general health promotion initiatives and some specific programs. The next phase of the study involved a training course on organizing groups and activities in the community. Another venture was to provide one-day workshops for health promotion workers in the various communities on food and diet. The goal of these workshops was to promote Asian foods as healthy. To complement this activity, cookery demonstrations were organized at a local community center. Based on the findings of the needs assessment, members of the SHARP team worked with the community leisure services personnel to develop services for the Muslim population and Asian women. Douglas (1996) concludes that there is a need to extend the methodology employed in SHARP to other communities, a goal that is often constrained by national policies.

MASS MEDIA PROGRAMS

Baric (1996) has provided an excellent review of the developments in the use of mass media as a vehicle for health education and health promotion. He has traced the developments in this area from the Knowledge–Attitude–Practice model, advanced shortly after the Second World War, to more recent models based on mass communication theories. Research indicates that mass media health promotion programs alone have limited value in producing an action or health behavior change (Baric, 1996; Bennett & Murphy, 1997). Baric (1996) suggests that the major advantage of mass media health promotion programs is that they act simultaneously on the population as a whole, and hence, have the potential to influence social norms of behavior. He suggests that the vast array of information available via a variety of media worldwide makes us aware of cultural differences and the fact that we live in a "global village." He argues that this results in the need for much more complex models of mass communication as a basis for health promotion programs. The implication is that these models have yet to be derived and evaluated. Bennett and Murphy (1997) draw a similar conclusion and suggest that social marketing and diffusion theory may provide a starting point.

At a more practical level, Lake (1996) has developed a workbook designed to help health professionals plan media campaigns. She provides practical examples in the HIV/AIDS area of health promotion. Naidoo and Wills (1998) have placed media approaches to health promotion in a broader context in their chapter on "Marketing Health." The complexity of planning mass media programs of health promotion is further complicated when cultural factors are considered. Lupton (1994) has argued that health promoters need to move from social psychological to sociocultural paradigms in designing mass media programs. Hubley (1993) has provided a comprehensive discussion of the many factors that must be considered when designing mass media health promotion programs for the many cultural groups around the world. His approach exemplifies the call of Lupton (1994) for a paradigm shift in the design of mass media health promotion programs. He discusses such topics as communication theory, popular media, the use of media, and the impact of politics. For example, he suggests that a number of folk media, such as storytelling, drama, song, and pictures, can be employed in health promotion media programs. He includes one chapter on planning culturally sensitive health promotion mass media programs.

Alcalay, Ghee, and Scrimshaw (1993) have described the process of designing prenatal care messages for Mexican women in Tijuana. Baseline data were collected to identify the specific information needs of the target population, the most appropriate communication approach, and how to develop culturally appropriate messages. The authors used ethnographic methods and surveys to gather the data and focus groups to design and pretest the media materials. A poster, calendar, pamphlet, and two popular songs for radio were developed as complementary media to meet the goals identified in the needs assessment. The pregnancy-related goals were to encourage early prenatal care, to inform about weight gain, to promote good nutrition and the use of vitamins, and to enhance the identification and management of risk factors. The authors reported that a number of private organizations had agreed to fund the production and dissemination of the materials.

While a number of authors have focused on media programs as independent vehicles of health promotion, others have argued that media programs should be integrated with other health promotion approaches to be effective (Baric, 1996; Naidoo & Wills, 1998; Ramirez, Villarreal, & Challela, 1999). This argument can be extended to many of the methods reviewed to this point, in that a multimethod approach involving a combination of appropriate methods to achieve health promotion goals is likely to be most effective. Macaulay et al. (1997) have reported the results of such a multimethod program directed toward diabetes prevention with a native community in Canada. Naidoo and Wills (1998) and their colleagues report on multimethod approaches to reduce accidents, to prevent coronary heart disease and strokes, to prevent cancer, and to promote sexual health and mental health. Ramirez et al. (1999) have presented a case study on a program of diabetes control for Mexican Americans in San Antonio, Texas, which combines a number of media approaches and the natural community support network. Their results are impressive.

HEALTH PROMOTION PROGRAM DEVELOPMENT AND EVALUATION

As with any other program in the health field, there is a need to follow established procedures in the development and evaluation of health promotion programs (Davies & MacDonald, 1998; Kline, 1999; Peberdy, 1997). Program development and evaluation are extensive topics in their own right. Space remaining in this chapter permits us simply to alert the reader to some of the specific resources in the health promotion area. Naidoo and Wills (1994) provide some discussion of needs assessment and program development in the health promotion area in general. Kline (1999) and Hubley (1993) have outlined the steps in program development in the health promotion field with particular reference to multicultural populations and other cultures, respectively. Kahn et al. (1975), Nolde and Smillie (1987), and Meegan and McCormick (1988) discuss some specific elements of health promotion program development with other cultures. General discussions of evaluation methods applied to health promotion programs are provided in Davies and MacDonald (1998), Peberdy (1997), and Naidoo and Wills (1994).

SUMMARY

The history and definition of health promotion have been reviewed in this chapter. The model of health and health promotion proposed by Seedhouse (1997) was presented as a meaningful approach to health promotion from a cultural perspective. The examples of individual, group, organizational, community, and media health promotion programs discussed in this chapter demonstrate the diversity of approaches and the many gaps to be filled by future health promotion programs. It is clear that the goal of "Health for All by 2000" was not met. Perhaps by 2050, many of the gaps will be reduced and health promotion from a cultural perspective will have come of age.

CASE STUDY

Thapa (1996) describes the work of CARE in Bajura, a district in Nepal, between 1990 and 1995. The program was under the Remote Area Basic Needs Project and the Ministry of Local Development. Community-based health workers were placed in several villages in the district. The health workers organized a number of local committees that were focused on agroforestry and the community infrastructure, and they provided primary health care. As a result of the program, most villages have at least one toilet, bridges have been built, and small-scale drinking water systems have been established. The villagers now cultivate and eat fresh vegetables and fruit. They have been trained in basic hygiene, and traditional birth attendants are providing more service to mothers during and after delivery. A number of educational and literacy projects were also emerging in the district. Thapa (1996) concludes by indicating that many fundamental changes have occurred in Bajura, one of the most impoverished districts in Nepal. Despite the changes, he concludes that "Bajura has a long way to go" (Thapa, 1996, p. 1246).

1. Based on the Foundations Theory of Health, what would you suggest the next goals in the CARE program should be?
2. How would you maintain the changes that have been made?
3. What elements would you include in a program to achieve the next set of goals in the program?
4. What measures would you use to evaluate the impact of these programs?

SUGGESTED READINGS

Gorin, S. S., & Arnold, J. (Eds.). (1998). *Health promotion handbook.* St. Louis, MO: Mosby.
Huff, R. M., & Kline, M. V. (Eds.). (1999). *Promoting health in multicultural populations: A handbook for practitioners.* Thousand Oaks, CA: Sage.
Naidoo, J., & Wills, J. (1994). *Health promotion: Foundations for practice.* London, UK: Baillière Tindall.
Naidoo, J., & Wills, J. (1998). *Practising health promotion: Dilemmas and challenges.* London, UK: Baillière Tindall.
Seedhouse, D. (1997). *Health promotion: Philosophy, prejudice and practice.* Chichester, UK: Wiley.

REFERENCES

Aboud, F. E. (1998). *Health psychology in global perspective.* Thousand Oaks, CA: Sage.
Aikins, M. K., Fox-Rushby, J., D'Alessandro, U., Langerock, P., Cham, K., New, L., Bennett, S., Greenwood, B., & Mills, A. (1998). The Gambian national impregnated bednet program: Costs, consequences and net cost-effectiveness. *Social Science and Medicine, 46,* 181–191.
Airhihenbuwa, C. O. (1994). Health promotion and the discourse on culture: Implications for empowerment. *Health Education Quarterly, 21,* 345–353.
Alcalay, R., Ghee, A., & Scrimshaw, S. (1993). Designing parental care messages for low-income Mexican women. *Public Health Reports, 108,* 354–362.
Alonzo, A. A. (1993). Health behavior: Issues, contradictions and dilemmas. *Social Science and Medicine, 37,* 1019–1034.
Anderson, R. T., Aaronson, N. K., Leplège, A. P., & Wilkins, D. (1996). International use and application of generic health-related quality of life instruments. In B. Spilker (Ed.), *Quality of life and pharmacoeconomics in clinical trials* (2nd ed., pp. 613–632). Philadelphia, PA: Lippincott–Raven.
Arnold, J., & Breen, L. J. (1998). Images of health. In S. S. Gorin & J. Arnold (Eds.), *Health promotion handbook* (pp. 3–13). St. Louis, MO: Mosby.
Baric, L. (1996). *Handbook for students and practitioners.* Altrincham, UK: Barnes Publications.
Bastien, J. W. (1990). The making of a community health worker. *World Health Forum, 11,* 368–372.
Bastien, J. W. (1994). Collaboration of doctors and nurses with ethnomedical practitioners. *World Health Forum, 15,* 133–137.
Bennett, P., & Murphy, S. (1997). *Psychology and health promotion.* Buckingham, UK: Open University Press.
Blaxter, M. (1990). *Health and lifestyles.* London, UK: Tavistock/Routledge.
Bowling, A. (1997). *Measuring health: A review of quality of life measurement scales* (2nd ed.). Buckingham, UK: Open University Press.
Buchanan, I. (1995). The purpose–process gap in health promotion. In D. Seedhouse (Ed.), *Reforming health care: The philosophy and practice of international health reform* (pp. 221–227). Chichester, UK: Wiley.

Calfas, K. J. (1998). Physical activity. In S. S. Gorin & J. Arnold (Eds.), *Health promotion handbook* (pp. 185–213). St. Louis, MO: Mosby.

Calfas, K. J., Long, B. J., Sallis, J. F., Wooten, W. J., Pratt, M., & Patrick, K. (1996). A controlled trial of physician counseling to promote the adoption of physical activity. *Preventive Medicine, 25,* 225–233.

Caplan, R. (1993). The importance of social theory for health promotion: From description to reflexivity. *Health Promotion International, 8,* 147–157.

Charles, M., Masihi, E. J., Siddiqui, H. Y., Jogarao, S. V., D'Lima, H., Mehta, U., & Britto, G. (1994). Culture, drug abuse and some reflections on the family. *Bulletin on Narcotics, 46,* 67–86.

Chen, P. C. Y. (1989). Health care in Sarawak's jungles. *World Health Forum, 10,* 190–192.

Cull, A. M. (1997). Cancer-specific quality of life questionnaires: The state of the art in Europe. *European Journal of Cancer, 33,* (Suppl. 6), S3–S7.

Cummins, R. A. (1996). The domains of life satisfaction: An attempt to order chaos. *Social Indicators Research, 38,* 303–328.

Davies, J. K., & MacDonald, G. (Eds.). (1998). *Quality, evidence and effectiveness in health promotion: Striving for certainties.* London, UK: Routledge.

Day, H., & Jankey, S. G. (1996). Lessons from the literature: Toward a holistic model of quality of life. In R. Renwick, I. Brown, & M. Nagler (Eds.), *Quality of life in health promotion and rehabilitation* (pp. 39–50). Thousand Oaks, CA: Sage.

de Viggiani, N. (1997). *A basis for health promotion.* London, UK: Distance Learning Center.

Diener, E., Emmons, R. A., Larsen, R. J., & Griffin, S. (1985). The Satisfaction With Life Scale. *Journal of Personality Assessment, 49,* 71–75.

Diener, E., Suh, E. M., Lucas, R. E., & Smith, H. L. (1999). Subjective well-being: Three decades of progress. *Psychological Bulletin, 125,* 276–302.

Douglas, J. (1996). Developing the Black and minority ethnic communities, health promotion strategies which address social inequalities. In P. Bywaters & E. McLeod (Eds.), *Working for equality in health* (pp.177–196). London, UK: Routledge.

Elder, J. P. (1987). Applications of behavior modification to health promotion in the developing world. *Social Science and Medicine, 24,* 335–349.

Epp, J. (1986). *Achieving health for all: A framework for health promotion.* Ottawa: Supply and Services Canada.

Evans, D. R. (1994). Enhancing quality of life in the population at large. *Social Indicators Research, 33,* 47–88.

Evans, D. R. (1997). Health promotion, wellness programs and quality of life. *Canadian Psychology, 38,* 1–12.

Evans, D. R., & Cope, W. E. (1989). *Quality of Life Questionnaire manual.* Toronto: Multi-Health Systems.

Evans, D. R., Burns, J. E., Robinson, W. E., & Garrett, O. J. (1985). The Quality of Life Questionnaire: A multidimensional measure. *American Journal of Community Psychology, 13,* 305–322.

Evans, D. R., Nesbitt, L. M. L., Pilgrim, A. E., Potts, S. M., & Albert, W. G. (1985). The Community Alcohol Use Scale: A scale for use in prevention programs. *American Journal of Community Psychology, 13,* 715–731.

Farquhar, M. (1995). Definitions of quality of life: A taxonomy. *Journal of Advanced Nursing, 22,* 502–508.

Fidler, K., & Costello, A. (1995). The role of doctors in influencing infant feeding practices in South India. *Tropical Doctor, 25,* 178–180.

Fitzgibbon, M. L., Stolley, M. R., Avellone, M. E., Sugerman, S., & Chavez, N. (1996). Involving parents in cancer risk reduction: A program for Hispanic American families. *Health Psychology, 15,* 413–422.

Frankish, C. J., Lovato, C. Y., & Shannon, W. J. (1999). Models, theories, and principles of health promotion with multicultural populations. In R. M. Huff & M. V. Kline (Eds.), *Promoting health in multicultural populations: A handbook for practitioners* (pp. 41–72). Thousand Oaks, CA: Sage.

Gorin, S. S. (1998). Future directions for health promotion. In S. S. Gorin, & J. Arnold (Eds.), *Health promotion handbook* (pp. 401–420). St. Louis, MO: Mosby.

Guthrie, G. M., Guthrie, H. M., Fernandez, T. L., Ruiz-Lambo, N. R., & Barba, C. V. C. (1987). Maternal and child health promotion in a developing country. *Education and Treatment of Children, 10*, 84–96.

Hamilton, J. (1995). Training for skills. *Medical Education, 29* (Suppl. 1), 83–87.

Hammond, R., & Yung, B. (1991). Preventing violence in at-risk African-American youth. *Journal of Health Care for the Poor and Underserved, 2*, 359–373.

Hays, P. A. (1995). Multicultural applications of cognitive–behavior therapy. *Professional Psychology: Research and Practice, 26*, 309–315.

Holtzman, W. H. (1997). Community psychology and full-service schools in different cultures. *American Psychologist, 52*, 366–380.

Holtzman, W. H., Evans, R. I., Kennedy, S., & Iscoe, I. (1987). Psychology and health: Contributions of psychology to the improvement of health and health care. *Bulletin of the World Health Organization, 65*, 913–935.

Hubley, J. (1993). *Communicating health: An action guide to health education and health promotion.* London: MacMillan.

Huff, R. M. (1999). Cross-cultural concepts of health and disease. In R. M. Huff & M. V. Kline (Eds.), *Promoting health in multicultural populations: A handbook for practitioners* (pp. 23–39). Thousand Oaks, CA: Sage.

Huff, R. M., & Kline, M. V. (1999a). Health promotion in the context of culture. In R. M. Huff & M. V. Kline (Eds.), *Promoting health in multicultural populations: A handbook for practitioners* (pp. 3–22). Thousand Oaks, CA: Sage.

Huff, R. M., & Kline, M. V. (Eds.). (1999b). *Promoting health in multicultural populations: A handbook for practitioners.* Thousand Oaks, CA: Sage.

Hussain, M. F. (1984). Race related illness in Vietnamese refugees. *International Journal of Social Psychology, 30*, 153–156.

Jackson, D. N. (1970). A sequential system for personality scale development. *Current Topics in Clinical and Community Psychology, 2*, 61–96.

Jones, L. (1997a). Promoting health: Everybody's business. In J. Katz & A. Peberdy (Eds.), *Promoting health: Knowledge and practice* (pp. 2–17). Basingstoke, UK: MacMillan.

Jones, L. (1997b). What is health? In J. Katz & A. Peberdy (Eds.), *Promoting health: Knowledge and practice* (pp. 18–36). Basingstoke, UK: MacMillan.

Kahn, M. W., Williams, C., Galvez, E., Lejero, L., Conrad, R., & Goldstein, G. (1975). The Papago Psychology Service: A community mental health program on an American Indian reservation. *American Journal of Community Psychology, 3*, 81–97.

Kelleher, C. (1998). Evaluating health promotion in four key settings. In J. K. Davies & G. Macdonald (Eds.), *Quality, evidence and effectiveness in health promotion: Striving for certainties* (pp. 47–67). London, UK: Routledge.

Kline, M. V. (1999). Planning health promotion and disease prevention programs in multicultural populations. In R. M. Huff & M. V. Kline (Eds.), *Promoting health in multicultural populations: A handbook for practitioners* (pp. 73–102). Thousand Oaks, CA: Sage.

Lake, C. (1996). *Health and the media.* Manchester, UK: The Open College.

Lalonde, M. (1974). *A new perspective on health for Canadians.* Ottawa: Government of Canada.

Long, B. J., Calfas, K. J., Wooten, W., Sallis, J. F., Patrick, K., Goldstein, M., Marcus, B., Schwenk, T., Carter, R., Torez, T., Polinkas, L., & Heath, J. (1996). A multisite field test of the acceptability of physical activity counseling in primary care: Project PACE. *American Journal of Preventive Medicine, 12*, 73–81.

Lupton, D. (1994). Consumerism, commodity culture and health promotion. *Health Promotion International, 9*, 111–118.

Macaulay, A. C., Paradis, G., Potvin, L., Cross, E. J., Saad-Haddad, C., McComber, A., Desrosiers, S., Kirby, R., Montour, L. T., Lamping, D. L., Leduc, N., & Rivard, M. (1997). The Kahnawake Schools diabetes prevention project: Intervention, evaluation, and baseline results of a diabetes primary prevention program with a Native community in Canada. *Preventive Medicine, 86,* 779–790.

MacDonald, G., & Davies, J. K. (1998). Reflection and vision: Proving and improving the promotion of health. In J. K. Davies & G. Macdonald (Eds.), *Quality, evidence and effectiveness in health promotion: Striving for certainties* (pp. 5–18). London, UK: Routledge.

Meegan, M., & McCormick, J. (1988, July 16). Prevention of disease in the poor world. *Lancet, #8603, 11,* (2), 152–153.

Naidoo, J., & Wills, J. (1994). *Health promotion: Foundations for practice.* London, UK: Baillière Tindall.

Naidoo, J., & Wills, J. (1998). *Practising health promotion: Dilemmas and challenges.* London, UK: Baillière Tindall.

Nolde, T., & Smillie, C. (1987). Planning and evaluation of cross-cultural health education activities. *Journal of Advanced Nursing, 12,* 159–165.

Nordenfelt, L. (1995). On the nature and ethics of health promotion: An attempt at a systematic analysis. In D. Seedhouse (Ed.), *Reforming health care: The philosophy and practice of international health reform* (pp. 185–197). Chichester, UK: Wiley.

Peberdy, A. (1997). Evaluating health promotion. In J. Katz & A. Peberdy (Eds.), *Promoting health: Knowledge and practice* (pp. 267–328). Basingstoke, UK: MacMillan.

Prochaska, J. O., & DiClemente, C. C. (1984). *The transtheoretical approach: Crossing traditional foundations of change.* Homewood, IL: Irwin.

Ramirez, A. G., Villarreal, R., & Challela, P. (1999). Community-level diabetes control in a Texas barrio. In R. M. Huff & M. V. Kline (Eds.), *Promoting health in multicultural populations: A handbook for practitioners* (pp. 169–187). Thousand Oaks, CA: Sage.

Rosenberg, R. (1995). Health-related quality of life between naturalism and hermeneutics. *Social Science and Medicine, 41,* 1411–1415.

Sarafino, E. P. (1998). *Health psychology: Biopsychosocial interactions* (3rd. ed.). New York: Wiley.

Seedhouse, D. F. (1986). *Health: The foundations of achievement.* Chichester, UK: Wiley.

Seedhouse, D. (1997). *Health promotion: Philosophy, prejudice and practice.* Chichester, UK: Wiley.

Stone, L. (1992). Cultural influences in community participation in health. *Social Science and Medicine, 35,* 409–417.

Suh, E., Diener, E., Oishi, S., & Triandis, H. C. (1998). The shifting basis of life satisfaction judgements across cultures: Emotions versus norms. *Journal of Personality and Social Psychology, 74,* 482–493.

Terborg, J. R. (1998). Health psychology in the United States: A critique and selective review. *Applied Psychology: An International Review, 47,* 199–217.

Thapa, S. (1996). Challenges to improving maternal health in rural Nepal. *Lancet, 347,* 1244–1246.

Vidaurre, J. (1994). Conscripts for health. *World Health Forum, 15,* 345–347.

Watson, D., Clark, L. A., & Tellegen, A. (1988). Development and validation of brief measures of positive and negative affect: The PANAS scales. *Journal of Personality and Social Psychology, 54,* 1063–1070.

Werna, E. (1996). United Nations Agencies' urban policies and health. In S. Atkinson, J. Songsore, & E. Werna (Eds.), *Urban health research in developing countries: Implications for policy* (pp. 11–30). Oxford, UK: CAB International.

Williams, R. G. A. (1983). Concepts of health: An analysis of lay logic. *Sociology, 17,* 185–204.

Winett, R. A. (1995). A framework for health promotion and disease prevention programs. *American Psychologist, 50,* 341–350.

World Health Organization (1946). *Constitution.* Geneva: Author.

World Health Organization (1978). *Report on the International Conference on Primary Health Care* (Alma Ata). Geneva: Author.

World Health Organization (1984). *Health promotion: A discussion document on concepts and principles.* Geneva: Author.

World Health Organization (1986). *Ottawa Charter for Health Promotion: An International Conference on Health Promotion* (Ottawa). Copenhagen: Author.

World Health Organization (1988). *Report on the Second International Conference on Health Promotion* (Adelaide). Geneva: Author.

World Health Organization (1991). *Report on the Third International Conference on Health Promotion* (Sundvall). Geneva: Author.

World Health Organization (1993). *Health for all targets: The health policy for Europe* (updated edition). Copenhagen: Author.

World Health Organization (1997). *Report on the Fourth International Conference on Health Promotion* (Jakarta). Geneva: Author.

World Health Organization (1998). *The World Health Report 1998: Life in the 21st century—a Vision for all.* Geneva, Switzerland: Author.

World Health Organization Quality of Life Group. (1993). Study protocol for the World Health Organization project to develop a quality of life assessment instrument (WHOQOL). *Quality of Life Research, 2,* 153–159.

World Health Organization Quality of Life Group. (1998). The World Health Organization Quality of Life Assessment (WHOQOL): Development and general psychometric properties. *Social Science and Medicine, 46,* 1569–1585.

Yee, B. W. K., Castro, F. G., Hammond, W. R., John, R., Wyatt, G. E., & Yung, B. R. (1995). Panel IV: Risk-taking and abusive behaviors among ethnic minorities. *Health Psychology, 14,* 622–631.

Yee, T. T., & Lee, R. H. (1977). Based on cultural strengths, a school primary prevention program for Asian-American youth. *Community Mental Health Journal, 13,* 239–248.

5

ADHERENCE TO
HEALTH CARE

HEATHER M. SHEARER AND DAVID R. EVANS

Department of Psychology
The University of Western Ontario
London, Ontario, Canada

Patient adherence to medical treatment is a much studied topic. Within the last decade alone, several thousand articles have addressed various issues related to adherence. The problem of nonadherence to treatment regimens affects health care practitioners in every field. Morbidity, clinical decisions, cost-effectiveness of health care, and clinical trials are all affected by adherence. The extent of non-adherence is very difficult to identify. A review of the literature indicates that adherence rates have changed very little over the past decade or more, and despite the development of several theories and the introduction of a number of interventions, the reported statistics show little change. There are no definite numbers for the prevalence of adherence. Estimates of variance range from 15 to 93% (Myers & Midence, 1998; Rand & Weeks, 1998; Dunbar-Jacob, Burke, & Puczynski, 1995). Adherence rates also vary according to disease classification. For instance, approximately one-third of patients fail to adhere to regimens for acute illnesses while 50–55% of patients do not adhere for chronic illnesses (Rapoff, 1999). When addressing lifestyle changes such as exercise, weight loss, or smoking cessation, the rates of nonadherence are even greater.

Little has been written on treatment adherence and culture and far less research has been reported on the topic (Meyerowitz, Richardson, Hudson, & Leedham, 1998; Smith, Lin, & Mendoza, 1993). Searches of the psychological and medical literature yielded about 30 references to the topic and of those only 12 provided any useful information. As a result, an effort has been made in this chapter to incorporate material from other areas, such as primary care and health promotion.

In substance, the content of the chapter is much more treatment adherence-oriented and far less culture and treatment adherence-oriented than we would have liked. If anything, the lack of material on culture and treatment adherence points to an area in need of urgent attention by researchers and practitioners.

While lack of attention to the topic may explain the paucity of literature on culture and treatment adherence, there are other possibilities. One explanation may rest in the individualist/collectivist dimension of different cultures, and another explanation may reside in differences in the cultural meaning of health and treatment. It could be that the individualistic focus of Western medicine and the freedom of the individual to participate in treatment may make adherence a more important problem in this system of health care. Alternatively, the spiritual nature of non-Western health systems may mean that participants are more likely to adhere to the prescriptions of indigenous spiritual healers, and hence, adherence to treatment is not a problem (Ashing-Giwa, 1999).

Anderson (1993) has suggested that there are at least three alternate hypotheses to explain why members of cultural groups other than the majority culture fail to adhere to treatment regimens. The first hypothesis, which is frequently proposed, is that the patient's cultural beliefs are a barrier to treatment adherence. Under this proposition, the practitioner must be culturally competent in order to negotiate a treatment plan that is culturally acceptable to the patient. The second hypothesis is that nonadherence occurs because of barriers such as lack of funds, lack of time, misunderstanding of the proposed treatment, and failure of the practitioner to validate the patient's understanding of the treatment. These and other similar barriers seem to be common across cultures. The third hypothesis is that the health care system is organized to favor the majority culture. This proposition suggests that the reason for nonadherence of patients from cultural groups other than the majority culture lies in a complex of social, political, and economic systems. Meyerowitz et al. (1998) have proposed a model that incorporates facets of each of these hypotheses in relation to culture, access, knowledge, attitudes, adherence behavior, and outcomes. This model may be a useful paradigm to guide the much needed research in this area.

Although a large amount of research has been produced, there is still a great deal of uncertainty and disagreement surrounding what is considered a proper definition for adherence. Several authors make the distinction between the terms "adherence" and "compliance" (Sarafino, 1998; Myers & Midence, 1998; Karoly, 1993). If the two terms are considered interchangeable, a general definition might refer to the degree to which a patient's behavior coincides with what his/her health practitioner has advised. Current theorists advocate the use of the term adherence rather than compliance. Sarafino (1998) indicates that compliance suggests a more subservient role for the patient in the patient–physician relationship. Noncompliance can be viewed as a deviant behavior for which the patient is fully to blame. Noncompliance represents the patient's lack of willingness to follow the physician's directives. According to this view, the power to decide on what action is appropriate is the realm of the physician, while the responsibility for action is that of the patient. Over the years, it has been argued that this definition is inadequate and does not account for several factors affecting health behaviors (Noble, 1998).

In contrast, the term "adherence" refers to much more active involvement in the treatment regimen relationship on the part of both the patient and physician. There is a greater emphasis on the patients' role in their decision to follow through with a particular regimen. In this conceptualization, the patient–physician relationship is viewed as more of a partnership, in which decisions and actions are negotiated versus dictated.

Another issue surrounding adherence is how it is defined in different cultures. Very little research has addressed adherence in cultures other than the West. Is our definition of adherence appropriate to the health behaviors observed in other societies? Ryan (1998) reported that laypeople in a small village in Cameroon first chose treatments which were less expensive and easier to administer. If their choices were not congruent with the health practitioner's primary recommendations, presumably they would be considered nonadherent. These same individuals were also found to use a number of different treatments in the hope that at least one would be effective. Even though choices were made in a very organized manner, one wonders how Western practitioners would classify this behavior. It is important to understand adherence, its meaning, and the related behaviors in the context of culture.

Most literature on adherence focuses on the underuse of medications. An equally important aspect of adherence is that of drug overadherence. This often occurs when a medication provides immediate relief of symptoms. For example, patients with chronic obstructive pulmonary disease or asthma may use more aerosol therapy than prescribed (Ries, 1993).

An individual may fully intend to follow the advice of the health practitioner and still not adhere to the recommendations. This may not be deviant behavior because the patient might be considering several factors when deciding to follow a treatment regimen. This behavior can be described as rational adherence or intelligent nonadherence (Raynor, 1998). In this construct, an individual makes a decision to adhere or not based on the net consequences and benefits (Raynor, 1998; Ries, 1993). These individuals are acting rationally when they fail to take their medication as directed. For instance, if a medication has undesirable side effects and the overall benefit of the treatment is low, nonadherence could be considered rational. At this point, the patient has made a rational decision which, among other things, affects his or her quality of life.

FACTORS AFFECTING ADHERENCE

By understanding why patients do or do not adhere to treatment regimens, interventions can be designed and put into action in order to improve adherence. With this understanding, morbidity, mortality, and related health care costs can be reduced. In reviewing the literature, there are certain areas which have received a great deal of attention with respect to their relation to adherence. Variables such as client characteristics, health care providers, disease, and regimen are commonly listed as obstacles to adherence. In this section of the chapter, adherence obstacles are examined under three general headings: patient characteristics; treatment factors; and patient–provider relationship.

PATIENT CHARACTERISTICS

Several demographic characteristics of individuals and their effects on adherence have been studied. In much of the reviewed research, demographic variables were reported to have minimal effect on adherence. Gender, marital status, socioeconomic status, and age (with the exception of adolescence) have all been found to have little or no effect on adherence (Dunbar-Jacob et al., 1995; Sarafino, 1998; Myers & Midence, 1998). Adolescents have been found to have lower adherence than younger children (Rapoff, 1999). This is perhaps explained by the fact that parents are largely responsible for their young children's treatment adherence. As children move through their teen years, the responsibility of adherence tends to shift from the parents to the teen.

The patient's knowledge about his or her disease and treatment is another characteristic related to adherence. There are inconsistent results relating knowledge and adherence, but generally, the more well informed patients are of their circumstances, the more likely adherence will be enhanced (Rapoff, 1999; Dunbar-Jacob et al., 1995). Patients need to be instructed about symptoms, treatments, and likely outcomes. In some acute illnesses, it is common for symptoms to be alleviated before the treatment course is finished. As a result, patients may feel they no longer need the medication and discontinue its use. In some cases, the illness returns shortly after or the body builds an immunity to that particular treatment so that it becomes less effective in the future. Knowledge is especially important when trying to introduce Western medicine in other cultures. Mull, Shear Wood, Gans, & Mull (1989) reported that only 5 out of 128 people interviewed in Pakistan attributed leprosy to germs. Many felt that an antagonistic diet, such as mixing hot and cold elements, produced the illness. Other causes were thought to be untruthfulness, ingratitude, and blasphemy against the gods. If the real cause could be explained and understood, perhaps those suffering from the illness might be more receptive to effective medical regimens.

Conflicting behavior patterns also deserve mention. Often when a patient begins a treatment regimen, behavior must be changed in order to produce effective adherence. This means that enjoyable behaviors might have to be changed or replaced. For example, medication schedules can interfere with sleep patterns if administration is required during the night or sleep period. Also, some drugs are associated with behavioral restrictions, such as not being able to operate a motorized vehicle. Not only is the regimen irritating in the fact that it interferes with established behavioral patterns, it is likely that nonadherence increases with its level of intrusiveness (Grunberg & Cousino Klein, 1998).

In general, humans have a need to make sense of and explain life experiences. When an individual is suffering from an illness, the quest for meaning and understanding is often magnified. Culturally shaped beliefs can play a major role in determining an individual's understanding and subsequent behavior in relation to seeking medical care and adherence to a regimen (Ashing-Giwa, 1999). If an individual has health beliefs which are inconsistent with the treatment paradigm being applied, it is likely that adherence to treatments will be affected. Conflicting beliefs, fear of not being able to access the health care system, and poor patient–physician relations are all possible reasons for suboptimal adherence (Pachter & Weller, 1993). In a study of inner-city Puerto Rican families with children being treated for asthma, three main factors influenced adherence. Educational interventions, supportive social environments, and good communication and relations with physicians all significantly improved adherence (Pachter & Weller, 1993). These factors are all addressed within this chapter.

Social support is often cited as having an influence on adherence. There is great variability in the levels and type of social support, depending on the culture. In many cultures, an individual does not make decisions alone (Huff & Kline, 1999a, 1999b, 1999c, 1999d, 1999e). Close family, friends, and community leaders are often influential. Working as a group, a decision is reached as to what course of treatment will be followed. For example, in a small village in Cameroon, family members are often included in the decision on health actions (Ryan, 1998). If the patient has a social network that is supportive, it is more likely that the individual will adhere to the treatment regimen. On the other hand, for those with little support, adherence rates are much lower. For individuals with leprosy, nonadherence is common. These patients are often disowned and shunned by their spouses, families, and communities. In fact, denial of the diagnosis is quite common and perhaps even understandable, considering the social consequences which follow diagnosis (Mull et al., 1989). Adherence issues should be discussed with patients and family members. The discussions should be aimed at educating all concerned, resolving fears about the illness and possible side effects from the treatment.

Differences in cultural beliefs surrounding the efficacy of medication is an important predictor of compliance. Despite the availability of western medicines, traditional herbal remedies continue to be used (Morgan, 1995). Lack of knowledge and past experience with Western medicine are some reasons cited for the use of traditional remedies. For instance, individuals affected by leprosy are often distressed by side effects of the medication. Sensations of heat, swelling, nausea, dizziness, and changes in skin color are all possible side effects of the treatment regimen (Mull et al., 1989). Individuals sometimes find these effects frightening and often discontinue treatment, revert back to traditional treatments, or both. M. Smith et al. (1993) also report that Asians and Hispanics are generally cautious about possible side effects of Western medicine. Perhaps these beliefs stem from experiences with herbal drugs which do not often induce side effects. There is also concern about possible toxic and addictive properties of medications and this could increase nonadherence, especially if the regimen is to be followed for an extended period of time.

All health care providers need to be educated about different forms of medication and treatment. In many cultures, both traditional healers and biomedically trained physicians can learn from each other. Western medicine might provide treatment for an illness for which there is no herbal remedy while traditional treatments might be less invasive and just as effective for other ailments. Traditional healers could also offer patients some reassurance with their familiar cultural input which might help offset the uneasiness of using a foreign treatment regimen. In any case, both types of practitioners should be aware if the patient is combining alternate forms of treatment. The interactions of the remedies could have antagonistic or augmentative results (M. Smith et al., 1993).

TREATMENT FACTORS

Patients are commonly blamed for their poor adherence to a treatment regimen. Health care providers must learn to look not only at patient characteristics but also at other factors which might influence adherence. It has been reported that personality characteristics are of less importance to adherence than are characteristics of treatment regimens (Kerns, Bayer, & Findley, 1999). As treatments become more complex, intense, long-term, and costly, adherence tends to decrease (Rapoff, 1999). Imagine the difficulty some individuals might have if required to take several drugs over the course of one day. Each drug has different instructions, dosage, and possible side effects. Intuitively, the greater the number of drugs and the more complex the regimens, the more likely that an individual will fail to adhere properly to the treatment course.

Unfortunately, many therapeutic and life-saving drugs have severe and unpleasant side effects. This alone can be a strong deterrent in adherence to a regimen. For example, consider a cancer patient who is being treated with antineoplastic drugs. These drugs can cause effects such as nausea, vomiting, seizures, and loss of taste and hearing (Grunberg & Cousino Klein, 1998). Morgan (1995) suggested that side effects experienced from anti-hypertensive medication was one of the factors that accounted for the low rate of adherence among Afro-Caribbean compared to White patients in inner London, England. Often, patients feel they must choose between the overall benefit of the drug and their quality of life while on the medication or treatment regimen (Morgan, 1995).

Cost of treatment can also be prohibitive for some individuals and families. Sarafino (1998) reported that there is disagreement among researchers as to whether cost plays a major role in adherence but with decreased funding and coverage for prescriptions, groups such as the elderly are having more difficulty affording prescriptions and other health-related expenses. Meyerowitz et al. (1998) suggested that income was a more important factor than culture in the adherence of African American and Hispanic patients to cancer treatments.

PATIENT–PROVIDER RELATIONSHIP

With the growing fiscal restraints in health care, physician–patient contact is likely to become more strained. Thus, providing thorough information about illness and treatments as well as the effects of adherence is important in increasing treatment effectiveness. The practitioners' communication skills and their attitudes toward the patient influence adherence. Health care workers who are warm and address their client's concerns are likely to have better rates of adherence. It is important to communicate with patients from other cultures in a culturally competent manner, which involves a knowledge of both the communication styles and the beliefs of the patient's culture (Evans et al., 1998; Morgan, 1995; M. Smith et al., 1993). Perceived clinic support was indicated as one of the most important variables that affect child immunization completion (Gore et al., 1999). Procedural aspects of a clinic, such as waiting time, affect a patient's adherence (Dunbar-Jacob et al., 1995). The patient–physician relationship as a form of intervention to improve adherence is discussed later in this chapter.

ADHERENCE THEORIES

Given the extent of suboptimal adherence to medical regimens across a variety of illnesses, it is not surprising that a great deal of research has been devoted to the explanation and prediction of health-related behaviors. Several theoretical frameworks have been proposed. In this section of the chapter, some of the major theories in adherence research are described and appraised.

THE TRANSTHEORETICAL MODEL

This model focuses on the adoption and maintenance of health behaviors and has two major dimensions. The "stages of change" construct represents a temporal dimension. Change is considered to be a process occurring over time versus simply an event (Prochaska, Johnson, & Lee, 1998). The model describes five stages of change required for a specific outcome. The first stage is *precontemplation.* The client is not aware of a need to change or does not intend to change. In the second stage, *contemplation,* the client is aware of a need to change and is considering it. By deciding to take some action in the future and having recently attempted change, although unsuccessfully, the client has entered into the *preparation* stage. *Action* is the fourth stage. At this point, the client is engaging in the new behavior but has not yet attained the outcome. The final step is *maintenance.* Here, the client reaches his/her goal and works to maintain the behavior over time. Change is often described as a cyclical versus linear pattern so there is the possibility of relapsing back to an earlier stage (Marcus, Rakowski, & Rossi, 1992). The progression through the five stages is often not linear. Individuals may cycle through the stages several times before being able to reach the maintenance phase.

Processes of change constitute the second major dimension of the transtheoretical model. These are overt and covert activities used to progress through the stages of change. Prochaska et al. (1998) identify 10 processes. These processes include consciousness-raising, dramatic relief, self-reevaluation, environmental reevaluation, self-liberation, social liberation, counter-conditioning, stimulus control, contingency management, and helping relationships. People use different processes at different stages of change (Prochaska et al., 1998). Processes are matched with stages of change. For example, helping relationships, counter-conditioning, stimulus control, and contingency management can all be grouped under the action and maintenance stages (Rapoff, 1999).

A concrete example of this model using Type II Diabetes is as follows. In the precontemplation stage, the patient either does not recognize the need to take medication or to adhere to the physician's recommendations to make diet and lifestyle changes or does not care; these individuals are content with their current status and do not realize the health implications. Once patients begin to understand the health problem and are unhappy with their current situation, the contemplation stage is reached. At this point, patients might realize that if they do not adhere to the recommendations, they might become insulin-dependent or develop other serious health problems. With the preparation stage, patients attempt to follow the regimen but are unsuccessful. Even so, additional action, such as consulting a health practitioner or trying to make better diet and lifestyle choices, will occur in the future. Once successful adherence is accomplished, patients become more committed to the changed behavior and the action stage is reached. In the final stage, an acceptable level of adherence has been reached and behavior focused on maintaining the current level of activity is initiated.

There has been some research that has examined intercountry and intercultural differences in stages of change with respect to health behaviors. None has been directed toward the subject of stages of change and adherence. Rakowski, Fulton, and Feldman (1993) evaluated the ability of the stages of change model to predict breast self-examination. They found no significant differences in the predictive value of the model among cultural groups. Laforge, Velicer, Richmond, and Owen (1999) compared the distribution across the stages of change of large samples of Americans and Australians for five health risk factors. Despite the large samples, they did not evaluate the effect of culture on the distributions. Distributions across stages for all of the risk factors were similar for Americans and Australians. In a study involving 1000 participants from each of the 15 countries in the European Union and their stage of change with respect to changing to a healthier diet, de Graaf, Van der Gaag, Kafatos, Lennernas, and Kearney (1997) found some differences in the distribution across stages for different countries. The results of these studies are suggestive, but research on the model and its utility in predicting adherence and ameliorating nonadherence is urgently needed.

THE HEALTH BELIEF MODEL

This theory focuses on threat perception and behavior evaluation. Threat perception can be separated into two components: perceived *susceptibility* to illness and *severity* of the illness. Behavior evaluation consists of beliefs surrounding the benefits of a specific health behavior as well as the costs or barriers of performing the behavior. Cues to action may evoke the health behavior if the individual has the appropriate beliefs. Social pressure, education campaigns, and perception of symptoms are just a few examples of cues. The final construct included in the Health Belief Model is the individual's *health motivation* (found in later versions of the model) (Sheeran & Abraham, 1996).

The components of the Health Belief Model can be applied to interventions promoting change. The Health Belief Model has been successfully used to predict one-time or more limited health behaviors, such as immunization and breast-cancer screening (Ashing-Giwa, 1999; Mermelstein, 1997). In the five studies that have investigated the applicability of the model to breast-cancer screening and that have included African Americans, two did not report separate results for African Americans, two found some utility of the model for this cultural group, and the final study suggested that accessibility and affordability were better predictors for the group (Ashing-Giwa, 1999). Health professionals using this model should emphasize personal susceptibility to disease/illness. For example, individuals should be targeted in the late fall for influenza immunizations. Emphasis should be placed on the fact that individuals (especially the elderly) are most susceptible for infection in the winter months and, thus, need to be immunized early on. Another way in which change can be promoted is to outline the severity of the consequences if an individual avoids certain immunizations. The elderly and parents of young children (elderly and youth are high-risk groups) could have the risk of illness, debilitation, and even death, which may result from nonaction, explained to them. The perceived benefits to action can also be reinforced during the discussion on consequences.

THEORY OF PLANNED BEHAVIOR

This theory emphasizes that intentions or decisions to behave in a specific way motivate health-related behaviors. The behavioral intentions are determined by three factors. Attitudes toward a behavior, perceptions of subjective norms to engage in a behavior, and perceptions of control to perform a behavior successfully are postulated as the components of behavioral intentions (Mermelstein, 1997). The link between intentions and behaviors can perhaps reflect the fact that individuals more often engage in behaviors they intend to perform.

Attitudes can have a major impact on behavior intentions (Mermelstein, 1997). A belief that an outcome is likely to be positive can strongly shape the attitude about the related health behavior. For example, if individuals know that taking medication will help with the management of chronic obstructive pulmonary disease, they will be more likely to partake in self-medication. Perceptions of subjective norms can also influence behavioral decisions. If adherence to medication regimens and treatments were considered a societal norm, the individual may be more likely to partake in these behaviors in order to reduce cognitive dissonance. Also, if significant others believe that a certain intervention is required, the individual may be more motivated to comply. For instance, a woman over the age of 60 who has never received a mammogram may be influenced to partake in one by societal norms and beliefs of important family members (i.e., husband, children).

Finally, the perceived behavior control of an individual is similar to the notion of self-efficacy and directly affects behavioral intentions. This relationship indicates that individuals are more likely to partake in behaviors over which there is perceived control (Conner & Sparks, 1996). One drawback of the Theory of Planned Behavior is that it does not account for a wider number of influences on an individual's health and behavior not involved in perception of control. Although the Theory of Planned Behavior involves a fairly common-sense approach, specific behavioral practices may aid in changing behaviors.

Research on the utility of the Theory of Planned Behavior in predicting adherence to various treatment regimens in specific cultural groups is extremely limited. Ashing-Giwa (1999) cites only one study on differences among cultures with respect to breast-cancer screening, and no cultural differences were significant. Jenings-Dozier (1999) concluded that the Theory of Planned Behavior was not adequate to predict the intention of African American women and Latinas to obtain a Pap smear. She suggested a model that also included social support and subjective norms. The sparsity of research on the application of the model to the adherence of members of various cultural groups to a variety of treatment regimens begs urgent attention.

MEASURING ADHERENCE

As previously mentioned, although adherence to medication regimens is highly studied, it is a poorly understood problem. Not only is there disagreement about the definition and measurement of adherence, but there are no clear statistics for the extent of nonadherence. Several methods have been used to study adherence, all of which have their inherent strengths and weaknesses. There is no one method which is applicable to all clinical and research situations and a combination of methods is often advisable for reliable results. Methods for measuring adherence can be broken down into two general groups. The first group to be discussed are the indirect measures. Clinician judgment, self-report, medication measurement, microelectronic measurement, and pharmacy database reviews are all forms of indirect measurement. Direct measurement is the second group of measures to be discussed. Biochemical analyses and direct observation are the two forms of direct measurement.

INDIRECT MEASURES

Clinician Judgment

The health care provider forms an impression of how well a patient is following the medical regimen (Rand & Weeks, 1998). This is best determined by asking open-ended, nonjudgmental questions. As previously mentioned, the physician's interviewing skills and quality of interaction are important factors in measuring and influencing adherence. The clinician's judgment affects the selected therapy and follow-up. Goldberg, Cohen, and Rubin (1998) reported that physicians actually have great difficulty in accurately appraising the adherence of their patients.

Self-Report

Interviews, patient-kept diaries, or structured questionnaires are used to keep track of adherence. These measures are generally inexpensive and provide greater detail of behaviors affecting adherence than do other forms of measurement. Although self-reports are cost effective and are applicable to a variety of clinical and research settings, there are important drawbacks to be considered. Both the interviewer's skill and question construction may affect the reliability of the results. The time frame between the behavior and reporting is also a factor. Cues to action and situations inhibiting adherence can be forgotten if not reported in a timely fashion. Demand characteristics may also be a factor. Patients may report a certain behavior or level of adherence which is not factual simply because they know that this is what the investigator is expecting (Rand & Weeks, 1998; Farmer, 1999; Dunbar-Jacob et al., 1995).

Medication Measurement

In this method, the number of pills or dosage units taken between each visit is counted. Inhaler use and use of liquid medicines can also be measured with this method. This is an objective and simple method but there are also some logistical concerns. Individuals are required to bring their medication with them at each visit and it is not uncommon for patients to forget to do this. They might also realize that their behavior is being monitored so they discard medication in order to appear adherent. This method does not provide information on accuracy of dosage or timing of medication. Also, this approach is very labor-intensive so it is done mostly in research settings (Rudd, 1993). Researchers should be aware of the effect culture has on patient's health beliefs. Some individuals may choose to stop taking prescribed medications and return to traditional remedies or may take both at the same time. This could alter measurement results and might even have an effect on the reported effectiveness of the clinical trial.

Pharmacy Database Review

This methodology provides information on the prescribed regimen, the amount of medication which is dispensed, and the timing between medication refills. This is an excellent source for measuring adherence across a wide range of regimens and illnesses. One of the major shortcomings with this method is that patients can confound the technique by using more than one pharmacy for their prescriptions and refills (Rand & Weeks, 1998). There is also no confirmation of consumption or whether the adherence is suboptimal.

Microelectronic Measurement

Electronic devices can be used to record the time and date of each medication use. A microprocessor is activated when opening a pill bottle, discharging inhaled medications, and releasing eye drops. Currently, there are two devices with widespread use. The Medication Event Monitoring System (MEMS) is used for regimens with pills or tablets. The microprocessor stores the date, time, and duration the bottle is open. The information is retrieved by an investigator at a later date. The Nebulizer Chronolog (NC) is used with inhalers. It replaces the plastic mouthpiece and records each depression as a use (Farmer, 1999). The primary advantage of this form of indirect measurement is that it provides continuous and reliable data on medication use. Even though this technology is expensive and not practical for studying large numbers of patients, it is an excellent source for longitudinal data on accuracy of adherence to regimens.

DIRECT MEASURES

Biochemical Analyses

These methods confirm and measure actual drug ingestion levels in blood, urine, or other bodily excretions. This is the only method which confirms that the medication has been taken. Biological markers can also be used to trace substances which are not evaluable by biochemical assays. This method is not effective for monitoring day-to-day adherence or the level of adherence (Dunbar-Jacob et al., 1995). Investigators should be aware that the presence of the drug in assays does not necessarily mean the patient is adherent. The patient may have begun to take the medication shortly before the clinic visit, but otherwise have suboptimal adherence. This is known as "white-coat compliance" (Farmer, 1999). Also, drug level is affected by an individual's metabolism and, thus, the interpretation of results is limited. When using this method, adherence is best assessed with repeated measures.

Directly Observed Therapy

Patients are directly observed when receiving their dose or treatment. Directly Observed Therapy was initially used in the treatment of tuberculosis (Rand & Weeks, 1998). This method has been shown to increase adherence, although it is not practical for most situations. Patients are still able to feign adherence by not swallowing the medication and removing it when no longer being observed.

Because of the shortcomings in each of these strategies, the use of multiple measures would be the optimal way to assess adherence and the behaviors influencing it. Investigators must also consider reactivity when measuring adherence. If patients are aware that their adherence to the medication regimen is being monitored, they may behave in an atypical manner.

STRATEGIES FOR ENHANCING ADHERENCE

Given the complex nature of adherence, the many factors that contribute to it, and the high proportion of persons that fail to embrace the appropriate interventions for their health situation, it is appropriate to devote some attention to strategies that can enhance adherence. Failure to adhere to a treatment regimen can be equated with resistance (Basco & Rush, 1996). However, it is more productive to approach a person's failure to adhere to an intervention from the perspective of enhancing cooperation with the treatment regimen (Evans et al., 1998). As Basco and Rush (1996) have pointed out, facilitating cooperation with a treatment plan consists of identifying and removing obstacles to adherence to the plan. One obstacle to appropriate adherence may be failure of the patient's health practitioner to follow practice guidelines.

Noble (1998) has identified a number of studies that demonstrate that health practitioners do not always adhere to treatment regimens and practice guidelines when treating patients. For example, studies by Yeo et al. (1994) and McMillan, Lockyer, Magnan, Akierman, & Parboosingh (1991) showed that physicians failed to follow guidelines for prescribing medication even when they were exposed to an educational program. Other studies reviewed by Myers and Midence (1998) also show that physicians often fail to follow correct prescription protocols and dietary advice when instructing their patients. Myers and Midence (1998) described studies that indicate that both physicians and nurses fail to adhere to infection-control procedures. For example, Anita-Obong, Young, and Effiong (1993) have identified the need to educate traditional birth assistants in Nigeria about hygienic practices in order to reduce neonatal tetanus. Dugan and Cohen (1998) have proposed a method of enhancing health practitioner adherence to practice guidelines, which is based on the stages of change model (Prochaska & DiClemente, 1982; Prochaska, DiClemente, & Norcross, 1992). They described the interventions that are potentially most effective for moving health practitioners through the stages of change from precontemplation to actively following practice guidelines. These considerations could be important in developing programs to train traditional health care providers.

Raynor (1998) has argued that the facilitation of adherence in patients depends upon the acquisition of knowledge and motivation to adhere. To these two should be added skills and support from one's family and/or community. Within each of these domains, there is a range of methodologies that have been employed to facilitate each. In the sections that follow, a brief discussion will be provided of approaches that have been developed to facilitate knowledge acquisition, motivate patients, assist patients to acquire requisite skills, and develop social support to enhance adherence to health regimens.

KNOWLEDGE ACQUISITION AND ADHERENCE

Despite the fact that physicians play an important role in the education of their patients concerning treatment regimens, they spend on average about 6% of the time that they see patients educating them (DiMatteo, 1993). As might be expected given this finding, exit interviews following physician visits indicate that patients generally have a poor understanding of the prescribed treatment regimen (Cromer, 1998). There is also evidence to suggest that patients are dissatisfied with the amount of information their physicians provide about their medical care (Noble, 1998). In addition Noble (1998) has observed that while physicians spend some time providing information and instructions, they spend little time checking how the information is received and what the patient wants to know.

One rationale for not providing information about side effects in particular is the belief that to do so will increase the probability that the patient will have side effects. Noble (1998) identified a number of studies that indicate that there is no evidence to support the belief that providing information about side effects increases their occurrence nor that it reduces adherence. The latter position is supported by other studies reviewed by Raynor (1998).

Noble (1998) concluded that a considerable body of research demonstrates that patients who understand their condition and the nature and purpose of their treatment are more likely to adhere to the treatment regimen. Basco and Rush (1996) have stated that, in order to adhere to treatment, individuals must understand (1) the purpose of the treatment, (2) the expected impact of the treatment, and (3) their responsibilities in the intervention. As noted earlier in the chapter, individuals must also posses the economic, personal, and social resources necessary to adhere to treatment. Basco and Rush (1996) have suggested including a discussion of these resources when interacting with patients about treatment regimens.

Cromer (1998) is another author who has stressed the importance of educational programs to increase adherence to treatment regimens. She suggested that the educational component should include information concerning the correct procedures necessary to effect the treatment protocol, a description of the outcome with and without adherence to the treatment protocol, and a description of the disease and its pathophysiology. She stressed that it is important that this educational activity be carried out within the sociocultural context of the patient.

While the content and organization of the information to be imparted to patients is important, the means of conveying the information is also important. A number of authors have commented on the means of conveying information in order to enlist patient cooperation and adherence. The majority of these recommendations are summarized here.

Communication Strategies to Enhance Understanding

• Orient patients to their medical condition and treatment options in terms that are understandable to them (DiMatteo & Lepper, 1998; Noble, 1998, Sheridan & Radmacher, 1992).

• Provide patients with a rationale for the treatment plan and evidence that it will work (Sheridan & Radmacher, 1992).

• Identify patients' misconceptions and interact with patients to clear them up (Basco & Rush, 1996; Noble, 1998).

• With cultural groups, respect traditional values and practices that might lead to failure to follow a treatment regimen and develop ways to accommodate these values and practices (Huff & Klein, 1999b).

• Use plain language that is at the patient's level and avoid jargon (DiMatteo, 1993; Noble, 1998; Sheridan & Radmacher, 1992; Thompson, 1998).

• Written material should be at the readability level of patients (Noble, 1998).

• Structure the information to be provided, and signal to the patient when a new segment of information is to be introduced (Noble, 1998).

• Provide information in an interactive manner, involving the patients as partners in the discussion of the material (Basco & Rush, 1996; DiMatteo & Lepper, 1998; Noble, 1998). Members of some cultures are less likely to feel comfortable with this form of relationship (Thompson, 1998). Huff and Kline (1999c) have stressed the use of active listening, open-ended questions, and attention to nonverbal cues when communicating with Asian Americans.

• Repeat important information (Noble, 1998).

• Communicate in a warm, caring manner that demonstrates positive regard, lack of tension, and nonverbal expressiveness (Basco & Rush, 1996; DiMatteo & Lepper 1998; Noble, 1998; Sheridan & Radmacher, 1992). Huff and Kline (1999b) have indicated that respect is a strong central value among American Indians and Alaska Natives. Thus, treating patients with kindness, equality, and goodness is important.

• It is important to provide information in terms that are compatible with the patient's cultural background (Cromer, 1998). For example, in Hispanic groups, respect is an important factor in relationships, as is the avoidance of conflict and achieving harmony (Huff & Klein, 1999).

Cromer (1998) noted that, in some cases, the health practitioner's information contradicts folk wisdom and competes with the patient's explanatory model of his or her health. She has suggested that it may be important to incorporate the treatment regimen into traditional practice. Aboud (1998), among others, has described a number of programs in Ethiopia and other countries in which treatment regimens have been incorporated into local delivery systems. Huff and Klein (1999a) have suggested that when working with African Americans, health practitioners should consider the learning styles of the target group and seek to develop educational approaches that reflect the ways of learning within these varied groups. They have suggested that the educational materials must reflect the relevant cultural values, themes, and literacy levels of the groups for which they are intended (Huff & Kline, 1999a, 1999b).

When designing educational materials for American Indian and Alaska Natives, Huff and Kline (1999b) have suggested that talking circles in conjunction with tribal stories may be useful and culturally appropriate vehicles. They have also suggested that, with these cultural groups, storytelling may be an appropriate educational medium. With Pacific Islander groups, Huff and Kline (1999e) have suggested the use of "talk-stories." Storytelling may also be an appropriate educational vehicle with several other cultural groups around the world (Hubley, 1993).

Role induction is one procedure that can be used to orient patients to treatment protocols. Walitzer, Derman, and Connors (1999) have reviewed several strategies that have been developed to increase the number of patients participating in psychotherapy. There is no reason why these procedures should not be used in other treatment domains. They review a number of studies that have demonstrated that role induction presented by interview, lecture, and film to both individuals and groups enhances involvement of patients in psychotherapy. Role induction is used to educate patients about the rationale for treatment, the treatment process, the expected outcome, and the responsibilities of the practitioner and the patient. Such an approach would seem very appropriate for patients requiring long-term and complex treatment, such as those for hypertension, diabetes, and cardiovascular disorders.

Another important issue in the provision of the educational component is the source of social influence. Raven (1988) has indicated that informational, expert, and self-referent sources of social influence are the most effective means of educating patients. In some cultures, health practitioners are not the most appropriate sources of social influence, in that they may not be seen as experts. For example, G. Smith et al. (1993) have suggested that traditional healers may be important in promoting oral rehydration therapy for diarrhea in rural Nicaragua. Huff and Klein (1999b) have suggested that employing and training tribal members among American Indian and Alaska Natives to facilitate educational programs is a valuable approach to facilitating implementation and adherence to programs. Similarly, with Asian American groups, they have suggested that trained neighborhood leaders and/or other community members be used to facilitate educational programs (Huff & Kline, 1999c).

DiMatteo (1993) reviewed a number of studies that indicate that patients forget much of what they are told verbally during visits to health care practitioners. Further, Sheridan and Radmacher (1992) have indicated that the greater the amount of verbal information provided, the more patients forget. Hence, an important component in the education of patients is written material (Cromer, 1998).

Written Information and Adherence

Increasingly, health professionals are providing treatment information in written form (Raynor, 1998). There are a number of reasons for this development: patients tend to forget verbal information; the provision of written information reduces the time the health professional must spend with patients; and treatment protocols are becoming more complex (Raynor, 1998). Raynor (1998) argues that the provision of general information about treatment, specific information about new procedures, and information that corrects misunderstandings, alters attitudes to treatment, and/or increases satisfaction with care all enhance adherence with treatment. In contrast, information on the risks of treatment, excessive information, and confusing information from multiple sources can all act to reduce adherence to treatment (Raynor, 1998).

Raynor (1998) points out that information from professionals is always filtered through the existing information and beliefs about treatment that patients already have. Much of the later information and beliefs come from prior experience, the media, family and friends, and one's culture. Recently, there has been an increase in the advertising of prescription drugs on television in North America and Europe. From a cultural perspective, the observation that prior experience, the media, family, and friends influence the decision-making process with respect to adherence to treatment is particularly important. Information provided in cultures in which the collective is more important than the individual must be directed toward the collective and take into account the lack of knowledge, misunderstandings, attitudes, and potential satisfaction of the collective.

Huff and Klein (1999d) have stressed that educational materials for Hispanic cultural groups must reflect relevant cultural values, themes, and learning styles of the groups for which they are designed. Information that is written in Spanish must be back-translated and pilot-tested to ensure that it conveys the intended message and is clear and understandable to the target group (Huff & Kline, 1999d). Huff and Klein (1999b) have suggested that when designing educational materials for American Indian and Alaska Native populations, it is important to incorporate traditional values, beliefs, and ways of life into the design of the materials while respecting differences among tribal groups. They make a similar suggestion for Asian American groups and Pacific Islander groups (Huff & Kline, 1999c, 1999e).

Raynor (1998) has observed that the label is the most important source of information for patients. One problem with labels is that their size limits the amount of information that can be provided. As with verbal information, the use of plain language on labels leads to more accurate understanding of the treatment regimen (Raynor, 1998). Next to the use of labels to provide information is the use of leaflets (patient information leaflets) and booklets.

Studies reviewed by Raynor (1998) clearly indicate that the provision of well-designed and written patient information leaflets, reinforced by verbal information provided by health professionals reviewing the material with patients, leads to greater knowledge of treatment information than either written or verbal information provided alone. The findings on the impact of the combined presentation of information on adherence are mixed. Raynor (1998) outlines studies of the effects of personalized medicine reminder charts for patients taking several medications on several occasions each day. Early studies suggest that this individualized approach leads to greater knowledge and adherence on the part of patients (Raynor, 1998).

Raynor (1998) suggested that there are three important elements that influence the impact of written material on patients. The three elements are the mode of delivery, the design, and the content of the written material. Raynor (1998) argued that written material has maximal effect when it is handed to the patient by the health professional, who then goes over the information, highlighting important points. The written information should contain clear headings, be concise, and use bulleted lists, bolded lower-case text for emphasis, and a familiar font with a size of at least 12 points. The use of the question-and-answer format is also suggested. Authors of the content should use simple words and short sentences, be specific, avoid jargon, use the active case, and phrase material positively (Raynor, 1998). Once developed, the written information should be piloted and amended as required before widespread use. Variants of the material should be developed to accommodate blind people, those that are illiterate, and those that speak languages other than that of the majority culture. Anecdotal evidence exists to suggest that pictorial labels enhance adherence with illiterate groups (Park & Jones, 1997).

Basco and Rush (1996) provided a method of developing a written plan with patients that defines the treatment plan(s), the anticipated obstacles to adherence, and the patient's plan(s) to overcome the obstacles. Three sections are included in this individualized treatment plan, as follows:

I, _____, plan to follow the treatment plans listed below.

[Specific actions to be followed by the patient are listed here]

I anticipate these problems in following my treatment plan.

[Specific problems with adherence anticipated by the patient are listed here]

To overcome these obstacles, I plan to do the following:

[Specific actions to overcome each obstacle are listed here] (Basco & Rush, 1996, p. 103).

The elements in each of these sections are developed using a problem-solving interaction between the health professional and the patient (Basco & Rush, 1996; Evans et al., 1998). First, the problems or obstacles to adherence are defined in operational terms. Next, the patient is asked to develop solutions to obstacles. Then, the feasibility of each solution is evaluated. The solution that is most acceptable to the patient and is most likely to work is selected. Once the plan is implemented, the efficacy of the solution is evaluated and, if necessary, alternative solutions are selected using the same approach.

MOTIVATION ENHANCEMENT AND ADHERENCE

Several authors have argued that an important aspect in enhancing motivation to adhere to treatment regimens is to have patients set their own treatment goals whenever possible (Basco & Rush, 1996; Evans et al., 1998). Basco and Rush (1996) have suggested that patients should be encouraged to set their own treatment goals, which should be simple and achievable. Subgoals can be used to attain larger more complex goals. The authors indicate that goals should be defined in sufficient detail to be easily acted upon and defined, such that attainment can be easily evaluated.

Miller and Rollnick (1991) define motivation in the context of treatment as "the probability that a person will enter into, continue, and adhere to a specific change strategy" (p. 19). From the perspective of this definition, it is easy to conceptualize what must be done to motivate patients to adhere to treatment regimens. In setting treatment goals, both patient and health practitioner must focus on what must be done to facilitate entry into treatment, continuation of treatment, and adherence to the treatment protocol. A useful framework for addressing the latter components of treatment is the stages of change model developed by Prochaska and DiClemente (1982) and Prochaska et al. (1992).

As noted previously, Prochaska and his colleagues (Prochaska & DiClemente, 1982; Prochaska et al., 1992; Prochaska et al., 1998) have identified several stages of change that individuals move through when changing their behavior, such as adopting a treatment regimen. The stages are precontemplation, contemplation, preparation, action, and maintenance. Walitzer et al. (1999) argue that patients cycle through these stages in a dynamic rather than a linear fashion. Hence, the motivation of the patient to participate in a treatment regimen can fluctuate from week to week or even hour to hour. In motivating patients to adhere to treatment, health practitioners must facilitate goal setting that takes account of where the patient is in this dynamic complex of stages of change. Goldstein, DePue, Kazura, and Niaura (1998) have provided an extended version of the Five A's approach to behavior change that is sensitive to the stage of change at which the patient is.

Motivational interviewing (Miller & Rollnick, 1991) has evolved from the stages of change model and has been used to treat alcohol abuse and a range of other mental health problems (Walitzer et al., 1999). Its applicability in motivating patients to adhere to other treatment regimens can be readily appreciated. The acronym FRAMES captures the components of motivational interviewing (Walitzer et al., 1999). The components when applied to adherence are *feedback* of diagnostic information, patient *responsibility* for adherence, *advice* about the treatment regimen, a *menu* of strategies to attain and/or maintain adherence, health practitioner *empathy,* and facilitation of patient *self-efficacy.* Motivational interviewing, as conceived, can take considerable time, up to 2 hours (Goldstein et al., 1998). A brief version of motivational interviewing for ambulatory care using fewer components has been described by Rollnick, Heather, and Bell (1992).

Increasingly, people are required to continue an intervention when they are feeling good and are symptom-free. However, as Basco and Rush (1996) have observed, patients frequently discontinue treatment when their symptoms have gone, even when they have been instructed to continue a longer course of treatment. The latter concern is of particular importance in the treatment of chronic conditions, such as hypertension, diabetes, and cardiovascular disorder. Basco and Rush (1996) indicated that even if people do not discontinue their program of treatment when they are feeling well, there is a tendency to be less motivated in adhering to the program. Another tendency is to modify the program to fit one's lifestyle.

Most people have been prescribed a course of antibiotics at some time in their life, which usually involves a course of treatment that is at least 10 to 14 days in length. Frequently, the symptoms of the disorder for which the antibiotics are prescribed disappear in 3 or 4 days. The natural reaction of patients is to discontinue the antibiotics at this point. Has your physician ever explained why you should continue the antibiotics after the symptoms have subsided? Sheridan and Radmacher (1992) describe the rationale for continuing the course of antibiotics. They indicate that, in the early period of taking the antibiotic, the weaker bacteria are destroyed and the symptoms disappear. However, if the antibiotics are stopped at this point the hardy bacteria may reproduce and the patient ends up with treatment-resistant infection (DiMatteo & Lepper, 1998). This phenomenon of having to continue treatment in the absence of symptoms is a challenge to the maintenance of treatment regimens in both acute and chronic conditions. It must be addressed in the maintenance stage of any treatment, if adherence is to be maintained.

Principles of behavior analysis have also been shown to enhance adherence with treatment regimens (Greenspoon, 1997). Greenspoon concluded that educational approaches to adherence were not particularly effective. He reviews research that suggests that the addition of such behavior-analytic techniques as social reinforcement, self-monitoring, and response cost are effective adjuncts in enhancing adherence. Some of these approaches are useful when parents are endeavoring to enhance adherence to treatment regimens in children. Putnam, Finney, Barkley, and Bonner (1994) showed that making written and verbal commitments to adhere to a 10-day antibiotic regimen enhanced adherence to the treatment. Greenspoon (1997) concludes his paper with a discussion of procedures that can be employed to assist patients to keep appointments. Elder (1987) has provided a useful description and discussion of the application of behavioral approaches to health concerns, such as malnutrition and communicable diseases, in developing countries. Huff and Kline (1999c) have suggested that behavioral interventions might be most appropriate with Asian American groups.

SKILL DEVELOPMENT AND ADHERENCE

Sheridan and Radmacher (1992) discuss the importance of providing skill training where necessary in order to facilitate adherence. They suggest that skill training may involve oral and written instructions and modeling on the part of the health practitioner. Modeling skills for patients is important when working with cultural groups, such as Asian American and Pacific Islander groups (Huff & Klein, 1999c, 1999e). Goldstein et al. (1998) describe the Patient-Centered Patient Education Model, which involves focusing on two forms of patient skills, instrumental and coping. Instrumental skills are those skills needed to effect change, such as using an inhaler or monitoring blood glucose. In contrast, coping skills are those required to maintain the treatment regimen. While little has been written about skill acquisition, it follows that adherence to health protocols will not occur if patients do not have the requisite skill(s).

SOCIAL SUPPORT AND ADHERENCE

Despite the fact that the family and, potentially, the patient's community are important in the adherence of the patient to a treatment regimen, little emphasis has been placed on this component. This is perhaps because of the importance of the individual in the majority culture in North America, the source of much of the literature on adherence to treatment. Sheridan and Radmacher (1992) underline the importance of the social support of family and other community agents in facilitating adherence to treatment regimens. Thompson (1998) describes the family systems approach to patient care, which recognizes the embeddedness of the patient in a family and social network. She stresses the importance of communicating with the patient and the family and social network. Goldstein et al. (1998), in describing various forms of patient-centered care, stress the importance of assessing and mobilizing the patient's social support system and resources. The importance of family dynamics and their impact on adherence has been discussed by Cromer (1998). She observed that cohesive families with effective communication support adherence, while dysfunctional families are associated with poor adherence. This proposition is supported in a study by Blumberg (1999), who found that lower levels of family cohesion in African American and Hispanic families led to poorer treatment regimen adherence among children and adolescents with type 1 diabetes.

Huff and Kline (1999d) have argued that culturally competent practice involves an understanding that family and family support is extremely important for Hispanic groups. Hence, family support must be considered in designing programs to enhance adherence among these cultural groups. Huff and Klein (1999d) have suggested that decisions associated with an individual's active participation in treatment among Hispanic populations might involve the head of the household, who will decide what is best for the family. Similar patterns of relationship and decision making in the family are described for Asian American groups (Huff & Kline, 1999c). Decisions by Asian Americans to seek health care and participate actively in treatment may involve the head of the household and other family members, who will make a decision in terms of what is best for the family. Hence, interventions that have a family rather than an individual focus are likely to be more effective. With American Indian and Alaska Native populations, Huff and Kline (1999b) have suggested that spiritual, cultural, and traditional healers be involved in the delivery of programs, including treatment regimens. With Pacific Islander groups, Huff and Kline (1999e) have suggested that when planning interventions, focusing on the family rather than the individual is important, and that the interpersonal dynamics within the family must be considered. They observe that many Pacific Islander groups are matriarchal and this fact should be considered in treatment planning.

SUMMARY

In this chapter, the definition of adherence to treatment is considered, factors affecting adherence are discussed, theories predicting adherence are reviewed, and procedures for measuring adherence are examined. In the latter half of the chapter, strategies for enhancing adherence to treatment are presented and discussed. What is most evident from the literature available is the paucity of studies devoted to cultural factors that impact upon adherence to treatment. This observation underlines the urgent need for studies investigating culture and adherence to treatment regimens.

CASE STUDY

Mr. Etap, a Native Canadian, was placed on medication for hypertension by his family physician. After several weeks, he informed his physician about several side effects he was experiencing and his difficulty deciding to stay on the medication. Although patients typically discontinue medication in these circumstances, Mr. Etap contacted his physician about these concerns. The physician had made it a practice to discuss treatment adherence with patients, and this made Mr. Etap comfortable discussing his concerns with the physician before discontinuing his medication. [This is a modified version of the case presented by Basco & Rush, 1996.]

1. What cultural values should the physician consider when discussing treatment adherence with Mr. Etap?
2. How might the physician involve the family in enhancing Mr. Etap's adherence to the treatment regimen?
3. Discuss the use of trained members of Mr. Etap's Canadian Native group in managing his adherence to treatment.

SUGGESTED READINGS

Farmer, K. C. (1999). Methods for measuring and monitoring medication regimen adherence in clinical trials and clinical practice. *Clinical Therapeutics. The International Journal of Drug Therapy, 21,* 1074–1090.

Huff, R. M., & Kline, M. V. (Eds.). (1999). *Promoting health in multicultural populations: A handbook for practitioners.* Thousand Oaks, CA: Sage.

Mull, J. D., Shear Wood, C., Gans, L. P., & Mull, D. S. (1989). Culture and "compliance" among leprosy patients in Pakistan. *Social Science & Medicine, 29,* 799–811.

Myers, L. B., & Midence, K. (Eds.). (1998). *Adherence to treatment in medical conditions.* Amsterdam: Harwood Academic Press.

Shumaker, S. A., Schron, E. B., Ockene, J. K., & McBee, W. L. (Eds.). (1998). *The handbook of health behavior change* (2nd ed.). New York: Springer.

REFERENCES

Aboud, F. E. (1998). *Health psychology in a global perspective.* Thousand Oaks, CA: Sage.

Anderson, J. M. (1993). Ethnocultural communities as partners in research. In R. Masie, L. L. Menseh, & K. A. McLeod (Eds.), *Health and cultures: Exploring the relationships: Vol. 1* (pp. 319–328). Oakville, Ontario: Mosaic Press.

Anita-Obong, O. E., Young, M. U., & Effiong, C. E. (1993). Neonatal tetanus: Prevalence before and subsequent to implementation of the Expanded Programme on Immunization. *Annals of Tropical Paediatrics, 13,* 7–12.

Ashing-Giwa, K. (1999). Health behavior change models and their socio-cultural relevance for breast cancer screening in African American women. *Women and Health, 28*(4), 53–71.

Basco, M. R., & Rush, A. J. (1996). *Cognitive–behavioral therapy for bipolar disorder.* New York: Guilford Press.

Blumberg, M. J. (1999). Impact of family factors on metabolic control and on regimen adherence in type 1 diabetes among Hispanic and African American adolescents. *Dissertation Abstracts International, 59,* 5570-B.

Conner, M., & Sparks, P. (1996). The theory of planned behaviour and health behaviours. In M. Conner & P. Norman (Eds.), *Predicting health behaviour* (pp. 121–162). Buckingham, UK: Open University Press.

Cromer, B. A. (1998). Compliance with health recommendations. In S. B. Friedman, M. Fisher, S. K. Schonberg, & E. M. Alderman (Eds.), *Comprehensive adolescent health care* (2nd ed., pp. 104–108). St Louis, MO: Mosby.

de Graaf, C., Van der Gaag, M., Kafatos, A., Lennernas, M., & Kearney, J. M. (1997). Stages of dietary change among nationally-representative samples of adults in the European Union. *European Journal of Clinical Nutrition, 51*(Suppl. 2), S47–S56.

DiMatteo, M. R. (1993). Expectations in the physician–patient relationship: Implications for patient adherence to medical treatment recommendations. In P. D. Blanck (Ed.), *Interpersonal expectations: Theory, research, and applications* (pp. 296–315). Cambridge, UK: Cambridge University Press.

DiMatteo, M. R., & Lepper, H. S. (1998). Promoting adherence to courses of treatment: Mutual collaboration in the physician–patient relationship. In L. D. Jackson & B. K. Duffy (Eds.), *Health communication research: A guide to developments and directions* (pp. 75–86). Westport, CT: Greenwood Press.

Dugan, E., & Cohen, S. J. (1998). Improving physicians' implementation of clinical practice guidelines: Enhancing primary care practice. In S. A. Shumaker, E. B. Schron, J. K. Ockene, & W. L. McBee (Eds.), *The handbook of health behavior change* (2nd ed., pp. 283–304). New York: Springer.

Dunbar-Jacob, J., Burke, L. E., & Puczynski, S. (1995). Clinical assessment and management of adherence to medical regimens. In P. M. Nicassio & T. W. Smith (Eds.), *Managing chronic illness: A biopsychosocial perspective* (pp. 313–349). Washington, DC: American Psychological Association.

Elder, J. P. (1987). Applications of behavior modification to health promotion in the developing world. *Social Science and Medicine, 24,* 335–349.

Evans, D. R., Hearn, M. T., Uhlemann, M. R., & Ivey, A. E. (1998). *Essential interviewing: A programmed approach to effective communication.* Pacific Grove, CA: Brooks/Cole.

Farmer, K. C. (1999). Methods for measuring and monitoring medication regimen adherence in clinical trials and clinical practice. *Clinical Therapeutics. The International Journal of Drug Therapy, 21,* 1074–1090.

Goldberg, A. I., Cohen, G., & Rubin, A. E. (1998). Physician assessments of patient compliance with medical treatment. *Social Science & Medicine, 47,* 1873–1876.

Goldstein, M. G., DePue, J., Kazura, A., & Niaura, R. (1998). Models for provider–patient interaction: Applications to health behavior change. In S. A. Shumaker, E. B. Schron, J. K. Ockene, & W. L. McBee (Eds.), *The handbook of health behavior change* (2nd ed., pp. 283–304). New York: Springer.

Gore, P., Madhavan, S., Curry, D., McClung, G., Castiglia, M., Rosenbluth, S. A., & Smego, R. A. (1999). Predictors of childhood immunization completion in a rural population. *Social Science & Medicine, 48,* 1011–1027.

Greenspoon, J. (1997). Compliance, health service, and behavior analysis. In P. A. Lamal (Ed.), *Cultural contingencies: Behavior analytic perspectives on cultural practices* (pp. 31–52). Westport, CT: Praeger.

Grunberg, N. E., & Cousino Klein, L. (1998). Biological obstacles to adoption and maintenance of health promoting behaviours. In S. A. Shumaker, E. B. Schron, J. K. Ockene, & W. L. McBee (Eds.), *The handbook of health behaviour change* (2nd ed., pp. 114–132). New York: Springer.

Hubley, J. (1993). *Communicating health: An action guide to health education and health promotion.* London, UK: MacMillan.

Huff, R. M., & Klein, M. V. (1999a). Tips for working with African American populations. In R. M. Huff & M. V. Kline (Eds.), *Promoting health in multicultural populations: A handbook for practitioners* (pp. 259–266). Thousand Oaks, CA: Sage.

Huff, R. M., & Kline, M. V. (1999b). Tips for working with American Indian and Alaska Native Populations. In R. M. Huff & M. V. Kline (Eds.), *Promoting health in multicultural populations: A handbook for practitioners* (pp. 327–334). Thousand Oaks, CA: Sage.

Huff, R. M., & Kline, M. V. (1999c). Tips for working with Asian American populations. In R. M. Huff & M. V. Kline (Eds.), *Promoting health in multicultural populations: A handbook for practitioners* (pp. 383–394). Thousand Oaks, CA: Sage.

Huff, R. M., & Kline, M. V. (1999d). Tips for working with Hispanic populations. In R. M. Huff & M. V. Kline (Eds.), *Promoting health in multicultural populations: A handbook for practitioners* (pp. 189–197). Thousand Oaks, CA: Sage.

Huff, R. M., & Kline, M. V. (1999e). Tips for working with Pacific Islander Populations. In R. M. Huff & M. V. Kline (Eds.), *Promoting health in multicultural populations: A handbook for practitioners* (pp. 189–197). Thousand Oaks, CA: Sage.

Jennings-Dozier, K. (1999). Predicting intentions to obtain a Pap smear among African American and Latina Women: Testing the theory of planned behavior. *Nursing Research, 48*(4), 198–205.

Karoly, P. (1993). Enlarging the scope of the compliance construct: Toward developmental and motivational relevance. In N. A. Krasnegor, L. Epstein, S. Bennett Johnson, & S. J. Yaffe (Eds.) *Developmental aspects of health compliance behaviour* (pp. 11–27). Hillsdale, NJ: Erlbaum.

Kerns, R. D., Bayer, L. A., & Findley, J. C. (1999). Motivation and adherence in the management of chronic pain. In A. R. Block, E. F. Kremer, & E. Fernandez (Eds.), *Handbook of pain syndromes: Biopsychosocial perspective* (pp. 102–121). Hillsdale, NJ: Erlbaum.

LaForge, R. G., Velicer, W. F., Richmond, R. L., & Owen, N. (1999). Stage distributions for five health behaviors in the United States and Australia. *Preventive Medicine, 28(1),* 61–74.

Marcus, B. H., Rakowski, W., & Rossi, J. S. (1992). Assessing motivational readiness and decision making for exercise. *Health Psychology, 11,* 257–261.

McMillan, D. D., Lockyer, J. M., Magnan, L., Akierman, A., & Parboosingh, J. T. (1991). Effect of educational programme and interview on adoption of guidelines for the management of neonatal hyperbilirubinemia. *Canadian Medical Association Journal, 144,* 707–712.

Mermelstein, R. J. (1997). Individual interventions: Stages of change and other health behavior models—The example of smoking cessation. In S. J. Gallant, G. P. Keita, & R. Royak-Schaler (Eds.), *Health care for women* (pp. 387–403). Washington, DC: American Psychology Association.

Miller, W. R., & Rollnick, S. (1991). *Motivational interviewing: Preparing people to change addictive behavior.* New York: Guilford Press.

Morgan, M. (1995). The significance of ethnicity for health promotion: Patients' use of anti-hypertensive drugs in inner London. *International Journal of Epidemiology, 24* (Suppl. 1), S79–S84.

Mull, J. D., Shear Wood, C., Gans, L. P., & Mull, D.S. (1989). Culture and "compliance" among leprosy patients in Pakistan. *Social Science & Medicine, 29,* 799–811.

Myers, L. B., & Midence, K. (1998). Concepts and issues in adherence. In L. B. Myers & K. Midence (Eds.), *Adherence to treatment in medical conditions* (pp. 1–24). Amsterdam: Harwood Academic Publishers.

Noble, L. M. (1998). Doctor–patient communication and adherence to treatment. In L. B. Myers & K. Midence (Eds.), *Adherence to treatment in medical conditions* (pp. 51–82). Amsterdam: Harwood Academic Press.

Pachter, L. M., & Weller, S. C. (1993). Acculturation and compliance with medical therapy. *Developmental and Behavioural Pediatrics, 14,* 163–168.

Park, D. C., & Jones, T. R. (1997). Medication adherence and aging. In A. D. Fisk & W. A. Rogers (Eds.), *Handbook of human factors and the older adult* (pp. 257–287). San Diego, CA: Academic Press.

Prochaska, J. O., & DiClemente, C. C. (1982). Transtheoretical therapy: Towards a more comprehensive model of change. *Psychotherapy: Theory, Research and Practice, 19,* 276–288.

Prochaska, J. O., DiClemente, C. C., & Norcross, J. C. (1992). In search of how people change: Applications to addictive behaviors. *American Psychologist, 47,* 1102–1114.

Prochaska, J. O., Johnson, S., & Lee, P. (1998). The transtheoretical model of behavior change. In S. A. Shumaker, E. B. Schron, J. K. Ockene, & W. L. McBee (Eds.), *The handbook of health behaviour change* (2nd ed., pp. 59–84). New York: Springer.

Putnam, D. E., Finney, J. E., Barkley, P. L., & Bonner, M. J. (1994). Enhancing commitment improves adherence to a medical regimen. *Journal of Consulting and Clinical Psychology, 62,* 191–194.

Rakowski, W., Fulton, J., & Feldman, J. (1993). Women's decision-making about mammography. *Health Psychology, 12,* 209–214.

Rand, C. S., & Weeks, K. (1998). Measuring adherence with medication regimens in clinical care and research. In S. A. Shumaker, E. B. Schron, J. K. Ockene, & W. L. McBee (Eds.), *The handbook of health behaviour change* (2nd ed., pp. 114–132). New York: Springer.

Rapoff, M. A. (1999). *Adherence to pediatric medical regimens.* New York: Kluwer Academic/Plenum Publishers.

Raven, B. H. (1988). Social power and compliance in health care. In S. Maes, C. D. Spielberger, P. B. Defares, & I. G. Sarason (Eds.), *Topics in health psychology* (pp. 229–244). Chichester, UK: Wiley.

Raynor, D. K. (1998). The influence of written information on patient knowledge and adherence to treatment. In L. B. Myers & K. Midence (Eds.), *Adherence to treatment in medical conditions* (pp. 83–111). Amsterdam: Harwood Academic Press.

Ries, A. L. (1993). Adherence in the patient with pulmonary disease. In J. E. Hodgkin, G. L. Connors, & C. W. Bell (Eds.), *Pulmonary rehabilitation* (2nd ed., pp. 86–101). Philadelphia: Lippincott.

Rollnick, S., Heather, N., & Bell, A. (1992). Negotiating behavior change in medical settings: The development of brief motivational interviewing. *Journal of Mental Health, 1,* 25–37.

Rudd, P. (1993). The measurement of compliance: Medication taking. In N. A. Krasnegor, L. Epstein, S. Bennett Johnson, & S. J. Yaffe (Eds.) *Developmental aspects of health compliance behaviour* (pp. 185–213). Hillsdale, NJ: Erlbaum.

Ryan, G. W. (1998). What do sequential behavior patterns suggest about the medical decision-making process?: Modeling home case management of acute illnesses in a rural Cameroonian village. *Social Science and Medicine, 46(2),* 209–225.

Sarafino, E. P. (1998). Using health services. In *Health psychology: Biopsychosocial interactions* (pp. 266–297). New York: Wiley.

Sheeran, P., & Abraham, C. (1996). The health belief model. In M. Conner & P. Norman (Eds.), *Predicting health behaviour* (pp. 23–61). Philadelphia, PA: Open University Press.

Sheridan, C. L., & Radmacher, S. A. (1992). *Health psychology: Challenging the biomedical model.* New York: Wiley.

Smith, G. D., Gorter, A., Hoppenbrouwer, J., Sweep, A., Perex, R. M., Gonzalez, C., Morales, P., Pauw, J., & Sandiford, P. (1993). The cultural construction of childhood diarrhoea in rural Nicaragua: Relevance for epidemiology and health promotion. *Social Science and Medicine, 36,* 1613–1624.

Smith, M., Lin, K., & Mendoza, R. (1993). "Nonbiological" issues affecting psychopharmacology:

Cultural considerations. In K. Lin, R. E. Poland, & G. Nakasaki (Eds.) *Psychopharmacology and psychobiology of ethnicity* (pp. 37–58). Washington, DC: American Psychiatric Press Inc.

Symister, P., & Friend, R. (1996). Quality of life and adjustment in renal disease: A health psychology perspective. In R. J. Resnick & R. H. Rozensky (Eds.), *Health psychology through the life span* (pp. 265–287). Washington, DC: American Psychological Association.

Thompson, T. L. (1998). The patient/health professional relationship. In L. D. Jackson & B. K. Duffy (Eds.), *Health communication research: A guide to developments and directions* (pp. 37–55). Westport, CT: Greenwood Press.

Walitzer, K. S., Dermen, K. H., & Connors, G. J. (1999). Strategies for preparing clients for treatment: A review. *Behavior Modification, 23,* 129–151.

Yeo, G. T., de-Burgh, S. P., Letton, T., Shaw, J., Donnelly, N., Swinburn, M. E., Phillips, S., Bridges-Webb, C., & Mant, A. (1994). Educational visiting and hypnosedative prescribing in general practice. *Family Practice, 11,* 57–61.

HEALTH PSYCHOLOGY AND CULTURE

SPECIFIC HEALTH CONCERNS

6

FROM THE HEARTLAND: CULTURE, PSYCHOLOGICAL FACTORS, AND CORONARY HEART DISEASE

BRIAN BAKER

Department of Psychiatry
University Health Network, and
University of Toronto
Toronto, Ontario, Canada

ALAN RICHTER

QED Consulting
New York, New York

SONIA S. ANAND

Divisions of Cardiology and General Medicine
McMaster University
Hamilton, Ontario, Canada

Coronary heart disease (CHD) is the leading cause of death worldwide, and accounts for 20% of all deaths in developing countries and 40% of all deaths in developed countries (Murray & Lopez, 1997). Given that CHD is a global phenomenon, there are marked country-to-country differences in the burden of CHD and in its determinants (Anand & Yusuf, 1998a; Bonow, Bohannon, & Hazzard, 1996). While the causes of CHD are multiple, a large body of research supports a group of factors, which are strongly associated with CHD ("conventional" risk factors), and there are many other factors for which data is accumulating in support of an association with CHD ("emerging" risk factors).

Although the heart and the mind have been linked for centuries, it is only recently that evidence has emerged in support of a relationship between certain emotional states and CHD (Frasure-Smith, Lesperance, & Talajic, 1993; Kawachi, Sparrow, Vokonas, & Weiss, 1994; Orth-Gomer, Rosengren, & Wilhelmsen, 1993). In this chapter, we will use the term "psychological factors" in a broad sense, to incorporate all factors of a psychological nature which impinge on the individual, including emotions, attitudes, and behavior. The inclusion of psychological factors allows the examination of lifestyle issues, which, in a narrow sense (such as diet or smoking), have been rather extensively investigated in respect to CHD. However, in a broad sense, and examined as behavioral or psychological phenomena, these factors are invariably complex and difficult to measure, and this makes the study of their association with CHD challenging.

Determining how psychological variables in relation to CHD vary among cultural groups presents further challenges and evaluating this interrelationship is still in its early stages. However, it is important to review the existing evidence to improve our understanding of ethnic and psychological factors and CHD, so that we may develop strategies which can be applied to multiple populations. Efforts to identify and modify conventional CHD risk factors have already resulted in substantial decreases in cardiac morbidity and mortality (Reddy & Yusuf, 1998). Similarly, elucidation of psychological and cultural factors and their impact on CHD have the potential to lead to interventions to reduce the burden of CHD. We will review briefly the major conventional and emerging risk factors for CHD and highlight the evidence for psychological and cultural variations in this context.

CORONARY HEART DISEASE

Vascular disease of the coronary, cerebral, and peripheral circulation is the most significant noncommunicable disease in the world and its underlying pathology is atherosclerosis (Reddy & Yusuf, 1998). Although some populations demonstrate a genetic predisposition to develop accelerated atherosclerosis, the vast majority of atherosclerotic disease is acquired through lifestyle behaviors, and its clinical manifestations appear in later life. Compelling observational data from several historical landmark studies (Kannel, Wilson, & Blair, 1985; Keys, 1980; Stamler, Wentworth, & Neaton, 1986) suggest that tobacco use, elevation of cholesterol, hypertension, and glucose intolerance are important causal risk factors for clinical vascular disease. Although each risk factor independently influences the development of atherosclerosis, the progression is increased when two or more risk factors are present simultaneously.

A risk factor is a factor which is associated with an increased likelihood that disease will develop at a later time. Risk factors may be modifiable (e.g., smoking, hypertension, obesity) or nonmodifiable (age and gender), and both categories are important to consider when determining an individual's baseline risk (Anand & Yusuf, 1998a). Apart from the major conventional risk factors for atherosclerosis (smoking, cholesterol, hypertension, diabetes), other risk factors such as overweight status, lifestyle factors such as physical inactivity, and menopausal status in women should also be considered. Emerging biologic risk factors such as elevated Lp(a), microalbuminuria, hyperhomocysteinemia, chlamydia infection, as well as psychological factors such as depression, anxiety, anger, and social support, require consideration, although their exact contribution to CHD has not been clearly elucidated.

PSYCHOLOGICAL FACTORS AND CHD

Emotional or behavioral factors are complex given that they cannot be easily reduced to discrete components such as smoking or high cholesterol, even though both these examples are seen as part of lifestyle behavior patterns. In recent years, there have been robust attempts to refine the measures used to evaluate psychological or behavioral factors and this has resulted in important findings which have been reported in the foremost medical journals (Frasure-Smith et al., 1993; Kawachi et al., 1994). An example of this is the use of the structured interview and specific self-report measures to diagnose depression, which has been shown repeatedly to link both minor and clinical depression with increased mortality post myocardial infarction.

While the evidence relating specific psychological factors and CHD outcome is not yet conclusive, there is mounting evidence of such associations in respect to depression, anger, social support, and, to a certain extent, anxiety. "Stress" and CHD is best dealt with by restricting the use of the term to either severe life stressors or stress in the context of the demands of daily life. There is some evidence that cardiac death is increased after catastrophes such as an earthquake but this may be counterbalanced by a decrease in subsequent cardiac deaths (Muller, Taylor, & Stone, 1989). In the context of daily stress, the work environment has received the most attention. The home environment, which includes often stressful marital and family relationships, has yet to come under the same sort of scrutiny (Schnall, Landsbergis, & Baker, 1994; Brisson et al., 1999).

As an introduction, we will describe the psychological factors for which there is the most evidence for an association with CHD and for which cultural factors have not yet been clearly identified: depression, anger, social support, and anxiety. While some cultural influences on these factors have been observed, evidence for their relevance in CHD remains speculative. It is very likely, though, that there will be differences in the cultural expression of certain psychological factors and this may impact on CHD outcome. For example, not only are there varying rates of major depression between European cultures, which also change over time (see the declining rate of suicide in Hungary), there appear to be different manifestations of depression across cultures (Kuo, 1984).

There is now evidence that depression may be linked to eventual cardiac outcome and this will be the focus of more extensive epidemiological studies in the future (Anda et al., 1993). Equally provocative have been the findings in the post-myocardial infarction population, albeit in sample sizes that are not large compared to average clinical trials in cardiology (Frasure-Smith et al., 1993). Depression, as diagnosed by structured interview, appears to be related to increased mortality in the 6 months post myocardial infarction, whereas mild depression (usually a score of 10 or more on the Beck Depression Inventory) is related to more long-term (18 months or 2 years) increase of cardiac mortality (Frasure-Smith, Lesperance, & Talajic, 1995).

The question of the overlap of depression and fatigue is not resolved and there have been European studies linking "vital exhaustion" after heart attack, which may reflect an amalgam of depression and fatigue, to increased mortality (Appels & Mulder, 1989). It is interesting that there have been different foci from European, as opposed to mostly North American, investigators which mirror the type of dilemma examined in this chapter: Is there a real difference around the world between individuals or are the investigators approaching the same subject from a different perspective?

After an initial flurry of reports linking Type A personality with CHD outcome, subsequent findings were inconclusive and even contradictory (Friedman & Rosenman, 1974; Shekelle et al., 1985). What now remains of the original Type A personality concept, which had essentially three components (competitive/striving, time urgency, and hostility), is the emergence of the hostility complex as, for the most part, showing a robust association with CHD outcome (Williams, 1987). Lack of social support has also frequently been found to be associated with CHD outcome, often as a mitigating rather than a direct factor (Orth-Gomer et al., 1993). Somewhat confusingly, different aspects of social support emerge (Seeman & Syme, 1987) rather than one particular component such as perceived support, number of social activities, or what is often considered the anchor of social support systems—the presence of a confidante. The more traditional cultures have retained the inviolability of the extended family in contrast to the "anomie" of westernized society, where the family has been pared down; however, there may be compensation in other forms (religious, recreational, political) in the community. Again, these factors have not been adequately studied in respect to CHD.

Anxiety as a risk factor for CHD outcome remains somewhat controversial. Follow-up studies with healthy subjects have shown that panic anxiety may be related to sudden cardiac death; however, the actual number of deaths has been small, the subjects always male, and the measure of anxiety has been based on relatively small scales (Kawachi et al., 1994; Fleet & Beitman, 1998). Furthermore, the impact of culture remains unexplored.

CULTURAL DIMENSIONS:
A THEORETICAL PERSPECTIVE

Recent studies in culture have highlighted the key dimensions for under-standing differences across cultures (see Hofstede, 1991, and Trompenaars, 1997). Dimensions of culture may apply to studies of psychological factors which impinge on coronary heart disease; examples are anger and social support, which are conducive to being understood better in terms of key dimensions of culture. Where anger may be framed in terms of competitiveness, time urgency, and hostility, both competitiveness and time urgency are part of the competi-tiveness–cooperation dimension and fixed versus fluid time dimension, respec-tively. Competitiveness/cooperation is closely aligned with the individualist/collectivist dimension of culture. Individualist cultures tend to be far more com-petitive, while collectivist ones tend to be more cooperative. Hofstede (1991) suggests that there is evidence from countries around the world which attests to the variability of the individualist/collectivist dimension. In simplified terms, North America and Western Europe tend to be individualist, while most of Asia, Africa, and South America tend to be more collectivist. This dimension of cul-ture also strongly correlates with the psychological factor of social support, in that collectivist cultures provide greater social support than individualist cultures. With regard to time orientation, time urgency can be understood in terms of the fixed–fluid dimension of culture. For example, fixed-time cultures (e.g., Bonn or Boston) mean 8:30 when they set a meeting for 8:30 and people from that cul-ture will be offended if anyone is late. In fluid-time cultures (e.g., Riyadh or Rio), it is understood and expected that an 8:30 meeting will begin around 9 or 9:30 and no one should be surprised or offended. The psychological factor of time urgency is clearly located at the "fixed-time" end of the spectrum.

Finally, it is suggested that there are two other key dimensions of culture that should have profound effects on the psychological factors that impact on coro-nary heart disease. The first dimension is called "Control versus Constraint" (see Trompenaars, 1997) and relates to Hofstede's Uncertainty Avoidance (or Han-dling Ambiguity) dimension. In the Control versus Constraint dimension at the control end of the spectrum, cultures believe that they are in complete control of their destiny (Sartre's existentialism would be an extreme example). At the other end of the spectrum, constraint characterizes cultures that believe that everything is destiny or fate (e.g., "it is all in the hands of God"). The midpoint is called balance—where cultures hold that they are constrained by some forces, but have some control over their fate. A hypothesis yet to be tested would be that control cultures tend to have higher anxiety and stress levels, which are factors affect-ing heart disease.

The other dimension of culture that may be hypothesized to impact on the psychological factors in relation to CHD discussed previously, is the dimension of "Neutral-Affect." This dimension can be understood in terms of people show-ing and sharing their feelings with others. In a neutral culture (e.g., Japan), one does not readily show one's feelings, while in an affect culture (e.g., Italy), one decidedly does display one's feelings. Again, a hypothesis yet to be tested is that neutral cultures tend to have higher anxiety and stress levels since they keep their emotions inside and have less opportunity for catharsis. Repression of emotions, particularly in the absence of psychological-mindedness (see alexithymia), has been associated with increased mortality in middle-aged men (Kauhanen, Kaplan, Cohen, Julkunen, & Salonen, 1996).

CULTURE AND CHD

A racial group refers to a population who shares a common gene pool and assumes that important genetic differences exist between racial groups. On the other hand, an ethnic group refers to a population who shares common cultural characteristics such as language, religion, and diet. Therefore, the concept of ethnicity relies more on a shared cultural definition of identity than solely on biologic similarity (Anand & Yusuf, 1998b). Variations in disease rates between populations may be explained by socioeconomic, sociocultural, biological, and genetic factors. Therefore, in studying variations in disease rates and risk factors between populations, classification by ethnic origin rather than race is desirable.

WORLDWIDE PATTERNS OF DISEASE

The major noncommunicable diseases are cardiovascular disease (CVD), cancer, and diabetes (WHO; World Health Organization, 1994). Noncommunicable diseases account for 75% of deaths in industrialized countries and 40% of deaths in developing countries (Berrios et al., 1997). Half of these deaths are due to CVD and total approximately 12 million deaths per year worldwide (Anand & Yusuf, 1998a). In most developed countries, CHD rates are declining due to CHD risk factor modification and improved secondary prevention strategies. However, in developing countries, an epidemiologic transition from acute infectious diseases to a rise in the major noncommunicable diseases is occurring. Reasons for this transition include increasing life expectancy associated with a decline in childhood and adult deaths from infections and an increase in the prevalence of CHD risk factors associated with industrialization and urbanization (Reddy & Yusuf, 1998). Population differences in the CHD mortality rates are influenced by geographical and environmental differences. Cultural variations in disease rates are closely tied to geographical patterns of disease. Often, the first clue that cultural variations in disease burden exist comes from observations made between countries. These geographical differences have provided many of the initial hypotheses of the association between lifestyle factors and CHD.

CULTURE, PSYCHOLOGY, AND CHD

There are inherent difficulties in drawing meaningful conclusions when examining the interaction of psychological factors, culture, and CHD. The first problem is the complexity and lack of refinement of each entity. The second problem derives from this complexity, which is the necessary overlap between factors, such as psychological and biological, an example of which is smoking, which can be examined on its own but is necessarily a component of lifestyle behavior. A third problem is distinguishing between putative causative factors. If, for example, there is evidence that migration of Japanese people to areas which are more westernized than their home country results in an incidence of CHD higher than is found usually in this population in Japan, it can be difficult to distinguish whether this is an important observation about migration or about this ethnic group in particular. Finally, the discussion of the influence of cultural and psychological factors on the course of CHD is confounded by the limited data that is available to adjust for psychological, ethnic, and cardiac factors. This necessarily constricts the discussion of evidence and requires that we focus on what data is actually available for review.

In spite of these limitations and the realization that the evidence for the interrelationship of culture, psychological factors, and CHD is necessarily preliminary, the examination of this interrelationship has potentially far-reaching consequences. This is because CHD impinges on the well-being of a large proportion of the world population, especially if the considerable impact—not only on the patients themselves but on their family members and support systems—is considered. This impact is in relation to both morbidity and death and the profound emotional effects.

POTENTIAL BIOLOGICAL BASES

In the study of cultural variation of CHD, given that people who share similar cultural practices share common genes for conventional risk factors such as diabetes or hypertension, it is also possible that genes exist which code for behavioral factors such as depression and hostility. Given that most phenotypes of traits for CVD are a consequence of gene–environmental interactions and not purely ascribed to one or the other, this same model is likely appropriate in considering behavioral factors as a consequence of gene and environmental interactions (Hegele, 1996). While the link to CHD remains speculative, it is pertinent to mention reactivity studies which have demonstrated a different pressor (elevated blood pressure) and epinephrine response to laboratory-induced stressors in hypertensive African American subjects as compared to Caucasian subjects or normotensive subjects in both groups (Mills, Berry, & Dimsdale, 1993). This suggests that racial or ethnic factors may operate selectively to affect a vulnerable population (those tending to develop risk factors for CHD or CHD itself).

TOBACCO

Cigarette smoking is a powerful and independent causal factor for the development of cardiovascular disease (Peto, Lopez, Boreham, Thun, & Heath, 1992). During the 1990s, tobacco consumption in developed countries caused about 30% of all deaths in the 35- to 69-year age group, making it the largest single cause of premature death. The risk of cardiovascular disease is increased 2.5- to 3-fold in smokers compared with nonsmokers, and again the relative impact of cigarette smoking is increased in younger age groups and less in older. However, there is encouraging evidence that preventive measures both before and after clinical manifestations of several diseases are worthwhile. Individuals who stop smoking before middle age subsequently avoid almost all the excess risk that they would have otherwise suffered, and even those who stop smoking in middle age (i.e., 35 years) are at significantly lower risk than those who continue to smoke. Although there is uncertainty about the effectiveness of clinical interventions to reduce smoking rates, a number of studies have demonstrated that physician counseling can change patient behavior even when the advice is translated through relatively simple messages; therefore, formal smoking-cessation counseling should be offered routinely to all smokers (Grundy et al., 1996). For those considered to be addicted, formal programs to deal with nicotine withdrawal and behavioral modification should be considered.

Smoking is a highly addictive behavior, observed throughout the world; however, it is more prevalent in some societies as compared to others. For example, there are high smoking rates in Eastern Europe as well as in certain countries of Western Europe and this, along with other factors (such as diets high in saturated fat), may account for the high rates of CHD observed in those communities. There has been an impressive reduction in CHD mortality in the United States following efforts at CHD risk factor modification (Hunink et al., 1997), of which smoking is a prime candidate because the opposition from the health lobby is "all or nothing." However, this is counterbalanced by the severely addictive nature of nicotine, coupled with a powerful tobacco industry and the alarming tendency of increased smoking habits observed in female adolescents and in women generally. It is interesting to observe that while the deleterious effects of smoking on vascular and pulmonary health is incontrovertible, the strength of this relationship may vary between cultural groups. Despite relatively high rates of smoking in countries such as Japan and China, the CHD morbidity and mortality is disproportionately low (WHO, 1994). However, rather than dismissing tobacco use as being unimportant in these groups, such observation should promote research into this phenomenon to try and understand the pathogenesis of atherosclerosis in these populations. More recently, it has been observed that in these populations, as the levels of serum cholesterol increase in the presence of high tobacco use, the rates of CHD proportionally increase also. This raises the possibility that the adverse effect of tobacco use becomes manifest in individuals with a certain level of serum cholesterol.

CHOLESTEROL

A vast body of epidemiologic studies has demonstrated a continuous and incremental relationship between serum cholesterol levels and CHD whereby the risk of CHD increases across the whole range of cholesterol values (Chen et al., 1991). One of the first studies to raise the importance of cholesterol as a CHD risk factor was the Seven Countries study, in which countries with high rates of CHD (such as Finland) and countries with low rates of CHD (such as Japan) were assessed for difference in mean cholesterol levels (Scandinavian Simvastatin Survival Study Group, 1994). Not surprisingly, the significant difference in mortality from CHD was highly correlated with the levels of serum cholesterol in the population. With the availability of the HMG–Co–A reductase inhibitors, the degree of cholesterol lowering in trials of 5 years duration is about 25%, and results show clear reductions (approx. 20%) in total mortality with cholesterol lowering (Collins et al., 1990).

BLOOD PRESSURE

Prospective epidemiologic data demonstrate that increased risk of cardiovascular disease (strokes, CHD, heart failure, and renal failure) due to elevated systolic or diastolic blood pressure is continuous and graded (Kannel, Dawber, & McGee, 1980). The Framingham data demonstrated a correlation between increasing blood pressure levels and CHD and a progressive increase in cardiovascular risk with every increment of systolic pressure (Appel et al., 1997). It is estimated that for a middle-aged man, 20 mm Hg higher systolic BP is associated with 60% greater cardiovascular disease mortality and a 40% higher all-cause mortality over 10 years. Furthermore, observational studies predict that reductions of diastolic BP of 5–6 mm Hg result in a reduction in stroke of 34% and CHD of 20–25%. A systematic overview of 14 randomized control trials involving 37,000 hypertensive patients treated with beta blockers or diuretics, with a mean decrease in diastolic blood pressure of 5–6 mm Hg over 5 years, led to a highly significant reduction of 42% of stroke incidence and a 14% reduction in CHD (Collins et al., 1990). Treatment of systolic hypertension in elderly patients also significantly reduces cardiovascular morbidity and mortality. Recently, the Dietary Approaches to Stop Hypertension (DASH) trial (Appel et al., 1997) tested the effects of a high fruit and vegetable and low-fat diet compared to a standard diet in individuals with a systolic blood pressure of < 160 mm Hg and diastolic pressure of between 80 and 95 mm Hg. Individuals who consumed at least 8 servings of fruits and vegetables per day demonstrated an impressive 11 mm reduction in systolic blood pressure compared to the standard diet group (Appel et al., 1997). Therefore, in both low risk and higher risk populations, it is important to recognize the continuous relationship between BP and the risk of CHD and stroke.

COMPLIANCE WITH ANTIHYPERTENSIVE TREATMENT

Much of the treatment of hypertension rests on the use of antihypertensive medication, a daily practice that is meant to continue for years on end, possibly for the whole life of the individual. The rates of compliance can be expected to vary widely between ethnic groups; however, it is often difficult to disentangle this phenomenon from differences in socioeconomic status. At least one-third of hospital admissions for heart failure result from noncompliance with therapeutic regimens, both dietary and pharmacologic. In chronic diseases, noncompliance with both lifestyle modification and medication regimens is a major health problem. Patients frequently stop taking their medications because they consider them ineffective or because they experience unpleasant side effects. In asymptomatic conditions, patients may believe they do not need the medication and may not even fill their prescription. If they do obtain the medications, they may forget to take them regularly. Educational efforts and behavioral techniques can improve patient compliance in chronic, asymptomatic conditions, but one of the most effective strategies remains improved patient–physician communication. In some western cultures, there is an improved attitude toward health compliance and this is related to better outcome for CHD in those communities (Hunink et al., 1997; Vartainen, Pusku, Pekkanen, Tuomilehto, & Jousilahti, 1994).

GLUCOSE INTOLERANCE

There is early evidence which suggests that glucose, like cholesterol and BP, share a continuous relationship with atherosclerosis (Gerstein & Yusuf, 1996). Diabetics are at a much higher risk of CVD and death for any given level of the other major cardiovascular risk factors compared with nondiabetics, with a risk of cardiovascular death three times higher across all ages, even after adjustment for serum cholesterol, hypertension and cigarette-smoking (Gerstein & Yusuf, 1996). Modest elevations of plasma glucose in a prediabetic range are associated with an increased risk of cardiovascular disease, as this risk rises progressively with the level of postprandial glucose and appears to be "continuous" over a broad range of glucose levels. The link between elevated glucose levels, insulin, and associated dyslipidemia to atherosclerosis is complex, and the exact mechanism by which these factors are proatherogenic has not yet been elucidated. There are substantial variations in the prevalence of Type II diabetes among ethnic groups (Iso, Komachi, Shimamato, & Iida, 1996). Populations who migrate from a traditional lifestyle of relatively low fat consumption and adequate physical activity to urban environments in which the percent of calories from fat is increased and physical activity is deceased are at high risk. For example, indigenous peoples from Mexico, native North Americans, and Australian Aborigines have among the highest rates of diabetes in the world (Howard et al., 1996). In addition, people of Asian origin (originating from India, China, Pakistan, and Bangladesh) develop excessive rates of diabetes when they migrate to urban environments (Iso et al., 1996). Opportunities for prevention of late-onset diabetes are greater because its development is associated with obesity and physical in-activity, and it usually has an adult onset. Given that these lifestyle factors vary by ethnic group, i.e., diet and physical activity, prevention strategies must be de-vised which are culturally sensitive and tailored to particular ethnic groups.

DIET

Diet is a productive area of focus in respect to the interaction of culture, psy-chological or behavioral factors, and CHD because there are few such areas for which all these entities have been carefully studied and controlled. Dietary prac-tices have been associated with elevated serum cholesterol, elevated blood pres-sure, glucose intolerance, obesity, and variations in coagulation factors, all of which may be associated with the development of CHD (Kesteloot & Joossens, 1994). As eating is an essential component of life, eating behaviors and dietary practices have strong social aspects and are influenced by social practices. Along with language, religion, and homeland affiliation, dietary habits have developed over the centuries and are often seen as quintessential components of ethnocul-tural identity.

Diets that are high in saturated fats are endemic in Western societies. These diets are directly related to the progress of CHD. In recent years in developed countries there have been attempts to reduce levels of saturated fats through di-etary change. In Finland, Poland, and the United States, the level of fats has shown a significant decrement and this is associated with improved cardiac out-come (Zatonski, 1996). In the 1990s, there has been a sharp increase of CHD in Eastern Europe, concomitant with marked socioeconomic and political changes. In contrast, the Japanese, who consume a diet low in saturated fat, show low prevalence of CHD as well as low rates of CHD mortality. However, serum cho-lesterol in the Japanese population has started to show elevations and, along with increasing urbanization and a recent persistent downswing in the economy, a re-versal of these trends may be expected (Iso et al., 1996). Similarly, a change of dietary habits seen with urbanization and other associated socioeconomic pres-sures in sub-Saharan blacks has been associated with increased LDL cholesterol and the incidence of CHD is also expected to rise.

Lower rates of CHD have been observed in specific populations and these have been linked to certain "protective" dietary factors. For example, it has long been noted that there is a lower incidence of CHD in southern as compared to northern countries of Europe. The Mediterranean diet has been raised as a pos-sible protective factor against CHD (Trichopolou & Lagiou, 1997). These diets are high in monounsaturated fats and antioxidants and also contain moderate consumption of alcohol, particularly wine, high consumption of fruits, grains, moderate consumption of dairy products, and low consumption of meat. There has been a similar interest in the diet in France, given the relatively low rate of CHD, with the consumption of alcohol as part of the regular diet and the re-peated finding of protection against CHD with the moderate consumption of alcohol (the equivalent of one to two glasses of wine per day) (Criqui & Ringel, 1994; Rimm & Ellison, 1995). Of interest, it is thought that the mortality rates of the French are not as low as expected due to increased death rates from other causes related to increased alcohol intake.

SEDENTARY LIFESTYLE

Regular exercise has demonstrable effects on improving health and cardiac outcome; conversely, a predominantly sedentary lifestyle can act to worsen progression of CHD (Kannel et al., 1985). This latter course can be observed in the move toward urbanization and adoption of a westernized lifestyle, which is increasing markedly, especially in the developing countries. An associated problem of reduced physical activity in the face of increased caloric intake is the development of obesity. As compared to their counterparts of European origin, certain migrant populations, such as North American aboriginal people and South Asians, appear to have a propensity to develop central obesity which is associated with glucose intolerance and is strongly associated with the development of CHD (Alpert, Goldberg Ockens, and Taylor, 1991; Anand & Yusuf, 1998b).

HEALTH COMPLIANCE

It is now recognized that it is very difficult to bring about changes to risk factors that can modify outcome in CHD. Even under the "optimal conditions" of the Multiple Risk Factor Intervention Trial (Shekelle et al., 1985), many subjects were unable to follow the dietary and smoking recommendations. However, in developed countries where there is more socioeconomic stability, there have been some concerted efforts made to ensure heart-healthy lifestyles to encourage risk factor modification and control. The latter includes the adherence to treatment regimens, such as the daily use of antihypertensive medication and careful control of diabetes. Risk factor modification includes smoking cessation, reduction of saturated fats in the diet, and regular exercise. Encouraging results are being seen in various communities where education and specific programs have been established. The improvements in mortality rates which have been noted in the United States and Finland and are also being observed in Eastern European countries (such as Poland) where a degree of economic stability has been obtained, and public health policy (e.g., restricting animal fats, increasing the supply of fruits and vegetables) has been promoted (Zatonski, 1996).

SOCIOECONOMIC STATUS AND DISEASE

Individuals' lifestyle practices are closely related to their socioeconomic status. It is a finding across all nations that all-cause mortality and morbidity follow a gradient across socioeconomic classes. Lower income and lower social status are associated with poorer overall health. Furthermore, human behavior is influenced by the social environment in which people live and work, and psychosocial work conditions may directly influence mortality independent of unhealthy lifestyle choices. Psychosocial work conditions such as job strain, as will be discussed, skill discretion, authority over decisions, and social support at work are important links in addition to social class and heart disease.

The Whitehall Studies demonstrated a relationship between inverse social gradient and CHD incidence and mortality, with higher rates seen in men of lower employment grade. This was attributed to the psychosocial work environment (Marmot & Theorell, 1988; Marmot et al., 1991). These studies were conducted with British civil servants. The difference in social class persisted despite controlling for smoking, blood pressure, and cholesterol. This evidence suggests that understanding the relationship between social position and coping abilities is important and requires investigation at a population level. Psychosocial characteristics such as working conditions may be, in part, responsible for the higher prevalence of cardiovascular disease in lower social classes, through influence on established biologic risk factors or by independent neuroendocrinal effects associated with stress. To be successful, risk-factor modification or lifestyle-changing interventions must be sensitive to differences in socioeconomic status and coping abilities.

Social class and economic status are recognized as correlates of CHD risk factors such as smoking, glucose intolerance, obesity, and lack of exercise. Health care seeking, access to medical therapies and hospital services, and compliance often can be directly related to socioeconomic status. This has been observed with African Americans and the underprivileged, where fewer diagnostic tests and cardiac procedures are performed compared to their white counterparts (Ghali, Cooper, Kowatly, & Liao, 1993; Geronimus, Bound, Waidmann, Hillemeier & Burns, 1996). In South Africa, where CHD is "epidemic" among the white and South Asian populations, inequalities of socioeconomic status, lifestyle, and access to health care dramatically contribute to differences in the prevalence and complications of hypertension (Seedat, 1996).

There is now a fairly extensive literature examining the evidence for the association of job strain and CHD, especially in men (Alfredsson, Spetz, & Theorell, 1985; Schnall et al., 1994). Job strain has been defined, following Karasek's (1979) model, as excessive job demands combined with limited job latitude. In an attempt to examine the reasons accounting for a CHD mortality which is four times greater in 50-year-old Lithuanian men as compared to their Swedish counterparts, unfavorable psychosocial risk factors were found in the Lithuanian sample, including higher job strain, lower social support at work, lower emotional support, and lower social integration (Kristensen et al., 1998). Understandably, there has been much interest in the phenomenon of "karoshi," or death from overwork, observed in Japan, which has been postulated to relate to Japanese production management or "lean production" (Nishiyama & Johnson, 1997). Efforts are now being made to reduce this form of apparent extreme job strain.

MIGRATION AND ACCULTURATION

Disentangling the effects of migration, acculturation, and urbanization on risk factors and the development of CHD presents challenges that are not easy to resolve, but some studies are persuasive in providing some evidence of the potential impact of cultural factors when people migrate from their place of origin to a foreign culture. The Ni-Ho San Study of Japanese migrants to Hawaii and San Francisco illustrates the effects of environmental influences. The age-adjusted CHD mortality rates were highest in California, intermediate in Hawaii, and lowest in Japan (Benfante, 1992). However, a further study of Japanese migrants in California revealed two subpopulations, those who had adopted western lifestyles and who were considered "acculturated" had CHD rates 2.5 to 5 times higher than a second group who had retained Japanese lifestyles very similar to those of Japanese living in Japan. This latter group was considered to be "relatively immune from the effects of sociocultural mobility even though they had experienced a major change in geographic and cultural circumstances" (Marmot & Syme, 1976; Syme, 1987)

Another revealing study was that of urban South Asians living in India who were compared to their siblings in the United Kingdom in respect to coronary risk factors (Bhatnagar et al., 1995). This showed that those who had emigrated from India had higher rates of obesity, systolic blood pressure, cholesterol, and fasting glucose than did their siblings in their home country. This, again suggests the deleterious effects of acculturation to a westernized lifestyle in respect to CHD; however a comparable trial as was shown with Japanese subpopulations in California, comparing those South Asians who adhered to their traditional lifestyle to those adopting a more westernized lifestyle would be even more persuasive in respect to understanding the impact of acculturation on CHD prevalence and outcome. Disentangling the effects of migration, acculturation, and urbanization on CHD risk factors and the development of CHD presents challenges that are not easy to resolve.

URBANIZATION

Throughout the world, there is a tendency for people to move to urban areas where work and services are often more available than in rural areas. Unfortunately, there are a number of reasons why living in the city may be bad for your health. It is not the environment alone that accounts for health-related problems, but rather the lifestyle that is entailed in living in the city. Dietary practices are usually less healthy, being higher in saturated fats and lower in fiber. Furthermore, work and leisure have tended to be more sedentary in the city than in the country, although this is counterbalanced by the recognition over recent decades, particularly in developed countries, of the health benefits of physical fitness, resulting in the healthy diet and physical fitness industries.

A repeated finding is the increased prevalence of conventional risk factors for CHD over time in urban populations. For example, in China, CHD rates increase by twofold in urban areas compared to rural areas (People's Republic of China–United States Cardiovascular & Cardiopulmonary Epidemiology Research Group, 1992). Risk factors for CHD, such as hypertension, serum cholesterol, and mean body mass index, were all lower in rural as compared to urban areas. Furthermore, epidemiological data revealed a striking urban–rural difference in the prevalence of CHD and CHD risk factors in South Asians living in India and abroad. As found in China, the difference was between a ninefold increase of CHD in urban as opposed to a twofold increase in rural areas over 20 years of study (Gupta & Gupta, 1996). There is a similar increase of CHD risk factors, apart from smoking, seen in the urban as compared to the rural areas of India. As more aboriginal people give up their traditional hunter-gatherer lifestyles and adopt urban lifestyles, the prevalence of CHD and CHD risk factors increases (Alpert et al., 1991). A similar pattern is seen in sub-Saharan Africa where the prevalence of CHD risk factors is low in rural areas and increases significantly in the urban areas. These examples may illustrate that people from certain cultures may be more vulnerable to the adverse effects of urbanization as compared to other cultures.

CONCLUSIONS

Health promotion in respect to risk factor modification has led to a reduction in CHD rates in Western countries; however, there remains a sharp discrepancy in these practices, as well as in health utilization in socially disadvantaged groups such as African Americans in the United States (Ghali et al., 1993). Rapid socioeconomic and political changes, increasing urbanization, and the adoption of a westernized lifestyle may contribute to the increasing rates of CHD in developing countries. Conventional and established risk factors, which may be influenced directly by lifestyle practices, are seen in varying degrees with different ethnic groups. These practices may aggravate or be protective in terms of CHD development. For example, on exposure to urban environments, certain ethnic groups are susceptible to certain physiological vulnerabilities (such as glucose intolerance) leading to the progression of CHD. These biological tendencies of ethnic groups in respect to CHD are of particular interest, because this may provide a physiological basis to explain the cultural difference found in CHD prevalence and outcome.

Due to the paucity of data, it is not possible to draw any definitive conclusions about the interrelationship between culture, psychological, factors and CHD. However, the information that we do have highlights the potential importance of this interrelationship. Our review delineates lifestyle behaviors such as dietary practices, that may be harmful or protective, variations in smoking behavior and sedentary lifestyle, efforts at health compliance, socioeconomic factors, and especially migration and acculturation as areas of focus in which to examine the effects of cultural influence, in relation to psychological or behavioral aspects, on CHD.

The literature suggests that large-scale studies on CHD outcome are needed that are well controlled and that target ethnic groups. The methodology of previous studies is weakened in that different cultures in different (rather than the same) environments are examined, which confounds the elucidation of the ethnic (as opposed to the environmental) influence on cardiac risk factors and outcome.

Cultural factors may also require more detailed qualification rather than a simple ethnic designation; examples are cultural practices adhered to and length of time in a new environment. In theory, the most productive ways to control for ethnic influences is to examine a similar population in a different environment, such as the South Asian sibling study, or otherwise to examine ethnically different populations in the same environment, such as the study of traditional and acculturated Japanese in California.

To address this need for multicultural studies using standardized methodology, an international study of acute myocardial infarction has been initiated in 54 countries including many of the developing countries. This study, called INTER-HEART, is sponsored by the World Health Organization and is based at McMaster University in Hamilton, Canada. In this case-control study, specific psychological and socioeconomic data are being collected, such as depression, locus of control, and emotional and physical stress. Results from this study are expected by the year 2001 (Yusuf, Ounpuu & Anand, 1999).

APPLICATION

Despite the limited nature of information available, we can observe that certain cultural practices may be protective or deleterious to CHD outcome and so recognize the potential importance of the interrelationship of cultural and behavioral factors in CHD. If we remain unaware of these factors, then information on CHD may be limited in its application to population groups other than the ones studied. Alternatively stated, as more research is conducted in countries with more resources, the findings generated may not be generalizable necessarily to other cultures. Obviously, more research which controls for these factors is required.

Following awareness and the accrual of more knowledge about cultural and behavioral effects on CHD is the need to provide this information to all concerned and affected parties. This next step is the education of both health professionals and the public. Education includes both providing greater cross-cultural knowledge and developing skill sets to effectively interact across cultures. The skill sets include cross-cultural communication as well as the ability to reconcile differences across the many dimensions of culture. Health care workers who are cognizant of the potential influence of cultural factors will need to incorporate this knowledge into their interventions and be able to communicate this to both patients and their families. Communication will be enhanced if this is expressed in the language of origin and by workers of the same ethnic background. However, this is not always possible nor is it necessarily desirable, particularly in multiethnic societies where cooperation between groups will be mutually advantageous. Thus, education can be extended to health care workers, patients, and their families, as well as the public, which may help to improve CHD outcome and also promote harmony between heterogeneous groups in society.

Interventions may be targeted to various population groups. For example, if certain dietary practices are deleterious to heart health, education of the particular group may allow modification of these current practices. Any change in a practice which has been an integral part of a group's lifestyle for generations will need to be approached with great sensitivity because resistance can be expected. The most practical solution needs to be sought; radical change is usually not required and is not realistically achievable. While the interrelationship of psychological and behavioral factors, ethnicity, and CHD is complex, further study may yield important approaches to improve outcome in a disease, which causes more deaths than any other.

SUMMARY

Cultural factors are of importance in health utilization, lifestyle practices, and physiological vulnerabilities in respect to the development of cardiovascular heart disease. Our understanding of the influence of psychological factors in this area is suggestive, but large, well-designed, and controlled studies are required to elucidate the potential interrelationships whose application, once established, would involve increased awareness through education of health professionals and the public. Evidence-based targeted interventions have the potential to benefit greatly the health of all segments of culturally diverse societies.

CASE STUDY

As the new coordinator of a post-discharge group program of cardiac patients and their partners, you are entrusted with the task of providing education and support in an 8-week series. The titles of sessions are Introduction, Cardiology, Nutrition, Physical Activity, Emergency Procedures, Psychological Aspects, Stress, and Wind-up (Source: Heart to Heart Program, Heart and Stroke Foundation of Ontario).

There are seven couples in your education and support group. They are from Toronto, a metropolitan area where the narrow majority of the population is immigrants. All of the couples have been carefully screened and found to be motivated and appropriate for the group. Three couples are locally born—one from an affluent area, one on social welfare, and an African

Canadian couple. Four are immigrant couples—one from Italy, one from India, one from China, and a recent arrival from Russia.

The challenge: How to successfully convey material and provide support to all members of the group at two points in time—the start of the series and for the sessions involving emotional aspects and dealing with stress. In response to questions raised with the vignette, the following answers may be considered:

1. At the start, the goal is to develop a sense of inclusiveness. How do you introduce and welcome each couple? You may emphasize the differences of the group by, for example, having participants greet each other in their appropriate way or asking them to share an idiom from their language/culture related to the heart. On the other hand, it may be preferable to simply allow each couple to relate their own experience of heart disease in terms of what actually happened to them, in order to promote an atmosphere of encouragement, support, and tolerance. At the same time, it is crucial to ensure that there is good comprehension and participation of all group participants, especially with regard to language diversity.

2. For the sessions where emotional issues are discussed, the moderator would benefit from reviewing the following questions: how may people be different in terms of their emotional awareness? their emotional experience? their emotional expressiveness? Culture may confer certain tendencies for groups, but stereotyping of individuals is counterproductive and will lead to false conclusions. Have each group member describe their emotional experience of the cardiac event and thereafter. A particular focus at this point is the spouse or support system whose role, particularly in the early weeks and months following the event, is an active and important one. An example is the common response of hypervigilance, which is normal in the aftermath of an event such as a heart attack (especially when the patient comes home), but can be deleterious to both patient and significant other and may vary among cultures and people generally. The moderator needs to make sure that key concepts such as "depression," "stress," "anxiety" are understood so that discussions of these concepts are intelligible to all.

ACKNOWLEDGMENTS

We acknowledge Rose Mayhew for administrative assistance and Brian Cameron for help with information retrieval.

SUGGESTED READINGS

Allen, R., & Scheidt, S. (1996). *Heart and mind*. Washington, DC: American Psychological Association.

Baker, B., & Newman, D. (2000). Guest Editors, Cardiology Special Issue. *Journal of Psychosomatic Research, 48(4,5),* 313–508.

Kleinman, A. (1980). *Patients and healers in the context of culture*. London: University of California Press.

REFERENCES

Alfredsson, L., Spetz, C. L., & Theorell, T. (1985). Type of occupation and near-future hospitalization for myocardial infarction and some other diagnoses. *International Journal of Epidemiology 14*, 378–388.

Alpert, J. S., Goldberg, R., Ockens, I. S., & Taylor, P. (1991). *Heart disease in Native-Americans, Cardiology, 78*, 3–12.

Anand, S., & Yusuf, S. (1998a). Ethnicity and vascular disease. In S. Yusuf, J. A. Cairns, A. J. Camm, E. L. Fallen, & B. J. Gersh (Eds.), *Evidence based cardiology* (pp. 329–352). London: BMJ Books.

Anand, S., & Yusuf, S. (1998b). Risk stratification for sympathetic atherosclerosis. In J. S. Ginsberg (Ed.), *Critical decisions in thrombosis and hemostasis* (pp. 179–189). Hamilton, Ontario: BC Decker Inc.

Anda, R., Williamson, D., Jones, D., Macera, C., Eaker, E., Glassman, A., & Marks, J. (1993). Depressed affect, hopelessness and the risk of ischemic heart disease in a cohort of U.S. adults. *Epidemiology, 4*, 285–294.

Appel, L. J., Moore, T. J., Obarzanek, E., Vollmer, W. M., Svetkey, L. P., Sacks, F. M., Bray, G. A., Vogt, T. M., Cutler, J. A., Windhauser, M. M., Lin, P. H., & Karanja, N. (1997). A clinical trial of the effects of dietary patterns on blood pressure. DASH Collaborative Research Group. *New England Journal of Medicine, 336*, 117–124.

Appels, A., & Mulder, P. (1989). Fatigue and heart disease: The association between fatigue and "vital exhaustion" and past, present and future coronary heart disease. *Journal of Psychosomatic Research, 33*, 727–738.

Benfante, R. (1992). Studies of cardiovascular disease and cause-specific mortality trends in Japanese American men living in Hawaii and risk factor comparisons with other Japanese populations in the Pacific region: A review. *Human Biology, 64*, 791–805.

Berrios, X., Koponen, T., Huiguang, T., Khaltaev, N., Puska, D., & Nissinen, A. (1997). Distribution and prevalence of major risk factors of noncommunicable diseases in selected countries: The WHO Inter-Health Programme. *Bulletin World Health Organization, 75*, 99–108.

Bhatnagar, D., Anand, I. S., Durrington, P. N., Patel, D. J., Wander, G. S., Mackness, M. I., Creed, F., Tomenson, B., Chandrashekhar, Y., & Winterbotham, M. (1995). Coronary risk factors in people from the Indian subcontinent living in west London and their siblings in India. *Lancet, 345*, 405–409.

Bonow, R. O., Bohannon, N., & Hazzard, W. (1996). Risk stratification in coronary artery disease and special populations. *American Journal of Medicine, 101*, 17S–22S.

Brisson, C., Laflamme, N., Moisan, J., Milot, A., Masse, B., & Vezina, M. (1999). Effect of family responsibilities and job strain on ambulatory blood pressure among white-collar women. *Psychosomatic Medicine, 61*, 205–213.

Chen, Z., Peto, R., Collins, R., MacMahon, S., Lu, J., & Li, W. (1991). Serum cholesterol concentration and coronary heart disease in population with low cholesterol concentrations. *British Medical Journal, 303*, 276–282.

Collins, R., Peto, R., MacMahon, S., Fiebach, N. H., Eberlein, K., Godwin, J., Qizilbash, N., Taylor, J. O., & Hennekens, C. H. (1990). Blood pressure, stroke and coronary heart disease. *Lancet, 335*, 827–838.

Criqui, M. H., & Ringel, B. L. (1994). Does diet or alcohol explain the French paradox? *Lancet, 344*, 1719–1723.

Fleet, R. P., & Beitman, B. D. (1998). Cardiovascular death from panic disorder and panic-like anxiety: A critical review of the literature. *Journal of Psychosomatic Research, 44*, 71–80.

Frasure-Smith, N., Lesperance, F., & Talajic, M. (1993). Depression following myocardial infarction. *Journal of the American Medical Association, 70,* 1819–1825.

Frasure-Smith, N., Lesperance, F., & Talajic, M. (1995). Depression and 18-month prognosis after myocardial infarction. *Circulation, 91,* 999–1005.

Friedman, M., & Rosenman, R. H. (1974). *Type A behavior and your heart.* New York: Knopf.

Geronimus, A. T., Bound, J., Waidmann, T. A., Hillemeier, M. M., & Burns, P. B. (1996). Excess mortality among blacks and whites in the United States. *New England Journal of Medicine, 335,* 1552–1558.

Gerstein, H. C., & Yusuf, S. (1996). Dysglycaemia and risk of cardiovascular disease. *Lancet, 347,* 949–950.

Ghali, J. K., Cooper, R. S., Kowatly, I., & Liao, Y. (1993). Delay between onset of chest pain and arrival to the coronary care unit among minority and disadvantaged patients. *Journal of the National Medical Association, 85,* 180–184.

Grundy, S. M., Greenland, P., Herd, A., Huebsch, J. A., Jones, R. J., Mitchell, J. H., Schlant, R. C., & Thomas, D. C. (1996). Cardiovascular and risk factor evaluation of healthy American adults. A statement for physicians by an Ad Hoc Committee appointed by the Steering Committee, American Heart Association (Review). *Circulation, 40,* 201S–208S.

Gupta, R., & Gupta, V. P. (1996). Meta-analysis of coronary heart disease prevalence in India. *Indian Heart Journal, 48,* 241–245.

Hegele, R. A. (1996). The pathogenesis of atherosclerosis. *Clinica Chimica Acta, 246,* 21–38.

Hofstede, G. (1991). *Cultures and organizations.* London: McGraw-Hill.

Howard, B. V., Lee, E. T., Fabsitz, R. R., Robbins, D. C., Yeh, J. L., Cowan, L. D., & Welty, T. K. (1996). Diabetes and coronary heart disease in American Indians: The Strong Heart Study. *Diabetes, 45,* S6–S13.

Hunink, M. G., Goldman, L., Tosteson, A. N., Mittleman, M. A., Goldman, P. A., Williams, L. W., & Tsevat, J. (1997). The recent decline in mortality from coronary heart disease, 1980–1990. *Journal of the American Medical Association, 277,* 535–542.

Iso, H., Komachi, Y., Shimamato, T., & Iida, M. (1996). *Trends for cardiovascular risk factors and disease in Japan: Prevention.* (Personal communication).

Kannel, W. B., Dawber, T. R., & McGee, D. L. (1980). Perspectives on systolic hypertension. The Framingham Study. *Circulation, 61,* 1183–1187.

Kannel, W. B., McGee, D., & Gordon, T. (1976). A general cardiovascular risk profile: The Framingham Study. *American Journal of Cardiology, 38,* 46–51.

Kannel, W. B., Wilson, P., & Blair, S. N. (1985). Epidemiological assessment of the role of physical activity and fitness in development of cardiovascular disease. *American Heart Journal, 109,* 876–885.

Karasek, R. (1979). Job demand, job decision latitude and mental strain: Implications for job redesign. *Administrative Science Quarterly, 24,* 285–307.

Kauhanen, J., Kaplan, G. A., Cohen, R. D., Julkunen, J. & Salonen, J. T. (1996). Alexithymia and risk of death in middle-aged men. *Journal of Psychosomatic Research, 41,* 541–549.

Kawachi, I., Sparrow, D., Vokonas, P. S., & Weiss, S. T. (1994). Symptoms of anxiety and risk of coronary heart disease. *Circulation, 90,* 2225–2229.

Kesteloot, H., & Joossens, J. V. (1994). Nutrition and international patterns of disease. In M. Marmot and P. Elliot (Eds.), *Coronary heart disease epidemiology* (pp. 152–165). New York: Oxford University Press.

Keys, A. (1980). *Seven countries: A multivariate analysis of death and coronary heart disease.* Boston: Harvard University Press.

Kristensen, M., Kucinskiene, Z., Bergdahl, B., Calkauskas, H., Urmonas, V., & Orth-Gomer, K. (1998). Increased psychosocial strain in Lithuanian versus Swedish men: The LiVicordia study. *Psychosomatic Medicine, 60,* 277–282.

Kuo, W. H. (1984). Prevalence of depression among Asian-Americans. *Journal of Nervous and Mental Disease, 172,* 449–457.

Marmot, M. G., & Syme, S. L. (1976). Acculturation and coronary heart disease in Japanese Americans. *American Journal of Epidemiology, 104,* 225–247.

Marmot, M., & Theorell, T. (1988). Social class and cardiovascular disease: The contribution of work. *International Journal of Health Services, 18,* 659–674.

Marmot, M. G., Smith, G. D., Stansfeld, S., Patel, C., North, F., Head, J., White, I., Brunner, E., & Feeney, A. (1991). Health inequalities among British civil servants: The Whitehall study. *Lancet, 337,* 1387–1393.

Mills, P. J., Berry, C. C., & Dimsdale, J. E. (1993). Temporal stability of task-induced cardiovascular, adrenergic, and psychological responses: The effects of race and hypertension. *Psychophysiology, 30,* 197–204.

Muller, J. E., Taylor, G. H., & Stone, P. H. (1989). Circadian variation and triggers of onset of acute cardiovascular disease. *Circulation, 79,* 733–743.

Murray, C. J., & Lopez, A. D. (1997). Mortality by cause for eight regions of the world: Global burden of disease study. *Lancet, 349,* 1269–1276.

Nishiyama, K., & Johnson, J. V. (1997). Karoshi—death from overwork: Occupational health consequences of Japanese production management. *International Journal of Health Services, 27,* 625–641.

Orth-Gomer, K., Rosengren, A., & Wilhelmsen, L. (1993). Lack of social support and incidence of coronary heart disease in middle-aged Swedish men. *Psychosomatic Medicine, 55,* 37–43.

People's Republic of China–United States Cardiovascular and Cardiopulmonary Epidemiology Research Group. (1992). An epidemiological study of cardiovascular and cardiopulmonary disease risk factors in four populations in the People's Republic of China. *Circulation, 85,* 1083–1096.

Peto, R., Lopez, A. D., Boreham, J., Thun, M., & Heath, C. (1992). Mortality from tobacco in developed countries: Indirect estimation from national vital statistics. *Lancet, 339,* 1268–1278.

Reddy, K. S., & Yusuf, S. (1998). The emerging epidemic of cardiovascular disease in developing countries. *Circulation, 97,* 596–601.

Rimm, E. B., & Ellison, R. C. (1995). Alcohol in the Mediterranean diet. *American Journal of Clinical Nutrition, 61,* 1378S–1382S.

Scandinavian Simvastatin Survival Study Group. (1994). Randomized trial of cholesterol lowering in 4444 patients with coronary heart disease: The Scandinavian Simvastatin Study (4S). *Lancet, 344,* 1383–1389.

Schnall, P. L., Landsbergis, P. A., & Baker, D. (1994). Job strain and cardiovascular disease. *Annual Review of Public Health, 15,* 381–411.

Seedat, Y. K. (1996). Ethnicity, hypertension, coronary heart disease and renal disease in South Africa. *Ethnicity and Health, 1,* 349–357.

Seeman, T. E., & Syme, S. L. (1987). Social networks and coronary artery disease: A comparison of the structure and function of social relations as predictors of disease. *Psychosomatic Medicine, 49,* 541–554.

Shekelle, R. B., Hulley, S. B., Neaton, J. D., Billings, J., Borhani, N., Gerace, T., Jacobs, D., Lasser, N., Mittlemark, M., & Stamler, J. (1985). The Multiple Risk Factor Intervention Trial (MRFIT) behavior pattern study II: Type A behavior and incidence of coronary heart disease. *American Journal of Epidemiology, 122,* 559–570.

Stamler, J., Wentworth, D., & Neaton, J. D. (1986). Is relationship between serum cholesterol and risk of premature death from coronary heart disease continuous and graded? Findings in 356,222 primary screenees of the Multiple Risk Factor Intervention Trial (MRFIT). *Journal of the American Medical Association, 256,* 2823–2828.

Syme, S. L. (1987). Coronary artery disease: A sociocultural perspective. *Circulation, 76,* 112–116.

Trichopolou, A., & Lagiou, P. (1987). Healthy traditional Mediterranean diet: An expression of culture, history and lifestyle. *Nutrition Reviews, 55,* 383–389.

Trompenaars, F. (1997). *Riding the waves of culture* (2nd ed.). Burr Ridge, IL: Irwin.

Vartainen, E., Pusku, P., Pekkanen, J., Tuomilehto, J., & Jousilahti, P. (1994). Changes in risk factors explain changes in mortality from ischaemic heart disease in Finland. *British Medical Journal, 309,* 23–27.

Williams, R. B. (1987). Refining the Type A hypothesis: Emergence of the hostility complex. *American Journal of Cardiology, 60,* 27J–32J.

World Health Organization. (1994). World health statistical annual 1994. Geneva, Switzerland: Author.

Yusuf, S., Ounpuu, S., & Anand, S. (1999). Global burden of cardiovascular disease. In K. K. Sethi (Ed.), *Coronary artery disease in Indians: A global perspective* (pp. 11–25). New Delhi: Cardiological Society of India.

Zatonski W. (December 5, 1996). *The development of Poland's health situation after 1988.* (Personal communication).

7

CULTURAL ASPECTS OF CANCER PREVENTION AND CONTROL

CAROLYN COOK GOTAY, MILES MURAOKA, AND JOAN HOLUP

Cancer Research Center of Hawaii
University of Hawaii
Honolulu, Hawaii

Over the past few decades, the United States has become increasingly culturally diverse, and this trend will continue and intensify in the coming century. In 1970, about one in eight persons belonged to an ethnic/racial minority group, a figure that had grown to one in four by the late 1990s. Non-Whites are projected to make up more than a third of the population by 2020, and slightly less than half by 2050. The groups expected to have the highest rates of increase are Hispanics and Asians and Pacific Islanders. In fact, Hispanics are predicted to add the largest number of people to the population and, after 2020, are projected to add more people to the United States every year than all other race/ethnic groups combined. Lin-Fu (1998) identified three reasons for these striking trends: "a dramatic rise in immigration from Latin America and Asia since the 1950's, resettlement of refugees from Cuba and Southeast Asia, and a higher fertility rate among minorities as compared to non-Hispanic whites" (p. 125). Changing U.S. demographics offers a challenge to the health care community to meet the needs of this diverse population with care that is both culturally sensitive and appropriate (Gordon, 1995).

Cancer constitutes one of the most serious health threats in the United States. Over the course of this century, cancer has become increasingly prevalent and, at present, it is the second leading cause of death (after heart disease), accounting for an estimated 553,000 deaths in 2001. More than 1.26 million new cancer cases are estimated in 2001. This number is likely to continue to grow as the population ages, since the majority of cancer cases are diagnosed in elderly people (Friis & Sellers, 1999). The financial impact of cancer is high. Overall annual costs are estimated at $108.2 billion, including direct medical costs and expenses associated with lost productivity and premature death. These figures do not include expenses that may be encountered by 8.9 million cancer survivors, many of whom live with permanent sequelae of the disease and treatment (all statistics from American Cancer Society, 2001).

This chapter focuses on culture's impact on individuals during the cancer experience. Although entire books have been written about "culture," no single definition of this concept is accepted by all social scientists (Okazaki & Sue, 1995; cf. Harris, 1983; LeVine, 1984; both cited in Thomas, 1988; Kagawa-Singer, 1994). In this chapter, our concept of culture includes the central areas thought to define a cultural group, encompassing shared common beliefs, ideas, experiences, knowledge, attitudes, and behaviors (Pachter, 1994), as all of these elements may pertain to variations in cancer experiences. We will attempt to characterize cultural patterns, although it is important to remember that there is considerable variability within cultures due to subgroup and individual differences. Large ethnic and cultural amalgamations such as "Asians and Pacific Islanders," a standard classification used by the U.S. census, homogenize individuals from nearly 30 Asian nations and 25 Pacific Island cultures into a single group (Lin-Fu, 1998), thus obscuring important cultural variation. In addition, the social science literature does not clearly distinguish ethnicity, race, and culture (Pasick, D'Onofrio, & Otero-Sabogal, 1996), and researchers have defined these constructs in differing ways (cf. Bates & Edwards, 1992; Eaton 1980; Phinney, 1990). Regardless of definition, these concepts are integrally related, and we will draw on relevant literature using any of these terms. Further, while there is promising, biologically oriented research into the link between cancer and membership in certain ethnic and/or racial groups (Elmore, Moceri, Carter, & Larson, 1998; Perera, 1997; Perkins, Cooksley, & Cox, 1996), racial and ethnic variation in biological events, such as genetics traits and/or susceptibility, is not discussed here.

In this chapter, we will discuss patterns of cancer in different ethnic groups; ethnic and cultural differences in knowledge, attitudes, and behaviors about cancer; cancer prevention, screening, and early detection; reactions to a diagnosis of cancer; and living with cancer. Our emphasis will be on the largest ethnic/racial subgroups in the United States (African Americans, Native Americans, Asians and Pacific Islanders, and Hispanics), and comparisons will be made to the majority (White) population wherever possible. Our use of the term Native Americans applies to both American Indian and Alaska Native populations. Wherever possible, we will provide an example of an intervention that has utilized cultural values in assisting individuals to prevent, detect, or cope with cancer.

PATTERNS OF CANCER IN CULTURALLY DIVERSE GROUPS

Table 7.1 summarizes information about cancer rates in different ethnic groups. Both incidence (rates of newly diagnosed cases) and mortality (death rates) are listed. Depending on the site of disease, different ethnic minorities in the United States experience disproportional rates of cancer incidence and mortality relative to Whites. For example, African Americans are diagnosed with prostate cancer at rates greatly exceeding those of any other group. Overall, Native Americans suffer greater mortality rates relative to their frequency of cancer diagnoses, implying that if they are diagnosed with cancer, they are more likely to die of it. While Asians and Pacific Islanders report markedly lower rates than do Whites for most cancers, they are comparable in the numbers of colorectal cancers that are diagnosed. Epidemiological data such as these provide provocative hypotheses about why one group may differ from another, and there is continuing research and discussion regarding how to explain the heterogeneity of cancer across ethnic groups (Meyerowitz, Richardson, Hudson, & Leedham, 1998).

TABLE 7.1   Incidence and Mortality Rates[a] by Ethnicity and Cancer Site[b]

Site	African American	Native American	Asian/ Pacific Islander	Hispanic[c]	White
INCIDENCE[d,e]					
All cancers	442.9	153.4	279.1	275.4	402.9
Breast	99.3	33.9	72.6	69.4	113.2
Colorectal	50.4	16.4	38.6	29.0	43.9
Lung/bronchus	73.9	18.6	35.8	27.6	55.9
Prostate	222.9	46.5	81.5	102.8	147.3
MORTALITY[d,e]					
All cancers	223.4	104.0	103.4	104.9	167.5
Breast	31.4	12.3	11.4	15.3	25.7
Colorectal	23.1	9.9	10.9	10.4	17.4
Lung/bronchus	60.5	28.8	23.7	19.9	49.3
Prostate	54.8	14.3	10.7	16.7	23.7

[a]Rates are per 100,000 population and are age-adjusted to the 1970 U.S. standard population.

[b]Adapted from Greenlee, R. T., Murray, T., Bolden, S., and Wingo, P. A. (2000).

[c]Hispanic is not mutually exclusive of White, African American, Asian/Pacific Islander, or Native American.

[d]Incidence data are from the 11 SEER areas; mortality data are from all states except Connecticut, Oklahoma, Louisiana, and New Hampshire.

[e]Data sources: NCI Surveillance, Epidemiology, and End Results Program, 1999 (incidence); Vital Statistics of the United States, 1999 (mortality).

Studies examining cancer incidence and mortality rates among individuals who have migrated to the U.S. may assist in identifying the relative contributions of lifestyle and the environment versus genetic/constitutional factors. Migrant studies provide the ability to examine cancer incidence and mortality rates among individuals who have moved to the United States, compared to United States rates (overall and in population subgroups) and rates in their country of origin, as well as effects due to the length of residence in the new country, age at time of migration, exposure to carcinogens in either environment, and other variables (Thomas & Karagas, 1996). In general terms, rates of cancers that occur infrequently in countries of origin tend to be higher in migrants, and rates of relatively common cancers in countries of origin appear to be lower among migrants (Thomas & Karagas, 1987). In addition, rates among migrants tend to approach those found in the general United States population with each succeeding generation. Migrant studies have been conducted primarily with Asians; fewer studies have examined the effects of migration in Hispanics and African Americans.

One factor that may account for the closer correspondence in cancer rates between immigrant groups and the general population with the passage of generations is acculturation. Acculturation refers to the process whereby an individual makes choices about adopting the beliefs, behaviors, and values of the host culture and retaining aspects of his/her native culture (Berry & Kim, cited in Kagawa-Singer, 1998). Measures of acculturation include the degree to which an individual uses his/her native language, number of years spent in the United States, ethnicity of close friends, and level of pride in one's heritage (e.g., Cuellar, Harris, & Jasso, 1980). Acculturation has been shown to increase cancer knowledge and decrease negative attitudes (e.g., Hubbell, Chavez, Mishra, & Valdez, 1996a, 1996b), and increase cancer screening rates (e.g., Yi, 1995). With respect to cancer risk factors, the majority of studies, most of which have been based in Hispanic populations, have indicated increasing acculturation is correlated with behaviors more like those in the dominant (White) culture; for example, more acculturated Hispanics were found to have dietary fat intake that was intermediate between that of less acculturated Hispanics and Whites (Otero-Sabogal, Sabogal, Perez-Stable, & Hiatt, 1995; Winkleby, Albright, Howard-Pitney, Lin, & Fortmann, 1994), and the same trends have been seen for smoking and alcohol use (Black & Markides, 1993; Elder et al., 1991; Marin, Perez-Stable, & Marin, 1989; Otero-Sabogal et al., 1995). Not all research is consistent in this area, however (cf. Elder et al., 1991; Klonoff & Landrine, 1996; Marin et al., 1989). The relationship between acculturation and cancer-related attitudes and behaviors will be discussed in the remainder of the chapter where information is available.

ETHNIC DIFFERENCES IN KNOWLEDGE, BELIEFS, AND ATTITUDES ABOUT CANCER

Numerous studies have documented lower levels of knowledge about risk factors and signs and symptoms of cancer in culturally diverse groups, including

African Americans (Breslow, Sorkin, Frey, & Kessler, 1997; Demark-Wahnefried et al., 1995; Jepson, Kessler, Portnoy, & Gibbs, 1991; Lipkus et al., 1996; Loehrer et al., 1991; Miller & Champion, 1997; Price, Colvin, & Smith, 1993; Smith, DeHaven, Grundig, & Wilson, 1997), Hispanics (Hubbell et al., 1996a, 1996b), Korean Americans (Kim, Yu, Chen, Kim, & Brintnall, 1998), Chinese Americans (Garcia & Lee, 1989; Mo, 1992), Vietnamese Americans (Jenkins, McPhee, Bird, & Bonilla, 1990; Pham & McPhee, 1992), Native Hawaiians (Blaisdell, 1998; LeMarchand & Kolonel, 1989), and American Samoans (Mishra, Luce-Aoelua, & Hubbell, 1998).

Some of the lack of knowledge in many of these studies reflects lack of information. For example, Kim et al. (1998) found that only 4 and 3% of 159 Korean American women correctly identified "unusual bleeding and discharge" and "a lump in breast," respectively, as abnormal signs that could indicate cancer. Jenkins et al. (1990) found that 13% of their sample of Vietnamese Americans had never heard of cancer, 27% did not know that smoking is a risk factor for cancer, and 28% believed that cancer is a communicable disease. While the minority populations were less knowledgeable than Whites in all studies that compared these groups, a large-scale ($N = 12,035$) national survey demonstrated that there were considerable deficits in knowledge about cancer risk in all groups, regardless of ethnicity. Low income and education (factors which are often correlated with minority group membership) were also related to less cancer knowledge (Breslow et al., 1997).

In addition to knowledge deficits, some misconceptions may reflect cultural attitudes about disease. For example, poor hygiene was cited as a cause for breast and cervical cancer by both Vietnamese (Pham & McPhee, 1992) and Hispanics (Hubbell et al., 1996a, 1996b), and Garcia and Lee's (1989) sample of Chinese Americans identified "dirt and filth" as causative agents for breast cancer. Martinez, Chavez, and Hubbell (1997) provide qualitative support that the women's response of "poor hygiene" referred to hygiene following sexual intercourse. The Hispanic women in studies by this group of investigators (Chavez, Hubbell, McMullin, Martinez, & Mishra, 1995; Hubbell et al., 1996b; Martinez et al., 1997) also identified numerous other aspects of sexual behavior as causative for cervical cancers; some of these reasons are supported by scientific evidence (e.g., multiple sexual partners), whereas others (e.g., birth control pills, abortions, having sex within 40 days of giving birth) are not. The heavy emphasis by these women on sexual causes led Martinez et al. to suggest that these women saw cancer in a moral context that may stem from their cultural and religious background.

Another common belief reported in studies of almost all culturally diverse groups is that of fatalism. African American men (Demark-Wahnefried et al., 1995; Price et al., 1993), women (Champion & Menon, 1997; Sung, Blumenthal, Coates, & Alema-Mensah, 1997), and adolescents (Price, Desmond, Wallace, Smith, & Stewart, 1988) tended to endorse beliefs such as "cancer is a death sentence" or "a person with cancer cannot be expected to live a normal life." Other studies have also reported Hispanics' fatalistic view toward cancer (Garcia & Lee, 1989). Perez-Stable, Sabogal, Otero-Sabogal, Hiatt, and McPhee (1992) found that attitudes toward cancer differed between Hispanics and Whites, such that a higher percentage of Hispanics believed that having cancer is life-ending, that cancer is God's punishment, or that one can do little to avoid cancer. Fatalistic beliefs have also been reported in Vietnamese (Pham & McPhee, 1992), Native Hawaiians (Blaisdell, 1998; Braun, Look, & Tsark, 1995), and American Samoans (Mishra et al., 1998).

Such beliefs may be deeply rooted in cultural views of health and illness. For example, Powe (1996) cites cultural, historical, and socioeconomic factors that have affected African Americans over generations that have given rise to these pessimistic perceptions. Perez-Stable et al. (1992) posited that the Hispanic cultural concept of *fatalismo,* the belief that one is helpless against the forces of fate, could account for Hispanic views about cancer. Uba (1992) describes the beliefs of Southeast Asian cultures in the context of medical problems. Illness and suffering are viewed as inevitable consequences of life and are to be accepted; for example, the Hmong (indigenous people of Laos) believe that the time of death is predetermined (Brainard & Zaharlick, 1989). It is clear how these views of life would engender fatalistic attitudes. African American cancer patients have been shown to have spiritual beliefs regarding the causes of cancer (Ashing-Giwa & Ganz, 1997).

Both lack of information and cultural beliefs may affect cancer-related behaviors. These attitudes and perceptions should be kept in mind as we consider cultural aspects of cancer prevention.

INTERVENTION BUILDING ON CULTURAL FACTORS TO ADDRESS KNOWLEDGE, BELIEFS, AND ATTITUDES ABOUT CANCER

Sabogal, Otero-Sabogal, Pasick, Jenkins, and Perez-Stable (1996) provided suggestions on developing culturally sensitive and appropriate printed health educational materials. The most important step is to gain an understanding of a group's subjective culture, which reflects beliefs, perceptions, attitudes, roles, social norms, expectancies, and values. This is accomplished by involving members of the target audience to help identify core cultural values through focus groups, in-depth interviews, and open-ended surveys. For example, Sabogal et al. (1996) found, through focus groups, that many minority groups stressed the importance of the family unit and its well-being. They incorporated this aspect in their cancer education materials for Hispanics and more traditional Chinese women. The cover of these materials featured pictures of three generations of family members as a way to promote interest. In addition, messages such as "I get an annual mammogram because I want to watch my daughter grow up" were used to educate Hispanic women of the importance of early detection; material targeted for Chinese women emphasized the importance of routine preventive practices so that the women can live longer for their family. Other suggestions to increase attention to these materials include extensive pretesting with various segments of the target population, use of attractive and simple layouts in low-literacy materials, avoidance of technical or complicated terminology, and use of visual materials to highlight major components of the message.

CANCER PREVENTION

It has been estimated that up to 70% of cancer mortality (Doll & Peto, 1981) and up to 90% of cancer incidence rates (Doll, 1998) may, in principle, be avoidable by altering lifestyle risk behaviors associated with cancer. Doll identified 17 factors that may be responsible for cancer mortality, including tobacco and alcohol consumption, pollution, occupation, physical inactivity, and diet, among others. According to the American Cancer Society, "smoking is the most preventable cause of death in our society" (American Cancer Society, 2001). Over 430,000 deaths per year in the United States could be attributed to smoking (during the 1990–1994 period), to both tobacco-related cancers (e.g., lung, esophagus, head and neck, bladder, cervical) and lung and heart disease. In this chapter, we will focus on ethnic and cultural differences in tobacco use, currently the aspect of cancer prevention about which most is known.

ETHNIC AND CULTURAL DIFFERENCES
IN TOBACCO USE

The most comprehensive and up-to-date review of tobacco use among culturally diverse groups in the United States is the 1998 Report of the Surgeon General (USDHHS, 1998), as summarized in Table 7.2. Unless otherwise noted, all of the data in this section are based on this report. The table indicates the raw and age-adjusted smoking rates are highest among Native American men and women; Asians and Pacific Islanders have the lowest rates, particularly in women. African Americans have rates comparable to Whites.

Although their smoking rates appear to be similar to or higher than those of Whites, minorities apparently smoke fewer cigarettes per day. Greater proportions of minorities smoke fewer than 15 cigarettes a day than Whites; greater percentages of Whites smoke 25 or more cigarettes a day than all other groups.

Previous-month smoking rates among high school seniors are also highest among Native Americans relative to the students in other groups. The relatively high rates among Asian and Pacific Islander female students is notable, given the low rates of smoking among adult Asian and Pacific Islander women and may reflect acculturation among the young women.

With respect to smokeless (chewing tobacco and snuff) and any tobacco (smokeless, cigarette, cigar, and pipe) use, Native Americans again have the highest rates. Another interesting finding is the high rate of smokeless tobacco

TABLE 7.2 Percentage of African American, Hispanic, Asian American/Pacific Islander, Native American/Alaska Native, and White Tobacco Use Data from the Surgeon General's Report on Tobacco Use among U.S. Racial/Ethnic Minority Groups

Percentage who reported:	African American			Hispanic			Asian American/ Pacific Islander			Native American/ Alaska Native			White		
	Total	Men	Women	Total	Men	Women	Total	Men	Women	Total	Men	Women	Total	Men	Women
Current cigarette smoking (Age-adjusted)[a]	26.5 (26.5)	31.4 (31.4)	22.7 (22.2)	18.9 (18.0)	22.9 (21.7)	15.1 (14.6)	15.3 (14.2)	25.1 (23.8)	5.8 (5.4)	39.2 (36.0)	45.4 (39.3)	34.2 (32.9)	25.9 (26.4)	27.6 (28.1)	24.4 (25.0)
Daily smoking intake[a]															
< 15 cigarettes	63.9	61.1	67.1	65.0	62.4	68.8	70.6	69.1	77.3	49.9	36.2	64.9	35.3	29.3	41.6
15–24 cigarettes	28.4	28.6	28.3	27.3	29.9	23.5	21.4	23.6	11.5	33.0	42.1	23.1	43.1	43.0	43.2
≥ 25 cigarettes	7.6	10.3	4.6	7.7	7.6	7.7	8.0	7.3	11.2	17.0	21.7	12.0	21.6	27.7	15.2
Smokeless tobacco use[b]	3.0	3.1	2.9	0.8	1.5	0.1	0.6	1.2	0.0	4.5	7.8	1.2	3.4	6.8	0.3
Any tobacco product use[b]	35.2	42.4	29.3	23.4	30.4	17.0	16.8	25.6	7.9	40.2	43.9	36.6	32.2	38.0	26.8
High school seniors who were previous-month smokers[c]		11.6	8.6		28.5	19.2		20.6	13.8		41.1	39.4		33.4	33.1

[a]National Center for Health Statistics, public use data tapes, 1994–1995 aggregate data.
[b]National Health Interview Survey, 1987 and 1991 aggregate data, Centers for Disease Control and Prevention, 1994.
[c]Bachman, Johnston, & O'Malley (1991), Institute for Social Research, University of Michigan, unpublished data.

use among African American women, whose rates are higher than Hispanic and Asian and Pacific Islander men.

Although as a whole, Asians and Pacific Islanders have the lowest smoking prevalence rates, rates for certain subgroups within this category exceed the rates for Whites. For example, rates of smoking in men ranged from 55% in Cambodians (USDHHS, cited in Moeschberger et al., 1997) and 56% in Vietnamese (Jenkins et al., 1990) to 72% in Laotians (Levin, Nachampassach, & Xiong, cited in Moeschberger et al., 1997). Native Hawaiians also have high smoking prevalence rates; prevalence was estimated at 34% of Native Hawaiians (USDHHS, cited in Li & Pawlish, 1998). Hawaiians were also found to smoke more cigarettes per day than other ethnic groups in Hawaii (Whites, Chinese, Japanese, and Filipinos) (Chung, Tash, Raymond, Yasunobu, & Lew, 1990).

HISTORICAL AND TRADITIONAL FACTORS: CULTURALLY DIVERSE GROUPS AND TOBACCO USE

The meanings, uses, and economic importance of tobacco have varied among ethnic populations originating from different locales and operating under different cultural circumstances. Understanding the history and traditions related to tobacco among United States ethnic populations may aid in understanding their current tobacco use.

African Americans

Tobacco has been a part of the experience of African Americans since early in the 1600s, when Africans were first brought to the Americas and employed in southern tobacco-growing plantations, and during and after the colonial period in tobacco manufacturing. Until the mid-1940s, many African Americans held low-paying jobs in tobacco-related work, although around the time of WWII, some companies began advertising to this population. By the end of the 1950s, African American men had surpassed White men in smoking prevalence (USDHHS, 1998).

Hispanics

Tobacco predated European colonization of Latin America and the Caribbean and played a prominent role in religious and healing practices, often used by shamans or spiritual leaders. Economically, tobacco manufacturing and trade have played a significant role in the Caribbean and Latin America, and Hispanics, primarily those of Cuban ancestry, have played a key role in the manufacturing of cigars in Florida factories. Currently, cigarette smoking is a social activity for Hispanics, consistent with cultural values of *personalismo* (the value placed on personal relations) and *simpatía* (a social mandate for positive social relations) (Marin, Marin, Perez-Stable, Sabogal, & Perez-Stable, 1990, cited in USDHHS, 1998).

Asians and Pacific Islanders

Tobacco was introduced to Asia by Europeans in the early 17th century, where, for example, in China it was mixed with opium and smoked. Later, tobacco was used medicinally in various areas. Currently, Asian countries produce the majority of the world's tobacco. Smoking is prevalent in Asia, and sharing cigarettes, particularly among males, is a positive social gesture. Cigarette smoking in Asia has been associated with sophistication and affluence and, as in the United States, is glamorized in advertising. Although these facts are known about Asian countries, relatively little information exists regarding the relationship between factors present in Asian countries and their effect on tobacco use in the United States among immigrant and United States-born populations (USDHHS, 1998).

Native Americans

Early documentation of the Americas found extensive farming and use of tobacco among native populations. Tobacco served many purposes, including ceremonial, religious, and medicinal functions. Examples include using tobacco as an offering of good luck in hunting, as a topical ointment, and to cleanse a room for rituals. Tobacco smoking, in particular, was prevalent during solemn occasions, such as when leaders met, and also was used between enemies after battle to signify a truce. Currently, tobacco has mixed meaning for native populations, as for some it has lost its attributes, while for others, there are still traditional uses and practices, for example, in powwows and other gatherings (USDHHS, 1998).

INTERVENTION BUILDING ON CULTURAL VALUES IN TOBACCO USE

Lichtenstein and Lopez (1999) developed and evaluated a program to enhance the tobacco-control policies of Northwest Indian tribes that was a joint activity of Oregon-based academic groups and the Northwest Portland Area Indian Health Board (NPAIHB). Half of the 39 participating area tribes received the consulting help immediately and half received consulting later, allowing for all tribes to be served and for scientific evaluation of the program.

Native American professional staff helped to develop the program, and consulting and evaluation staff always identified themselves as NPAIHB employees, bolstering perceptions that the project was at least partly "Native American-owned." Native American colleagues were assumed to know best how to work with the tribes, and distinctions were made between traditional uses of tobacco and habitual recreational use. The consultation process involved each tribe's receiving a tobacco policy workbook that explained the importance of tobacco use policies, gave guidelines for choosing, developing, and implementing a policy, and included policy examples. Tribal representatives were also invited to a workshop and provided with additional follow-up materials, including examples and drafts policies that could be tailored to suit the tribe's needs and supplementary Native American-specific materials on smoking cessation.

Existing tribal policies were evaluated and classified before the intervention as either smoke-free, moderately-restrictive, or lenient/no policy within areas common to all tribes (tribal council meetings, work areas, and private offices). After the program intervention, policies were stronger, and more tribes were smoke-free in common areas, with the number of tribes having smoke-free policies in all three common areas more than doubling by the conclusion of the program.

USE OF SCREENING TESTS

Although cultural/ethnic "minorities" have lower or comparable cancer incidence rates relative to Whites, they suffer from disproportionately higher death rates due to some cancers. Part of this discrepancy has been attributed to lower utilization of routine screening tests and, consequently, being diagnosed when cancers are already more advanced and less curable. Well-established and widely available screening modalities and recommendations for their use have been developed for some common cancers. These include clinical breast examination and mammogram screening for breast cancer, which are recommended annually for all women 50 years and older (United States Preventive Services Task Force, 1995) and Papanicolaou (Pap) screening for cervical cancer, which is recommended for all women who are sexually active and/or are 18 years and older (National Cancer Institute, 1998). Established screening tests for colorectal cancer include fecal occult blood testing and flexible sigmoidoscopy; although these tests are recommended, they are not yet in widespread use (The Centers for Disease Control, 1996). A test reflecting blood levels of prostate-specific antigen (PSA) is widely available to test for prostate cancer, although its efficacy is still being investigated in clinical trials and its use as a screening test is not recommended by the United States Preventive Services Task Force (1995). For other common cancers, such as lung cancer, unfortunately, no screening tests are currently available.

In this section, we will examine studies investigating the screening for breast and cervical cancer—the areas where most ethnic-specific data are available—and culturally linked influences on screening. Comprehensive population-based data on self-reported use of clinical breast examination, mammography, and Pap test are available from the National Health Interview Survey, conducted annually by the National Center for Health Statistics of the Centers for Disease Control. Currently, the most recent data available that report screening test use by ethnic group are for 1994, and Table 7.3 provides a summary of this information for adherence to screening recommendations. In addition to screening adherence, the numbers of individuals ever receiving a screening test is informative. The most recent data providing this information for most of the target ethnic groups (although not Native Americans) was collected by Hiatt et al. (1996) in the San Francisco Bay area. The data in this study ($N = 4228$) were collected at about the same time as data in the CDC survey; comparable time periods are important to consider, since there has been considerable temporal change in the use of

TABLE 7.3   Use of Cancer Screening Tests by Ethnicity (% Receiving Test)

Screening test	African American	Native American	Asian/ Pacific Islander	Hispanic	White
		Ever receiving screening[a]			
Clinical breast exam	96	NA	60	89	98
Mammogram	90	NA	61	80	93
Pap test	98	NA	56	76	99
		Adherent to recommendations[b]			
Mammogram and clinical breast exam in past 2 years	56	53	46	50	56
Pap test in past 3 years	84	73	66	74	76

[a]Hiatt et al. (1996).
[b]Centers for Disease Control, May–June, 1999.
NA = Not available.

mammography over the past 10 years, with many more women receiving mammograms over time (cf. Breen & Kessler, 1994).

With respect to clinical breast examination, high percentages (89% or higher) of African American, Hispanic, and White women have had at least one such examination, although rates were somewhat lower (60%) in Asians and Pacific Islanders. The pattern was similar for women reporting ever having received a mammogram; 80% or more of African American, Hispanic, and White and 61% of Asian and Pacific Islander had received at least one mammogram. With respect to obtaining a clinical breast examination and mammogram within recommended intervals, women in all ethnic groups were similar, ranging from 46% of Asians and Pacific Islanders to 56% of African American and White women.

Rates for receipt of Pap tests indicate that almost all African American and White women have had at least one Pap smear, with somewhat lower rates in Hispanic women (76%) and considerably lower (56%) among Asians and Pacific Islanders. With respect to adherence with Pap testing, African Americans had the highest rates (84%), with Native Americans, Hispanics, and Whites reporting similar figures (73, 74, and 76%, respectively) and Asians and Pacific Islanders being somewhat lower (66%).

There are some commonalities across these data. Asians and Pacific Islanders report the lowest rates for ever receiving any of the screening tests and for being adherent with obtaining screening at recommended intervals. The less than optimal adherence rates point out that there is considerable room for improvement in all groups. In addition, adherence rates are more similar across ethnic groups than are rates for ever receiving a test, implying that the most significant ethnocultural barriers to screening may lie in motivating and enabling women to get their first screening exam. Subsequent adherence to recommendations may be affected by common factors that affect women of all ethnic groups in a similar fashion.

FACTORS AFFECTING SCREENING

Structural barriers such as cost of tests (e.g., Maxwell, Bastani, & Warda, 1997, 1998; Pham & McPhee, 1992), no health insurance (e.g., McPhee et al., 1997), transportation difficulties (e.g., Kelly et al., 1996), and lack of time and inconvenience (e.g., Friedman et al., 1995) negatively affect screening rates. These issues particularly affect women of lower socioeconomic status, and cut across all racial/ethnic groups. Indeed, Hoffman-Goetz, Breen, and Meissner (1998) found that less-educated and lower-income women, including Whites, had very low rates of breast and cervical cancer screening tests.

Affective barriers, which have more of a cultural/ethnic basis than do structural barriers, may also be important to minority women. For example, many Asian (e.g., Maxwell et al., 1998) and Hispanic (Jennings, 1997) women report being embarrassed when undergoing breast and cervical cancer screening tests. Cultural beliefs about personal modesty and morality have been noted by Martinez et al. (1997) among Hispanic women and by Mo (1992) among Chinese women. Issues of embarrassment may also engender preferences to obtain medical services from female physicians by Vietnamese (Tosomeen, Marquez, Panser, & Kottke, 1996), Chinese (Lovejoy, Jenkins, Wu, Shankland, & Wilson, 1989), and Hispanic (Saint-Germain & Longman, 1993) women.

Anxiety about cancer has also been shown to be associated with low clinical breast examination and Pap test screening rates among Hispanic women (Lobell, Bay, Rhoads, & Keske, 1998), and low mammography rates among African American women (Friedman et al., 1995). Dibble, Vanoni, and Miaskowski (1997) reported that mammography-related radiation fears (e.g., fear of radiation preventing future mammograms) were higher among Asians, Hispanics, and Pacific Islanders relative to White women. Fear of pain associated with mammograms was high in African American and Hispanic women (Stein, Fox, & Murata, 1991).

Other barriers to screening involve incorrect or inadequate knowledge concerning screening tests or cancer in general among Vietnamese (e.g., Yi, 1998), Hispanic (e.g., Morgan, Park, & Cortes, 1995), and African American (e.g., Sung, Blumenthal, Coates, & Alema-Mensah, 1997) women. McPhee et al. (1996) noted that the patriarchal family system has ill prepared Vietnamese women to deal with issues outside this network. They are often isolated and alienated from the host society and, along with limited English proficiency, may not be able to benefit from public health information promoted in the community at large.

Lack of a preventive health orientation has been documented in a number of studies (e.g., Lovejoy et al., 1989; Uba, 1992). Beliefs that breast cancer screening tests are not necessary in the absence of symptoms have been found in Filipino women who had low rates of screening (Maxwell et al., 1997). Fatalistic attitudes about cancer (noted previously) also contribute to low rates of screening. Chavez, Hubbell, Mishra, and Valdez (1997) found that cancer fatalism was an independent predictor of Pap test use among Hispanic women; Hispanic immigrants were more likely to hold fatalistic attitudes toward cancer and were less likely to have received a Pap test than were Hispanic women born in the United States.

Degree of acculturation and associated factors, such as English language proficiency and length of United States residency, also affect screening rates, with the more acculturated having higher rates of clinical breast examinations (e.g., Wismer et al., 1998; Yi, 1994), mammograms (e.g., Longman, Saint-Germain, & Modiano, 1992; O'Malley, Kerner, Johnson, & Mandelblatt, 1999), and Pap smears (e.g., Harmon, Castro, & Coe, 1996; Yi, 1995).

Social support and social ties were found to predict mammography use in older African American women (Kang & Bloom, 1993). African American women who reported having many friends and relatives and those active in church activities were more likely to have received mammograms. Similarly, Suarez, Lloyd, Weiss, Rainbolt, and Pulley (1994) found that the number of close friends was the most important predictor of mammography and Pap smear prevalence among Hispanic women.

INTERVENTION BUILDING ON CULTURAL VALUES FOR CANCER SCREENING

Of all areas of cancer control interventions, programs to increase screening in culturally diverse groups have received the most attention. A number of interventions build on social ties between individuals in the same ethnic group, thus increasing social support, providing role models, and reinforcing shared cultural values. Culturally tailored programs have been based in African American, Hispanic, Native American, Vietnamese, and Native Hawaiian communities (see Gotay and Wilson, 1998, for a review). An example of one such program was reported by McAlister et al. (1995) and Ramirez et al. (1995), who studied the impact of a program called "Programa a Su Salud" (Program for Your Health) on Mexican American women in San Antonio. This intervention was modeled after a program that had led to smoking reductions in a similar population and included the mass media (print, radio, and television) to disseminate information that showed role models engaging in desired behaviors (e.g., newspaper articles featuring a Hispanic woman who had obtained a mammogram). Within their social networks, volunteers also distributed monthly community bulletins and other print materials, which contained consistent screening messages. The impact of this program was evaluated by comparing changes in breast and cervical screening before and after the program among women who had never had a mammogram or a Pap test, compared to Mexican American women in another Texas city

(Houston). Significant increases were seen for mammography and marginally significant increases for Pap tests in the women who had been exposed to the intervention.

THE CANCER DIAGNOSIS

COMMUNICATION OF A CANCER DIAGNOSIS AND PROGNOSIS

Considerable cultural variation exists about the desirability of telling a patient that s/he has cancer. While nearly all practicing United States physicians currently disclose a cancer diagnosis (Novack et al., 1979), the assumption that "truth-telling" is or should be a universal practice, either nationally or globally, has been contested (Ali, 1996; Blackhall, Murphy, Frank, Michel, & Azen, 1995; Carrese & Rhodes, 1995; Orona, Koenig, & Davis, 1994). For the majority of Japanese physicians, it is standard practice to withhold a cancer diagnosis, since physicians traditionally have believed that it is their professional responsibility to assume the burden of knowledge regarding patients' poor prognoses and simultaneously protect them from this knowledge (Delvecchio-Good, Good, Schaffer, & Lind, 1990). Mitchell's (1998) review of numerous studies that relate to disclosure and cancer demonstrates widely differing disclosure patterns among countries, as well as differences within the United States among cultural groups.

African American and White patients have been found to differ strikingly from members of other cultural groups in their preference for truth-telling. In a stratified quota sample ($N = 800$) enrolling participants from senior centers, Blackhall et al. (1995) found that African Americans (88%) and Whites (87%) were significantly more likely than Korean Americans (47%) and Mexican Americans (65%) to believe that patients should be told the truth about the diagnosis and prognosis of a terminal condition and were less likely to believe that patients should make the decision regarding life-prolonging measures. The authors attribute the differing attitudes toward truth-telling to family-centered belief models in Korean Americans' and Mexican Americans' cultures where nondisclosure is seen as protective, and autonomy is not viewed as empowering but rather as burdensome. This traditional Asian world-view toward nondisclosure is further detailed in Muller and Desmond's (1992) case study of a Chinese family whose mother was terminally ill with cancer. While the Chinese family wanted little or no information transmitted to the patient, the physicians, operating in a value system dominated by patient autonomy, wanted open and direct discussion. Similar cases with Chinese families have been documented elsewhere (Koenig & Gates-Williams, 1995). These differing cultural values have resulted in communication breakdown and the development of mutual mistrust and frustration (Dodd, Chen, Lindsey, & Piper, 1985).

Religion, acculturation, and gender may also influence patterns of disclosure. Hispanic families' religious beliefs may allow for miracles such that the family may still wish to focus on cures rather than a poor, medical prognosis. Acculturation may also play a role in nondisclosure of a cancer diagnosis. For example, Spinetta (cited in Schaefer, 1983) attributes Hispanic families' reluctance to tell a child a cancer diagnosis to the fact that in their country of origin, cancer usually means death. Gender differences may also affect disclosure. Orona et al.'s (1994) participant-observation and qualitative study of seven economically disadvantaged patients shows that for some Hispanics, open discussion between members of the opposite sex about certain types of cancers affecting reproductive regions, such as the uterus, ovaries, prostate, or testes, can seem impolite and inappropriate.

Privacy is also strongly valued in many cultures. Even though African Americans may generally prefer disclosure of a diagnosis to patients, Ashing-Giwa and Ganz's (1997) study involving in-depth interviews with African American informants ($N = 12$) demonstrated a tendency among African Americans to treat cancer as a private manner not readily discussed with close relatives and friends. In Native Americans, privacy is highly valued also and, as a result, cancer may not be discussed in native communities, with consequent isolation of Native American cancer patients (Kaur, 1996). Even long-term survivors may never tell others about their diagnosis. Therefore, the only individuals known to have cancer may be those who die, thus contributing to a sense of fatalism in these communities.

CULTURAL SENSITIVITY IN COMMUNICATION

In addition to deciding whether to tell patients they have cancer, cultural issues affect how information is best communicated. Many patients feel that they need time to understand what they are being told, and physicians may be viewed as too abrupt or insensitive by some patients. In a study of African American late-stage breast cancer patients ($N = 34$), Mathews, Lannin, and Mitchell (1994) indicated that a straightforward diagnosis and immediate planning of treatment was so offensive that six women walked out of the clinic at the point of diagnosis and never returned. Hodge, Fredericks, and Rodriguez (1996) identify a similar issue from the perspective of Native Americans. Whereas providers may prefer direct communication, many Native Americans, particularly women, have an indirect style that may be misunderstood as an unwillingness of the patient to participate in her own care. From the patient perspective, providers can be perceived as too busy and uncaring to listen to a patient's symptoms. Further, care must be taken to avoid infusing further negativity into the illness event in Native American communities. Carrese and Rhodes's (1995) in-depth interviews among Navajo informants ($N = 34$) uncovered a strong theme of avoiding thinking or speaking in a negative way. Of the 22 informants who were asked about advance care planning, 19 stated or implied that it was a dangerous violation of traditional Navajo values and way of thinking.

Communication patterns within families are also important concerns. The notion of family differs greatly by cultural group (Tseng & Hsu, 1991). The conception of "family" ranges from the traditional notion of the North American "nuclear family," composed of parents and children, to a much broader definition held by many other cultural groups that includes grandparents, cousins, and even ancestors. Culture mediates the power differentials within families, dictating domestic roles and, among other things, who among family members make most decisions (Gotay, 1996). Several studies have compared family structure and communication in different cultural groups. Becker, Beyene, Newsom, and Rodgers (1998) found that Hispanic and Filipino extended families played a considerable role in caregiving and decision-making, particularly compared to African Americans, and Orona et al. (1994) found the same phenomenon for Hispanic and Chinese families compared to Whites.

Treatment decision making can become complicated when cultural patterns dictate that the family instead of the physician or patient takes responsibility for treatment decisions (Sawyers & Eaton, 1992), especially when predominant family orientations and a strong collectivist identity can turn a patient's illness into a family illness (Sagara & Pickett, 1998; Nilchaikovit, Hill, & Holland, 1993). Muller and Desmond's (1992) case presentation of a Chinese family details the turmoil between health care professionals and a family over the care given to their mother, who was diagnosed as terminally ill with metastatic lung cancer. According to traditional Chinese culture, when a person's illness is life-threatening, it is assumed that the practitioner will talk to the family rather than the patient and that the family will take responsibility for treatment decisions. In this case, the differing expectations of the Chinese family and physicians about responsibility for decision making led to painful conflicts. The physicians, overriding the wishes of the family, wrote a "do not resuscitate" order for the patient, leaving the family hurt and upset.

Other unique communication patterns have been identified in Asian families. Orona et al. (1994) described dynamics among Chinese families who chose, knowing the reality of the situation, to maintain a tacit agreement not to acknowledge the underlying illness as cancer and to live in an "as if" world, primarily for the protection of the patient. Kagawa-Singer (1993) also found the practice of "as if," which the author depicted as patients' positive use of denial. Particularly with the Japanese American patients in the study, by avoiding open discussion of the disease "the patients seemed to feel that they were reducing the impact of the experience on their families . . . and it seemed to reduce unnecessary discomfort for their family and friends in a situation which could not be changed" (p. 302). One Japanese American male patient in the study held a public persona in which he did not acknowledge that he knew his diagnosis, although through private discussion it was apparent that the man did know of his cancer. Through "not knowing," he could continue with his daily routine and avoid awkwardness and maintain harmony in his family. Japanese American families may maintain a typically Japanese communication style which is subtle, nonverbal, and generally less direct than what is typical with many Americans (Sagara & Pickett, 1998).

INTERVENTION BUILDING ON CULTURAL FACTORS
IN COMMUNICATION

The Royal Children's Hospital in Melbourne, Australia, has developed a "cultural consultation service" to work with immigrant families seeking Western medical treatment. Eisenbruch and Handelman (1990) detailed the case of a Cambodian family with a child with a prognosis of terminal brain cancer. The family had limited prior exposure to Western medicine and held beliefs regarding treatment that differed starkly from those of the health care staff. For example, anesthesia posed a problem, as the family feared that with each use, their child's life would be reduced by 25 years. This was a major threat to their lives because anesthesia was required two or three times for operations. The cultural consultation service educated the staff about the family's concerns and beliefs and helped allay the family's fears by reminding them that their child actually "belongs to Buddha." Additionally, sensitivity was allowed during the family's informing the child of his terminal prognosis. Buddhists with a fatal illness may want to accumulate merit before dying, to help improve the patient's next incarnation. Thus, the family, rather than informing the child directly, let him learn of his prognosis during a merit-making ceremony, which was a supportive situation. The family's beliefs regarding causes for the disease were based in Buddhist notions of karma, as well as house spirits; these beliefs were respected and listened to with interest by the staff. This case demonstrates that with appropriate steps in the health care process, karma and other non-Western religious beliefs about the etiology of cancer do not necessarily preclude or contradict the use of standard medical treatments. This family, although never espousing etiological ideas based on Western biomedicine, complied with all treatment protocols and enabled their child to receive the best available Western health care.

LIVING WITH CANCER

Culture continues to influence patient and family well-being during the period of cancer treatment and recovery (Die Trill and Holland, 1993). Cultural differences related to the (noncancer specific) illness process have been investigated elsewhere (Nilchaikovit et al., 1993). However, although there is considerable literature on psychological and social adjustment to cancer, coping strategies, and quality of life in cancer patients and families (Classen, Koopman, Angell, & Spiegel, 1996; Dunkel-Schetter, Feinstein, Taylor, & Falke, 1992; Ganz, 1994; Gotay & Muraoka, 1998; Helgeson & Cohen, 1996; Irvine, Brown, Crooks, Roberts, & Browne, 1991; King et al., 1997; Tope, Ahles, & Silberfarb, 1993), surprisingly, very few studies have investigated whether cancer-specific outcomes vary according to ethnicity or culture.

Kagawa-Singer (1993) conducted semi-structured interviews with American-born Japanese ($N = 25$) and White ($N = 25$) cancer patients drawn from 8 private practices to determine interpretations of the cancer experience and coping styles. Both groups were found to hold the same goal, namely, to maintain a sense of self-integrity. However, fewer Japanese American men reported disturbance in their lives (29%) than did White men (83%), despite the fact that the Japanese American men were more likely to have more widespread, metastatic cancer. Kagawa-Singer (1993) theorized that these differences result from differences in cultural sanctions regarding the acceptability of dependency, as there appears to be more socially sanctioned means for Japanese American men to be both physically and emotionally dependent and accept nurturing. In contrast, Japanese American women reported almost twice the degree of distress (64%) than did White women (34%). The author suggests this results from the Japanese American woman's difficulty in accepting dependency, as in her role of mother she is the usual nurturer.

Kagawa-Singer, Wellisch, and Durvasula's (1997) study of White ($N = 12$), Chinese American ($N = 11$), and Japanese American ($N = 11$) breast cancer survivors found that both age and acculturation affected communication of distress. Older women, particularly older Asian women, were less likely to report depression. Less acculturated women reported fewer psychosocial problems and more medical problems than more acculturated Asian women, whose responses were similar to those of the White women. In addition, the White women were three times more likely to request help than were Japanese Americans and two times more likely than Chinese Americans to do so. These findings follow the authors' (culturally based) discussion relating to normative Western therapeutic modes of sharing aspects of experience, rather than the more indirect mode with minimal expression found among Asians. However, counter to the authors' hypothesis, Asian women did not appear to express more somatic distress than did White women.

Gotay, Holup, and Muraoka (1999) investigated well-being in multiethnic cancer survivors ($N = 704$) of Filipino, Hawaiian, Japanese, and White ancestry who were identified through a population-based cancer registry. Measures included standardized questionnaires of stress, depression, and affect. Multivariate analyses controlling for sociodemographic and clinical variables indicated that ethnicity was significantly related to stress, depression, and positive affect, primarily due to better outcomes in Japanese survivors. These findings imply that Japanese survivors may have experienced fewer problems and/or that they were less willing to admit to and discuss problems.

Only a few studies have focused on African Americans. Musick, Koenig, Hays, and Cohen (1998) investigated the relationship between religion and depression in African Americans ($N = 1636$) and Whites ($N = 1371$); their sample included individuals who had cancer, another chronic disease, or were disease-free. Results indicated that religious activity (as reflected in attendance at church services) was correlated with less depression for African Americans and particularly for cancer patients. The authors postulate that, historically, African American churches have served an important supportive role for their parishioners that is particularly helpful during a stressful event, such as cancer diagnosis and treatment.

Ashing-Giwa, Ganz, and Petersen's (1999) study of African American ($N = 117$) and White ($N = 161$) long-term breast cancer survivors found univariate differences between the groups on several standardized measures of quality of life, with African Americans expressing poorer quality of life, general self-rated health, and stress. However, in multivariate analyses controlling for demographic variables and life stress, no ethnic differences were found. The authors suggest that socioeconomic status, life stress, comorbidity, and living situation are important predictors of quality of life in breast cancer patients. This study points out the importance of considering additional variables that may be correlated with ethnicity, rather than concluding that differences among ethnic groups are due to ethnicity per se.

INTERVENTION BUILDING ON CULTURAL FACTORS IN LIVING WITH CANCER

To date, very few culturally tailored interventions to help patients living with cancer have been reported. Miano, Rojas, and Trujillo (1996) implemented a culturally-sensitive cancer support group for Hispanic patients after traditional support groups proved to be inappropriate for the Hispanic community. Hispanic cultural values were found to be incompatible with usual support group objectives such as developing insight, personal sharing, and intimate disclosure. For example, Miano et al. cited research showing Hispanics' preference for focusing on the present and coming up with concrete solutions, and noted issues of "saving face," dignity, and confidence. These factors interfered with patient participation in standard support groups. Noting the "inherent social nature of this population" (p. 201), the culturally-appropriate support group meetings (conducted in Spanish) were presented as informal get-togethers, where patients could obtain information, education, and support. The name of the program was called "Platicas y Merienda," which essentially means talk/conference and afternoon snack/break. The objective was to have patients become better acquainted with each other and to form informal social support networks. Feedback from participants was generally positive.

DISCUSSION

In this chapter, we have provided an overview of the ways that consideration of ethnic and cultural issues is important to understanding cancer. At each step in the continuum of cancer—from prevention, to screening, diagnosis, and living with cancer—culture has a significant influence on cancer-associated events. Cultural factors can elucidate understanding of variables, such as levels of knowledge, tobacco use, and use of screening tests, as well as variations in response to cancer, such as communication preferences and quality of life. Consideration of cultural factors including communication styles, beliefs, and values has been an important component of interventions directed at specific minority populations described here. Despite increased interest in cultural aspects of cancer prevention and control, considerable challenges lie ahead for both research and practice in this area. We will discuss several questions that need to receive attention in the future.

HOW DO CULTURAL FACTORS AFFECT REACTIONS TO CANCER THERAPY?

There is very little information available about how minority cancer patients respond to cancer therapy, how differences in symptoms are experienced, and how cultural beliefs and values may affect their reactions. The primary therapies used to treat cancer (e.g., surgery, radiation therapy, and chemotherapy) are powerful and have multiple side effects, including amputation (for surgery) and nausea, vomiting, and fatigue (for radiation and chemotherapy). In addition, the tumor itself may generate effects such as pain, while the experience of being diagnosed and treated for cancer may affect psychological status and disrupt family and employment activities. All of these areas may be affected by cultural factors.

HOW DO CULTURAL FACTORS AFFECT CANCER SURVIVORSHIP?

Many more cancer patients are living for extended periods or even being cured of cancer. This is a recent phenomenon: only one in five cancer patients survived five or more years in 1930 (Ganz, 1990), but today, this proportion has increased to approximately six in ten (American Cancer Society, 2001). Although considerable data are beginning to emerge about the long-term impact of cancer on survivors (Saleeba, Weitzner, & Meyers, 1996; Wyatt & Friedman, 1996), virtually no information has been reported on how quality of life may vary in cancer survivors in different ethnic groups. However, cultural factors, such as views of illness etiology, fatalism, and family concerns, may have a profound influence on cancer rehabilitation and survivor well-being, and such information will be critical in the future (Gotay & Muraoka, 1998).

HOW DO CULTURAL FACTORS AFFECT THE DEVELOPMENT OF SUPPORTIVE INTERVENTIONS FOR CANCER PATIENTS?

Considerable scientific data have demonstrated that psychosocial interventions provide positive benefits for cancer patients (Andersen, 1992). Such interventions include behavioral interventions, nonbehavioral counseling and therapy, informational and educational methods, and organized peer support (Meyer & Mark, 1995). However, since few non-White patients have participated in such studies (Meyer & Mark, 1995), information is not available about which approaches are more effective in different minority groups, what additional strategies may be warranted, and how existing models could be modified to make them more appropriate for additional populations. In addition to obvious concerns, such as making interventions available in the patient's preferred language, other cultural factors may affect whether an intervention is culturally sensitive. For example, based on evidence about communication styles reviewed in this chapter, it seems reasonable to assume that the direct and open communication that often characterizes support groups may not be as comfortable or supportive for Asian or Native American patients as it is for White patients. More investigation of such questions is warranted.

HOW CAN CULTURAL INFLUENCES BE DISTINGUISHED FROM ASPECTS OF SOCIOECONOMIC STATUS?

Minority ethnic group membership is linked disproportionately with low socioeconomic status. Certain cancer-related outcomes, such as knowledge about cancer and cancer prevention, may be a function of low levels of education. Other outcomes, such as use of screening tests, may be directly linked to lack of health insurance and lack of transportation to health care facilities. Living in poverty and associated stressors may affect the priority of cancer prevention and control in the context of other pressing concerns. Developing appropriate interventions requires distinguishing variation due to ethnic and cultural factors from those due to economic considerations.

WHAT IMPACT DOES CULTURAL BLENDING HAVE ON CANCER-RELATED VARIABLES?

Over the past several decades, metropolitan areas in the United States have become increasingly multicultural (Frey & Farley, 1996). The state of Hawaii may represent a case study in multiculturalism of the future, for not only is the population composed of many different ethnic groups, but also there is no majority ethnicity. Four ethnic groups make up 73% of Hawaii's 1.15 million residents: Japanese (19%), Hawaiian/part Hawaiian (19%), Caucasian (22%), and Filipino (13%) (State of Hawaii, 1999). Since most residential neighborhoods and social groups in Hawaii tend to be heterogeneous in terms of ethnic representation, most Hawaii residents' lifestyles include aspects of various cultural heritages. Further, in 1998, nearly one in two marriages in the state is between individuals of different ethnic/racial backgrounds (State of Hawaii, 1999). Thus, future populations will reflect a blending of cultural and racial heritages, and being able to assess ethnicity and its effects on cancer-related outcomes, as well as to design interventions targeted to any single ethnic or cultural group, will pose challenges. Instead of relying on ethnic or racial labels, researchers and program planners will increasingly be tasked with learning more about what culture means in terms of attitudes, behaviors, and preferences for interventions in order for programs to be culturally sensitive.

HOW DO CULTURAL PATTERNS PERSIST AND CHANGE OVER TIME?

Acculturation has frequently emerged as an important influence on cancer-related knowledge and attitudes and screening behaviors. Some aspects of acculturation seem to occur rapidly when immigrants move to a new location. However, other aspects of culture may persist indefinitely. In fact, immigrants may retain cultural practices that were standard in their country of origin at the time of immigration, even though those practices change over time in the parent country. Distinguishing between aspects of culture that quickly change and those that continue to exert a long-lasting impact on cancer-related attitudes and behaviors is an important and understudied area of research.

DO CANCER-RELATED CONCERNS REFLECT UNIQUE CULTURAL ISSUES?

Cancer presents a distinct health threat. It is one of the most feared diseases, the treatments are highly toxic, and it is often fatal. It is possible that a diagnosis of cancer mobilizes individuals to return to the core values of their ancestors and, thus, reflects an intensified impact of cultural factors on coping with disease. On the other hand, the effects of culture may be similar across health problems and concerns.

SUMMARY

Questions such as those listed here provide opportunities to contribute to both cultural and health research. Cancer provides an excellent model for examining a full spectrum of behavioral questions, ranging from how to promote healthy lifestyles through to how to assist individuals coping with disease, whether they are survivors or in terminal phases of disease. The fact that 1500 Americans die of cancer each day stands as a stark reminder of the need for research, as well as its tremendous potential to make a positive difference.

CASE STUDY

Cancer statistics indicate that Native Hawaiians are more than three times as likely to die of breast cancer than are women of Japanese ancestry in Hawaii, due, in part, to the fact that Native Hawaiian patients are diagnosed at a more advanced stage than patients of other ethnicities (LeMarchand & Kolonel, 1989). Community representatives, health professionals, and scientific researchers worked collaboratively to develop, implement, and evaluate an intervention to increase the use of cervical and breast screening in a Native Hawaiian community (Matsunaga, et al., 1996). The intervention—referred to as a Kokua Group—consisted of education and support delivered by trained health educators in a group setting. The groups incorporated traditional Hawaiian values of Kokua (defined as a mutual willingness to help, to help without an expectation of return, and without having to be asked), Aloha (Love), and Lokahi (Harmony), among others, and was conducted using a structured curriculum presented in "talk story" fashion. The Kokua Groups were led by specially trained community residents, and recruitment built on preexisting social bonds among community members. Five hundred women participated in the groups. Questionnaires measuring cancer-related knowledge, attitudes, and behaviors were administered before and after group participation.

Kokua Group participants demonstrated significant positive changes in knowledge, attitudes, and behavioral intentions before and after the group. With respect to behavioral intentions, significant changes were found for both Pap tests and mammograms: women moved along the continuum of behavioral change toward the objective of getting regular Pap tests or mammograms. Increases in intentions to obtain the screening tests were likely influenced by gains in knowledge during the Kokua Group and also by increases in confidence to negotiate successfully in the health care system. This approach, which is anchored in the mores of the community in which it is based, offers the prospect of reducing breast and cervical cancer mortality in this population (Banner et al., 1999; Gotay et al., 2000).

1. How were cultural values reflected in this intervention?
2. How could this approach be adapted to a different ethnic group?

ACKNOWLEDGMENTS

The preparation of this chapter was partially supported by awards from the National Institute of Aging (AG 16601) and the National Cancer Institute (Supplement to N01 CN 77001).

SUGGESTED READINGS

Gotay, C. C. (1996). Cultural variation in family adjustment to cancer. In L. Baider, C. L. Cooper, & A. Kaplan De-Nour (Eds.), *Cancer and the family* (pp. 31–52). West Sussex, UK: Wiley.
Hiatt, R. A., Pasick, R. J., Perez-Stable, E. J., McPhee, S. J., Engelstad, L., Lee, M., Sabogal, F., D'Onofrio, C. N., & Stewart, S. (1996). Pathways to early cancer detection in the multiethnic population of the San Francisco Bay Area. *Health Education Quarterly, 23* (Supplement), S10–S27.
Meyerowitz, B. E., Richardson, J., Hudson, S., & Leedham, B. (1998). Ethnicity and cancer outcomes: Behavioral and psychosocial considerations. *Psychological Bulletin, 123,* 47–70.

Nilchaikovit, T., Hill, J. M., & Holland, J. C. (1993). The effects of culture on illness behavior and medical care: Asian and American differences. *General Hospital Psychiatry, 15,* 41–50.

REFERENCES

Ali, N. S. (1996). Providing culturally sensitive care to Egyptians with cancer. *Cancer Practice, 4,* 212–215.

American Cancer Society. (2001). *Cancer facts & figures–2001.* Atlanta, GA: Author.

Andersen, B. L. (1992). Psychological interventions for cancer patients to enhance the quality of life. *Journal of Consulting and Clinical Psychology, 60,* 552–568.

Ashing-Giwa, K., & Ganz, P. A. (1997). Understanding the breast cancer experience of African-American women. *Journal of Psychosocial Oncology, 15,* 19–35.

Ashing-Giwa, K., Ganz, P. A., & Petersen, L. (1999). Quality of life of African-American and white long term breast carcinoma survivors. *Cancer, 85,* 418–426.

Bachman, J. G., Johnston, L. D., & O'Malley, P. M. (1991). *Monitoring the future: Questionnaire responses from the nation's high school seniors.* Ann Arbor, MI: Survey Research Center, Institute for Social Research, University of Michigan.

Banner, R. O., Gotay, C. C., Matsunaga, D. S., Hedlund, N., Enos, R., Issell, B. F., & DeCambra, H. (1999). The effects of a culturally-tailored intervention to increase breast and cervical cancer screening in Native Hawaiians. In C. S. Glover & F. S. Hodge (Eds.), *Native outreach: A lay report to American Indian, Alaska Native, and Native Hawaiian Communities* (pp. 45–55). Bethesda, MD: National Cancer Institute.

Bates, M. S., & Edwards, W. T. (1992). Ethnic variations in the chronic pain experience. *Ethnicity and Disease, 2,* 63–83.

Becker, G., Beyene, Y., Newsom, E. M., & Rodgers, D. V. (1998). Knowledge and care of chronic illness in three ethnic minority groups. *Family Medicine, 30,* 173–178.

Black, S. A., & Markides, K. S. (1993). Acculturation and alcohol consumption in Puerto Rican, Cuban-American, and Mexican-American women in the United States. *American Journal of Public Health, 83,* 890–893.

Blackhall, L. J., Murphy, S. T., Frank, G., Michel, V., & Azen, S. (1995). Ethnicity and attitudes toward patient autonomy [see comments]. *Journal of the American Medical Association, 274,* 820–825.

Blaisdell, R. K. (1998). Culture and cancer in Kanaka Maoli (Native Hawaiians). *Asian American and Pacific Islander Journal of Health, 6,* 400.

Brainard, J., & Zaharlick, A. (1989). Changing health beliefs and behaviors of resettled Laotian refugees: Ethnic variation in adaptation. *Social Science and Medicine, 29,* 845–852.

Braun, K. L., Look, M. A., & Tsark, J. A. (1995). High mortality rates in Native Hawaiians. *Hawaii Medical Journal, 54,* 723–729.

Breen, N., & Kessler, L. (1994). Changes in the use of screening mammography: Evidence from the 1987 and 1990 National Health Interview Surveys. *American Journal of Public Health, 84,* 62–67.

Breslow, R. A., Sorkin, J. D., Frey, C. M., & Kessler, L. G. (1997). Americans' knowledge of cancer risk and survival. *Preventive Medicine, 26,* 170–177.

Carrese, J. A., & Rhodes, L. A. (1995). Western bioethics on the Navajo reservation. Benefit or harm? [see comments]. *Journal of the American Medical Association, 274,* 826–829.

Centers for Disease Control. (1996). *Behavioral Risk Factor Surveillance System* (Online Prevalence Data). Available: http://www2.cdc.gov/nccdphp/brfss/index.asp.

Centers for Disease Control. (May–June, 1999). [On-line source]. National Center for Health Statistics, National Health Interview Survey. Available: http://raceandhealth.hhs.gov/TOC.HTM.

Champion, V., & Menon, U. (1997). Predicting mammography and breast self-examination in African American women. *Cancer Nursing, 20,* 315–322.

Chavez, L. R., Hubbell, F. A., McMullin, J. M., Martinez, R. G., & Mishra, S. I. (1995). Structure and meaning in models of breast and cervical cancer risk factors: A comparison of perceptions among Latinas, Anglo women, and physicians. *Medical Anthropology Quarterly, 9,* 40–74.

Chavez, L. R., Hubbell, F. A., Mishra, S. I., & Valdez, R. B. (1997). The influence of fatalism on self-reported use of Papanicolaou smears. *American Journal of Preventive Medicine, 13,* 418–424.

Chung, C. S., Tash, E., Raymond, J., Yasunobu, C., & Lew, R. (1990). Health risk behaviors and ethnicity in Hawaii. *International Journal of Epidemiology, 19,* 1011–1018.

Classen, C., Koopman, C., Angell, K., & Spiegel, D. (1996). Coping styles associated with psychological adjustment to advanced breast cancer. *Health Psychology, 15,* 434–437.

Cuellar, I., Harris, L. C., & Jasso, R. (1980). An acculturation scale for Mexican American normal and clinical populations. *Hispanic Journal of Behavioral Sciences, 2,* 199–217.

Delvecchio-Good, M., Good, B. J., Schaffer, C., & Lind, S. E. (1990). American oncology and the discourse on hope. *Culture, Medicine and Psychiatry, 14,* 59–79.

Demark-Wahnefried, W., Strigo, T., Catoe, K., Conaway, M., Brunetti, M., Rimer, B. K., & Robertson, C. N. (1995). Knowledge, beliefs, and prior screening behavior among blacks and whites reporting for prostate cancer screening. *Urology, 46,* 346–351.

Die Trill, M., & Holland, J. (1993). Cross-cultural differences in the care of patients with cancer: A review. *General Hospital Psychiatry, 15,* 21–30.

Dibble, S. L., Vanoni, J. M., & Miaskowski, C. (1997). Women's attitudes toward breast cancer screening procedures: Differences by ethnicity. *Women's Health Issues, 7,* 47–54.

Dodd, M. J., Chen, S., Lindsey, A. M., & Piper, B. F. (1985). Attitudes of patients living in Taiwan about cancer and its treatment. *Cancer Nursing, 8,* 214–220.

Doll, R. (1998). Epidemiological evidence of the effects of behavior and the environment on the risk of human cancer. *Recent Results in Cancer Research, 154,* 3–21.

Doll, R., & Peto, R. (1981). The causes of cancer: Quantitative estimates of avoidable risks of cancer in the United States today. *Journal of the National Cancer Institute, 66,* 1191–1308.

Dunkel–Schetter, C., Feinstein, L. G., Taylor, S. E., & Falke, R. L. (1992). Patterns of coping with cancer. *Health Psychology, 11,* 79–87.

Eaton, W. W. (1980). *The sociology of mental illness.* New York: Praeger.

Eisenbruch, M., & Handelman, L. (1990). Cultural consultation for cancer: Astrocytoma in a Cambodian adolescent. *Social Science and Medicine, 31,* 1295–1299.

Elder, J. P., Castro, F. G., de Moor, C., Mayer, J., Candelaria, J. I., Campbell, N., Talavera, G., & Ware, L. M. (1991). Differences in cancer-risk-related behaviors in Latino and Anglo adults. *Preventive Medicine, 20,* 751–763.

Elmore, J. G., Moceri, V. M., Carter, D., & Larson, E. B. (1998). Breast carcinoma tumor characteristics in black and white women. *Cancer, 83,* 2509–2515.

Frey, W. H., & Farley, R. (1996). Latino, Asian, and black segregation in United States metropolitan areas: Are multiethnic metros different? *Demography, 33,* 35–50.

Friedman, L. C., Webb, J. A., Weinberg, A. D., Lane, M., Cooper, H. P., & Woodruff, A. (1995). Breast cancer screening: Racial/ethnic differences in behaviors and beliefs. *Journal of Cancer Education, 10,* 213–216.

Friis, R. H., & Sellers, T. A. (1999). *Epidemiology for public health practice.* (2nd ed.). Gaithersburg, MD: Aspen Publishers, Inc.

Ganz, P. (1990). Abolishing the myths: The facts about cancer. In F. Mullan & B. Hoffman (Eds.), *An almanac of practical resources for cancer survivors* (pp. 7–30). Mount Vernon, NY: Consumers Union.

Ganz, P. A. (1994). Quality of life and the patient with cancer: Individual and policy implications. *Cancer, 74* (4 Suppl), 1445–1452.

Garcia, H. B., & Lee, P. C. Y. (1989). Knowledge about cancer and use of health care services among Hispanic- and Asian-American older adults. *Journal of Psychosocial Oncology, 6,* 157–177.

Gordon, A. K. (1995). Deterrents to access and service for blacks and Hispanics: The Medicare Hospice Benefit, healthcare utilization, and cultural barriers. *Hospice Journal, 10,* 65–83.

Gotay, C. C. (1996). Cultural variation in family adjustment to cancer. In L. Baider, C. L. Cooper, & A. Kaplan De-Nour (Eds.), *Cancer and the family* (pp. 31–52). West Sussex, UK: Wiley.

Gotay, C. C., & Muraoka, M. Y. (1998). Quality of life in long-term survivors of adult-onset cancers. *Journal of the National Cancer Institute, 90,* 656–667.

Gotay, C. C., & Wilson, M. E. (1998). Social support and cancer screening in African American, Hispanic, and Native American women. *Cancer Practice, 6,* 31–37.

Gotay, C. C., Banner, R. O., Matsunaga, D. S., Hedlund, N., Enos, R., Issell, B. F., DeCambra, H. (2000). The impact of a culturally-appropriate intervention to increase breast and cervical screening among Native Hawaiian women. *Preventive Medicine, 31,* 529–537.

Gotay, C. C., Holup, J., & Muraoka, M. (1999, March). *Predicting well-being in multi-ethnic cancer survivors.* Poster presentation at the National Cancer Institute Conference on Research Challenges and Opportunities for the New Millennium. Bethesda, MD.

Greenlee, R. T., Murray, T., Bolden, S., and Wingo, P. A. (2000). Cancer statistics, 2000. *CA, 50,* 7–33.

Harmon, M. P., Castro, F. G., & Coe, K. (1996). Acculturation and cervical cancer: Knowledge, beliefs, and behaviors of Hispanic women. *Women's Health, 24,* 37–57.

Helgeson, V. S., & Cohen, S. (1996). Social support and adjustment to cancer: Reconciling descriptive, correlational, and intervention research. *Health Psychology, 15,* 135–148.

Hiatt, R. A., Pasick, R. J., Perez-Stable, E. J., McPhee, S. J., Engelstad, L., Lee, M., Sabogal, F., D'Onofrio, C. N., & Stewart, S. (1996). Pathways to early cancer detection in the multiethnic population of the San Francisco Bay Area. *Health Education Quarterly, 23* (Supplement), S10–S27.

Hodge, F. S., Fredericks, L., & Rodriguez, B. (1996). American Indian women's talking circle: A cervical cancer screening and prevention project. *Cancer, 78* (7 Suppl.), 1592–1597.

Hoffman-Goetz, L., Breen, N. L., & Meissner, H. (1998). The impact of social class on the use of cancer screening within three racial/ethnic groups in the United States. *Ethnicity and Disease, 8,* 43–51.

Hubbell, F. A., Chavez, L. R., Mishra, S. I., & Valdez, R. B. (1996a). Differing beliefs about breast cancer among Latinas and Anglo women. *Western Journal of Medicine, 164,* 405–409.

Hubbell, F. A., Chavez, L. R., Mishra, S. I., & Valdez, R. B. (1996b). Beliefs about sexual behavior and other predictors of Papanicolaou smear screening among Latinas and Anglo women. *Archives of Internal Medicine, 156,* 2353–2358.

Irvine, D., Brown, B., Crooks, D., Roberts, J., & Browne, G. (1991). Psychosocial adjustment in women with breast cancer. *Cancer, 67,* 1097–1117.

Jenkins, C. N., McPhee, S. J., Bird, J. A., & Bonilla, N. T. (1990). Cancer risks and prevention practices among Vietnamese refugees [published erratum appears in Western Journal of Medicine 1990 Sep;153(3):331]. *Western Journal of Medicine, 153,* 34–39.

Jennings, K. M. (1997). Getting a Pap smear: Focus group responses of African American and Latina women. *Oncology Nursing Forum, 24,* 827–835.

Jepson, C., Kessler, L. G., Portnoy, B., & Gibbs, T. (1991). Black–white differences in cancer prevention knowledge and behavior. *American Journal of Public Health, 81,* 501–504.

Kagawa-Singer, M. (1993). Redefining health: Living with cancer. *Social Science and Medicine, 37,* 295–304.

Kagawa-Singer, M. (1994). Cross-cultural views of disability. *Rehabilitation Nursing, 19,* 362–365.

Kagawa-Singer, M. (1998). Cancer and Asian American cultures. *Asian American and Pacific Islander Journal of Health, 6,* 383–399.

Kagawa-Singer, M., Wellisch, D. K., & Durvasula, R. (1997). Impact of breast cancer on Asian American and Anglo American women. *Culture, Medicine and Psychiatry, 21,* 449–480.

Kang, S. H., & Bloom, J. R. (1993). Social support and cancer screening among older black Americans. *Journal of the National Cancer Institute, 85,* 737–742.

Kaur, J. S. (1996). The potential impact of cancer survivors on Native American cancer prevention and treatment. *Cancer, 78,* (7 Suppl.), 1578–1581.

Kelly, A. W., Fores-Chacori, M., Wollan, P. C., Trapp, M. A., Weaver, A. L., Barrier, P. A., Franz, W. B., III, & Kottke, T. E. (1996). A program to increase breast and cervical cancer screening for Cambodian women in a midwestern community. *Mayo Clinic Proceedings, 71,* 437–444.

Kim, K., Yu, E. S., Chen, E. H., Kim, J., & Brintnall, R. A. (1998). Colorectal cancer screening: Knowledge and practices among Korean Americans. *Cancer Practice, 6,* 167–175.

King, C. R., Haberman, M., Berry, D. L., Bush, N., Butler, L., Dow, K. H., Ferrell, B., Grant, M., Gue, D., Hinds, P., Kreuer, J., Padilla, G., & Underwood, S. (1997). Quality of life and the cancer experience: The state-of-the-knowledge. *Oncology Nursing Forum, 24,* 27–41.

Klonoff, E. A., & Landrine, H. (1996). Acculturation and cigarette smoking among African American adults. *Journal of Behavioral Medicine, 19,* 501–514.

Koenig, B. A., & Gates-Williams, J. (1995). Understanding cultural difference in caring for dying patients. *Western Journal of Medicine, 163,* 244–249.

LeMarchand, L., & Kolonel, L. N. (1989). Cancer Epidemiology and prevention. In E. Wegner (Ed.), *Social process in Hawaii: Vol. 32. The health of Native Hawaiians: A selective report on health status and health care in the 1980's* (pp. 134–148). Honolulu, HI: University of Hawaii Press.

Li, F. P., & Pawlish, K. (1998). Cancers in Asian Americans and Pacific Islanders: Migrant studies. *Asian American and Pacific Islander Journal of Health, 6,* 123–129.

Lichtenstein, E., & Lopez, K. (1999). Enhancing tobacco control policies in Northwest Indian Tribes. In National Cancer Institute, *Native outreach: A report to American Indian, Alaska Native, and Native Hawaiian Communities* (pp. 57–65). National Institute of Health, MA: Office of Special Populations Research.

Lin-Fu, J. S. (1998). Advances in genetics: Issues for United States racial and ethnic minorities: An Asian American and Pacific Islander perspective. *Community Genetics, 1,* 124–129.

Lipkus, I. M., Rimer, B. K., Lyna, P. R., Pradhan, A. A., Conaway, M., & Woods-Powell, C. T. (1996). Colorectal screening patterns and perceptions of risk among African-American users of a community health center. *Journal of Community Health, 21,* 409–427.

Lobell, M., Bay, R. C., Rhoads, K. V., & Keske, B. (1998). Barriers to cancer screening in Mexican-American women [see comments]. *Mayo Clinic Proceedings, 73,* 301–308.

Loehrer, P. J., Sr., Greger, H. A., Weinberger, M., Musick, B., Miller, M., Nichols, C., Bryan, J., Higgs, D., & Brock, D. (1991). Knowledge and beliefs about cancer in a socioeconomically disadvantaged population. *Cancer, 68,* 1665–1671.

Longman, A. J., Saint-Germain, M. A., & Modiano, M. (1992). Use of breast cancer screening by older Hispanic women. *Public Health Nursing, 9,* 118–124.

Lovejoy, N. C., Jenkins, C., Wu, T., Shankland, S., & Wilson, C. (1989). Developing a breast cancer screening program for Chinese-American women. *Oncology Nursing Forum, 16,* 181–187.

Marin, G., Perez-Stable, E. J., & Marin, B. V. (1989). Cigarette smoking among San Francisco Hispanics: The role of acculturation and gender. *American Journal of Public Health, 79,* 196–198.

Martinez, R. G., Chavez, L. R., & Hubbell, F. A. (1997). Purity and passion: Risk and morality in Latina immigrants' and physicians' beliefs about cervical cancer. *Medical Anthropology, 17,* 337–362.

Mathews, H. F., Lannin, D. R., & Mitchell, J. P. (1994). Coming to terms with advanced breast cancer: Black women's narratives from eastern North Carolina. *Social Science and Medicine, 38,* 789–800.

Matsunaga, D. S., Enos, R., Gotay, C. C., Banner, R. O., DeCambra, H., Hammond, O. W., Hedlund, N., Ilaban, E. K., Issell, B. F., & Tsark, J. A. (1996). Participatory research in a Native Hawaiian community: The Wai`anae cancer research project. *Cancer, 78,* 1582–1586

Maxwell, A. E., Bastani, R., & Warda, U. S. (1997). Breast cancer screening and related attitudes among Filipino-American women. *Cancer Epidemiology Biomarkers and Prevention, 6,* 719–726.

Maxwell, A. E., Bastani, R., & Warda, U. S. (1998). Mammography utilization and related attitudes among Korean-American women. *Women's Health, 27,* 89–107.

McAlister, A. L., Fernandez-Esquer, M. E., Ramirez, A. G., Trevino, F., Gallion, K. J., Villarreal, R., Pulley, L. V., Hu, S., Torres, I., & Zhang, Q. (1995). Community level cancer control in a Texas barrio: Part II–Base-line and preliminary outcome findings. *Journal of the National Cancer Institute Monographs, 18,* 123–126.

McPhee, S. J., Bird, J. A., Davis, T., Ha, N. T., Jenkins, C. N., & Le, B. (1997). Barriers to breast and cervical cancer screening among Vietnamese-American women. *American Journal of Preventive Medicine, 13,* 205–213.

McPhee, S. J., Bird, J. A., Ha, N., Jenkins, C. N. H., Fordham, D., & Le, B. (1996). Pathways to early cancer detection for Vietnamese women: Suc khoe la vang! (Health is Gold!). *Health Education Quarterly, 23* (Supplement), S60–S75.

Meyer, T. J., & Mark, M. M. (1995). Effects of psychosocial interventions with adult cancer patients: A meta-analysis of randomized experiments [see comments]. *Health Psychology, 14,* 101–108.

Meyerowitz, B. E., Richardson, J., Hudson, S., & Leedham, B. (1998). Ethnicity and cancer outcomes: Behavioral and psychosocial considerations. *Psychological Bulletin, 123,* 47–70.

Miano, L. Y., Rojas, M. S., and Trujillo, M. (1996). Platicas y merienda: Reaching Spanish-speaking patients in an oncology setting. *Cancer Practices, 4,* 199–203.

Miller, A. M., & Champion, V. L. (1997). Attitudes about breast cancer and mammography: Racial, income, and educational differences. *Women's Health, 26,* 41–63.

Mishra, S. I., Luce-Aoelua, P., & Hubbell, F. A. (1998). Identifying the cancer control needs of American Samoans. *Asian American and Pacific Islander Journal of Health, 6,* 277–285.

Mitchell, J. L. (1998). Cross-cultural issues in the disclosure of cancer. *Cancer Practice, 6,* 153–160.

Mo, B. (1992). Modesty, sexuality, and breast health in Chinese-American women. *Western Journal of Medicine, 157,* 260–264.

Moeschberger, M. L., Anderson, J., Kuo, Y. F., Chen, M. S., Jr., Wewers, M. E., & Guthrie, R. (1997). Multivariate profile of smoking in Southeast Asian men: A biochemically verified analysis. *Preventive Medicine, 26,* 53–58.

Morgan, C., Park, E., & Cortes, D. E. (1995). Beliefs, knowledge, and behavior about cancer among urban Hispanic women. *Journal of the National Cancer Institute Monographs, 18,* 57–63.

Muller, J. H., & Desmond, B. (1992). Ethical dilemmas in a cross-cultural context: A Chinese example. *Western Journal of Medicine, 157,* 323–327.

Musick, M. A., Koenig, H. G., Hays, J. C., & Cohen, H. J. (1998). Religious activity and depression among community-dwelling elderly persons with cancer: The moderating effect of race. *Journals of Gerontology: Psychological Sciences and Social Sciences, 53,* S218–S227.

National Cancer Institute (1998). *Pap tests: A healthy habit for life* (NIH Publication No. 98-3213): National Institutes of Health, Public Health Service.

Nilchaikovit, T., Hill, J. M., & Holland, J. C. (1993). The effects of culture on illness behavior and medical care: Asian and American differences. *General Hospital Psychiatry, 15,* 41–50.

Novack, D. H., Plumer, R., Smith, R. L., Ochitill, H., Morrow, G. R., & Bennett, J. M. (1979). Changes in physicians' attitudes toward telling the cancer patient. *Journal of the American Medical Association, 241,* 897–900.

Okazaki, S., & Sue, S. (1995). Methodological issues in assessment research with ethnic minorities. *Psychological Assessment, 7,* 367–375.

O'Malley, A. S., Kerner, J., Johnson, A. E., & Mandelblatt, J. (1999). Acculturation and breast cancer screening among Hispanic women in New York City. *American Journal of Public Health, 89,* 219–227.

Orona, C. J., Koenig, B. A., & Davis, A. J. (1994). Cultural aspects of nondisclosure. *Cambridge Quarterly of Healthcare Ethics, 3,* 338–346.

Otero-Sabogal, R., Sabogal, F., Perez-Stable, E. J., & Hiatt, R. A. (1995). Dietary practices, alcohol consumption, and smoking behavior: Ethnic, sex, and acculturation differences. *Journal of the National Cancer Institute Monographs, 18,* 73–82.

Pachter, L. M. (1994). Culture and clinical care: Folk illness beliefs and behaviors and their implications for health care delivery. *Journal of the American Medical Association, 271,* 690–694.

Pasick, R. J., D'Onofrio, C. N., & Otero-Sabogal, R. (1996). Similarities and differences across cultures: Questions to inform a third generation for health promotion research. *Health Education Quarterly, 23* (Supplement), S142–S161.

Perera, F. P. (1997). Environment and cancer: Who are susceptible? *Science, 278,* 1068–1073.

Perez-Stable, E. J., Sabogal, F., Otero-Sabogal, R., Hiatt, R. A., & McPhee, S. J. (1992). Misconceptions about cancer among Latinos and Anglos. *Journal of the American Medical Association, 268,* 3219–3223.

Perkins, P., Cooksley, C. D., & Cox, J. D. (1996). Breast cancer: Is ethnicity an independent prognostic factor for survival? *Cancer, 78,* 1241–1247.

Pham, C. T., & McPhee, S. J. (1992). Knowledge, attitudes, and practices of breast and cervical cancer screening among Vietnamese women. *Journal of Cancer Education, 7,* 305–310.

Phinney, J. (1990). Ethnic identity in adolescents and adults: Review of research. *Psychological Bulletin, 108,* 499–514.

Powe, B. D. (1996). Cancer fatalism among African-Americans: A review of the literature. *Nursing Outlook, 44,* 18–21.

Price, J. H., Colvin, T. L., & Smith, D. (1993). Prostate cancer: Perceptions of African-American males. *Journal of the National Medical Association, 85,* 941–947.

Price, J. H., Desmond, S. M., Wallace, M., Smith, D., & Stewart, P. M. (1988). Differences in black and white adolescents' perceptions about cancer. *Journal of School Health, 58,* 66–70.

Ramirez, A. G., McAlister, A., Gallion, K. J., Ramirez, V., Garza, I. R., Stamm, K., de la Torre, J., & Chalela, P. (1995). Community level cancer control in a Texas barrio: Part I–Theoretical basis, implementation, and process evaluation. *Journal of the National Cancer Institute Monographs, 18,* 117–122.

Sabogal, F., Otero-Sabogal, R., Pasick, R., Jenkins, C., & Perez-Stable, E. J. (1996). Printed health education materials for diverse cultures: Lessons learned from Vietnamese and Latina communities. *Health Education Quarterly, 23* (Supplement), S123–S141.

Sagara, M., & Pickett, M. (1998). Sociocultural influences and care of dying children in Japan and the United States. *Cancer Nursing, 21,* 274–281.

Saint-Germain, M. A., & Longman, A. J. (1993). Breast cancer screening among older Hispanic women: Knowledge, attitudes, and practices. *Health Education Quarterly, 20,* 539–553.

Saleeba, A., Weitzner, M., & Meyers, C. (1996). Subclinical psychological distress in long-term survivors of breast cancer: A preliminary communication. *Journal of Psychosocial Oncology, 14,* 83–93.

Sawyers, J. E., & Eaton, L. (1992). Gastric cancer in the Korean-American: Cultural implications. *Oncology Nursing Forum, 19,* 619–623.

Schaefer, D. S. (1983). Issues related to psychosocial intervention with Hispanic families in pediatric cancer setting. *Journal of Psychosocial Oncology, 1,* 39–46.

Smith, G. E., DeHaven, M. J., Grundig, J. P., & Wilson, G. R. (1997). African-American males and prostate cancer: Assessing knowledge levels in the community. *Journal of the National Medical Association, 89,* 387–391.

State of Hawaii. (1999). *Hawaii state data book.* Honolulu, HI: Department of Business, Economic Development and Tourism.

Stein, J. A., Fox, S. A., & Murata, P. J. (1991). The influence of ethnicity, socioeconomic status, and psychological barriers on use of mammography. *Journal of Health and Social Behavior, 32,* 101–113.

Suarez, L., Lloyd, L., Weiss, N., Rainbolt, T., & Pulley, L. (1994). Effect of social networks on cancer-screening behavior of older Mexican-American women. *Journal of the National Cancer Institute, 86,* 775–779.

Sung, J. F., Blumenthal, D. S., Coates, R. J., & Alema-Mensah, E. (1997). Knowledge, beliefs, attitudes, and cancer screening among inner-city African-American women. *Journal of the National Medical Association, 89,* 405–411.

Thomas, D. (1988). *Distinguishing culture and ethnicity in research involving ethnic minorities.* Paper presented at the Heterogeneity in Cross-Cultural Psychology, the Ninth International Conference for the International Association for Cross-Cultural Psychology, Newcastle.

Thomas, D. B., & Karagas, M. R. (1987). Cancer in first and second generation Americans. *Cancer Research, 47,* 5771–5776.

Thomas, D. B., & Karagas, M. R. (1996). Migrant studies. In D. Schottenfeld & J. F. Fraumeni (Eds.), *Cancer epidemiology and prevention* (2nd ed., pp. 236–254). New York: Oxford University Press.

Tope, D. M., Ahles, T. A., & Silberfarb, P. M. (1993). Psycho-oncology: Psychological well-being as one component of quality of life. *Psychotherapy and Psychosomatics, 60,* 129–147.

Tosomeen, A. H., Marquez, M. A., Panser, L. A., & Kottke, T. E. (1996). Developing preventive health programs for recent immigrants. *Minnesota Medicine, 79,* 46–48.

Tseng, W.-S., & Hsu, J. (1991). *Culture and family.* Binghamton, NY: Haworth Press.

Uba, L. (1992). Cultural barriers to health care for southeast Asian refugees. *Public Health Reports, 107,* 544–548.

USDHHS. (1998). *Tobacco use among United States racial/ethnic minority groups—African Americans, Mexican Indians and Alaskan Natives, Asian Americans and Pacific Islanders, and Hispanics: A report of the Surgeon General.* Atlanta, GA: Centers for Disease Control and Prevention, National Center for Chronic Disease Prevention and Health Promotion, Office of Smoking and Health.

U. S. Preventive Services Task Force. (1995). *Guide to clinical preventive services, 2nd ed.* Washington, DC: United States Department of Health and Human Services.

Winkleby, M. A., Albright, C. L., Howard-Pitney, B., Lin, J., & Fortmann, S. P. (1994). Hispanic/white differences in dietary fat intake among low educated adults and children. *Preventive Medicine, 23,* 465–473.

Wismer, B. A., Moskowitz, J. M., Chen, A. M., Kang, S. H., Novotny, T. E., Min, K., Lew, R., & Tager, I. B. (1998). Mammography and clinical breast examination among Korean American women in two California counties. *Preventive Medicine, 27,* 144–151.

Wyatt, G., & Friedman, L. L. (1996). Long-term female cancer survivors: Quality of life issues and clinical implications. *Cancer Nursing, 19,* 1–7.

Yi, J. K. (1994). Breast cancer screening practices by Vietnamese women. *Journal of Women's Health, 3,* 205–213.

Yi, J. K. (1995). Acculturation, access to care and use of preventive health services by Vietnamese women. *Asian American and Pacific Islander Journal of Health, 3,* 31–41.

Yi, J. K. (1998). Acculturation and Pap smear screening practices among college-aged Vietnamese women in the United States. *Cancer Nursing, 21,* 335–341.

8

CULTURALLY TAILORING HIV/AIDS PREVENTION PROGRAMS: WHY, WHEN, AND HOW

ANITA RAJ AND HORTENSIA AMARO

School of Public Health
Boston University
Boston, Massachusetts

ELIZABETH REED

Department of Endocrinology
Brigham and Women's Hospital
Boston, Massachusetts

The HIV/AIDS pandemic has had a negative impact on millions of people across the world. The Joint United Nations Programme on HIV/AIDS (UNAIDS, 1997) estimates that 30.6 million adults and children worldwide were living with HIV/AIDS at the end of 1997. The Centers for Disease Control (CDC, 1999) reported that, through June 1998, an estimated 350,000 adults and children were living with HIV/AIDS in the United States. Although HIV/AIDS has had an impact on all nations and all communities, certain nations and groups have been harder hit than others. Over 90% of current HIV/AIDS cases are in developing countries, with sub-Saharan Africa holding one-third of the total number of HIV/AIDS cases in the world (UNAIDS, 1997). In industrialized countries such as the United States, lower-income, culturally diverse groups report higher seroprevalence rates than are found among the higher-income, majority populations. Among American men, African Americans and Hispanics account for 60% of reported HIV cases; among women, African Americans and Hispanics account for 78% of reported cases (CDC, 1999). These findings are particularly staggering as African Americans make up only 12.1% and Hispanics only 11.4% of the U.S. population (U.S. Bureau of the Census, 1999).

Handbook of Cultural Health Psychology
195
Copyright © 2001 by Academic Press.
All rights of reproduction in any form reserved.

The disproportionate impact of HIV/AIDS within the United States has not been felt solely by racial/ethnic "minority" groups. Men who have sex with men (MSMs), injection drug users (IDUs), sexually active adolescents, and women who have sex with men have also been heavily hit by this health crisis. Again, the racial/ethnic minority groups within these populations have been the most severely affected (CDC, 1999). Further, these groups continue to be hard hit, despite the fact that they reside in a country that is not only wealthy, but also capable of providing access to the most advanced HIV-related medical technologies available. Global analysis of who is most directly affected by the HIV/AIDS pandemic yields diverse groups with a single common point: They are marginalized within their societies. Whether oppressed because of race, class, gender, or nonconformity to socially prescribed behaviors (e.g., MSMs, IDUs, or commercial sex workers [CSWs]), each of these hardest-hit groups is composed of second-class citizens from both the macro level (developing world versus industrialized world) to the micro level (poor individual versus wealthy individual).

Because the most oppressed groups are at greatest risk for HIV/AIDS, prevention efforts must be focused on multiple levels if the pandemic is to be controlled. Specifically, there must be a systemic intervention designed to reduce marginalization of hard-hit groups; smaller-level change cannot be sustained without such larger-level social change. However, systemic change is a long-term goal; because thousands die daily, we also need shorter-term solutions. Smaller interventions designed to improve HIV-risk reduction among groups with high seroprevalence rates are necessary for more immediate results. The purpose of this chapter is to identify specific issues and strategies relevant to groups at higher risk for HIV/AIDS. Identification of these issues and strategies is important not only to guide subsequent program development and research tailored to these groups but also to model the process by which cultural tailoring can occur. For the purpose of this chapter, we focus on cultural groups in the United States for whom higher HIV seroprevalence rates are reported. We have focused on the United States due to the country's higher overall seroprevalence, its cultural diversity, its disproportionate seroprevalence rates, and the authors' familiarity with United States subpopulations.

THE NEED FOR CULTURALLY
TAILORED PROGRAMS

What is culture? The *Oxford American Dictionary* (Ehrlich, Flexner, Carruth, & Hawkins, 1980) defines culture as "the customs and civilization of a particular people or group" (p. 155). Anthropologists describe culture as a "set of guidelines (both explicit and implicit) which individuals inherit as members of a particular society (or group) and which tells them how to view the world, how to experience it emotionally, and how to behave in it . . ." (Helman, 1994, p. 2). Public health defines culture as "including mores, norms, and ideologies of an individual or a community which has a profound effect on their response to health education and health promotion" (Modeste, 1996, p. 27). All of these meanings define culture as social doctrines taken on by a group, and this group may be based on any unifying social phenomenon: race/ethnicity, gender, class, religion, sexual orientation, region, national origin, age, and so forth.

Within any society there are numerous cultures and subcultures, and any given individual can be affiliated with multiple cultures and subcultures. For example, American cultures include those of a variety of racial/ethnic groups, immigrant culture, women's culture, adolescent culture, lesbian culture, and college culture, just to name a few. An individual living in the United States may be an African American female who is also an immigrant, an adolescent, a lesbian, and in college; thus, her cultural makeup as an individual may be composed to varying degrees of all of these cultures as well as the overall American culture. Hanson (1992) acknowledges that culture is not developed from a rigid set of instructions, but rather from "a framework through which actions are filtered or checked as individuals go about daily life" (p. 3). People may have similar cultural backgrounds and not behave in similar manners. Therefore one's behavior may be influenced by ethnic background as well as other factors, such as socioeconomic status, sex, age, length of time living in particular residence, and level of education (Hanson, 1992).

Helman (1994) states that culture must always be viewed in social context (historical, economical, political) and will always be influenced by outside forces. As mentioned previously, certain cultural groups have been harder hit by the HIV/AIDS pandemic because of the oppression under which many of these groups exist. However, American HIV-prevention programs do not always target these marginalized cultural groups, despite epidemiological data demonstrating need. For example, among MSMs, 5-year increases in AIDS rates are highest among American Indian/Alaskan Natives (Sullivan, 1995); yet, there are no publications on the existence of HIV-prevention programs for this subpopulation.

Although culture can mean many things, in the United States it is often defined as race/ethnicity due to the diversity of racial/ethnic groups as well as the history and continued existence of racial hierarchy within the country. Consequently, racial/ethnic groups are the primary defined cultures of people in the United States, and racial/ethnic identity is one of the most common ways in which individuals define themselves. Further, ethnic identity development and subsequent exploration, knowledge, and acceptance of one's cultural group have been linked to healthier psychological development of individuals in marginalized racial/ethnic groups (Atkins, Morten, & Sue, 1983; Cross, 1978; Helms, 1990; Kim, 1981; Marcia, 1966; Phinney, 1989, 1993). However, in the United States there tends to be an oversimplification of the term culture when used in reference to one's ethnicity. When one looks at the manner in which groups are classified under race/ethnicity in the United States, five primary groups emerge: African American, Hispanic, Caucasian, Native American/Alaskan, and Asian/Pacific Islander. However, individuals who identify themselves as Hispanic may be Dominican, Puerto Rican, Mexican, Cuban, or of many other possible national origins, many of which have very different cultural practices or characteristics. Therefore, it is important to note the existence of subpopulations within these five primary groups that often differ in cultural attitudes, behaviors, and other characteristics. Despite these intragroup differences, race/ethnic affiliation has been identified and defined in the United States as a factor that identifies people at increased risk for HIV. For the purpose of this chapter, cultural groups will be defined as racial/ethnic groups.

WHY MUST PROGRAMS BE CULTURALLY TAILORED?

The importance of cultural sensitivity in HIV-prevention programs is commonly discussed among HIV/AIDS researchers (Auerbach, Wypijewska, & Brodie, 1994). Because AIDS and behaviors related to HIV transmission (e.g., sex, injection drug use) are taboo across many cultures and the meaning of AIDS- and HIV-related behaviors may be different across cultures, many HIV researchers and practitioners argue that cultural tailoring is absolutely necessary for effective intervention. Individually based behavioral theory, commonly used in HIV prevention efforts in the United States, also operates differently for different ethnic groups, with such theory more predictive of HIV risk for Caucasian Americans than for Hispanic Americans, African Americans, and Asian Americans (Steers, Elliot, Nemiro, Ditman, & Oskamp, 1996). Further, Wyatt, Forge, and Guthrie (1998), in their study with African American, Hispanic (Mexican origin), and Caucasian women, found that there were different patterns of sexual risk-taking for each racial/ethnic group. This reinforces the need for development of programs that meet the needs of specific groups.

Although few researchers dispute the need for culturally sensitive programs, some researchers argue that, within HIV research and practice, culture has been used to characterize risk groups in a way that further marginalizes the people in these groups (Schiller, Crystal, & Lewellen, 1994). These authors state that "the widespread interest in culture as an explanatory variable in describing the evolution of the epidemic . . . has tended to reflect a usage of culture that. . . portrays AIDS as a disease residing in distant and separate populations" (p.1337). This framework has not only characterized groups such as gay men or lower income ethnic minority women as high-risk groups, it has also allowed the HIV-prevention needs of so-called "low-risk groups," such as adolescents and women in longer-term relationships, to be ignored.

Further, research that overgeneralizes runs the risk of perpetuating stereotypes. Research on MSMs has focused primarily on middle-class Caucasian men who frequent bars; research on IDUs has focused primarily on African American men residing in lower-income urban communities. These defined high-risk groups perpetuate stereotypes that are not consistent with reality: sexually active gay men are not majority Caucasian middle-class, and IDUs are not majority African American men (Schiller et al., 1994). In addition, some racial/ethnic subgroups are clumped in research analyses in a way that negates groups' different immigration histories, cultural practices, and societal labels. This is most notably true among Hispanics and Asian Americans. Among Asian Americans, for example, the Vietnamese are more likely than Asian Indians to have immigrated to the United States based on refugee status, with resulting different economic opportunities, levels of support, and subsequent HIV-risk factors. Yet, services provided do not take into account such historical context, much less issues of diversity in language and culture. Although cultural tailoring is clearly needed to provide better programs for all people, it must also be conducted in a way that does not overgeneralize or promote stereotypes, increasing marginalization for already marginalized groups.

Cultural competence is required to provide ethical and effective cultural tailoring of programs. The Department of Health and Human Services (HHS) defines cultural competence as a "set of academic and interpersonal skills that allow individuals to increase their understanding and appreciation of cultural differences and similarities within, among, and between groups" (Office for Substance Abuse Prevention, 1992, pp. 3–4). Further, this guide concludes that in order to assure cultural competence, the community in question must be involved in the development of interventions. Lynch (1992), in her guide to development of cross-cultural competence, offers a psychological approach to understanding cultural competence. She states that "although it may be impossible to feel or experience what someone else is feeling, becoming more culturally competent can help interventionists understand, appreciate, and support families more directly" (p. 36).

Why Are Programs Not Being Culturally Tailored?

Despite the prioritization of culturally tailored programs and culturally competent researchers in the theoretical literature, the intervention literature continues to reveal few examples. This appears to be the case for two major reasons. First, the field of public health has historically ignored oppressed groups until their health costs have an impact on less marginalized groups. In addition, culture is a fluid concept and difficult to capture for an entire group of individuals.

The culture of a group constructs the way its members think and feel about disease prevention and wellness promotion (Hahn, 1995). Historically, however, much of our public health work has been based on decisions from researchers and institutions that are not part of the cultural groups for which the efforts were designed. Thus, the culturally based needs of groups on these issues may not have been reflected by the public health efforts. For example, many of the public health decisions made to curb the spread of AIDS among gay males in the early 1980s did not stem from the grassroots efforts of gay males who knew the needs of their community. Instead, decisions came from heterosexually focused public policymaking. For example, rather than setting up condom distribution and education in New York bathhouses, bathhouses were simply shut down (Schilts, 1987). This is part of the social context in which HIV transmission and public health work occurs, and the example reflects what happens when dominant culture is pitted against marginalized cultures, such as gay male culture.

Fluidity of culture and cultural identification also increase the difficulty of culturally tailoring programs. As stated earlier, an individual can simultaneously be a member of various cultural groups. Tailoring programs to meet the needs of culturally diverse groups requires capturing the common cultures as well as addressing the diverse cultures within populations of the group. This becomes an increasingly difficult endeavor as populations become increasingly diverse. Further, for each affiliation that marginalizes individuals or groups, individuals become harder to reach. For example, homeless women in the United States might have minimal access to media campaigns promoting HIV-risk reduction, but homeless women with no English skills have even less access, due to the lack of non-English media messages available. Finally, fluidity of cultural identification can also result in changes within a cultural identity as well as among cultural identities of an individual; this can be a consequence of assimilation and acculturation.

Thus, even though cultural tailoring may be necessary for HIV-prevention programs, it is also a difficult task as our models for approaching culture and HIV-risk are so problematic. In our next sections, we will review the research on HIV-risk factors and interventions for the following four primary racial/ethnic groups: African American, Hispanic, Asian American, and American Indian/Alaskan Native. However, in order to prevent the continuing misrepresentation of culture as uniform within groups, we will approach each group, whenever possible, by identifying the literature on subgroups within the larger racial/ethnic group. To minimize length and maximize the review of cultural issues, this chapter will focus on sexual risk factors for HIV infection because sex is the primary means of HIV transmission for all populations discussed.

HIV RISK FACTORS FOR SPECIFIC RACIAL/ETHNIC GROUPS

HIV SEXUAL RISK FACTORS FOR AFRICAN AMERICANS

African American Women

The vast majority of research looking at risk factors for African Americans has been conducted with lower-income African American women residing in urban environments. This research was designed to assess women's risk via heterosexual contact by identifying correlates of condom use among these sample populations. Consistent with behavioral theories such as Social Cognitive Theory (Bandura, 1977, 1989), Health Belief Model (Becker, 1974; Becker & Joseph, 1988), and Theory of Reasoned Action (Ajzen & Fishbein, 1980; Fishbein & Ajzen, 1975), individually based risk factors were associated with increased frequency of condom use for this population. These factors included women's behavioral intentions (Sikkema, Heckman, & Kelly, 1997; St. Lawrence et al., 1998), their perceived risk/susceptibility (Sikkema et al., 1997; Sikkema et al., 1995), and their sexual self-efficacy (Sikkema et al., 1995). Another individually based factor, women's attitudes toward safer sex, was associated with less condom use, with many women viewing condoms as "unnatural" or "less arousing" (Eldridge, St. Lawrence, Little, Shelby, & Brasfield, 1995; Sikkema et al., 1997; St. Lawrence et al., 1998; Wingood & DiClemente, 1998c). Adolescent African American girls also reported noncondom use because of unavailability; they did not carry condoms themselves, viewing condom carrying as the male's role (Fullilove, Fullilove, Haynes, & Gross, 1990).

In addition to these individually based factors, social influences from peers and partners have also been shown to have an impact on condom use among African American women. Perceptions of peer norms regarding condom use (Sikkema et al., 1995; St. Lawrence et al., 1998) and perceived peer approval of condom use (St. Lawrence et al., 1998) appear to be associated with increased condom use among African American women. With regard to relationship factors, most studies reveal that African American women in longer-term or monogamous relationships were more likely to engage in condom use (Sikkema et al., 1997; Wingood & DiClemente, 1998b), even when the longer-term partner was at higher risk (Wagstaff et al., 1995). Among women with steady partners, specific partner influences affect African American women's condom use. Women who communicate with their partner were more likely to engage in condom use (Sikkema et al., 1997; St. Lawrence et al., 1998; Wingood & DiClemente, 1998b). However, gender-based power dynamics in relationships and in society also affect women's ability to negotiate for condom use, use condoms in their relationships, or both. Studies show that African American women who do not assertively negotiate condom use (Wingood & DiClemente, 1998b) or who fear partner reaction to condom use (Mays & Cochran, 1988) are less likely to use condoms. Further, when women have a history of sexual abuse, they are more afraid of partner reaction to condom use (Wingood & DiClemente, 1998a) and less likely to use condoms (Kalichman, Williams, Cherry, Belcher, & Nachimson, 1998; Wingood & DiClemente, 1998a).

Although the discussed risk factors are important to address HIV risk for African American women, these risk factors are less ethnocentric in their approach. In contrast, Fullilove et al.'s (1990) qualitative study with adolescent and adult African American women in California was designed to look at culturally specific African American roles related to sexuality and HIV risk for women. Consistent with studies in Caucasian women (Holland, Ramazanoglu, Scott, Sharpe & Thompson, 1992), Fullilove et al. (1990) found that her sample of African American women defined women with "Madonna/whore" labels. However, these labels vary slightly in definition from those used in dominant Caucasian culture. For participants of Fullilove et al.'s (1990) study, the term "whore" means a woman who gives sex casually without a relationship or exchanges sex for money or drugs. Both of these behaviors are referred to as "tossin," and women who engage in these behaviors are called "tossups." The tossups engage in sex practices that "good girls" do not, for instance oral sex. The first group of women engages, by definition, in high-risk behavior; by cultural definition, they also are considered at high risk.

For the African American teenagers in Fullilove et al.'s (1990) study, the major trait of the whore is her drug use, generally viewed as crack use. Crack use affects her reputation, behavior, and sexual risk. Interestingly, older women did not mention drug use in their discussions; historical context of women's roles and African American roles was the more central influence of their sexual attitudes and behavior. Fullilove et al. (1990) note that crack use is becoming increasingly important in increasing African American women's HIV risk. One recent study with African American women had findings consistent with this view. It found that crack users were significantly more likely to have multiple partners, to have a history of multiple sexually transmitted diseases (STDs), and to engage in inconsistent condom use than were nondrug users or users of alcohol or marijuana (Raj et al., 1997).

In contrast to the whore, the "Madonna" is not a "tossup." These women stay within the proper sexual norms, which define sexual assertiveness or female initiation of sex as unacceptable. Of note is that fact that these norms are also associated with reduced likelihood of condom use among African American women (Wingood & DiClemente, 1998b). Consistent with findings from other studies with African American adolescents and women (Holland et al., 1992; Whitehead, 1997), women and girls in the Fullilove et al. (1990) study viewed sex as the consummation of the relationship. They felt that a true relationship is characterized by deep trust, and that trust implies "take a chance" and do not use condoms. For teens, this involved even greater risk because respectable sexual behavior for this group meant staying faithful even when the partner is not. Thus, for African American women the Madonna as well as the whore may be at increased HIV risk, but for different reasons.

Another facet of a culturally specific twist on gender-specific HIV risk relates to women's desire to be in a relationship. Women gain status and self-esteem from their intimate relationships with male partners (Baker-Miller, 1993), and so women are invested in having that relationship. Both Fullilove et al. (1990) and Wingood, Hunter, and DiClemente (1993) found that African American women want a relationship with an African American man. These researchers feel the shortage of African American men may make these girls and women more willing to cope with problem issues with an African American male partner so that the relationship can be maintained. Participants of Fullilove et al.'s study (1990) also reported resentment of the women's movement. They perceived it as a White women's effort that cost African American women relationships with their African American male partners by demanding power for themselves. Fullilove et al. (1990) go on to describe the paradox of how African American men are losing their economic power in society, yet subsequently gaining more power in their relationships with African American women. It is these power differentials that increase women's vulnerability to sexual HIV risk from their male partners.

African American Men

Although there is a great deal published on HIV risk among African American women at risk through their heterosexual relationships, there is a paucity of literature on HIV risk among African American men who have sex with women (MSWs). Further, most of the literature on sexual risk among adult African American MSWs has focused on substance users and STD-clinic patients rather than community-based populations. The lack of focus on sexual risk among MSWs may be due to the fact that, both biologically and statistically, men are less likely to become infected by a woman than are women likely to become infected by a man (Brunswick & Flory, 1998; CDC, 1999). The lack also may be attributed to general absence of attention given to the health needs of African American men by the field of public health. This lack of information is particularly notable because HIV risk appears to be higher among African American men than men of other racial/ethnic heritage in the United States. Although African American male adolescents report greater condom use than do males of other racial/ethnic backgrounds, they also report earlier onset of intercourse and greater number of partners by age 19 (Sonenstein, Pleck, & Ku, 1991). Further, as noted for African American women, there continues to be a disproportionate number of African American men living with HIV/AIDS (Centers for Disease Control, 1999).

For both adult and adolescent African American males, individually based psychosocial variables, such as attitudes, self-efficacy, risk perceptions, and behavioral intentions, are related to HIV risk taking (Ford & Norris, 1995; Dolcini, Coates, Catania, Kegeles, & Heuck, 1998; Whitehead, 1997). Again, stigmatization of condoms as something used in more casual situations was reported by African American adolescent males (Gilmore, DeLamater, & Wagstaff, 1996). Studies with African American men in New York also revealed that men with greater multiple partnering, a history of paying for sex, or both were also more likely to become infected with HIV (Brunswick & Flory, 1998). These findings demonstrate that theoretically generated risk factors are associated with increased risk, but that contextual factors are equally important.

In findings similar to those found in research with African American women, the relationship between substance abuse and HIV risk is often noted in studies with African American men. In fact, most of the studies on MSWs and sexual risk focus on male substance abuse. Studies with young African American men reveal that those who use crack were more likely to report multiple sexual partnering (Hudgins, McCusker, & Stoddard, 1995; Word & Bowser, 1997), which is associated with higher likelihood of seropositivity (Brunswick & Flory, 1998). African American men who smoke crack are also more likely to engage in injection drug use (Tortu et al., 1998), as well as more likely to engage in sex with other IDUs (Word & Bowser, 1997). They also report higher likelihood of engagement in sex trade (Elwood, Williams, Bell, & Richard, 1997; Hudgins et al., 1995; Word & Bowser, 1997) and higher likelihood of engagement in unprotected sex during sex trade (Tortu et al., 1998). Again, the existence of crack abuse has intensified the HIV risk among lower-income African Americans.

Gender issues for African American MSWs also affect HIV risk for these men. A recent qualitative study (Gilmore et al., 1996) with African American adolescent males revealed that they feel at risk from women due to their general distrust of women. These male adolescents are concerned that women will trick them into impregnating the partner or will intentionally infect them with HIV. At the same time, they feel that if a partner asks to use condoms, she is either infected or does not trust him. Whitehead's (1997) study with adult African American males also revealed that the idea of women initiating sexual discussion disconcerts men. These findings are consistent with beliefs African American women hold about men, and, as mentioned previously, these beliefs decrease the likelihood of female-initiated safer sex.

Whitehead (1997) suggests that African American men's investment in these gender roles stems from their lack of sociopolitical and economic power in society. According to Whitehead (1997), males get power from respectability (i.e., economic power, following rules, and competing successfully) and reputation (i.e., sexual prowess, defying authority, and winning by outsmarting). However, he states that African American men are only sanctioned reputation. Thus, they monopolize the power they are sanctioned. For sexual prowess, this means multiple partnering and controlling sexual activity. For defying authority, this means engaging in sexual risk and, in relation to that, substance abuse. These actions place themselves and their partners at increased HIV risk.

According to Whitehead (1997), these issues have heightened in importance since the addition of crack use. In the 1980s, as economic power became more difficult to obtain in lower-income African American communities, drug use and violence increased. While crack sales, as well as the sale of other drugs, provided economic power, more and more African American men went to jail. African American women in Whitehead's studies reported increasing frustration with African American men's inability to provide financial contribution. African American men reported increased frustration with African American women's desire for material gain. The result has been that older African American women with children, rent, and financial responsibilities are less likely to be in relationships, and younger African American women without financial obligations are dating older African American men. Whitehead found that African American men with lower sociopolitical and economic power reported dating younger women because they can more easily afford the women's needs, and they can also maintain more power in the relationship.

As noted previously, another facet of crack use that relates to sexual risk is sex trade and prison. In both cases, sexual activity with male partners occurs for men who may not otherwise identify themselves as gay or bisexual. Wright (1993) found that some African American men are heterosexuals who engage in sex with men to satisfy their sexual or economic needs. Wright (1993) suggests that men such as these may maintain their heterosexual identity to themselves by always being the "inserter" rather than the "insertee" during sexual encounters with men. This is consistent with findings from Linn et al. (1989) that demonstrate, unlike Caucasian men, African American men did not view insertive anal sex as necessarily indicating acceptance of or involvement with homosexuality. These findings are also consistent with those of Stokes, Vanable, and McKirnan (1996), which found that African American men receiving insertive anal intercourse were more accepting of their gay or bisexual identity and more involved with the gay community.

The need for African American MSMs to identify themselves as heterosexual, even when they might be gay or bisexual, may be attributed to the pervasive antigay sentiment in African American communities (Hays & Peterson, 1994; Peterson, 1992; Wright, 1993) as well as society. Stokes, Vanable, and McKirnan (1996) found that African American MSMs perceive their communities as antigay, and Stokes and Peterson (1998) found that young African American MSMs feel they must live a double life to avoid victimization. Consistent with these findings, recent studies show that African American MSMs are less likely than Caucasian MSMs to disclose their common sex behaviors (McKirnan, Stokes, Doll, & Burzette, 1995; Stokes, McKirnan, & Burzette, 1993; Stokes, McKirnan, Doll, and Burzette, 1996). This increases HIV risk because, according to a study from Peterson et al. (1992), African American men with greater discomfort disclosing their homosexual behavior are less likely to engage in condom use.

Among gay-identifying men, African American men report a variety of emotional and mental health concerns that may place them at increased risk for HIV. African American men find it difficult to be involved in either the gay community or the African American community without having to sacrifice part of themselves (Stokes & Peterson, 1998). Most major cities have a "gay area." However, gay African American men tend to remain in the African American communities because "gay areas" are often predominantly Caucasian, which means they are more expensive and, potentially, more racist; these areas may also not be available to them due to housing discrimination. Doll, Peterson, Magana, and Carrier (1991) also suggest that African American MSMs may stay in their own racial/ethnic communities to maintain their "closet" status. However, remaining in African American communities that are often antigay also creates problems. A recent study with young African American MSMs revealed that many of these men face constant homophobia and internalize the homophobia; this reduces their self-esteem and their investment in keeping themselves healthy (Stokes & Peterson, 1998). These authors also found that some of these men avoid displaying interest in HIV education for fear of disclosure. However, they are unlikely to have a steady partner due to difficulty in maintaining a long-term closeted relationship. Further, they are likely to have casual sexual relationships with men to build their self-esteem and to provide themselves with some sense of connectedness. The result is that African American gay men perceive themselves as being at less risk for HIV than do Caucasian gay men (Stokes, Vanable, & McKirnan, 1996). Yet, in some regions of the country, African American men report higher seroprevalence rates than do Caucasian gay men (Lemp et al., 1994).

HIV RISK FACTORS FOR HISPANICS

The Hispanic population in the United States is quite diverse and varies greatly in HIV risk by country of birth and place of residence in the United States (Diaz, Buehler, Castro, & Ward, 1993; COSSMHO, 1991). This population is also diverse in socioeconomic status, although research has primarily focused on lower-income, urban communities. Further, research with Hispanics is relatively more recent, despite the fact that HIV/AIDS has disproportionately affected this community almost from the start of the epidemic.

The states with the highest rates of AIDS cases among Hispanics are concentrated in the northeastern area of the United States (e.g., Massachusetts, Rhode Island, Connecticut, New Jersey, New York, and Washington, DC) and Puerto Rico (CDC, 1997). The major Hispanic groups that reside in the United States Northeast are Puerto Ricans, Dominicans, and Cubans, suggesting that these groups of Hispanics may be at highest risk. The southwestern states, where most Mexican American women and men live, have a much smaller number of reported AIDS cases. One explanation for the apparent higher prevalence of AIDS among Hispanics living in the eastern areas of the United States and Puerto Rico may be that they reside in the areas that have the highest prevalence of AIDS cases in the population at large (Amaro, 1988). Another explanation may be that Puerto Rican women and men have higher rates of lifetime and current use of illicit drugs than do Mexican Americans or Cubans, therefore increasing their risk of HIV infection (Amaro, 1988). Diaz and Klevens (1997) found that among Hispanic participants who reported having AIDS, Puerto Rican men were more likely to have injected drugs than other groups in the study (Central American and Mexican). Therefore, it is important to note the different HIV risk factors within subgroups of the American Hispanic population.

Traditional cultural values, religious beliefs, and gender roles have often been cited as factors affecting HIV-related risk taking among Hispanics. Although these values may play a role in setting norms, other factors, such as socioeconomic status and structural characteristics of the service delivery system, are also important in determining attitudes and behavior regarding reproduction, sexuality, and HIV prevention (Amaro, 1988). For example, although many Hispanics are Roman Catholic, studies suggest that rather than strictly adhering to Catholic doctrine concerning birth control, most Hispanic women use contraception (Amaro, 1988). In addition, the lower rates of contraception use among Hispanic women when compared with Caucasian women appear to be due more to socioeconomic factors rather than to religious opposition to contraceptives (Amaro, 1988; Gurak, 1980). Lack of knowledge about contraception and reproduction, as well as the linguistic and cultural inappropriateness of services, are also factors that decrease the effective use of contraceptives among Hispanic women (Amaro, 1988). Therefore, although cultural values may affect community norms, they are not the sole contributors to increased HIV risk in Hispanic communities.

Structural issues also appear to place Hispanic populations in the United States at greater risk for HIV infection. Hispanics are more likely than Caucasians to suffer from poor or no housing, insufficient food and clothing, and inadequate access to health services (Gordon-Bradshaw, 1987). Hence, there may be more focus among Hispanics on basic and immediate needs of survival (e.g., shelter, food, safety, employment/economic security) rather than HIV/AIDS prevention (Mays and Cochran, 1988; Kalichman, Kelly, & Hunter, 1992). Further, Mays and Cochran (1988) suggest that even if these communities perceived AIDS as a risk, they may lack the resources to reduce their risk due to linguistic and economic barriers to health care access. Again, structural issues need to be addressed to meet more fully the needs of Hispanic communities. However, in addition to these macro-level approaches, it is also important to address micro-level issues within Hispanic communities.

Hispanic Women

The majority of the existing literature and research looking at risk factors for Hispanics has focused on lower-income, urban women. As with African American women, much of this research has focused on individually based factors for HIV risk, including knowledge, attitudes, and perceptions regarding condom use.

Studies assessing HIV knowledge among Hispanic women indicate that these women have limited knowledge of how HIV is transmitted and how transmission can be prevented (Amaro & Gornemann, 1996; Kalichman et al., 1992); however, knowledge does appear to vary according to the participant's sociodemographic profile. Less knowledgeable women tend to be less acculturated (Nyamathi, Bennet, Leake, Lewis, & Flaskerud, 1993) and less educated (Aruffo, Coverdale, & Vallbona, 1991; McCaig, Hardy, & Winn, 1991) and to reside in communities with lower HIV/AIDS incidence (McCaig et al., 1991). Hispanic women also report low HIV risk perceptions and negative attitudes toward safer sex practice (Catania et al., 1992), again with less acculturated women reporting more negative attitudes and lower risk perceptions (Nyamathi et al., 1993; Marks, Kantero, & Simoni, 1998).

Studies with Hispanic women have revealed that condoms are viewed as making sex less pleasurable and condom use implies infidelity or distrust in male partners (Carovano, 1991). These women believe that condoms do not need to be used within the context of an intimate relationship with a steady partner (Catania et al., 1994; Marin, Tschann, Gomez, & Gregorich, 1998) and that sex without a condom is an expression of greater love (Pivnick, 1993). Consistent with these attitudes, Yep (1992a) found that Hispanic women reported unprotected sex with their partners even when they knew that their partners were infected with HIV because unprotected sex symbolized love and intimacy (Yeakley & Gant, 1997).

Clearly low levels of knowledge, low HIV risk perceptions, and negative attitudes toward safer sex are increasing HIV risk for Hispanic women, especially among less acculturated women, because they have even lower knowledge and HIV risk perceptions (Nyamathi et al., 1993; Marks et al., 1998). However, more highly acculturated Hispanics are at increased risk as well, because they are more likely to become infected through drug use or sex with multiple partners (Nya-mathi et al., 1993). Substance abuse is becoming increasingly common in the Hispanic community, with cocaine use more prevalent among Hispanics than among Caucasian Americans (SAMHSA, 1999). As mentioned in the discussion of African American women, drug-using Hispanic women are more likely to have the additional risks factors of multiple sex partners, exchanging sex for money, and often, less control over use of condoms (Turner & Solomon, 1996). Condom use among drug-using Hispanic women is affected by both situational factors, including residence and economic stability, as well as social factors such as relationship power dynamics and gender roles (Mays & Cochran, 1988). For poor, drug-using women, the fear of being without a male partner may outweigh the fear of HIV infection (Mays & Cochran, 1988). In addition, for Hispanic women who are poor, practice substance abuse, or both, sex may also function as a source of employment, a method for establishing trust in a relationship, or as a way to obtain emotional or financial support (Mays & Cochran, 1988). Fur-ther, for these women, emotional and physical violence, including assault, rape, murder, street violence, demands of a drug habit, and limited economic possi-bilities, often hinder and come before women's efforts to protect themselves against HIV infection (Romero-Daza, Weeks, & Singer, 1998).

The issue of substance abuse and HIV risk for Hispanic women clearly re-veals the role of the male partner in women's risk; however, this role exists re-gardless of the woman's substance abuse history. As seen in the African Ameri-can community, negative perceptions of condom use by male partners are often a barrier to women's risk reduction practices (Catania et al., 1992). Rather than viewing condoms as a means of preventing infection, many Hispanic males per-ceive condoms as signifying disease (Weeks, Schensul, Williams, Singer, & Grier, 1995), which many women fear may result in male abandonment or vio-lence. Weeks et al. (1995) found that some women feared violent repercussions by male partners in response to condom negotiation, and Mays and Cochran (1988) found a small subset of Hispanic women who were actually physically or verbally assaulted in response to requests for partners to use condoms. Often, women who are in relationships marked by male violence experience isolation and lowered self-esteem, which may keep them from even contemplating HIV prevention in their relationship (Amaro & Gornemann, 1996).

Partner awareness of female contraceptive attitudes can also result in less con-dom use among these women (O'Donnell, San Doval, Vornfett, & O'Donnell, 1994). There is a stereotype of the Hispanic woman as a "breeder." However, Amaro (1988) found that many Hispanic women prefer moderately sized rather than large families, and thus, they use contraception (Amaro, 1988). In addition, female sterilization has been reported to be alarmingly high among Puerto Rican women (Schensul, Borrera, Backstand, & Guarnaccia, 1982), in part, due to un-ethical public health practice. O'Donnell et al. (1994) suggest that Hispanic men who believe their female partners are using contraception are less willing to use a condom. Fleisher, Senie, Minkoff, and Jaccard (1994) additionally found that, among Hispanics, condom use was more likely to be successful if used for contraceptive reasons rather than for disease prevention. Given that the most common form of HIV prevention is the male condom, it is not surprising that condom use does not happen unless the male decides it should happen. Deren, Shedlin, and Beardsley (1996) found that even when Hispanic women have concerns about HIV and discuss these concerns with partners, rates of condom use remain low.

Male control over decision making regarding condom use can be attributed directly to culturally prescribed gender roles. *Machismo,* the traditionally prescribed male Hispanic gender role, enforces male control of sexual decision making; in contrast, Hispanic women are expected to remain passive and subservient to the decisions of male partners (Amaro & Gornemann, 1996). *Machismo* also reinforces male promiscuity, whereas proper Hispanic women are expected to be ignorant about sex and serve as "gatekeepers" to sexual activity (Erickson, 1998). A Hispanic woman who carries condoms may be viewed as "prepared for sex" and, thus, believed to be promiscuous and undesirable (Mays & Cochran, 1988; Weeks et al., 1995). This gender- and culture-based script for sexual relations places Hispanic women at increased risk for HIV, regardless of their knowledge and skills, in situations where their partners are unwilling to use condoms (Amaro & Gornemann, 1996; Flaskerud, Uman, Lara, Romero, & Taka, 1996).

Hispanic Men

Similar to research concerning HIV risk factors for African American populations, literature on Hispanic populations is largely concerned with risk factors for women. The literature on Hispanic men focuses primarily on MSMs, with less emphasis on MSWs. Again, this is probably based on biological and statistical risk (Brunswick & Flory, 1998; CDC, 1999).

Sexual risk taking appears to be very high among Hispanic MSWs. Multiple sex partners, including sex with prostitutes, has also been reported to be relatively higher among populations of Hispanic men than among Caucasian men (Kim, Marmor, Dubin, & Wolfe, 1993; Caetano & Hines, 1995). This is especially true among Hispanic men who are unmarried, younger (between the ages of 18 and 21), better educated, lower in income, and highly acculturated (Sabogal, Faigeles, & Cantania, 1993). Hispanic men who have multiple partners report low condom use with secondary partners and even lower rates of condom use with primary partners (Sabogal et al., 1993). Reported rates of condom initiation among Hispanic MSWs also appears to be low, regardless of whether the sexual encounter was casual or steady (Forrest, Austin, Valdes, Fuentes, & Wilson, 1993).

Individually based risk factors appear to be an issue for Hispanic MSWs. HIV knowledge is not high among Hispanic MSWs; but even when AIDS knowledge is high, condom use appears to be sporadic (Forrest et al., 1993). Low risk perceptions are also common among Hispanic MSWs (Forrest et al., 1993). Forrest et al. (1993) found in his sample of lower-income Hispanic MSWs in California that low HIV risk perceptions remained, even in men who engaged in sex with higher risk partners. Hispanic MSWs also reported low self-efficacy for condom use with a main partner (Marin et al., 1998). Further, alcohol consumption, as well as use of other drugs, all of which are becoming increasingly common among Hispanics (SAMHSA, 1999), also decrease condom use among these men (Weinstock, Lindan, Bolan, Kegeles, & Hearst, 1993; Caetano and Hines, 1995).

Whereas individually based risk factors have been well documented among Hispanic MSWs, less research has been conducted to determine the influence of partners and perceptions of cultural norms. Based on literature with Hispanic women, Hispanic male control of condom use appears to be the norm. However, Weinstock et al. (1993) found that female influence does have some impact on male decision making, because Hispanic MSWs are more likely to use condoms if their partners want to use them. In addition, the cultural norm of male sexual knowledge and control, while highly disadvantageous for Hispanic women, may be useful to increase safer sex practice among Hispanic men.

Research with Hispanic MSMs has also been more recent than work with African American and Caucasian MSMs. This research is obviously late in coming, as young Hispanic MSMs account for a large percentage of AIDS cases among MSMs in the United States (Denning, Jones, & Ward, 1997). Diaz, Stall, Hoff, Daigle, and Coates (1996) suggest that the actual proportion of Hispanic MSM cases may be even higher than estimated, ranging from 59% among Mexican Americans to 70% among Cuban Americans. Yet, despite these high infection rates, lack of condom use remains common among this population. Diaz et al. (1996) found that, among Hispanic males who engaged in anal intercourse (38% of the sample), 67% had unprotected sex with primary partners and 44% had unprotected sex with casual partners in the past 30 days.

Risk factors for unsafe sex among Hispanic MSMs are similar to those seen in other populations that have been discussed. Individually based factors include lower safer sex intentions, lower self-efficacy, lower sexual self-control, and substance abuse during sexual encounters (Diaz et al., 1996). Historical factors also influence risk; Carballo-Dieguez and Dolezal (1995) found that history of childhood sexual abuse among MSMs increases the likelihood of engaging in receptive anal intercourse without protection. The primary dyadic factor that has been addressed is involvement with a primary partner. Similar to other populations, Hispanic MSMs are less likely to use condoms with primary partners (Diaz et al., 1996), again revealing that false security in relationships is placing people at increased risk for infection.

The primary cultural factor that affects Hispanic MSMs is the conservatism that promotes homophobia and prevents Hispanic MSMs from disclosing their sexual orientation (Flaskerud et al., 1996). Many gay Hispanic men may not identify as such due to severe stigmatization and alienation, where coming out may be seen as shameful to family members (Flaskerud et al., 1996; O'Donnell et al., 1994). Therefore, in a culture that provides and cherishes strong family ties, one's sexual orientation may not be disclosed in order to protect the family from dishonor or shame. Studies indicate that some Hispanic men do not identify as gay or bisexual, but report having sex with both men and women (Flaskerud et al., 1996; Lehner & Chiasson, 1998). Further, Izazol-Licea et al. (1991) have found that condom use is significantly lower in cities with more conservative attitudes about homosexuality. These findings suggest that Hispanic MSMs may be placing themselves as well as their partners at risk for HIV transmission.

HIV RISK FACTORS FOR ASIAN AMERICANS
AND PACIFIC ISLANDERS

Although American Asian/Pacific Islanders (APIs) compose a large segment of the United States population, little is known about their HIV risk, due to gaps in the ways that surveillance data are collected and reported. One major problem in data collection and reporting is that the demographic group termed API is not uniformly defined. Many states consolidate Asian/Pacific Islanders and Native Americans in their reporting to Centers for Disease Control (Sy, Chng, Choi, & Wong, 1998). In addition, Filipinos, one of the largest API groups, are often included with Hispanics due to common Spanish surnames, with the possible result of falsely reducing API seroprevalence rates (Sy et al., 1998). Further, Asian/Pacific Islanders as a classification is problematic because the term represents extremely diverse peoples. Asian/Pacific Islanders are diverse in race, ethnicity, language, culture, and even geographical location or origin; some Asian/ Pacific Islanders live in their culture of origin (e.g., Guam, Hawaii), whereas some do not (e.g., China, India, Vietnam). These poor data collection and reporting techniques maintain our lack of understanding of how HIV is having an impact on American Asian/Pacific Islander communities.

Lack of inclusion of Asian/Pacific Islanders in HIV community organizing efforts is, in part, responsible for this poor classification system. Recent research indicates that APIs have been kept out of many state and local HIV-prevention community planning groups and are rarely prioritized in HIV prevention efforts (Bau, 1998). Consequently, many of the HIV prevention efforts that are currently being made are focused around organizing the community to develop a response. Unfortunately, these organizing efforts are not national but occur primarily on the West Coast, in Hawaii, and in a few states in the Northeast (Chng, Sy, Choi, Bau, & Astudillo, 1998). These regions are not the only areas with high Asian/ Pacific Islander concentrations. Further, much of the prevention work that is being done has not been based on community needs assessment, and, to date, no prevention programs for Asian/Pacific Islanders have been formally evaluated for outcome effects, although process evaluations are common (Chng et al., 1998). The result is that we have minimum data on HIV risk in the API community and few effective interventions to address this risk.

Although numerous HIV prevention programs exist across the United States, the vast majority do not target API communities. Most HIV prevention messages offered are not made in Asian/Pacific Islanders' languages (Sy et al., 1998), and strategies offered are not necessarily culturally appropriate or specific. For instance, peer educators and outreach workers are effective education tools for most mainstream United States communities; however, Asian/Pacific Islanders prefer professional health care providers rather than peers or outreach workers as their educators (Loue, Lloyd, & Phoombour, 1996). As a result, HIV prevention programs have been developed that primarily target the general Asian/Pacific Islanders population, Asian/Pacific Islanders gay men, and Asian/Pacific Islanders youth (Chng et al., 1998), negating the needs of women. Certain API ethnic/cultural groups have also been disproportionately excluded in Asian/Pacific Islanders organizing efforts. Asian Indians, for example, are a large ethnic group in the United States, but no program has been developed specifically for them (Chng et al., 1998). In addition, most HIV service programs for Asian/Pacific Islanders have come from gay initiatives (Chng et al., 1998). Chng et al. (1998) suggest that this has resulted in Asian/Pacific Islanders maintaining low risk perceptions—viewing HIV as a gay disease. As a result of the prioritization of certain API groups in HIV prevention efforts, most of the research conducted with Asian/Pacific Islanders has tended to focus on East and Southeast Asians in general, Asian/Pacific Islander MSMs, and Asian/Pacific Islander adolescents.

General Asian/Pacific Islanders Population

Most Asian/Pacific Islanders HIV/AIDS cases are in metropolitan areas with large Asian populations (Sy et al., 1998); consequently, much of the research with Asian/Pacific Islanders has also been conducted in metropolitan areas. This research has been primarily conducted with East and Southeast Asians and has often used convenience sampling (Choi, Coates, Catansia, Lew, & Chow, 1995). These studies have found that safer sex behaviors, such as HIV testing, condom use, and safer sex communication with partners, are not common among Asian/Pacific Islanders (Gock & Ja, 1995; Nemoto et al., 1998; Sy et al., 1998; Yep, 1993). APIs appear to have one of the lowest rates of HIV testing in the United States (Nemoto et al., 1998; Sy et al., 1998), although this may be a consequence of the increased likelihood of this population to seek private physicians. Lack of condom use also appears to be common among APIs. A recent study with majority East and Southeast Asian APIs in San Diego found that 73% reported unprotected sex with multiple partners. In addition, safer sex discussions with partners are assumed to be infrequent in API communities because discussions of sex and illness are taboo in many API cultures (Chang, 1993; Gock & Ja, 1995).

In addition to the prevalence of HIV-risk practices, recent studies have also found low HIV knowledge (Loue et al., 1996) and negative HIV-related attitudes (Loue et al., 1996; Sy et al., 1998) to be common in Asian/Pacific Islanders communities. A recent study of APIs in San Diego found that they felt AIDS was a consequence of doing bad things, with 13% feeling that quarantine was appropriate for HIV-positive people (Loue et al., 1996). These attitudes keep HIV/AIDS hidden in Asian/Pacific Islander communities (Yep, 1993) and stigmatize both APIs living with HIV/AIDS and their families (Loue et al., 1996). Further, such stigmatization of HIV/AIDS may have an impact on HIV reporting to CDC. Specifically, female HIV-positive Asian/Pacific Islanders report higher contraction rates from blood-derived products. There is no reason that this should be the case, and Sy et al. (1998) suspect that greater stigma leads to misrepresentation of information, furthering difficulties in interpreting API epidemiologic data.

Asian/Pacific Islander MSMs

The majority of HIV research in the Asian/Pacific Islander communities has been with MSMs aged 25 to 44 years, due to the highest incidence of Asian/Pacific Islanders HIV infections among this population (Centers for Disease Control, 1999). Asian/Pacific Islander MSMs have been hardest hit in the Midwest, South, and West, all regions with larger Asian/Pacific Islanders communities and metropolitan areas more accepting of gays and lesbians (Sullivan, 1995). Recent studies reveal that, unlike Caucasian MSMs, Asian/Pacific Islander MSMs continue to have an increasing incidence of HIV/AIDS (Centers for Disease Control, 1999), with certain API groups, such as Filipinos, being harder hit (Loue et al., 1996). Nonetheless, Asian/Pacific Islander MSMs remain largely ignored by HIV prevention efforts (Sy et al., 1998). The few studies that do exist are composed of relatively small sample sizes and rely on convenience samples.

Recent reviews of epidemiologic studies with Asian/Pacific Islanders found seroprevalence rates ranging from 1.4 to 27.8%, based on recruitment, data collection, regional location, and sample. Overall, the studies indicate that HIV is a major issue for Asian/Pacific Islander MSMs (Nemoto et al., 1998; Sy et al., 1998). Similarly, incidence rates of HIV-risk behavior range from study to study. Choi et al. (1996) and Lemp et al. (1994) found that 27 to 29% of Asian/Pacific Islander MSMs had engaged in unprotected anal intercourse in the past 6 months. In contrast, Matteson (1997) found that only 17% of Asian/Pacific Islanders in his study had done so. Differences in findings cannot be attributed to working with different Asian/Pacific Islander ethnic groups because both studies were conducted with predominantly Chinese and Filipino men, but differences may be attributed to regional differences or recruitment procedures. Choi et al. (1995, 1996) and Lemp et al. (1994) conducted their studies in California with men who identified themselves as gay; Matteson (1997) conducted his study in a midwestern city with men who had sex with men but did not necessarily identify themselves as gay. Further complicating the issue is the role of substance abuse. Choi et al. (1996) found that Asian/Pacific Islander MSMs who used drugs were 5.5 times more likely than nondrug users to engage in unprotected anal intercourse, and substance abuse may have been more common in the California samples. Nonetheless, unprotected anal intercourse does appear to be an issue for Asian/Pacific Islander MSMs, especially for Asian/Pacific Islander MSMs who engage in drug use.

In addition to a high incidence of unprotected intercourse, Choi et al.'s studies (1995, 1996) with API MSMs found that 95% had multiple partners in the past 5 years and 59% had multiple partners in the past 3 months. Further, 11% of his sample had engaged in sex trade. Placing API MSMs at even greater risk is the high prevalence of hepatitis B among these men. Sexually transmitted diseases such as hepatitis B place individuals at greater risk for contracting HIV. While risk taking appears to be high among Asian/Pacific Islander MSMs, Choi et al. (1995, 1996) also found that 78% of their gay-identified Asian/Pacific Islanders sample had been tested for HIV infection. This finding indicates that awareness of risk is increasing among Asian/Pacific Islander MSMs. Nonetheless, despite high HIV knowledge among Asian/Pacific Islander MSM samples that were majority Japanese, Chinese, or Filipino (Choi et al., 1995; Yep, 1992b), researchers suggest that Asian/Pacific Islander MSMs do not have sufficient cognitive skills to practice safer sex (Yep, 1992b; Choi et al., 1995, 1996).

In addition to the influence of knowledge and cognitive skills on safer sex practice among Asian/Pacific Islander MSMs, many researchers have identified cultural factors that prevent these men from engaging in HIV-risk reduction. In particular, family and cultural issues maintain their high risk. Gay men and lesbian Asian Americans feel that their communities deny the existence of homosexuality (Carrier, Nguyen, & Su, 1992). Consequently, there is also denial and lack of acceptance of homosexuality in Asian/Pacific Islander families (Choi & Kumekawa, 1998). Thus, many Asian/Pacific Islander MSMs do not disclose to their families because it would mean family shame (Choi & Kumekawa, 1998). Closeted MSMs have less access to needed HIV-prevention information and will be less inclined to seek out or keep such information for fear of being discovered.

Additional family pressures for MSMs include Asian/Pacific Islanders family responsibility to get married, have children, and carry on the family name (Choi & Kumekawa, 1998). Being a first son creates even more difficulty because it is their responsibility to assume care of the family (Ona, Cadabes, & Choi, 1996). These rigid family roles result in many young MSMs having two lives. Many MSMs engage in more casual and less safe sexual encounters due to difficulties sustaining a relationship in such circumstances (Choi & Kumekawa, 1998). Further, the stress and guilt from living these two lives lead to low self-esteem, self-hatred, depression, social inhibition, and insecurities for young Asian/Pacific Islander MSMs, which may place them at greater risk for engaging in unsafe sex. Choi et al. (1995) found that APIs with greater discomfort with being gay reported higher HIV risk.

Discomfort with their Asian/Pacific Islander communities does appear to force some men away, but often they do not feel comfortable in the gay male community either. Although Matteson (1997) found that Asian/Pacific Islander MSMs were more likely to choose gay friends over Asian friends, many gay Asian/Pacific Islanders are wary of the predominantly Caucasian gay male community and feel issues for MSMs of color and immigrant MSMs are ignored

(Choi & Kumekawa, 1998) Ona et al. (1996) also found that many Asian/Pacific Islander MSMs had experienced negative stereotyping, marginalization, and objectification by the mainstream gay community.

As seen with African American and Hispanic MSMs, there is a sense of Caucasian focus in the mainstream gay community that defines beauty as Caucasian and large, an unattainable standard for many Asian/Pacific Islander MSMs (Choi & Kumekawa, 1998). Asian/Pacific Islanders feel that the mainstream gay community stereotypes them as smart, asexual, lower risk, monogamous, subservient, and the receptive anal sex partner (Choi & Kumekawa, 1998; Ona et al., 1996). These perceptions not only result in depression and lowered self-esteem in API MSMs, they also result in internalized oppression that can increase HIV risk. Matteson (1997) found that most Asian/Pacific Islander MSMs prefer non-Asian partners as they are "more attractive." This often results in Asian/Pacific Islander MSMs partnering with older, Caucasian men, which can create a power differential based on both age and race/ethnicity that may place Asian/Pacific Islander MSMs at greater risk for HIV. Although race of partner did not predict risk for Asian/Pacific Islander MSMs, role-specific sexual practices (feminine–receptive, masculine–insertive) may be associated with relationships marked by power differential and, consequently, may place Asian/Pacific Islander MSMs at greater risk.

Another major issue for MSM Asian/Pacific Islanders is the diversity, and subsequent conflict, within these groups. For example, many Asian/Pacific Islander MSMs are bisexual rather than gay. Matteson (1997) found that many bisexuals feel forced to be either gay or straight, because neither group is accepting of bisexuals. Thus, when maintaining bisexual identification, these Asian/Pacific Islanders may also be unable to access needed HIV risk reduction information because they are often not targeted by HIV prevention programs (Chng et al., 1998). This is of particular concern because bisexual APIs engage in riskier behavior than do heterosexual Asian/Pacific Islanders (Matteson, 1997). In addition to diversity in sexual orientation, there is also diversity in acculturation and sexual identification. Carrier et al. (1992) found two distinct groups of Vietnamese MSMs: Vietnamese gays (acculturated and gay-identified) and Vietnamese homosexual outsiders (unacculturated or with no clear sexual identification). These groups had difficulties with each other, which complicates developing an HIV prevention program, even for MSMs of the same ethnic heritage. Thus, prevention messages must take into account intragroup differences when developing plans of action.

Asian/Pacific Islander Adolescents

Although the majority of HIV interventions in the United States have been developed for adolescents, HIV research with Asian/Pacific Islander adolescents has been relatively scarce. Again, much of this work has focused on East and Southeast Asians. Much of the research that has been done shows that API adolescents report lower HIV knowledge than do other students (DiClemente, Zorn,

& Temoshok, 1987; Horan & DiClemente, 1993; Strunin, 1991; Seage et al., 1991), especially knowledge related to HIV transmission and prevention (Horan & DiClemente, 1993). Researchers posit that this is a consequence of less sexual health discussion between API parents and children. Hou and Basen-Enquist (1997) found APIs do communicate less about sexual health issues with parents than do Caucasian students. Research also shows Asian/Pacific Islander adolescents initiate sexual activity later than most American children (Cochran, Mays, & Leung, 1991). However, once started, Asian/Pacific Islander adolescents engage in unsafe sex at the same rates as other students (Hou & Basen-Enquist, 1997). Further, Hou and Basen-Enquist (1997) found that sexually active Asian/Pacific Islanders were also more likely to have multiple partners than were Caucasian students. Like Caucasian students, Asian/Pacific Islanders were also less likely to use condoms during sex after alcohol or drugs had been used, although they were less likely to use alcohol or drugs before sex than were Caucasian students. Again, rational–empirical models are useful in explaining HIV risk among Asian/Pacific Islander adolescents; however, such minimal research provides no real information on the influence of culture or context.

HIV RISK FACTORS FOR NATIVE
AMERICANS/ALASKANS

There is a general paucity of literature on HIV risk among Native Americans/Alaskan Natives. Mortality due to HIV infection among Native American/Alaskan Natives appears to be infrequent and is 0.4 times the rate of mortality due to HIV for all races in the United States (Department of Health and Human Services, 1997). For young adults 13 to 24 years of age, Native American/Alaskan Natives represent 1% of the cumulative AIDS cases and 1% of the cases reported in 1997 (CDC, 1997). However, this lower rate does not signify that HIV prevention should not be addressed for this population. Rather, under-recognition of the HIV/AIDS problem may be occurring due to limited access to any health care or to adequate health care for the people defined as Native.

United States 1990 Census data show higher rates of poverty (32% Native American/Alaskan versus 13% all races), unemployment (16 versus 6% all races), and school dropout rate (65% high-school graduates versus 75% all races) among Native Americans and Alaskan Natives. These rates indicate fewer resources and less access to health care for this population, which have been found to be significant factors in increasing rates of HIV transmission in other American communities. The presence of these factors should serve as impetus for HIV prevention work in Native American/Alaskan communities in order to determine if low rates are accurate and to maintain low rates if they truly exist.

Native American and Alaskan Women

The majority of the literature concerning Native American and Alaskan women focuses on risks related to drug use. Substance abuse is disproportionately high among Native Americans (SAMHSA, 1999). Studies also suggest that Native Americans who use drugs are more likely than other racial/ethnic groups to inject drugs (Fisher, Cagle, & Wilson, 1993; Metler, Conway, & Stehr-Green, 1991), thus increasing their risk for HIV. Female Native American drug users were more likely than women of other racial/ethnic groups to have sex partners who were IDUs (Fenaughty et al., 1998). CDC data for 1996 (CDC, 1996) indicate that there is a higher rate of HIV infection among Native American and Alaskan Native women (56%) from heterosexual transmission with an IDU partner than there is for any other racial/ethnic group (Hispanics 40%, African Americans 33%, Caucasians 37%, Asians/Pacific Islanders, 20%).

Further increasing risk is that fact that condom use is low among sex partners of IDUs. Fenaughty et al. (1998) found that Native women who were sex partners of drug users reported a lower rate of condom use than did any other racial/ethnic group in Anchorage. Fenaughty et al. (1998) also found that Native American women were more than twice as likely as Native American men to have never used condoms for vaginal and anal sex in a 30-day period. The difference in reported condom use is, in part, due to the fact that many Native American women reported having a Caucasian male partner; it was with these partners that there was less condom use (Fenaughty et al., 1998). Although research is beginning to assess risk among Native American/Alaskan women, no published research to date has assessed specific risk factors for this group.

Native American and Alaskan Men

Whereas there is minimal research on Native American and Alaskan women, there is even less on Native American and Alaskan men. Again, the literature that does exist for this group does not focus on HIV risk factors. This is particularly alarming because MSMs report the highest incidence of HIV/AIDS among all groups of Native Americans (CDC, 1998); further, Native American MSMs have been disproportionately affected by the epidemic, even among other MSM populations (CDC, 1999).

OVERVIEW OF HIV RISK FOR CULTURALLY DIVERSE GROUPS

Overall, research on HIV risk for different racial/ethnic populations reveals that far more research is needed before any true conclusions can be reached on what constitutes risk for the different groups. Many populations, such as Native American and Alaskans, have only barely been addressed in the literature. For other populations, such as Hispanics, research has been conducted more with certain Hispanic populations than others, limiting the ability to generalize findings. And even in cases where more broad-scale research is occurring, such as with African American communities, research has focused on specific economic class (e.g., lower income) and regional (e.g., urban) groups and neglected the needs of African Americans who do not fit those stereotypical groupings. Further, overall, there has been a shameful paucity of research conducted across racial/ethnic groups on sexual HIV risk for MSWs. This lack of research not only negates the needs of men, but it also further reinforces the concept of sole female responsibility for reducing sexual risk in heterosexual dyadic relationships.

Nonetheless, findings from this literature review do yield important information for those interested in developing and evaluating effective HIV-prevention programs for minority racial/ethnic groups. Among the samples in which HIV risk was assessed, regardless of group affiliation (e.g., women, MSMs, adolescent males), individually based risk factors predicted by rational–empirical theories are consistently associated with increased risk in the studied population. These risk factors include safer sex intentions, HIV risk perceptions, positive outcome expectancies from safer sex, lower negative outcome expectancies from safer sex, safer sex self-efficacy, and low substance use self-efficacy. However, consistent with findings from Amaro and Hardy-Fanta (1995), historical, relationship, and sociocultural factors not addressed by rational–empirical theories influence risk as well.

Historical factors include a history of physical or sexual abuse, as well as a history of risk taking. These appear to be more of an issue for women and MSMs than for MSWs; however, this association may due to lack of research on this factor in MSWs. Relationship factors include steady relationship status and partner attitudes toward safer sex; these seem to be important regardless of gender. Partner abuse is a major issue observed in the literature with women, but it is not discussed in the literature with men. With regard to MSWs, this can be attributed to the fact that females are more likely to be victimized by a partner than are males (Greenfield, 1998). However, for MSMs, the lack of association between partner violence and HIV risk may also be due to lack of research on the subject.

Significant sociocultural factors differ according to the specific racial/ethnic group, as well as to the subgroups within the racial/ethnic group (e.g., MSMs, women who have sex with men, incarcerated youth). Nonetheless, there do appear to be some overlapping issues across racial/ethnic groups. Women, regardless of racial/ethnic group, appear to be influenced by gender-based power differentials in relationships. MSMs, regardless of racial/ethnic group, appear to be influenced by the stigmatization of homosexuality. Last, adolescents, regardless of racial/ethnic group, engage in sexual risk taking in conjunction with other risk-taking behaviors.

A Review of HIV Interventions for Specific Racial/Ethnic Groups

Although the need for HIV interventions for specific racial/ethnic groups is clear, there has been a paucity of literature on effective HIV interventions targeting these populations. For the purpose of this chapter, we are defining effective HIV interventions as those that resulted in significant behavioral change (e.g., increased condom use, safer sex negotiation, or HIV testing) among program participants. The following is a review of studies of evaluated HIV-prevention efforts for specific racial/ethnic groups in the United States that did result in significant sexual risk reduction among intervention participants. The majority of the studies included in this review targeted lower-income groups residing in urban settings whose primary risk factors for HIV infection were related to risky sexual activity with casual or long-term partners. Excluded from this review were interventions aimed primarily at IDUs or CSWs. Computer-based searches of Medline and PsycLit were conducted from January 1999 to August 1999 to identify articles published in peer-reviewed professional journals that met the inclusion criteria; 11 studies were identified (See Table 8.1).

CHARACTERISTICS OF
COGNITIVE–BEHAVIORAL INTERVENTIONS

As seen in Table 8.1, cognitive–behavioral group interventions are the most common type of intervention resulting in behavioral change across populations addressed. Cognitive–behavioral group interventions are generally grounded in Social Cognitive Theory (Bandura, 1977, 1989) and involve HIV education and skills training to produce behavioral change. The content and strategies of these types of interventions are based on the constructs of Social Cognitive Theory. Behavioral capabilities to engage in risk reduction are influenced by increasing knowledge and skill building. Health education videos and lectures on HIV prevention and transmission, as well as condom use modeling and practice, are ways to increase such capabilities. Outcome expectancies are the individual's expected results of engaging or not engaging in safer sex; these can include expected negative partner response to condom use or health risk results of nonuse of condoms. This construct can be influenced by cognitive rehearsal, in which the participant verbally or mentally processes how to deal effectively with a potentially risky sexual encounter. Personalizing risk via video or presentation of an HIV-positive peer or HIV statistics on the affiliated population of intervention participants also influences outcome expectancies of unsafe sex practice. Self-monitoring and coping skills can be influenced by identifying triggers of sexual risk taking such as substance abuse or depression, as well as identifying ways to cope with such triggers. An example of the latter may be avoiding sex when depressed or intoxicated or carrying condoms to bars. Self-efficacy, the real or perceived ability to engage in a behavior, can be influenced by role-play exercises in which participants act out safer sex behaviors, such as sexual risk-reduction negotiation. Behavioral reinforcement may be provided by facilitators and group members supporting a participant's desire to practice safer sex or her actual safer sex practices. Participants' environment and situation relates to whether the individual has or perceives having a social environment or sexual situation conducive (free of barriers) to safer sex practice. This construct is generally supported by distribution of free condoms, which improves both affordability and accessibility to them. Partner intervention to promote safer sex could also be used to facilitate condom use by influencing the situation or context of the safer sex prac-

Author	Sample characteristics	Recruitment strategies	Intervention content	Intervention strategies
Kalichman et al. (1996)	• African American women (N = 92) in Milwaukee • Mean age = 33 • Not in monogamous relationship • Note: 72% of recruited eligible women elected to participate in the intervention	• Street outreach • Fliers to housing projects and social service agencies	• Self-management: environment rearrangement, cognitive restructuring, behavior modification, identification of and coping with triggers • Sexual communication: assertiveness, refusal, negotiation • HIV transmission, prevention, illness	• Education and skills building: cognitive rehearsal, roleplays, condom practice, video, discussion
Kalichman et al. (1993)	• African American women (N = 106) in Chicago • Mean age = 32.1 • Lower income, less educated, 80% single; 96% with kids	• Outreach at Family Community Resource Center • Fliers in community	• HIV transmission and prevention • Impact of HIV on African American communities, families, and children	• Video
DiClemente & Wingood (1995)	• African American women (N = 128) in San Francisco • Sexually active • Age 18–29	• Street outreach	• Ethnic and gender pride • HIV risk-reduction information • Sexual self-control • Sexual assertiveness and communication skills • Condom use skills • Partner norms supportive of condom use	• Education and skills building: discussion, video, role-plays, modeling
Peterson et al. (1996)	• African American gay and bisexual men (N = 318) from San Francisco • 18 years+ • Not diagnosed with AIDS	• Recruited from gay bars, erotic book-stores, & bathhouses • Outreach at CBOs • Ads and referrals	• HIV transmission and prevention information • Gay self-identity • Development of social support • Sexual communication • Behavior management	• Education and skills building: Videos, games, role-plays, group discussion
Jemmott et al. (1992)	• African American adolescents (N = 157) in Philadelphia • Mean age = 14.6	• Outpatient clinic recruitment • 10–12 grade assemblies • Outreach at YMCA	• HIV transmission and prevention • Sexual and IDU risk	• Education and skills building: games, role-plays, videos, and brochures

Study design	Intervention and comparison group structures	Cultural tailoring strategies	Facilitators/ staff	Study results
• RCT • Pretest, 3 month follow-up • 95% of sample retained for 3 month follow-up	• 4 groups: (a) education session and 3 communication skills sessions; (b) 1 education session and 3 behaviorial self management sessions; (c) 1 education session, 1½ communications skills sessions, and 1½ behavioral self management sessions; (d) 4 education sessions • 1 session/week for 4 weeks • Small groups	• Defined as culture and gender-tailored • Not specified	• Co-facilitators: 1 African American woman and 1 White male	• Groups receiving communication skills training reported higher unsafe sex refusal rates and higher safer sex communication with partner at 3-month follow-up • The group receiving communications skills and self-management skill training reported the lowest rates of unprotected sex at 3 month follow-up
• RCT • Pretest, 2 week follow-up • 71.7% of sample retained for 2 week follow-up	• 3 videos: (a) Comparision 1: Surgeon General gives info on HIV statistics, AIDS, sexual and IDU risk; White woman gives info on HIV myths; (b) Comparison 2: 3 Black women give the same information as above; (c) Intervention: 3 Black women present HIV education and HIV in the Black community • Small groups	• Use of African American presenters • Focus on African American community • Based on pilot work with focus groups	• N/A	• Intervention participants were more likely to view AIDS as a personal threat, more likely to discuss HIV/AIDS with friends, and more likely to request condoms
• RCT • Pretest, 3 month follow-up • Retention rates were 90.6% (intervention), 82.9% (comparison), and 57.5% (control)	• 3 groups: (a) Intervention: education and skills building for 5 sessions (1/week); (b) Comparison: Education for 1 session; (c) Control: waitlist control • Intervention based on Social Cognitive Theory and Theory of Gender and Power • 5 session program (1/week) • Small groups	• Community members helped develop curriculum • Afrocentric poetry, art, and images used in the curriculum • Afrocentric dialogue used in the curriculum	• Peer educators	• Intervention group revealed increased consistent condom use, greater sexual self-control, greater sexual communication and assertiveness, more positive safer sex partner norms as compared with the comparison and control groups
• RCT • Pretest, 12 month, and 18 month follow-ups • 53% and 58% completed 12 and 18 month follow-ups	• 3 groups: (a) Intervention: HIV education and skills building for 3 sessions, (1 session/week, 1 hr/session); (b) Comparison: HIV education and skills building for 1 3-hour session; (c) Control: waitlist control • Intervention based on AIDS Risk Reduction Model • Small groups	• Curriculum and related materials were pilot tested with African American homosexual and bisexual men	• Co-facilitators: • African American gay males • Trained health educators	• Intervention participants reported the greatest reduction in unprotected anal intercourse at the 12 and 18-month follow-ups, but program effects were not statistically significant
• RCT • Pretest, posttest, 3 month follow-up • Retention rate for the 3 month follow-up was 96%	• Age specific groups: Intervention: (a) AIDS education and skills building; (b) Comparison: career opportunities • Both groups were 1 session for 5 hours • Small groups	• All materials had been extensively pilot tested • African American facilitators	• Trained adult facilitators (male and female)	• At 3 month follow-up, intervention participants reported less frequent sex, less unprotected sex, less anal sex, less multiple partnering, and lower likelihood of a relationship with a non-monogamous partner as compared with comparison group

(continues)

TABLE 8.1 (*continued*)

Author	Sample characteristics	Recruitment strategies	Intervention content	Intervention strategies
Galbraith et al. (1996) Stanton et al. (1996)	• African American adolescents & preadolescents (N = 383) from an Eastern city • Age 9–15 • 56% male • 68% sexually experienced	• Outreach at Community Recreation Centers in lower income neighborhoods • Snowball sampling into peer groups of recruitees	• Facts about AIDS, STDs, birth control, and human development • Sexual decision making • Cultural integration	• Education and skills building
Jemmott et al. (1998)	• African American adolescents (N = 659) in Philadelphia • Mean age = 11.8 • 53% female	• Outreach to 6th and 7th graders from 3 middle schools in lower income neighborhoods	• HIV transmission and prevention information • How to use condoms	• Education and skills building: group discussion, videos, games, brain storming, experiential exercises, and condom practice
St Lawrence et al. (1995)	• African American adolescents (N = 246) in Jackson, MS • No symptoms of HIV/AIDS • Mean age = 15.3 • 72% female	• Recruited from lower income clinics	• HIV transmission and prevention • Condom skills • Sexual decision making • Behavioral management • Sexual communication	• Education and skills training: lecture, games, role-plays, condom practice, peer support, presentations from HIV+ teens
Sellers et al. (1994)	• Latino teens (N = 586) from Boston & Harford • Age 14–20 • 94% Puerto Rican	• Community outreach in neighborhoods with large Latino populations • 84% response rate	• Promote condom use • Increase knowledge of how to use a condom	• Condom distribution • Brochures • PSAs
Zimmerman et al. (1997)	• Mexican gay and bisexual men (N = 92) • Mean age of 25 years • Diverse SES	• Recruited from bars, restaurants • Street outreach	• HIV transmission and prevention info • Plan a HIV community intervention	• Group discussion • Social action to develop & implement a community intervention
Choi et al. (1995, 1996)	• API gay men (N = 329) from San Francisco • 37% Chinese, 34% Filipino, 29% other • Age 18 or older • Non-IDU	• Recruited from Gay API CBOs and street fairs	• Positive gay and API self-identity • Social support • Safer sex info • Eroticize condoms • Sexual communication	• Education and skills building: lecture, discussion, group sharing, scenarios, and role-playing

Study design	Intervention and comparison group structures	Cultural tailoring strategies	Facilitators/ staff	Study results
• RCT (stratified) friendship groups were randomized) • Pretest, posttest, 6, 12, 18-month follow-ups • 91%, 88%, 94% retention at 6, 12, 18 month follow-ups	• 2 groups: (a) Intervention: HIV education and skills; (b) Comparison group: films on HIV and discussion • Intervention based on Social Cognitive Theory & Protection Motivation Theory • 8 weeks, 1/wk, 90 min • Small groups: stratified by age, gender, and sex experience	• Needs assessment research conducted • Community members on research team • Community advisory board was included	• Community members recruited from CBOs facilitated groups • Age 16–47 • Diverse in education & work experience	• Intervention group more likely to use condoms and more effective birth control, including oral contraception with condoms
• RCT • Pretest, 3, 6, and 12-month follow-ups	• 3 groups: (a) Intervention: HIV education and skills building; (b) Comparison: abstinence education; (c) Control: health issues not related to HIV • Small groups stratified by gender and age	• Program pilot tested on target population • African American adult and peer facilitators used	• Trained and experienced adult facilitators • Trained peer facilitators: 56% female	• Intervention participants reported more consistent condom use at 3 mo follow-up and higher frequency of condom use and less unsafe sex at 3, 6, 12 month follow-ups • Intervention participants reported less frequent sex at 6 and 12-month follow-ups (among sexually active)
• RCT • Pretest, 2, 6, and 12 month follow-ups	• 2 groups: (a) Intervention: HIV education and skills building for 8 weeks (1 session/week); (b) Comparison: HIV education for 1 session • Small groups sessions were 2 hours in length	• Afrocentric videos used • African American HIV+ youth presented	• Not specified	• Intervention group less likely to become active • Intervention males reported less unprotected sex • 100% of intervention participants stopped unprotected anal sex • Intervention participants increased condom use; effect dissipated for males at 12 month follow-up
• Matched cities • Pretest and posttest • Retention rates were 92.8% (intervention) & 90.7% (control)	• Community-based intervention program • 18 month program • Conducted in schools, CBOs, clinics, homes	• None	• Trained peer leaders	• Intervention participants were more likely to have a condom in their possession, less likely to become sexually active, less likely to multiple partner • Frequency of sex did not increase as a consequence of this program
• Quasi-experimental: Participants unwilling to be in the intervention were placed into the Comparison group • Retention rates: N/A	• 2 groups: (a) Intervention Group: HIV discussion and social action, met once a week for 8 months, 2–3 hours/session; (b) Control group • Intervention based on Empowerment Model	• Community members as coordinators, lay health educators, curriculum developers • Needs assessment	• Coordinators: 2 gay men trained in HIV/AIDS, community assessment, recruitment, facilitation	• Intervention participants reported more frequent condom use • The intervention group mobilized community support of the community action effort • Participants developed greater knowledge about community resources
• RCT • Pretest and 3 month follow-up • Retention rate was 78% (Those lost to follow-up were more likely to be intervention participants Filipino, HIV−)	• 2 groups: (a) Intervention group: HIV education and skills building; (b) Control group: waitlist control • Intervention based on Health Belief Model, Theory of Reasoned Action, and Social Cognitive Theory	• Discussed racism and homophobia • Intervention materials were pilot-tested on target population	• Co-facilitators: trained outreach worker and trained community volunteer	• Intervention participants were more likely to report a reduction in number of sex partners • Chinese and Filipino intervention participants reported a significantly higher reduction in unprotected anal intercourse at 3 month follow-up

tice. All of these constructs overlap and combine with the desired behavior to operate in a reciprocally deterministic fashion. In other words, there is a dynamic interaction of person, environment, and behavior that creates behavioral change; cognitive–behavioral interventions are designed to address each of these levels via the discussed constructs to produce behavioral change among intervention participants.

REVIEW OF INTERVENTIONS

Interventions with African Americans

The majority of HIV interventions for African Americans were conducted with women and adolescents. The three programs with women (DiClemente & Wingood, 1995; Kalichman et al., 1993; Kalichman, Rompa, & Coley, 1996) all included HIV transmission and prevention information. However, two of the programs involved multisession cognitive behavioral groups with education, skills building, and group discussion (DiClemente & Wingood, 1995; Kalichman et al., 1996), whereas the other program used only a video to educate participants (Kalichman et al., 1993). Although the program with the video did affect participants' condom negotiation skills (Kalichman et al., 1993), the cognitive–behavioral programs resulted in increased condom use and sexual assertiveness (DiClemente & Wingood, 1995; Kalichman et al., 1996). Kalichman et al. (1996) additionally found that participants receiving both sexual communication skills training and behavioral self-management training (sexual self-control) were most likely to reduce their risk behaviors.

All programs for women described themselves as culturally tailored. However neither Kalichman et al. (1996) nor DiClemente and Wingood (1995) described their tailoring strategies other than to define them as both culture- and gender-specific. DiClemente and Wingood (1995) did use community members to assist with curriculum development and peer African American facilitators for program implementation; they stated that an ethnic pride component was included in their curriculum. In contrast, Kalichman et al. (1993) offered a more complete description of the cultural tailoring strategies they used in their video. They not only used African American presenters, they also focused on themes important to African American women. These themes, which were identified in pilot research with their target population, included the impact of HIV on African American communities, families, and children. Although increased condom use was not a result of the program, one major outcome was that participants were more likely to discuss HIV/AIDS with others subsequent to program participation.

Only one study with African American males was found to result in behavioral change; this program focused on intervening with African American MSMs. Peterson et al. (1995) used a multisession cognitive–behavioral group intervention to promote risk reduction in this population. Study results revealed that intervention participants reported the greatest reduction in unprotected anal intercourse at 12- and 18-month follow-ups, but program effects were not statistically significant. The study also described their program as culturally tailored. How-ever, descriptions were limited to pilot testing the curriculum and related mate-rials on the target population and using peer facilitators (African American gay males).

Again, we note that African American MSWs are not addressed in the pub-lished interventions. Kalichman, Rompa, and Coley (1997) did evaluate a pro-gram for African American MSWs. The evaluation compared a traditional, non-tailored, four-session cognitive–behavioral program with a culturally tailored four-session program that included a video and discussions. The culturally tai-lored program incorporated themes important to African American men, which were based on pilot research with the target population. The first theme involved risk recognition: African American men were beginning to recognize their risk, in part as a consequence of Magic Johnson's disclosure about his HIV serosta-tus. The second theme involved individual survival: Personal survival in a racist society was their primary goal, and a program would need to meet their needs in helping them survive for them to be interested in attending. Study results re-vealed no significant differences between groups, as neither group increased con-dom use. Furthermore, 45% of participants dropped out of the programs, with no significant differences between groups in terms of dropout rates. However, dropouts were more likely to be younger and to use condoms; they were less likely to have been tested for HIV.

Although this study was not successful in reducing HIV risk, the study find-ings are very important because it is the only published evaluation study with African American MSWs. The authors postulate that the culturally tailored in-tervention did not work because the HIV prevention messages were embedded within larger, more salient issues (e.g., unemployment, violence, drug abuse) for these men, such that the program further reinforced HIV as a secondary or ter-tiary concern for the African American participants. The authors also suggest tar-geting younger men separately from men aged 30 or older, as younger men may have been lost to intervention due to the lack of developmental tailoring. Al-though these younger men appear to have low risk perceptions, they felt the pro-gram was more useful for adolescents than for themselves.

Kalichman et al. (1997) also suggest that, unlike African American women and MSMs, African American MSWs may be more comfortable in one-on-one cognitive–behavioral training than in group interventions, such as those proven successful in men's smoking cessation. Further, they say cognitive–behavioral skills training that emphasizes negotiation skills may be less useful for MSWs because they are more likely to control condom use in the first place. Hence, di-verse interventions will need to be studied before effective intervention content and strategies for African American MSWs can be defined.

In contrast to work with African American males, studies with African Amer-ican adolescents proved more successful. All programs for this group used cog-nitive–behavioral groups to reduce participants' HIV risk (Galbraith et al., 1996; Jemmott, Jemmott, & Fong, 1992; Jemmott, Jemmott, Faan, & Fong, 1998; Stanton, Li, Galbraith, Feigelman, & Kaljee, 1996; St. Lawrence et al., 1995). One program was solely for males (Jemmott et al., 1992), whereas the others were for both males and females. All programs, including the solely male program, resulted in increased risk reduction. Risk reduction included less frequent sex, less multiple partnering, less anal sex, fewer risky partners, more condom use, and less unprotected sex (Galbraith et al., 1996; Jemmott & Jemmott, 1992; Jemmott et al., 1998; Stanton et al., 1996; St. Lawrence et al., 1995). Although these programs for adolescents resulted in reduction in unsafe sex, they did not change participants' sexual activity. St. Lawrence et al. (1995) found that, among nonsexually active adolescents, participants of the 8-week intervention group were less likely to initiate sexual activity than were 1-session program participants.

Although the cognitive–behavioral groups appear to be effective in producing behavioral change among African American adolescents, cultural tailoring may not have been the cornerstone of these programs. As with previously discussed programs, pilot testing was conducted for needs assessment and to check program materials; African American facilitators were used (Galbraith et al., 1996; Jemmott & Jemmott, 1992; Jemmott et al., 1998; Stanton et al., 1996). Developmental tailoring appears to have been common as well, including the use of adolescent facilitators, educational games, and combining contraceptive and HIV-prevention education (Galbraith et al., 1996; Jemmott & Jemmott, 1992; Jemmott et al., 1998; Stanton et al., 1996; St. Lawrence et al., 1995). However, specific cultural tailoring strategies outside of pilot testing and inclusion of community members and peers were not mentioned in any of the reviewed programs.

Interventions with Hispanics

The review of programs for Hispanics revealed that none of the evaluated programs for Hispanic women or Hispanic MSWs resulted in significant behavioral risk reduction. However, there was one program for adolescents (Sellers, McGraw & McKinlay, 1994) and one for gay men (Zimmerman, Valles, Suarez, De la Rosa & Castro, 1997) that used community-level approaches to reduce individual risk. The program for adolescents (Sellers et al., 1994), composed mostly of Puerto Rican teens, used condom distribution, brochures, and public service announcements in predominantly Hispanic communities. Participants of the intervention were significantly more likely to have a condom in their possession and less likely to multiple partner than were participants in the control city; no impact on actual condom use was mentioned. Similar to St. Lawrence et al.'s (1995) program with African American adolescents, participants of this intervention were also less likely to become sexually active. Zimmerman et al.'s (1997) program with Mexican gay and bisexual men was also community-based, built on Empowerment Theory (Friere, 1970). This program educated participants in HIV transmission and prevention information and then, via discussion groups, facilitated the men's development of an HIV intervention for gay Hispanic men in their community. The program was tailored to participants by including community members as program coordinators, lay health educators, and curriculum developers; specific cultural tailoring strategies were not mentioned. Participants reported more frequent condom use and greater knowledge of community resources; they also mobilized community support for their program efforts. Both of these community-level programs appear to be effective in promoting risk reduction among Hispanic adolescents and gay males without specific cultural tailoring. These findings may suggest that community versus cognitive–behavioral approaches may be more culturally suitable for Hispanic populations.

Interventions with American Asian/Pacific Islanders

Only one evaluated program resulting in behavioral change has been conducted with Asian/Pacific Islanders, and it focused on API gay men (Choi et al., 1995, 1996). No HIV-prevention programs for Asian/Pacific Islanders women, MSWs, or adolescents were found in the literature. The evaluated program for gay APIs was cognitive–behavioral in its approach and had mostly Chinese and Filipino participants. As seen with other cognitive–behavioral programs, focus was on education and communication and self-management skills building. The program was culturally tailored to include discussions of racism against Asian/Pacific Islanders. However, the cultural tailoring was tied to tailoring for gay males. Focus of discussions was on how gay APIs were viewed by the larger gay male community as well as the larger API community. Overall, program participants were significantly more likely to reduce their multiple partnering. Among Chinese and Filipino intervention participants, reduced unprotected intercourse was also observed as a consequence of program participation.

Summary of Findings

Despite the need for HIV-prevention efforts targeting specific minority racial/ethnic populations, a review of the literature revealed that studies demonstrating effective HIV interventions for these groups are rare. For Native Americans and Alaskan Natives, they are nonexistent. The majority of studies found in the literature search were for African Americans. Most were with African American women and adolescents. In contrast, no programs were found for Hispanic or API women. Only one program was found for Hispanic adolescents, and none for API adolescents. Further, African American MSMs, Hispanic MSMs, and API MSMs each had only one study evaluating a program targeting their group. Clearly, present program research is not meeting the needs of diverse American racial/ethnic populations.

Nonetheless, this review of the literature does yield important findings. First, it reveals that, consistent with HIV-risk factor research literature demonstrating the importance of individually based interventions, cognitive–behavioral groups do appear to be somewhat effective in reducing HIV risks for African American women, African American adolescents, African American MSMs, and Asian/Pacific Islanders gay men. However, due to minimal follow-up in most studies, long-term effects from such programs cannot be determined. Community-level approaches appear to be effective with Hispanic communities as well. Second, tailoring programs involves not just racial/ethnic cultural tailoring but also tailoring to subpopulations such as women, MSMs, and adolescents. Accounting for issues such as gender-based power differentials for women, homophobia for MSMs, and developmental risk taking for adolescents, for instance, will be important across racial/ethnic groups. Third, cultural tailoring, absent or minimally mentioned in most programs, appears not to be a consequence of specific strategies previously identified by researchers. This tailoring appears to be more a result of pilot research with the target population as well as inclusion of community members in the program development, implementation, and research processes.

CONCLUSION AND IMPLICATIONS

Although HIV/AIDS continues to have a disproportionately high impact on racial/ethnic minority groups in the United States (CDC, 1999), there is increasing recognition that HIV-prevention programs must be better tailored to meet effectively the needs of these groups. Consequently, culturally tailored programs are commonly discussed as an important and necessary component of HIV-prevention efforts. Unfortunately, culturally tailored programs appear to be discussed more frequently in the theoretical literature than in the empirical literature, demonstrating that, in practice, cultural tailoring is more a rarity than a norm.

The vast majority of literature and interventions focusing on HIV prevention for racial/ethnic minority populations in the United States has been conducted primarily with lower-income, urban African American and Hispanic women, adolescents, and MSMs. This is very likely due to the higher rates of HIV infection within these communities. However, this focus increases the invisibility of members of these racial/ethnic groups who do not fit the stereotypic socioeconomic profile; it also negates the HIV risk of unacknowledged subgroups such as MSWs. In addition to the lack of focus on certain African American and Hispanic subpopulations, there is little literature focusing on HIV prevention within other racial/ethnic communities—ones that may have lower rates of HIV infection but do demonstrate a high prevalence of risk behaviors (e.g., APIs, Native Americans/Alaskans). Thus, our understanding of the needs of the various racial/ethnic minority populations and subpopulations is minimal, although the need to work with these communities is great.

Despite the paucity of literature on HIV risk factors for racial/ethnic minority groups, studies conducted with these populations do reveal certain findings. Individual risk factors (e.g., safer sex intentions, HIV risk perceptions, self-efficacy, attitudes towards safer sex) appear to affect risk across racial/ethnic groups and subpopulations (e.g., women, MSMs, adolescents). In addition, sociocultural factors related to the dyadic relationship, peer influence, historical experience, and societal power also have an impact on risk; however, these factors naturally differ by group and subpopulation. Finally, racial/ethnic cultural factors and social phenomena also influence risk for members of the populations we have addressed. These cultural factors are intertwined with cultural factors related to subpopulation affiliation. For instance, the stigmatization of homosexuality within the Hispanic community may keep gay Hispanic men from accessing HIV-prevention information for fear of disclosure. All of these risk factors must be addressed to meet the HIV-prevention needs at every level for these target populations.

The literature review of existing interventions resulting in significant behavioral change again reveals a paucity of research conducted with racial/ethnic minority populations. As with the HIV risk factor literature, programs focused primarily on lower-income, urban populations. Thus, it is not possible to generalize the findings from these studies. Nonetheless, there does seem to be some indication that cognitive–behavioral group intervention programs that address individually based risk factors are effective in producing behavioral change in some groups, including lower-income African American women and adolescents, African American MSMs, and API gay men. Community-based approaches to HIV prevention appear to work with Hispanic MSMs and adolescents, although they do not have a strong impact on condom use. Overall, the findings indicate that, with the help of the target population, effective interventions can be developed for many subpopulations of racial/ethnic minority groups. However, within each cultural group subpopulation, there may exist the need for different HIV-prevention strategies.

The majority of programs critiqued did not mention specific strategies of cultural tailoring for groups. Often, definitions of cultural tailoring were restricted to pilot testing of intervention materials and inclusion of community members in program development and implementation. However, given the consistency with which these strategies were used in reviewed programs, the importance of these strategies cannot be understated. Programs that discussed more specific culturally tailored strategies had focused on making their health messages relevant to the target population. Relevant messages were based on themes important to the target population, and these themes were generated via pilot testing, often done with focus groups. In addition to a relevant message, it appears that a relevant messenger was important, too. Peers, community members, and members of the same gender, age, sexual orientation, and racial/ethnic group often served as facilitators for the reviewed programs. Thus, culturally tailored program messages and message providers may be the cornerstone of cultural tailoring, but this tailoring can only occur based on previous research with the target population.

IMPLICATIONS

Review of this literature yields important implications for future HIV-prevention efforts with racial/ethnic minority communities.

1. Programs must be culturally tailored to meet the needs of the target population better. However, such efforts must be applied in ways that do not serve to further marginalize members of these populations. This will require including members of these populations in the program development, implementation, and evaluation processes, such that they, rather than the researchers, own these processes.

2. Cultural tailoring efforts should be based on previous research with the target populations.

   a. Previous research must include review of the research literature as well as pilot testing with the target population.

   b. Pilot testing should involve both quantitative (closed-ended questionnaires) and qualitative (open-ended questions) research to determine the following: What are the needs of the target population? What are the issues important to the target population? To what type of health messages would the target population be most likely to respond? To what type of messenger and message system would the target population be most likely to respond?

3. Various cultural affiliations (e.g., gender, age, sexual orientation), including racial/ethnic identity, must be addressed to attend fully to the concerns of all groups. Due to the fact that any individual may be affiliated with any number of cultures (e.g., African American, gay male, rural), group tailoring needs to address multiple cultures.

4. Program participants must be actively involved in the cultural tailoring process. No program can be fully tailored to a program population due to fluidity of culture and diversity of cultural affiliation. Thus, programs must be created to allow for program tailoring during the program process. Only this can ensure that participants of any program can get their needs met.

SUMMARY

While both HIV researchers and practitioners support the need for more culturally tailored HIV-prevention research and programs, the published literature suggests that there has been a paucity of such programs implemented and evaluated. This is the case for a variety of reasons, including a historic ignoring of the needs of marginalized groups, the fluidity of culture, as well as the difficulties of culturally tailoring programs to a multicultural society. However, research on various racial/ethnic minority groups underscore the need as well as the ability to culturally tailor programs to better meet the needs of these populations, though this research also emphasizes the gaps in literature for racial/ethnic groups, such as Native Americans, as well as for other specific populations, such as men who have sex with women (MSWs).

Based on this review of the literature, it is clear that HIV prevention as a field must be more active in addressing the needs of multicultural populations (i.e., populations diverse in race/ethnicity, class, gender, and risk), especially those of marginalized groups. With regard to program development and implementation, this will mean responding to the needs of the population served by including members of the target population and by considering cultural issues of the population throughout the program development and implementation processes. With regard to program evaluation, this will involve use of standard components in terms of content and strategies but simultaneously program flexibility, so participants can further tailor the programs to suit their needs.

CASE STUDY

Erica and Felix started dating when Erica was 18 and Felix was 27. They fell in love and began living together. Erica became close to Felix's mother and sister. During Erica and Felix's relationship, Felix told Erica that he wanted a baby. When she was 21 and he was 29, they had a son named Mario. However, soon after Erica brought Mario home, he began to get repeated infections. Finally, the doctor suggested to Erica that she and her son should get tested for HIV. Test results showed that both Erica and Mario were HIV-positive. Erica immediately told Felix that he might have the virus, too. That was when Erica found out that Felix had known that he had HIV before they were ever together; further, his mother, and sister knew. Felix, his mother, and his sister also knew that he could infect her if they had unprotected sex. But Erica felt she understood why they kept the secret. It made sense that Felix and his family wanted him to have a baby before he died, and they did not know that the baby could get HIV. She also understood why Felix's mother and sister would want to protect him; he was the only man in their family. Erica loved Felix, and she forgave him. She was also hopeful that her baby would not remain HIV-positive because the doctors told her that some babies become HIV-negative after they are 18 months old. Nonetheless, Erica's parents severed all ties with her once they found out that she, her boyfriend, and her child were HIV-positive. After Mario was 18 months old, Erica got him tested again; he was still positive. Erica became depressed, blaming herself for the baby's illness. She felt that, as the baby's mother, it was her responsibility to keep her baby healthy; she felt she had failed her child. Eventually, her depression became so severe she was sent to a mental health institute for 3 weeks. As soon as she was released, she stopped dealing with her depression and just focused on taking care of Mario and Felix. Erica worked from 4 to 11 p.m. every evening waiting tables to keep her family together, and her days were spent taking care of her child and her husband. Felix quit work to take care of the baby, although the baby usually stayed with Felix's mother during the day. When Mario was 3, Erica found out that Felix had an affair and infected one of her friends. Again, Felix's family knew of his infidelity, but said nothing either to Erica or the friend. Erica found it more difficult to forgive Felix and his family for this, but she did not leave. She loved Felix and they had a child together; also, there was nowhere for her to go. Soon, Felix became sicker, and his mother took care of both him and the baby while Erica worked.

When Erica was not working, she took care of both her husband and her child. Recently, Erica became ill, too. She went to the doctor and found that her T-cell count was low. She was diagnosed with AIDS. Erica says the hardest thing for a woman with HIV is dealing the cocktails that knock her out; these keep her from being able to take care of her family. Currently, Erica and her family live day to day, just trying to survive.

1. How did culture play a role in Erica's HIV infection? What types of culture were involved—gender, race/ethnicity, familial culture?

2. Where could intervention have occurred such that Erica would not have become HIV-positive? What types of risk factors put Erica at increased risk for getting HIV?

3. How can cultural ideologies that increase HIV risk be addressed in a way that is not victim-blaming or culture-blaming? How could cultural factors work to increase resiliency?

Note: This case study was provided by Ana Lamarche, HIV Program Coordinator for Martha Eliot Health Center, Boston, Massachusetts. The names have been changed to ensure the anonymity of the family.

SUGGESTED READINGS

Feldman, D. A. (Ed.). (1991). Culture and AIDS. New York: Praeger.
Herdt, G., & Lindenbaum, S. (Eds.) (1992). *The time of AIDS: Social analysis, theory, and method.* Newbury Park, CA: Sage.

REFERENCES

Ajzen, I., & Fishbein, M. (1980). *Understanding attitudes and predicting social behavior.* Englewood Cliffs, NJ: Prentice Hall.
Amaro, H. (1988). Considerations for prevention of HIV infection among Hispanic women. *Psychology of Women Quarterly, 12,* 429–443.
Amaro, H., & Gornemann, I. (1996). Hispanic women and AIDS: Knowledge, attitudes, behaviors, and barriers to prevention. Unpublished manuscript.
Amaro, H., & Hardy-Fanta, C. (1995). Gender relations in addiction and recovery. *Journal of Psychoactive Drugs, 27,* 325–337.
Aruffo, J. F., Coverdale, J. H., & Vallbona, C. (1991). AIDS knowledge in low-income and minority populations. *Public Health Reports, 108,* 115–119.
Atkins, D., Morten, G., & Sue, D. W. (1983). *Counseling American minorities.* Dubuque, IA: Wm. C. Brown.
Auerbach, J. D., Wypijewska, C., & Brodie, H. K. H. (Eds.). (1994). *Understanding the determinants of HIV risk behavior.* AIDS and Behavior: An integrated approach (pp. 78–123). Institute of Medicine. Washington, DC: National Academy Press.
Baker-Miller, J. (1993). The development of women's sense of self. In J. V. Jordan, J. Baker-Miller, I. P. Stiver, & J. L. Surrey (Eds.), *Women's growth in connection* (pp. 11–26). New York: Guildford Press.
Bandura, A. (1977). Perceived self-efficacy: Toward a unified theory of behavioral change. *Psychological Review, 84,* 191–215.

Bandura, A. (1989). Perceived self-efficacy in the exercise of control over AIDS infection. In V. M. Mays, G. W. Albee, & S. F. Schneider (Eds.), *Primary prevention of AIDS* (pp. 128–141). London, UK: Sage.

Bau, I. (1998). Asians and Pacific Islanders and HIV prevention community planning. *AIDS Education and Prevention, 10* (Suppl. A), 77–93.

Becker, M., & Joseph, J. (1988). AIDS and behavioral change to avoid risk: A review. *American Journal of Public Health, 78,* 384–410.

Becker, M. H. (1974). The health belief model and sick role behavior. *Health Education Monographs, 2,* 409–419.

Brunswick, A. F., & Flory, M. J. (1998). Changing HIV infection rates among an African American community cohort. *AIDS Care, 10,* 267–281.

Caetano, R., & Hines, A. M. (1995). Alcohol, sexual practices, and risk of AIDS among blacks, Hispanics, and whites. *Journal of Acquired Immune Deficiency Syndrome and Human Retroviruses, 10,* 554–561.

Carballo-Dieguez, A., & Dolezal, C. (1995). Association between history of childhood sexual abuse and adult HIV risk sexual behavior in Puerto Rican men who have sex with men. *Child Abuse and Neglect, 19,* 595–605.

Carovano, K. (1991). More than mothers and whores: Redefining the AIDS prevention needs of women. *International Journal of Health Services, 21,* 131–142.

Carrier, J., Nguyen, B., & Su, S. (1992). Vietnamese American sexual behaviors and HIV infection. *Journal of Sex Research, 29,* 409–419.

Catania, J., Coates, T., Golden, E., Dolcini, M., Peterson, J., Kegeles, S., Siegel, D., & Fullilove, M. (1994). Correlates of condom use among black, Hispanic, and white heterosexuals in San Francisco: The AMEN longitudinal survey. *AIDS Education and Prevention, 6,* 12–26.

Catania, J. A., Coates, T. J., Kegeles, S., Fullilove, M. T., Peterson, J., Marin, B., Siegel, D., & Hulley, S. (1992). Condoms use in multi-ethnic neighborhoods of San Francisco: The population-based AMEN (AIDS in multi-ethnic neighborhoods) study. *American Journal of Public Health, 82,* 284–287.

Centers for Disease Control (1996). *HIV/AIDS Surveillance Report: United States HIV and AIDS cases reported through December 1995.* Year End Edition, 7(1).

Centers for Disease Control (1997). *HIV/AIDS Surveillance Report: United States HIV and AIDS cases reported through December 1996.* Year End Edition, 8(1).

Centers for Disease Control (1999). *HIV/AIDS Surveillance Report: United States HIV and AIDS cases reported through June 1998.* Midyear Edition, 10(1).

Centers for Disease Control (1998). HIV/AIDS among American Indians and Alaskan Natives—United States, 1981–1997. *Morbidity and Mortality Weekly Reports, 47,* 154–160

Chang, R. (1993). *U.S. national Asian and Pacific Islander HIV /AIDS agenda.* San Francisco, CA: Asian Pacific AIDS Coalition.

Chng, L. C., Sy, F. S., Choi, S. T., Bau, I., & Astudillo, R. (1998). Asian and Pacific Islander American HIV community-based organizations: A nationwide survey. *AIDS Education and Prevention, 10* (Suppl. A), 48–60.

Choi, K.-H., & Kumekawa, E. (1998). Environmental influences and sexual risk-taking among young Asian and Pacific Islander men who have sex with men. Unpublished raw data. In K. H. Choi, G. A. Yep, & E. Kumekawa (Eds.), HIV prevention among Asian and Pacific Islander men who have sex with men: A critical review of theoretical models and directions for future research. *AIDS Education and Prevention, 10* (Suppl. A), 19–30.

Choi, K.-H., Coates, T. K., Catansia, J. A., Lew, S., & Chow, P. (1995). High HIV risk among gay Asian and Pacific Islander men in San Francisco. *AIDS Journal, 9,* 306–307.

Choi, K.-H., Lew, S., Vittinghoff, E., Catania, J. A., Barrett, D. C., & Coates, T. J. (1996). The efficacy of brief group counseling in HIV risk reduction among homosexual Asian and Pacific Islander men. *AIDS, 10,* 81–87.

Cochran, S. D., Mays, V. M., & Leung, L. (1991). Sexual practices of heterosexual Aisan-American young adults: Implications for risk for HIV infection. *Archives of Sexual Behavior, 24,* 381–393.

COSSMHO (Coalition of Hispanic Health and Human Service Organizations). (1991). *HIV/AIDS: The impact on Hispanics in selected states.* Washington, DC: Author.

Cross, W. (1978). The Thomas and Cross models of psychological nigressence: A literature review. *Journal of Black Psychology, 4,* 13–31.

Denning, P. H., Jones, J. L., & Ward, J. W. (1997). Recent trends in the HIV epidemic in adolescent and young adult gay and bisexual men. *Journal of Acquired Immune Deficiency Syndrome and Human Retroviruses, 16,* 5, 374–379.

Department of Health and Human Services, Public Health Service, Indian Health Service. (1997). *Trends in Indian health—1996.* Rockville, MD: Department of Health and Human Services, Public Health Service, Indian Health Service.

Deren, S., Shedlin, M., & Beardsley, M. (1996). HIV-related concerns and behaviors among Hispanic women. *AIDS Education and Prevention, 8,* 335–342.

Diaz, T., & Klevens, M.(1997). Differences by ancestry in sociodemographics and risk behaviors among Latinos with AIDS. The Supplement to HIV and AIDS Surveillance Project Group. *Ethnicity and Disease, 7,* 200–206.

Diaz, T., Buehler, W., Castro, K. G., & Ward, J. W. (1993). AIDS trends among Hispanics in the United States. *American Journal of Public Health, 83,* 504–509.

Diaz, R., Stall, R., Hoff, C., Daigle, D., & Coates, T. (1996). HIV risk among Latino gay men in the southwestern United States. *AIDS Education and Prevention, 8,* 415–428.

DiClemente, R. J., & Wingwood, G. M. (1995). A randomized controlled trial of an HIV sexual risk-reduction intervention for young African–American women. *Journal of American Medical Association, 274,* 1271–1276.

DiClemente, R. J., Zorn, J., & Temoshok, L. (1987). The association of gender, ethnicity, and length of residence in the Bay area to adolescents' knowledge and attitudes about acquired immunodeficiency syndrome. *Journal of Applied Social Psychology, 17,* 261, 230.

Dolcini, M. M., Coates, T. J., Catania, J. A., Kegeles, S. M., & Heuck, W. W. (1998). Multiple sex partnering and their psychosocial correlates: The population-based AIDS in multiethnic neighborhood AMEN) study. *Health Psychology, 14,* 1, 22–31.

Doll, L. S., Peterson, J., Magana, J. R., & Carrier, J. M. (1991). Male bisexuality and AIDS in the United States. In R. Tielman, M. Carballo, & A. Hendricks (Eds.), *Bisexuality and HIV/AIDS* (pp. 27–39). Buffalo, NY: Prometheus.

Ehrlich, E., Flexner, S. B., Carruth, G., & Hawkins, J. M. (Eds.) (1980). *Oxford American Dictionary.* New York: Oxford University Press.

Eldridge, G. D., St. Lawrence, J. S., Little, C. E., Shelby, M. C., & Brasfield, T. L. (1995). Barriers to condom use and barrier method preferences among low income African American women. *Women and Health, 23,* 73–89.

Elwood, W. N., Williams, M. L., Bell, D. C., & Richard, A. J. (1997). Powerlessness and HIV prevention among people who trade sex for drugs ("strawberries"). *AIDS Care, 9,* 273–284.

Erickson, P. (1998). Cultural factors affecting the negotiation of first sexual intercourse among Latina adolescent mothers. *International Quarterly of Community Health Education, 18,* 121–137.

Fenaughty, A. M., Fisher, D. G., Cagle, H. H., Stevens, S., Baldwin, J. A., & Booth, R. (1998). Sex partners of Native American drug users. *Journal of Acquired Immune Deficiency, 17,* 275–282.

Fishbein, M., & Ajzen, I. (1975). *Belief, attitude, intention and behavior: An introduction to theory and research.* Reading, MA; Addison-Wesley.

Fisher, D. G., Cagle, H. H., & Wilson, P. J. (1993). Drug use and HIV risk in Alaska Natives. *Drugs and Society, 7,* 107–117.

Flaskerud, J. H., Uman, G., Lara, R., Romero, L., & Taka, K. (1996). Sexual practices, attitudes, and knowledge related to HIV transmission in low income Los Angeles Hispanic women. *Journal of Sex Research, 33,* 343–353.

Fleisher, J. M., Senie, R. T., Minkoff, H., & Jaccard, J. (1994). Condom use relative to knowledge of sexually transmitted disease prevention, method of birth control, and past or present infection. *Journal of Community Health, 19,* 395–407.

Ford, K., & Norris, A. E. (1995). Factors related to condom use with casual partners among urban African American and Hispanic men. *AIDS Education and Prevention, 7,* 494–503.

Forrest, K. A., Austin, D. M., Valdes, M. I., Fuentes, E. G., & Wilson, S. R. (1993). Exploring norms and beliefs related to AIDS prevention among California Hispanic men. *Family Planning Perspectives, 25,* 111–117.

Friere, P. (1970). *Pedagogy of the oppressed.* New York: Seabury Press.

Fullilove, M. T., Fullilove, R. E., Haynes, K., & Gross, S. (1990). Black women and AIDS prevention: A view towards understanding the gender rules. *The Journal of Sex Research, 27,* 46–64.

Galbraith, J., Ricardo, I., Stanton, B., Black, M., Feigelman, S., & Kaljee, L. (1996). Challenges and rewards of involving community in research: An overview of the "Focus on Kids" HIV risk reduction program. *Health Education Quarterly, 23,* 383–394.

Gilmore, S., DeLamater, J., & Wagstaff, D. (1996). Sexual decision-making by inner city Black adolescent males: A focus groups study. *Journal of Sex Research, 33,* 363–371.

Gock, T. S., & Ja, D. Y. (1995). Providing substance abuse treatment to Asian Pacific clients. In O. Amulerli-Marshall (Ed.), *Substance abuse treatment in the era of AIDS 2* (pp. 223–249). Rockville, MD: Center for Substance Abuse Treatment.

Gordon-Bradshaw, R. (1987). A social essay on special issues facing poor women of color. *Women and Health, 12,* 243–259.

Greenfield, L. (1998). Violence by intimates: Analysis of data on crimes by current or former spouses, boyfriends, and girlfriends. *Bureau of Justice Statistics Fact Book.* Washington, DC: United States Department of Justice.

Gurak, D. T. (1980). Assimilation and fertility: A comparison of Mexican American and Japanese American women. *Hispanic Journal of Behavioral Sciences, 2,* 219–239.

Hahn, R. A. (1995). *Sickness and healing: An anthropological perspective.* New Haven, CT: Yale University Press.

Hanson, M. (1992). Ethnic, cultural, and language diversity in intervention settings. In E. Lynch & M. Hanson (Eds), Developing cross-cultural competence: A guide for working with young children and their families (pp. 3–21). Baltimore, MD: Paul H. Brookes Publishing Co.

Hays, R. B., & Peterson, J. L. (1994). HIV prevention for gay and bisexual men in metropolitan cities. In R. J. DiClemente & J. L. Peterson (Eds.), *Preventing AIDS: Theory and methods of behavioral interventions* (pp. 267–296). New York: Plenum.

Helman, C. G. (1994). *Culture, health and illness: An introduction for health professionals* (3rd ed.). Oxford, UK: Butterworth-Heinemann.

Helms, J. (1990). *Black and white racial identity: Theory, research and practice.* New York: Greenwood.

Holland, J., Ramazanoglu, C., Scott, S., Sharpe, S., & Thompson, R. (1992). Risk, power, and possibility of pleasure: Young women and safer sex. *AIDS Care, 4,* 273–283.

Horan, P. F., & DiClemente, R. J. (1993). HIV knowledge, communication, and risk behaviors among white, Chinese-, and Filipino-American adolescents in a high-prevalence AIDS epicenter: A comparative analysis. *Ethnicity and Disease, 3,* 97–105.

Hou, S.-I., & Basen-Enquist, K. (1997). Human immunodeficiency virus risk behavior among White and Asian/Pacific Islander high school students in the United States: Does culture make a difference? *Journal of Adolescent Health, 20,* 68–74.

Hudgins, R., McCusker, J., & Stoddard, A. (1995). Cocaine use and risky injection and sexual behavior. *Drug and Alcohol Dependence, 37,* 7–14.

Izazol-Licea, J., Valdespino-Gomez, J., Gortmaker, S., Townsend, J., Becker, J., Palacios-Martinez, M., Mueller, N., & Sepulveda, J. (1991). HIV-1 seropositivity and behavioral sociological risks among homosexual and bisexual men in six Mexican cities. *Journal of Acquired Immune Deficiency Syndrome, 4,* 614–622.

Jemmott, J. B., Jemmott, L. S., & Fong, G. T. (1998). Abstinence and safer sex HIV risk-reduction interventions for African–American adolescents. *Journal of American Medical Association, 279,* 1529–1536.

Jemmott, J. B., Jemmott, L. S., & Fong, G. T. (1992). Reduction in HIV risk-associated sexual behaviors among Black male adolescents: Effects of an AIDS prevention intervention. *American Journal of Public Health, 82,* 372–377.

Kalichman, S. C., Kelly, J., & Hunter, T. (1992). Perceptions of AIDS susceptibility among minority and nonminority women at risk for HIV infection. *Journal of Consulting and Clinical Psychology, 60,* 725–732.

Kalichman C. S., Kelly, J. A., Hunter, T. L., Murphy, D. A., & Tyler, R. (1993). Culturally tailored HIV/AIDS risk-reduction messages targeted to African-American urban women: Impact on risk sensitization and risk reduction. *Journal of Consulting and Clinical Psychology, 61,* 291–295.

Kalichman, C. S., Rompa, D., & Coley, B. (1996). Experimental component analysis of a behavioral HIV/AIDS prevention intervention for inner-city women. *Journal of Consulting and Clinical Psychology, 64,* 687–693.

Kalichman, S. C., Rompa, D., & Coley, B. (1997). Lack of positive outcomes from a cognitive–behavioral HIV and AIDS prevention intervention for inner-city men: Lessons from a controlled pilot study. *AIDS Education and Prevention, 9,* 299–313.

Kalichman, S. C., Williams, E. A., Cherry, C., Belcher, L., & Nachimson, D. (1998). Sexual coercion, domestic violence, and negotiating condom use among low-income African American women. *Journal of Women's Health, 7,* 371–378.

Kim, J. (1981). The process of Asian-American identity development: A study of Japanese-American women's perceptions of their struggle to achieve positive identities. Doctoral dissertation, University of Massachusetts (cited in J. S. Phinney. A three stage model of ethnic identity development in adolescence. In M. B. Bernal & G. P. Knight (Eds.) (1993), *Ethnic identity: Formation and transmission among Hispanics and other minorities* (pp. 61–79). New York: State University of New York.

Kim, M. Y., Marmor, M., Dubin, N., & Wolfe, H. (1993). HIV risk-related sexual behaviors among heterosexuals in New York City: Associations with race, sex, and intravenous drug use. *AIDS, 7,* 409–414.

Lehner, T., & Chiasson, M. A. (1998). Seroprevalence of human immunodeficiency virus type 1 and sexual behaviors in bisexual African American and Hispanic men visiting a sexually transmitted disease clinic in New York City. *American Journal of Epidemiology, 147,* 269–272.

Lemp, G. F., Hirozawa, A. M., Givertz, D., Nieri, G. N., Anderson, L., Lindegren, M. L., Janssen, R. S., & Katz, M. (1994). Seroprevalence of HIV and risk behaviors among young homosexual and bisexual men. The San Francisco/Berkeley Young Men's Study. *Journal of American Medical Association, 272,* 449–454.

Linn, L. S., Speigal, J. S., Mathews, W. C., Leake, B., Lien, R., & Brooks, S. (1989). Recent sexual behaviors among homosexual men seeking primary care. *Archives of Internal Medicine, 149,* 2685–2690.

Loue, S., Lloyd, L. S., & Phoombour, E. (1996). Organizing Asian Pacific Islanders in an urban community to reduce HIV risk: A case study. *AIDS Education and Prevention, 8,* 381–393.

Lynch, E. (1992). Developing cross-cultural competence. In E. Lynch & M. Hanson (Eds), *Developing cross-cultural competence: A guide for working with young children and their families* (pp. 22–43). Baltimore, MD: Paul H. Brookes Publishing Co.

Marcia, J. (1966). Development and validation of ego-identity status. *Journal of Personality and Social Psychology, 3,* 551–558.

Marin, B. V., Tschann, J. M., Gomez, C. A., & Gregorich, S. (1998). Self-efficacy to use condoms in unmarried Latino adults. *American Journal of Community Psychology, 26,* 53–71.

Marks, G., Cantero, P. J., & Simoni, J. M. (1998). Is acculturation associated with sexual risk behaviors? An investigation of HIV-positive Latino men and women. *AIDS Care, 10,* 283–295.

Matteson, D. R. (1997). Sexual and homosexual behavior and HIV risk among Chinese-, Filipino-, and Korean-American men. *Journal of Sex Research, 34,* 93–104.

Mays, V., & Cochran, S. (1988). Issues in the perception of AIDS risk and risk reduction activities by black and Hispanic/Latina women. *American Psychologist, 43,* 949–957.

McCaig, L. F., Hardy, A. M., & Winn, D. M. (1991). Knowledge about AIDS and HIV in the United States adult population: Influence of the local incidence of AIDS. *American Journal of Public Health, 81,* 1591–1595.

McKirnan, D. J., Stokes, J. P., Doll, L., & Burzette, R. G. (1995). Bisexually active men: Social characteristics and sexual behavior. *Journal of Sex Research, 32,* 64–75.

Metler, R., Conway, G. A., & Stehr-Green, J. (1991). AIDS surveillance among American Indians and Alaska Natives. *American Journal of Public Health, 81,* 1469–1471.

Modeste, N. N. (1996). *Dictionary of public health promotion and education: Terms and concepts.* Thousand Oaks, CA: Sage.

Nemoto, T., Wong, F. Y., Ching, A., Chng, C. L., Bouey, P., Henrickson, M., & Sember, R. E. (1998). HIV seroprevalence, risk behaviors, and cognitive factors among Asian and Pacific Islander men who have sex with men: A summary and critique of empirical studies and methodological issues. *AIDS Education and Prevention, 10,* (Suppl. A), 31–47.

Nyamathi, A., Bennet, C., Leake, B., Lewis, C., & Flaskerud, J. (1993). AIDS-related knowledge, perceptions, and behaviors among impoverished minority women. *American Journal of Public Health, 83,* 65–71.

O'Donnell, L., San Doval, A., Vornfett, R., & O'Donnell, C. (1994). STD prevention and the challenge of gender and cultural diversity: Knowledge, attitudes, and risk behaviors among black and Hispanic inner-city STD patients. *Sexually Transmitted Diseases, 21,* 137–148.

Office for Substance Abuse Prevention (1992). *Cultural competence for evaluators: A guide for alcohol and other drug abuse prevention & practitioners working with ethnic/racial communities.* Rockville, MD: Author.

Ona, F. F., Cadabes, C., & Choi, K. H. (1996). [Focus groups with gay Asian and Pacific Islander men in San Francisco]. In Choi, K-H, Yep, G. A., & Kumekawa, E. (1998). HIV prevention among Asian and Pacific Islander men who have sex with men: A critical review of theoretical models and directions for future research. *AIDS Education and Prevention, 10* (Suppl. A), 19–30.

Peterson, J. L. (1992). Black men and their same-sex desires and behaviors. In G. Herdt (Ed), *The culture of gay men* (pp. 147–164). Thousand Oaks, CA: Sage.

Peterson, J. L., Coates, T. J., Catania, J., Hauck, W. W., Acree, M., Daigle, D., Hillard, B., Middleton, L., & Hearst, N. (1995). Evaluation of an HIV risk reduction intervention among African-American homosexual and bisexual men. *AIDS, 10,* 319–325.

Peterson, J. L., Coates, T. J., Catania, J., & Hauck, W. W. (1996). Evaluation of an HIV risk-reduction intervention among African American heterosexual and bisexual men. *AIDS, 10,* 319–325.

Peterson, J. L., Coates, T. J., Catania, J. A., Middleton, L., Hilliard, B., & Hearst, N. (1992). High-risk sexual behavior and condom use among gay and bisexual African American men. *American Journal of Public Health, 82,* 1490–1494.

Phinney, J. S. (1989). Stages of ethnic identity development in minority group adolescents. *Journal of Early Adolescence, 9,* 34–49.

Phinney, J. S. (1993). A three-stage model of ethnic identity development in adolescence. In M. B. Bernal & G. P. Knight (Eds.), *Ethnic identity: Formation and transmission among Hispanic and other minorities* (pp. 61–79). New York: State University of New York.

Pivnick, A. (1993). HIV infection and the meaning of condoms. *Culture, Medicine, and Psychiatry, 17,* 431–453.

Raj, A., Marsh, S., DeLuca, N., Wingood, G. M., & DiClemente, R. J. (1997). Gender differences in HIV risk-related behaviors among a community-based sample of African American drug users and non-drug users. Presented at the 1997 American Public Health Association Conference, Indianapolis, IN.

Romero-Daza, N., Weeks, M., & Singer, M. (1998–1999). Much more than HIV! The reality of life on the streets for drug-using sex workers in inner city Hartford. *International Quarterly of Community Health Education, 18,* 107–119.

Sabogal, F., Faigeles, B., & Cantania, J. A. (1993). Data from the National AIDS Behavioral Surveys. II. Multiple sexual partners among Hispanics in high risk cities. *Family Planning and Perspectives, 25,* 257–262.

SAMHSA (Substance Abuse and Mental Health Statistics). (1999). *Summary findings from the 1998 National Household Survey on Drug Abuse.* Office of Applied Studies: Substance Abuse and Mental Health Statistics.

Schensul, S. L., Borrera, V., Backstand, J., & Guarnaccia, P. (1982). A model of fertility control in a Puerto Rican community. *Urban Anthropology, 11,* 81–99.

Schiller, N. G., Crystal, S., & Lewellen, D. (1994). Risky business: The cultural construction of AIDS risk groups. *Social Science and Medicine, 38,* 1337–1346.

Schilts, R. (1987). And the Band Played On: Politics, people, and the AIDS epidemic. New York, NY: St. Martin's Press.

Seage, G., Mayer, K. H., Lenderking, W. R., Wold, C., Gross, M., Goldstein, R., Cai, B., Heeren, T., Seigal, D., & Lazarus, N. (1991). AIDS knowledge, attitudes and behavior among inner city, junior high school students. *Journal of School Health, 61,* 160–165.

Sellers, D. E., McGraw, S. A., & McKinlay, J. (1994). Does the promotion and distribution of condoms increase teen sexual activity? Evidence from an HIV prevention program for Latino youth. *American Journal of Public Health, 84,* 1952–1959.

Sikkema, K. J., Heckman, T. G., & Kelly, J. A.(1997). HIV risk behaviors among inner-city African American women. *Women's Health: Research on Gender, Behavior, and Policy, 3,* 3–4, 349–366.

Sikkema, K. J., Koob, J. J., Cargill, V. C., Kelly, J. A., Disederato, L. L., Roffman, R. A., Norman, A. D., Shabazz, M., Copeland, C., Winett, R. A., Steiner, S., & Lemke, A. L. (1995). Levels and predictors of HIV risk behavior among women in low income public housing developments. *Public Health Reports, 110,* 707–713.

Sonenstein, F. L., Pleck, J. H., & Ku, L. C. (1991). Levels of sexual activity among adolescent males in the United States. *Family Planning Perspectives, 21,* 162–167.

St. Lawerence, J. S., Brasfield, T. L., Jefferson, K. W., Alleyne, E., Bannon R. E., & Shirley, A. (1995). Cognitive-behavioral intervention to reduce African-American adolescents' risk for HIV infection. *Journal of Consulting and Clinical Psychology, 63,* 221–237.

St. Lawrence, J. S., Eldridge, G. D., Reitman, D., Little, C. E., Shelby, M. C., & Brasfield, T. L. (1998). Factors influencing condom use among African American women: Implications for risk reduction interventions. *American Journal of Community Psychology, 26,* 7–28.

Stanton, B. F., Li, X., Galbraith, J., Feigelman, S., & Kaljee, L. (1996). Sexually transmitted diseases, human immunodeficiency virus, and pregnancy prevention: Combined contraceptive practice among urban African-American early adolescents. *Archives of Pediatric and Adolescent Medicine, 150,* 17–24.

Steers, W. N., Elliot, E., Nemiro, J., Ditman, D., & Oskamp, S. (1996). Health beliefs as a predictor of HIV-preventive behavior and ethnic differences in prediction. *The Journal of Social Psychology, 136,* 99–110.

Stokes, J. P., & Peterson, J. L. (1998). Homophobia, self-esteem, and risk for HIV among African American men who have sex with men. *AIDS Education and Prevention, 10,* 278–292.

Stokes, J. P., McKirnan, D. J., & Burzette, R. G. (1993). Sexual behavior, condom use, disclosure of sexuality, and stability of sexual orientation in bisexual men. *Journal of Sex Research, 30,* 203–213.

Stokes, J. P., McKirnan, D. J., Doll, L., & Burzette, R. G. (1996). Female partners of bisexual men: What they don't know might hurt them. *Psychology of Women Quarterly, 20,* 267–284.

Stokes, J. P., Vanable, P. A., & McKirnan, D. J. (1996). Ethnic differences in sexual behavior, condom use, and psychosocial variables among Black and White men who have sex with men. *Journal of Sex Research, 33,* 373–381.

Strunin, L. (1991). Adolescents' perceptions of risk for HIV infection: Implications for future research. *Social Sciences Medicine, 32,* 221–228.

Sullivan, P. S. (1995). AIDS in men who have sex with men: Trends in racial/ethnic groups. Paper presented at the Gay Men of Color HIV Prevention and Research Summit, San Francisco, CA.

Sy, F. S., Chng, C. L., Choi, S. T., & Wong, F. Y. (1998). Epidemiology of HIV and AIDS among Asian and Pacific Islanders. *AIDS Education and Prevention, 10* (Suppl. A), 4–18.

Tortu, S., Goldstein, M., Deren, S., Beardsley, M., Hamid, R., & Zeik, K. (1998). Urban crack users: Gender differences in drug use, HIV risk, and health status. *Women's Health, 27,* 177–189.

Turner, N. H., & Solomon, D. J. (1996). HIV risks and risk reduction readiness in hard-to-reach, drug-using African American and Mexican American women: An exploratory study. *AIDS Education and Prevention, 8,* 236–246.

UNAIDS. (1997). Report on the global HIV/AIDS epidemic: Estimates as of December 1997. Presented at the United Nations, Geneva, Switzerland, November, 1997.

U.S. Bureau of the Census (1999). Residential population of the U.S.: Estimates by sex, race, Hispanic origin with median age (updated December 28, 1998). U.S. Census website.

Wagstaff, D. A., Kelly, J. A., Perry, M. J., Sikkema, K. J., Solomon, L. J., Heckman, T. G., & Anderson, M. S. (1995). Multiple partners, risky partners, and HIV risk among lower income urban women. *Family Planning Perspectives, 27,* 241–244.

Weeks, R. W., Schensul, J., Williams, S., Singer, M., & Grier, M. (1995). AIDS prevention for African American and Latina women: Building culturally and gender-appropriate interventions. *AIDS Education and Prevention, 7,* 251–263.

Weinstock, H. S., Lindan, C., Bolan, G., Kegeles, S. M., & Hearst, N. (1993). Factors associated with condom use in a high risk heterosexual population. *Sexually Transmitted Diseases, 21,* 14–20.

Whitehead, T. (1997). Urban low-income African American men, HIV/AIDS, and gender identity. *Medical Anthropology Quarterly, 11,* 411–447.

Wingood, G. M., & DiClemente, R. J. (1998a). Rape among African American women: Sexual, psychological, and social correlates predisposing survivors to risk of STD/HIV. *Journal of Women's Health, 7,* 77–84.

Wingood, G. M., & DiClemente, R. J. (1998b). The influence of psychosocial factors, alcohol, drug use on African American women's high risk sexual behavior. *American Journal of Preventive Medicine, 15,* 54–59.

Wingood, G. M., & DiClemente, R. J. (1998c). Partner influences and gender-related factors associated with noncondom use in young adult African American women. *American Journal of Community Psychology, 26(1),* 29–51.

Wingood, G. M., Hunter, G. D., & DiClemente, R. J. (1993). A pilot study of sexual communication and negotiation among young African American women: Implications for HIV prevention. *Journal of Black Psychology, 19,* 190–203.

Word, C. O., & Bowser, B. (1997). Backround to crack cocaine addiction and HIV high risk behavior: The next epidemic. *American Journal of Drug and Alcohol Abuse, 23,* 67–77.

Wright, J. W. (1993). African American male sexual behavior and the risk for HIV infection. *Human Organization, 52,* 421–431.

Wyatt, G. E., Forge, N. G., & Guthrie, D. (1998). Family constellation and ethnicity: Current and lifetime HIV-related risk taking. *Journal of Family Psychology, 12,* 93–101.

Yeakley, A., & Gant, L. (1997). Cultural factors and program implications: HIV/AIDS interventions and condom use among Latinos. *Journal of Multicultural Social Work, 6,* 3, 47–71.

Yep, G. A. (1992a). Communicating the HIV/AIDS risk to Hispanic populations: A review and integration. *Hispanic Journal of Behavioral Sciences, 14,* 403–420.

Yep, G. A. (1992b). The effects of community-based HIV and AIDS education and prevention messages on knowledge, beliefs, attitudes and behavioral enactment skills among Asian men. Proceedings of the Ninth Annual Intercultural and International Communication Conference in May, Miami, FL, 19–22.

Yep, G. A. (1993). Health beliefs and HIV prevention: Do they predict monogamy and condom use? *Journal of Social Behavior and Personality, 8,* 507–520.

Zimmerman, M. A., Valles, J. R., Suarez, E., De la Rosa, G., & Castro, A. M. (1997). An HIV/AIDS prevention project for Mexican homosexual men: An empowerment approach. *Health Education & Behavior, 24,* 177–190.

9

PAIN FROM THE
PERSPECTIVES OF
HEALTH PSYCHOLOGY
AND CULTURE

CHRISTINE T. KOROL AND
KENNETH D. CRAIG

Department of Psychology
University of British Columbia
Vancouver, British Columbia, Canada

Unlike other health concerns addressed in this volume, pain is a universal experience, shared by persons of all ages in all cultures and throughout the long history of *Homo sapiens*. Virtually no one avoids this powerful feature of human existence, including the neonate (Anand & Craig, 1996; Korol, Goodman, Merchant, & Lawrence, 2001), young children (McGrath & Unruh, 1987), people with intellectual disabilities (LaChapelle, Hadjistavropoulos & Craig, 1999) and elderly people with dementia (Hadjistavropoulos et al. 1998) or in the terminal stages of life (Ferrell & Ferrell, 1996). This life span perspective and contrast across people with different capacities for cognitive functioning demonstrates the substantial individual differences in the nature of the pain experience and its expression, despite its ubiquity. Perhaps less obvious are the dramatic individual differences associated with the diverse cultural heritages to be observed on this planet because people grow up imbued with their culture's distinctive patterns of thought and behavior.

In this chapter, we will define pain, impairment, and disability and provide a primer in biological models of pain, describe socialization of pain experience and pain expression, illustrate earlier findings of cross-cultural variation, and develop a model for assessment and treatment of pain with diverse cultures.

PAIN, IMPAIRMENT, AND DISABILITY

The human capacity to experience pain evolved because it was adaptive and increased the probability of survival and procreation. In the case of acute pain associated with injuries and many diseases, the functions of pain are obvious. It almost invariably provokes withdrawal or escape from tissue stress and injury. However, there are no apparent benefits of chronic pain, such as headache, arthritis, or persistent back pain. Indeed, with longstanding and recurrent pain, the warning purpose appears ludicrous and avoidance or escape are improbable, with efforts to accomplish this futile. Its impact upon the health, personal life, vocational capacities, and family well-being of the person are almost always destructive (Bonica, 1979).

Complex psychological mechanisms can be observed in both acute and chronic pain. People are born well equipped to experience, become motivated by, and act on injuries or diseases instigating this usually feared and avoided state. These ancient dispositions are encoded in the DNA structures all persons inherit. Variation in genetic structures would account for some of the dramatic differences in individual behavioral response to painful events. But the human capacity for adaptive response also includes a remarkable ability to learn and understand one's environment, to benefit from the experiences of others with whom one is closely associated, and to develop socially constructed adaptive strategies for solving life demands. The demands to enhance, maintain, or restore health are more important than any other life demands. Hence, we constantly seek out and attempt to use pertinent information. In consequence, the manner in which we actually experience pain and act upon it is renewed for each person because it reflects socialization in the individual's unique familial and cultural background.

A widely accepted and influential definition of pain developed by the International Association for the Study of Pain characterizes it as "an unpleasant sensory and emotional experience associated with actual or potential tissue damage, or described in terms of such damage" (Merskey & Bogduk, 1994). This potent subjective experience usually is a tumultuous confusion of sensations, feelings, thoughts, and images that command attention and are disruptive of ongoing activity. While of great importance to the person in pain, the subjective experience can only become known to others through verbal and nonverbal signals. Individuals attending the needs of those in pain can provide care only to the extent that they are able to accurately interpret expressions of distress as indicative of pain. For the clinician, a detailed description of pain is necessary when it becomes the focus of treatment (e.g., chronic musculoskeletal back pain, fibromyalgia, or palliative care for terminal cancer pain) or when the nature of the pain provides important diagnostic information (e.g., abdominal pain signaling appendicitis). Clinicians can encounter major challenges if treatment requires a patient's complete and thorough description of pain and the patient has a different cultural background, even when the clinician and client share the same language. The importance of language and pain even leads to difficulties in attempting cross-cultural comparisons of pain because various languages provide a completely different vocabulary for descriptions of noxious stimuli. The different languages may vary in the number of words they use to describe pain, as well as in the emotional content of pain descriptors. It can also be unclear how these linguistic differences shape the meaning of a particular noxious event.

There is substantial scope for variation in the experience and expression of pain as a result of different personal, familial, and cultural backgrounds. The meaning of pain, the emotional distress experienced, the cognitive and behavioral coping skills exercised, and the manner in which pain is communicated to others in an effort to secure help are heavily influenced by socialization. The relatively unique social system in which any given individual is born and grows up provides innumerable learning opportunities about pain. Questionable notions about pain, for example, as a sensory experience symptomatic of injury or disease, that are dominant in Western cultures, do not always prevail in all other societies (Tu, 1980) and emotional reactions of fear or anger are not the only possibilities (Craig, 1999). Indeed, sexual arousal and pleasure are possibilities for people with masochistic predilections. Considerable variation in coping skills has been documented also, with some people described as displaying great fortitude and others as engaging in hysterical overreaction. Note that these encapsulated descriptions are value-laden. One could otherwise characterize these same people as foolhardy or sensibly seeking care. Finally, the skills necessary to access and optimize delivery of help from the health care system are culture specific. They invariably require the considerable training available to those who grow up in a culture, leaving those less well indoctrinated experiencing difficulties accessing the health care system. The skills are often taken for granted, with their importance only becoming conspicuous when people do not know how to exercise them.

Important distinctions should be recognized among *pain, impairment,* and *disability*. Impairment has been defined by the World Health Organization (WHO) as "any loss or abnormality of psychological, physiological, or anatomical structure or function," and disability, as defined by the WHO, refers to "any restriction or lack of ability to perform an activity in the manner or within the range considered normal for a human being." Pain refers to the subjective experience of distress, as defined previously, impairment refers to damage to psychological and biological systems, and disability refers to inability to engage in usual life tasks. They are not identical. Pain without identifiable physical damage is not unusual, particularly in the case of chronic pain, and physical damage can occur without pain. Pain usually is associated with disability, but people in pain can be remarkably resilient and maintain active involvement in daily activities despite distress. All levels of personal and physical functioning and the role of sociocultural factors relating to them require assessment to understand the role of pain in an individual's life.

The potential for committing errors in the pain assessment process because of insensitivity to one's own or others' cultural norms is considerable. Cultural factors not only influence how people attach meaning to the experience of pain, but they influence how we perceive pain in others. This emphasizes the importance of a match between the expectations and understandings of people in pain and their caregivers. Health practitioners have a responsibility to be familiar with the cultural backgrounds that shape their patients' understanding and response to pain. A culture that places a high priority on stoicism and honor might discourage any form of acknowledgment of an individual's personal discomfort (e.g., Sargent, 1984). However, the clinician should not equate a stoical approach to physical discomfort with absent or diminished experience. Nor does a voluminous, emotional display of distress necessarily signal profound subjective distress. There is always potential for discordance between the experience of pain and its expression, verbal and nonverbal.

As a further precaution, clinicians should not presume that stereotypic characterizations of pain displayed by contrasting ethnic and cultural groups represent individuals within those groups. There remains considerable variation within cultural groups, dependent upon additional sources of variation in pain experience and expression, such as the individual's biological inheritance, socialization, current life circumstances, and other contextual factors. Group differences are often small, relative to variation within the group, and overlap between groups is usually substantial. Many people in a cultural group that is usually characterized as intolerant to pain are likely to endure more pain than are people in a group described as quite tolerant. The cultural stereotypes of patterns of pain experience and expression, which will be described, are likely not as informative as an individual's personal narrative regarding their understanding of the underlying causes and potential treatments for their pain. The stereotypes may provide some hypotheses concerning an individual's likely background and pattern of response, but they are no substitute for a thorough history and description of the person's underlying beliefs and attitudes.

MODELS OF PAIN

The theorist proposing a model of pain is challenged to describe the biological foundations of a complex, multidimensional experience that is related to but neither predicted by the magnitude of tissue damage nor the observed behavioral distress. The model must recognize the potential for exacerbation, modulation, and amelioration through biological interventions, such as pharmacological or surgical treatment, as well as sociobehavioral and psychological influences (McGrath & Unruh, 1987; Zeltzer, Anderson, & Schechter, 1990).

From the time of the ancient Greeks until the ascendancy of empirical medical knowledge in the late 19th and 20th centuries, pain had been construed as an emotion—the opposite of pleasure. Descartes' 17th century mechanistic models of biological functioning (Melzack & Wall, 1988), and later biomedical research in sensory physiology, progressively led to the dominance of conceptual models of pain as a sensory experience that varied in intensity with the relative amount of tissue damage. This view led to the neglect of thoughts and feelings as components of the pain experience. The scientific emphasis has been upon the complexities of the biology of nociception, or the afferent processing of information signaling tissue stress and damage. The broader perspective that prevails today generally recognizes that only after the nociceptive afferent input is processed in the brain in the context of memories and the immediate situation can the experience of pain, with all its overtones, emerge.

Two early theories, the Specificity and Pattern theories of pain, are examples of models of pain that embraced the notion that the experience of pain was the sole result of nociceptive sensory input (Melzack & Wall, 1988).

SPECIFICITY THEORY

This theory was first proposed by Descartes in 1664 and, unfortunately still is taught frequently as fact in modern neurology textbooks (Melzack & Wall, 1988). Basically, specificity theory maintains that there is a specific set of cutaneous receptors that deliver nociceptive signals directly to the brain. Four distinct types of cutaneous receptor specific to cold, warm, touch, and pain stimuli were believed to relay sensory information directly to the appropriate center in the cortex.

This theory led to three primary assumptions relating to the experience of pain: (1) receptors are differentiated and specialized; (2) each sensory site beneath the skin surface contained a single specific receptor; and (3) there was a one-to-one relationship between the intensity of a particular stimulus and the psychological experience of pain. Of these three assumptions, only the first, that receptors are specialized, has received empirical support.

Basically, nerves consist of three classes: (1) sensory afferent, (2) motor axons that cause muscle contraction, and (3) sympathetic axons for autonomic functions, such as sweating and blood flow (Bonica, 1990a). Within the first class, there are four major types of cutaneous receptors that are classified according to their conduction velocity, the type of stimulus that evokes a response, and response characteristics (Bonica, 1990a; Melzack & Wall, 1988). These include (1) Type I A receptors, connected to large myelinated afferents. They respond to mechanical stimuli, have a high threshold for heat, and are thought to signal pain of long duration; (2) Type II A receptors, connected to small myelinated afferents. They respond to mechanical and heat stimuli and are believed to play a role in the first sensation of pain; (3) receptors connected to the large unmyelinated C-fibers that respond to mechanical and heat stimuli and certain chemicals; and (4) receptors that respond to cold.

Although these receptors are somewhat specialized, they are not unimodal and may respond to one or more different types of stimuli. Furthermore, there is no simple relationship between the type of nerve fibers stimulated and the actual experience of pain. Thus, there are many qualities of the pain experience that remain unexplained by this theory that focuses upon sensory parameters.

PATTERN THEORY

In contrast to specificity theory, pattern theory suggests that the experience of pain is the result of a specific pattern of neuronal impulses from undifferentiated receptors, rather than from specific receptors (Bonica, 1990b). Thus, it was believed that when cutaneous receptors received extreme stimulation from the periphery, the pattern of that stimulation would be interpreted, in the cortex, as pain (Bonica, 1990b; Melzack & Wall, 1988; Wall, 1989). This early theory of pain again suggested that the sensory experience directly corresponds to the nature and magnitude of external stimulation. Therefore, there was no room for important factors, such as affective, cognitive, and contextual variables, that play important roles in the pain experience. There clearly was room for added theoretical developments.

GATE CONTROL THEORY

The gate control theory of pain, proposed by Melzack and Wall (1965), has had a significant impact on our understanding of clinical pain because it addressed various explanatory gaps neglected by sensory specific theories and incorporated both biological and psychological mechanisms (Melzack & Wall, 1988). Basically, Melzack and Wall (1965) posited the existence of a "gating mechanism" located in the substantia gelatinosa layer of the spinal cord dorsal horn. This gate is believed to modulate nociceptive input entering the central nervous system from the periphery. Both large- and small-diameter afferent neural fibers terminate in the substantia gelatinosa, with the gating process influenced by the relative amount of neural input received from the two types of fibers. That is, Melzack and Wall (1965) concluded that nociceptive and somaesthetic signals compete with each other and that innocuous stimulation activates interneuronal systems (both opioid and nonopioid) that inhibit transmission of nociceptive signals to the central nervous system. This component of the gate control formulation of pain led to the development of a number of clinical interventions, such as transcutaneous electrical nerve stimulation (Fowler-Kerry & Lander, 1987) and dorsal column stimulation (Krainick & Thoden, 1984). These interventions have been shown to reduce pain significantly when compared to the use of "placebo" machines that did not deliver any afferent neuronal stimulation.

In addition to postulating a spinal gating mechanism in the dorsal horns, Melzack and Wall (1965) proposed a specialized set of fibers, projecting to brainstem and cortical structures, which activate various psychological processes related to affect, cognition, and attention. Once activated, central control processes were thought to influence the spinal gating mechanism through descending efferent projections. For example, cognitive processes, as influenced by memory of previous pain experiences, culture, anxiety, and attention, are thought to mediate the spinal gating mechanism through pyramidal fibers that project to the dorsal horns (Melzack, 1986).

Inclusion of a description of descending mechanisms provided a plausible physiological explanation for psychological factors observed to influence the perception of pain. For example, soldiers wounded on the battlefield are more likely to present with lower pain levels than do civilians with similar injuries (Beecher, 1955). This facet of the gate control model supported inclusion of cognitively based coping strategies in self-management training programs offered to pain patients (e.g., Turk & Melzack, 1992).

Biological formulations of pain have become progressively more sophisticated in recent decades with the discovery of endorphins, or naturally occurring opioids capable of modulating nociceptive afferent input (Fields & Basbaum, 1999), the mapping of complex neurophysiological systems extending beyond the gate control system, and the discovery of central sensitization and windup effects that sustain nociceptive activity long after the physical insult has been terminated (e.g., Coderre, Katz, Vaccarino, & Melzack, 1993). Despite these advances, efforts to understand the biology of pain have only begun to address its complexities. For example, while we have an increasingly good appreciation of the nociceptive afferent systems that transmit sensory-discriminative information to the brain, the physiology of the cognitive, affective, and social parameters of pain remains poorly understood. The new brain-imaging technologies are beginning to demonstrate a dramatically broad range of involvement of different brain structures during pain experience (Casey, in press; Ingvar & Hsieh, 1999).

PSYCHOLOGICAL PARAMETERS

Paralleling the increasing understanding of the biology of pain has been increased sophistication in our appreciation of psychological mechanisms. Initial attempts to account for dramatic individual differences in pain and other somatic complaints posited explanatory roles for personality constructs or traits. For example, a distinction was proposed between individuals classified as "repressors," those who choose to ignore physical symptoms, and "sensitizers," those who scan for changes in their physical condition. Repression/sensitization was deemed a stable personality trait, and predictions in somatic focus were made on this basis (Byrne, 1961).

There was some argument as to which style would be more adaptive. Some argued that because repression is a less mature defense mechanism, it should be maladaptive (cf. Byrne, 1961). However, researchers reported equivocal results. For example, repressors were found to experience fewer side effects or symptoms when coping with stressful situations (Schultheis, Peterson, & Selby, 1987; Steptoe & O'Sullivan, 1986; Ward, Leventhal, & Love, 1988). Nevertheless, the argument seems moot because the personality traits themselves require explanation as to their origins, and substantial cross-situational variability can be observed in pain, suggesting the traits are not as stable as believed.

A more useful concept of individual variation, contingent upon situational factors, along the dimensions of monitoring and blunting has been proposed by Miller (1979a,b, 1989; Miller & Mangan, 1983). Monitoring reflects the degree to which individuals seek out information about an upcoming aversive event. Blunting, on the other hand, is the degree to which individuals ignore, reevaluate, or rationalize threat-relevant information. The use and success of a particular style is described as depending upon certain situational aspects (Miller, 1979a,b). First, if the situation were predictable, scanning for threat-relevant information would be useful, because lack of danger signals would tell the person that he or she could relax. A second situational variable that makes monitoring more desirable would be the controllability of the situation. If the individual could control certain aspects of the aversive event, scanning for information would help moderate the impact of the event by permitting use of controlling measures. This work demonstrates how the search for psychological factors moderating pain experience and behavior turned to cognitive and perceptual mechanisms.

ATTENTION

The degree to which individuals are focused upon or distracted from their physical symptoms predicts whether the symptoms will be noticed or perceived as distressing. For example, Pennebaker (1983) found that individuals who were externally focused on activities or surroundings were less likely to express discomfort about a variety of somatic complaints. Pennebaker (1980) also reported that the degree to which people attend to physical symptoms varied with attention to an interesting or boring event. Participants watching a movie were more likely to notice scratching or tickling in their throats, as measured by coughing, during boring events than during the interesting segments. Eccleston, Crombez, Aldrich, and Stannard (1997) found in a more recent study that chronic pain patients who presented with both high pain intensity and high somatic awareness performed poorly on an attention-demanding cognitive task compared to participants with similar pain intensity but low somatic awareness. Thus, attentional mechanisms are important moderators of pain experience and behavior.

EMOTIONS AND PHYSICAL SYMPTOMS

Practitioner and patient focus upon pain sensation often leads to neglect of emotional and mood states, even though it is the emotional distress that is the most compelling and undesirable feature of pain (Craig, 1999). Acute pain is often associated with fear and anxiety and depression with chronic pain (Sternbach, 1986), with the totality of the pain experience dependent upon the severity of emotional distress. Treatment interventions often benefit from explicit attention to emotional processing of the pain experience. Mood has also been seen as an important determinant of whether an individual will attend to or report pain. Salovey and Birnbaum (1989) examined the relationship between self-reported mood, ratings of general health, and the report of physical symptoms. Their results demonstrated that individuals in a positive mood were more likely to rate themselves as healthy and present with fewer somatic complaints than were individuals in a negative mood.

COMMUNICATION MODELS OF PAIN

The emphasis on pain as a subjective experience fails to recognize the social importance of both the experience and its expression. This can be pursued from the many perspectives provided by communication models of pain (Craig, Lilley, & Gilbert, 1996; Prkachin & Craig, 1995). The experience of pain may be highly distressing and difficult, but others cannot render aid unless they can appreciate the distress (Craig, Prkachin, & Grunau, in press). The experience must be encoded in observable signs, verbal or nonverbal, to be understood by others. In turn, the observer will bring schemata for interpreting the meaning and significance of the suffering person's distress and act upon this understanding. The response of others is perhaps no more important for survival than during the earliest days, weeks, and months of life, when the newborn and infant are wholly dependent upon others (Craig, 1998), although the dependency remains when people are injured or ill and increases in the frail elderly. Certain social manifestations of pain appear to have evolved solely because of their communicative function. Thus, pain language, paralinguistic vocalizations signaling painful distress, such as crying or moaning, and facial grimaces specific to pain (Craig et al., in press) enhance species survival because they are effective in enlisting aid or because they convey warnings to conspecifics.

SOCIALIZATION OF INDIVIDUAL DIFFERENCES IN PAIN EXPRESSION

Human adaptation to the dramatically different ecological systems on this planet has been accomplished largely through development of specialized cooperative social systems, or cultures. Vast differences in customs, mores, and languages illustrate this diversity. They reflect needs and propensities to organize experience and behavior in order to adapt in the best possible way to both physical and social environmental demands. Customs and practices relating to physical health and survival share this diversity and there is a bewildering array of health-oriented practices, ranging from those often referred to as Western medicine to a host of procedures often described today as complementary and alternative practices. These are not to be dismissed lightly. Native use of willow bark gave rise to aspirin and the derivative of the opium poppy, morphine, still represents the most commonly used postoperative analgesic used today. When evaluated for their effectiveness from the perspective of the canons of science applied to empirically validate interventions (cf. Dobson & Craig, 1998), many may prove to be less than optimal, but they represent the "best practice" to have emerged from their originating societies. Given a cultural consensus that they are the best practices available, there would be firm commitments to ensuring their application and perpetuation.

Protecting children from physical threat and teaching them to avoid risk or to seek help are seen by parents as a pivotal responsibility defining the quality and success of their role as parents (Craig, 1986). Children learn through complex sources what events are likely to be painful, how the experience feels, the impact of various actions, and social expectations as to how they should behave to optimize the impact of the interventions of others. Perhaps most obvious and powerful would be learning through direct experience, for example, when a child accidentally burns him- or herself or when a tummy ache attacks. Perhaps less obvious is the instruction provided when parents vigorously intercede when the child is in danger—parents almost invariably vigorously interact with the child to promote physical safety and children who do not immediately conform are likely to be admonished repeatedly and subjected to severe discipline. But of even greater importance are the opportunities for observational learning that permit children to learn health behavior in general, and pain behavior in particular, as they witness the behavior of others who are in pain (Craig, 1986). In so doing, familial and cultural expectations concerning how one should behave will be inculcated in the child (Sargent, 1984). While there undoubtedly are immutable, hard-wired characteristics of the experience of pain, it also is a social construction requiring appreciation through the lens of the family and the culture in which the individual has grown up and is embedded.

ILLNESS AND SYMPTOM SCHEMATA

Recent research on how people recognize and interpret physical symptoms and health threats is instructive. An individual's cognitive representation of illness and physical symptoms or implicit models of illness, or schemata (Lau & Hartman, 1983; Markus, 1977; Neisser, 1976; Pennebaker, 1983), are known to influence coping with illness and such factors as whether a person pays attention to anomalous bodily experience, decides to seek treatment for symptoms, adheres to a particular treatment regimen, or even returns to work following a painful incident (cf. Lacroix, 1991; Leventhal & Nerenz, 1983; Leventhal, Meyer, & Nerenz, 1980; Mechanic, 1962; Leventhal, E. A., Leventhal, H., Robitaille, & Brownlee, 1999; Leventhal, Idler, & Leventhal, 1999; Clemmey & Nicassio, 1997). For example, whether an individual interprets a pain in the chest as indigestion or a heart attack has dramatic implications for how that individual responds to that symptom. One could contemplate the meanings of chest pain that would have prevailed prior to discovery of the cardiovascular system or in cultures not exposed to Western medicine and its belief systems. Many people hold naive assumptions about the causes and potential cures for their medical conditions (e.g., believing you can catch a cold from going outside without a jacket or that hypertension increases when you are experiencing stress). Chronic pain, in particular, is a difficult concept for both lay individuals and some professionals to grasp, given the dominance of sensory-oriented perspectives.

In reference to medical populations, Lacroix (1991) defined schemata as (1) a belief in the relatedness of a variety of physiological and psychological functions, which may or may not be objectively accurate; (2) a cluster of sensations, symptoms, emotions, and physical limitations in keeping with that belief; (3) a naive theory about the mechanisms that underlie the relatedness of the elements identified in (2); and (4) implicit or explicit prescriptions for corrective action (p. 97).

Schemata tend to operate automatically and serve to make sense of the plethora of events available by selective attention to those that are pertinent to the schemata. In the domain of somatic perception, they are described as incorporating (1) the label or name attached to a given cluster of symptoms, (2) the expected consequences, including the impact of the illness on daily activities and the treatment required, (3) the expected time course of the illness, (4) the presumed causes responsible for the onset of the illness, and (5) the appropriate cure—how and whether the illness can be treated (Lau & Hartman, 1983; Leventhal & Nerenz, 1983). For example, Lau, Bernard, and Hartman (1989) found that those individuals who held clear beliefs about an illness label and thought a cure for that particular illness was possible reported being more likely to seek medical treatment when they were ill than were individuals whose illness representations did not contain clear illness labels or cure components. Schemata can be seen to be self-regulatory and self-perpetuating. They not only provide patients with a guide for organizing information about one's physical symptoms, they also direct patients to monitor for particular symptoms which are consistent with their understanding of their medical condition (Markus & Wurf, 1987; Pennebaker, 1983).

BEHAVIORAL DIFFERENCES AND THE MEANING OF PAIN ACROSS CULTURES

The illness schemata model provides a useful strategy for identifying lay assumptions about pain in culturally diverse patient populations (Leventhal, Leventhal et al., 1999; Edman & Kamboka, 1997). Longstanding approaches to characterizing different ethnic groups have focused upon behavioral differences.

SPECIFIC DIFFERENCES BETWEEN VARIOUS CULTURAL GROUPS

Numerous studies have described how different cultural groups vary in their reports of pain intensity and in pain behaviors. Illustrative studies are described here. It is important to note that these descriptions provide only very general stereotypes and neglect personal idiosyncrasies. The methodologies used either employed experimental pain paradigms, where healthy participants were asked to indicate their pain thresholds and tolerances, or examined differences among pain patients on various assessment instruments. These studies do little to explain why the differences exist or how culture affects the interpretation of noxious somatic events.

One of the first studies to compare members of different ethnic groups was undertaken by Tursky and Sternbach (1967). In their study, 15 housewives belonging to one of four different ethnic groups (Yankee, Irish, Jewish, and Italian) were interviewed and given electric shocks of increasing intensity. There were no differences in threshold required to first detect the stimulus, but there were differences in pain tolerance. Tursky and Sternbach (1967) also reported differences in attitudes toward pain that were consonant with the psychophysical results, "Yankees have a phlegmatic, matter-of-fact orientation toward pain; Jews express a concern for the implication of pain and a distrust of palliatives; Italians express a desire for pain relief and the Irish inhibit expression of suffering and concern for the implications of pain."

A more recent study (Edwards & Fillingham, 1999) compared African American and Caucasian American participants' responses to thermal pain. There were no differences between these groups in warmth thresholds, pain thresholds, or pain intensity ratings. However, the African American participants had lower pain tolerance and rated the thermal stimuli as more unpleasant than did Caucasian subjects. The authors concluded that it is the affective–motivational component of the pain experience that varies between these two groups rather than the sensory aspects. Note that self-report measures confound the actual experience with the willingness to report the experience.

Lawlis, Achterberg, Kenner, and Kopetz (1984) studied 60 patients with chronic "spinal" pain from three ethnic groups (Caucasian American, Mexican American, and African American). Muscle ischemia was used to induce pain, with participants reporting pain threshold, tolerance, and when the ischemic pain matched their chronic pain. Two observers also rated the magnitude of pain behavior displayed during the experimental task. The results demonstrated that Mexican Americans reported the highest level of pain when chronic pain was matched to the ischemic event, but they were judged as not presenting with an "exaggerated" pain response. Caucasian Americans reported less spinal pain but had a lower pain tolerance than did the Mexican Americans. The African American group did not differ from either group on any of the measures of pain.

These studies used experimental paradigms, while others have sought to uncover ethnic group differences in the pain experience using clinical samples. Jordan, Lumley, and Leisen (1998) compared Caucasian American and African American women with rheumatoid arthritis (RA) in terms of their primary coping strategies and reports of control over pain, pain severity, activity levels, and affective states. They found no differences between the groups in pain severity or negative affect. However, African Americans presented with lower activity levels and relied on distraction and praying/hoping more than did the Caucasian

American group. Caucasian Americans, in turn, tended to ignore pain as a means of coping. Given the large number of measures included without correction for experimentwise error, a number of the differences may have been spurious.

Bates and Rankin-Hill (1994) investigated the relationship between locus of control and ethnicity in chronic pain patients from six different ethnic groups (Old American, Latino, Italian, French Canadian, Irish, and Polish). They were able to predict locus of control on the basis of cultural identity for all but the Old American group, and locus of control subsequently predicted ratings of pain intensity. However, the direction of the relationship between locus of control and pain intensity was not the same for each of the ethnic groups (e.g., an internal LOC was associated with higher pain ratings in the Old American and Polish groups in contrast to the other four groups).

While these studies reported differences among members of ethnic groups, other studies have failed to find similar differences. For example, Flannery, Sos, and McGovern (1981) failed to find any differences in pain severity or behavior following an episiotomy among five ethnic groups in the United States: African American, Italian, Jewish, Irish, and Anglo-Saxon Protestant. Similarly, Pfefferbaum, Adams, and Aceves (1990) found no differences in ratings of pain severity or behavior during an invasive procedure in Caucasian and Hispanic children with cancer. They did note that Hispanic parents reported higher levels of anxiety than the Caucasian parents did. Gaston-Johansson, Albert, Fagan and Zimmerman (1990) compared intensity ratings attached to the words "pain," "ache," and "hurt" made by Hispanics, American Indians, African Americans, and Caucasian Americans. All four groups rated "pain" as the most intense descriptor followed by "hurt" and "ache." No differences were found between groups in the intensity ratings attached to each of these words.

These studies provide evidence that some differences can be identified among cultural groups in the experience and expression of pain, but the meaning of the findings is complex. The piecemeal approach makes it difficult to understand processes responsible for the differences. The samples, for example, African Americans, Caucasians, or Latinos, must have been heterogeneous groups in the first instance, and, if they were not, one wonders whether representative sampling was achieved. Assimilation of people with different ethnic backgrounds into the prevailing culture would be variable, depending upon whether the participants were recent immigrants. Quasi-experimental, cross-sectional designs are always questionable as to whether group differences represent a causal variable and lead one to question whether findings can be attributed to ethnic variation or other differences among the groups. We simply end up with a catalogue of sometimes unreplicated and contradictory cultural variations (e.g., this group has higher pain intensity ratings, while this group uses distraction, while this group presents with more pain complaints). A simple awareness of these group differences is of little help for a clinician working with an individual patient with a different cultural background.

NARRATIVE APPROACHES

An examination of illness narratives or beliefs shared among members of a particular culture, as reflecting the schemata they share, may be more useful in understanding group differences. If clinicians were aware of the schemata employed by patients, interventions could be tailored in a culturally sensitive manner. Lack of cooperation, limited treatment adherence, and health practitioner frustration often can be attributed to incompatibility of the patient's and practitioner's perspectives on illness.

Western Beliefs about Pain and Illness

Communities within the developed world, influenced by European perspectives on health, share certain beliefs about illness and pain that are not necessarily matched by those of patients from communities with different backgrounds and heritages. Patterns of health care consultation reflect the dominant schemata in Western communities. When people believe that their symptoms warrant medical consultation, they typically visit their primary care physician. The expectation is that after a physical examination, some diagnostic tests, and a careful review of the symptoms, the physician will provide a diagnosis, prescribe a remedy to cure the ailment, and give some indication as to the time course of the problem. In turn, health care providers expect patients to fully disclose their symptoms and to follow treatment recommendations. These expectations are usually met, as most medical problems are resolved, through intervention or natural healing, and both the patient and physician feel satisfied.

However, when the best treatments have proven ineffective and a condition persists beyond expected time limits, the situation becomes more complicated for both parties. The physician may wish to conduct a more thorough assessment by ordering invasive and expensive diagnostic tests, making referrals to numerous specialists, and using more aggressive interventions, such as surgery. Patients often receive conflicting opinions about diagnosis and treatment recommendations, with none resolving the problem, feel compelled to attempt more drastic solutions, continue to solicit other opinions when interventions fail, and rely on alternative and ineffective remedies or medications until a solution is found.

Most Western health care providers without specific training in chronic pain conditions and patients tend to view the body mechanistically. If there is a symptom such as pain, there must be an underlying cause that can be identified and fixed. If this approach is unsuccessful, there is a risk that both patients and physicians will resort to dangerous analgesic regimens despite potentially harmful side effects and the diminishing efficacy of drugs when patients develop tolerance to their effects. Guidelines for the use of opioids with persistent, nonmalignant pain have only recently been published and are not widely applied (Canadian Pain Society, 1998).

Within Western cultures, a clear distinction often is made between the mind and body. One disadvantage has been that both health care providers and patients may be resistant to the position that psychological factors play a role in the development and maintenance of chronic pain and related disability. Psychologists working in pain clinics often are confronted with skepticism and hostility from patients who fear they have been sent to a psychologist whose purpose is to determine whether the pain is "all in their heads." Psychologists must alleviate these concerns by affirming the reality of the patient's experience and educating the patient and the referral source as to the contributions of psychological factors to the experience of pain and related disability. A discussion of the impact of persistent pain on the individual's daily activities is often a good beginning, given the substantial probability of work stress, deterioration in family life, and changes in mood. This can be followed with a discussion of the individual's personal background, the variable success of coping strategies, and the potential for more effective coping. The assertion that the pain "is all in your head" is most likely to be made by health care practitioners using outmoded sensory specificity models of pain that accommodate well to dualistic thinking. They do not recognize that all pain is subjective experience with complex determinants and do not appreciate that medical science has not discovered somatic generators for large numbers of people suffering chronic pain.

South Asian Beliefs about Illness

Within the past decade, there has been a considerable influx of South Asian immigrants to Western Canada and a subsequent need on the part of health care providers to become familiar with the expectations of these patients concerning the medical system and the function of health care providers. Individuals in this broad category may come from India, Pakistan, or Nepal and speak a variety of languages including Hindu, Punjabi, or Urdu. Upon arrival in Canada, immigrants must take jobs, often requiring physical labor, because they cannot speak the host language well enough to perform accustomed jobs. Once injured, they must rely on an unfamiliar medical system, as well as cope with the stress of not being able to provide for their families, circumstances that can exacerbate disability and stress.

Again, health care providers need to be aware of dominant cultural beliefs regarding the medical system and the treatment of illness. In a series of studies, Dalal and colleagues identified a number of central themes in South Indian patients regarding both the causes and cures of various medical conditions. In a study of 70 male Hindu tuberculosis patients, Dalal and Singh (1992) reported that the most frequent causal attributions were made to God's will and karma, whereas recovery was attributed to God and the skill of the physician. They also noted a positive relationship between perceived control over the disease and psychological adjustment. These findings were replicated in a study of 132 Hindu cervical cancer patients (Kohli & Dalal, 1998). Here, the most common causal attributions included fate, God's will, and karma.

It is noteworthy that the relationship between patients and physicians in India is considerably more formal than in North America. Physicians in India make specific treatment recommendations that are typically passively accepted by their patients. This can create difficulties in North American pain clinics, where there are expectations that patients will take an active role in their rehabilitation by identifying personal treatment goals, experimenting with various coping strategies, and pursuing exercise programs that may improve physical functioning but not pain levels. Clinicians may need to adopt a more directive stance and emphasize their expertise when working with South Asian patients.

East Asian Beliefs about Illness

East Asian patients comprise as ethnically diverse a population as South Asian patients. Recent immigrants to Canada may come from countries such as China, Hong Kong, Vietnam, or Taiwan. There inevitably are notable differences in languages, health care systems, and personal backgrounds, often reflected in the factors influencing the decision to immigrate, ranging from civil unrest, desire to leave a communist society, persecution of a dominant minority, extreme poverty, or opportunities for economic gain (Assanand, Dias, Richardson, & Waxler-Morrison, 1990).

Western health care providers often subscribe to misconceptions that East Asian patients tend to somatize distress and are reluctant to report symptoms of psychological conflict that play a role in both the cause and the maintenance of their health concerns. In a frequently cited study, Kleinman (1982) investigated the symptoms of patients diagnosed with *Shenjing Shuairuo* (neurasthenia), literally translated as "neurological weakness." Neurasthenia is a frequently diagnosed ailment in China. It is included in the *International Classification of Diseases, Version 10 (ICD-10)*, with symptoms including fatigue, headache, dizziness, gastrointestinal discomfort, and other somatic complaints. Kleinman (1982) conducted extensive diagnostic interviews with 100 patients diagnosed with neurasthenia at a psychiatric outpatient clinic at the Hunan Medical College. He reported that 87 of these patients met DSM–III diagnostic criteria for a major depressive disorder, 69 were diagnosed with various anxiety disorders, and 44 were diagnosed with chronic pain syndrome. He also found that the majority of these patients showed some improvement when prescribed antidepressant medication. Kleinman (1982) characterized neurasthenia as a "special form of somatization" and argued that neurasthenia and major depressive disorders were both cultural constructions of a similar set of symptoms.

This study conducted two decades ago continues to influence Western perceptions of Chinese patients. It is frequently assumed that the Chinese, and East Asians in general, find it more acceptable to obtain help for somatic complaints than to receive a psychiatric diagnosis or that somatic complaints are a culturally acceptable means of obtaining support. However, the study has been controversial and other prominent investigators have challenged many of its assumptions (Lee, 1997; Chun, Enomoto, & Sue, 1996). Lee (1997) noted that the diagnostic criteria for a somatoform disorder require physical symptoms without an identifiable physical cause and in the absence of acknowledged psychological symptoms. Lee states that this diagnosis makes little sense in a culture that does not ascribe to notions of mind–body dualism. In traditional Chinese medicine, the illness is conceived as a disruption of energies or an imbalance of yin and yang. Various human problems can lead to this imbalance, resulting in physical illness. Therefore, when asked, Chinese patients will report symptoms of psychological distress and will readily accept recommendations related to stress reduction. Given this more holistic view of illness, a diagnosis of somatoform disorder makes little sense to either Chinese psychiatrists or their patients.

Other reasons for the suppression of reports of psychological symptoms have been proposed. Some Chinese patients are reluctant to report psychological symptoms for fear of bringing shame upon their families. Others focus on physical symptoms because they believe those are the only symptoms of interest to the physicians. Many Chinese turn to other sources for assistance with symptoms of psychological distress, including consulting family members or friends or practicing meditation, with discussion of psychological symptoms not seeming appropriate with physicians. However, these response biases are shared with many patients reared in Western traditions. Lee (1997) also attributes reluctance to report psychological symptoms to China's overburdened health care system, where physicians must focus on physical symptoms of immediate concern.

CULTURALLY COMPETENT CARE

Given an understanding of the processes whereby pain comes to be experienced and expressed in a manner that reflects the person's family and culture, the clinician then must develop strategies for working with culturally diverse populations. How can one identify a patient's understanding of their pain condition, clarify misconceptions, if necessary or appropriate, and develop a treatment plan that is congruent with the individual's pain beliefs and attitudes? The culturally competent clinician needs at his or her disposal an assessment method that would discover the patient's personal schemata for the symptoms he/she is experiencing, and intervention strategies that use this information to work toward culturally appropriate treatment goals. The final component of this chapter addresses the challenges of providing culturally sensitive care by illustrating components of the treatment and intervention processes that would reflect this care.

ASSESSMENT

The clinician needs to uncover personal understandings or idiosyncratic beliefs about pain and illness and the explanatory model for the current episode through any line of inquiry that will be informative. Primarily, this would require interviews with the patient or significant others and should include specific inquiry about subculture and familial perspectives. It could include consultation of archival records. Given that most people have difficulty fully understanding their particular medical condition, careful identification of erroneous beliefs is an important endeavor even for those with similar cultural backgrounds.

Regardless of cultural background, obtaining a concise narrative of a patient's understanding of their medical condition is a necessary beginning to understanding the client's perspective and will enhance the therapeutic relationship. A strong therapeutic alliance would make them more open to treatment options and encourage openness to their adopting a self-management approach to pain management. Generally, a clinical interview begins with a clear description of when the pain began or the circumstances of an accident. Careful attention is paid to the language used to describe the nature of the patient's injuries and its correspondence to medical accounts of those injuries. Further inquiries lead to what the patient believes is wrong with them, what physicians have told them, and whether they agree with this account. Explanatory beliefs about their condition that are antithetical to clinician accounts or treatment goals can interfere with treatment progress. For example, a patient who feels that her back is fragile and could "snap" like a twig is probably not going to progress with active physiotherapy and perhaps would feel increased anger with therapists who were not aware of her fears. The patient's beliefs about the role of Western medicine, folk remedies, or traditional healers may also hold the key to recovery. All interventions patients have tried to control their pain should be determined. A familiarity with traditional interventions would be helpful, as some patients may not spontaneously reveal nonmedical remedies for fear of ridicule. A checklist of possible interventions can assist patients to remember what they have tried in the past.

A final area of assessment can examine disability or the impact of pain on the patient's life. Objective indicators, such as return to work and the ability to carry out other functional activities, are useful indicators of the severity of a patient's condition. Questions such as "What is the worst thing about having pain?" may provide meaningful treatment goals. Patients may report an inability to prepare family meals, pain during sex, or being unable to kneel during religious services. It is useful to ask what areas of their life have been left untouched by pain to establish functional abilities that have remained intact. Initially, most patients respond that pain interferes with every part of their life. However, specific inquiry (e.g., do they still love their children as much or can they still enjoy their hobbies) may help to identify parts of their life where they still enjoy some degree of control.

TREATMENT

Self-management pain programs require patients to educate themselves and to reduce dependency on medications and physicians. This stands in stark contrast to typical treatment in Western cultures that foster reliance on the physician to "fix" the condition. Clinicians in self-management programs often spend many hours when patients enter the program educating them about their responsibilities and informing them that they will be the primary agents of change. Typically, these programs are multidisciplinary and include team members from psychology, physiotherapy, general practice, medical specialities, pharmacy, occupational therapy, kinesiology, and vocational counseling. In addition to exercise and gradual return-to-work programs, the self-management of pain often contains a large educational component. Patients are taught multidimensional models of pain, for example, the gate control theory, how their thoughts influence their pain, relaxation techniques to reduce pain, coping strategies, how to increase physical activity despite pain, the influence of emotions on pain, family influences, and the function of pain behavior in the maintenance of chronic pain conditions.

Needless to say, this approach differs substantially with most patients' previous encounters with the health care system. Many patients who believe their treatment team thinks their pain is all in their head are skeptical that cognitive coping strategies will be helpful, doubt the value of medication reduction programs, and question the value of relaxation training. Clinicians often spend time diffusing resistance of this type. Reasons for not participating in groups, exercising, or practicing relaxation techniques must be determined from the patient. Therapists should not assume that the patient is merely being "difficult" or "lazy," an attribution associated with inappropriate stereotypes for some cultural groups. It is the responsibility of the therapist to understand and clarify patient misconceptions about the program and to adapt the program to suit individual needs, regardless of the cultural background of the patient, as the self-management approach requires patients to adopt a radically different perspective on pain control.

WORKING WITH TRANSLATORS

The need to use translators perhaps epitomizes the complexities of culturally competent care. These are often needed in rehabilitation centers. New immigrants usually must accept work that requires manual labor, with the attendant increased risk of injury. Careful planning on the part of the therapist can prevent problems from arising. Family members, typically, should not serve as the translators. They also may have difficulty speaking English, misunderstand questions, misinterpret answers, and censor or volunteer too much personal information without consent. There also are private issues in families that are difficult to discuss with relatives, for example, issues of the impact of pain on the marital relationship or sexual functioning. Problems may also arise when the translator is not a family member. Professional translators can disagree with therapeutic protocols or suggest options that are inconsistent with a self-management approach. They may feel the treatment team is "too hard" and sabotage the treatment goals as patient advocates. Translators also may engage patients in irrelevant conversations or talk for the patient instead of reporting what the patient has said.

To circumvent these challenges, the therapist must establish firm expectations concerning the translator's role and ensure a strong therapeutic alliance within the triad. Translators should understand they play an important role in helping the patient understand the treatment goals and important ethical issues such as confidentiality. The therapist can prepare translators for some of the difficult emotional issues to be discussed and help them to feel comfortable with difficult topics. There should be an understanding among all parties as to how therapy will proceed with a third person in the room. Both the translator and the patient need to understand that the translator should remain detached and simply communicate what the therapist and patient are saying, word for word. Typically, a good translator will respond verbatim by saying things in the first person (e.g., "my" pain radiates down my leg; "I feel depressed"; or "I cry every day"). While the challenges of working with a translator are considerable, they are not insurmountable.

SUMMARY

In this chapter, the concepts of pain, impairment, and disability were discussed. In addition, three biological models of pain were described: the Specificity Theory, the Pattern Theory, and the Gate Theory. Psychological parameters and cultural variations in the experience and expression of pain were also discussed. Finally, a culturally competent model of care for the assessment and treatment of pain was presented. The culturally competent care model requires assessment and intervention methods that explore personal schemata for pain symptoms and the establishment of treatment goals that are based on the client's/patient's cultural experience and expression of pain.

CASE STUDY

Preepi was injured when she slipped on a wet floor while she was carrying a stack of dishes in the restaurant where she worked two years ago. She has been unable to work since her injury and complains of severe low back pain and numbness down her right leg. She was 52 at the time she was first assessed in a multidisciplinary pain program and presented as severely disabled (e.g., she was only able to stand or sit for 5 minutes at a time, had severely decreased range of motion and little strength, and relied primarily on her family to help her with her activities of daily living). She reported through a Punjabi interpreter to the psychologist on the team that her mother-in-law and her two teenage children took care of household chores for her, and her husband was very helpful because he would rub her back and bring her pain medication. Despite support from her family, Preepi felt guilty about not being able to care for her family, reported that it was God's will that she suffer, and was resigned to the fact that, after two years, she would probably always suffer. Upon careful assessment, Preepi was diagnosed as depressed with several vegetative features and occasional suicidal ideation. She was admitted to the Chronic Pain Management Program in the clinic, and the treatment team noted that they would have to pay special attention to the many factors contributing to her continued disability (e.g., family solicitousness, resignation and helplessness, depressed mood, and sedentary lifestyle).

The first activity in the treatment program involved the identification of personal goals that the patients would like to achieve by the time they were discharged from the program. This was done in a group setting with each patient being given a large piece of paper and a felt pen. Most patients in the group identified goals such as "walk for 30 minutes every day," "play with my children without hurting myself," or "return to work." Despite encouragement from her interpreter, Preepi's paper was blank at the end of the session. Later, in a session with the psychologist, Preepi reported that she could not think of any goals and felt she could not know what to hope for because she was not an expert in this area. The psychologist then decided to take a more directive approach with Preepi, specifically outlining the ways the program would help her and providing her with a list of goals that she might like to achieve. Preepi then selected a number of treatment goals that were suggested (e.g., she decided that she would like to be able to make dinner for her family).

Once the physiotherapy component of the program began, new problems began for Preepi. Patients were required to exercise in the pool and were told to bring bathing suits for the following day. But on the first day, they would begin their cardio-exercise training program in the clinic's gym. The physiotherapist had designed an individual exercise program for each of the patients when they had undergone assessment and instructed each patient on how to begin their exercise program. Preepi instantly excused herself from the area of the treadmills and exercise bikes and went to the bathroom. Twenty minutes later, the physiotherapist and interpreter left to investigate. They found Preepi in the washroom definitely not wanting to come back to the gym. She admitted that she did not want to exercise in front of the men and that she could not possibly wear a bathing suit the following day. The physiotherapist decided to place one of the exercise bikes in an area of the clinic that could be curtained off. In addition, Preepi was told that she did not have to wear a bathing suit, but that it was extremely important to her treatment program that she do her pool exercises. Instead, she agreed to wear a longsleeved T-shirt and longer shorts.

Preepi continued to improve in the Chronic Pain Management Program, as long as the team members continued to identify the reasons for her nonparticipation that occurred occasionally throughout the program. Inevitably, it was due to her discomfort or embarrassment, rather than an unwillingness to listen to the team's recommendations. Her family also responded well to the psychologist's explicit instructions to let Preepi take care of herself, not to bring her pain medications, and to ignore any pain behaviors (e.g., sighing, wincing). The physician on the team reinforced this point by writing out some of these recommendations on a prescription pad (which one of the children translated and posted on the refrigerator).

At the end of the treatment program, Preepi was walking for 20 minutes every day, entered a gradual return to work program at the restaurant she had worked at two years ago, and was making dinner for her family twice a week.

1. Imagine that you are the psychologist on the treatment team and the rest of the team believes that Preepi is simply being nonadherent and "difficult." How might you convince them of the importance of taking cultural factors into account?

2. What are some of the ways that Preepi's family could be included in her treatment? Would this be beneficial?

3. What are some of the factors that make it difficult for a person from another culture to explain why they might be uncomfortable with a particular treatment regimen?

ACKNOWLEDGMENT

Preparation of this chapter was supported by research grants from the Social Sciences and Humanities Research Council of Canada to Kenneth D. Craig.

SUGGESTED READINGS

Craig, K. D. (1999). Emotions and psychobiology. In P. D. Wall & R. Melzack (Eds.), *Textbook of pain* (4th ed, pp. 331–343). Edinburgh, UK: Churchill Livingstone.

Leventhal, H., Benyamini, Y., Brownlee, S., Diefenbach, M., Leventhal, E., Patrick-Miller, L., & Robitaille, C. (1997). Illness representations: Theoretical foundations. In K. J. Petrie & J. A. Weinman (Eds.), *Perceptions of health and illness: Current research and applications* (pp. 19–46). Amsterdam: Harwood Academic Publishers.

Waxler-Morrison, N., Anderson, J., & Richardson, E. (Eds.) (1990). *Cross-cultural caring: A handbook for health professionals.* Vancouver, BC: University of British Columbia Press.

REFERENCES

Anand, K. J. S., & Craig, K. D. (1996). Editorial: New perspectives on the definition of pain. *Pain, 67,* 3–6.

Andrew, J. M. (1970). Recovery from surgery, with and without preparatory instruction for three coping styles. *Journal of Personality and Social Psychology, 15,* 223–226.

Assanand, S., Dias, M., Richardson, E., & Waxler-Morrison, N. (1990). The South Asians. In N. Waxler-Morrison, J. Anderson, and E. Richardson (Eds.), *Cross-cultural Caring: A handbook for health professionals* (pp. 141–180). Vancouver: University of British Columbia Press.

Bates, M. S., & Rankin-Hill, L. (1994). Control, culture and chronic pain. *Social Science and Medicine, 39,* 629–645.

Beecher, H. K. (1955). The powerful placebo. *Journal of the American Medical Association, 159,* 1602–1606.

Bonica, J. J. (1979). Important clinical aspects of acute and chronic pain. In R. E. Beers & E. C. Bassett (Eds.), *Mechanisms of pain and analgesic compounds* (pp. 15–29). New York: Raven Press.

Bonica, J. J. (1990a). History of pain concepts and therapies. In J. J. Bonica (Ed), *The management of pain* (2nd ed., pp. 2–17). Philadelphia, PA: Lea & Febiger.

Bonica, J. J. (1990b). Anatomic and physiologic basis of nociception and pain. In J. J. Bonica (Ed), *The management of pain* (2nd ed., pp. 28–49). Philadelphia, PA: Lea & Febiger.

Byrne, D. (1961). The repression–sensitization scale: Rationale, reliability, and validity. *Journal of Personality, 29,* 334–349.

Canadian Pain Society (1998). Use of opioid analgesics for the treatment of chronic noncancer pain: A consensus statement and guidelines from the Canadian Pain Society. *Pain Research and Management, 3,* 197–208.

Casey, K. (in press). The future of diagnostic imaging in pain assessment (MRI, PET, SPECT). In D. C. Turk & R. Melzack (Eds.), *Handbook of pain assessment* (2nd Ed). New York: Guilford.

Chun, C.-A., Enomoto, K., & Sue, S. (1996). Health care issues among Asian Americans. In P. M. Kato & T. Mann (Eds.), *Handbook of diversity issues in health psychology* (pp. 347–365). New York: Plenum Press.

Clemmey, P. A., & Nicassio, P. M. (1997). Illness self-schemas in depressed and nondepressed rheumatoid arthritis patients. *Journal of Behavioral Medicine, 20,* 273–290.

Coderre, T. J., Katz, J., Vaccarino, A. I., & Melzack, R. (1993). Contribution of central neuroplasticity to pathological pain: Review of clinical and experimental evidence. *Pain, 52,* 259–285.

Craig, K. D. (1986). Pain in context: Social modelling influences. In R. A. Sternbach (Ed), *The psychology of pain* (2nd ed., pp. 67–96). New York: Raven Press.

Craig, K. D. (1998). The facial display of pain. In G. A. Finley & P. J. McGrath (Eds.), *Measurement of pain in infants and children* (pp. 103–122). Seattle, WA: IASP Press.

Craig, K. D. (1999). Emotions and psychobiology. In P. D. Wall & R. Melzack (Eds.), *Textbook of pain* (4th ed., pp. 331–343). Edinburgh, UK: Churchill Livingstone.

Craig, K. D., Lilley, C. M., & Gilbert, C. A. (1996). Social barriers to optimal pain management in infants and children. *Clinical Journal of Pain, 17,* 247–259.

Craig, K. D., Prkachin, K., & Grunau, R. V. E. (in press). The facial expression of pain. In D. C. Turk & R. Melzack (Eds.), *Handbook of pain assessment* (2nd ed.). New York: Guilford Press.

Dalal, A. K., & Singh, A. K. (1992). Role of causal and recovery beliefs in the psychological adjustment to a chronic disease. *Psychology and Health, 6,* 193–203.

Dobson, K. S., & Craig, K. D. (Eds.). (1998). *Empirically supported therapies: Best practice in professional psychology.* Thousand Oaks, CA: Sage Publications.

Eccleston, C., Crombez, G., Aldrich, S., & Stannard, C. (1997). Attention and somatic awareness in chronic pain. *Pain, 72,* 209–215.

Edman, J. L., & Kamboka, V. A. (1997). Cultural differences in illness schemas: An analysis of Filipino and American illness attributions. *Journal of Cross-Cultural Psychology, 28,* 252–265.

Edwards, R. R., & Fillingham, R. B. (1999). Ethnic differences in thermal pain responses. *Psychosomatic Medicine, 61,* 346–354.

Ferrell, B. R., & Ferrell, B. A. (1996). Pain in the elderly. Seattle: IASP Press.

Fields, H. L., & Basbaum, A. I. (1999). Central nervous system mechanisms of pain modulation. In P. Wall & R. Melzack (Eds.), *Textbook of pain* (4th ed, pp.309–330). Edinburgh, UK: Churchill Livingstone.

Flannery, R. B., Sos, J., & McGovern, P. (1981). Ethnicity as a factor in the expression of pain. *Psychosomatics, 22,* 39–50.

Fowler-Kerry, S., & Lander, J. (1987). Management of injection pain in children. *Pain, 30,* 169–175.

Gaston-Johansson, F., Albert, M., Fagan, E., & Zimmerman, L. (1990). Similarities in pain descriptions of four different ethnic-culture groups. *Journal of Pain and Symptom Management, 5,* 94–100.

Hadjistavropoulos, T., LaChappelle, D., MacLeod, F., Hale, C., O'Rourke, N., & Craig, K. D. (1998). Cognitive functioning and pain reactions in hospitalized elders. *Pain Research and Management, 3,* 145–151.

Ingvar, M., & Hsieh, J-C. (1999). The image of pain. In P. Wall & R. Melzack (Eds.), *The textbook of pain* (4th ed., pp. 215–233). Edinburgh, UK: Churchill-Livingstone.

Jordan, M. S., Lumley, M. A., & Leisen, J. C. C. (1998). The relationships of cognitive coping and pain control beliefs to pain and adjustment among African-Americans and Caucasian women with rheumatoid arthritis. *Arthritis Care and Research, 11,* 80–88.

Kleinman, A. (1982). Neurasthenia and depression: A study of somatization and culture in China. *Culture, Medicine and Psychiatry, 6,* 117–190.

Kohli, N., & Dalal, A. K. (1998). Culture as a factor in causal understanding of illness: A study of cancer patients. *Psychology and Developing Societies, 10,* 115–129.

Korol, C. T., Goodman, J. T., Merchant, P., & Lawrence, J. (2001). Contextual influences on the facial expression of pain in the neonatal intensive care unit. Submitted for publication.

Krainick, J. U., & Thoden, U. (1984). Dorsal column stimulation. In P. D. Wall & R. Melzack (Eds.), *The textbook of pain* (pp. 701–705). Edinburgh, UK: Churchill Livingstone.

LaChapelle, D., Hadjistavropoulos, T., & Craig, K. D. (1999). Pain measurement in persons with intellectual disabilities. *Clinical Journal of Pain, 15,* 13–23.

Lacroix, J. M. (1991). Assessing illness schemata in patient populations. In J. A. Skelton & R. J. Croyle (Eds.), *The mental representations of health and illness: Models and applications* (pp. 103–219). New York: Springer-Verlag.

Lau, R. R., & Hartman, K. A. (1983). Common sense representations of common illnesses. *Health Psychology, 2,* 167–185.

Lau, R. R., Bernard, T. M., & Hartman, K. A. (1989). Further explorations of common-sense representations of common illnesses. *Health Psychology, 8,* 195–219.

Lawlis, G. F., Achterberg, J., Kenner, L., & Kopetz, K. (1984). Ethnic and sex differences in response to clinical and induced pain in chronic spinal pain patients. *Spine, 9,* 751–754.

Lee, S. (1997). A Chinese perspective of somatoform disorders. *Journal of Psychosomatic Research, 43,* 115–119.

Leventhal, H., & Nerenz, D. R. (1983). A model for stress research with some implications for the control of stress disorders. In D. Meichenbaum & M. Jarenko (Eds.), *Stress reduction and prevention* (pp. 5–38). New York: Plenum Press.

Leventhal, H., Idler, E. L., & Leventhal, E. A. (1999). The impact of chronic illness on the self system. In R. J. Contrada & R. D. Ashmore (Eds.), *Self, social identity, and physical health: Interdisciplinary explorations* (pp. 185–208). New York: Oxford University Press.

Leventhal, E. A., Leventhal, H., Robitaille, C., & Brownlee, S. (1999). Psychosocial factors in medication adherence: A model of the modeler. In D. C. Park, R. W. Morrell, & K. Shifren (Eds.), *Processing of medical information in aging patients* (pp. 145–165). Mahwah, NJ: Erlbaum.

Leventhal, H., Meyer, D., & Nerenz, D. (1980). The common sense representation of illness danger. In S. J. Rachman (Ed.), *Contributions to medical psychology* (Vol. 2, pp. 7–30). New York: Pergamon Press.

Markus, H. (1977). Self-schemata and processing information about the self. *Journal of Personality and Social Psychology, 35,* 63–79.

Markus, H., & Wurf, E. (1987). The dynamic self-concept: A social psychological perspective. *Annual Review of Psychology, 38,* 299–337.

McGrath, P. J., & Unruh, A. M. (1987). *Pain in children and adolescents.* Amsterdam: Elsevier.

Mechanic, D. (1962). The concept of illness behavior. *Journal of Chronic Disease, 15,* 189–194.

Melzack, R. (1986). Neurophysiological foundations of pain. In R. A. Sternbach (Ed.), *The psychology of pain* (2nd ed., pp. 27–48). New York: Raven Press.

Melzack, R., & Wall, P. D. (1965). Pain mechanisms: A new theory. *Science, 150,* 971–979.

Melzack, R., & Wall, P. D. (1988). *The challenge of pain.* Harmondsworth, UK: Penguin Books.

Merskey, H., & Bogduk, N. (Eds.). (1994). *Classification of chronic pain. Descriptions of chronic pain syndromes and definitions of pain terms.* New York: Elsevier.

Miller, S. M. (1979a). Controllability and human stress: Method, evidence and theory. *Behaviour, Research and Therapy, 17,* 287–304.

Miller, S. M. (1979b). When is a little information a dangerous thing? Coping with stressful events by monitoring vs. blunting. In S. Levine & H. Ursin (Eds.), *Coping and health* (pp. 145–170). New York: Plenum Press.

Miller, S. M., & Mangan, C. E. (1983). Interacting effects of information and coping style in adapting to gynecologic stress: Should the doctor tell all? *Journal of Personality and Social Psychology, 45,* 223–236.

Neisser, U. (1976). *Cognition and reality.* San Francisco, CA: Freeman.

Pennebaker, J. W. (1980). Perceptual and environmental determinants of coughing. *Basic and Applied Social Psychology, 1,* 83–91.

Pennebaker, J. W. (1983). Accuracy of symptom perception. In A. Baum, S. E. Taylor, and J. Singer (Eds.), *Handbook of psychology and health* (Vol. 4, pp. 189–218). Hillsdale, NJ: Erlbaum.

Pfefferbaum, B., Adams, J., & Aceves, J. (1990). The influence of culture on pain in Anglo and Hispanic children with cancer. *Journal of the American Academy of Child and Adolescent Psychiatry, 29,* 642–647.

Prkachin, K. M., & Craig, K. D. (1995). Expressing pain: The communication and interpretation of facial pain signals. *Journal of Nonverbal Behavior, 19,* 191–205.

Salovey, P., & Birnbaum, D. (1989). Influence of mood on health-relevant cognitions. *Journal of Personality and Social Psychology, 57,* 539–551.

Sargent, C. (1984). Between death and shame: Dimensions of pain in Bariba culture. *Social Sciences and Medicine, 19,* 1299–1304.

Schultheis, K., Peterson, L., & Selby, V. (1987). Preparation for stressful medical procedures and person x treatment interactions. *Clinical Psychology Review, 7,* 329–352.

Steptoe, A., & O'Sullivan, J. (1986). Monitoring and blunting coping styles in women prior to surgery. *British Journal of Clinical Psychology, 25,* 143–144.

Sternbach, R. A. (1986). *The psychology of pain.* New York: Raven Press.

Tu, W. (1980). A religiophilosophical perspective on pain. In H. W. Kosterlitz & L. Y. Terenius (Eds.), *Pain and society* (pp. 63–78). Weinheim, Germany: Verlag.

Turk, D. C., & Melzack, R. (1992). The measurement of pain and the assessment of people experiencing pain. In D. C. Turk & R. Melzack (Eds.), *Handbook of pain assessment* (pp. 3–14). New York: Guilford Press.

Tursky, B., & Sternbach, R. A. (1967). Further physiological correlates of ethnic differences in reponses to shock. *Psychophysiology, 4,* 67–74.

Waddell, G., & Turk, D. C. (1992). Clinical assessment of low back pain. In D. C. Turk & R. Melzack (Eds.), *Handbook of pain assessment* (pp. 15–36). New York: Guilford Press.

Wall, P. D. (1989). Introduction. In P. Wall & R. Melzack (Eds.), *Textbook of pain* (2nd ed., pp. 1–18). New York: Churchill Livingston.

Ward, S. E., Leventhal, H., & Love, R. (1988). Repression revisited: Tactics used in coping with a severe health threat. *Personality and Social Psychology Bulletin, 14,* 735–746.

Zeltzer, L. K., Anderson, C. T. M., & Schechter, N. L. (1990). Paediatric pain: Current status and new directions. *Current Problems in Pediatrics, 20,* 411–486.

10

CULTURAL ISSUES IN
SUICIDAL BEHAVIOR

SHAHÉ S. KAZARIAN* AND EMMANUEL PERSAD†

*Departments of Psychology and Psychiatry
†Department of Psychiatry
The University of Western Ontario
London, Ontario, Canada

Suicide is a major public health problem confronting the international community. Suicide is the fifth leading killer in Canada and the ninth in the United States. The age-adjusted suicide rate in 1992 in Canada was 13.0 per 100,000. This represents a total of 3709 suicide deaths and accounts for 1.9% of all deaths in the country. The age-adjusted suicide rate in 1991 in the United States was 11.4 per 100,000. This represents a total of 30,810 suicide deaths and accounts for 1.4% of the total number of deaths in the country (U.S. Bureau of the Census, 1994). More recent data, i.e., 1997, show the suicide rate in Canada to be 12.3 per 100,000 (Statistics Canada, Catalogue No. 82F0075XCB) and 11.4 in the United States (Centers for Disease Control and Prevention, http://www.cdc.gov/ncipc/factsheets/suifacts.htm). Crosby, Cheltenham, and Sacks (1999) estimated the 12-month incidence of suicidal ideation, planning, and attempts among United States adults. They found that 5.6% of the survey respondents reported suicidal ideation. This represents about 10.5 million adults in the United States. The study also found that 2.7% of the respondents (representing about 2.7 million people) reported making a specific suicide plan. Finally, the study found that 0.7% (about 700,000) respondents reported making a suicide attempt. Crosby et al. (1999) estimated 36 suicide attempts for every one completed suicide. They also estimated the *direct* costs associated with hospitalized suicide attempts to be over $882 million.

In many other countries of the world, suicide is among the eight leading causes of death. In England, suicide accounts for 8.5 and 3.8% of years of life lost before the age of 64 years for males and females, respectively. In addition to the personal tragedy that it portrays and the kaleidoscope of human emotions that it evokes, suicide engulfs considerable economic resources from the health and mental health care systems, sustains an everlasting burden on its survivors, and defies societal pronouncement of victory over its morbidity.

International attention on suicidal behavior has increased over the past two decades. The World Health Organization (WHO) identified suicide as a programmatic target for the European region (Faria, 1992). Target 12 stipulated "sustained and continuing reduction of the current rising trends in suicide and attempted suicide" through improvements in three areas. The first pertained to societal factors that are sources of strain on individuals (e.g., unemployment and social isolation). The second related to the strengthening of the abilities of individuals to cope with life events through education and social support. The third consisted of training of service providers in health and social services for effectiveness in dealing with people at high risk for suicide.

Identification of suicide as a multidimensional societal problem, the establishment of national research into the causes of suicide, and the development of effective prevention and intervention approaches have also been recommended in Canada and the United States (Garland & Zigler, 1993; Health Canada, 1987, 1994).

In the present chapter, we discuss the interface between cultural psychology and the psychology of suicidal behavior, with a view to engendering consideration of a more culturally relevant suicide theory, research, and practice.

DEFINITION OF SUICIDAL BEHAVIOR

Two opinions have been offered on the origin of the word "suicide." The first represents derivation from the word *suist,* meaning "a selfish man," and the second from the Latin word *suicidium,* comprising the two root words, *sui* meaning "himself or herself" and *cedo* meaning "to give up." According to Barraclough and Shepherd (1994), the term suicide was coined by Sir Thomas Browne and used for the first time in the published edition of his book, *Religio Medici,* in 1643.

Historical landmarks in suicidal behavior are presented in Table 10.1. Suicide has been viewed variously as a rational "honorable exit," exemplified in the death of Socrates. It has also been portrayed as an act of martyrdom, as an act that commands condemnation, denial of funeral rites, and excommunication, as a sinful act, as a triple crime (murder, high treason, and heresy), as an illness, and as a symptom of mental illness. Philosophic writers of the 17th and 18th centuries who disfavored the free-choice conception of suicide opposed the use of the term. Rather, they emphasized its criminal nature and referred to suicide as self-murder, self-homicide, self-slaughter, and self-killing (Barraclough & Shepherd, 1994).

TABLE 10.1   Historical Landmarks in Suicidal Behavior

399 B.C.	View of suicide as a rational "honorable exit"
350	View of suicide as a detrimental act in cultures that value community welfare
33 A.D.	View of suicide as martyrdom
65	Consideration of quality of life in rational suicide
400	View of suicide as a sinful act
1643	The first printed use of the term *suicide* in English
1751	Decriminalization of suicide in Germany
1763	View of suicide as an illness
1838	View of suicide as a symptom of mental illness
1897	Publication of Emile Durkheim's *Le Suicide*
1906	Founding of the Antisuicide Bureau of Salvation Army (London, England) and the National Save-a-Life League (New York)
1910	Psychoanalytic Association Conference on Suicide (Vienna)
1928	Founding of Refuge for People "Tired of Living" (Vienna)
1953	Opening of First Samaritan Branch in Central London (England)
1955	Founding of the Suicide Prevention Centre (Vienna)
1958	Establishment of the Los Angeles Suicide Prevention Center, the first in the United States
1960	International Association for Suicide Prevention and Crisis Intervention (Vienna)
1968	American Association of Suicidology
1971	Publication of journal *Life Threatening Behavior*
1972	Decriminalization of suicide in Canada
1975	Renaming of *Life Threatening Behavior* to *Suicide and Life-Threatening Behavior*
1981	Meeting of Working Group on Changing Patterns in Suicide Behavior (Greece)
1984	Health for All in the Year 2000–European Strategy
1985	Youth Suicide Prevention Act (United States)
1985	Incorporation of Canadian Association for Suicide Prevention
1986	WHO/EURO Working Group on Preventive Practices in Suicide
1987	WHO/EURO Multicenter Study on Parasuicide
1989	Consultation on Strategies for Reducing Suicidal Behavior (Hungary)
1990	Meeting of Third European Symposium on Suicidal Behavior and Risk Factors
1991	Publication of Derek Humphrey's *Final Exit*
1993	Decriminalization of suicide in Ireland
1997	Establishment of Arthur Sommer Rotenberg Chair in Suicide Studies (Canada)

Suicidal behavior has generally been viewed as a continuum, from ideation to gesture to attempt to completion (Crosby et al., 1999; Garland & Zigler, 1993; Silverman & Maris, 1995). Suicidal ideation refers to thought or wish to die. Rescuability and lethality are used to differentiate between suicidal gestures and suicidal attempts. Suicidal gestures, or parasuicide, are deliberate nonlethal acts of self-harm in contexts of high likelihood of rescuability and with intent to evoke environmental effects such as sympathy or attention for the failed suicide (cry for help). Suicidal attempts are lethal self-inflicted acts with intent to die and minimal likelihood for rescuability. Suicide completions are deaths by suicide. While suicidal behavior is conceptualized as a continuum, "it is yet to be demonstrated that this continuum is continuous for every individual in every situation" (Silverman & Maris, 1995). In addition, the "factors that move an individual along the continuum (if, in fact, there truly is such a linked continuum) from ideation, through intent and plan, to execution of a self-destructive or life-threatening behavior" are yet to be elucidated (Silverman & Maris, 1995). Finally, suicide has been reconceptualized as a "unidimensional continuum from positive life-enhancing to negative life-threatening behaviors" (Lewinsohn, Rohde, & Seeley, 1996, p. 35). This view of suicidal behavior suggests a psychology of suicidal behavior that focuses not only on "reasons for dying" (i.e, motivational and risk factors for suicide) but also on "reasons for living." As Jobes and Mann (1999) have described, integration of the reasons for dying approach to suicide and the reasons for living approach enables better understanding of the "gestalt of the suicidal mind" (p. 98). Needless to say, the integrated approach to suicidal behavior requires consideration of both positive life-enhancing and negative motivational and "risk factor" indicators in suicide assessment, treatment, and prevention.

TYPES OF SUICIDE

Suicides have been committed by single individuals or have involved two or more people. Dyadic or group suicides have been manifested in family suicides, cult suicides, pact suicides, mass suicides, and murder–suicides. The Canadian Press (1991) reported the tragic case of a murder–suicide. A man who returned home from work on an early Tuesday morning found his 31-year-old wife, Sukwant Dulai, and 5-year-old daughter hanging in the basement. He also found his 2-year-old daughter wandering in the house with marks on her neck, suggestive of an attempted hanging. Ms. Dulai had called Ms. Sanichara, her boss, on the previous Saturday to tell her that her "marriage was finished." Ms. Sanichara had arranged to meet with Ms. Dulai on the Monday before Ms. Dulai was found dead.

Takahashi (1989) has offered a plausible explanation for parent–child suicide pacts or parent–child murder–suicides. He has suggested that Asians, particularly those influenced by Confucian teachings, tend to internalize aggression rather than openly reveal hostility toward others. Takahashi (1989) has attributed the common occurrence of parent–child suicide pacts in Asian culture or parent–child murder–suicides to the combined effects of strong bonds among Asian family members and the release of the unexpressed aggression on other members of the family.

Suicides have also been known to occur in clusters. Suicide clusters are imitative and subject to the "contagion effect." Cluster suicides occur in Western and non-Western cultures in addition to being more common among Aboriginal youth than in the North American general population (Kirmayer, 1994). Cluster suicides have been linked to depictions of suicide in the media, including newspapers, movies, soap operas (Fekete & Schmidtke, 1995; Gould & Shaffer, 1989; Health Canada, 1994; Phillips, 1989; Platt, 1987, 1989), and, more recently, to the Internet. McGran (1997) reported the double suicide of a 21-year-old man from Chicago and a 24-year-old woman from Orillia, Canada, who developed a relationship on the Internet. The couple were found dead in a hotel in Toronto from an overdose. Evidently, they had used a recipe of drugs and pills they had also found on the Internet.

METHODS OF SUICIDE

Some methods of suicide are culturally universal (e.g., use of firearms) while others are culture-specific (e.g., setting oneself on fire). Shiang et al. (1997) reported that Asian Americans in the city of San Francisco predominantly used hanging to complete suicide whereas those of European American heritage (Caucasian) predominantly used the gunshot method. Taylor and Wicks (1980) described two theories that explain the choice of methods among suicide victims: lethality of intent and differential socialization with firearms. Shiang et al. (1997), on the other hand, offered a self-construal theory for explaining the relationship between culture and method of suicide. The authors interpreted the choice of hanging in the Asian American group "in terms of cultural construals of self as interconnected," i.e., the perception of suicide in Asian culture as an interpersonal act. Similarly, Hendin (1995) attributed the high rate of use of drowning in Norway to the centrality of the sea in the Norwegian conscious and unconscious psyche. Nevertheless, the association between suicide and self-orientation (i.e., independent-self and interdependent-self) has been inferred rather than tested directly.

EPIDEMIOLOGY OF SUICIDAL BEHAVIOR

The epidemiology of suicide has been considered from both intercultural and intracultural perspectives, such comparative studies dating back to the early 20th century (Yap, 1958). The intercultural perspective entails comparisons of suicide rates among nations. The intracultural approach comprises of comparisons among diverse cultural groups within a culturally pluralistic context. There are four important issues associated with the intercultural and intracultural approaches to the epidemiology of suicide. While both approaches allow examination of cultural similarities and differences, Takahashi (1997) observed the excessive emphasis on cultural differences in culture and suicide research, "thus running the risk of increasing prejudice toward different cultures and reinforcing overgeneralizations" (p. 137). Second, Hovey and King (1997) pointed out the epidemiologic reliance on completed suicides. They have suggested increased focus on research that relates culture to the full continuum of suicidal behavior. Third, there is merit to considering culture-specific methodologies in the epidemiologic approach to understanding suicidal behavior, such as the use of personal documents in the form of personal narratives or storytelling in Inuit culture (Leenaars, Anawak, & Taparti, 1998). Finally, the epidemiologic research on suicide has taken an ethnic approach rather than a cultural approach. In the ethnic approach, two or more ethnic groups are selected without a theoretical rationale for comparison purposes. In the cultural approach, two or more ethnic groups are selected on the basis of theoretical dimensions for comparative purposes (Lonner & Adamopoulos, 1998; van deVijver & Leung, 1998). Individualism/collectivism represents an example of a cultural dimension (Kagitcibasi, 1998). Levine and Norenzayan (1999) have cited evidence of a higher rate of suicide in individualistic cultures than in those that are collectivistic.

INTERCULTURAL STUDIES OF COMPLETED SUICIDES

Caution is required in interpreting variations in suicide rates among different countries. Moscicki (1995) has pointed out that worldwide and standardized criteria for the classification and reporting of suicide deaths are nonexistent. Moscicki (1995) has also observed that the quality of such data is highly variable.

A number of studies have examined completed suicide rates in different countries and factors that are associated with rates of suicides (WHO, 1993; La Vecchia, Lucchini, & Levi, 1994; Lester, 1997a; Sakinofsky & Leenaars, 1997). Except for the People's Republic of China, suicide rates across nations are higher for males than females (La Vecchia et al., 1994; Shiang, 1998; WHO, 1993). Additionally, suicide rates are more favorable in less developed areas of the world. Also, upward trends in most industrialized nations for adolescents, young adults, and the elderly are observed. Finally, indigenous people, gays and lesbians, persons in custody, and individuals with a past history of suicide (personal or familial) are shown to be at high risk for suicide.

Explanations for international differences in completed suicide rates are varied (Lester, 1997a). They include physiological factors (e.g., differences in neurotransmitters, such as serotonin), psychological factors (e.g., mood disturbances and alcohol and drug abuse), compositional factors (e.g., population differences in the proportion of those at high risk for suicide, such as the elderly), and social variables (e.g., social integration).

INTRACULTURAL STUDIES OF COMPLETED SUICIDES

Caution is required in interpreting variations in intracultural completed suicide rates. Intracultural studies fail to operationally define such terms as race, ethnicity, minority, majority, White, and Caucasian. A related concern is the interchangeable use of terms, e.g., ethnicity and race. A second concern is neglect of the heterogeneity of the racial or ethnic groups under investigation. The third concern relates to known difficulties associated with random sample selection of cultural groups for comparison purposes. A fourth concern relates to inferences drawn from intracultural studies on suicide. A common practice is confounding race and ethnicity with biological and socioeconomic factors. An equally common practice is drawing causal statements from a correlational methodology, i.e., attributing observed differences between and within racial or ethnic groups to the "independent" effect of race or ethnicity.

Among the earlier intracultural studies on suicide is that of Strauss and Strauss (1953) from Sri Lanka. The authors compared the suicide rates of seven cultural groups and found that of the European group to be the highest (80.0 per 100,000). Strauss and Strauss (1953) attributed the high rate of suicide for the European group to their alien status in Sri Lanka and their social isolation.

The Group for the Advancement of Psychiatry (1989) reviewed available data on suicide among five major cultural groups in the United States. The Group stated, "Most dramatic are the substantially higher aggregate rate of suicide among Native Americans and the lower rates among Blacks, Puerto Ricans, and Mexican-Americans. The rates for Chinese- and Japanese-Americans are lower than the national figures, but not strikingly dissimilar" (Group for the Advancement of Psychiatry, 1989, p. 96). More recently, Shiang (1998) examined suicides among racial groups (African Americans, Asians, Caucasians, Hispanics, and Native Americans) in San Francisco for a 10-year period (1987–1996). Shiang (1998) found the absolute numbers of completed suicides for African Americans, Hispanics, and Native Americans to be strikingly small. Shiang (1998) also found important differences and similarities among the cultural groups. For example, the use of firearms as a means of suicide was common to all the racial groups in the study.

While African American men and women show overall lower rates of suicide, the suicide rates for African Americans have witnessed a significant rise in the past five decades (Chance, Kaslow, Summerville, & Wood, 1998), such that the suicide rates for African American men in the 25–34 and 75–84 age groups are similar to those of "Whites." Risk factors and protective factors for suicide in African Americans have been identified (Gibbs, 1997; Neeleman, Wessely, & Lewis, 1998). Risk factors included being male, substance use, psychiatric disorders, family/interpersonal conflict, antisocial behavior, and homosexuality. On the other hand, factors that mitigate the risks of suicidal behavior include religiosity, older age, southern residence, and social support (see also Early, 1992).

Garland and Zigler (1993) examined suicide rates in the United States from 1966–1988 for 15- to 19-year-olds and found that Native American youth showed the highest suicide rates of any ethnic group in the country. The authors, nevertheless, recognized the great variability in suicide rates across Native American communities. Garland and Zigler (1993) indicated that the high suicide rates for

Native American adolescents were associated with high rates of substance use, unemployment, availability of firearms, and child neglect and abuse. The authors identified cultural values, stress and discrimination, self-destructive behaviors other than suicide (e.g., victim-precipitated homicides), and social support networks as explanatory factors for the cultural differences in suicide rates. Lester (1997b) confirmed the significant roles that acculturation and cultural conflict assume in precipitating suicidal behavior among Native Americans (see also EchoHawk, 1997). Clarke, Frankish and Green (1997) identified consistencies across the United States, Canada, Australia, and New Zealand and cautioned against the "nativity is destiny" view. Rather, Clarke et al. (1997) argued that the increased suicide rates among indigenous adolescents were due to the social milieu in which First Nations people generally have found themselves.

Unlike in the United States, national, population-based data on suicide rates by "race" are not available in Canada. It is worth noting that the Canadian pattern of higher suicide rates in males, in the younger and older age groups, and in Aboriginal people is consistent with those of their neighbors to the south. In relation to the indigenous people in Canada, Aboriginal suicide occurs at two or three times the rate of nonaboriginal suicides (Health Canada, 1987), with wide variations in rates between communities and higher rates among the youth (Gotowiec & Beiser, 1993).

SUICIDAL IDEATION, GESTURES, AND ATTEMPTS

A number of international studies have reported prevalence rates for suicidal ideation, suicidal gestures, and suicidal attempts (Schmidtke et al., 1996; Weissman et al., 1999). Schmidtke et al. (1996) showed that for the 1989–1992 period, the average age-standardized rates of suicide attempts were highest for males in Helsinki (314 per 100,000 population) and for females in Cergy-Pontoise, France (462 per 100,000 population). The lowest rates of suicide attempts for both males and females were in Guipuzcoa, Spain (45 per 100,000 population for males and 69 per 100,000 population for females). Weissman et al. (1999) reported greater cross-cultural variations in rates of suicide ideation than rates for suicide attempts.

Prevalence rates on suicide ideation, gestures, and attempts in North America are based on community household surveys, telephone surveys of injury-related topics, or studies on specialized treatment programs (Crosby et al., 1999; Weissman et al., 1999). Crosby et al. (1999) reported no significant difference in the 12-month incidence rates of suicidal ideation and suicidal plan by Latino origin. Prevalence rates in North America for gestures and attempts have been comparable to European figures (Sakinofsky & Leenaars, 1997). Nearly 80% of suicide completers are men and the majority of attempters, regardless of country, race, or ethnicity, are women (Moscicki, 1995). Attempts are reported less frequently among African Americans than Anglo Americans; and in comparison to non-black/non-Hispanic adults, risk for attempted suicide is lower in both African American and Spanish American adults.

CULTURAL ATTITUDES TOWARD
SUICIDAL BEHAVIOR

Suicide has been in evidence in every time period in recorded history and in almost every culture around the world. It is depicted, and reasons for its committal described, in tribal folklore, Greek tragedies, religious, philosophical, and historical writings, literature, modern soap operas, and rock music. The Eskimo elderly have committed suicide to relieve burden on their families; South American Indians for fear of conquest; African tribal members for aborting slavery; North American Indigenous people for avoiding placement on reservations; Chinese for dealing with harassment and humiliation during the Cultural Revolution; Armenians for fear of rape and torture during the 1915 Armenian genocide; and Jews for escaping Nazi invasion and Nazi concentration camps.

RELIGION AND SECULAR LAW

Religion has been a critical factor in shaping attitudes toward suicide. Suicide in the Muslim religion is a forbidden act (Headley, 1983) because it is considered sinful and against the will of God. The command ". . . and commit not suicide" is in *Sura* 4 of the Koran (Everyman, 1997, p.52). Muslims who are healthy and sane and who commit suicide are considered infidels, having turned away from their religion and brought disgrace and dishonor upon the family. While individuals who commit suicide may be denied burial in Muslim cemeteries, such denials occur very rarely. The families of those who commit suicide are not criticized nor are they censured for the suicidal act. Similarly, attitudes of Muslims toward the ill, especially the mentally ill, who commit suicide are understanding, as are attitudes toward those who attempt suicide. The tolerant and sympathetic attitudes toward suicide attempters are due to the attribution of the suicide attempts to distress and a signal for the need for external assistance and support. Nevertheless, suicides hurt Muslim families psychologically and economically (Headley, 1983), and families may conceal such acts to preserve family reputation, social ranking within the community, and marriageability of their children.

The Jewish religious and social laws with respect to suicide are as forbidding as those of the Muslim religion. The Code of Jewish Law asserts that no one is so wicked as the one who commits suicide and that destroying one human life is akin to destroying a whole world (cited in Headley, 1975, p. 216). Individuals who commit suicide are unlikely to resurrect on judgment day and gain entry to the Promised Land. The personal shame and attention drawn to the Jewish family from the suicidal act are significant issues for surviving families, in addition to difficulties associated with burial arrangements. Suicide is sanctioned only to enable people to avoid a painful or disgraceful demise or forced abandonment of the Jewish faith (Stillion & McDowell, 1996).

Eastern religious beliefs (e.g., Buddhist, Hindu) have also shaped attitudes toward suicide. Followers of these religions tend to be less devout than those of the Muslim religion in addition to believing in the life cycle of reincarnation and rebirth (Ko & Kua, 1996). As described earlier, suicide in Eastern cultures may represent a collective rather than an individual act. The importance of the collective versus individual view of suicide is illustrated in the case of a Japanese American woman who walked into the ocean with her two children to commit family suicide after discovering that her husband was having an affair. The woman's infant and 4-year-old both drowned, and she was accused of murder and jailed. The Japanese American community, however, rallied to her support because they sympathized with her effort to resolve her dilemma through suicide. The Japanese American community perceived her action as a Japanese suicide rather than an American murder (Group for the Advancement of Psychiatry, 1989).

Attitudes about suicide in Christianity have evolved over time, as have secular laws with respect to individuals who commit suicide. Suicide is denounced as a mortal sin early in the history of Christianity and declared a crime against God, punishable in Hell. Dante placed those who committed suicide with murderers in the seventh circle of the Inferno, the ninth circle being the lowest and closest to the Devil. In addition to condemnation by the church, legal sanctions were instituted to supplement religious prohibitions against suicide, and suicide was criminalized in the Middle Ages. In the absence of derangement or reputational considerations (e.g., rape), the bodies of those who committed suicide were dragged through the streets, hung naked upside-down for public view, and impaled on a stake at a public crossroads. They were also denied burial in the church or city cemetery. In England, the suicide victims' assets were forfeited, and the surviving families were severely stigmatized, the widows and children formally censured, and the family's property confiscated (Neeleman, 1996).

In the 18th century, suicide was viewed as an act of lunacy rather than a criminal act even though the stigmatization, shame, and taboo associated with suicide remained invariant. Suicide was decriminalized in Germany in 1741, France in 1791, Holland in 1810, Norway in 1842, Austria in 1852, Denmark in 1868, Finland in 1910, England and Wales in 1961, Hong Kong in 1967, and Ireland in 1993 (Neeleman, 1996). Decrmininalization of suicide in the United States occurred in various states at various times. In Canada, the criminality of attempted suicide was abolished in 1972 while the criminality of assisted suicide or its counseling was sustained in Section 241 of the Criminal Code (Health Canada, 1994). While suicide nowadays is still viewed as a sinful act or as morally wrong, the two acts, physician-assisted suicide and euthanasia (i.e., physician "killing" by either omission or commission), popularized by Dr. Jack Kevorkian, continue to be the subject of considerable debate nationally and internationally (see also Hendin, 1995, 1999).

Kelleher, Chambers, Corcoran, Williamson, and Keeley (1998) studied the relationship between the existence of religious sanctions against suicide and the aggregate suicide rates reported to the WHO. While the average reported rates for countries with religious sanctions were lower than those for countries without sanctions, particularly for females, factors other than the existence of sanctions seem to influence suicide rates. Kelleher et al. (1998) identified two such variables. The first was the reliability of the reported rates of suicide. Kelleher et al. (1998) suggested that the recording and reporting procedures of suicide rates may be affected by the existence of sanctions. Second, the authors indicated that distinctions in suicide rates among the different religious denominations seem to have been somewhat blurred, particularly in relation to Catholics and Protestants. Kelleher et al. (1998) observed that Catholics in certain societies show a higher reported suicide rate than the majority of Protestant churches.

CULTURAL BELIEFS AND PRACTICES

Invaluable contributions to the exploration of cultural beliefs, practices, and help-seeking behavior in the context of suicide have been those of Farberow (1975), Headley (1983), and Reynolds, Kalish, and Farberow (1975). Reynolds et al. (1975) reported that African Americans and Mexican Americans attributed suicide to mental illness, more so than Anglo Americans and Japanese Americans. Mexican Americans and Japanese Americans also considered the suicide victim cowardly, a finding Reynolds et al. (1975) attributed to the collectivistic orientation of the Mexican and Japanese cultures. Reynolds et al. (1975) also reported that African Americans, Anglo Americans, and Japanese Americans viewed nonserious threats of suicide as general calls for help and attention. Mexican Americans, on the other hand, perceived such acts as need for help from a professional or a priest. Finally, Reynolds et al. (1975) reported that all four cultural groups endorsed the police as their first choice of intervention with a person they knew was seriously considering suicide. Excluding for African Americans, the priest was the favored second choice for contact for Anglo Americans, Japanese Americans, and Mexican-Americans.

CONCEPTUAL MODELS OF
SUICIDAL BEHAVIOR

As pointed out by Garland and Zigler (1993), "the search for the etiology of suicide spans many fields of study, from the molecular level of biochemistry to the celestial level of astronomy" (p. 171). In the present section, medical/psychiatric, sociological, psychological, and cultural models of suicide are discussed briefly.

MEDICAL/PSYCHIATRIC MODEL

The medical model relies on diagnosis and medical–psychological conditions as causal explanations for suicide. In this model, the act of self-destruction is viewed as "a disease or necessarily the manifestation of disease." Studies on risk factors in suicidal behavior indicate that close to 90% of completed suicides have a diagnosable psychiatric condition at the time of death (Duberstein & Conwell, 1997).

Genetic, neuroendocrine, and neurophysiological studies have provided support for a biological diathesis for suicidal behavior (Roy, Nielson, Rylander, Sarchiapone, & Segal, 1999). Several family studies found a significant association of a positive family history for suicide and suicidal behavior in those patients who committed suicide (Farberow & Simon, 1969). Roy (1983) found that a family history of suicide significantly increased the risk for an attempted suicide in a wide variety of diagnostic groups. Roy (1983) further indicated that almost half of those with a family history of suicide had themselves attempted suicide.

Egeland and Sussex (1985) have found that, in their study of the Amish community in Pennsylvania, suicide was a relatively rare event and that over a period of 100 years in which 26 suicides occurred, 75% of those suicide victims were found to cluster in four family pedigrees, each containing a heavy loading for affective disorders and for suicide.

There is an increase in the risk for suicide in monozygotic twins compared with dizygotic twins (Roy, Segal, Centrewall, & Robinette, 1991). Similarly, clinical data from twin and adoption studies support the genetic susceptibility to suicide (Roy et al., 1999).

Neuroendocrine and neurophysiological studies have suggested that low concentrations of the serotonin metabolite 5-hydroxy-indol-acetic-acid (5-HIAA) have been associated with suicidal behavior (Arango, Underwood, & Mann, 1997; Mann, Oquendo, Underwood, & Arango, 1999). In their review of several studies on the biology of suicide, Arango et al. (1997) and Mann et al. (1999) have suggested that alteration of the neurotransmitters serotonin and norepinephrine support the hypothesis that low levels of these neurotransmitters appear to be associated with suicidal behavior. Further, there is a suggestion in their reviews that neurotransmitter abnormality in the ventral prefrontal cortex appears to play a role in suicidal behavior. This hypothesis is, in part, supported by the belief that this particular brain region provides behavioral inhibition and that a compromised ventral prefrontal cortex may result in a predisposition to suicidal behavior. The relationship between medical or physical disorders and suicide has been of increasing interest, particularly in view of the emergence of chronic life-threatening illnesses such as HIV/AIDS as well as other chronic and debilitating illnesses. It is important that patients with serious physical illnesses be fully assessed for the presence of a psychiatric disorder which may contribute to suicidal behavior. Research in this area is also greatly needed (Hendin, 1999).

SOCIOLOGICAL THEORIES

The most influential sociological theory of suicide has been that of the French sociologist Emile Durkheim (1897/1951). According to Durkheim (1897/1951), vulnerability to suicide is a function of social integration. Individuals who are not integrated into any religious, communal, or family group are vulnerable to suicide. Vulnerability to suicide is even higher for individuals whose previous pattern of social integration is challenged or disrupted. Durkheim (1897/1951) has described four explanatory types of suicide (altruistic, egoistic, anomic, and fatalistic) in addition to consideration of social categories (e.g., age, sex, marital status, and religion) for the identification of individual vulnerability to suicide. For example, individuals who are single, divorced, or Protestant are identified as more vulnerable to suicide than those who are married and Catholic. Durkheim (1897/1951) has rejected consideration of psychological, psychiatric, biological (heredity), climatic, or cultural factors in suicide.

PSYCHOLOGICAL THEORIES

Psychological approaches to suicide have varied and include the psychoanalytic–psychodynamic, behavioral, cognitive, and humanistic–existential perspectives. The most influential psychoanalytic–psychodynamic theory of suicide has been that of Sigmund Freud. While Durkheim (1897/1951) discovered suicide outside people (i.e., in their social context), Freud and his followers found it deep in the individual psyche. According to Freud, anger and the repressed desire to kill a lost loved object when self-directed can lead to depression and can serve as a motivator for suicide. Freud has been as guilty in his neglect of culture as Durkheim. Freud's view of suicide as disguised murder and his stress on intrapsychic factors have precluded meaningful consideration of social and cultural influences on suicidal behavior.

More recent psychological perspectives on suicidal behavior have considered multidimensional causes of suicide within a diathesis–stress model (Blumenthal & Kupfer, 1988; Lewinsohn et al., 1996; Mann, Wateraux, Haas, & Malone, 1999). For example, Blumenthal and Kupfer (1988) identified four determinants of suicidal behavior: predisposing risk factors, risk factors, protective factors, and precipitating factors. Predisposing risk factors include genetic/family history, biological factors (e.g., perinatal insults), and personality traits (e.g., impulsivity). Risk factors provide vulnerability for suicidal behavior and entail environmental considerations and exposure to suicide in addition to psychiatric conditions, such as mood disorders, anxiety, substance-use disorders, and posttraumatic stress disorders. Protective factors include cognitive flexibility, positive social support, hopefulness outlook, and treatment for psychiatric or personality disorder. Precipitating factors entail availability of methods for suicide and proximal life events, including those perceived as humiliating. In their threshold model of suicidal behavior, Blumenthal and Kupfer (1988) suggested that stressful events can put a person with preexisting biological and social–psychological vulnerabilities over the edge.

CULTURAL MODELS

Research in anthropology, transcultural psychiatry, cross-cultural psychology, and cultural psychology suggest that "cultural practices are much more important than previously thought in determining day-to-day behavior, including the patterns that a person chooses to complete suicide" (Shiang, 1998, pp. 345–346). While considerable progress has been made in the advancement of theoretical models for suicidal behavior, conceptual consideration of the interface between culture and suicide has been a recent phenomenon (Conners, 1994; Griffith, Berry, Foulks, & Wintrob, 1989; Group for the Advancement of Psychiatry, 1989; Hovey & King, 1997). The cultural models have applied the concepts of acculturation and acculturative stress to mental health, in general, and to suicide in particular.

Berry and Kim (1987, 1988) and Williams and Berry (1991) have presented a conceptual framework for the relationship between acculturation and mental health. Berry and Kim (1987) proposed that stressors may result from varying experiences of acculturation and that "varying levels of acculturative stress may become manifest as a result of acculturation experience and stressors" (p. 494). Acculturative stress refers to stress that emanates from and has its source in acculturation. Cognitive, emotional, and behavioral indicators of acculturative stress include identity confusion, depression, anxiety, feelings of alienation and marginality, and heightened psychosomatic symptoms. In the acculturation–mental health model, the following variables that mediate acculturation and mental health have been identified: characteristics of the dominant or host culture (pluralism, tolerance for diversity, multiculturalism ideology), the type of the acculturating group (indigenous people, ethnocultural groups, immigrants, refugees, sojourners), the phase of acculturation (precontact, contact, conflict, crisis, and adaptation), mode of acculturation (assimilation, integration, separation, and marginalization), the sociocultural characteristics of the acculturation group (age, sex, marital status, employment, education, social support, settlement pattern, stratification, entry status, and status mobility), and the psychological characteristics of the acculturating individual (prior knowledge of host culture, congruity between expectations and realities, values and beliefs, and attitudes toward mode of acculturation). These factors are seen as "buffers" in the reduction of acculturative stress. For example, a refugee with an integrational mode of acculturation is likely to experience more acculturative stress in an intolerant and assimilationist host culture than in a host culture that is tolerant and integrationist in policy.

The mediating role of acculturation in suicidal behavior has been supported empirically. For example, higher rates of suicide are seen in cultural groups in their countries-of-settlement than in those in their counties-of-origin. Similarly, there is evidence for convergence over time in suicide rates between "minority" and "majority" cultural groups in culturally pluralistic communities. Finally, mode of acculturation and suicide are correlated. These trends and associations have been replicated in North America (Group for Advancement of Psychiatry, 1989; Lester, 1997b; Trovato, 1986) and Australia (Hassan, 1995). Trovato (1986) examined the relationship between acculturation and suicide mortality in Canada and, using multiple regression analysis, he supported the following two important hypotheses: the greater the degree of ethnic assimilation in host culture, the higher the suicide rate; and the greater the degree of ethnic community integration with the host culture, the lower the suicide mortality (Trovato, 1986). Trovato concluded that "the fact that the ethnic community integration factor is found to be a strong inhibitor of suicide in relation to assimilation suggests that ethnic members may assimilate in some dimensions, but at the same time, ethnic community affiliations play a dominant role in preventing psychological distress and suicide. Multiculturalism provides an indirect buffer to this tendency by promoting the importance of ethnicity."

Hovey and King (1997) have extended the acculturation–mental health model of Berry and colleagues to suicidal *ideation*. In their Model of Acculturative Stress, Depression, and Suicidal Ideation, Hovey and King (1997) have suggested that level of acculturation (little to much) "leads to varying levels of acculturative stress, and that elevated levels of acculturative stress may result in significant levels of depressive symptoms and suicidal ideation" (p. 93). Thus, acculturative stress may lead to depression or suicidal ideation and depression itself may lead to suicidal ideation. Following Berry and his colleagues, Hovey and King (1997) have also listed factors "that possibly moderate levels of acculturative stress, depression, and suicidal ideation." The list of factors include family cohesiveness, social support, socioeconomic status, premigration adaptive functioning (e.g., self-esteem, coping, psychiatric status), motives for the move (e.g., voluntary versus involuntary), cognitive variables (e.g., attitudes toward acculturation), age at immigration, generation in new community, and degree of cultural pluralism in host or dominant culture.

The Hovey and King (1997) Model of Acculturative Stress, Depression, and Suicidal Ideation has been a significant development in addressing cultural issues in suicidal ideation. Nevertheless, their model has three major limitations. First, it is an acculturation model of suicidal ideation rather than a cultural model of suicidal behavior. In this respect, it excludes consideration of other dimensions of culture (e.g., individualism–collectivism) as predisposing risk factors, risk factors, and precipitating factors in suicidal behavior. As the model focuses on suicidal ideation, it is silent on other aspects of suicidal behavior (i.e., attempts and completions). Second, it considers acculturation as a unidimensional experience (from little to much) influencing acculturative stress rather than a bidimensional process, i.e., identification with heritage culture and host culture. The bidimensional model of acculturation also considers acculturation orientations at the *individual* level (integration, assimilation, separation, and marginalization) and at the *host culture* level (integration, assimilation, segregation, and exclusion). The focus on acculturative orientations is consistent with more recent conceptualization of acculturation processes and outcomes (Berry, 1998; Berry & Kim, 1987; Bourhis, Moise, Perreault, & Senecal, 1997; Kazarian, 1997).

The third limitation of the Model of Acculturative Stress, Depression, and Suicidal Ideation, as described by Hovey and King (1997), is that it oversimplifies the relationship between acculturative stress, depression, and suicidal ideation. In their model, depression and suicidal ideation are described as the inevitable consequences of acculturative stress. However, it is known that depression and suicidal ideation are only two possible outcomes of acculturative stress. Other outcomes of acculturative stress include identity confusion and psychosomatic complaints. Finally, Hovey and King (1997) describe suicidal ideation as resulting from depression and fail to consider hopelessness as a mediating factor between clinical depression and suicidal ideation.

In Fig. 10.1, we present a cultural model of suicidal behavior. In this model, we consider suicidal behavior in the context of the interactive effect of individual and host culture acculturation orientations and include aspects of culture other than those specific to acculturation. In relation to acculturation, and consistent with Berry and Kim's (1987) and Bourhis et al.'s (1997) formulations, we suggest that acculturative stress is more likely in contexts in which the individual and host-culture acculturative orientation profiles are conflictual rather than consensual, i.e., a *negative* outcome is not inevitable. The latter is important and consistent with the reality that individuals from diverse cultures adapt successfully to host cultures and become model citizens in their adopted countries (Berry & Kim, 1987). In the Cultural Model of Suicidal Behavior, we also pro-

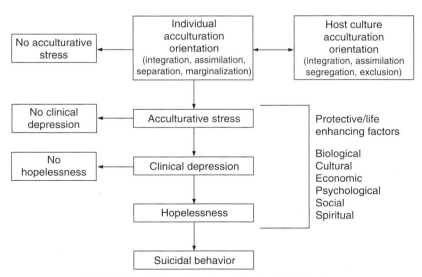

FIGURE 10.1   Cultural model of suicidal behavior.

pose that a probabilistic relationship exists between an individual's acculturative orientation and the level of acculturative stress experienced. More specifically, and consistent with empirical evidence, we suggest that mode of acculturation is correlated with acculturative stress, as defined by Berry and Kim (1987) and Berry, Kim, Minde, and Mok (1987). Berry and Kim (1987) have shown the acculturation attitude of integration is associated with less acculturative stress than the acculturative attitudes of separation, assimilation, and marginalization.

In the cultural model of suicidal behavior, we also consider the threshold concept and allow an outcome for acculturative stress other than clinical depression. More specifically, we propose that acculturative stress that is above an individual's threshold may result in clinical depression or physical, psychological, and social outcomes other than depressed mood. It is as yet unclear why the consequences of acculturative stress vary across individuals. It is likely that cultural factors interact with biological and personality attributes and lead to individual differences in outcomes. In the cultural model of suicidal behavior, we also incorporate hopelessness as a mediating factor between clinical depression and suicidal behavior. Inclusion of hopelessness in the model is consistent with findings of a strong association between stable levels of hopelessness and suicidal behavior (Beck, Steer, Kovacs, & Garrison, 1985; Beck, Steer, Beck, & Newman, 1993; Beck, Brown, Steer, Dahlsgaard, & Grisham, 1999).

Finally, we offer a comprehensive list of factors that are likely to mediate the relationship between acculturation and suicidal behavior. These include biological, economic, psychological, social, cultural, and spiritual components. In terms of culture, we propose consideration of aspects of culture other than acculturation, because most empirical cultural research on suicidal behavior has been based on models of acculturation. While research on acculturation and suicidal behavior has contributed significantly to our understanding of suicide, and while such research should continue, there also needs to be research and practice focus on aspects of culture other than acculturation. Aspects of culture that require greater attention in suicide research and practice are individualism–collectivism, construals of the self (e.g., autonomous versus interdependent), and self-disclosure. For example, qualitative (being direct versus beating around the bush, or circumstantial) and quantitative (eager to talk versus reticent) styles of communication among individuals from diverse cultures assume important mediating roles in suicidal behavior and have important implications for the diagnosis of suicidal behavior and its management (Takahashi, 1989).

SUICIDE PREVENTION, INTERVENTION, AND POSTVENTION

It should be underscored that a high proportion of individuals from diverse cultures adapt successfully as citizens, immigrants, or refugees and never engage in suicidal behavior. Nevertheless, health care providers and mental health professionals do encounter individuals from diverse cultural groups and refugees with mental health issues, including suicidal behavior (Kazarian, Mazmanian, Sussman, & Persad, 1993). Consequently, the cultural competence of health professionals in suicide research and practice is an imperative.

In collaboration with an interdisciplinary team (V. Sharma, psychiatrist, S. Holbert, Clinical Nurse Specialist, K. White, Staff Development, and K. McDermott, psychologist), the present authors surveyed the educational needs of mental health professionals (medical staff, nursing, occupational therapists, psychologists, social workers, vocational counselors) in two provincial (state) psychiatric hospitals for suicide assessment, intervention, prevention, and postvention (i.e., aftermath of suicide). Respondents were asked to indicate their level of need for a suicide in-service program (1=Not at All, 6=Very Much So) for the purpose of refining their knowledge and skills in dealing with the suicidal patient. Respondents were also instructed to write down suggestions for specific topics for inclusion in each of the four areas of suicide assessment, suicide intervention, suicide prevention, and suicide postvention.

A summary of the suggestions of the respondents is provided in Table 10.2. Of interest is the negative finding with respect to culture. Even though 91.2% of the respondents ($n=136$) endorsed the need for a suicide in-service program for the purpose of refining their knowledge and skills in dealing with suicide, none of them identified the need for inclusion of cultural issues in the development and implementation of such a comprehensive initiative. These findings suggest that culture is not in the "minds" or schema of mental health professionals, and training initiatives are required to promote incorporation of cultural issues in suicidal behavior curricula. This is particularly important in a health context, in which understanding the cultural values and beliefs of individuals and their acculturation experiences is a prerequisite for a culturally competent and ethically sound approach to suicide prevention, intervention, and postvention research and practice.

SUICIDE PREVENTION

Suicide prevention programs aim at reducing the incidence and prevalence of suicidal behavior. In a write-up on the Internet, David Gunnell has attributed the first recorded suicide prevention initiative to Plutarch's (46–110 AD) report of an approach in the Greek city of Miletus in which an epidemic of suicide among young women was aborted by the public display of the naked bodies of those committing suicide.

Taylor, Kingdom, and Jenkins (1997) have listed 13 common themes associated with suicide prevention strategies: public education, media, school-based programs, detection and treatment of depression and other mental disorders, alcohol and drugs, somatic illness, enhanced access to mental health services, assessment of attempted suicide, postvention, crisis intervention, work and unemployment, training, and reduced access to lethal methods. Taylor et al. (1997)

TABLE 10.2 Suggested Topics of Mental Health Professionals for a Suicide
In-service Program

Suicide assessment
Definition of suicidal behavior (e.g., difference between suicide attempt, self-harm, and self-abuse)
Symptoms, early warning signs, risk factors, incidence, and other pertinent statistics
Techniques for assessing various components and overall level of risk for making a lethal attempt
Standardized assessment approaches including history taking
Assessment tools and checklists

Suicide intervention
Specific techniques—what to say one-on-one, what to do, and ongoing evaluation of risk
Interventions that make client/patient safe so that hospital is not necessary
What can you do and what can't you do to intervene?
Psychosocial support, physical therapies, underlying diagnoses, managing crisis situations
Helping family members with people who threaten and don't follow through

Suicide prevention
Management of depression including screening and appropriate referral
How to talk about suicide; define actions that can be suggested to prevent suicide
Risk assessment, stress management, dealing with anger and frustration
Information with respect to helping people to live with mental illness
Training in the management of the borderline personality disorders
Support services available in community
Education of patients/clients, staff, family, and community

Suicide postvention (aftermath of suicide)
Critical stress debriefing for treatment team, other patients, and client's family
Psychiatric postmortem
Support for family and staff
Teaching staff and patients how to cope with a suicidal event, dealing with guilt and loss
Need for bereavement/grief counseling and support group for staff, patients and families, etc.
How to contain and deal with rage and anger of significant other
How to deal with children whose parents have suicided

---

have also identified three levels of national action to reduce suicide: nations with comprehensive strategies, those with national preventive programs, and nations without national action. The United States is a nation with a national preventive program whereas Canada is a nation without a national program.

SUICIDE PREVENTION PROGRAMS

Traditionally, comprehensive suicide prevention programs have consisted of several interrelated components, including public education, environmental suicide-proofing, suicide prevention centers, and school-based suicide prevention initiatives. Public education programs have been devised to increase public awareness, and improve individual life skills and coping, and media relations with respect to the possible imitative effect of suicide coverage. Suicide prevention councils across the continent have assumed an important role in advocacy and public awareness initiatives. Environmental suicide-proofing approaches have taken the form of stricter gun-control laws, creation of environmental barriers for preventing suicides committed by jumping in the transit system, and limitations to easy accessibility to "attractive hazards" (e.g., the Golden Gate Bridge in San Francisco).

Suicide prevention centers (crisis intervention, 24-hour telephone "lifelines" or "hot lines") have been established in numerous countries including Australia, England, Canada, the United States, Japan, Taiwan, Singapore, and India. The first telephone hot line programs were introduced in the late 1950s (Shneidman & Farberow, 1957) to allow trained volunteers to "tune in" to the distress of callers, to "talk them out of suicide," and to inform them of the availability of professional help. A suicide-prevention challenge that has confronted the global community is the Internet. In response to an Internet-related double suicide in Toronto, the Canadian Association for Suicide Prevention designed and introduced a new website (http://www.sympatico.ca/masecard) to "try to deal with suicide in an on-line world" (McGran, 1997).

Comparative studies on the effectiveness of suicide prevention centers in non-Western cultures are not known even though their use for a variety of reasons (e.g., family problems, marital discord, parental difficulties, unhappy love affairs, and financial hardships) has been documented (Headley, 1983). Studies on the effectiveness of suicide prevention centers (crisis or suicide hotlines) in Western cultures have focused on the characteristics of the users of these services and the impact of the services on rates of suicidal behavior. The available evidence indicates that the most frequent "customers" of suicide prevention centers are young white women (Dennis & Kirk, 1976) and that suicide prevention centers tend to reduce the suicide rates in their specific clientele (Diekstra & Kerkhof, 1994). While there is increasing recognition for the need for multilingual and diversity-focused suicide prevention initiatives, culturally competent models for service development, training, research, and evaluation continue to be lacking.

School-based suicide education programs have been developed to target high-risk adolescents, to inform adolescents of the "warning signs" of suicide (e.g., giving away one's notes when one is doing well in a course, a change in grades) as a means of helping them develop the "third ear" for suicide detection and to teach them how and where to refer an individual who seems suicidal. Nevertheless, arguments for and against the development and implementation of school-based suicide prevention programs for adolescents continue to prevail (Hazell & King, 1996). Of additional concern in a multicultural context is the lack of consideration of cultural models in the development, implementation, and evaluation of school-based suicide prevention programs. In their survey of youth suicide prevention efforts in the 50 states, Metha, Weber, and Webb (1998) were able to identify only a limited number of school-based suicide prevention initiatives with special emphasis on cultural diversity and the needs of special populations.

Diekstra and Kerkhof (1994) reviewed the effectiveness of school-based suicide prevention programs and drew the following distressing conclusion:

> . . . there is little evidence that the programmes have the desired effect on knowledge
> and attitudes towards suicidal behaviour [see also Garland & Zigler, 1993] and there is
> some suggestive evidence that programmes may increase the percentage of students that
> see suicide as a possible solution of problems (p. 150).

They concluded that there was no clear-cut evidence to suggest that the programs
had any effect on the suicidal or help-seeking behavior of the participants.

Metha et al. (1998) analyzed youth suicide prevention initiatives in 50 states
for effectiveness and drew conclusions similar to those of Garland and Zigler
(1993). Garland and Zigler recommended that suicide prevention initiatives focus on social problems most closely associated with suicidal behavior: delinquency, truancy, substance abuse, teen pregnancy, and family distress, in addition to professional education for educators and health and mental health service
providers, firearm management, media education with respect to suicide, identification and treatment of youth at high risk for suicide, crisis intervention and
treatment for suicide attempters, and educational involvement of policymakers.

Even though there is a paucity of nonschool-based and culturally formulated
suicide prevention programs, model programs exist. A diversity-based health
promotive program is the Multicultural Women's Community Development Project (Kazarian, 1993; see also Kazarian & Kazarian, 1998). This project targets
newcomers and refugee women and is funded by Canadian Heritage, the Canadian Ministry of Citizenship, and the United Way. The main goals of the project
have been cultural integration and promotion of health in women from diverse
cultures in a local community by consideration of four health determinants: individual competence, empowerment, social support, and community support systems. The project focuses on acculturation and improving the quality of life for
recent immigrant and refugee women and their families in the following life domains: social, employment, housing, nutrition, family, leisure, and self-esteem.
The structure (train the trainer) and process (group approach) of the project allows integration of women from various cultures in the host culture, fosters effectiveness in dealing with individual acculturation issues of marginalization and
separation, and promotes consideration of life-enhancing attitudes and behaviors.
A highly successful activity is an annual four-day camping event, involving
women and children from diverse cultures and a local Girl Scouts organization
(L. Z. Kazarian, August 14, 1999). While the project has focused primarily on
women from diverse cultures and their families, it has equal application to multicultural children, youth, and the elderly. A number of suicides have been
aborted through identification and appropriate referral (Kazarian, 1993).

In view of the accumulating evidence in support of an association between
both child abuse and neglect and suicidal behavior, and posttraumatic stress
disorder and suicide comorbidity (Adams & Lehnert, 1997; Wagner, 1997),
theoretically driven research and suicide prevention initiatives for children and

families are required. Research consideration needs to be given to identifying the similarities and differences between trauma- and nontrauma-related suicidal behaviors and impact analysis of suicide prevention initiatives with abused and neglected children (Vicky-Veitch Wolfe, May 20, 1999). Consideration also needs to be given to developing and implementing culturally relevant national community-based screening approaches for identification of depression and intervention against suicide (Jacobs, 1999) among the youth, adults, and the elderly.

Training is an important requirement for suicide prevention. In Canada, a multidisciplinary team of professionals from the province of Alberta has assumed a leadership role in suicide prevention training. Ramsay, Cooke, and Lang (1990) have described the development, implementation, and test marketing of the Alberta Suicide Prevention Programs in Canada, the United States (The California Suicide Intervention Training program), and such countries as Australia, England, Germany, The Netherlands, and Hong Kong. As part of the Alberta programs, a Training for Trainers course has been prepared for large-scale dissemination of a standardized curriculum approach to suicide prevention training. An important strength of the Training for Trainers course is that it can be adapted to various cultural groups (e.g., Hispanic communities in California and Native Canadians in Canada) in pluralistic communities.

The Alberta-based Suicide Intervention Workshop consists of a two-day workshop organized at local communities, at the conclusion of which participants receive certificates for participation (Living Works Education Inc., not dated). The workshop schedule is inclusive of an Attitude Module, a Knowledge Module, a Model to Guide Intervention, and a Resources for Persons at Risk and Caregivers Module. Nevertheless, an important factor that needs to be considered in the further refinement of the Suicide Intervention Workshop is increased focus on cultural diversity in the context of suicidal behavior. The need to include the culture–suicide interface is predicated on two assumptions: those attending the Suicide Intervention Workshop represent the variety of cultures in North America and participants in the courses are likely to encounter suicidal issues in individuals from a variety of cultures.

In culturally pluralistic contexts, developmental, diversity-oriented, and health promotive policies are essential for culturally competent training, implementation, and evaluation of suicide prevention initiatives. Local, state (provincial), national, and international organizations with a multicultural mandate and a mandate for suicide prevention have a vital role to play in this context. Such organizations include Multicultural Councils, Multicultural Community Health Developers, Associations for Suicide Prevention, the American Suicide Foundation, the International Work Group on Death, Dying, and Bereavement, the International Association for Suicide Prevention, the International Union for Health Promotion and Education, the World Federation for Mental Health, Suicide Chairs, and the variety of the WHO Working Groups on suicidal behavior.

SUICIDE INTERVENTION

Intervention refers to short-term management of suicidal crises and long-term care and treatment of those at high risk for suicide (Health Canada, 1994). There are two fundamental components to suicide intervention: assessment and treatment. The most desirable form of intervention is the early identification of those individuals who are at high risk for suicide. From the foregoing, it is clear that suicidal behavior is a complex biopsychosociocultural phenomenon and in order to identify those at risk as well as to provide meaningful intervention, a complete psychiatric, psychological, and social assessment is crucial. It is also important to arrive at a determination as to the presence of a treatable condition which may be associated with the suicidal behavior. This is particularly true of the major psychiatric disorders such as mood disorders, including mixed state, schizophrenia, and other psychotic disorders (Sharma, Persad, & Kueneman, 1998). The assessment process of risk factors should also arrive at a clear understanding of the degree of risk that is present in any particular individual. It is important, therefore, that the first step in intervention is to provide the individual at risk with a secure environment, such as an inpatient psychiatric program.

As recommended by several authors (Lewinsohn et al., 1996; Bongar et al. 1998), suicidal behavior should be assessed routinely at intake and at management transitions, including discharge, leaves of absence from hospital, committals, and staff shift changes. At a minimum, a comprehensive assessment (Beck et al., 1999; Shiang, 1998) should include diagnosis, previous history of treatment, history of suicide attempts, family history of suicide, sociodemographic factors, and employment status. The assessment should also entail cultural beliefs, practices, and rules regarding health, mental health, death, suicide, construal of self, self-disclosure, and communication of affect, premigration, migration, and postmigration processes and outcomes, including acculturation orientation and acculturative stress.

Finally, a comprehensive assessment should focus on the individual's inner experience of suicide, warning signs of suicide, and level of risk for suicide. Warning signs are indicators of potential suicidal risk. They convey messages that suicide may be in the mind of the individual assessed in addition to being an invitation for external assistance (i.e., cries for help). Evaluation of level of risk for suicide entails determination of the immediacy of the suicide risk. Three predictive factors of the risk that an actual attempt or suicide might occur are current suicide plan, past suicidal behavior, and availability of resources (Farberow, Heilig, & Litman, 1994; Ramsay, Tanny, Tierney, & Lang, 1994). Individuals are high at risk for suicide in contexts in which they convey a current plan for suicide (i.e., they identify methods and means of doing themselves in, they express preparing or having already prepared a plan, and they describe a time frame for implementing the plan), they have attempted suicide before or have experienced the death by suicide of a significant other in their lives, and they have inadequate or unavailable external supports in the form of family, friends, financial security, satisfying jobs, access to professional help, positive role models, and affiliation with church, school, or other social institutions. Needless to say, assessment is an ongoing process and individuals suspected of risk for suicide require an effective strategy for intervention.

Ramsay et al. (1994) have described a suicide intervention model comprising three phases and six intervention tasks. In the Exploration phase, the skills of engagement and identification are critical for helping individuals to discuss their problems in a climate of trust and to identify the issue of suicide. In the Understanding phase, inquiry and assessment skills are applied to elucidate the nature of the current suicidal crisis, to evaluate the level of risk for suicide, and to determine availability of resources. In the Action phase, contracting a plan and plan implementation strategies are used to prevent the immediate risk of suicide.

Identification of risk factors and warning signs for suicide provide no guarantees for prediction. Nevertheless, a variety of interviews and psychological measures have been developed and may be of benefit in the assessment of suicidal behavior and the determination of factors associated with suicide (Range & Antonelli, 1990; Maris, 1991; Yufit, 1991; Kral & Sakinofsky, 1994; Sommers-Flanagan & Sommers-Flanagan, 1995). A list of useful instruments for assessing suicidal behavior is provided in Table 10.3. As has been warned by clinicians (Beck et al., 1999; Jobes & Mann, 1999), a patient's inner experience should be considered the "gold standard" of clinical evaluation, and a patient's status for risk for suicide should "never be based on a score of a single scale."

An important feature of two of these measures, the Life Attitude Schedule (LAS; Lewinsohn et al., 1995) and the Reasons for Living versus Reasons for Dying Assessment (Jobes & Mann, 1999), are their inclusion of both positive life-enhancing or "reasons for living" indicators and negative life-threatening behaviors or "reasons for dying" indicators in the assessment of suicide. It is important to underscore that the application of available suicide assessment interviews and scales have been examined in the context of Euro North American culture. Consequently, individual difference factors (e.g., language limitations, cultural and motivational differences) and procedural variables (i.e., task and form appropriateness and psychological equivalence) should be considered in the use of these instruments with individuals from diverse cultural groups and their further psychometric development (Butcher, Nezami, & Exner, 1998).

There is now increasing attention on the biological and psychosocial treatment of suicide even though the cultural perspective to suicide intervention continues to be in an embryonic stage. Western-based treatments vary in modality, theoretical orientation, and context. Suicidal individuals may be treated on an individual, group, or family basis, and as inpatients, outpatients, or both (Retterstol, 1993; Litman, 1994; Chiles & Strasahl, 1995; Stillion & McDowell, 1996; Rhodes & Links, 1998; Jamison & Baldessarini, 1999). Approaches to treatment in these contexts may entail crisis intervention, biological strategies, psychoanalytic or dynamic psychotherapies, cognitive–behavioral interventions (e.g.,

TABLE 10.3   Instruments for the Assessment of Suicidal Behavior

Beck Depression Inventory–II (Beck, Steer, & Brown, 1996)

Beck Hopelessness Scale (Beck & Steer, 1988)

Beck Scale for Suicide Ideation (Beck & Steer, 1993)

Clinical Assessment for Suicide Survivors (Nodin Counselling Services, 1993; also available in Oji-Cree)

College Student Reasons for Living Inventory (Westefeld, Badura, Kiel, & Scheel, 1996)

Firestone Assessment of Self Destructive Thoughts (Firestone & Firestone, 1996)

Life Attitudes Schedule (Lewinsohn et al., 1995)

Los Angeles Suicide Prevention Center Scale (Farberow, Heilig, & Litman, 1994)

Measure of Adolescent Potential for Suicide (Eggert, Thompson, & Herting, 1994)

Multi-Attitude Suicidal Tendencies Scale (MAST; Orbach et al., 1991; also available in French)

Reasons for Attempting Suicide (Holden, Kerr, Mendonca, & Velamoor, 1998)

Reasons for Living Inventory (Linehan, Goodstein, Nielsen, & Chiles, 1983; also in Chinese)

Reasons for Living Inventory vs. Reasons for Dying (RFL/RFD)

Assessment (Jobes & Mann, 1999)

Self-Harm Inventory (Sansone, Wiederman, & Sansone, 1998)

Suicide Assessment Checklist (Rogers, Alexander, & Subich, 1994)

Suicide Assessment Scale (Stanley, Traskman-Bendz, & Stanley, 1986; also in Italian)

Suicide Ideation Questionnaire (Reynolds, 1987)

Suicide Intent Scale (Pierce, 1981; also available in Italian)

Suicide Opinion Questionnaire (Domino, Moore, Westlake, & Gibson, 1982)

Suicide Probability Scale (Cull & Gill, 1988)

problem-solving; Pollock & Williams, 1998), humanistic–existential therapies, and family therapies. The aim of all of these treatment approaches is to prevent further suicidal behavior.

Crisis intervention refers to brief therapies with a view to identifying and resolving the immediate crisis confronting the suicidal individuals and mobilizing their resources in the community. Weaver and Wodarski (1995) examined the meanings of crisis intervention and culture and identified three principles for bridging the cultural gap in serving culturally diverse people in crisis: familiarity with cultural norms, characteristics, and history; awareness of service providers of their own world-views and cultural influences; and consideration of culture in the assessment and intervention processes.

Biological interventions inclusive of electroconvulsive therapy, antipsychotic medications, antidepressants, lithium and mood stabilizers, focus on diagnosable psychiatric disorders (mood disorders, schizophrenia, and comorbid abuse of alcohol or other substances), borderline personality disorder, and posttraumatic stress disorder. There is substantial evidence to suggest that individuals who commit suicide are usually depressed. However, it is also evident that a significant proportion of depressed individuals remain either untreated or undertreated.

The choice of antidepressants in treating a depressed suicidal patient requires careful thought. There is a suggestion in the literature that some antidepressants, for example, those that are serotonergic, may be effective in improving a depressed mood compared with the nonserotonergic antidepressants but that the suicidal risk and successful attempts appear to increase with the use of the serotonergic antidepressants.

It is also stated that the likelihood of the serotonergic antidepressants producing restlessness and inner turmoil can increase the risk of suicidal acts. It is well known that the risk of suicide tends to increase with the apparent improvement in the patient's mood and it is speculated that the reason for this is that the recovering depressed patient may then have the energy to carry out their suicidal ideations, because these tend to diminish at a slower rate than the change in mood. It should also be noted that some antidepressants, especially the nonserotonergic group, can be lethal when taken in overdose. This is particularly true of the older generation tricyclic antidepressants.

The most effective intervention for a depressed patient who is suicidal is electroconvulsive therapy (ECT). This form of treatment is often left as a last resort. However, it is to be noted that in addition to its effectiveness in providing a faster response, follow-up rates of suicide appear to be significantly reduced following ECT versus with antidepressants.

The use of antidepressant medication in treating depression remains the first-line treatment. However, no antidepressant, at this point, is especially "antisuicidal." Some of the newer mood stabilizers, such as carbamazepine and lithium, have been reported to reduce the risk of suicide over time.

Finally, ethnicity is an important factor to consider in the use of any drugs, especially those with psychiatric features. It is well established that individuals of Asian origin metabolize drugs differently than do those from other racial groups. The reason suggested for this difference is based on the low levels of enzymes in the liver required to break down these drugs including antidepressants and other psychiatric drugs. It follows from this fact, therefore, that lethality as well as side effects from antidepressants will vary, depending on the racial group taking the medications. For a detailed discussion on this topic, refer to a special issue on ethnicity in the pharmacologic treatment process (*Psychopharmacology Bulletin,* 1996).

Cognitive–behavioral interventions are individual or group-based therapies with a common focus on depression, depressogenic cognitions and behaviors, and social competence. The Adolescent Coping With Depression program is an example of a cognitive–behavioral group intervention for depressive adolescents (Lewinsohn et al., 1996). Adolescents are exposed to the application of a variety of skill-development strategies (e.g., control of negative ideation and problem solving), with a view to increasing their sense of control over their mood. In some cases, a combination of two or more of these interventions would be more effective.

While there is supportive evidence on the positive impact of biological and psychosocial interventions on functional status and quality of life, more research evidence is required to support their effectiveness in suicide prevention and to demonstrate their specific effect on risk for suicide (Baldessarini & Jamison, 1999). In addition, the inadequate consideration of cultural factors in the assessment and treatment of suicidal behavior needs to be rectified. A paradigmatic shift from the biomedical model to the biopsychosociocultural model may also be necessary. The establishment of chairs in suicide studies, such as the Arthur Sommer Rotenberg Chair in Suicide Studies at the University of Toronto (Links, 1998), and the development of networks with national and international organizations are important for supporting and promoting collaborative and coordinated approaches to suicide research and practice within a holistic framework.

Efforts to support a paradigmatic shift in the health care system are beginning to emerge. For example, a number of multicultural health service programs have been instituted in hospitals in North America to assist patients in negotiating their way through a maze of linguistic and cultural barriers (Lechky, 1992). Nevertheless, experiences of cultural insensitivity abound. Lechky (1992) relates the case of a daughter with an excellent command of the English language who was asked by hospital staff to act as an interpreter for her parents, one of whom was being treated for cancer. The daughter became depressed and suicidal as the physician relied on her to interpret and convey all the medical information to her parents, including the "bad" and potentially devastating news that went with it. Pope and Vasquez (1991) reported that a suicidal Spanish-speaking woman came to the emergency room "talking of pills." The physician, who spoke limited Spanish, "obtained what he thought was her promise not to attempt suicide and sent her back to her halfway house." It was later discovered that the woman "had been saying that she had already taken a lethal dose of pills and was trying to get help" (p. 167).

An understanding of the world-view of the suicidal person is a prerequisite for effective cultural intervention. In comparing intervention practices of Western and Asian cultures, Takahashi (1989) has asserted that Western service providers operate on the basis of a linear logic, i.e., they are straightforward, open, and direct with their patients and expect similar conduct from them. Asian patients, on the other hand, operate on a logic that is circular, i.e., their communication with service providers is subtle, indirect, and reticent with respect to self-disclosure. Takahashi (1989) and Shiang (1998) have also observed that Western service providers are likely to be individualistic in their orientation. They value in their patients autonomy, personal control, and the belief that the mind and the body are two separate systems and require separate interventions. The Western construal of the self as an independent agent is limiting in that it focuses on the "personal cause" of suicide, i.e., it views suicide as an independent, autonomous act and a manifestation of a "problem in the mind," requiring treatment from the mental health system of care (Shiang, 1998). In contrast, Asian patients are likely to be collectivistic in orientation. They value the good of the group over that of the individual and hold the belief that the mind and the body are parts of one system. The Asian construal of the self as an interdependent agent assigns suicide a "social cause," i.e, a relational problem involving the suicidal individual, the family, and the community (Shiang, 1998). It also dissociates suicide from mental abnormality and sanctions somatic expression of psychological problems.

Differences between service providers and patients in world-views, self construals, patterns of self-disclosure, and behavioral expectations are likely obstacles to effective suicide intervention processes and outcomes. As pointed out by Shiang (1998), clinician cultural competence is an issue that requires continued exploration.

SUICIDE POSTVENTION

Shneidman (1973) coined the term "postvention" to recognize the need for helping friends and families of suicide victims. Postvention approaches are important in a variety of contexts (family, health care professionals, schools, workplaces)(Berman, 1995; Kleespies, 1993). For example, Kleespies (1993) estimated that 40% of psychology trainees have a patient suicide (11.3%) or a patient suicide attempt (29.1%) during their training tenure and suggested a health-promotive approach to their education.

Postvention approaches have taken several forms and include direct services to the suicide bereaved, psychological autopsies, and context-based response protocols (e.g., schools) to suicide deaths (Blanchard, Blanchard, & Rolls, 1976; Catone & Schatz, 1991; Farberow, 1994; Mishara, 1995). Direct help for coping with grief is available in the form of individual, family, or group counseling, survivor support groups, and self-help groups (e.g., Core & Core, 1996). Nevertheless, there is evidence suggesting that bereavement support groups may be perceived as stigmatizing, precluding involvement of suicide survivors in them (Levy & Derby, 1992). Consideration of culture in the assessment and counseling of suicide survivors may contribute to acceptability and effectiveness. A model approach in this regard is the bereavement counseling program of the Sioux Lookout First Nations Health Authority (Nodin Counselling Services, 1993).

SUMMARY

Suicidal behavior is a public health problem of international magnitude. Theories of the causes of suicidal behavior have ranged from the biological to the social–psychological. Efforts to understand suicidal behavior have also taken a "reasons for dying" approach while neglecting a "reasons for living" approach to complement it. Race and ethnicity have been the historical dominant approaches to the culture and suicide interface. This narrow approach has neglected consideration of broader cultural dimensions and processes in suicidal behavior. A shared understanding of nomenclature and a shift from the atheoretical ethnicity approach to the cultural approach in suicide research and practice are required. Embrace of culture and the life-enhancing perspective to the research and practice of suicidal behavior are likely to contribute to better understanding of the "gestalt of the suicidal mind," to increase the prediction of suicidal behavior, and to improve individual, family, and community well-being.

CASE STUDY

The Canadian Press (1998) reported the case of a suicidal Belgian woman whose life was saved by her French Canadian "Internet Big Brother." Gabriella (not her real name) was a young Belgian woman. She was married and had three children. She had connected with Gabriel, a French Canadian man, on the Internet, and had chatted with him about "everything and nothing." Over the course of two months, Gabriella had developed what Gabriel described as a "big brother" relationship with him. This entailed confiding in Gabriel and asking him for advice. Over a two-week period, however, Gabriel began noticing a change in the tone of the messages he was receiving from Gabriella. One Sunday night, Gabriella sent Gabriel a farewell letter. In the letter, she indicated the time when she planned to commit suicide. She also included in the letter a message that she wanted relayed to her husband and suggestions for her children's future. On receiving the suicidal note from Gabriella, Gabriel and his wife decided to help save her life. They phoned police in Brussels and gave Gabriella's family name and the Belgian town in which she resided. That was all the information he had on Gabriella. About an hour later, Gabriel learned that Gabriella had been found. Evidently, Gabriella had been a bit angry initially but had accepted the external help and mobilization of her familial support system.

The following assumptions are necessary in a discussion of this particular vignette:

1. Internet use appears to facilitate intimate yet anonymous interaction.

2. Information is shared which is not accompanied by the usual sense of responsibility between communicators.

3. When sharing certain kinds of information and certain quality of interactions, there are boundary issues that will become evident for professionals.

4. This phenomenon is now transglobal.

In response to questions raised with the vignette, the following answers might be considered:

1. There is obviously a moral obligation to "do something" in response to receiving information as described. However, the individuals who were respondent were quite effective in preventing what seemed to have been a determined act of suicide.

2. What are the issues associated with the use of the Internet as a medium for suicide assessment, intervention, prevention, and postvention? The

Internet is one example where this kind of interaction may take place. Other technologies are being employed in providing mental health interventions. These include phone counseling and telepsychiatry. However, strict guidelines would be required that would include training requirements as well as consideration of national jurisdictions with respect to professional standards of practice. It is also self-evident that cultural and social distinctions need to be respected.

SUGGESTED READINGS

Fuse, T. (1997). *Suicide, individual and society.* Toronto: Canadian Scholars Press.
Group for the Advancement of Psychiatry (1989). *Suicide and ethnicity in the United States.* New York: Brunner/Mazel Publishers.
Kosky, R. J. et al. (1998). *Suicide prevention: The global context.* New York: Plenum Press.
Leenaars, A. A., Wenckstern, S., Sakinofsky, I., Dyck, R. J., Kral, M. J., and Bland, R. C. (Eds.) (1998). *Suicide in Canada.* Toronto: University of Toronto Press.

REFERENCES

Adams, D. M., & Lehnert, K. L. (1997). Prolonged trauma and subsequent suicidal behavior: Child abuse and combat trauma reviewed. *Journal of Traumatic Stress, 10,* 619–634.
Arango, V., Underwood, M., & Mann, J. (1997). Biological alterations in the brain stem of suicides. *The Psychiatric Clinics of North America, 20,* 581–593.
Baldessarini, R. J., & Jamison, K. R. (1999). Effects of medical interventions on suicidal behavior: Summary and conclusions. *Journal of Clinical Psychiatry, 60* (Suppl. 2), 117–122.
Barraclough, B., & Shepherd, D. (1994). A necessary neologism: The origin and uses of suicide. *Suicide and Self-Defeating Behavior, 24,* 113–126.
Beck, A. T., & Steer, R. A. (1988). *Manual for Beck Hopelessness Scale.* San Antonio, TX: Psychological Corporation.
Beck, A. T., & Steer, R. A. (1993). Manual for the Beck Scale for Suicidal Ideation. San Antonio, TX: Psychological Corporation.
Beck, A. T., Brown, G. K, Steer, R. A., Dahlsgaard, K. K., & Grisham, J. R. (1999). Suicide ideation at its worst point: A predictor of eventual suicide in psychiatric outpatients. *Suicide and Life-Threatening Behavior, 29,* 1–9.
Beck, A. T., Steer, R. A., Beck, J. S., & Newman, C. F. (1993). Hopelessness, depression, suicide: Ideation and clinical diagnosis of depression. *Suicide and Life-Threatening Behavior, 23,* 139–145.
Beck, A. T., Steer, R. A., & Brown, G. K. (1996). Manual for the Beck Depression Inventory-II. San Antonio, TX: Psychological Corporation.
Beck, A. T., Steer, R. A., Kovacs, M., & Garrison, B. (1985). Hopelessness and eventual suicide: A 10-year prospective study of patients hospitalized with suicidal ideation. *American Journal of Psychiatry, 142,* 559–563.
Berman, A. L. (1995). "To engrave herself on all our memories, To face her body into our lives": The impact of suicide on psychotherapists. In B.L. Mishara (Ed.), *The impact of suicide* (pp. 85–99). New York: Springer Publication Company, Inc.
Berry, J. W. (1998). Acculturation and health. In S. S. Kazarian & D. R. Evans (Eds.), *Cultural clinical psychology: Theory, research and practice* (pp. 39–57). New York: Oxford University Press.
Berry, J. W., & Kim, U. (1987). Comparative studies of acculturative stress. *International Migration Review, 21,* 491–511.

Berry, J. W., Kim, U., Minde, T., & Mok, D. (1987). Comparative studies of acculturative stress. *International Migration Review, 21,* 491–511.

Berry, J. W., & Kim, U. (1988). Acculturation and mental health. In P. Dasen, J. W. Berry, & N. Sartorius (Eds.), *Health and cross-cultural psychology: Toward applications* (pp. 207–236). London, UK: Sage.

Blanchard, T. D., Blanchard, E. L., & Rolls, S. (1976). A psychological autopsy of an Indian adolescent suicide and implications for community services. *Suicide and Life Threatening Behavior, 6,* 3–10.

Blumenthal, S. J., & Kupfer, D. J. (1988). Clinical assessment and treatment of youth suicide. *Journal of Youth and Adolescence, 17,* 1–24.

Bongar, B., Berman, A. L., Maris, R. W., Silverman, M. M., Harris, E. A., & Packman, W. L. (1998). *Risk management with suicidal patients.* New York: Guilford Press.

Bourhis, R. Y., Moise, L. C., Perreault, S., & Senecal, S. (1997). Towards an interactive acculturation model: A social psychological approach. *International Journal of Psychology, 32,* 369–386.

Butcher, J. N., Nezami, E., & Exner, J. (1998). Psychological assessment of people in diverse cultures. In S. S. Kazarian & D. R. Evans (Eds.), *Cultural clinical psychology: Theory, research and practice* (pp. 61–105). New York: Oxford University Press.

Canadian Press (December 18, 1991). Mother, daughter found hanged. *The London Free Press,* A6.

Canadian Press (January 25, 1998). Quebecer uses Internet to avert woman's suicide in Belgium. *Toronto Star,* A5.

Catone, W. V., & Schatz, M. T. (1991). The crisis movement: A school's response to the event of suicide. *School Psychology International, 12,* 17–23.

Chance, S. E., Kaslow, N. J., Summerville, M. B., & Wood, K. (1998). Suicidal behavior in African American individuals: Current status and future directions. *Cultural Diversity and Mental Health, 4,* 19–37.

Chiles, J. A., & Strasahl, K. (1995). *The suicidal patient: Principles of assessment, treatment and case management.* Washington, DC: American Psychiatric Press.

Clarke, V. A., Frankish, C. J., & Green, L. W. (1997). Understanding suicide among indigenous adolescents: A review. *Injury Prevention, 3,* 126–134.

Conners, E. (1994). First Nations and Inuit communities. In Health Canada, *Suicide in Canada: Update of the Report of the Task Force on Suicide in Canada* (pp. 92–93). Ottawa, ON: Ministry of National Health and Welfare.

Core, C. A., & Core, D. M. (Eds.) (1996). *Handbook of childhood death and bereavement.* New York: Springer Publishing Company, Inc.

Crosby, A. E., Cheltenham, M. P., & Sacks, J. J. (1999). Incidence of suicidal ideation and behavior in the United States, 1994. *Suicide and Life-Threatening Behavior, 29,* 131–140.

Cull, J. G., & Gill, W. S. (1988). *Suicide Probability Scale (SPS) manual.* Los Angeles, CA: Western Psychological Services.

Dennis, R. E., & Kirk, A. (1976). Survey of the use of crisis intervention centres by the Black population. *Suicide and Life Threatening Behavior, 6,* 101–105.

Diekstra, R. F. W., & Kerkhof, J. F. M. (1994). The prevention of suicidal behaviour: A review of effectiveness. In S. Maes, H. Leventhal, & M. Johnson (Eds.), *International review of health psychology* (pp. 145–165). New York: Wiley.

Domino, G., Moore, D., Westlake, L., & Gibson, L. (1982). Attitudes toward suicide: A factor analytic approach. *Journal of Clinical Psychology, 38,* 257–262.

Duberstein, P. R., & Conwell, Y. (1997). Personality disorders and completed suicides: A methodological and conceptual review. *Clinical Psychology: Science and Practice, 4,* 359–376.

Durkheim, E. (1897/1951). *Suicide: A study in sociology.* New York: Free Press.

Early, K. E. (1992). *Religion and suicide in the African-American community.* Westport, CT: Greenwood Press.

EchoHawk, M. (1997). Suicide: The scourge of Native American people. *Suicide and Life-Threatening Behavior, 27,* 60–67.

Egeland, J., & Sussex, J. (1985). Suicide and family loading for affective disorders. *Journal of American Medical Association, 254,* 915–918.

Eggert, L. L., Thompson, E. A., & Herting, J. R. (1994). A Measure of Adolescent Potential for Sui-
  cide (MAPS): Development and preliminary findings. *Suicide and Life-Threatening Behavior, 24,*
  359–381.
Everyman. (1994). *The Koran.* London, UK: Author.
Farberow, N. L. (1975). *Suicide in different cultures.* Baltimore, MD: University Park Press.
Farberow, N. L. (1994). The Los Angeles Survivors' after-suicide program. In E. S. Shneider, N. L.
  Farberow, & R. E. Litman (Eds.), *The psychology of suicide: A clinician's guide to evaluation
  and treatment* (Rev. ed., pp. 171–186). Northvale, NJ: Jason Aronson, Inc.
Farberow, N., & Simon, M.(1969). Suicide in Los Angeles and Vienna. *Public Health Report, 84,*
  389–403.
Farberow, N. L., Heilig, S. M., & Litman, R. E. (1994). Evaluation and management of suicidal persons.
  In E. E. Shneidman, N. L. Farberow, & R. E. Litman (Eds.), *The psychology of suicide: A clinician's
  guide to evaluation and treatment.* (Rev. ed., pp. 99–118). Northvale, NJ: Jason Aronson, Inc.
Faria, J. G. S. (1992). Introduction. In P. Crepet, G. Ferrari, S. Platt, & M. Bellini (Eds.), *Suicidal
  behaviour in Europe: Recent research findings* (pp. 9–12). Rome: John Libbey CIC srl.
Fekete, S., & Schmidtke, A. (1995). The impact of mass media reports on suicide and attitudes toward
  self-destruction: Previous studies and some new data from Hungary and Germany. In B. L. Mishara
  (Ed.), *The impact of suicide* (pp. 142–155). New York: Springer Publication Company, Inc.
Firestone, R. W., & Firestone, L. A. (1996). *Firestone Assessment of Self Destructive Thoughts man-
  ual.* San Antonio, TX: Psychological Corporation.
Garland, A. F., & Zigler, E. (1993). Adolescent suicide prevention: Current research and social pol-
  icy implications. *American Psychologist, 48,* 169–182.
Gibbs, J. T. (1997). African-American suicide: A cultural paradox. *Suicide and Life-Threatening Be-
  havior, 27,* 68–79.
Gotowiec, A., & Beiser, M. (Winter, 1993). Aboriginal children's mental health: Unique challenges.
  Canada's Mental Health, 7–11.
Gould, M. S., & Shaffer, D. (1989). The impact of suicide in television movies: Evidence of imita-
  tion. In R. F. W. Diekstra, R. Maris, S. Platt, A. Schmidtke, & G. Sonneck (Eds.), *Suicide and
  its prevention: The role of attitude and imitation* (pp. 331–340). Leiden, The Netherlands: E. J.
  Brill.
Griffith, E., Berry, J. W., Foulks, E., & Wintrob, R. (1989). *Suicide and ethnicity.* New York:
  Brunner/Mazel.
Group for the Advancement of Psychiatry (1989). *Suicide and ethnicity in the United States.* New
  York: Brunner/Mazel.
Hassan, R. (1995). *Suicide explained: The Australian experience.* Victoria, Australia: Melbourne Uni-
  versity Press.
Hazell, P., & King, R. (1996). Arguments for and against teaching suicide prevention in schools. *Aus-
  tralian and New Zealand Journal of Psychiatry, 30,* 633–642.
Headley, L. (1975). Jewish suicide in Israel. In N. L. Farberow (Ed.), *Suicide in different cultures*
  (pp. 215–230). Baltimore, MD: University Park Press.
Headley, L. A. (1983). *Suicide in Asia and the Near East.* Berkeley, CA: University of California
  Press.
Health Canada (1987). *Suicide in Canada.* Ottawa, ON: Minister of National Health and Welfare.
Health Canada (1994). *Suicide in Canada.* Ottawa, ON: Ministry of National Health and Welfare.
Hendin, H. (1995). *Suicide in America: New and expanded edition.* New York: Norton.
Hendin, H. (1999). Suicide, assisted suicide and medical illness. *Journal of Clinical Psychiatry, 60*
  (Suppl. 2), 46–50.
Holden, R. R., Kerr, P. S., Mendonca, J. D., & Velamoor, V. R. (1998). Are some motives more linked
  to suicide proneness than others? *Journal of Clinical Psychology, 54,* 569–576.
Hovey, J. D., & King, C. A. (1997). Suicidality among acculturating Mexican-Americans: Current
  knowledge and directions of research. *Suicide and Life-Threatening Behavior, 27,* 92–103.
Jacobs, D. G. (1999). Depression screening and intervention against suicide. *Journal of Clinical Psy-
  chiatry, 60* (Suppl. 2), 42–45.

Jamison, K. R., & Baldessarini, R. J. (1999). Effects of medical interventions on suicidal behavior. *Journal of Clinical Psychiatry, 60* (Suppl. 2), 4–6.

Jobes, D. A., & Mann, R. E. (1999). Reasons for living versus reasons for dying: Examining the internal debate of suicide. *Suicide and Life-Threatening Behavior, 29,* 97–104.

Kagitcibasi, C. (1998). Individualism and collectivism. In J. W. Berry, M. H. Segall, & C. Kagitcibasi (Eds.), *Cross-cultural psychology: Social behavior and applications: Vol. 3* (pp. 1–50). Needham Heights, MA: Allyn & Bacon.

Kazarian, L. Z. (1993). *Multicultural Women's Community Development Project: Service delivery model and outcome.* Paper presented at the Multicultural Health Coalition Provincial Conference as part of a workshop chaired by Shanthi Radcliffe on Immigrant–Refugee Settlement: Implementing a Healthy Coordinated Approach, Kingston, Ontario, September 9–10.

Kazarian, L. Z. (August 14, 1999). Summer camp for newcomer immigrant families. (Personal communication).

Kazarian, S. S. (1997). The Armenian psyche: Genocide and acculturation. *Mentalities, 12,* 74–87.

Kazarian, S. S., & Kazarian, L. Z. (1998). Cultural aspects of family violence. In S. S. Kazarian & D. R. Evans (Eds.), *Cultural clinical psychology: Theory, research and practice* (pp. 316–347). New York: Oxford University Press.

Kazarian, S. S., Mazmanian, D., Sussman, S., & Persad, E. (1993). Countries of origin of patients and professional staff in a mental hospital. *Canadian Journal of Psychiatry, 28,* 694.

Kelleher, M. J., Chambers, D., Corcoran, P., Williamson, E., & Keeley, H. S. (1998). Religious sanctions and rates of suicide worldwide. *Crisis, 19,* 78–86.

Kirmayer, L. (1994). Suicide among Canadian Aboriginal people. *Transcultural Psychiatric Research Review, 31,* 3–58.

Kleespies, P. M. (1993). The stress of patient suicidal behavior: Implications for interns and training programs in psychology. *Professional Psychology: Research and Practice, 24,* 477–482.

Ko, S. M., & Kua, E. H. (1996). Ethnicity and elderly suicide in Singapore. In J. L. Pearson & Y. Conwell (Eds.), *Suicide and aging: International perspectives* (pp. 177–185). New York: Springer Publishing Company, Inc.

Kral, M. J., & Sakinofsky, I. (1994). Clinical model for suicide risk assessment. *Death Studies, 18,* 311–326.

La Vecchia, C., Lucchini, F., & Levi, F. (1994). Worldwide trends in suicide mortality, 1955–1989. *Acta Psychiatrica Scandinavica, 90,* 53–64.

Lechky, O. (1992). Cultural awareness part of the health care agenda at Toronto Hospital. *Canadian Medical Association Journal, 146,* 2212–2214.

Leenaars, A. A., Anawak, J., & Taparti, L. (1998). Suicide among the Canadian Inuit. In R. J. Kosky & H. S. Hadi (Eds.), *Suicide prevention: The global context* (pp. 111–120). New York: Plenum Press.

Lester, D. (1997a). Suicide in an international perspective. *Suicide and Life-Threatening Behavior, 27,* 104–111.

Lester, D. (1997b). Suicide in America: A nation of immigrants. *Suicide and Life-Threatening Behavior, 27,* 50–59.

Levine, R. B., & Norenzayan, A. (1999). The pace of life in 31 countries. *Journal of Cross-Cultural Psychology, 30,* 178–205.

Levy, L. H., & Derby, J. F. (1992). Bereavement support groups: Who joins, who doesn't, and why. *American Journal of Community Psychology, 20,* 649–662.

Lewinsohn, P. M., Langhinrichsen-Rohling, L., Rohde, S., Seeley, J. R., & Chapman, J. (1995). The Life Attitude Schedule: A scale to assess adolescent life-enhancing and life-threatening behaviors. *Suicide and Life-Threatening Behavior, 25,* 458–474.

Lewinsohn, P. M., Rohde, P., & Seeley, J. R. (1996). Adolescent suicidal ideation and attempts: Prevalence, risk factors, and clinical implications. *Clinical Psychology: Science and Practice, 3,* 25–46.

Linehan, M. M., Goodstein, J. L., Nielsen, S. L., & Chiles, J. A. (1983). Reasons for staying alive when you are thinking of killing yourself: The Reasons for Living Inventory. *Journal of Consulting and Clinical Psychology, 51,* 276–286.

Links, P. S. (1998). Suicidal behaviour. *Canadian Journal of Psychiatry, 43,* 783.

Litman, R. E. (1994). Long-term treatment of chronically suicidal patients. In E. S. Shneidman, N. L. Farberow, & R. E. Litman (Eds.), *The psychology of suicide: A clinician's guide to evaluation and treatment* (Rev. ed., pp. 119–131). Northvale, NJ: Jason Aronson, Inc.

Living Works Education Inc. (not dated). *Suicide intervention workshop.* Calgary, Alberta: Author.

Lonner, W. J., & Adamopoulos, J. (1998). Culture as antecedent to behavior. In J. W. Berry, W. H. Poortinga, & J. Pandey (Eds.), *Cross-cultural psychology: Social behavior and applications: Vol. 1* (pp. 43–84). Needham Heights, MA: Allyn & Bacon.

Mann, J. J., Oquendo, M., Underwood, M. D., & Arango, V. (1999). The neurobiology of suicide risk: A review for the clinician. *Journal of Clinical Psychiatry* (Suppl. 2), 7–11.

Mann, J. J., Waternaux, C., Haas, G. L., & Malone, K. M. (1999). Toward a clinical model of suicidal behavior in psychiatric patients. *American Journal of Psychiatry, 156,* 181–189.

Maris, R. W. (1991). Assessment and prediction of suicide. *Suicide and Life-Threatening Behavior, 21,* 1–17.

McGran, K. (March 11, 1997). Relationship begun on Net leads to double suicide. *The London Free Press,* A5.

Metha, A., Weber, B., & Webb, L. D. (1998). Youth suicide prevention: A survey and analysis of policies and efforts in the 50 States. *Suicide and Life-Threatening Behavior, 28,* 150–164.

Mishara, B. L. (Ed.) (1995). *The impact of suicide.* New York: Springer Publication Company, Inc.

Moscicki, E. K. (1995). Epidemiology of suicidal behavior. *Suicide and Life-Threatening Behavior, 25,* 22–55.

Neeleman, J. (1996). Suicide as a crime in the UK: Legal history, international comparisons and present implications. *Acta Psychiatrica Scandinavica, 94,* 252–257.

Neeleman, J., Wessely, S., & Lewis, G. (1998). Suicide acceptability in African- and White Americans: The role of religion. *Journal of Nervous and Mental Disorders, 186,* 12–16.

Nodin Counselling Services (1993). *Bereavement counselling program: Clinical assessment for suicide survivors.* Sioux Lookout First Nations Health Authority: Author.

Orbach, I., Milstein, I., Har-Even, D., Apter, A., Tyano, S., & Elizur, A. (1991). A multi-attitude suicide tendency scale for adolescents. *Psychological Assessment, 3,* 398–404.

Phillips, D. P. (1989). Recent advances in suicidology: The study of imitative suicide. In R. F. W. Diekstra, R. Maris, S. Platt, A. Schmidtke, & G. Sonneck (Eds.), *Suicide and its prevention: The role of attitude and imitation* (pp. 279–312). Leiden, The Netherlands: E. J. Brill.

Pierce, D. W. (1981). The predictive validation of a suicidal intent scale: A five year follow up. *British Journal of Psychiatry, 139,* 391–396.

Platt, S. (1987). The aftermath of Angie's overdose: Is soap (opera) damaging your health. *British Medical Journal, 294,* 954–957.

Platt, S. (1989). The consequences of a televised soap opera drug overdose: Is there a mass media imitation effect? In R. F. W. Diekstra, R. Maris, S. Platt, A. Schmidtke, & G. Sonneck (Eds.), *Suicide and its prevention: The role of attitude and imitation* (pp. 341–359). Leiden, The Netherlands: E. J. Brill.

Pollock, L. R., & Williams, M. G. (1998). Problem solving and suicidal behavior. *Suicide and Life-Threatening Behavior, 28,* 375–387.

Pope, K. P., & Vasquez, M. J. T. (1991). *Ethics in psychotherapy and counselling: A practical guide for psychologists.* San Francisco: Jossey-Bass, Inc.

Psychopharmacology Bulletin (1996). Ethnicity in the pharmacologic treatment process. *Psychopharmacology Bulletin, 32,* 181–289.

Ramsay, R. F., Cooke, M. A., & Lang, W. A. (1990). Alberta's suicide prevention training programs: A retrospective comparison with Rothman's developmental research model. *Suicide and Life-Threatening Behavior, 20,* 335–351.

Ramsay, R. F., Tanny, B. L., Tierney, R. J., & Lang, W. A. (1994). *Suicide intervention handbook.* Calgary, AB: Living Works Education Inc.

Range, L. M., & Antonelli, K. B. (1990). A factor analysis of six commonly used instruments associated with suicide among college students. *Journal of Personality, 55,* 804–811.

Rettersol, N. (1993). *Suicide: A European perspective.* New York: Cambridge University Press.

Reynolds, D. K., Kalish, R. A., & Farberow, N. L. (1975). A cross-ethnic study of suicide attitudes and expectations in the United States. In N. L. Farberow (Ed.), *Suicide in different cultures* (pp. 35–50). Baltimore, MD: University Park Press.

Reynolds, W. M. (1987). *Suicide Ideation Questionnaire.* Odessa, FL: Psychological Assessment Resources.

Rhodes, A. E., & Links, P. S. (1998). Suicide and suicidal behaviours: Implications for mental health services. *Canadian Journal of Psychiatry, 43,* 785–791.

Rogers, J. R., Alexander, R. A., & Subich, L. M. (1994). Development and psychometric analysis of the Suicide Assessment checklist. *Journal of Mental Health Counselling, 16,* 352–368.

Roy, A. (1983). Features associated with suicide attempts in depression: A partial replication. *Journal of Affective Disorders, 27,* 35–38.

Roy, A., Nielson, D., Rylander, G., Sarchiapone, M., & Segal, N. (1999). Genetics of suicide in depression. *Journal of Clinical Psychiatry, 60* (Suppl. 2), 12–17.

Roy, A., Segal, N., Centrewall, D., & Robinette, D. (1991). Suicide in twins. *Archives of General Psychiatry, 48,* 29–32.

Sakinofsky, I., & Leenaars, A. A. (1997). Suicide in Canada with special reference to the difference between Canada and the United States. *Suicide and Life-Threatening Behavior, 27,* 112–126.

Sansone, R. A., Wiederman, M. W., & Sansone, L. A. (1998). The Self-Harm Inventory (SHI): Development of a scale for identifying self-destructive behaviors and borderline personality disorder. *Journal of Clinical Psychology, 54,* 973–983.

Schmidtke, A., Bille-Brahe, U., DeLeo, D., Kerkhof, A., Bjerke, T., Crepet, P., Haring, C., Hawton, K., Lonnqvist, J., Michel, K., Pommerereau, X., Querejeta, I., Phillipe, I., Salander-Renberg, E., Temesvary, B., Wasserman, D., Fricke, S., Weinacker, B., & Sampaio-Faria, J. G. (1996). Attempted suicide in Europe: Rates, trends and sociodemographic characteristics of suicide attempters during the period 1989–1992, results of the WHO/EURO Multicentre Study on Parasuicide. *Acta Psychiatrica Scandinavica, 93,* 327–338.

Sharma, V., Persad, E., & Kueneman, K. (1998). A closer look at inpatient suicide. *Journal of Affective Disorders, 47,* 123–129.

Shiang, J. (1998). Does culture make a difference? Racial/ethnic patterns of completed suicide in San Francisco, CA 1987–1996 and clinical applications. *Suicide and Life-Threatening Behavior, 28,* 338–354.

Shiang, J., Blinn, R., Bongar, B., Stephens, B., Allison, D., & Schatzberg, A. (1997). Suicide in San Francisco, CA: A comparison of Caucasian and Asian groups, 1987–1994. *Suicide and Life-Threatening Behavior, 27,* 80–91.

Shneidman, E. S. (1973). *Deaths of man.* New York: New York Times Book Co.

Shneidman, E. S., & Farberow, N. L. (1957). *Clues to suicide.* New York: Blakison.

Silverman, M. M., & Maris, R. W. (1995). The prevention of suicidal behaviors: An overview. *Suicide and Life-Threatening Behavior, 25,* 10–21.

Sommers-Flanagan, J., & Sommers-Flanagan, R. (1995). Intake interview with suicidal patients: A systematic approach. *Professional Psychology: Research and Practice, 26,* 41–47.

Stanley, B., Traskman-Bendz, L., & Stanley, M. (1986). The suicide assessment scale: A scale evaluating change in suicidal behavior. *Psychopharmacology Bulletin, 22,* 200–205.

Stillion, J. M., & McDowell, E. E. (1996). *Suicide across the life span.* Bristol, PA: Taylor & Francis.

Strauss, J. H., & Strauss, M. A. (1953). Suicide, homicide and social structure in Ceylon. *American Journal of Sociology, 58,* 461–469.

Takahashi, Y. (1989). Mass suicide by members of a Japanese church. *Suicide and Life-Threatening Behavior, 19,* 289–296.

Takahashi, Y. (1997). Culture and suicide: From a Japanese psychiatrist's perspective. *Suicide and Life-Threatening Behavior, 27,* 137–145.

Taylor, M. C., & Wicks, J. W. (1980). The choice of weapons: A study of suicide by sex, race and region. *Suicide and Life-Threatening Behavior, 10,* 142–149.

Taylor, S. J., Kingdom, D., & Jenkins, R. (1997). How are nations trying to prevent suicide? An analysis of national suicide prevention strategies. *Acta Psychiatrica Scandinavica, 95,* 457–483.

Trovato, F. (1986). Suicide and ethnic factors in Canada. *International Journal of Social Psychiatry, 32,* 55–64.

U. S. Bureau of the Census (1994). *Statistical abstract of the United States 1994 (114th edition).* Washington, DC: Author.

van de Vijver, F. J. R., & Leung, K. J. (1998). Methods and data analysis of comparative research. In J. W. Berry, W. H. Poortinga, & J. Pandey (Eds.), *Cross-cultural psychology: Social behavior and applications: Vol. 1* (pp. 257–300). Needham Heights, MA: Allyn & Bacon.

Wagner, B. M. (1997). Family risk factors for child and adolescent suicidal behavior. *Psychological Bulletin, 121,* 246–298.

Weaver, H. N., & Wodarski, J. S. (1995). Cultural issues in crisis intervention: Guidelines for culturally competent practice. *Family Therapy, 22,* 213–223.

Weissman, M. M., Bland, R. C., Canino, G. J., Greenwald, H. G., Hwu, J. P. R., Karam, E. G., Lee, C. K., Lellouch, J., Lepine, J. P., Newman, S. C., Rubio-Stipec, M., Wells, J. E., Wickramatne, P. J., Wittchen, H. U., & Yeh, E. K. (1999). Prevalence of suicide ideation and suicide attempts in nine countries. *Psychological Medicine, 29,* 9–17.

Westefeld, J. S., Badura, A., Kiel, J. T., & Scheel, K. (1996). Development of the College Student Reasons for Living Inventory with African Americans. *Journal of College Student Psychotherapy, 10,* 61–65.

Williams, C. L., & Berry, J. W. (1991). Primary prevention of acculturative stress among refugees: Application of psychological theory and practice. *American Psychologist, 46,* 632–641.

Wolfe, V. V. (May 20, 1999). Suicide and post-traumatic stress disorder. A half-day professional development presentation of the London–Middlesex Suicide Prevention Council, London, Ontario, Canada.

World Health Organization (WHO). (1993). *1992 world health statistics annual.* Geneva, Switzerland: Author.

Yap, P. M. (1958). *Suicide in Hong Kong with special reference to attempted suicide.* New York: Oxford University Press.

Yufit, R. I. (1991). Suicide assessment in the 1990's. *Suicide and Life-Threatening Behavior, 21,* 152–163.

PART

III

HEALTH PSYCHOLOGY

ISSUES WITH SPECIFIC
CULTURAL GROUPS

11

CULTURE AND LATINO ISSUES IN HEALTH PSYCHOLOGY

HECTOR BETANCOURT AND JOSÉ L. FUENTES

Department of Psychology
Loma Linda University
Loma Linda, California

Some of the main issues relevant to health psychology in the Latino population are not specific to health. These are issues relevant to the study of culture in human behavior in general, but they are particularly important in understanding health behavior in a multicultural society. First, some of the problems associated with the study of culture and ethnicity in mainstream American psychology must be considered. This is important in order to fully understand the limitations of the psychological knowledge on which health research, interventions, and policies are often based. Second, some characteristics of nondominant ethnic populations, such as intragroup diversity, socioeconomic status, and levels of acculturation, which are particularly important for Latinos in the United States, should be taken into consideration if interventions and policy decisions are to be successful.

In the first section of this chapter, we address some of the general aspects concerning the study of culture in mainstream psychology. We also address intragroup diversity in cultural background, socioeconomic status, and levels of acculturation, all of which are issues relevant to the study and practice of health psychology in general and of Latinos in particular. Then, we focus on some of the issues specific to health psychology in the Latino population. Due to space limitations, we cover only some areas, particularly those that serve to illustrate the kinds of health concerns relevant to this population as observed in the United States.

GENERAL CONSIDERATIONS

THE STUDY OF CULTURE AND ETHNICITY
IN PSYCHOLOGY

Mainstream American psychology has traditionally neglected the study of culture and cross-cultural psychology has been criticized for being rather segregated from mainstream psychology. In addition, cross-cultural research as well as the psychological study of ethnic minority issues have been criticized for neglecting theoretical and methodological developments (Betancourt & Lopez, 1993). This reality appears to be changing (Goldberger & Veroff, 1995; Peplau & Taylor, 1997). However, the current body of knowledge in psychology is still, to a large extent, ethnocentric. In many areas, the role that culture plays in understanding human behavior—including the fact that often psychological knowledge represents just one instance of how psychological processes determine behavior, within a particular cultural context—is often ignored. Hence, theories and principles seen as scientific, in fact, lack the universality that is expected of scientific laws.

This reality creates the likelihood that the knowledge on which culturally diverse health policies are based is founded, in fact, predominantly on studies of Anglo American subjects functioning within the context of an Anglo American culture. This knowledge is, to a great extent, produced by Anglo American scholars who have only lived in an Anglo American culture. Furthermore, they generally know little about other cultures and are mostly unaware of how their understanding of their subjects' behavior, as well as their own, may be, at least in part, a function of their own culture. From a scientific perspective, such knowledge, representing only one instance of psychological and behavioral functioning as observed within the context of one particular culture, ignoring the role of culture, would not be appropriate to explain health behavior issues in a multicultural society.

Within this context, it is important to note that developments in numerous areas, such as disease prevention and health promotion, are making it impossible for American psychologists to continue assuming universality when this knowledge is based on culture-specific research. Other advances, such as increased awareness of the changes in U.S. demographics, advancements in electronics and communications technology, and manifestations of a global economy, are among the factors that contribute to this new interest in a culturally diverse knowledge base. This could be the case particularly in areas such as health psychology, where psychologists may be as aware as public health professionals of the importance of culture to understanding health behavior and illness. In contrast to the "parochial" views that have characterized American psychologists, health professionals have long been dealing with the challenges of disease prevention and health promotion at the local and international levels. This has made cultural, economic, and human diversity at all levels more salient and difficult to ignore. This may serve to enhance awareness among psychologists concerning the importance of including culture in their research, theories, and interventions.

DIVERSITY OF THE LATINO POPULATION

Another aspect of general interest in the study of health issues in the Latino population is the diversity of groups included in this categorization, in terms of various aspects of their social, economic, and cultural background and reality. This within-group diversity appears to be something of which mainstream scholars and policymakers appear to have little awareness. Intragroup variations, such as those concerning culture, socioeconomic status, and access to health care and education, are often ignored in research and intervention in areas such as health promotion, education, and policymaking affecting nondominant ethnic groups. In fact, most of the demographic information often used, which has been obtained from sources such as the U.S. Federal Government, could be misleading, unless the limitations concerning within-group diversity are considered.

The study and practice of health psychology in a multicultural population necessitates the use of data concerning the intrinsic diversity of the population. The system of classification that has been employed in the United States when studying population trends is misleading in terms of the cultural characteristics not only of Latinos but also of other groups often considered homogeneous, such as Asian Americans.

In the case of Latinos, the term "Hispanic" is particularly misleading in that it is used to include people from all Spanish-speaking countries, irrespective of differences such as cultural values and beliefs, education, socioeconomic status, or level of acculturation. In fact, this is one of the inherent factors contributing to the erroneous impression of social and cultural homogeneity among Latinos of various backgrounds. The dominance of the Spanish language, which has led some to categorize all Latino Americans as "Hispanic," creates the erroneous impression that Latino people are generally homogeneous in regard to beliefs, practices, socioeconomic and educational status, and ethnic identity.

It seems that the term "Latino," more than "Hispanic," serves as a convenient reference to include all of the U.S. population that comes from the various regions and countries of Latin America. This also includes individuals whose ethnicity is rooted in the regions of the U.S. that were originally Latin American, such as California and Texas. Although Spanish is the native language for most Latino groups—which may still create the impression of homogeneity—awareness of the fact that Latinos come from many different Latin American countries and regions, which include different ethnicities, cultural traditions, socioeconomic backgrounds, and languages, make the diversity of this population more obvious. Moreover, since, from a health behavior perspective, culture and ethnicity—more than language—influence psychological processes and behavior, we propose that the use of the term "Latino" is more appropriate when addressing this population but especially in the context of psychological research and practice.

The facade homogeneity attributed to this population also ignores the fact that migrational patterns of Latinos in the United States have resulted in the formation of communities that are often overrepresented by one dominant subculture. For example, Mexican American immigrants have a strong presence in southern California and Texas, while in the greater Miami area, there is a larger contingency of Cuban American immigrants. New Jersey and New York, on the other hand, have strong contingents of Dominican and Puerto Rican immigrants.

To some extent, the concentration or dominance of one or another of the Latino groups in a particular region not only creates the impression of homogeneity at the federal but also at the state level. This impression of homogeneity at the regional level hides the diversity associated with the presence of other Latino subgroups in the same region. For instance, distinctive cultural, educational, and socioeconomic characteristics of Latinos from Puerto Rico, Cuba, Central, and South America might be ignored in the study of Latino health issues in California and the Southwest.

In regard to health data for Latinos, there are serious questions as to how valid the data are in representing the Latino populace. For example, it was not until the 1970s that the United States census separated the data from the Latino population from the data from those categorized as "White" (Hayes-Bautista, 1992). Consequently, discriminating data compiled prior to 1970 with reference to Latinos is not available. More current data from the National Center for Health Statistics (NCHS) has improved in that there is a stronger effort made to include other cultural categories under the term Hispanic. However, the problem remains that in order to apply statistical measures and analysis to this population, there is the underlying assumption that Hispanic is a valid, reliable, and measurable category in which the data are representative of all Latino groups and subcultures.

The implications of employing broad arbitrary classifications, based largely on linguistic or phenotypic characteristics, can have a profound effect on social, political, and health related policymaking decisions. Just as an example, a study conducted by Sorlie, Rogot, and Johnson (1992) found that while racial classification on death certificates and self-identification of a knowledgeable family member correlated highly (>98%) for Anglo and African Americans, discrepancies were observed in this classification with Asian, Pacific Islander, Latino, and Native Americans. If death certificates are used to report on cause of death, then it is likely that incidence rates for terminal illness, accidents, crime, and the like are inaccurate and nonrepresentative of some cultural groups, including Latinos.

ACCULTURATION

An important characteristic of the Latino and other groups experiencing a steady influx of new immigrants is the various levels and forms of acculturation observed within the corresponding population. Acculturation studies have been criticized for using indirect measures of level of acculturation instead of actually measuring the cultural variables of interest (see Betancourt & Lopez, 1993). However, if research includes the assessment of relevant cultural variables, such as health-related value orientations and beliefs, a better understanding of the cultural processes that enhance or prevent positive health outcomes, such as adaptation and resiliency, may be possible (Zambrana, 1995). The study of such processes, including cultural variables and levels of acculturation, is one way in which the study of issues concerning the health behavior of Latinos (or other ethnic groups) can serve to advance the understanding of the role of culture and acculturation in health psychology in general.

In addition, the study of the process, forms, and levels of acculturation in groups such as Latinos may be as important in understanding health behavior and outcome as the direct study of cultural influences in health behavior and outcome. For example, Berry (1990) provides a model of classification that is based on varieties of acculturating groups rather than on phenotypic, linguistic, or geographic distinctions. Under this classification system, people are divided into five groups that are particularly relevant to the understanding of acculturation among Latinos and other nondominant ethnic groups in the United States. *Ethnic groups* refer to individuals who identify with and exhibit a common heritage in the second and/or subsequent generations after immigration. *Native peoples* refer to people who are indigenous (aboriginal) to the land and were present prior to settlement, in the case of North America, European settlement. In the case of the United States, this would include people of Native American Indian descent. In parts of Texas, New Mexico, Arizona, and California, some people of Mexican and Spanish descent could also be considered *native peoples,* given that they were present well over 100 years prior to Anglo colonization. *Immigrants* and *refugees* are similar in that they are both considered to be first-generation immigrants. However, immigrants are more likely to have emigrated from their country in quest of a better way of life. On the other hand, refugees may have emigrated due to persecution, political unrest, or other negative factor from within their own culture. Finally, the term *sojourners* applies to people who have emigrated but have a distinct purpose and or time period after which they intend to return to their country of origin.

The process of acculturation for groups such as Latinos can be complex and mediated by numerous factors, including circumstances and previous experiences as well as those encountered in the new society by groups and individuals. One example is found in mobility. As presented by Berry (1990), mobility refers to fluidity of contact with the new culture as well as the voluntariness of this contact (Berry, Kim, Minde, & Mok, 1987; Berry 1990). It is proposed that sojourners are individuals who are in temporary contact with the dominant culture and, thus, lack a permanent social support network. The net result of this contact is likely to be characterized by more health problems. Both immigrants and sojourners are more likely to be in voluntary contact with the dominant group. However, immigrants are more likely to establish a relatively more permanent contact with the dominant society, thus resulting in a stronger social support network, which may well mediate a reduction in acculturative stress. As such, this may account for a lower propensity to exhibit stress-related health problems.

One advantage to this classification system may be its tendency to be more inclusive and less exclusive in regard to ascribing membership to the dominant group. However, this categorical depiction is equally inadequate in generalizing health trends and subsequent needs both within and among all groups in question. At this point, the *construct* of acculturation can take on a significant role in understanding health and other population trends.

Regarding strategies or attitudes of acculturation, Berry, Poortinga, Segall, and Dasen (1992) provide a parsimonious structural framework from which to evaluate how an individual has accommodated to the dominant culture. This theory proposes four primary strategies: assimilation, integration, separation, and marginalization.

Strategies of acculturation present meaningful dynamics to the study of health and psychology in that they are likely to be more representative of the needs of individuals. However, it should be pointed out that individuals can routinely utilize multiple strategies of acculturation in different roles. That is, an individual may resort to a strategy of integration in her work and employment while remaining separate in her religious views.

SOCIOECONOMIC STATUS (SES)

Among the more profound limitations in addressing Latino health needs is the failure to control for socioeconomic status (SES) within the Latino cultures. While SES cannot account for poor health indicators on its own, numerous studies support the tenet that higher income and education—both measures of SES—are often associated with better health outcomes (Williams & Collins, 1995). One example of how SES may contribute to better health outcomes is found in the study by Wagner and Schatzkin (1994), who found that the mortality rate of women with breast cancer was significantly lower for women who reside in high SES counties as compared to women who reside in low SES counties.

General population trends suggest that Latinos, as a group, continue to be overrepresented in low SES statistics. From 1980 to 1996, the median household income increased by an average of 10.5% for "non-Latino White" and African American households, but Latino households saw a decline of 4% in median household income during this same period. Black and Latino households were more likely to be at or near poverty level, compared to non-Latino Whites and Asian Americans. In fact, African Americans and Latinos had a poverty rate that was 3.3 times higher than that of non-Hispanic Whites.

However, while accounting for socioeconomic status may indeed meet the standard of necessity, studies on the incidence of low birth weight strongly suggest that it lacks evidence for establishing sufficiency. For example, statistics have shown that women with low socioeconomic status tend to have a higher incidence rate for low birth weight (i.e., less than 2500 grams). Based on this evidence, it makes intuitive sense that Latinas would fall at risk for having infants with low birth weight. However, Fig. 11.1 shows that while Latinas as a whole

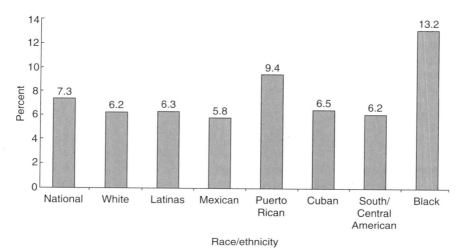

FIGURE 11.1   Percent of low birth weight.

generally have a low incidence rate for low birth weight, Mexican American women have the lowest incidence of low birth weight of any population group. This is ironic, especially when taking into consideration that the Mexican American women have similar SES to that of African American women. Also, this graphic shows that while Latinas average a good overall incidence rate for low birth weight, Puerto Rican American women have an incidence rate that is nearly 50% higher than the average for Latinas and nearly 29% higher than the national rate. This is second only to African American women, who have an incidence rate that is over 80% higher than the national rate.

SPECIFIC HEALTH PSYCHOLOGY ISSUES

In order to address health concerns of Latinos, it is important to consider the potential changes that Latinos experience. Health data has clearly suggested that across most health indicators, low socioeconomic status, among other variables, is associated with higher health risks. Latinos show patterns of health access to health care and mortality rates that differ from the overall population (Johnson et al., 1996). Consequently, it is important to consider the larger social environment and intragroup diversity of Latinos when studying health. For example, in the southern part of Florida, Cubans are heavily involved in the political process, including healthcare. However, not all Latino groups are equally involved or united in regional areas where they may be concentrated and, as such, require that specific attention be given to their health needs.

Perhaps some of the problem in the disparity of knowledge can be explained by an erroneous assumption of what is considered to be common knowledge. For

example, the belief that exercise is good for you may be understood and generally accepted; however, the definition of exercise lacks consensus. Someone educating Latinos who have physically strenuous jobs on the importance of exercise may likely encounter the position that they do enough exercise on their job,
or perhaps that because they exert so much energy, a diet with higher fat content
is of little relevance.

Before proceeding with the presentation of specific health psychology issues
and their implications within the Latino population, we encourage the reader to
consider the following key points before generalizing conclusions. First, it is important to note that prior to the 1970 census, there were no relevant statistics kept
for Latinos. In fact, the current Vital Statistics reports continue to lack adequate
representation of all minority groups, including Latinos. Second, within the context of diversity, some of the health issues presented are more relevant to some
Latino groups than others (e.g., incidence of low birth weight is considerably
higher in Puerto Rican American than in Mexican American women). Third, the
reality of acculturation clearly contributes to health issues within the Latino communities. For example, in areas such as coronary heart disease, Latinos tend to
decrease in health status as they acculturate to the dominant culture. Also,
women, specifically Mexican American women who adhere to their cultural beliefs, generally tend to have better health outcomes than do those who acculturate. Finally, it is clear that Latinos have critical health issues that, indeed, place
them at higher risk than other ethnic groups. Examples of these critical issues include the incidence rate of diabetes and AIDS.

CORONARY HEART DISEASE

Despite efforts aimed at preventing heart disease, this remains the major killer
in the United States. Because heart disease is influenced by numerous factors, it
is important to consider these when making inferences as to its incidence rate.
Some of the major risk factors for developing coronary heart disease include
smoking, diabetes, overweight, sedentary lifestyle, and diet. Health statistics
consistently demonstrate that people of lower socioeconomic status have a higher
incidence rate for each of these risk factors when compared with people of
higher socioeconomic status. Of the ethnic minority groups studied over the last
10 years, Latinos are the only group that continues to show decline in SES. Consequently, it would be logical to assume that Latinos are among those falling at
risk for coronary heart disease, a fact that is, indeed, true.

A common misconception about diet can be found in perceptions about Mexican food. There is the assumption that Mexicans routinely eat the type of diet
that we see in popular restaurants with Mexican motif. However, this would be
the equivalent of taking a Thanksgiving dinner and generalizing that this represents a typical meal for the Anglo American family. The health problem for Latinos and their diet is that, as they acculturate, they generally tend to move away
from a more healthy traditional diet and consume more fast food. With the in-

troduction of fast food comes the gradual reduction of fresh fruits and vegetables and homecooked legumes, which are often a staple of many Latino diets.

The acquisition of a more Anglo American lifestyle also plays a significant role in the health decline of the Latino populace. The concept of *siesta* is one that is not easily transferable to the fast pace of westernized societies. The fast pace of life has often taken women out of the home, thus making the time-saving consumption of fast food a necessity. There is also a more sedentary lifestyle, where walking is not as common, given the need for the Latino family to keep up with the fast pace of the dominant culture. Often, it is necessary for both parents to work in order to make ends meet. This further contributes to the decentralization of the family, a major source of support for Latinos.

Stress is also known to play a significant role in the development and expression of coronary heart disease. Acculturation does not come without experience of stress. These stressors are exacerbated by the gradual deterioration of the family, leaving the individual to make difficult choices. To choose the family may be honorable but could well result in problems assimilating into the new dominant culture. Conversely, moving toward assimilation could result in alienation from his family and, thus, a loss of support. Stress can also be experienced by having to balance many variables in a new culture that is more foreign and perhaps more complex than the individual anticipated.

For example, access to health care is often not available for Latinos, even if they are gainfully employed. The high cost of medical care makes it prohibitive to seek out preventative care, thus resulting in more acuity by the time a physician is consulted. In the home country where health care is not as advanced, there is a network of folk healers that often fill this need, or the family resorts to herbal and other folkloric remedies that have been passed down through generations. However, accessing this type of network may be difficult and there is also a scarcity of sources where these supplies could be found and purchased.

HIV/AIDS

Even though the AIDS virus does not discriminate in regard to victims, analysis of health data shows that Latinos are disproportionately overrepresented among AIDS cases. Recent census data suggest that Latinos account for approximately 12% of the population in the United States. However, they account for more than 17% of AIDS cases, a rate that is second only to African Americans.

Latinos account for over 11% of the male population in the United States. Latinas make up about 10.4% and Latino children about 9.7%. However, Latino males account for over 17% of AIDS cases, Latinas about 20.2%, and Latino children represent an astonishing 23.1%. This means that nearly one in every four pediatric AIDS cases involves a Latino child. Compared to their non-Hispanic White counterparts, Latino males are three times more likely to contract AIDS, while Latinas are about 6.5 times more likely to contract AIDS (Organizations, 1998).

Unfortunately the trend toward disproportionate representation of AIDS cases in Latinos has steadily increased since 1987. This trend, combined with the fact that Latinos are among the fastest growing group in the United States, points toward the critical need to address prevention and health education campaigns that are specific to the needs of this population. However, statistics suggest that regional considerations should be weighed in developing prevention and intervention programs.

For example, the most common forms of AIDS transmission for Latinos are men having sex with men and intravenous drug use. Consequently, if an AIDS prevention program were constructed based on these demographics, it would make sense to strongly address homosexual male relationships. However, a closer look at this data shows that Massachusetts, New Jersey, New York, and Puerto Rico have a reported incidence rate of AIDS transmission through intravenous drug use that is three times higher than male homosexual intercourse. Thus, it would seem necessary that prevention programs in these states should place a significant emphasis on educating Latinos on the dangers of intravenous drug use.

The question of how we can reach Latinos with lifesaving information on AIDS prevention is as diverse as the population itself. Not only are there regional considerations, but also cultural beliefs, practices, and customs that, if not addressed, could hinder rather than advance progress. For example, a recent survey conducted by the Kaiser Family Foundation (1998) shows that most Latinos (77%) are aware that there is no cure for AIDS. However, from another perspective, this also means that approximately 23% of Latinos surveyed believe that either there is a cure for AIDS or are not sure whether a cure for AIDS exists. In the general population, 1 in 20 people believe that there is a vaccine for AIDS. Antithetically, 1 of 5 Latinos expressed a belief that there was a vaccine for AIDS. This obvious discontinuity in knowledge points toward the need to examine the nature and extent of prevention and intervention programs to see why they are not having commensurate results with Latinos.

Television and radio appear to be the most popular and influential media from which Latinos obtain information about AIDS. Compared to the general population, Latinos are more likely to hear information about AIDS from TV news programs at a rate that is 25% higher; 68% higher from TV entertainment programs; 61.5% higher from radio, talk, or call-in shows; and 100% higher from other radio programming. Generally speaking, Latinos who are primarily Spanish-speaking are more likely to obtain their information through TV and radio compared to English-speaking Latinos, who appear to get more of their information from newspapers and magazines.

CANCER

There is some available data that suggests that risk for cervical and breast cancer is higher in low socioeconomic status population groups (Suarez & Siefert,

1998; Wagner & Schatzkin 1994). This presents a particularly critical problem when working with Latinas, given that they are among the poorest members of society. For both of these types of cancer, early detection and intervention is critical to improve outcome. However, given that Latinas generally have less access to health care services, the probability of their being included in screening programs is lower than other groups. Additionally, level of acculturation may also play a mediating role in access to health care. Hubbell, Chavez, Mishra, and Valdez (1996) suggest that Latinos who are not acculturated appear to be at higher risk for not using health care services in a preventative manner. Instead, they are more likely to access services when the condition is more grave. However, Laws and Mayo (1998) suggest that acculturation, ethnicity, or level of education fail to predict utilization of mammography.

Patient education plays a critical role in health prevention programs, which means that patients need to have access to their physician in order to obtain the necessary information. For example, self-administered breast examinations can be very helpful in early detection of breast cancer. However, without routine visits to health care, the likelihood of learning and applying these techniques is significantly reduced.

In the case of cervical cancer, the issue of cultural beliefs also becomes important. Martinez, Chavez, and Hubbell (1997) suggest that within the Latino culture, the concept of promiscuity overrepresents the risks associated with cervical cancer. That is, Latinas are more likely to believe that if they are not promiscuous, they are not at any higher risk for cervical cancer. This suggests the need to educate Latinas on the other factors that contribute to cervical cancer and the importance of getting routine medical checkups to increase the likelihood of early detection.

DIABETES

Previously, it was implied that Latinos with low levels of acculturation, as a whole, tend to have better health outcomes in specific areas. However, diabetes is clearly one of the areas where Latinos, especially those of Mexican descent, are considerably more at risk than other population groups. By some estimates, Latinos are nearly two times more likely to have diabetes when compared to non-Latino Whites.

Among the more significant trends of diabetes in the Latino culture is the fact that young Latinos are being diagnosed with Type II diabetes at an alarming rate. Typically, Type II diabetes is not diagnosed until the individual is an adult. However, Latino children are being diagnosed with this type of diabetes with increasing frequency.

It is estimated that nearly 6% of the population in the United States has diabetes. However, of the nearly 16 million people estimated to have diabetes, approximately one-third have yet to be diagnosed. The highest prevalence for diabetes is found in persons over 65 years of age. In this age group, it is estimated that over 18% have this disorder. Those over 20 years of age have a prevalence rate of just over 8%. Those under the age of 20 have the lowest incidence rate, at well under 1%.

Diabetes can be classified into four different types. Type I or insulin-dependent diabetes mellitus (IDDM) accounts for 5 to 10% of persons with diabetes. As the name implies, persons with Type I diabetes require insulin injections to manage their blood-sugar levels. Persons with insulin-dependent diabetes mellitus are more likely to develop the disease early in life. In fact, this type of diabetes used to be referred to as juvenile-onset diabetes.

Type II or noninsulin-dependent diabetes mellitus (NIDDM) accounts for 90 to 95% of persons diagnosed with diabetes. Persons with noninsulin-dependent diabetes mellitus are not dependent on insulin and are more likely to develop this condition later in life. However, it should be noted that both types of diabetes can occur in the very young or the very old (Miller-Keane, 1992).

Gestational and other specific types of diabetes account for a significantly smaller percentage of diabetes cases. Gestational diabetes occurs in 2 to 5% of all pregnancies and generally subsides after the termination of pregnancy. Hispanic women are among those at higher risk for developing gestational diabetes. Obesity also increases the risk for this type of diabetes. There is also an increased risk of developing Type II diabetes later in life for women with a history of gestational diabetes. Other specific types of diabetes account for less than 2% of all diagnosed cases of diabetes (National Diabetes Data Group, 1995).

PAIN: A LIFESPAN APPROACH

Management of pain is complicated, given the propensity of diversity in its etiology. This factor is confounded by how the individual experiences and expresses his experience of pain. From the perspective of professionals, pain rarely presents itself in a manner that is subject to direct measurement. Consequently, the degree of pain an individual should experience is largely based on inferences made from the type of injury sustained, determined by range of motion, biofeedback readings, grip strength, responses to questionnaires, and a plethora of other techniques, approaches and/or instruments. Furthermore, culture can also influence how pain is expressed and managed within the context of the identified patient's family.

Chronic pain presents challenges to the individual and family alike. Given the important role of family in the Latino cultures, the biopsychosocial model provides a functional paradigm from which to address pain management. The biological origins of pain are diverse and have significant variance. Back pain, joint pain, muscle pain, and other experiences of pain often have biological antecedents which are readily diagnosed. Magnetic resonance imaging and other technological advances have afforded ample opportunity to observe where pain may be present. However, there are numerous situations where this determination cannot be substantiated biologically. There are other circumstances where the degree of pain expressed by an individual is not consistent with bioanatomical evidence.

As is the case with other cultures, education on the medical or biological nature of the pain disorder is an important part of the healing mechanism for Latinos. At times, language can become a significant barrier in communicating with the Latino family. A common way around that has been for medical doctors to use a family member to translate the information to the patient or other members of the family. However, there may be times when young children are relied on for translation since they are more familiar with the English language. Unless these children are adults, professionals are likely to better serve the needs of their Spanish-speaking patients by requesting that the family bring with them an adult to provide the translation.

Psychological factors are strong moderating variables to the experience of pain. Prior research has informed that stress can be manifested physically through muscle tension and other biological markers. From a cognitive behavioral perspective, stress can be ameliorated by changing the cognitions of how the individual interprets and responds to stressful events. Prolonged experience of stress has a higher probability of decreasing healthy psychological adjustment which, in turn, could result in feelings of depression, anxiety, and other psychological problems. The prolonged experience of stress could be a consequence of unemployment, physical stress directly related to the pain disorder, familial stress resulting from change in roles, and acculturative stress that results from the process of acculturating into a new dominant society.

Even though Latinos are the fastest growing group in the United States, their demographics suggest that, as a whole, their economic and educational status has decreased in the past few years. Combined with the fact that Latinos tend to be underrepresented in regard to having medical insurance, a long-term pain disorder presents significant psychological challenges.

Because demographics show that Latinos are less likely to complete high school or college compared to other minority groups, it is logical to assume that they are more likely to be employed in jobs that require physical labor. Such jobs provide little opportunity for the body to heal. For those who have an employer that pays for disability or worker's compensation insurance, there is some source of income while they are incapable of working. However, even while gainfully employed, many Latino families have difficulty meeting their basic needs. The inability to provide for the family may subject the Latino male to an additional source of stress.

DISEASE PREVENTION AND HEALTH PROMOTION

Disease prevention and health promotion are important components of health psychology. However, health promotion is promulgated within the context of culture and family. The structure for Latino families is centripetal in that the tendency is to draw its members in rather than push them toward independence. Consequently, health promotion may be more successful with Latinos if more emphasis were placed on family involvement (Fitzgibon, Stolley, Avellone, & Sugerman, 1996). In fact, across many cultures, the family serves as the central medium by which values, beliefs, and customs are passed on (Bagley, Angel, Dilworth-Anderson, Liu, & Schinke, 1996), a dynamic from which Latinos are not exempt. Understanding the needs of the Latino cultures is important, especially when considering that this group could very well make up one-fourth of the entire United States population within the first half of the 21st century.

However, even though the Latino community continues to grow, it is failing to make gains in its socioeconomic demographics. The Latino community is relatively young but continues to be overrepresented in poverty and low levels of education, both of these being variables that have been linked to health outcomes. It is estimated that as many as one-third of Latinos do not have health insurance and, thus, have limited access to health care. Given this lack of quality health care, it is more likely that this subgroup of Latinos will seek out medical care only when their condition is more advanced, or only when they are experiencing a medical emergency. This level of access to health care is likely to result in poor access to preventative programs that can help decrease the acuity of their health needs, not to mention that the cost of care is much higher for the individual and for the society at large.

SUMMARY

The first part of this chapter deals with some of the general aspects of the study of culture in mainstream psychology that are relevant to the study and practice of health psychology with nondominant ethnic groups in a multicultural society. Then, issues such as the intragroup diversity of Latino Americans and other nondominant groups in the U.S. are discussed. Health data and statistics on some of the relevant health concerns of this population are used to illustrate the fact that some of the health issues presented are relevant to some, but not to other, Latino groups. In addition, general issues, such as patterns of immigration and acculturation, are considered in relation to health issues, such as coronary heart disease. Also, misconceptions about the health of Latino groups are contrasted with actual data. For example, data showing that, in many cases, the health of Latino groups deteriorates with acculturation are used to illustrate some of the complex effects of acculturation. Specifically, as Latino groups acculturate, they move away from healthier traditional diets and adopt aspects of the Anglo American lifestyle that contribute to their health decline.

The final part of the chapter focuses on specific health psychology issues of particular interest in dealing with the various Latino groups. Coronary heart disease, HIV/AIDS, cervical cancer, diabetes, and chronic pain management are among the topics considered in order to illustrate the kinds of health psychology issues that concern Latinos. Such issues are seen as important for a cultural approach to health psychology research and practice with this population.

CASE STUDY

Marcos, a 5-year-old Latino boy, was admitted to a rehabilitation unit in a major teaching hospital in Southern California. He had sustained a closed head injury as a result of an automobile accident. The nature of his injuries required him to undergo surgery and intensive rehabilitation services to help him return to a more normal level of functioning.

Marcos's family was involved throughout the course of his treatment and was present at all therapies. A member of the family, either immediate or extended, was present in his room at all times. His parents and the majority of the family spoke only Spanish. Since no official translator was provided, explanation of forms and procedures were translated only when a Spanish-speaking staff member was available. Occasionally, a cleaning person who happened to be at hand did this. Sometimes, when it came to making decisions about Marcos's care, the physician would talk to the mother and ask questions, all in English. According to his report, she was very agreeable to everything and never asked questions of him.

After several weeks of treatments, the team began to express concern that the family was hindering the process of therapy more than they were helping. For example, one of the tasks addressed in his therapy was dressing skills. However, whenever Marcos's mother was with him, she would proceed to assist Marcos in dressing, something he was capable of doing.

Not understanding what was happening and what was the boy's fate, the family turned to a Latino staff member in another unit, who was not involved in Marcos's care but was bilingual. In asking her colleagues to assist her in providing information to the family, she noticed that the presence of family members at all times appeared to bother some of the staff. Also, some of the therapists appeared to be unhappy with the "interference" of the mother with "unnecessary" assistance to the boy. However, after talking with the family, she realized that they did not know what was being done, why, and what the outcome would be. They felt that Marcos was not welcome in the hospital and were afraid that nobody cared enough to do the best that could be done to help him. They indicated that the doctor appeared not to care whether or not they understood him and whether or not they had any concerns. They were also concerned that what they saw as the therapists' hostility toward the family could put Marcos at risk for neglect or not getting the best treatment possible for his condition. This was a powerful deterrent for them to ask questions.

When Marcos's therapies extended beyond four weeks, the father became more assertive and reluctant to agree to additional therapies. He insisted more and more on outpatient services. Despite the persistence on the part of the medical team in informing the father on the importance and necessity of the treatments, the father remained insistent on discharge. Even though all members of the family expressed agreement with the recommendations of the medical team, none was observed to challenge the position of the father.

A bilingual/bicultural staff member from another unit was asked to translate and mediate in meetings with the family. A full explanation of Marcos's condition and treatment needs was given to the family by the physician and translated into Spanish by the mediator. With the assistance of the bilingual mediator, the family could ask questions and express their concerns in Spanish. The negative attitude of the therapists toward the mother's assisting Marcos was explained to the family and the mother explained to the staff her understanding of motherhood and family. It became apparent that she understood perfectly that he was capable of dressing himself and that her behavior had nothing to do with objecting to the therapy or antagonizing the therapists. It had more to do with her perceived responsibility to satisfy the needs of the boy, comforting him and making him feel protected, particularly under conditions of high uncertainty and perceived hostility.

1. How do familism and related cultural value orientations, such as collectivism/individualism, serve to explain some of the behavioral phenomena observed in this case? Identify some aspects of the case (e.g., the attitude and behavior of the mother, the reaction of the therapists, the attitude and behavior of the physician, the father, the extended family) that could be explained on the basis of these or other cultural characteristics of Latinos and other Mediterranean cultures.

2. Based on the cultural factors involved in this case, identify aspects of the Anglo-dominated health care system, institutions, and personnel which could be changed in order to better serve the needs of the emerging majority population represented by Latinos and the other nondominant ethnic groups in states like California.

3. From a health psychology perspective, if you were a member of the staff, what culturally sensitive suggestions would you make to the physician, the other members of the staff, and the hospital?

SUGGESTED READINGS

Betancourt H., & Lopez, S. (1993). The study of culture, ethnicity and race in American psychology. *American Psychologist, 48,* 629–637.

Furino, A. (Ed.). (1992). *Health policy and the Hispanic.* Boulder, CO: Westview Press.

Geisinger, K. (Ed.). (1992). *Psychological testing of Hispanics.* Washington, DC: American Psychological Association.

Goldberger, N., & Veroff, J. (Eds.). (1995). *The culture and psychology reader.* New York: New York University Press.

Padilla, A. (Ed.). (1995). *Hispanic psychology: Critical issues in theory and research.* Thousand Oaks, CA: Sage.

Zambrana, R. E. (Ed.). (1995). *Understanding Latino families: Scholarship, policy, and practice.* (Vol. 2). Thousand Oaks, CA: Sage.

REFERENCES

Bagley, S. P., Angel, R., Dilworth-Anderson, P., Liu, W., & Schinke, S. (1996). Panel V: Adaptive health behaviors among ethnic minorities. *Health Psychology, 14,* 632–640.

Berry, J. W. (1990). Psychology of acculturation: Understanding individuals moving between cultures. In R. W. Brislin (Ed.), *Applied cross cultural psychology* (pp. 232–253). Newbury Park, CA: Sage.

Berry, J. W., Kim, U., Minde, T., & Mok, D. (1987). Comparative studies of acculturative stress. *International Migration Review, 21,* 491–511.

Berry, J. W., Poortinga, Y. H., Segall, M. H., & Dasen, P. R. (1992). *Cross-cultural psychology: Research and applications.* New York: Cambridge University Press.

Betancourt, H. M., & Lopez, S. R. (1993). The study of culture, ethnicity, and race in American psychology. *American Psychologist, 48,* 629–637.

Fitzgibon, M. L., Stolley, M. R., Avellone, M. E., & Sugerman, S. (1996). Involving parents in cancer risk reduction: A program for Hispanic American families. *Health Psychology, 15,* 413–422.

Goldberger, N. R., & Veroff, J. B. (Eds). (1995). *The culture of psychology reader.* New York: New York University Press.

Hayes-Bautista, D. E. (1992). Latino health indicators and the underclass model: From paradox to new policy models. In A. Furino (Ed.), *Health policy and the Hispanic* (pp. 32–47). Boulder, CO: Westview Press.

Hubbell, F. A., Chavez, L. R., Mishra, S. I., & Valdez, R. B (1996). Differing beliefs about breast cancer among Latinas and Anglo women. *Western Journal of Medicine, 164,* 405–409.

Johnson, K. W., Anderson, N. B., Bastida, E., Kramer, B. J., Willimas, D., & Wong, M. (1996). Panel II: Macrosocial and environmental influences on minority health. *Health Psychology, 14,* 601–612.

Kaiser Family Foundation (May, 1998). Kaiser Family Foundation national survey of Latinos on HIV/AIDS. Menlo Park, CA: Atlantic Information Services.

Laws, M. B., & Mayo, S. J. (1998). The Latina breast cancer control study, year one: Factors predicting screening mammography utilization by urban Latina women in Massachusetts. *Journal of Community Health, 23,* 251–267.

Martinez, R. G., Chavez, L. R., & Hubell, F. A. (1997). Purity and passion: Risk and morality in Latina immigrants' and physicians' beliefs about cervical cancer. *Medical Anthropology, 17,* 337–362.

O'Toole, M. (Ed.). (1992). *Miller-Keane: Encyclopedia and dictionary of medicine, nursing and allied health* (5th Ed.). Philadelphia, PA: Saunders.

National Diabetes Data Group. (1995). *Diabetes in America.* Bethesda, MD, National Institutes of Health.

Organizations, N.C.O.H.H.A.H.S. (1998). HIV/AIDS: The impact on Hispanics [on-line]. Available http://www.cossmho.org.

Peplau, L. A., & Taylor, S. E. (Eds). (1997). *Sociocultural perspectives in social psychology: Current readings.* Upper Saddle River, NJ: Prentice Hall.

Sorlie, P. D., Rogot, E., & Johnson, N. J. (1992). Validity of demographic characteristics on the death certificate. *Epidemiology, 3,* 181–184.

Suarez, Z. E., & Siefert, K. (1998). Latinas and sexually transmitted diseases: Implications of recent research for prevention. *Social Work Health Care, 28,* 1–19.

Wagner, D. K., & Schatzkin, A. (1994). Temporal trends in the socioeconomic gradient for breast cancer mortality among U.S. women. *American Journal of Public Health, 84,* 1003–1006.

Williams, D. R., & Collins, C. (1995). U.S. economic and racial differences in health: Patterns and explanations. *Annual Review of Sociology, 21,* 349–386.

Zambrana, R. E. (Ed.). (1995). *Understanding Latino families: Scholarship, policy, and practice.* Thousand Oaks, CA: Sage.

12

HEALTH ISSUES IN NORTH AMERICAN PEOPLE OF AFRICAN HERITAGE

SHAHÉ S. KAZARIAN

Departments of Psychology and Psychiatry
The University of Western Ontario
London, Ontario, Canada

Health psychologists are recognizing the value of incorporating cultural diversity into their research and practice. Two comparable approaches to health status and health determinants have emerged in North America. In Canada, the population health model is followed as an approach to comparing the health status and the determinants of the health of subpopulations within the larger segment of society. On the other hand, in the United States, the cultural diversity approach to health outcome and factors influencing health behavior has evolved (Kato & Mann, 1996). Similar to the population health model, the primary focus of the cultural diversity approach to health is population heterogeneity. The model allows consideration of health status and health determinants in contexts that define the dimensions of population diversity. Health psychologists with a population health or cultural diversity perspective address health science and practice issues as they relate to age, gender, cultural (or ethnic) groups, and sexual orientation. They examine intra- and intergroup similarities and differences within a population in relation to health status indicators and health risk behaviors in an effort to assesses health outcomes and to elucidate biopsychosociocultural and physical environmental mechanisms that underlie health status universals or disparities.

The focus of the present chapter is on the health issues of North American people with an African heritage. The chapter focuses on health status issues in both African Canadians and African Americans and explanatory models for the known disparities in health outcomes. In discussing health issues among African

North Americans, it is important to note that African Americans are not the same as African Canadians (Foster, 1996). The implication of sociohistorical differences between the two groups for health psychologists is that "what works with African Americans in the United States may not work with African Canadians in Canada." Similarly, the common belief among North Americans of European descent that African North American culture is no different than Anglo American culture because of colonization and assimilation is negated (Airhihenbuwa, 1995). The implication of the recognition of cultural differences between the two groups is that disease prevention and health promotion strategies that work with North Americans of European descent may not work with North Americans of African heritage.

HEALTH ISSUES OF AFRICAN CANADIANS

DEMOGRAPHICS OF AFRICAN CANADIANS

In Canada, visible minority for census purposes is defined as "persons, other than Aboriginal peoples, who are non-Caucasian in race or non-white in color." (Statistics Canada, 1997, p. 9). Arabs and West Asians, Blacks, Chinese, Filipinos, Koreans, Japanese, Latin Americans, South Asians, Southeast Asians, and Pacific Islanders are all considered to be in the category "visible minority." While there are issues in the use of the term *minority,* it is used in this chapter for consistency with existing literature and avoidance of terminological confusion. "Landed immigrant" is defined in the Canada census as an individual who has been granted the right to live in Canada permanently. "Immigrant population" is defined as people who are, or have been at one time, landed immigrants. Finally, "recent immigrant" is defined as a person who has immigrated to the country within the past 5 years.

According to Census Canada 1996, African Canadians (Blacks) constituted 2.01% of the population of Canada (see Table 12.1). This figure is likely an underestimate, because it excludes two groups of individuals: those classified in the census data as "visible minority not included elsewhere" and those who reported more than one visible minority (e.g., black and South Asian).

In 1996, the largest African Canadian communities were in Ontario and Quebec, followed by Alberta, British Columbia, Nova Scotia, and Manitoba. African Canadians were the largest visible minority group in Montreal (122,320, 30.5%), the third largest visible minority group in the Toronto census metropolitan area (274,935, 20.5%), and the eighth largest visible minority group in Vancouver (16,400, 2.9%). Halifax and the census metropolitan area of Ottawa–Hull were also home to sizable African Canadian communities. African Canadians composed 54% of the visible minority population of Halifax and 27% of those in Ottawa–Hull. A total of 16,780 individuals from Jamaica immigrated to Toronto between 1991 and 1996 (3.8% of total recent immigrants for Toronto), 13,195 (3.0%) from Guyana, and 11,375 (2.6%) from Trinidad and Tobago (Statistics

TABLE 12.1   African Canadian (Black) Population in Canada

Country/province	N	% of total population	% of "visible minority" population
Canada	573,860	2.01	17.9
Alberta	24,915	0.93	9.2
British Columbia	23,275	0.63	3.5
Manitoba	10,775	0.98	13.9
New Brunswick	3,120	0.43	39.0
Newfoundland	595	0.11	15.6
Northwest Territories	225	0.35	13.5
Nova Scotia	18,105	2.01	57.8
Ontario	356,220	3.35	21.2
Prince Edward Island	265	0.20	17.4
Quebec	131,970	1.87	30.4
Saskatchewan	4265	0.44	15.8
Yukon Territory	120	0.39	12.1

Extracted from Statistics Canada (1998).

Canada, 1997). According to the 1996 Canada census, Jamaica (86,910, 4.9% of total and recent immigrants for Toronto) and Guyana (60,705, 3.4%) were among the top 10 places of birth for total immigrants and recent immigrants in Toronto (Statistics Canada, 1997). On the other hand, the Francophone nation of Haiti was among the top 10 places of birth for total immigrants (43,075, 7.3%) and recent immigrants (9995, 7.4%) in Montreal (Statistics Canada, 1997).

A BRIEF HISTORY OF AFRICAN CANADIANS

Traditionally, Canadian history has not embraced African Canadian history. For example, there is very little, if any, historical coverage of Canadian blacks in Leacock's (1941) *Canada* or in the centennial publication, *Canada One Hundred 1867–1967* (Dominion Bureau of Statistics, 1967). Nevertheless, the history of African Canadians is embedded in ignoble aspects of Canadian history. Settlement of Blacks in Canada predates the Confederation of 1867 (Foster, 1996; Stone, 1998). The French brought slaves from Africa to Canada in the early 1600s. Settlers were also given explicit permission to import more slaves from Africa in 1689. Rebellious slaves in Jamaica, Maroons, were exiled in Nova Scotia in 1796, while Blacks from California were invited to settle on Vancouver Island in 1859. Slavery was legalized in what is now Canada in 1709. It was abolished in Upper Canada (Ontario) in 1793 and the rest of British North America in 1834, 125 years after its legalization and 33 years before confederation (Stone, 1998).

At the time of confederation (1867), there were 21,000 Africans residing in Canada. The first wave of blacks to arrive in Canada was a heterogeneous group of people. Some were slaves brought by the United Empire Loyalists fleeing the

American Revolution of 1775 to settle in Ontario, Lower Canada (Quebec) and Nova Scotia. Some were fugitive slaves. They considered Canada the North Star and took the Underground Railroad to escape into Canada. Others were United Empire Loyalists. The Black Loyalists were promised tangible rewards for fighting for the British against the United States republicans, a promise that continues to beg fulfillment.

Many of the fugitive slaves "used railroad terms to veil their exodus from bondage" and settled in the two counties of Southwestern Ontario, Essex and Kent. Located east of Detroit and Windsor, Chatham became the largest center of fugitive Blacks in the province, while Buxton became the most successful self-supporting black community in Canada in 1849 (Bilski, 1992). Interestingly, isolated cases of black settlement in various parts of the country were also reported. For example, a Barbadian, Joe Fortes, settled in Vancouver as early as 1885 (Foster, 1996).

Historically, British America (Canada) imported and welcomed all "alien races" (i.e., those who were non-English or non-French) in "accord with the traditional doctrines of liberty, of the open-door, the traditional British privilege of refuge for exiles of all complexion and color" (Leacock, 1941, p. 209). However, the discovery of the "Asiatic peril," i.e., the perceived dangers inherent in unrestricted immigration of Chinese to British Columbia, prompted the Dominion Government to enact an 1886 statute which enabled it to check Chinese immigration by an admission tax of $50 (Canadian). The 1886 act was likely the precursor to a culture-biased immigration policy that lasted for eight decades and favored "European alien races" and disfavored "alien races" with "complexion and color." Change in the Canadian immigration policy commensurate with that of the United States, occurred in the 1960s. Unlike its predecessor, the new immigration policy represented a rainbow policy in that it extended an open door and equally welcoming arms to people of all complexions and colors.

Post-confederation, several waves of Black immigration occurred to various parts of the country with concentrations in urban centers, inclusive of Toronto, Montreal, Winnipeg, and Vancouver. Generally speaking, French-speaking Blacks (e.g., Haitians) settled by the thousands in Montreal, following the Quebec government's preference for French-speaking immigrants. On the other hand, English-speaking Blacks from the Caribbean and the African continent showed a preference to settle in English-speaking urban centers. Major waves of Black immigration also occurred in the five decades after World War II. From 1950 to 1990, Caribbean and African immigrants served the (cheap) labor needs of Canadians. The late 1980s and the 1990s saw the last major wave of Blacks come to Canada. The Black settlers were mainly refugees from a variety of African countries, including Somalia and Eritrea, countries characterized by famine, political repression, and turmoil.

African Canadians are not homogeneous with respect to language, values, beliefs, or behaviors. Differences in acculturating groups (native-born African

Canadian versus immigrant versus sojourner), language (French and English), country-of-origin (Caribbean Islands versus Africa), and mode of settlement (refugee versus immigrant) are factors that accentuate cultural diversity within the African Canadian community. At present, three main permanent-settler groups represent the African Canadian communities in Canada: the indigenous Black Canadians (Nova Scotian Blacks), the Caribbean communities (Caribbean immigrants), and settlers from the African continent (African immigrants).

Nova Scotian African Canadians are descendants of Blacks from Jamaica (Maroons), Barbados, and the United States, having lived in North America for several generations (Foster, 1996). While the prejudice they and those living in Ontario experienced was probably similar to that in the States, a psychologically significant difference was that "they were protected under the law" (Bilski, 1992). Their long tradition of fighting for civil rights paved the way for subsequent waves of immigration from Africa and the Caribbean. The Caribbean group constitutes the largest African Canadian community in Canada. The earliest wave of Caribbean immigration to Canada occurred after the First World War, and settlement was mainly in Halifax and Winnipeg. The third group, African immigrants, are a small but heterogeneous group of Africans who have settled in Canada, as immigrants, recent immigrants, or refugees. The numerical dominance of the Caribbean group has contributed to the evolution of an African Canadian community that is diverse but considerably culturally similar to Caribbean culture. As in other acculturating groups, intergenerational difference among African Canadians is a source of tension and conflict for the community at large.

ADAPTATION OF AFRICAN CANADIANS

African Canadians are not the same as African Americans, nor is their diversity and history the same as those of African Americans. African Canadians are not blacks from Africa and the Caribbean who have been Americanized by the American culture (Forster, 1996). While their African heritage is a significant source of bonding for the two groups, the history of African Canadians and their experiences are different from those of individuals living in the United States. For example, the black church in Canada has not evolved into the status of the black church in America. The powerful image of the "strong black church that has a long history and deep roots in a population, black and white, that has been around for centuries" is not applicable in the African Canadian context (Foster, 1996). Consequently, the role of the black church in the lives of African Canadians is not as pervasive as that of the black church in the United States. The profound assertion that African Canadians are not the same as African Americans underscores the inherent risks in importing an African American knowledge base uncritically. It also highlights the importance of focusing on Canadian-made solutions to African Canadian health and related issues rather than applying American-made solutions in a Canadian context.

African Canadians describe a sense of pride in their Africanness and consider their blackness as a visible sign of their direct lineage to the motherland, Africa. African Canadians have a different sensitivity and a well-developed sense of pride because of where they came from before arriving in Canada. However, a common experience has been a segregationist host culture attitude and behavior, the consequence of which has been lack of opportunity for full participation and self-actualization. For example, Toronto's African Canadians, who account for more than 75% of the Canadian black population, disproportionately occupy low-paying jobs (clerical, manufacturing, and services) and live in low-income communities (annual income of $25,000 or less). African Canadians are subjected to discrimination and unfair and unjust treatment on the basis of the color of their skin or their Caribbean accent. Common experiences include segregation, discriminatory hiring practices, and police impatience, intolerance, and superiority. The historical discriminatory treatments against African Canadians in various parts of the country, especially in the areas of employment and housing, have been documented. These have taken the form of exclusion, harassment, physical assaults, excessive use of force by police, including shootings of young black people, and overrepresentation of African Canadians in the criminal justice system. For example, a taxi company fired its Haitian drivers on the pretext that it was losing business to companies with an unwritten "employ white only" policy (Frances, Jones, & Smith, 1996). Employment is a critical issue for African Canadians. The daily hardships of many immigrant professionals who spend their time walking the streets of major Canadian cities looking for work is common knowledge to all those who have an open eye on settlement issues. Individuals who have higher education (physicians, engineers, and lawyers) from their countries of origin drive taxis or wash dishes for a living in urban centers. Even African Canadians, when compared with Canadian Canadians with Canadian university degrees, fail to secure meaningful jobs for themselves.

However, African Canadians acknowledge that their segregation experiences in Canada are not the same as those experienced by African Americans in the United States, neither do they resemble those associated with the Aboriginal people in Canada. They perceive their experiences of racism and discrimination from the host culture to be qualitatively different from those of their African American counterparts. In the United States, racism is described as overt or blatant while in Canada it is described as benign racism, i.e., "racism with a smile on its face" (Foster, 1996). Racism in Canada is also described as "silk-glove racism," in contrast to the "iron-fist racism" of the United States (Omar Aguilar, December 1, 1999, personal communication).

African Canadians are torn between the acculturation strategies of integration and separation. Their perception is that the political system treats them as outsiders or interlopers, despite their presence for over 400 years. They also believe that the dominant culture is determined to keep them powerless. Needless to say, the conflict between the African Canadian acculturation orientation and that of the host culture is of profound consequence not only to individual African Canadians but also to the host culture generally. The negative outcomes of failure to integrate on individual and societal levels include disillusionment, especially on the part of the youth and the elderly, illegal means of survival, violence, trouble with the law, consideration of the option of separation rather than integration, marginalization (alienation from the African Canadian community and the community-at-large), demoralization, and an everlasting yearning for "back home."

The acculturation experience of African Canadians underscores the importance of considering the interactional nature of psychological acculturation (Bourhis, Moise, Perreault, & Senecal, 1997), i.e., the interaction between host-culture acculturation orientation (segregationist, in this case) and the individual acculturation orientation (integrationist, in this case). Needless to say, the outcome of the interaction is conflictual and seemingly in favor of the host culture. Confronted with the chronic conflict, African Canadians are continuing their integration strategies or are considering (or have already decided on) an acculturative orientation different from that of integration. Assimilation is not a favored option. Despite conscious and unconscious attempts, it is difficult to make the visible skin color invisible. The remaining available options are marginalization and separation. While the number of African Canadians likely to become marginalized is not known, and the number of those likely to choose psychological separation from the host culture is not known, the shift to acculturation strategies other than integration highlights the importance of considering acculturation processes and outcomes interactively and longitudinally. To identify African Canadians as an "unacculturated lot" ignores the historical role that the host culture plays in the integration or cultural alienation of its nondominant citizens.

While African Canadians have found their new life in Canada a considerable improvement over life in their countries of origin, adaptation to the host culture has been anything but a "smooth sail," particularly in times of economic downturns or slowdowns. African Canadians have had a presence in Canada for over 400 years. They have chosen Canada and have made it their home for a variety of reasons. While African Canadians have settled in Canada for the purpose of integration with the host culture, their efforts have been frustrated by segregationist attitudes and practices. Two major factors serve as barriers to the ideal of African Canadian adaptation to Canadian culture. The first relates to the visible skin color of the African Canadian, and the second relates to the host-culture ideology respecting immigrants generally, and people of color specifically. The visible skin color of African Canadians accentuates their "different" status and racializes their relationship with the English and French Canadian host people. The anti-immigrant and pro-white sentiments of select but "established" Canadians generally, and their negative assumptions about the humanity of the African Canadian particularly, precludes opportunities for African Canadians for full participation and integration in host culture and citizenry and compromises their psychological well-being and health.

HEALTH STATUS AND HEALTH DETERMINANTS
OF AFRICAN CANADIANS

The health of African Canadians has not been the subject of extensive study nor has the subject of their health beliefs and practices. For example, the first health report prepared by the Federal, Provincial, and Territorial Advisory Committee on Population Health (1996) did not examine health status and factors that influence health in the context of the culturally diverse groups in the country as a whole or at the provincial and territorial level. Rather, population health was examined in the context of time trends (e.g., rate of improvement in the health of Canadians over time), international comparisons (level of health in Canada as compared to health indicators in other countries), equality (differences in health as they relate to age, sex, living and working conditions, income and social status, education, Aboriginal health, and the provinces), potential for health improvement, and influences on health (living and working conditions, physical environment, personal health practices and skills, health services, and biology and genetics). Consequently, the first report on the health of Canadians (Federal, Provincial, & Territorial Advisory Committee on Population Health, 1996) was silent on the issue of culture and health and offered no specific information on the health status of African Canadians.

Similarly, the *Wealth and Health, Health and Wealth* reports based on the findings of the Ontario Health Survey (Warren, 1994) assessed the importance of several social and economic determinants of the health of Ontarians generally, but failed to consider these issues within a cultural framework. More specifically, the report examined health in relation to income, education, healthy families (e.g., functional versus dysfunctional), healthy workplaces (e.g., workplace stress, income security), supportive social environments (e.g., social support, feeling loved and appreciated), healthy physical environments (environmental pollution), and the burden of ill health on individuals, families, and societies. The major findings of the report are summarized in Table 12.?.

On the other hand, the health status and factors that influence the physical and psychological well-being of visible minorities (inclusive of African Canadians) were examined in the second report of the Federal, Provincial, and Territorial Advisory Committee on Population Health (1999), *Toward a Healthy Future: Second Report on the Health of Canadians.* The health status indicators and the health determinants that were considered in the second report are summarized in Table 12.3.

In analyzing and reporting on the health status of the Canadian population, the Advisory Committee followed a population health framework. Population health "refers to the health of a population as measured by health status indicators and as influenced by social, economic, and physical environments, personal health practices, individual capacity and coping skills, human biology, early child development, and health services" (p. 174). It is important to recognize that the population health approach places emphasis and examines the interactions between health determinants over the life course for the purpose of pattern identification and application of the knowledge base for policy development and im-

TABLE 12.2 Summary of Major Findings of *Wealth and Health, Health and Wealth*

Income and health: As income increases, so does health. The "poverty is not good to your health" finding holds true for smokers and nonsmokers (i.e., smokers in poverty are less healthy than rich smokers, and nonsmokers in poverty are less healthy than wealthy nonsmokers), for sedentary individuals and those who exercise regularly, and for those with limited formal education and those with postsecondary education.

Education and health: As education increases, so does health. The positive effect of education on health is independent of income or health risk behaviors.

Healthy families: Members of healthy families are more likely to be healthy themselves.

Healthy workplaces: As employee workplace stress increases, so does the ill health and absenteeism of the employee.

Supportive social environments: Supportive social environments (i.e., high levels of social support, active social lives, being loved and appreciated, and being cared for) are more conducive to positive health.

Healthy physical environments: One out of three individuals surveyed reported adverse effects on their health from environmental pollution.

The burden on ill health: Self-ratings of health are related to health problems, service utilization, and income. People with high ratings of positive health are less likely to have health problems, to use health care services, and to live in poverty.

Extracted from Warren (1994).

plementation. While the focus of population health on the interplay between health determinants is theoretically sound, the omission of culture in its definition is paradoxical and conceptually limiting, particularly, in culturally diverse health population contexts, such as Canada. It also ignores completely the pervasive role that culture assumes in human behavior generally and health behavior particularly.

The Federal, Provincial, and Territorial Advisory Committee on Population Health (1999) acknowledged that the report could not fully address the diversity of Canada's population. For example, the database used did not capture health measures for cultural or socioeconomic subpopulations within the various jurisdictions (provinces) under study. Nevertheless, in comparison to the first report, the second report of the Federal, Provincial, and Territorial Advisory Committee on Population Health (1999) placed appreciably greater theoretical and empirical emphasis on gender and socioeconomic factors in the context of health status and health determinants. The second report also considered a developmental approach to health by focusing on healthy child development. In addition, the report expanded on the analysis of the role of the physical environment in health. Finally, it contained information on the use of alternative health services, including acupuncturist, homeopath, herbalist, and spiritual healer.

The greater theoretical and empirical emphasis placed on the role of diversity in health is manifest in the Federal, Provincial, and Territorial Advisory Committee on Health Status (1999) consideration and examination of the relationship

TABLE 12.3   Health Status Indicators and Health Determinants

Health status indicators	Key health determinants
Self-rated health	Income and income distribution
Psychological well-being	Education and literacy
Sense of coherence	Working conditions (e.g., work stress)
Self-esteem	The social environment (e.g., social support,
Mastery	violence in the home and community)
Selected diseases	Healthy child development
Chronic diseases	
Depression	Physical environment (e.g, ozone depletion,
HIV/AIDS	air, water, food, environmental toxins)
Injuries	Built environment (e.g., exposure to tobacco
Disability and activity limitations	smoke, transportation, housing)
Major causes of death	Personal health practices (e.g., physical
Cardiovascular disease	activity, healthy eating, tobacco use, illicit
Cancer	drug use, gambling)
Unintentional injuries	Health services (e.g., health service
Suicide	expenditures, access to services, availability
Homicide	of alternative health services)
Infant mortality	Biology and genetic endowment
Deaths attributable to smoking	
Life expectancy at birth	
Potential years of life lost	
Human development index*	

Extracted from Federal, Provincial, and Territorial Advisory Committee on Population Health (1999).

*A composite measure (life expectancy, educational attainment, and adjusted income) used by the United Nations. In 1998, three additional measures were added to the index—the Human Poverty Index, the Gender-Related Development Index, and the Gender-Empowerment Measure.

between settlement status, ethnicity, visible minority, and acculturation and health status and health determinants. In relation to health status, the Federal, Provincial, and Territorial Advisory Committee on Population Health (1999) was able to analyze immigrant status in terms of only two indicators: disability and activity limitations, and life expectancy at birth. The Advisory Committee reported that immigrants to Canada were less likely than those born in Canada to have any long-term disability. The Advisory Committee also reported that immigrants contributed to the overall life expectancy rate of the country, i.e., immigrants, particularly those from non-European countries, had lower mortality rates and higher life expectancies than did their Canadian-born counterparts. The Advisory Committee also summarized published data that showed that chronic diseases in 1994–1995 were less common among immigrants (50%) generally and non-European immigrants (37%) particularly than among the Canadian-born population (57%) and that acculturation in the form of length of settlement was positively related to prevalence of chronic disease, i.e., as the duration of stay of immigrants in Canada increased, so did the prevalence of chronic diseases.

The Federal, Provincial, and Territorial Advisory Committee on Population Health (1999) analyzed and reported on the relationship of health determinants to cultural factors within the confines of the available data. In addition to demonstrating that health and income were correlated (i.e., low-income Canadians are more likely to suffer illnesses and die early), the Federal, Provincial, and Territorial Advisory Committee on Population Health (1999) reported that Aboriginal people and visible minority populations were more likely to live in low-income situations. For example, it was found that in 1995, "36% of the visible minority population in Canada and 45% of children under the age of 6 in visible minority families were in a low income situation" (p. 47). Similarly, the Federal, Provincial, and Territorial Advisory Committee on Population Health (1999) showed a link between health and unemployment (those with high rates of unemployment being health disadvantaged) and reported high rates of unemployment among First Nations People, the visible minority population, and people with physical and psychological disabilities.

The population health approach and the findings on the health determinants in the Canadian context have important implications for the physical and psychological health, and overall well-being of Canadians generally, and the diverse cultural groups such as African Canadians, particularly. The conceptual framework followed is also consistent with the life-course and multidimensional model applied to explicating health outcomes among African Americans in the United States (Jackson & Sellers, 1996).

HEALTH ISSUES OF AFRICAN AMERICANS

DEMOGRAPHICS OF AFRICAN AMERICANS

The total African American population residing in the United States in 1997 was about 34 million (total 33,947,000; male=16,121,000, female =17,826,000). Thus, 12.7% of citizens of the U.S. are African Americans (Centers for Disease Control and Prevention, 1999). It is estimated that, in the 21st century (i.e., year 2050) the U.S. population will be made up of approximately 53% White, 25% Latino, 14% Black, 8% Asian/Pacific Islander, and 2% American Indian.

As with African Canadians, heterogeneity in the African American population in the United States needs to be recognized and taken into consideration in addressing health issues. The intragroup variations in history and culture contribute to variation in health belief systems and health behaviors and necessitate their consideration for culturally competent health practice and a health outreach inclusive of all African Americans (McBarnette, 1996).

HEALTH STATUS AND HEALTH DETERMINANTS
OF AFRICAN AMERICANS

African Americans have made important gains in their health status over time. Their mortality, natality, and morbidity rates in certain areas were appreciably better in 1997 than in 1990. For example, the life expectancy of African American males improved between 1995 and 1997 in that they are now likely to live 2 years longer than before. As can be seen in Table 12.4, the overall morbidity rate for African Americans has declined, as have rates of specific morbidity indicators.

Despite the positive trends in certain health outcome indicators, African Americans continue to show health disadvantage relative to Anglo Americans (Centers for Disease Control and Prevention, 1999). The exception to this rule is the consistently lower overall suicide rate for African Americans for at least the past 9 decades and chronic obstructive pulmonary disease since 1985. In relation to mortality, African Americans live 6 years less than do Anglo Americans (life expectancy of 71.1 years for African Americans and 77.1 years for Euro Americans). African American men live 7 years less and African American women 5

TABLE 12.4 Age-adjusted Death Rates* for Selected Causes of Death for African Americans and Anglo Americans

Cause	African American 1990	African American 1997	Anglo American 1997
All causes	789.2	705.3	456.5
Natural causes	701.3	632.7	409.7
Diseases of heart	213.5	185.7	125.9
Ischemic heart disease	113.2	96.3	82.5
Cerebrovascular disease	48.4	42.5	24.0
Malignant neoplasms	182.0	165.2	122.9
Respiratory system	54.0	47.9	38.4
Colorectal	17.9	16.8	11.6
Prostate	35.3	31.4	12.6
Breast	27.5	26.7	18.9
Chronic obstructive pulmonary disease	16.9	17.4	21.7
Pneumonia and influenza	19.8	17.2	12.4
Chronic liver disease and cirrhosis	13.7	8.7	7.3
Diabetes mellitus	24.8	28.9	11.9
HIV	25.7	24.9	3.3
External causes	87.8	72.6	46.8
Unintentional injuries	39.7	36.1	29.6
Motor vehicle-related injuries	18.4	16.8	15.9
Suicide	7.0	6.3	11.3
Homicide & legal intervention	39.5	28.1	4.7

Extracted from Centers for Disease Control and Prevention (1999).
*Deaths per 100,000 resident population.

years less than their Anglo American counterparts (67.2 years for African American males, 74.7 years for African American women, 74.3 years for Anglo American males, and 79.9 for Anglo American females). Similarly, the infant mortality rate in 1997 for African Americans was twice the infant mortality rate for Anglo Americans (14.1 deaths per 1000 live births for African Americans versus 6.1 deaths per 1000 live births for Anglo Americans). In terms of natality, the rate of low birth weight (less than 2500 grams) for African Americans was twice that of Anglo Americans (13.01 for African Americans versus 6.46 for Anglo Americans). In relation to morbidity, the death rate of African Americans from natural and external causes is 1.5 times higher than that of Anglo Americans. The top five killers of African Americans are diseases of the heart, malignant neoplasms, cerebrovascular diseases, unintentional injuries, and diabetes mellitus. The top five killers of Anglo Americans are diseases of the heart, malignant neoplasms, cerebrovascular diseases, chronic obstructive pulmonary diseases, and unintentional injuries.

Several factors have been identified to explain the disproportionate risk for negative health outcomes among African Americans relative to Anglo Americans (see Table 12.5). These explanations relate to biology, socioeconomic factors, psychosocial issues, individual lifestyles, the health beliefs and behaviors of African Americans, and issues in the health care delivery system (Airhihenbuwa,

TABLE 12.5 Factors Associated with the Health Inequalities of African Americans

Biological factors
Innate biological differences (sometimes in favor of Anglo Americans)
Genetic predisposition to certain diseases

Socioeconomic factors
Low levels of income, education, occupation, and wealth

Psychosocial factors
High general stress, acculturative stress, or race-related stress

Individual lifestyle
High-fat diets, smoking cigarettes, unprotected sex, failure to use safety belts, sedentary lifestyle
    (e.g., excessive television viewing), alcohol consumption, use of illicit drugs

Physical environment
Overrepresentation in "high risk" occupations (e.g., exposure to toxic chemicals), "environmental
    racism," i.e., racial biases in the distribution of environmental hazards

Health beliefs and behavior
Fatalistic or helpless attitude, a strong sense of the present but not the future, active folk medicine
    system (i.e., reliance on folk healers), underutilization of formal health care system, delay in
    seeking health care

Health care delivery system
Unaffordability, inaccessibility, barriers to health care, underrepresentation of African Americans
    as health providers, culturally insensitive system, discriminatory practices (inferior quality
    service to African Americans)

1995; Bailey, 1991; Jones & Rice, 1987; Jackson & Sellers, 1996; McBarnette, 1996; Ostrove, Feldman, & Adler, 1999; Sylvester, 1998; Williams, Yu, Jackson, & Anderson, 1997). For example, a number of studies have shown the adverse effects of racial discrimination on physical health and psychological well-being (Williams et al., 1997). These findings and those that demonstrate the negative effects of economic disadvantage on health underscore the need for consideration of a multidimensional perspective to understanding health issues in African Americans, rather than an approach that blames the "messenger," i.e., the individual or group with health issues. In the latter perspective, health problems are attributed solely to people's individual lifestyles or cultural characteristic, such as their racial group. The messenger-blaming approach also ignores the profound effects that historical, cultural, social, and economic realities have on individual and group behavior generally and health behavior particularly.

Finally, the messenger-blaming approach turns a deaf ear to the negating effects that an intolerant host culture has on the physical and psychological well-being of its nondominant citizens or groups of citizens. At the basic level, a multifactorial view of the health of African Americans dictates a quality of life that is not heavenly but one that meets their need for an improved standard of living, nutrition, and education; meaningful, nonhazardous, and secure employment; decent housing with safer water and adequate income; and a host culture that is tolerant of the different shades of skin colors of its citizens.

Jackson and Sellers (1996) offered a conceptual model that elucidates the mechanism underlying the disparity in health among African Americans. The multidimensional life-course framework described by those researchers identifies micro-level (individual), meso-level (interpersonal), and macro-level (societal) factors as three variables that influence health outcome. The individual or micro-level dimension focuses on demographic factors, such as age and sex, biological and psychological vulnerabilities, and individual risk factors. The interpersonal or meso-level dimension, on the other hand, addresses a range of intermediary-level variables, inclusive of socioeconomic and employment factors and familial and neighborhood considerations. Finally, the macro-level dimension refers to racialization and racism processes. Jackson and Sellers (1996) refer to racialization as a process in which a particular group is defined as a race and group differences are attributed to biological endowments. Similarly, Jackson and Sellers (1996) define racism as an ideology that categorizes and ranks various racial groups on the dimension of superiority. A racist ideology serves the purpose of sustaining and justifying individual and institutional discrimination toward the "inferior" racial group.

The importance of the multidimensional life course model is that it places health outcomes within structural and sociohistorical contexts rather than exclusively in the realm of racial biology or individual behavior. The implication of the life-course and multidimensional model, as in the population health approach, is that focus on the micro-level (e.g., individual lifestyle or health-risk behaviors) is insufficient to understand health status outcomes in African Americans. Rather, the health outcomes need to be examined longitudinally and interactively at all three levels, i.e., micro-, meso-, and macro-levels.

Consistent with the multidimensional framework to health is the recognition at the national level that elimination of existing racial and ethnic disparities in health in the United States requires a multidimensional approach, including focus on such underlying issues as poverty, environmental hazards in homes and neighborhoods, lack of access to quality health care, and needs-based prevention programs (http://raceandhealth.hhs.gov). In his radio address on February 21, 1998, and per the nation's health action agenda for the 21st century, "Healthy People 2010," President William Clinton committed the nation to the ambitious goal of eliminating racial and ethnic disparities in health by the year 2010. Consistent with the nation's prevention agenda, "Healthy People 2000," the President identified six areas of health status that are targeted for elimination of racial and ethnic disparities. These are mortality, cancer screening and management, cardiovascular disease, diabetes, HIV/AIDS, and immunization.

HEALTH BELIEFS AND PRACTICES
OF AFRICAN AMERICANS

European folklore, Greek classical medicine, Western scientific medicine, Voodoo religion, African folklore, Christianity, and Native American traditions have all influenced African American health beliefs and practices (Bailey, 1991). Semmes (1996) identified four historical antecedents to the health beliefs and practices of African Americans: classical African medicine (African medical traditions), traditional African medicine (diverse health and healing practices that are indigenous to Africans on the continent and African immigrants), slave medicine in the United States, and postslavery African American health beliefs and practices. Semmes (1996) suggested that, in the historical analysis of African American health beliefs and practices, there has been a tendency to ignore the significant contributions that African and African American medical traditions have made to Anglo American medicine and to emphasize the magico-religious components of African and African American health traditions.

The Health Acculturation Model described in Chapter 1 of this book provides a useful conceptual framework for understanding African American health beliefs and practices. As slaves, African Americans imported African medicine to the host culture. For example, female African American slave doctors prevented and cured worms, malaria, croup, pneumonia, colds, teething discomfort, and measles by using drugs prepared from plants (Bailey, 1991). African American slaves were also exposed to the medical care of the host country. In the process of adaptation to the host health culture, African slaves used the *integrational* approach to health acculturation, i.e., they merged their African medicinal culture with the medicinal cultures of the host country. The outcome of the health acculturation process is an African American health culture that treats the individual biologically and spiritually (Bailey, 1991). As importantly, the bidirectional nature of the health acculturation process allowed an African influence on Anglo American health beliefs and practices. Consequently, African American health beliefs and practices are not totally culture-bound. Rather, some aspects of African American health behavior represent universals, i.e, they are shared by all segments of the North American population. For example, the practice of seeking advice from lay practitioners for remedies and the use of alternative medicine for health problems are common to African Americans, as they are to Anglo Americans and other cultures in the United States.

African American retention of African health beliefs and practices can be understood in the context of their adaptive and survival values (Bailey, 1991). European medicine was not made available to Africans in enslavement in South America, the Caribbean and North America in the 1500s and 1600s. African Americans were also exposed to continued oppression and a hostile social environment and relied on culturally adaptive health strategies to meet their health needs. In the 1700s and 1880s, their health beliefs and practices assumed similarity to those governed primarily by the Voodoo or Vodoun religious life of the African natives. The Voodoo medicine practiced by African Americans consisted of three major components (Bailey, 1991): the mystical (supernatural aspects of health, including spells and spirits), the psychological (emotional support to the individual), and the herbal and folk medicine. Oppression and continued lack of access or denial to Anglo American medical care sustained reliance on Voodoo medicine for biological and spiritual treatment in the South. The massive migration of African Americans to the North in the mid-1800s and early 1900s resulted in exposure to new health practices and less reliance on Voodoo medicine. For example, many African Americans in Detroit relied entirely on alternative health practitioners, variously known as traditional folk healers, "herb doctors," or Divine Healers, to meet their needs for treatment. Traditional African American health beliefs and practices continued to be an integral part of the African American health care strategy since they provided a meaningful alternative for health care and assumed a significant role in maintaining their cultural identity (Bailey, 1991).

The contemporary African American health world-view has been shaped by the limitations of Western medicine, as has the use of alternative medicine in North American society generally. The prevailing Western biomedical perspective to health has failed to address adequately the religious, spiritual, and metaphysical domains of African American life, dimensions that are central to African American health culture. It is important to underscore the overall disenchantment of North Americans generally with the biomedical model of care and its limitations in meeting their need for a holistic approach to health. In the case of African Americans, the biopsychosocial model of health is also considered limited because it fails to acknowledge explicitly the profound role of culture and spirituality in health. For African Americans, health is primarily a state of harmony or balance, a resource that transcends reliance solely on physical health. In view of the inherent limitations in Western scientific medicine, African American cultural scholars consistently challenge the application of the prevailing biomedically based treatment and/or behavior change models to disease prevention and health promotion for African Americans (Airhihenbuwa, 1995).

African Americans are not homogeneous with respect to their beliefs regarding the cause of disease, their experience of illness, their health-seeking behavior, or their adherence to treatment. In his study of Detroit African Americans, Bailey (1991) identified two etiological principles that guided their beliefs regarding the cause of disease. In the personalistic view, disease was attributed to spiritual agents, such as ghosts, souls, deities, or devils, or human agents with extraordinary powers such as witches, shamans, or priests. In the naturalistic view, disease was attributed to the interaction between internal impersonal and external factors, i.e., disharmony with nature. The assertion made by Willie, a 56-year-old African American that his "blood is probably high today because it's a little chilly outside and I'm getting older" represented a naturalistic belief of disease causation. As African American conception of health is holistic and embedded in the physical, spiritual, interpersonal, and environmental domains, a biopsychosociocultural–spiritual perspective represents a more complete health model for them.

IMPLICATIONS FOR CULTURALLY COMPETENT HEALTH CARE

Health attitudes (beliefs, emotions, and behaviors) are culture-bound rather than culture-free. In addition, African American culture is not the same as Anglo American culture. Consequently, the understanding of African American culture forms the foundation for a culturally competent approach to meeting the health needs of people of African heritage and to eliminating disparities in their health status. Core cultural values and culturally based health schema influence the experience of illness and health-seeking behavior (use of lay practitioners, use of folk treatments) and reflect the embeddedness of health within cultural, social (family and community), and spiritual domains. Core cultural values of people with African heritage include an emphasis on state of wellness or normality rather than pathology, on extended family, on collectivism rather than individualism, on respect for age, on lifestyle that is acquiescent to nature, and on oral tradition (Airhihenbuwa, 1995). Similarly, the personal and cultural beliefs and practices of African Americans and the factors that are operative in their health inequality need to be considered in the development and implementation of culturally competent health interventions, disease prevention approaches, and health promotion strategies.

SUMMARY

Health issues in African Canadians and African Americans are discussed following two approaches to the study of health and health determinants: population health and cultural diversity. In examining health issues in African Canadians, the assertion is made that African Canadian culture and African American culture are, in many respects, different, even though they share the same African cultural heritage. It is argued that African Canadians are a heterogeneous group of people but that they experience similar acculturation challenges in the host culture. While the health status of African Canadians has not been the focus of extensive research, the population health studies have important implications in understanding their health status and the factors that influence their health outcome.

African American culture is not the same as Anglo American culture. In addition, African American health culture is an integration of African medicine and Western medicine. While Anglo American health beliefs and practices are biomedical, Africa American health beliefs and practices are biopsychosociocultural–spiritual, a view that is consistent with African American definition of health as a state of harmony or balance. African Americans show disparity in health status relative to Anglo Americans. Factors that contribute to their health inequality are biology, socioeconomic indicators, psychosocial issues, health-risk behaviors, the physical environment, health beliefs and practices, and the health care delivery system. As health attitudes (cognitions, affect, and behavior) are culture-bound, health care practices, disease prevention approaches, and health promotion strategies require a cultural foundation for effectiveness. Consideration of personal and cultural beliefs and practices, core cultural values, and factors that are operative in health disparity is central to a culturally competent paradigm to address health issues in North American people of African heritage.

CASE STUDY

Martha is a 60-year-old African American woman with a history of essential hypertension. She believes that her health is her responsibility and not that of health providers. She also believes that she was "in tune" with her body and would seek health care professionals, as her mother did, only as a last resort. At present, she is under the care of a physician. She claims that she has difficulty understanding the medical explanations he offers but says nothing because she has been raised to never question authority figures. In addition to adhering to the medication prescribed to her by her physician, Martha uses folk medicine without his knowledge. She uses sassafras and herbal teas with the belief that they flush all impurities from her system. She purchases folk substances from grocery stores or from alternative/folk health practitioners (e.g., herbalists and magic store vendors). She neglects to tell her physician about her use of folk medicine for fear that he would disapprove of her actions.

1. How are Martha's health beliefs and practices influencing her health behavior generally and her interaction with the health care system particularly?

2. If you were to prescribe a culturally competent health care approach to Martha, what would your strategy entail?

3. How might you approach the prevention of disease in an African American or an African Canadian community?

SUGGESTED READINGS

Bailey, E. J. (1991). *Urban African American health care.* Lanham, MD: University Press of America, Inc.

Foster, C. (1996). *A place called heaven: The meaning of being Black in Canada.* Toronto: Harper/Collins.

Jackson, J. S., & Sellers, S. L. (196). African-American health over the life course: A multidimensional framework. In P. M. Kato & T. Mann (Eds.), *Handbook of diversity issues in health psychology* (pp. 301–317). New York: Plenum Press.

Landrine, H., & Klonoff, E. A. (1996). *African American acculturation: Deconstructing race and reviving culture.* Thousand Oaks, CA: Sage.

Semmes, C. E. (1996). *Racism, health, and post-industrialism: A theory to African-American health.* Westport, CT: Praeger.

REFERENCES

Airhihenbuwa, C. O. (1995). *Health and culture: Beyond the Western paradigm.* Thousand Oaks, CA: Sage.

Bailey, E. J. (1991). *Urban African American health care.* Lanham, MD: University Press of America, Inc.

Bilski, A. (July 6, 1992). Race to freedom. *Macleans, 58.*

Bourhis, R. Y., Moise, L. C., Perreault, S., & Senecal, S. (1997). Towards an interactive acculturation model: A social psychological approach. *International Journal of Psychology, 32,* 369–386.

Centers for Disease Control and Prevention (1999). *Health, United States, 1999.* Hyattsville, MD: U. S. Department of Health and Human Services.

Dominion Bureau of Statistics (1967). *Canada one hundred 1867–1967.* Ottawa, ON, Canada Queen's Printer and Controller of Stationery.

Federal, Provincial, and Territorial Advisory Committee on Population Health (1996). *Report on the health of Canadians.* Ottawa, ON, Canada: Ministry of Supply and Services Canada.

Federal, Provincial, and Territorial Advisory Committee on Population Health (1999). *Toward a healthy future: Second report on the health of Canadians.* Ottawa, ON, Canada: Minister of Public Works and Government Service Canada.

Foster, C. (1996). *A place called heaven: The meaning of being Black in Canada.* Toronto: Harper/Collins.

Frances, R. D., Jones, R., & Smith, D. B. (1996). *Destinies: Canadian history since Confederation.* Toronto: Harcourt-Brace Canada.

Jackson, J. S., & Sellers, S. L. (1996). African-American health over the life course: A multidimensional framework. In P. M. Kato & T. Mann (Eds.), *Handbook of diversity issues in health psychology* (pp. 301–317). New York: Plenum Press.

Jones, W., & Rice, M. (1987). Black health care: An overview. In W. Jones & M. Rice (Eds.), *Health care issues in black America: Policies, problems and prospects* (pp. 3–20). New York: Greenwood Press.

Kato, P. M., & Mann, T. (Eds.). (1996). *Handbook of diversity issues in health psychology.* New York: Plenum Press.

Leacock, S. (1941). *Canada: The foundations of its future.* Montreal: The House of Seagram.

McBarnette, L. S. (1996). African American women. In M. Bayne-Smith (Ed.), *Race, gender, and health* (pp. 43–67). Thousand Oaks, CA: Sage.

Ostrove, J. M., Feldman, P., & Adler, N. E. (1999). Relations among socioeconomic status indicators and health for African-Americans and Whites. *Journal of Health Psychology, 4,* 451–463.

Semmes, C. E. (1996). *Racism, health, and post-industrialism: A theory to African-American health.* Westport, CT: Praeger.

Statistics Canada (November 4, 1997). *Immigrants and citizenship.* The Daily, Catalogue No. 11-001E, p. 7.

Statistics Canada (February 17, 1998). *Ethnic origin and visible minorities.* The Daily, http://www.statcan.ca/Daily/English/980217/d980217.htm. Ottawa, ON: Author.

Stone, S. D. (February 28, 1998). The immigrants. *The Globe and Mail,* p. D7.

Sylvester, J. L. (1998). *Directing health messages toward African Americans: Attitudes toward health care and the mass media.* New York: Garland Publishing.

Warren, R. (1994). *Wealth and health, health and wealth.* Toronto: Queen's Printer for Ontario.

Williams, D. R., Yu, Y., Jackson, J. S., & Anderson, N. B. (1997). Racial differences in physical and mental health. *Journal of Health Psychology, 2,* 35–351.

13

HEALTH PSYCHOLOGY

AND THE NATIVE

NORTH AMERICAN

CLIENT

GEORGE S. RENFREY

Phoenix C & D
Barrie, Ontario, Canada

RENDA R. DIONNE

Indian Child and Family Services
Temecula, California

Health psychology is concerned with the promotion and maintenance of health, the prevention and treatment of illness, and the determination of factors relating to good health and the causes of disease (Matarazzo, 1980). According to the College of Psychologists of Ontario, "Health psychology is concerned with psychology's contribution to the promotion and the maintenance of good health, and the prevention and the treatment of illness. Applied heath psychology practitioners may, for example, design and conduct programs to help individuals stop smoking, lose weight, manage stress, or stay physically fit" (College of Psychologists of Ontario, 1993).

The health psychology field has grown in popularity in recent years. In 1990, health psychology was the most popular area of clinical research in APA-accredited clinical psychology doctoral programs (Mayne & Sayette, 1990). Despite the growing popularity of this discipline, however, little has been investigated in the area of cross-cultural sensitivity and sociocultural influences in the development and treatment of health-related problems. The importance of cultural sensitivity in the area of health psychology is encompassed by Diaz-Guerrero's statement, "If you wish to help a community improve its health you must learn to think like the people of that community" (Diaz-Guerrero, 1984, p. 167). To serve a population of people, one has to understand the people and the cultural context within which they live. Culture is most simply defined as a set of beliefs and practices, a way of thinking and relating, a way of conceptualizing the world to enable a people to govern their behavior and adapt to their surroundings in the best possible way.

Currently, the health and mental health fields are dominated by Euro-Western cultural values and scientific thinking. Within this mind-set, Western technology and concepts of health and wellness are viewed as superior to their non-Western counterparts. Native North American healing technology, concepts, and cultural value systems, though they have served their people well for thousands of years, are usually disregarded as primitive or otherwise inferior (Swinomish Tribal Mental Health Project, 1991). It is argued here that, to the extent that this holds true, the field of health psychology will not realize its potential in serving the Native populations of North America.

In this chapter, we will discuss both the diversity of Native people and the common ideologies, shared history, and perceptions of illness and health that constitute the Native viewpoint. We will also address clinical issues relevant to the practitioner working with Native people and specific health-related issues that Native people face. Finally, we will propose a culturally congruent model for health psychologists practicing within Native North American communities, a model that holds at its center the beliefs and values of the people served.

We believe that a brief note on terminology is in order at this point. The reader should be aware that there are a variety of terms used to describe the Aboriginal peoples of North America and their political and social systems. Although the terms "Native American" and "Native North American" are often considered politically correct in the United States, they are more at home in academe than in the Native communities themselves and are not typically used in Canada. The term "Indian" has received criticism by many, but it is, in fact, a legal designation in both Canada and the United States and is preferred by many Native people and tribal governments. The term "tribe" is commonly used in the United States to refer to a sovereign Aboriginal nation in the same way as the terms "First Nation" and "Band" are used in Canada, and is also used more colloquially to refer to a large grouping of Native people according to shared language and culture. Some have objected to the term on varied grounds, but it is important to realize that there is no consensus, even among Native people, on the most appropriate ways to refer to them and their cultures. With this in mind, we have used the terms "Native" and "Aboriginal" to refer to the peoples and their cultures, the term "community" in place of the terms "tribe" and "band," and the term "nation" to refer to a grouping of people on the basis of a shared language and culture. It is hoped that this will avoid confusion and offense.

NATIVE WORLD-VIEW AND HISTORY

If one is to begin to understand the Native person and gain insight into Native culture, one must begin by understanding a Native world-view and value system. Aboriginal cultures, like all intact cultures, had spiritual/cultural teachings that, upon close examination, provided the knowledge and understanding necessary to living a healthy and fulfilled life. When we, as Native people, seek to know who we are today, our elders often tell us that if we are to come to know this, we must first understand where we have come from. This is the primary focus of this section and its purpose is to provide the reader with a brief historic/cultural context of the Native experience.

Before any meaningful discussion of the Native culture, it is important to consider the exceptional amount of diversity that Native people represent. In 1988, LaFromboise (1988) pointed out that there were 511 federally recognized Native groups and 365 state-recognized communities in the United States alone. This has increased slightly since then with the inclusion of newly recognized community groups. There were once an estimated 1000 languages from 56 linguistic groups spoken by Aboriginal people in the Americas (McNickle, 1975, as cited by Thompson, Walker, & Silk-Walker, 1993; Powell, 1966, as cited by Thompson, Walker, & Silk-Walker, 1993), and more than 200 distinct Native American languages are still spoken (LaFromboise, 1988). Further, traditional Native North Americans can differ from one another in their cultures as widely as their Eurasian counterparts (Attneave, 1985; Levine & Lurie, 1970; Tefft, 1967). Since more than 60% of Aboriginal people in the United States and Canada have a mixed ethnic heritage, and since they can range from very traditional in alliance and custom to full acculturation to the dominant culture, regardless of blood quantum (Trimble, 1990), the situation is even more complex.

Despite the cultural losses over the past 507 years, Hodgkenson (1990) has estimated that Aboriginal people, who represent about 1% of the United States population, represent about 50% of the cultural diversity of the United States. Canadian figures likely parallel this. It follows, then, that stereotypes of Native people, though common, invariably fall short of describing any particular person or community group, and making generalizations across community groups should be avoided. Nevertheless, Native people share a similar history of European contact and its long-standing impact on communities and several general issues are likely to have relevance across community groups. There are also shared ideologies and values, which often differ dramatically from their Western counterparts. Much of the subsequent discussion is based on these commonalities, and an attempt has been made to identify community-specific information that may not apply to all Native groups.

In times past, it was through the creation stories that Native people learned who and what they were, where they came from, what their purpose on this earth was, and what their relationships to other living beings and the rest of creation were. Through these same teachings and teaching stories, they were given behavioral endorsements and admonitions on how to live in balance with the natural world; with other human beings; within community, clan, and family; and within one's self. To varying degrees, these same teachings are used to this day. Within the Ojibwa traditions, there are teachings that describe the stages and challenges of life that rival those of Western psychology in their completeness and utility, teachings that establish the roles of men and women, teachings that tell us how to raise our children in a good way. Teachings also provided and continue to provide understandings of disease and means of healing, many of which rival modern medicine and behavioral science. These conceptualizations of health and illness are holistic, as a rule. For example, among communities of the western plains, the medicine wheel is a symbol representing balance and harmony. It is composed of a circle divided into four quadrants, each of which can represent many aspects of life, including health. In terms of health, the quadrants might represent balance among the emotional, physical, mental, and spiritual aspects of a person. With each quadrant would come teachings about how to achieve growth in that realm and how to achieve balance in life. Being out of balance is synonymous with health and mental health problems.

Although communities are diverse, there are some fundamental values that they hold in common. Understanding the shared values that are relevant to the psyche of the Native client and to behaviors impacting health is imperative in establishing cultural congruence. Values relevant to health psychology include a strong spiritual orientation, a group orientation, the importance of respect and noninterference, living in harmony, nonmaterialism, and conceptualizations of lifestyle factors.

SPIRITUAL ORIENTATION

Spirituality is a critical element of Aboriginal existence that is often overlooked by Western practitioners. All aspects of life are seen as having a spiritual basis. This was stated well by Dan Foster (1997), who paraphrased an elder in saying, "We are spiritual beings on a physical journey." Things of the spirit were "known" to be as real and as important as things of the physical world. There is another Aboriginal saying that one of the present authors heard some years ago in Michigan, though its exact origins are unknown. "There are two worlds that we must deal with: the world of that which we see and touch, and then there is the real world." The latter refers to the spirit world. This captures the perceived importance of things of the spirit. All living things are conceptualized as having spirit, as are some objects, such as rocks, that Westerners think of as inanimate. Within the Ojibwa traditions, life itself is the very process of the spirit experiencing the physical world. This deems all life sacred and mandates that all living things must be treated with respect and honor. Even the process of hunting and gathering food is ritualized to include the acknowledgment that our plant and animal relatives willingly sacrifice their lives so that people can live. People in return are supposed to honor the plants and animals and be thankful for their sacrifice. A health promotion program acknowledging the sacredness of the food we eat could reinforce a mindful approach to eating.

INDIVIDUALISM AND GROUP ORIENTATION

Related to this is the notion that we come to this physical world with a larger purpose of experiencing the beauty of creation. We also have a special, individual purpose that we need to rediscover and fulfill. Accordingly, each of us is on a solitary spiritual journey that no one can question or dictate. It was and is a common practice for individuals seeking clarity about their spiritual or physical journey to fast and pray in isolation and what would come to that person was often not spoken of in any detail. It was a personal link between the individual and the spirit world. Although it is commonly believed that Aboriginal people were group-oriented and conformist, closer examination suggests we were group-oriented individualists. This is an important point for the health care worker to realize because if an approach to facilitating behavioral change is perceived as being controlling or overly directive in any way, it will not sit well with many Native people, who have retained this individualistic orientation and a belief in noninterference.

RESPECT AND NONINTERFERENCE

Another hint of the Native world-view can be gleaned from the eloquent expression, "All creation stories are true." Although this statement was heard by one of the authors in a traditional Ojibwa ceremony, it seems to be a fairly common belief across tribal groups and it certainly speaks to the notion of respect for the teachings and ways of others. It also has deeper meanings that, if thought through in the fashion of meditating upon a Zen koan, might lead one closer to the inner psyche of the Native person. It touches upon the notion of noninterference, wherein it is believed that one should not interfere with the life path or beliefs of another person or people. Diversity in culture and teachings was acknowledged to be a part of the natural order of things, much like the diversity of plant and animal life. There is a common belief that the Creator gave all the people of the earth a place to live and care for and teachings by which to live. It is not considered appropriate by many traditionals for non-Native people to be following or even to know of the teachings given to Native people because they have their own teachings and have a responsibility to know and follow them. This again denotes the notion of respect for others' differences.

LIFE AS HARMONIOUS

Another aspect common in Aboriginal traditions is the value of cooperation and harmony, as opposed to competition and conflict. Life on earth was thought to be a massive cooperative venture. All things lived in balanced cooperation, living lives in a sacred and respectful manner. For example, the natural succession of plant and animal life into a disturbed space would be considered a result of a cooperative, coordinated effort on the part of the species involved, rather than the result of Darwinian competition. To many tribal groups, other animal and plant beings were thought of as elder brothers and sisters and were thought to always be looking out for Native people as one might a younger sibling. There is a basic assumption that all creation, all life, continues to seek good relationships with humankind, and this is a part of the broader belief that life is good and proper when things are in "balance," when there is "harmony." This lies in stark contrast to the Darwinian viewpoint of biological, social, and economic relationships that dominates Western thought.

NONMATERIALISM

Another common aspect of Native cultures is a nonmaterialistic orientation. For example, very ancient Ojibwa teachings dictated that the (Ojibwa) people are not to own anything other than the spiritual path they were given to follow. This contrasts with Western notions of ownership of property and was the cause of misunderstanding and conflict between early European colonizers and Native people. This nonmaterial orientation is related to the value traditionally placed on sharing and cooperation. The good of the individual was intrinsically tied to the good of the family, clan, and community. Accordingly, if one had more than one needed, the rest was to be given away. In some tribal groups, status within the community could be increased through generosity, a fact that colonists took such advantage of on the West Coast of Canada that the Canadian Government once banned some of the traditional potlatch giveaways of the Coastal communities in a paternalistic attempt to save the Indians from their own generosity.

LIFESTYLE FACTORS—HEALTH-PROMOTING DIETARY AND EXERCISE HABITS

The traditional teachings, to our knowledge, rarely, if ever, provided a basis for healthy eating and exercise habits. Although games and sports appear to have been a passion with many communities, and the practice of basic hunting skills was very common, we have never come across a description of formalized exercise and organized dietary regimens and have never encountered such in the traditional teachings, though our knowledge of the teachings is limited. This makes sense if you consider that in primal cultures, whether hunting and gathering or agricultural, many of these practices are dictated by necessity. All available food sources would have been utilized, not for the sake of a balanced diet but for the sake of survival. Likewise, everyday tasks of living would likely have provided men and women with sufficient exercise to promote and maintain basic fitness.

ILLNESS AND HEALING

For many tribal groups, the natural order of things on the Native Life Road was health and happiness. Illness, then, was often viewed as a loss of balance within the individual and a loss of harmony with the outer world. Seen as a result of falling away from the life road, there was a tendency to ponder what the ill person had done, or what someone close to them had done to bring on the illness. Though this may sound superstitious, Western thought on illness and healing appears to be incorporating this perspective itself, particularly within the holistic or alternative medicine fields. This translates to an ownership of health that can be both productive and destructive. To the extent that one's health was seen as a function of how much in balance a person was living, this is good. To the extent that one's health was seen as a function of other people's behavior, there are potential negative consequences to deal with, particularly regarding self-efficacy. At the extreme, illness was also seen as sometimes resulting from "bad medicine," the use of spiritual power to bring harm to others. To this day, among many traditional and nontraditional Native people, there are often thoughts and concerns about people doing bad medicine. It is clear that much of this is a form of internalized racism that is partially the result of the Christian churches' early efforts to increase fear of traditional spirituality. Nevertheless, it is a common enough element in Aboriginal etiological thinking to keep in mind when working with individuals on health-related issues.

Healing was often seen in traditional culture as the result of divine intervention, though not always directly through a supreme power. Plants and other "elders" had the ability to heal the ill if the conditions were set right. In the 1970s, Virgil Vogel identified 170 botanical drugs previously discovered and used by Indian communities in pre-European times, including curare, quinine, ipecac, and digitalis (Vogel, 1970). Although many Native herbal remedies have proven effective from a Western pharmacological perspective, there is much more to it than this, for the plants were considered to have life, knowledge, and wisdom. To restore balance to the ill person, that person must come into good relationship with the healing plant. A spiritual connection needed to be made with the plant and with intervening spirits for healing to take place. In this sense, all healing was and is spiritual.

It should be evident from this brief overview that there were wide differences between the world-views of Native people and the European colonizers that first arrived in North America. In addition, European American policies aimed at extermination, isolation, and assimilation led to widespread destruction within Native communities. Differences in values systems and colonization gave rise to many misunderstandings and certainly made Native people vulnerable to exploitation and abuse. The changes that most community groups experienced as a result of colonization is best described as a holocaust.

A HISTORY OF LOSS AND TRAUMA

"We are the Borg. Lower your shields and surrender your ships. We will add your biological and technological distinctiveness to our own. Your culture will adapt to service us. Resistance is futile" (Braga & Moore, 1996). In the popular television and movie series, "Star Trek–Next Generation," there is a race of beings, half biological and half technological, that expands its way through the galaxy by absorbing other races and cultures by force, through its superior technology. The depiction of the Borg is a compelling analog to Western civilization from the perspective of the Aboriginal people of North America and possibly from the perspective of aboriginal people around the world who have retained some connection with ancient traditions.

Much has been written about the effects of colonization on Native people, and there exists a wide chasm between the version of history traditionally promoted by Western schools and media and the version known to Native people. There has been a narrowing of the chasm in recent years, with many Westerners rethinking the realities of the colonization of the continent and what it has meant to Native people. However, a backlash also exists as such attempts to review historic assumptions are sometimes condemned as "revisionist." For the most part, the perception of many Native people is that the dominant culture within North America has been built on the backs and through the blood of Native people and that its members today live in ignorance and denial of this historic reality. Accordingly, there is a perceived gulf of understanding that will be hard for many nonnative people to bridge.

On the gross scale of effects, Native populations suffered large declines upon colonization. It has been argued that these declines were brought about largely by disease rather than military intervention (Dobyns, 1983), as an estimated five-sixths of some tribal populations died of infectious diseases passed on by Europeans during early contact (Lawson, 1937). However, some epidemics were initiated through the gifting of disease-infected blankets, possibly the earliest documented use of biological warfare (Vogel, 1972). Brief descriptions of some of the other effects of colonization are provided in the following.

LAND TAKEOVERS

One has only to look at a map of North America and remind oneself that not many years ago, 100% of the land resources belonged to Aboriginal people to recognize the greatness of their loss. For any culture living close to the earth, this means a loss of soul; loss of connection, meaning, and identity; and loss of ability to make a living. Forced removal and relocation also took their toll on Native populations and cultures (Brown, 1970; Vogel, 1972).

POLITICAL CONTROL

Traditional political systems were replaced by Euro-based systems that conflict with basic Native values and principles. This resulted in a loss of the interdependence that served Native people well and by which they governed themselves for thousands of years. This, combined with the divide-and-conquer tactics used by Western governments, resulted in a state of social and political conflict and strife that dominates many of our First Nations communities to this day.

SPIRITUAL CONTROL

Through church and state, traditional spiritual practices were effectively banned, and a war of propaganda was waged against traditional values and beliefs. This resulted in a loss of traditional practices and connection with the Creator and all life. Most importantly, it resulted in a loss of connection with the spiritual inner self and, therefore, identity, the good life, meaning, and healing. Loss of respect for the original teachings that sustained Native people for thousands of years has meant a philosophical/spiritual vacuum for many and a loss of the good and healthful life for most.

FORCED EDUCATION

Forced education resulted in loss of language and cultural practices and forced acculturation to ways antagonistic to being Native. Forced removal of Indian children from their parents and communities to attend boarding schools had a devastating effect on generations of Native children (e.g., Driver, 1969; Goldstein, 1974; Kleinfeld & Bloom, 1977). The boarding schools resulted in a loss of connection between parents and children and a degradation in parenting skill over generations. This is still felt today and is often cited as a key problem within Native populations (Horejsi, Craig, & Pablo, 1992). Within these boarding schools, Native children experienced emotional, physical, sexual, and spiritual abuse. This has been a key factor identified in intergenerational posttraumatic stress disorder (Duran & Duran, 1995).

LOSS OF A TRADITIONAL LIFESTYLE AND RACISM

An Anishinaabe spiritual leader in North Dakota related to one of the authors that, "Before the white man came here, this land was good. Since he came, there has been nothing but abuse: abuse of land, abuse of animals, abuse of people." Similarly, an elder in California stated, "When they took away our bows and arrows, they took away our right to be men." Poverty has been a major factor in reservation communities. Low employment rates and limited means to follow traditional lifestyles has manifested in the form of a sedentary lifestyle on reservations or within urban ghettos. In regard to exercise and dietary habits, without any preexisting traditions of formal exercise and diet regulation, the loss of traditional means of living and eating meant that the people were left with a vacuum of health-enhancing behaviors. This, combined with the introduction of commodities, such as flour, lard, and cheese, has resulted in unhealthy eating and exercise habits that, over the past three or four generations, have become the norm. As a result, the incidence rates for diabetes and heart disease have increased radically for most Native groups. The Navajo, a well-cited example, experienced a dramatic increase in obesity and diabetes within a relatively short period of time following the introduction of such lifestyle changes (e.g., Hoy,

Light, & Megill, 1995). Also, overt, covert, and institutional racism functioned to further wound the Native spirit and degrade self-esteem. When a culture is oppressed, the qualities of the aggressor are sometimes internalized, thus perpetuating the abuse. Internalized racism is a pervasive problem in many Native communities and within our urban centers (Duran & Duran, 1995).

INTERGENERATIONAL POSTCOLONIAL STRESS
DISORDER (PCSD)

A holocaust took place on this continent that continues to impact Native American communities today. One way this impact manifests is through Postcolonial Stress Disorder (Duran & Duran, 1995). Eduardo Duran conceptualizes some of the common problems in Native communities, such as emotional numbing, anxiety, depression, violence, and alcoholism, as manifestations of unresolved anger and grief resulting from historical trauma.

CULTURAL REVITALIZATION

In spite of this attempt to eliminate Native American culture, Native North Americans are incredibly resilient and resourceful people. In spite of 500 years of attempted genocide, many of our cultures remain strong. There is a revitalization movement in Native communities today. People are learning their traditional languages, participating in traditional ceremonies and cultural activities, and honoring the wisdom of their ancestors. In 1976, the Self Determination Act was passed, granting Native Americans the right to determine their own health care. Since the passage of that act, many communities have developed their own health care plans in the United States. In Canada, the Medical Services Branch of Health Canada is currently negotiating health transfer payments that will place the responsibility of providing health care, mental health care, and preventive health care more directly in the hands of First Nations. When this process is complete, each First Nation will have the responsibility to provide such services to its members as it sees fit and much of this will likely be done through contracting with outside service providers.

IMPLICATIONS FOR HEALTH PSYCHOLOGY

UNDERUTILIZATION OF SERVICES AND
CULTURAL SENSITIVITY

Native North Americans, especially those in rural settings, are often underserved by health and mental health professions (e.g., Manson, 1982; Trimble, 1990). The lack of ready access to quality health and mental health services is not specific to rural Aboriginal people, but the isolation and economic realities of reservation life often exacerbate the sorts of problems found in many rural settings. The availability of quality health and mental health services can also be a serious problem for many urban Native people, particularly in the United States, where there is no universal health care coverage and special services for Native people are often nonexistent or severely overstressed.

Another factor in not receiving adequate health and mental health care is that Native people often underuse those services that are available to them (Sue, 1990; Sue, 1977; Sue, Allen, & Conaway, 1978). Cited reasons for not using available mental health services include perceptions that Western-based services are biased, often conflict with traditional values, beliefs, and preferences, and are otherwise insensitive to the needs of Native people (cf. Hippler, 1975; LaFromboise, 1988; LaFromboise, Trimble, & Mohatt, 1990; Manson & Trimble, 1982; Trimble, 1981). In regard to seeking Western medical treatment, there appear to be three main factors that may cause difficulty for many Native people. These have to do with divergent cultural paradigms, traumatic historical factors, and overgeneralization of medical research findings based on European American norms.

In terms of different cultural paradigms, illness is a sociocultural construct which influences the conceptualization of etiology, treatment, and prevention. The different ways Aboriginal and Western cultures conceptualize this construct might undermine the acceptability of Western diagnoses, treatments, and prevention strategies to the Native client. Comparisons between Western and Native American healing practices illustrate this point. Mainstream society adheres to a disease model for conceptualizing illness. In this model, bacteria or viruses are seen as causing many forms of illness. Treatment is primarily physiological and the patient is typically treated alone. The physician uses scientific means to diagnose and treat the problem and is viewed as curing the patient. On the other hand, most Native cultures have traditionally followed a more holistic model of health care (Champagne, 1994). Treatment addresses the mind, body, and spirit of the person and is often conducted within the context of family and community. Illness is traditionally seen as stemming from both natural and supernatural causes. The traditional healer is viewed as a catalyst evoking the assistance of spirits from plants, animals, and the spirit world for healing. The patient is seen as mutually involved in healing. Traditional healers had a multitude of responsibilities for both individuals and the community. To the extent that a Native person or group adheres to this more traditional perspective, the restricted focus and perspective of Western medicine might be expected to decrease the number of individuals seeking help for conditions that are not acute emergencies. This may also reduce compliance with treatment regimens in general. As the reader might expect, this is an area where the health psychologist with a more holistic approach can complement medical care.

In addition to divergent paradigms, there exists a historic distrust of Western medicine that has its roots in colonization. Initially, European presence in America brought widespread disease to Native American communities. Widespread loss of life through warfare and illness resulted in many Native Americans turning to European American medical practitioners to cure the white man's diseases. When these efforts were unsuccessful, they tried to return to their communities and were thwarted through efforts of missionaries and governmental systems whose goal was assimilation. In California, for example, Native Americans were coerced into being baptized in order to receive medical treatment and, when they wanted to return to their villages, they were forbidden to do so. If they fled, they were pursued and entire villages were punished if they allowed the person to stay (Champagne, 1994). Eventually, the United States government made treaties with Native Americans that usually included provisions for health care in exchange for ceding their lands. The treaties also placed many tribal groups in isolated areas and left them in conditions of extreme poverty, increasing the likelihood that they would experience more health problems and be limited to inadequate health services. In addition, many forms of healing ceremonies were outlawed until recently. It is a historic irony that the United States was supposed to have been founded with the notion of freedom of religion, yet traditional Native American spirituality was outlawed until the 1980s. The people were removed from sacred healing grounds and many healers died, depriving traditional people of their healing practices. The Canadian experience, though possibly less blatant, was no less racist and destructive.

In more recent times, one of the hardships brought to Native people by Western medicine in both the United States and Canada was the sterilization of Native women. For years, medical practitioners on both sides of the border were known to sterilize Native women during childbirth or other operations, often without the informed consent of the women. Though this has presumably stopped in recent years, one of the authors recently treated a Native woman in her mid-30s who had never had children. This woman had asked a physician, under emotional duress, to perform a hysterectomy as a form of birth control and the physician promptly complied, reportedly without any counsel about its implications. Other clients have reported to this author that their physicians have repeatedly encouraged them to have tubal ligations. One can easily conclude that subtle and overt racism has characterized the medical care received by Native people by some practitioners and that this continues, at least in subtle form, to this day. Again, this historic reality, embedded in the minds of most Native people, might be expected to affect help-seeking behavior and compliance, particularly in cases that do not involve an acute emergency.

Western medicine and health psychology do have much to offer Native people, but these historic realities do result in special challenges to service delivery at times. For example, it is clear that the introduction of Western exercise and dietary habits into Aboriginal lifestyles can complement the traditional ways that a tribal group might have retained without inherent conflict. However, for some Native people, particularly those attempting to return to the traditions, embracing the habits of other cultures is sometimes resisted. Accordingly, if healthy eating habits and exercise regimens are presented outside of an Aboriginal framework, they may be seen as another form of acculturation pressure and thus ridiculed or otherwise resisted. A case in point: one of the authors was told in fun by a traditional man from Manitoulin Island that there were once several non-Native teachers working on his home reserve. The teachers used to jog during their lunch breaks and people would often poke fun of this, calling them "Joginoshuk." (The Ojibwa/Odawa word for White people in their dialect is pronounced "zhoginoshuk.") Accordingly, attitudes about adopting lifestyle patterns that are clearly not Aboriginal in origin should be assessed and addressed. Also, when possible, targeted lifestyle changes should be framed through a Native perspective. In the case of running, for example, community members could be reminded that before the reservation systems, Native people valued strong running ability because of its utility and survival value. Adopting running into one's lifestyle, therefore, could then be recognized as a return to tradition, rather than as adopting another practice of the dominant culture.

Western practitioners will also need to consider the role of spirituality in their work. One can expect that the spiritual orientation within traditional culture will be found, to some extent, in most Native clientele, even though it may have become disconnected from the original teachings that gave rise to it. For many, it is believed that the creator gave Aboriginal people all the teachings to live a good and healthy life and that for every illness that exists, there is a cure that was provided. Being aware of and open to traditional healing alternatives will enable the provider to build rapport, increase belief in the perceived utility of the services provided, and ensure integrated services. Also, traditional teachings and beliefs, particularly among those who are traditional and knowledgeable about them, are often key influences in the Native person's behavior and yet they are sometimes not talked about. In other words, the behavioral health care provider, particularly if nonnative, may have to work with the effects of traditional beliefs on client behavior without being fully aware of them. Suggestions for dealing with this problem are made later in the chapter.

Finally, the effects of postcolonial stress need to be considered when providing services, particularly those that attempt to effect behavioral changes. As we well know, with individuals who have been exposed to multiple traumata, to chronic life stress that has not been in their immediate control, and to other soul-wounding experiences, a form of chronic, low-grade depression and a sense of learned helplessness can be expected. Because of this, health-related issues might not be within their immediate locus of concern and may be perceived to be beyond the individual's personal control. Therefore, motivational factors may need to receive special attention.

In summary, many Native people do not have access to quality health and mental health services and often underutilize those that are available because of perceived isolation, conflicts with held values and beliefs, and historical distrust. As Renfrey (1992) has argued, however, some cases of underutilization may have the function of preventing further erosion of culture and, hence, may be beneficial in the long run. As previously discussed, well-intentioned churches and government organizations caused widespread destruction to Native communities in efforts to "help them." Mental health programs which lack cultural sensitivity are at risk for perpetuating this abuse. If behavioral health services are to be offered to Aboriginal people and their communities then, it is considered critical that they be culturally congruent and applied with cultural sensitivity, as defined by Szapocznik, Scopetta, and King (1978). Szapocznik et al. (1978) stated that cultural sensitivity is "a treatment mode built on a set of therapeutic assumptions that complement the patient's basic value structure." Today, the devastating pandemics of infections following contact with Europeans have been largely replaced by metabolic and behaviorally modulated conditions closely associated with the acculturation process, such as diabetes, obesity, alcohol abuse, injuries, cancer, and heart disease (Rhoades, 1996), all health problems related to unhealthy lifestyles. Accordingly, the health psychologist has a potentially important role to play in the promotion and maintenance of health within our Aboriginal populations.

PROVIDING SERVICES

Given the above historic and world-view perspective, the reader should now have an appreciation for the nature of the cultural gulf that exists between many Native people and most nonnatives. The following section is written to further familiarize the reader with a number of practical issues that may arise in providing services to Native people and briefly discuss specific health issues that are likely to be targeted by the health psychologist. Finally, a recommended approach to service delivery will be outlined.

GENERAL ISSUES IN WORKING WITH NATIVE CLIENTS

Diversity and the Native American/Canadian Cultural Identity and Expression Scale

Due to heterogeneity among communities, it is important to be familiar not only with a particular community's unique features but also with the level of acculturation of a particular individual. Many of the issues discussed in this chapter will apply to a particular person in proportion to his/her level of acculturation and deculturation. The greater the acculturation to the dominant culture and deculturation from the traditional culture, the less a client will present special needs where cultural awareness and sensitivity are critical. The opposite is, of course, true, as well. Accordingly, some determination of acculturation status of an individual or range of status for a group is a recommended as a first step to providing effective services. Though this can be done superficially through simple questions, such as, "What role does your Native culture play in your life," more formal determinations may be called for, particularly when establishing service programs for communities.

The Native American/Canadian Cultural Identity and Expression Scale is offered as one attempt to provide a means of assessing levels of acculturation, deculturation, and preferred cultural expressions. It is provided in the Appendix, along with a usage manual and scoring template. Though not an instrument intended to be used in all applications of health psychology, it is provided to give the reader ideas about what factors to assess that may prove relevant to research or clinical applications.

THE BELIEF AND VALUES FACTORS

Despite the cultural diversity that exists among Native people, there are some commonalities in beliefs and values among tribal groups (cf. Attneave, 1982; Cooley, 1977; French, 1989; Herring, 1990; Ho, 1987; Renfrey, 1992; Spang, 1965; Tafoya, 1981, 1989). Some of these were discussed in more detail in the previous section but the commonalities generally identified as important include (1) present-time orientation, (2) harmony with nature, (3) cooperative relationships with others, (4) sharing, (5) respect for elders, (6) noninterference with others, (7) resentment of authority, (8) strong sense of autonomy, (9) nonmaterialism; (10) focus on the extended family, and (11) holism, wherein spirit, mind, body, community, and environment are interrelated and inseparable. Recognizing these and how they might impact the provision of services is important. For example, recognizing that many Native people may have a different appreciation for time would help prepare the provider to be flexible regarding appointment scheduling, length of meetings or sessions, and early or late arrivals. Sticking too rigidly to Western time constraints may widen the gulf between the provider and the Native client. Similarly, recognizing the value placed on noninterference, personal autonomy, and the mistrust of authority might help the provider to avoid presenting herself or her services in a manner that will be offensive or might otherwise damage rapport and trust. The importance of taking a holistic approach to intervention will be discussed later.

COMMUNICATION STYLE

It may prove difficult at times for the non-Native provider to establish rapport with many Native people because of the historic factors previously discussed and ongoing cultural conflicts. In such cases, the effects of counselor ethnicity may be at least partially attenuated if s/he employs culturally appropriate communication skills (Dauphinais, Dauphinais, & Rowe, 1981). Since the communications style of many Native people has been characterized as being *high-context* in nature (see Hall, 1976), it often relies more heavily on nonverbals and shared meanings than does that of the dominant culture (Sue, 1990). It follows, then, that significant differences in verbal and especially nonverbal communication between the nonnative provider and the Native client could impede communication and the development of trust and rapport (Sue & Sue, 1977; Sue, 1990). The reader might familiarize herself with such nonverbal components as handshakes (typically gentle), eye contact (often lower in frequency and duration), preferred physical distancing (often slightly greater) through careful observation and consultation with community informants.

Verbal components are also important to consider. For example, one might expect to encounter differences in pause time, which is usually slightly to significantly longer (Tafoya, 1989; Trimble & Hayes, 1984), and in a tendency to talk around a sensitive subject rather than directly address it (e.g., Sue, 1990). The style of conveying one's expertise can also have an impact and we can look to the literature on counseling Native people to help here. Although some authors have identified a directive approach as effective in providing counseling to Native people (e.g., Herring, 1990; Spang, 1965; Tafoya, 1989), others (e.g., French, 1989; Renfrey, 1992) have suggested that an overly directive approach might be resisted because of the values often placed on personal autonomy, noninterference, and mistrust of authority, especially of the nonnative provider. What might prove to be an effective compromise is the use of open-ended injunctions and the provision of behavioral options for the client to choose from. Regarding the latter, providing several examples of actions that others often find helpful in dealing with the issue at hand and then inviting the client to determine for himself whether any might be useful to him is a particularly effective strategy from counseling and therapy that can be applied to the health psychology field.

As with nonverbal communication differences, the reader might become familiar with differences in verbal components for a particular client or community by careful observation and consultation. This can be a lengthy and difficult task; however, provided that one has a respectful attitude toward both the client and the cultural differences, a reasonable approach to such situations would be to simply be one's self, communicate openly, and be open to admitting to and learning from one's mistakes. Without underestimating the importance of cultural differences, the reader should take some solace in recognizing that we are more alike than we are different.

USE OF TRADITIONAL INTERVENTIONS
AND RESOURCES

As previously argued, traditional healing practices can be effective for treating diverse mental, physical, and spiritual problems and may be preferred by many Native people. This is not to say that health psychology has nothing to offer our Native communities. It is our belief that Western and traditional healing complement each other and that a combination of both methods is the most promising approach to impacting health-related issues. As argued by Renfrey (1992), the use of traditional healing methods for many health problems is, arguably, appropriate when the client is traditional or when such methods might otherwise be effective. Even when a conventional intervention is the treatment of choice, supplementation by a traditional counterpart could improve therapist and treatment credibility, treatment compliance and outcome, and/or enhance prevention efforts (Ho, 1987; Jilek & Todd, 1974; LaFromboise et al., 1990;

Manson & Trimble,1982; Rappaport & Rappaport, 1981; Trimble & Hayes, 1984). It has also been suggested that collaboration with traditional healers and elders can be an effective avenue for the Western practitioner (e.g., Attneave, 1974; Bergman, 1973; Dinges, Trimble, Manson, & Pasquale, 1981; LaFromboise et al., 1990; Rappaport & Rappaport, 1981; Renfrey, 1992; Trimble & Hayes, 1984). Since traditional healers and elders usually hold positions of respect within their communities, forming a collaborative relationship with them can also help the Western provider to overcome the mistrust/acceptance barrier a little sooner than would otherwise be the case.

So, it would seem advisable for anyone providing direct interventions or consultations to Native communities to establish working, collaborative relations with traditional healers and elders. Aside from providing direct service themselves, traditional providers can also provide acculturation/training for the Western practitioner and ongoing consultation (cf. Delgado, 1979).

PROVIDER PREPARATION

There is no substitute for direct experience in this area. The health psychology practitioner cannot expect to become optimally effective immediately with a Native clientele without experience in working with Native people individually and with Native communities. This presents a dilemma for the would-be practitioner because opportunities for work with First Nations people and communities at a training level can be hard to come by. Accordingly, most practitioners who do find themselves serving Aboriginal communities and individuals will likely find themselves in the midst of it, feeling ill-prepared or, worse, feeling fully prepared and competent when they are not.

In preparing to work with Native people and communities, the practitioner is expected to be professional and effective and, in many ways, this is the bottom line. The would-be provider could establish contacts with Native people in advance and learn something of the people and culture to be served. Elders, traditional providers, and Aboriginal front-line workers should be effective contacts, in most cases. As per professional competency guidelines, for those practitioners who do not have experience working with this population, it will be important to seek supervision and ongoing consultation as needed with practicing psychologists and other health care professionals who serve our First Nations communities, particularly those who are Native themselves. Finally, being the best human being you can be is a largely unrecognized and underrated form of preparation for service. It is our belief that living a balanced lifestyle and being in good relationship with one's self and the world is critical to providing helpful services to our communities because it likely means that one is living with balance and that is congruent with Aboriginal traditions. Native people, because of our history, are usually pretty good at assessing what a person is really all about and it is not through what a person says or does not say, but rather through a sensing of the person as a whole. If you're a good human being with good intentions, it will help smooth out the bumps of your own acculturation to Native ways.

SPECIFIC HEALTH ISSUES

Much health and medical treatment for Native North Americans has been based on values systems and research findings of European American/Canadian culture. Some authors have argued that epidemiological data for Native people can be misleading because large differences exist in incidence rates among tribal groups, with some yielding lower than national averages and others higher (Barter & Barter, 1974; May & Dizmang, 1974; Shore, 1974; Westermeyer, 1974). This makes identifying patterns specific to Native Americans as a group challenging. However, there are broad trends that have been identified.

In general, there has been a shift in Aboriginal disease patterns, from acute infectious diseases to those of a more chronic and dangerous nature, and an increase in the prevalence of diseases and conditions with a strong behavioral component. Native North Americans have higher rates of morbidity and mortality for many health problems than do European Americans, which may be partially related to higher rates of unemployment and lower educational achievement and income (Rhoades, 1996). Native North Americans living on or near reservations die before the age of 45 at higher rates than do European Americans (Kimball, Goldberg, & Oberle, 1996). On average, three out of eight Native people die before their 45th birthday compared to one out of eight other Americans (Prieto, 1989). Overall, the health status of Native people tends to lag behind that of other Americans (Kimball et al., 1996). In comparison with European Americans, Grossman, Krieger, Sugarman, and Forguera (1994) conducted a study comparing rural and urban Native North Americans with European Americans on health measures related to prenatal risk factors, birth outcomes, age-specific mortality, cause-specific mortality, and communicable diseases. They found great disparities between urban Native North Americans and European Americans across almost every health dimension. Overall, urban Native people had lower birth weights, more infant mortality, and more delayed prenatal care than European Americans. They also had higher rates of hepatitis A and B, tuberculosis, more age-specific mortality rates except among the elderly, and more cause-specific mortality rates than European Americans. For example, Natives had higher rates of heart disease, unintentional injury, cerebral cerebrovascular disease, sexually transmitted diseases, chronic liver disease, and cirrhosis. They also had higher rates of unintentional injury, homicide, alcohol-related deaths, and tooth decay (LeMaster & McConnell, 1994). These higher rates of health-related problems are largely due to the high risk factors stemming from both individual and other social and environmental conditions (Kimball et al., 1996).

The causes of these health problems are a debated issue. However, core reasons often cited relate to the acculturation and deculturation stress wrought by the dominant European American culture (e.g., Christie & Halpern, 1990; Dozier, 1966; French, 1989; Jilek, 1974; Leighton & Hughes, 1961; Mail, 1989; May & Dizmang, 1974). According to this position, the effects of trauma and loss that colonization has inflicted on Aboriginal people across generations has lead to widespread health problems. Assimilation increased exposure to risk factors for disease. Although communities differ in terms of prevalence of risk factors and diseases, they share a common history of colonization, which had a similar impact on all Native people. For example, prior to colonization, many communities smoked only in moderation for medicinal or spiritual purposes. Other communities did not know about tobacco until the Europeans introduced it (Pego, Hill, Solomon, Chisholm, & Ivey, 1995). Alcohol use was nonexistent. Increasing rates of obesity, hypertension, and Type II diabetes are attributed to changes in diet and activity superimposed on a genetic predisposition (Zimmet, 1992). Furthermore, the attempted destruction of traditional cultural values, practices, and means of material support (deculturation) has left many Native people caught between conflicting cultures. As a result, many find themselves in a socially and economically untenable position. The resulting personal and interpersonal stressors then precipitate diverse health and mental health problems.

Following is a brief discussion of the three major risk factors related to chronic disease among Native Americans: tobacco use, alcohol use, and obesity. A brief discussion follows on diabetes, heart disease, and cancer. Finally, the potential utility of life skills development in promoting healthy lifestyles among Native people is explored.

ALCOHOL AND DRUG ABUSE

Alcohol abuse tends to be higher, on average, for Native Americans than for other ethnic groups (e.g., Bachman et al., 1991; Dozier, 1966; Lewis, 1982; Shore, 1974; Weibel, 1982; Weisner, Weibel-Orlando, & Long, 1984; Welte & Barnes, 1987). Alcohol-related deaths are higher among Native Americans than in the general United States population and continue to be the leading cause of mortality. A high-risk environment, flamboyant drinking styles, and risky postdrinking behavior all contribute to these higher death rates (May, 1994). While, Native American males tend to drink more than other groups, both male and female Native Americans begin drinking at a younger age, drink enough to pass out more often, and exhibit more risky behavior, such as drinking and driving, than do other groups (Kimball et al., 1996). Native American adolescents ranked highest in per capita alcohol consumption, percentage of heavy drinkers, number of times drunk, and number of alcohol-related problems when compared to other adolescent minority and nonminority groups (Welte & Barnes, 1987). May (1994) distinguishes alcohol-abusive drinking patterns, which include more sporadic binge drinking, and alcohol-dependent drinking styles, which are more chronic. He found that most Native Americans exhibited the alcohol-abusive drinking pattern. This pattern is associated with more motor vehicle accidents, other accidents, suicides, and homicides. Younger Native Americans, aged 15–35, tend to drink sporadically, to be at higher risk for alcohol-related injury, arrest, and death, and to have a higher blood alcohol content. The more chronic drinkers tend to be downwardly mobile, socially marginal, unemployed, and to have higher incidents of cirrhosis of the liver. Chronic liver disease and cirrhosis are the leading causes of death related to alcohol abuse (LeMaster & McConnell, 1994).

TOBACCO ABUSE

The Center for Disease Control (1992) reported that Native Americans had higher rates of tobacco use than did European Americans under age 35 but tended to smoke less heavily. They also found that Native American women smoked more than Native American men and Native Americans have the highest rates of tobacco use of any group (see also Center for Disease Control, 1992; Schinke, Moncher, Holden, Botvin, & Orlandi, 1989; Schinke et al., 1988). Tobacco use was particularly high among communities in the Northwest region of the United States, in reservation communities, and among Native college students. Tobacco use is associated with conditions such as cardiovascular disease, lung cancer, cancers of the larynx, bronchus, trachea, and pancreas, and fetal and infant morbidity and mortality (Pego et al., 1995).

OBESITY

One study found that both male and female Native Americans had higher rates of obesity than the general population on four reservations in Washington. Obesity in adolescents among the Navajo was found to be three times that expected among European American adolescents. Obesity is a risk factor for cardiovascular disease, diabetes, and hypertension. The introduction of starchy foods into reservation communities is one example of the effects of European contact on Native people leading to health risks. Some health problems stem from similar social and environmental conditions, such as communities sharing the introduction of alcoholism, poverty, and starchy foods. Other common health problems Native Americans face are diabetes and heart disease.

DIABETES

Although, in Canada, diabetes was very rare among First Nations people before the 1940s, it has grown to be a major health problem, affecting over 20% of the population. Similarly, among the Navajo diabetes was almost unheard of in the 1930s. By 1989, it was diagnosed in 17.2% of Navajos, aged 20–74. This is 2.5 times the average United States rate (Sugarman, Hickley, Hall, & Gohdes, 1990). In the United States, the average incidence for diabetes is twice as high among Native Americans as among the general United States population. It has been reported to be as high as 70% within the Pima population (Knowler et al.,

1991). Type II diabetes increases cardiovascular risk by a factor of two to four. Hypertension is also strongly associated with obesity and diabetes (Rhoades, 1996). Risk for hypertension is increased by factors such as excess sodium consumption, high body mass index, central obesity, intra-abdominal fat excess, and alcohol consumption, all modifiable features (Havas et al., 1996). These risk factors are high within many Native American communities.

HEART DISEASE AND DIET

Heart disease is the leading cause of death for adult Native American men and women nationwide (Havas et al., 1996). Risk factors contributing to heart disease include smoking, obesity, a high-fat diet, and physical inactivity. Five major risk factors for cardiovascular disease are obesity, diabetes, hypertension, hypercholesterolemia, and smoking (Campos-Outcalt et al., 1995). Cerebrovascular disease is the fourth leading cause of death and higher than the United States total. Death rates for hypertension and atherosclerosis are approaching the United States average.

CANCER

Cancer is relatively new to Native American populations. Overall incidence rates for cancer among Native Americans are lower than for European Americans but rates are increasing in communities where cancer has been studied (Joe & Justice, 1992). Cancers of the gallbladder, invasive cervical cancer, and stomach cancer are high in many Native American communities and cancers of the liver and nasopharynx are high in Alaska (Nutting et al., 1993).

LIFE SKILLS DEVELOPMENT

Quite possibly the most promising area for the health psychology practitioner to focus on is life skills development. Most areas covered in this discussion are amenable to a life skills approach because they all involve learned behaviors and their use or disuse. Such an approach has been shown to be effective in ameliorating several forms of behavioral problems among Native people. For example, LaFromboise and Howard-Pitney (1995) demonstrated the efficacy of a life skills development curriculum in impacting factors that contribute to suicide among Zuni high school students. This approach has also been shown to be effective in reducing tobacco abuse (e.g., Holden, Botvin, & Orlandi, 1989; Schinke et al., 1990) and alcohol abuse (e.g., Gilchrist, Schinke, Trimble, & Cvetkovich, 1987; Schinke et al., 1988). Also, to the extent that stress is a functional component of behavior-related health problems, a life skills approach that includes stress management might be expected to contribute to an overall intervention. Accordingly, life skills development is recommended here as an approach for those areas in the field where enhanced skills can be expected to directly or indirectly impact health-related behaviors.

In summary, practitioners need to be knowledgeable about research conducted on Native people, particularly on the specific communities with which they work. Caution must be used in generalizing results from epidemiological research on nonnative populations to Native populations and in generalizing across tribal groups. Shifting health-related problems for Native people from acute infectious diseases, prevalent since European contact, to more chronic, degenerative conditions are due, to a large extent, to lifestyle factors and are amenable, therefore, to behavioral interventions. Accordingly, the health psychologist is well positioned to serve this special population and its needs. Behavioral interventions aimed at altering health-related behaviors do, however, need to be culturally sensitive and applied in a culturally appropriate fashion.

RECOMMENDED APPROACHES

At present, there is insufficient research-based outcome data on the effects of health-promoting interventions on Native North American people to identify an approach of choice. The differences in tribal belief systems and levels of acculturation among Aboriginal populations also makes such global determinations tenuous. General approach issues can be addressed, however, and a creative, flexible approach can be suggested.

CULTURAL/HISTORIC AWARENESS

It is recommended that the health psychologist preparing to serve a Native community familiarize herself with the specific cultural/tribal mores and values, to the extent possible. Though the generalities discussed are good guidelines, specific information should be sought and used as much as possible. Also, the professional is advised to familiarize herself with the local history of the group served. Often, this will provide a more useful historic context for understanding the specific target problems and will likely enhance sensitivity and rapport. Related to this, investigating the history of the targeted behavioral/health-related problems will likely provide important clues on how to reverse them. It may prove possible to address the targeted health issues through reversing, if possible, the changes that brought them about. Finally, a sensitive and informal assessment of the political factors and social dynamics that may affect implementation and outcome of the service plan is advised. Caution must be used, to avoid being becoming involved in political situations. Because there are often strong social dynamics that compel neutral parties to take sides in issues, involvement in tribal politics can guarantee failure of the project.

INVOLVE THE COMMUNITY

Involving the community is imperative to gaining support for health promotion efforts. Diaz-Guerrero (1984, p. 165) has suggested that behavioral health be introduced to members of traditional cultures in groups by teachers, parents, spiritual organizations, and other agencies recognized by the people. This is consistent with the clinical wisdom of health and mental health workers serving our First Nations. It is also consistent with the emphasis placed on demonstrated community input and support for projects under funding consideration from varied government agencies.

One of the most successful, well-documented community-based mental health interventions to date is the Zuni Life Skills Development Curriculum, developed by LaFromboise (see LaFromboise & Howard-Pitney, 1995) and later converted into a more intertribal intervention package (LaFromboise, 1992). The curriculum was commissioned by the Zuni tribe to address rising rates of youth and young adult suicide within their community. In its development, community input into the content was used extensively to ensure cultural congruence and community support. One of the authors working in a First Nations community bore witness to the quick demise of several well-thought-out service delivery plans that held great promise in addressing critical health and mental health needs, simply because the planners did not include avenues for community input and feedback in the development of the plans. Fostering cooperation among the varied governing and service entities within Aboriginal communities in health promotion projects should be a high priority. Unless all parties that have a voice within the community can agree on the need for and focus of programs for social change and healing and can form a working arrangement for cooperation, the project may fail. Accordingly, whenever an intervention plan is to be developed, it is recommended that the planners identify all possible players and incorporate their input and cooperation. Focus groups usually prove useful for this purpose.

CULTURAL CONGRUENCE

Intervention approaches should be culturally relevant and sensitive because of the strong role culture plays in shaping health-related attitudes and behaviors (LeMaster & McConnell, 1994). Having Native leadership in planning, implementing, and interpreting programs, utilizing community focus groups to develop and modify programs, and including community members or known and respected service providers in the implementation of the plan is recommended. Native communities have used innovative methods to ensure cultural sensitivity, such as involving the community to create a subculture to provide maintenance of a healthy lifestyle (Health, Wilson, Smith, & Leonard, 1987), utilizing traditional activities in physical exercise and traditional foods in diets (Harris, Davis, Ford, & Tso, 1988) and incorporating knowledge about the historical (Parker, 1990) and spiritual components of substances like tobacco and alcohol. To make programs specific to particular populations, some communities have developed material at local levels (May & Hymbaugh, 1989) and incorporated a detailed knowledge of the particular tribal history, culture, and current epidemiological factors within the community.

TRAINING NATIVE PRACTITIONERS

Champagne (1994) suggested that encouraging and providing assistance for Native Americans to become physicians trained in both Western medicine and traditional healing might help to bridge the gap between Western medicine and traditional health practices. The authors concur with this, though training in the healing arts of both cultures is so rigorous, it seems unlikely that many would opt to attempt this. A similar suggestion can be made to support a greater study of psychology by Native people. Several excellent recruitment programs for professional psychology currently exist in the United States and they are helping to add new American Indian professional psychologists to the ranks each year. A corresponding program does not seem to exist in Canada, at present.

USE OF TRADITIONAL HEALERS AND ELDERS

In many tribal groups, traditional healers continue to provide for their people. In Western terms, their roles are diverse and may include diagnostics, herbal medicine, lifestyle counseling, psychological and spiritual counseling, birthing assistance, traditional teaching, and spiritual healing. Western medicine has come to see the importance of herbs in treating illness and factions within Western psychology and psychiatry have acknowledged the efficacy of indigenous counseling and psychotherapy for years (e.g., Frank, 1973; Wallace, 1958). Many Native people use both Western health/mental health practitioners and traditional healers, and many First Nations and urban Native organizations try to provide access to both. There is a logic to this that should be clear to the reader by now. There is also a logic to integrating the services of traditional providers into the services of the health psychologist, when feasible, though it is important to remember that some Native people are resistant to and even fearful of traditional services so it is important to check out client preferences.

EMPIRICAL KNOWLEDGE AND RESEARCH

When possible, empirical knowledge should be taken into account when designing programs (May, 1994). This is often challenging, given the limited number of studies conducted on Native populations and the heterogeneity among communities. A conference on cancer in Native Americans addressed several areas which need the attention of further research studies. The areas were defined as (1) the need to determine similarities and differences among communities, (2) the need to determine the similarities and differences between Native Americans and European Americans, (3) the need to identify what is known in terms of research with Native Americans, (4) the need to address problems of developing culturally sensitive strategies, (5) the need to address prevention strategies, (6) the need to identify major research gaps, and (7) the need to determine research priorities and directions (Joe & Justice, 1992).

BEHAVIORAL STRATEGIES

In regard to theoretical orientations, Renfrey (1992) has argued that a cognitive–behavioral framework is a convenient vehicle with which to render individual and community-based interventions. Behavioral approaches to health promotion have yielded some positive results within Native communities. For example, using behavioral strategies, such as imparting knowledge about a given topic, providing training in problem-solving related to the topic, and improving communication skills, led to fewer problems with unplanned pregnancy, substance abuse, and psychological stress among Native American adolescents (Schinke, Schilling, Palleja, & Zayas, 1987). However, the cultural myopia of the cognitive–behavioral field may prevent it from realizing its potential in this area. Differences in Native values, beliefs, communication styles, and problem-solving approaches may lead to resistance in completing homework assignments, behavioral contracting, and other such behavioral approaches. Special care must be taken to ensure personal ownership of the proposed behavioral strategies to reduce the probability of shaming and failure's becoming part of the therapeutic experience and to avoid further erosion of cultural values and strengths. The professional who does use a cognitive–behavioral approach should strive to employ it with sophistication and finesse. For example, Bobo, Gilchrist, Cvetkovich, Trimble, and Schinke (1988) developed a culturally sensitive skills enhancement program for the prevention of substance abuse among Native American adolescents in the Pacific Northwest. They gained community acceptance and improved substance-abuse knowledge and skills to manage peer pressure.

Although, a problem-solving, solution-based approach is generally recommended with Native American populations, a Jungian framework is more congruent with the nature of Aboriginal understandings and teachings (cf. Duran & Duran, 1995). More important than the theoretical underpinnings of a community intervention are the congruence of the intervention itself with community beliefs, values, and preferences and the sensitivity with which it is implemented. When we approach health from a Native perspective, we recognize that physical illness is a result of being out of balance in the world and it offers a valuable teaching opportunity in which we must learn to achieve greater harmony with ourselves and the world. From a Native perspective, illness is not just about the individual; it is about "all our relations," including the plant, animal, human, and spirit people. An elder in California stated, "When we dirty the water, we cause our children to give birth to deformed babies. We must understand the importance of our mother earth to our own health if we are to survive as a people." In a Native American community in California, a group of Native people came together and created a vision for the future generations. In that vision, the following message was stated: "We need to show more love to our family members— children and spouses—and teach them our way of life. Teach them to respect our mother earth, the land, the water, and everything that is upon the earth. We need to teach them our Native language, who they are. We need to teach them our traditional ways of life so that they can carry them on and pass them down to their children, and so forth, generation after generation." This vision was symbolically beaded into a quilt, which is hung in the reservation clinic (Dionne, 1997). This vision signifies the importance of honoring the Native culture for its intrinsic wisdom in achieving health and balance. In this vision is the understanding that illness is a much more encompassing concept than a mere incapacity due to infection, injury, inheritance, or indulgence. Instead, the concept of the relationship between human beings and the universe (Mail, McKay, & Katz, 1989) is emphasized. This understanding is critical for the health psychologist who is working with Native people. To be successful in serving Native communities, we consider it important to adopt an ethno-medical understanding (Mail et al., 1989) in which Native conceptualizations of illness and health are understood and addressed and the strengths within the community are identified and utilized.

Lastly, it is critical to emphasize harm reduction for professionals coming into Native communities. At an Indian Psychology conference, an elder, Art Blue (1997), stated, "The most important principle in working within Indian communities is to DO NO HARM." Brownlee (1978) identified some questions that help to utilize the community's strengths and determine the impact of interventions within the community. The following questions are recommended for the health professional to consider in working within Native communities:

- What beliefs and practices in the health area are beneficial to health? Are harmful to health? Should harmful beliefs and practices be changed?
- What are the functions of various health beliefs and practices? How are various beliefs and practices linked to one another? What meaning do they have to those who practice them? Do the individual beliefs and practices link together to form a meaningful whole?
- Are suggestions for changes of certain health beliefs and practices realistic, considering the total situation? What effects or repercussions may certain changes in health beliefs and practices have on other areas of life?
- When posing changes in health beliefs and practices, is it possible to develop innovations that fit in easily with the existing culture? Emphasize continuity with old traditions?

Consideration of these questions can help guide the practitioner through the difficult but highly rewarding task of serving Native people and their communities.

SUMMARY

In this chapter, we have discussed the diversity of the Aboriginal people of North America, as well as the common ideologies, shared history, and perceptions of illness and health that are common among them. We have briefly addressed some of the ways that the colonization of North America over the past 500 years has decimated Native cultures and some of the ways this has impacted health-related behaviors. We have argued that the cultural and sociopolitical differences that often exist between the dominant culture and Native groups can significantly affect the perception, relevance, and acceptance of behavioral health interventions. This, it is argued, can lead to low utilization and compliance rates and, hence, act to reduce the overall effectiveness of our interventions. We have also discussed some of the critical health issues that many Native groups face that may be addressed by health psychology, as well as many practical issues that can confront the practitioner working with Native people. Finally, a culturally congruent model for health psychologists was outlined, based on the position that effective services will be congruent with the beliefs and values of the people served.

Many of the issues covered in this chapter are more broadly relevant to providing behavioral health services to the culturally and ethnically different, in general. The demand for cultural sensitivity and relevance in our health delivery systems is increasing as we are called upon to provide effective interventions for this country's growing minority populations and for the international community. It is appropriate that health psychologists begin turning their research and professional activities to developing culturally congruent interventions and delivery systems that will address the behavioral health problems of the ethnically and culturally different on their own terms, based on sound, empirical principles.

CASE STUDY

The client, Lilian, was a 47-year-old Aboriginal female referred to one of the authors through a First Nation Health Centre for the assessment and treatment of depression. She presented with depressed mood, sleep onset delays of up to 3 hours, reduced interest in previously enjoyed activities, low energy, and feelings of worthlessness. Lilian had suffered a stroke 9 months earlier that had affected the strength and use of her right limbs but had reportedly left her cognitive faculties intact. At intake, she had not yet made a complete recovery and had not returned to her previous employment. According to her medical records at the Health Centre, she was diagnosed with significant disease of the coronary arteries but had not suffered from an identifiable heart attack. She had high blood pressure that was not being controlled by her regimen of medication, and she was about 25% above her recommended body weight. In addition, Lilian had worked with a dietician and occupational therapist since her stroke, but her progress in losing weight and regaining the strength and use of her limbs was slower than hoped for.

At the start of working with this client, the author took time to develop rapport, talk about general issues on the reserve, and talk about his own background and relationship to the community. Lilian was then invited to share her concerns. After she revealed that she had suffered a stroke and that she was still having difficulties doing things she used to, the author shared general information about the common effects of stroke, the challenges of recovery, and the ways in which a stroke might affect a person's lifestyle and

mood. She acknowledged that the stroke had affected her lifestyle in many
of the ways presented, but she stated, "I'll just have to manage it. It happened and there's no sense in getting upset about it." It was not until our second session that she began to talk more openly about how her stroke had affected her at a deeper, emotional level. During the initial session, the author
also asked Lilian about what her physicians and other health care providers
had done for her and what regimens they had prescribed. Further, she was
asked which of these she found to be helpful and which not. This was rather
impersonal information and proved to be easy for Lilian to talk about.

It became evident that Lilian was not adhering to the health care plans
developed for her. She did not take her medications as prescribed: she took
her anticoagulant medication per instructions, took her blood pressure medications only as she felt she might need them, and had ceased taking a prescribed antidepressant. She made a few temporary changes to her diet to reduce fat and salt, but had largely reverted back to her old diet. Lilian also
began a course of occupational therapy but suspended it because she did not
feel it was helping her. She was asked about other health-related habits and
she acknowledged that she had a drinking problem at one time but only
drank two or three times per month since her stroke. When she did drink,
however, she would do so to intoxication. She also stated that she smoked
cigarettes for over 20 years but had quit completely about 8 years earlier.
When asked about using traditional medicines or ceremonies for her condition, she stated that friends and relatives had suggested she see a traditional
healer and that she had declined. Lilian is nontraditional and tends to avoid
ancestral ceremonies and medicines. Finally, Lilian's own beliefs about why
the stroke occurred were explored. She stated that she wasn't yet sure but
thought that it might have been something she had done, though she wasn't
sure what that might be, or that it might have been something in the water
or food. Later, during our sixth session, she alluded to the possibility that
someone might have put it on her, referring to the possibility that it was the
result of bad medicine.

Regarding Lilian's history, she and her three siblings and four half-
siblings were raised on her mother's Central Ontario First Nation reserve
and were enrolled members of that community. Her mother was Ojibwa and
her father was Odawa from another First Nation. She and her three siblings
had full-blood quantum, while her half-siblings had 3/4-blood quantum.
Until his death when Lilian was 10 years of age, her father was absent from
home for long periods because his seasonal employment in fishing, timber-
cutting, and hunting took him away for weeks at a time. When Lilian's father was home, he and her mother would often fight and become embroiled
in alcohol-related violence. At other times, her mother was often absent from
the home for three or four days at a time. Lilian was the second oldest child
and the oldest daughter and was compelled to assume many parental
responsibilities from about age 8 years on. She also reported a history of
sexual abuse by several relatives, from age 5 to 11 years.

The client had her first child at 17 years of age but the child's father took
no responsibility in the child-rearing. This is about the same age at which
she began to smoke cigarettes and abuse alcohol several times per month.

From age 17 years to 32, she had a total of 3 children and, at the time of intake, had 5 grandchildren. She was in a relationship of 6 years at intake to a nonnative man who was 6 years her junior. She had supported herself and her children through various unskilled jobs over the years. She lived on the reserve with her partner, her 20-year-old son, and his partner and 2 children, and her own 15-year-old daughter. Lilian had been the only household member with steady employment until she suffered her stroke and had not been able to return to work. Although she received a regular disability payment, financial concerns were a source of stress for her, as were conflicts with her partner and the impact of living in overcrowded conditions.

The client was seen by the author for 12 hours over 10 sessions. Central to our work was a culturally congruent cognitive–behavioral treatment for depression, which integrated traditional values and beliefs and elements of a few of the "old stories." Concurrent with this, the client was encouraged to reexamine her self-care choices and nonintrusive psycho-education was employed. The latter took the form of sharing relevant information with the client and allowing her to extract her own meaning and applications from it. It also included more direct information about how medications and her other health care plans work and why consistency is important.

Regarding Lilian's health care choices, it seemed that her inconsistency in taking her prescribed medication resulted from a combination of not appreciating the importance of consistency, of not trusting the effects of some of the medications, and of experiencing side effects. To address this, Lilian's sovereignty to choose what medications she would use and not use was validated, but she was apprised of the importance of informing her physician of any side effects experienced or any planned changes in her regimen ahead of time. She expressed a reluctance to bring this up with her physician and exploration suggested that her physician tended to tell her in no uncertain terms what medication she needed to take and how often. Accordingly, she felt rather controlled and intimidated by him. Brief work was done with her to help her to understand communication-style differences and to generate ways of handling herself with her physician and other health care providers. This proved useful because she was able to discuss her medication concerns with her physician and by the end of our work, she was compliant with an altered regimen. It also became evident that she found the approach taken by her occupational therapist to be too blunt in telling her what she should and shouldn't do. The author consulted with her therapist and Lilian was subsequently able to return to her therapy. Regarding her dietary changes, Lilian's dietician was experienced with Aboriginal clients and her approach with Lilian was very appropriate. It appears, however, that her family tended to complain about dietary changes and were generally unsupportive of them. Lilian and her partner took much of the responsibility for meal preparation in the home and neither had the patience to prepare two types of meals. Accordingly, her reduced fat and salt diet was not adhered to after a few weeks of trying it. This problem proved to be the most difficult to work through but a suggested home visit and session with the family by the dietician did result in some appropriate changes in diet and food preparation habits within the home.

Lilian's depression did show significant improvement over the course of our work. She had tried another antidepressant for a few months but stopped taking it too because of side effects and refused to try another one. It is unclear whether her drinking pattern altered over the time she was seen. She was advised of the damaging effects of excess alcohol consumption on her heart and blood vessels and she did report reducing consumption to one or two drinks per session. This was unconfirmed. Finally, Lilian's beliefs about the cause of her stroke were addressed. Although no belief was challenged, appropriate responses to each possibility were examined and she developed a plan to prevent a subsequent stroke according to each.

At last contact, one year after intake, Lilian's blood pressure had stabilized, her weight was within 10% of recommendation, and she had made continued progress in recovery from her stroke. She was reportedly looking to return to work.

1. How might Lilian's birth order and early experiences have influenced her behavior and choices, to the detriment of her physical and emotional health?

2. How might Lilian's cultural background, particularly regarding her values and world-view, have influenced her adherence to the recommendations from her health care providers and contributed to her sources of stress?

3. With hindsight, if you were charged with coordinating Lilian's health care immediately after her stroke, what approach(es) might you have taken?

SUGGESTED READINGS

Brown, D. (1970). *Bury my heart at Wounded Knee: An Indian history of the American West.* New York: Holt, Rinehart and Winston.

Duran, E., & Duran, B. (1995). *Native American postcolonial psychology.* Albany, NY: SUNY Press.

Frank, J. D. (1973). *Persuasion and healing: A comparative study of psychotherapy.* Baltimore, MD: Johns Hopkins University Press.

LaFromboise, T. D., & Howard-Pitney, B. (1995). The Zuni life skills development curriculum: Description and evaluation of a suicide prevention program. *Journal of Counseling Psychology, 42,* 479–486.

LaFromboise, T. D., & Rowe, W. (1983). Skills training for bicultural competence: Rationale and application. *Journal of Counseling Psychology, 30,* 589–595.

Ross, R. (1992). *Dancing with a ghost: Exploring Indian reality.* Toronto, ON: McClelland & Stewart.

Schinke, S. P., Orlandi, M. A., Botvin, G. J., Gilchrist, L. D., Trimble, J. E., & Locklear, V. S. (1988). Preventing substance abuse among American Indian adolescents: A bicultural competence skills approach. *Journal of Counseling Psychology, 35,* 87–90.

REFERENCES

Attneave, C. L. (1974). Medicine men and psychiatrists in the Indian health service. *Psychiatric Annals, 4,* 49–55.

Attneave, C. L. (1982). American Indians and Alaska Native families: Emigrants in their own homeland. In M. McGoldrick, J. K. Pearce, & J. Giordano (Eds.), *Ethnicity and family therapy* (pp. 55–83). New York: Guilford.

Attneave, C. L. (1985). Practical counseling with Native American Indian and Alaska Native clients. In P. Pedersen (Ed.), *Handbook of cross-cultural counseling & therapy* (pp. 135–140). Westport, CT: Greenwood Press.

Bachman, J., Wallace, J., O'Malley, P., Johnston, L., Kurth, C., & Neighbors, H. (1991). Racial/ethnic differences in smoking, drinking and illicit drug use among high school seniors. *American Journal of Public Health, 81,* 372–377.

Barter, E. R., & Barter, J. T. (1974). Urban Indians and mental health problems. *Psychiatric Annals, 4,* 37–43.

Bergman, R. (1973). Navajo medicine and psychoanalysis. *Human Behavior, 2,* 8–15.

Blue, A. (1997). *Talk given at the Society for Indian Psychologists.* Logan, UT.

Bobo, J. K., Gilchrist, L. D., Cvetkovich, G. T., Trimble, J. E., & Schinke, S. P. (1988). Cross cultural service delivery to minority communities. *Journal of Community Psychology, 16,* 263–272.

Braga, B., & Moore, R. D. (1996). *Star Trek: First contact.* Paramount Pictures.

Brown, D. (1970). *Bury my heart at wounded knee: An Indian history of the American West.* New York: Holt, Rinehart and Winston.

Brownalee, A. T. (1978). *Community, culture and care: A cross cultural guide for health workers.* St. Louis, MO: Mosby.

Campos-Outcalt, D., Ellis, J., Aicken, M., Valencia, J., Wunsch, M., & Steele, L. (1995). Prevalence of cardiovascular disease risk factors in a Southwestern Native American tribe. *Public Health Report, 110,* 742–748.

Center for Disease Control (1992). Cigarette smoking among American Indian and Alaskan Natives—Behavioral Risk Factor Surveillance System, 1987–1991. *Morbidity and Mortality Weekly Report, 42,* 861–864.

Champagne, D. (1994). *Native America: Portrait of the peoples.* Detroit, MI: Visible Ink Press.

Christie, L., & Halpern, J. M. (1990). Temporal constructs and Inuit mental health. *Social Sciences and Medicine, 30,* 739–749.

College of Psychologists of Ontario (1993). *Applying for registration as a psychologist.* Toronto, ON: Author.

Cooley, C. R. (1977). Cultural effects in Indian education: An application of social learning theory. *Journal of American Indian Education, 17,* 21–27.

Dauphinais, P., Dauphinais, L., & Rowe, W. (1981). Effects of race and communication style on Indian perceptions of counselor effectiveness. *Counselor Education and Supervision, 21,* 72–80.

Delgado, M. (1979). Therapy Latino style: Implications for psychiatric care. *Perspectives in Psychiatric Care, 17,* 107–115.

Diaz-Guerrero, R. (1984). Behavioral health across cultures. In J. D. Matarazzo, S. M. Weiss, J. A. Herd, & S. M. Weiss (Eds.), *Behavioral health: A handbook of health enhancement and disease prevention* (pp. 164–178). New York: Wiley.

Dinges, N. G., Trimble, J., Manson, S., & Pasquale, I. (1981). Counseling and psychotherapy with American Indians and Alaska Natives. In A. J. Marsella & P. Pedersen (Eds.), *Cross-cultural counseling and psychotherapy* (pp. 243–276). Elmsford, NY: Pergamon.

Dionne, R. (1997). *The beading circle.* Torres Martinez Reservation.

Dobyns, H. F. (1983). *Their number become thinned.* Knoxville, TN: University of Tennessee Press.

Dozier, E. P. (1966). Problem drinking among American Indians: The role of sociocultural deprivation. *Quarterly Journal of Studies on Alcohol, 27,* 72–87.

Driver, H. E. (1969). *Indians of North America* (2nd ed., revised). Chicago, IL: University of Chicago Press.

Duran, E., & Duran, B. (1995). *Native American postcolonial psychology.* Albany, NY: SUNY Press.

Foster, D. (June 22, 1997). Tenth Annual Convention of American Indian Psychologists and Graduate Students, Logan, UT. Personal communication.

Frank, J. D. (1973). *Persuasion and healing: A comparative study of psychotherapy.* Baltimore, MD: Johns Hopkins University Press.

French, L. (1989). Native American alcoholism: A transcultural counseling perspective. *Counseling Psychology Quarterly, 2,* 153–166.

Gilchrist, L. D., Schinke, S. P., Trimble, J. E., & Cvetkovich, G. T. (1987). Skills enhancement to prevent substance abuse among American Indian adolescents. *International Journal of Addictions, 22,* 869–879.

Goldstein, G. S. (1974). The model dormitory. *Psychiatric Annals, 4,* 85–92.

Grossman, D. C., Krieger, J. W., Sugarman, J. R. & Forguera, R. A. (1994). Health status of urban Indians and Alaska Natives: A population based study. *Journal of the American Medical Association, 2,* 845–850.

Hall, E. T. (1976). *Beyond culture.* New York: Anchor Press.

Harris, M. B., Davis, S. M., Ford, V. L., & Tso, H. (1988). The checkerboard cardiovascular curriculum: A culturally oriented program. *Journal of School Health, 58,* 104–107.

Havas, S., Fujimoto, W., Close, N., McCarter, R., Keller, J., & Sherwin, R. (1996). The NHLBI Workshop on Hypertension in Hispanic Americans, Native Americans, and Asian/Pacific Islander Americans. *Public Health Reports, 3,* 451–458.

Health, G. W., Wilson, R. H., Smith, J., & Leonard, B. E. (1987). Community based exercise and weight control—Diabetes risk reduction and glycemic control in Zuni Indians. *American Journal of Clinical Nutrition, 53,* S1642–S1644.

Herring, R. D. (1990). Understanding Native-American values: Process and content concerns for counselors. *Counseling and Values, 34,* 134–137.

Hippler, A. E. (1975). Thawing out some magic. *Mental Hygiene, 59,* 20–24.

Ho, M. K. (1987). *Family therapy with ethnic minorities.* Beverly Hills, CA: Sage.

Hodgkenson, H. L. (1990). *The demographics of American Indians: One percent of the people; Fifty percent of the diversity.* Washington, DC: Institute for Educational Leadership, Inc., Center for Demographic Policy.

Holden, G. W., Botvin, G. J., & Orlandi, M. A. (1989). American Indian youth and substance abuse: Tobacco use problems, risk factors, and preventive interventions. *Health Education Research, 4,* 137–144.

Horejsi, C., Craig, B. H. R., & Pablo, J. (1992). Reactions by Native American parents to child protection agencies: Cultural and community factors. *Child Welfare League of America, 71,* 329–342.

Hoy, W., Light, A., & Megill, D. (1995). Cardiovascular disease in Navajo Indians with Type 2 diabetes. *Public Health Report, 110,* 87–93.

Joe, J. R., & Justice, J. W. (1992). Introduction: Proceedings of the first national conference on cancer in Native Americans. *American Indian Culture and Research Journal, 16,* 9–20.

Jilek, W. (1974). Indian healing power: Indigenous therapeutic practices in the Pacific Northwest. *Psychiatric Annals, 4,* 13–21.

Jilek, W., & Todd, N. (1974). Witchdoctors succeed where doctors fail: Psychotherapy among Coast Salish Indians. *Canadian Psychiatric Association Journal, 19,* 351–356.

Kimball, E. H., Goldberg, H. I., & Oberle, M. W. (1996). The prevelence of selected risk factors for chronic disease among American Indians in Washington state. *Public Health Reports, 3,* 264–271.

Kleinfeld, J., & Bloom, J. (1977). Boarding schools: Effects on the mental health of Eskimo adolescents. *American Journal of Psychiatry, 134,* 411–417.

Knowler, W. C., Pettitt, D. J., Saad, M. F., Charles, M. A., Nelson, R. G., Howard, B. V., Bogardus, C., & Bennett, P. H. (1991). Obesity in the Pima Indians: Its relationship and magnitude with diabetes. *American Journal of Clinical Nutrition, 53,* S1543–S1551.

LaFromboise, T. D. (1988). American Indian mental health policy. *American Psychologist, 43,* 388–397.

LaFromboise, T. D. (1992). *American Indian life skills development curriculum.* Madison, WI: University of Wisconsin Press.

LaFromboise, T. D., & Howard-Pitney, B. (1995). The Zuni life skills development curriculum: Description and evaluation of a suicide prevention program. *Journal of Counseling Psychology, 42,* 479–486.

LaFromboise, T. D., Trimble, J. E., & Mohatt, G. V. (1990). Counseling intervention and American Indian tradition: An integrative approach. *The Counseling Psychologist, 18,* 628–654.

Lawson, J. (1937). *History of North Carolina (1714).* Durham, NC: Garret and Massie.

Leighton, A. H., & Hughes, J. H. (1961). Cultures as causative of mental disorder. In A. H. Leighton & J. H. Hughes (Eds.), *Roundtable on causes of mental disorders: A review of epidemiological knowledge* (pp. 341–383). New York: Milbank Memorial Fund.

LeMaster, & McConnell, C. M. (1994). Health education interventions among Native Americans: A review and analysis. *Health Education Quarterly, 2,* 521–538.

Levine, S., & Lurie, N. O. (1970). *The American Indian today.* Baltimore, MD: Penguin.

Lewis, R. G. (1982). Alcohol and the Native American: A review of the literature. In National Institute on Alcohol Abuse and Alcoholism (Ed.), *Alcohol and health monograph 4: Special population issues* (pp. 315–328). Washington, DC: U.S. Government Printing Office.

Mail, P. D. (1989). American Indians, stress, and alcohol. *American Indian and Alaska Native Mental Health Research, 3,* 7–26.

Mail, P. D., McKay, R. B., & Katz, M. (1989). Expanding practice horizons: Learning from American Indian patients. *Patient Education and Counselling, 13,* 91–102.

Manson, S. M. (Ed.). (1982). *Topics in American Indian mental health prevention.* Portland, OR: Oregon Health Sciences University Press.

Manson, S. M., & Trimble, J. E. (1982). American Indian and Alaska Native communities: Past efforts, future inquiries. In L. R. Snowden (Ed.), *Reaching the underserved: Mental health needs of neglected populations* (pp. 143–163). Beverly Hills, CA: Sage.

Matarazzo, J. D. (1980). Behavioral health and behavioral medicine: Frontiers for a new health psychology. *American Psychologist, 35,* 807–817.

May, P. A. (1994). The epidemiology of alcohol abuse among American Indian: The mythical and real properties. *American Indian Culture and Research Journal, 18,* 121–143.

May, P. A., & Dizmang, L. H. (1974). Suicide and the American Indian. *Psychiatric Annals, 4,* 22–28.

May, P. A., & Hymbaugh, K. J. (1989). A macrolevel fetal alcohol syndrome prevention program for Native Americans and Alaska Natives: Description and evaluation. *Journal of the Studies of Alcohol, 50,* 508–518.

Mayne, T., & Sayette, M. (1990). *Insiders guide to graduate programs in clinical psychology: 1990/1991.* New York: Guilford.

Nutting, P. A., Freeman, W. L., Risser, E. R., Helgerson, S. D., Paisano, R., Hisnanick, J., Beaver, S. K., Peters, I., Carney, J. P., & Speers, M. A. (1993). Cancer incidence among American Indians and Alaska Natives, 1980–1987. *American Journal of Public Health, 83,* 1589–1598.

Parker, L. (1990). The missing component in substance abuse prevention efforts: A Native American example. *Contemporary Drug Problems, 17,* 251–270.

Pego, C. M., Hill, R. F., Solomon, G. W., Chisholm, R. M., & Ivey, S. E. (1995). Tobacco, culture, and health among American Indians: A historical review. *American Indian Culture and Research Journal, 19,* 143–164.

Prieto, D. O. (1989). Native Americans in medicine: The need for Indian healers. *Academic Medicine, 64,* 388–389.

Rappaport, H., & Rappaport, M. (1981). The integration of scientific and traditional healing. *American Psychologist, 36,* 774–781.

Renfrey, G. S. (1992). Cognitive–behavior therapy and the Native American client. *Behavior Therapy, 23,* 321–340.

Rhoades, E. R. (1996). American Indians and Alaska Natives—Overview of the population. *Public Health Reports, 3,* 49–50.

Schinke, S. P., Moncher, M. S., Holden, G. W., Botvin, G. J., & Orlandi, M. A. (1989). American Indian youth and substance abuse: Tobacco use problems, risk factors and preventive interventions. Special Issue: Smoking. *Health Education Research, 4,* 137–144.

Schinke, S. P., Orlandi, M. A., Botvin, G. J., Gilchrist, L. D., Trimble, J. E., & Locklear, V. S. (1988). Preventing substance abuse among American Indian adolescents: A bicultural competence skills approach. *Journal of Counseling Psychology, 35,* 87–90.

Schinke, S. P., Orlandi, M. A., Schilling, R. F., Botvin, G. J., Gilchrist, L. D., & Landers, C. (1990). Tobacco use by Native Indian and Alaska Native people: Risks, psychosocial factors, and preventive intervention. *Journal of Alcohol & Drug Education, 35,* 1–11.

Schinke, S. P., Schilling, R. F., Gilchrist, L. D., Ashby, M. R., & Katajima, E. (1987). Pacific Northwest Native American youth and smokeless tobacco use. *International Journal of Addiction, 22,* 881–884.

Schinke, S. P., Schilling, R. F., Palleja, J., & Zayas, L. H. (1987). Prevention research among ethnic–racial minority group adolescents. *Behavior Therapist, 10,* 151–155.

Shore, J. H. (1974). Psychiatric epidemiology among American Indians. *Psychiatric Annals, 4,* 56–66.

Spang, A. (1965). Counseling the Indian. *Journal of American Indian Education, 5,* 10–15.

Sue, D. W. (1990). Culture-specific strategies in counseling: A conceptual framework. *Professional Psychology: Review and Practice, 21,* 424–433.

Sue, D. W., & Sue, D. (1977). Barriers to effective cross-cultural counseling. *Journal of Counseling Psychology, 24,* 420–429.

Sue, S. (1977). Community mental health services to minority groups: Some optimism, some pessimism. *American Psychologist, 32,* 616–624.

Sue, S., Allen, D. B., & Conaway, L. (1978). The responsiveness and equality of mental health care to Chicanos and Native Americans. *American Journal of Community Psychology, 6,* 137–146.

Sugarman, J. R., Hickley, M., Hall, T., & Gohdes, P. (1990). Prevalence of diagnosed hypertension among diabetic Navajo Indians: The changing epidemiology of diabetes mellitus among Navajo Indians. *Western Journal of Medical Science, 153,* 140–145.

Swinomish Tribal Mental Health Project (1991). *A gathering of wisdoms—Tribal mental health: A cultural perspective.* La Conner, WA: Swinomish Tribal Community.

Szapocznik, J., Scopetta, M. A., & King, O. E. (1978). Theory and practice in matching treatment to the special characteristics and problems of Cuban immigrants. *Journal of Community Psychology, 6,* 112–122.

Tafoya, T. (1981). Dancing with Dash-Kayah: The mask of the cannibal woman. *Parabola, 6,* 6–11.

Tafoya, T. (1989). Circles and cedar: Native Americans and family therapy. *Journal of Psychotherapy and the Family, 6,* 71–98.

Tefft, S. K. (1967). Anomy, values, and cultural change among teen-age Indians: An exploration. *Sociology of Education, 40,* 145–157.

Thompson, J. W., Walker, R. D., & Silk-Walker, P. (1993). Psychiatric care of American Indian and Alaska Natives. In A. C. Gaw (Ed.), *Culture, ethnicity, and mental illness* (pp. 189–243). Washington, DC: American Psychiatric Press.

Trimble, J. E. (1981). Value differentials and their importance in counseling American Indians. In P. Pedersen, J. Draguns, W. Lonner, & J. Trimble (Eds.), *Counseling across cultures* (pp. 203–226). Honolulu, HI: University of Hawaii Press.

Trimble, J. E. (1990). Application of psychological knowledge for American Indians and Alaska Natives. *Journal of Training & Practice in Professional Psychology, 4,* 45–63.

Trimble, J. E., & Hayes, S. A. (1984). Mental health intervention in the psychosocial contexts of American Indian communities. In W. A. O'Connor & B. Lubin (Eds.), *Ecological approaches to clinical and community psychology* (pp. 293–321). New York: Wiley.

Vogel, V. J. (1970) *American Indian medicine.* OK: University of Oklahoma Press.

Vogel, V. J. (1972). *This country was ours: A documentary history of the American Indian.* New York: Harper & Row.

Wallace, A. F. C. (1958). Dreams and wishes of the soul: A type of psychoanalytic theory among the seventeenth century Iroquois. *American Anthropologist, 60,* 234–248.

Weibel, J. C. (1982). American Indians, urbanization, and alcohol: A developing urban Indian drinking ethos. In National Institute on Alcohol Abuse and Alcoholism (Ed.), *Alcohol and Health Monograph 4: Special Population Issues* (pp. 315–328). Washington, DC: U.S. Government Printing Office.

Weisner, T., Weibel-Orlando, J. C., & Long, J. (1984). Serious drinking, white man's drinking, and teetotaling: Drinking levels and styles in urban American Indian populations. *Journal of Studies on Alcohol, 45,* 237–250.

Welte, J. W., & Barnes, G. M. (1987). Alcohol use among adolescent minority groups. *Journal of Studies on Alcohol, 48,* 328–336.

Westermeyer, J. (1974). "The drunken Indian": Myths and realities. *Psychiatric Annals, 4,* 29–36.

Zimmet, P. Z. (1992). Challenges in diabetes epidemiology—From West to the rest. Kelly West Lecture, 1991. *Diabetes Care, 15,* 232–299.

APPENDIX

Native American/Canadian Cultural Identity and Expression Scale

Prepared by George S. Renfrey

Purpose: As a Native Canadian (North American Indian), your cultural identity and how you express it may have several meanings for you, and you may belong to more than one ethnic/cultural group. The following questions are designed to examine variations in Native cultural identity and expression.

Directions: The scale will take you about 10 minutes to complete. Please answer all of the questions, keeping in mind that there are no right or wrong answers. What is important is how you **really** feel, not how you think you **should** feel. For each item, simply circle the number that best describes how much you agree or disagree with the statement, using the scale below [1 (*strongly agree*) to 5 (*strongly disagree*)]. If you have trouble selecting an answer, your first impression may be your best guide.

1: Strongly Disagree   2: Disagree   3: Neutral
4: Agree   5: Strongly Agree

1. My identity as Native (North American Indian) is very important to me 1 2 3 4 5

2. My identity as a member of the dominant culture is very important to me 1 2 3 4 5

3. I identify with and value characteristics of several cultures 1 2 3 4 5

4. I fit well within my Native culture 1 2 3 4 5

5. Though I have much to learn, I am comfortable with my knowledge of Native traditions. 1 2 3 4 5

6. I fit well within the dominant culture 1 2 3 4 5

7. I have learned what I need to live in the dominant culture . 1 2 3 4 5

8. I feel firm and confident in my ethnic/cultural identity. . . . 1 2 3 4 5

9. I sometimes feel confused about my cultural identity. 1 2 3 4 5

10. It is important for Native children to learn of their culture and traditions 1 2 3 4 5

11. Taking part in Native cultural/community events is important to me 1 2 3 4 5

12. I hope to always live and work where I can be part of a
    Native community 1 2 3 4 5

13. I am strongly committed to my Native traditions. 1 2 3 4 5

14. Participating in social/cultural/sporting events of the
    dominant culture is important to me. 1 2 3 4 5

15. I strive to be a success in the dominant culture 1 2 3 4 5

16. I have felt singled out or treated unfairly at times because
    I am Native 1 2 3 4 5

17. I sometimes feel conflicted about my values and actions
    within my traditional Native culture. 1 2 3 4 5

18. I sometimes feel conflicted about my values and actions
    within the dominant culture. 1 2 3 4 5

19. Participating in traditional Native ceremonies is important
    to me. 1 2 3 4 5

20. My traditional Native spiritual teachings are important
    to me. 1 2 3 4 5

21. If I had a health problem I might seek the help of a
    Native medicine person. 1 2 3 4 5

22. When I die, I want a traditional Native burial ceremony . . 1 2 3 4 5

23. Participating in the spiritual services of the dominant
    culture (e.g., Christian) is important to me 1 2 3 4 5

24. The spiritual teachings of the dominant culture (e.g.,
    Christianity) are important to me. 1 2 3 4 5

25. For a health problem, I would only seek the help of a
    recognized medical professional. 1 2 3 4 5

26. When I die, I want a dominant culture burial (e.g.,
    Christian). 1 2 3 4 5

27. I follow spiritual teachings that are neither traditional–
    Native nor of the dominant culture. 1 2 3 4 5

28. My aunts, uncles, and grandparents played an important
    part in my upbringing. 1 2 3 4 5

29. I seek input from my relatives or Native elders when I
    have problems or make major decisions 1 2 3 4 5

30. Most of my friends are Native. 1 2 3 4 5

31. Wealth is best measured by what you have given others. . . 1 2 3 4 5

32. I believe children should be raised within an extended family 1 2 3 4 5

33. If I were to marry (or marry again), I would prefer a traditional Native ceremony 1 2 3 4 5

34. I was raised by my parents/guardians without much influence from other relatives. 1 2 3 4 5

35. Most of my friends are non-Native. 1 2 3 4 5

36. Acquiring money and personal possessions is important to me. 1 2 3 4 5

37. The ideal family consists of parents and their children. . . . 1 2 3 4 5

38. If I were to marry (or marry again), I would want a dominant culture ceremony 1 2 3 4 5

39. Learning and using my traditional Native language is important to me 1 2 3 4 5

40. Please rate your fluency in the following languages (1=None to 5=Fluent)

 a. Traditional Native language 1 2 3 4 5

 b. English 1 2 3 4 5

 c. Other [Specify: _____] 1 2 3 4 5

41. How much do you think in the following languages (1=None to 5=Almost all of the time)

 a. Traditional Native language 1 2 3 4 5

 b. English 1 2 3 4 5

 c. Other [Specify: _____] 1 2 3 4 5

If you are also a member of a non-Native minority group (e.g., Hispanic or Asian Canadian), please answer the following questions; otherwise, skip to the demographics section below.

42. My identity as another (non-Native) minority person is very important to me. 1 2 3 4 5

43. I fit well within another (non-Native) minority culture. . . . 1 2 3 4 5

44. I have learned what I need to live in another (non-Native) minority culture 1 2 3 4 5

45. Participating in the social/cultural/sporting events of another minority culture is important to me 1 2 3 4 5

46. I strive to be an accepted member of another (non-Native) minority culture 1 2 3 4 5

Demographics

A. Gender: Male _____ Female _____.
B. Age: ___.
C. Do you live ON _____ or OFF _____ a reservation? (please check one).
D. What is the name of the community where you live? _____.
E. How would you describe your ethnic/cultural heritage? (Native, Native &
   European, Native & African, etc.) _____.
F. What is (are) your First Nation affiliation(s)?_____
   _____ Status / Registered? Yes _____ No _____
   _____ Status / Registered? Yes _____ No _____

   Comments: (Is there anything more you would like to share with us?)

Native American/Canadian Cultural Identity and Expression Scale Manual and Scoring Sheet

Prepared by George S. Renfrey

Purpose of Scale Development

The Native American/Canadian Cultural Identity and Expression Scale was designed to assess the status of persons of Native American/Canadian ancestry on key acculturation and deculturation factors. The scale is thought to provide information useful for both research and social/health service delivery. Caution must be used, however, when applying Western standards of what is a normal and desirable lifestyle to the culturally different.

Philosophy of Scale Development

The scale was developed along the philosophy that Native people differ widely in the degree of deculturation from their traditional Native cultures and the degree of acculturation to the European culture that dominates much of North America. It was constructed in recognition that interactions between these two factors account for many problems that Native people face. Though much has been said of the failure of indigenous people to adapt to Western culture, it is recognized here that the desire of Native people to adapt as such varies widely, and that the loss of traditional ways of being may well create at least as many problems. Accordingly, the present scale attempts to assess both desired and realized levels of adaptation to both cultures. To this end, perceptions of cultural striving, competence, and comfort are assessed. Also, questions relating to language competence, spirituality, and family values provide a collateral assessment. It is also recognized that most Native people are of mixed ancestry and that sometimes the success of their adaptation to another minority culture may affect overall well-being. Accordingly, separate items are provided to help determine the level of desired and realized adaptation to another minority culture. Subscales are provided to assess the perceived level of cultural integration, identity lucidity or confusion, and cultural conflict. Within the scale, the term "Native" is used in place of "Native Canadian" or "North American Indian" to reflect the most common usage by Native people.

Administration

The scale is a self-report measure and should be completed in a quiet setting without distractions or time pressure. The scale is self-explanatory and most items are Likert-like. It can be administered individually, in groups, through one-to-one interactions, or through mailings. It may be helpful, when possible, to provide the instructions with examples on a one-to-one basis and to be available to troubleshoot problems if they arise.

Scoring and Interpretation

The completed scale can be scanned for key items according to the intent of the administrator. It is recommended, however, that the provided scoring scheme be used to realize the full potential of the scale. Item scanning is recommended to aid interpretation. The provided scheme combines thematically related questions (e.g., language competence), though administrators are free to formulate combinations to reflect their own notions. The scale is scored by simply totaling the endorsed scores for clustered items. These raw scores can be used as is, averaged, or can be entered into the provided template for a visual representation. The template is scaled, thereby providing a visual average, and allows direct comparisons of complementary themes (e.g., commitment to traditional versus dominant versus other minority cultures). Where the themes might apply to another minority culture (e.g., identity importance), a three-scale figure is provided, with both Native Canadian and the other minority culture placed to contrast the dominant culture,

Item Clusters

The Likert-like questions that make up the Native American/Canadian Cultural Identity and Expression Scale are clustered below according to broad themes (e.g., Personal Identification) and more specific themes (e.g., identification as Native). The purpose of each specific theme is stated.

A. Personal Identification

a. To assess the degree of personal identification as Native Canadian.
   1. My identity as Native (North American Indian) is very important to me.
b. To assess degree of identification with dominant culture.
   2. My identity as a member of the dominant culture is very important to me.
c. To assess degree of personal identification as another, non-Native minority.
   42. My identity as another (non-Native) minority person is very important to me.

B. Cultural Confidence and Comfort

a. To assess the perceived competence and comfort with Native culture.
   4. I fit well within my Native culture.
   5. Though I have much to learn, I am comfortable with my knowledge of Native traditions.
b. To assess perceived competence and comfort with the dominant culture.
   6. I fit well within the dominant culture.
   7. I have learned what I need to live in the dominant culture.
c. To assess perceived competence and comfort with another minority culture.

43. I fit well within another (non-Native) minority culture.
44. I have learned what I need to live in another (non-Native) minority culture.

C. Cultural Commitment

a. To assess degree of commitment to following/preserving Native traditions.
   10. It is important for Native children to learn of their culture and traditions.
   11. Taking part in Native cultural/community events is important to me.
   12. I hope to always live and work where I can be part of a Native community.
   13. I am strongly committed to my Native traditions.
b. To assess degree of commitment to following/fitting into the dominant culture.
   14. Participating in social/cultural/sporting events of the dominant culture is important to me.
   15. I strive to be a success in the dominant culture.
c. To assess degree of commitment to following/fitting into a non-Native minority culture.
   45. Participating in the social/cultural/sporting events of another minority culture is important to me.
   46. I strive to be an accepted member of another (non-Native) minority culture.

D. Spirituality

a. To assess adherence to traditional beliefs.
   19. Participating in traditional Native ceremonies is important to me.
   20. My traditional Native spiritual teachings are important to me.
   21. If I had a health problem, I might seek the help of a Native medicine person.
   22. When I die, I want a traditional Native burial ceremony.
b. To assess adherence to the spiritual traditions of the dominant culture.
   23. Participating in the spiritual services of the dominant culture (e.g., Christian) is important to me.
   24. The spiritual teachings of the dominant culture (e.g., Christianity) are important to me.
   25. For a health problem, I would only seek the help of a recognized medical professional.
   26. When I die, I want a dominant culture burial (e.g., Christian).
c. To assess adherence to other, non-Native and non-dominant spiritual beliefs.
   27. I follow spiritual teachings that are neither traditional-Native nor of the dominant culture.

E. Social/Family Values

a. To assess exposure and adherence to common traditional familial/social values.

    28. My aunts, uncles, and grandparents played an important part in my upbringing.

    29. I seek input from my relatives or Native elders when I have problems or make major decisions.

    30. Most of my friends are Native.

    31. Wealth is best measured by what you have given others.

    32. I believe children should be raised within an extended family.

    33. If I were to marry (or marry again), I would prefer a traditional Native ceremony.

b. To assess exposure and adherence to dominant familial/social values.

    34. I was raised by my parents/guardians without much influence from other relatives.

    35. Most of my friends are non-Native.

    36. Acquiring money and personal possessions is important to me.

    37. The ideal family consists of parents and their children.

    38. If I were to marry (or marry again), I would want a dominant culture ceremony.

F. Language

To assess importance, fluency, and usage of Native language, and the fluency and usage of English and any other language spoken. The latter may be relevant to the adaptation to another minority culture.

    39. Learning and using my traditional Native language is important to me.

    40. Please rate your fluency in the following languages (1=None to 5=Fluent)

a. Traditional Native language _____

b. English _____

c. Other [Specify: _____]

    41. How much do you think in the following languages (1=None to 5=Almost all of the time)

a. Traditional Native language _____

b. English _____

c. Other [Specify: _____]

G. Identity Firmness

a. To assess lucidity or firmness of identity.

    8. I feel firm and confident in my ethnic/cultural identity.

H. Identity Confusion

a. To assess level of identity confusion.
   9. I sometimes feel confused about my cultural identity.

I. Multiculturalism

a. To assess self-perceived multiculturalism, an indication of cultural integration.
   3. I identify with and value characteristics of several cultures.

J. Cultural Conflict

a. To assess perceived cultural conflict.
   16. I have felt singled out or treated unfairly at times because I am Native.
   17. I sometimes feel conflicted about my values and actions within my traditional Native culture.
   18. I sometimes feel conflicted about my values and actions within the dominant culture.

K. Demographics

A. Gender: Male ___ Female____.
C. Age: ___.
C. Do you live ON ___ or OFF ___ a reservation? (please check one).
D. What is the name of the community where you live? _____.
E. How would you describe your ethnic/cultural heritage? (Native, Native and European, Native and African, etc.) _____.
F. What is (are) your First Nation/Tribal affiliation(s)?

_____ Status/Registered? Yes ___ No ___.

_____ Status/Registered? Yes ___ No ___.

NACCIES Scoring

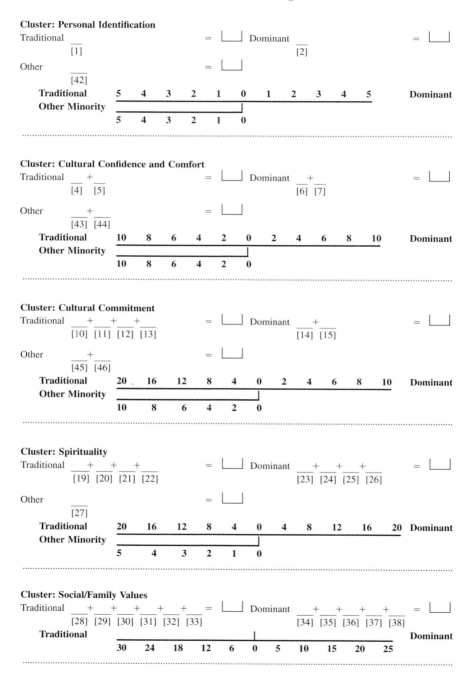

Cluster: Personal Identification

Traktional ___   = ⌊__⌋ Dominant ___   = ⌊__⌋
     [1]   [2]

Other ___   = ⌊__⌋
     [42]

Traditional	5	4	3	2	1	0	1	2	3	4	5	Dominant
Other Minority												
	5	4	3	2	1	0						

Cluster: Cultural Confidence and Comfort

Traditional ___ + ___   = ⌊__⌋ Dominant ___ + ___   = ⌊__⌋
     [4]   [5]   [6]   [7]

Other ___ + ___   = ⌊__⌋
     [43]   [44]

Traditional	10	8	6	4	2	0	2	4	6	8	10	Dominant
Other Minority												
	10	8	6	4	2	0						

Cluster: Cultural Commitment

Traditional ___ + ___ + ___ + ___   = ⌊__⌋ Dominant ___ + ___   = ⌊__⌋
     [10] [11] [12] [13]   [14] [15]

Other ___ + ___   = ⌊__⌋
     [45]   [46]

Traditional	20	16	12	8	4	0	2	4	6	8	10	Dominant
Other Minority												
	10	8	6	4	2	0						

Cluster: Spirituality

Traditional ___ + ___ + ___ + ___   = ⌊__⌋ Dominant ___ + ___ + ___ + ___   = ⌊__⌋
     [19] [20] [21] [22]   [23] [24] [25] [26]

Other ___   = ⌊__⌋
     [27]

Traditional	20	16	12	8	4	0	4	8	12	16	20	Dominant
Other Minority												
	5	4	3	2	1	0						

Cluster: Social/Family Values

Traditional ___ + ___ + ___ + ___ + ___ + ___ = ⌊__⌋ Dominant ___ + ___ + ___ + ___ + ___ = ⌊__⌋
     [28] [29] [30] [31] [32] [33]   [34] [35] [36] [37] [38]

| Traditional | | | | | | | | | | | | Dominant |
| | 30 | 24 | 18 | 12 | 6 | 0 | 5 | 10 | 15 | 20 | 25 | |

Cluster: Language

Native   __ + __ + __   = ⊔   English   __ + __   = ⊔
      [39] [40a] [41a]   [40b] [41b]

Other   __ __   = ⊔
      [40c] [41c]

Traditional	15	12	9	6	3	0	2	4	6	8	10	**Dominant**
Other Minority	10	8	6	4	2	0						

Identity Firmness:

Firmness   __   = ⊔   **Identity Confusion:**   __   = ⊔
     [8]   [9]

Firmness   5   4   3   2   1   0   1   2   3   4   5   **Confusion**

Multiculturalism:

__   = ⊔   0   1   2   3   4   5
[3]

Cultural Conflict:

__ + __ + __   = ⊔   0   3   6   9   12   15
[16] [17] [18]

14

HEALTH BELIEFS AND EXPERIENCES IN ASIAN CULTURES

XINYIN CHEN AND LEORA C. SWARTZMAN

Department of Psychology
The University of Western Ontario
London, Ontario, Canada

Understanding the biological, psychological, and social factors responsible for human health and illness has been an important focus of Asian (particularly Chinese) cultures. Although Asian cultures differ from each other in their emphasis and scope, Confucianism and Taoism play a predominant role in driving the conceptualization of health and medicine, not only in China, but also in many South Asian countries, such as Japan, Korea, Singapore, Indonesia, and Vietnam. An important feature of Chinese culture is that health issues are often interpreted and discussed in a broad context, in terms of their connections with internal emotional functioning and their interactions with social relationships, societal norms and values, and ecological factors. Whereas Taoism is concerned mainly with how one lives in relation to one's natural setting, Confucianism is concerned mainly with how one lives in one's social context.

More specifically, unlike the Western beliefs that we are in control of our own health and are held responsible for our illnesses (i.e., victim blaming) (Brownell, 1991; Taylor & Brown, 1988), Taoism emphasizes the importance of passive attitudes, such as "no-action" and internal peacefulness, for physical and psychological harmony and well-being. It is believed that to pursue many material possessions, beautiful colors, and even sound may lead to desires and confusions, which, in turn, may cause behavioral and psychological disturbances. Thus, one should remain unattached to things such as fame and wealth. In addition, according to Taoism, softness, tenderness, and weakness are the desirable attributes of life whereas firmness, strength, and stiffness are the undesirable concomitants of death. Thus, it is beneficial for health to remain flexible and take "no action" in daily life.

According to Confucianism, good health is achieved through active social participation (Ho & Lisowski, 1997). In fact, achieving individual health is a goal that is secondary to maintaining social harmony, upholding moral standards, and obeying social rules. The highest moral principles include *ren* (perfect virtue, benevolence, humanity), *yi* (righteousness), *li* (propriety, proper conduct), *zhi* (wisdom and knowledge), and *xin* (trustworthiness). According to Confucianism, one should always follow the five moral principles, even if it means sacrificing one's life, when one's own personal interests are in conflict with the principles. It has been argued that Chinese medicine is the "art of ren" (Ho & Lisowski, 1997). Thus, conformity to moral and social standards is essential to achieving health and a meaningful life.

In this chapter, we will outline the understanding and interpretation of health and illness that stems from these Taoist and Confucist traditions and will discuss how the cultural context shapes both collective and individual health behaviors, and health-related experiences in traditional and contemporary Chinese societies. For the increasing number of Asians who immigrate to the West (i.e., North America and Europe), the contrast between the dominant Western models of health and illness (the biomedical model) and their traditional Asian models can be a source of confusion. Thus, in the final section of the chapter, we discuss the implications of Chinese health ideologies for understanding the health and health service utilization patterns of Asian immigrant populations to the West, particularly North America. We will first briefly review the tenets of the biomedical model—the "lay" Western model of health and illness—to serve as a counterpoint to the traditional Chinese health model.

THE WESTERN BIOMEDICAL MODEL

Historically, the dominant paradigm of Western medical science has been the biomedical model. The biomedical model is based on two fundamental assumptions: reductionism and materialism. Reductionism refers to the view that an individual can be understood by studying his or her smallest constituent parts. From this perspective, illness can be understood by examining biochemical processes (Engel, 1977). Materialism is the view that individuals are physical beings whose existence and functions can be explained solely by the principles of physiology, anatomy, and biochemistry. Thus, the model leaves no room within its framework for the social, cultural, psychological, or behavioral dimensions of disease.

About 20 years ago, Engel (1977) proposed the biopsychosocial model as an alternative to the biomedical model in Western medicine. According to the biopsychosocial model, health and illness are determined by the interplay among biological, psychological, and social aspects of a person's life. It is unclear, however, to what extent the biopsychosocial model has gained acceptance and is being practiced in Western medicine. It is believed that this model has remained in the realm of ideology rather than becoming a general guide to daily practice (Blount & Bayona, 1994; Denig, Haaijer-Ruskamp, Wesseling, & Versluis, 1993; Sadler & Hulgus, 1992).

HEALTH BELIEFS IN CHINESE CULTURE: A HOLISTIC PERSPECTIVE

The philosophical basis for Chinese medicine and health conceptions is that human beings live between heaven and earth (i.e., a macrocosm) and comprise a miniature universe within themselves (i.e., microcosms). Moreover, health is believed to be achieved by maintaining the body in harmony with respect to internal psychological functions as well as external social and ecological conditions. The first systematic description of the holistic perspective on health appeared in Huang Di Nei Jing (the Emperor Huang's Manual of Corporeal Medicine), which was written over 2500 years ago. The general holistic view on the links between the human beings and internal and external factors and key constructs, such as Qi (vital energy) and the channels of the body, still serves as the primary framework for Chinese health and medical theories and practices today. According to Lin (1981), the importance of the correspondence between the microcosm and macrocosm (that is, that which is observed in nature should also be reflected in the human body) and dynamic balancing (or harmony) are the most central Chinese health constructs. Unlike the Western notions of homeostatic physiological negative feedback loops (Guyton, 1976) and self-regulatory behavior (see Schwartz, 1979; Leventhal, Zimmerman, & Gutmann, 1984), which focus on homeostatic forces largely within an individual, the Chinese holistic model addresses the balance and movement of internal forces (i.e., psychological and physical factors) as well as the harmony between forces within the individual and contextual conditions.

"YIN-YANG" AND "WU XING"

In Chinese culture, health and disease are directly associated with the balance of Yin and Yang, which are presumed to be polar opposites. Yin represents the passive and receding aspect of nature whereas Yang represents the active, advancing aspect of nature. It is believed that Yin and Yang exist at the emotional, physical, interpersonal/societal, and ecological levels. The experience of misery and sadness (emotions), the function of kidney (physical status), water, and night (natural conditions) are typical examples of Yin. In contrast, fiery temperament and hyperactivity, liver, fire, and daytime are examples of Yang. The two forces are thought to be interdependent, and the imbalance between them results in disease. Through the interactions and movements of Yin and Yang, physical functions interchange and transform from one state to another.

Wu Xing, as indicated in Fig. 14.1 and Table 14.1, represents the five states (or phases) in the functions of living beings. Each phase is reflected in an element in nature, a season, a part of the body, and a psychological function. The five elements are connected with and interact with each other. Each element may facilitate and inhibit the function of another element within its level. For example, water facilitates the growth of wood, which, in turn, facilitates the power of fire. Earth or soil can inhibit the movement of water, which, in turn, may inhibit fire. There are other processes among the five elements, such as mutual regulation (the effect of facilitation and inhibition of each element may be restrained by other factors) (Lin, 1981). Similar patterns of interactions may be identified among the five organs, seasons, colors, and emotions. According to the model, for example, joy or happiness may facilitate desire and inhibit grief or worry whereas fear may facilitate anger and inhibit joy. Other emotions may similarly affect each other. In addition to the mutual influence and regulation among the elements, the function at one level (e.g., ecological level) influences, and is influenced by, the movement and transition at other levels (e.g., physical level). In the section that follows, we will further discuss views about the relation between physical conditions and psychological functions in Chinese culture, given that they serve as an important basis for Chinese health beliefs and experiences.

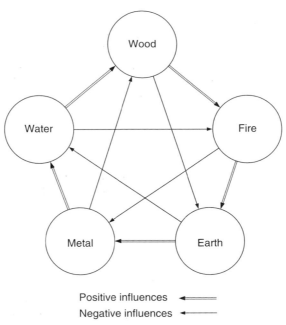

Positive influences ⇐══
Negative influences ←——

FIGURE 14.1　The "Five Elements" Model.

TABLE 14.1   Five Elements in Nature and the Human Body

Five elements	Wood	Fire	Earth	Metal	Water
Organs	Liver	Heart	Spleen	Lung	Kidney
Face	Eye	Tongue	Mouth	Nose	Ear
Body	Nerve	Blood	Muscle	Skin	Bone
Emotions	Anger	Joy	Worry	Grief/sad	Fright/fear
Taste	Sour	Bitter	Sweet	Pungent	Salty
Seasons	Spring	Summer	Between seasons	Autumn	Winter
Directions	East	South	Middle	West	North
Environmental factors	Wind	Heat	Dampness	Dryness	Cold
Color	Green	Red	Brown	White	Black

RELATIONS BETWEEN PHYSICAL FUNCTIONS AND EMOTIONS

According to the Chinese holistic model, physical and psychological functions are an integral part of the same system of the body. Emotions are completely tied in with specific body activities, both of which are subject to external influences, including the passage of seasons, changes in the weather, and other natural conditions, such as wind, cold, heat, moisture, and dryness (Kaptchuk, 1983). For example, the heart not only controls the circulation of blood, it also "keeps" the mind. Thus, the heart, not the brain, is believed to play a major role in mental functioning. Dysfunctions of the heart, which may be detected by purplish-red or swollen tongue, may lead to coma, insomnia, amnesia, dream-disturbed sleep, poor memory, and mental derangement. The kidney is seen as a place to reserve "essential spirit." Dysfunction of the kidney, which may be caused by excessive sexual activity, may lead to dizziness, fear, and feverish sensation. The lung and stomach are believed to produce vital energy, *Qi*. Dysfunction of either of them may weaken or diminish *Qi* and slow down vital processes of life. The typical psychological symptoms associated with diminished *Qi* are excessive worry and sadness. In addition, liver dysfunction is often manifested as irritability and anger, and problems with the spleen are associated with desire and "thinking too much" (Hammer, 1990).

It is important to note that the relations between the physical and psycho-emotional functions of the human body are presumed to be bidirectional and transactional in nature (Lin, 1981). Physical dysfunction of an organ may cause emotional problems and emotional disturbances may, in turn, be the origins of physical problems. For example, liver problems may result in irritability. Overindulgence in alcohol and tobacco may cause accumulation of heat, which turns into fire. The fire, which may affect the liver, further causes a distended sensation in the head, a headache, red eyes, a bitter taste in the mouth, and a flushed face. Damage caused by fire in the liver also causes impairment of its ability to provide a free flow of Qi and, thus, may lead to irritability. On the other hand, it is also the case that excessive joy or excessive fright may injure the heart, causing palpitations and insomnia. Anger and emotional frustration may cause liver dysfunction, dizziness, chest congestion, and pain in the upper abdomen. Excessive grief, sadness, and "overthinking" may cause dysfunction of spleen and stomach. Fear can make kidney Qi descend and may cause control problems in urination. Excessive anxiety and anger may also cause poor circulation of blood, which may, in turn, cause a tumor (Hammer, 1990; Ho & Lisowski, 1997).

EXTERNAL AND INTERNAL CAUSES OF DISEASE: THE IMPORTANCE OF A HEALTHY LIFESTYLE

As noted earlier, physical health, according to the Chinese holistic model, is not only determined by one's emotional functioning, but also subject to social–ecological influences. Internal factors include seven emotions: joy, anger, sadness, worry, grief, fear, and fright. Each of the emotions may affect the flow of Qi and Yin–Yang balance in organs. Heart and liver seem to be most susceptible to emotional disturbance because their normal functions are more dependent on emotional harmonies (Hammer, 1990; Kaptchuk, 1983). There are six external or exogenous factors, including wind, cold, fire or heat, dampness, dryness, and hotness. Among them, wind and fire may have the most pervasive effects on health, particularly when they are combined with other conditions, such as coldness and dryness.

The influences of external social and ecological conditions and internal emotions are often mediated by one's lifestyle; health is maintained when a person lives in harmony with social and ecological conditions and attains inner psychological balance. Accordingly, a healthy lifestyle is important in achieving these goals. Among various activities in daily life, particular attention is paid to diet and physical activity. Diet is important because it is presumed to affect the function of the stomach and spleen, which are responsible for transforming food into Qi and blood. An irregularity in the quantity and quality of food is thought to disrupt body harmony. Too much raw food can strain the Yang aspect of the spleen and generate internal cold dampness, which may result in abdominal pain, diarrhea, or weakness. Fatty and greasy food, alcohol, or sweets can produce dampness and heat. The importance of diet for health is widely recognized by ordinary Chinese people. It is commonly believed in China that some food (e.g., lamb) may produce "heat," while others (e.g., many fruits) may generate "cold" in the body and that some food (e.g., ginger) may facilitate Yang, while others (e.g., leafy green vegetables) may help Yin.

Similarly, physical activity is considered helpful for the flow of *Qi* and the development of strength in the body. However, physical activity should be done in moderation; excessive activity, including heavy labor, is thought to be harmful to health. It is believed that one should be active in the morning, during the spring, and in one's youth (Yang times), but one should rest in the evening, during the winter, and in one's old age (Yin times). Moreover, different types of exercise are recommended for individuals at different life stages. For example, whereas adolescents and youth are encouraged to participate in active sports, aged and weak people may improve their health by engaging in mild and controlled movement, such as Tai Chi.

Exercise and diet appeared to be seen as primary strategies for achieving health historically as well. In a medical book found in a tomb in Mawangdui, Chang Sha, dated from 168 B.C.E., during the Qi and Han dynasties (221 B.C.E.–220 C.E.) or perhaps earlier, a healthy diet and exercise were recommended for the preservation of health (e.g., Ho & Lisowski, 1997). Thus, as indicated by Kaptchuk (1983), knowledge of diet and exercise has been, and continues to be, part of the cultural model of "how to live" in Chinese society.

The focus on lifestyle as an important health determinant is also evident in Western culture, both currently (Brandt, 1997; Leichter, 1997) as well as historically (Thomas, 1997). In fact, the emphasis on a "healthy" (low fat, low sugar, high fiber) diet and physical exercise and fitness is so strong, particularly in the United States, that Leichter (1997) refers to it as "Lifestyle Correctness" and a form of "secular morality."

The focus on ecological conditions as determinants of health, however, is far stronger in traditional and contemporary Chinese culture than it is in the West. In the Mawangdui writings, living in a clean and remote environment with fresh air (such as in the mountains) was emphasized. Moreover, in a recent article written by Xie (1999), it is indicated that approximately 40% of deaths in the country are due to "unusual" weather or climate conditions. To reduce the risk, Xie (1999) recommends that the public be made aware of effective strategies to deal with the potential effects of adverse weather conditions. For example, persistent and high temperature, humidity, and heavy rain during the period from June to August in most areas of China is thought to cause irritability, fatigue, and dramatic changes in appetite and sleeping patterns. The typical physical conditions resulting from this type of weather include arthritis, skin problems, and respiratory (lung) and gastrointestinal (stomach) problems (Xie, 1999). Moreover, it is believed that humid and wet weather may facilitate the growth of bacteria, which may contaminate food, leading to epidemic diseases.

COLLECTIVISM AND HEALTH-RELATED EXPERIENCES

The holistic perspective emphasizes not only ecological and social influences on individual physical and psychological health, but also the significance of individual health and illness conditions for the functioning of larger macro-level group, social, and global systems. Health problems of individual members may damage the well-being of the collective, such as the family and the community, as well as the harmony of environmental and societal organization. The consequence of health and diseases is often evaluated in terms of their effects on the collective. Accordingly, plans and decisions concerning health care and prevention and treatment of illness are made from a collective perspective.

Collectivistic principles, which are established based mainly on Confucian doctrines, indicate that achieving and maintaining social order and stability are the primary concerns in the society. The interests of the individual are considered to be subordinated to those of the collective. Selfishness, including seeking individual benefit at the expense of group interests and indifference to group interests, is regarded as a cardinal evil (Ho, 1986; King & Bond, 1985). Individual behaviors that may threaten group functioning and the well-being of the collective are strictly prohibited.

In collectivistic cultures, health issues are often viewed in terms of their significance for collective well-being and functioning. This may be reflected in two different, and sometimes contradictory, considerations for how health care and medical practices are organized. First, since collective success is usually represented by the well-being of the majority of group members, health-related policies, plans, and actions at the societal level must focus on how the health issue is relevant to the public. Second, the collective in Asian cultures is typically hierarchical in structure. Thus, decisions about various issues, including health issues, are often made by individuals with a high status, and health care services are sometimes provided on a selective, discriminatory basis. For example, in a family, greater attention may be paid to the health conditions of the members who are regarded as important for the family (e.g., the father who may provide the most financial support to the family, senior family members who represent authority, and boys who carry on the family name). Similarly, individuals who have a high social–political status and are considered "valuable" in the society (e.g., officials, famous scientists) may receive special treatment in health care. In contrast, health problems of ordinary people may be neglected, given that their loss may not threaten the functioning of the collective. This hierarchical system of health care is often supported by all group members, including those who receive the fewest benefits, because they believe that the system is necessary for the improvement of the collective welfare.

Collectivism not only affects the judgment of valued health outcomes in terms of the collective well-being, but also prescribes the manner in which public health is achieved. Health care and practices are often decided by the group, and public health policies are established and implemented forcefully from a collective perspective. For example, members of a group (e.g., a work unit or an institute) are sometimes required to participate in a collective medical examination; failure to comply may be considered an indication of a negative political attitude toward the collective. Students from elementary schools to universities are required to do morning exercise collectively, because it is believed that exercise is necessary for the enhancement of the national health status. Similarly, middle-aged and older people may be required to learn Tai Chi for the good of the collective. Again, these health promotion activities are sometimes considered "political tasks." In addition, health information is provided through aggressive public education campaigns, through a range of outlets (television, radio, magazines, newspapers), in the classroom, and sometimes in public venues, such as parks and stores.

Personal self-care, health habits, and health-risk behaviors in China are driven as much (if not more) by concerns for the collective as by concerns for oneself. Concerns for the collective, such as family, may be a protective factor that reduces individual risk behaviors. Thus, the use of illegal substances, high-risk sexual behaviors, and suicide are looked down upon less because of their consequences for the individual than because they can bring shame to the family. As a result, these behaviors are generally low in Chinese societies (Chen, Greenberger, Lester, Dong, & Guo, 1998). Concern for the reputation of the family and ancestors is critical because it is believed that taking care of one's own health is an important part of the fulfillment of filial piety; one has no right to damage any part of the body because it comes from, and belongs to, one's parents. One striking demonstration of this collectivistic stance is a comment, reported by Nilchaikovit, Hill, and Holland (1993) of an Asian woman on the topic of suicide. She notes that one has no right to commit suicide because, "Your life is not yours, as many people like to think. You cannot grow up without the help of others, your family, your friends, the society, and many others. You owe your life to others and you cannot just take it away without affecting and hurting other people. Thus you have no right to take your own life without the consent of the others involved" (p. 42). Thus, it has been noted that an effective strategy to motivate Asian patients to cooperate and comply with treatment might be to try to convince them of the significance of treatment and therapy for the fulfillment of their role obligation in the family (Nilchaikovit et al., 1993).

Since individual behaviors are seen to have an impact on the group, other members of the group can often serve in an effective monitoring and assisting role. It is common for members of Chinese families to be involved in each other's personal affairs. Since health and illness are regarded as relevant to everybody in the family, decisions about health care and treatment are almost always made by the whole family. Thus, in working with Asian patients, it is important to discuss the treatment plans with family members and include them in every major decision (Nilchaikovit et al., 1993). Similarly, teachers and peers may play an important role in students' health-related activities in the school. Physical and health education is one of the three primary tasks (along with moral and intellectual education) in Chinese schools (Chen, Chen, Kaspar & Noh, 2000); performance of group members in this area is important for the evaluation of group functioning.

Collectivism is reflected in interdependence and mutual support, not only at the family level, but also at the community level. This is particularly so in rural areas of China because there is no public or private health insurance for peasants (who comprise over 80% of the population in the country). Among the peasants, members of the community are often called upon to provide suggestions and to make contributions (including financial) to the individual or the family that suffers from health problems.

HEALTH EXPERIENCES OF CHINESE PEOPLE

The Western biomedical model focuses on the "objective" biological processes underlying diseases and illness from an analytic perspective. Health problems are often regarded as an episodic deviation caused by micro-level, natural, etiological agents, such as genes, viruses, bacteria, and hormones (Amstrong & Swartzman, 1999; Landrine & Klonoff, 1994). Diseases are considered preventable and treatable by interventions in biomedical and physiological processes, especially with the assistance of advanced technology (Nilchaikovit et al., 1993). However, the diagnosis and treatment of health problems can be conducted only by "experts" who have received systematic training in medical and health areas (Nilchaikovit et al., 1993).

Since the Chinese holistic model emphasizes the associations between health conditions and emotional functions, lifestyles, interpersonal relationships, and social and ecological factors, it is necessary for ordinary people to understand the causes and processes of health and illness and to exert health care and illness prevention in daily life. Indeed, it has been found that Chinese people are likely to describe disease in terms of "internal imbalance," "blocked Qi," "excess cold," or "excess heat" (Quah & Bishop, 1996). Similar results were found in a study conducted by Amstrong and Swartzman (1999). In the following sections, we will focus specifically on how Chinese beliefs about the associations between somatic conditions and psychological functions are involved in health-related experiences.

EMOTIONAL CONTROL AND SELF-RESTRAINT

The holistic perspective in Chinese culture indicates that strong emotional reactions may be harmful for individual physical health; excessive experiences of emotions, such as anger and sadness and even positive emotions such as joy, may be pathogens or internal pathological factors that cause organic dysfunction (Bond & Hwang, 1986; Hammer, 1990; Luo, 1996). Further, Confucianism holds that self-control in both emotional and behavioral reactions in social interactions is necessary for the establishment and maintenance of harmonious social relationships and group functioning and for the development of "ideal" personality. As a result, individuals are encouraged to restrain and control their emotions. Unlike Western cultures, in which emotional catharsis is encouraged, Chinese culture emphasizes the suppression of emotions as an adaptive coping strategy

(Lin, 1981). Emotional control and inhibition may be learned through a number of ways, including meditation or mental exercise. From a developmental perspective, it is believed that individuals are more capable of inhibiting and regulating their emotions with increasing experience and age. Thus, emotional restraint is considered an index of social and psychological maturity. Mature people are often described in Chinese literature as emotionally "flat" and unresponsive to provocative, challenging, or stressful situations, which is sometimes considered a psychopathological symptom in the West (Nilchaikovit et al., 1993). In contrast, individuals who are emotionally sensitive and reactive are viewed by the Chinese as incompetent and even abnormal (e.g., Luo, 1996).

Emotion inhibition is evident during a very early period of development in Chinese children. It has been found that Chinese infants and toddlers are significantly more emotionally restrained than North American children (Camras et al., 1998; Chen, Hastings, Rubin, Chen, Cen, & Stewart, 1998; Freedman, 1974; Kagan et al., 1994). For example, Chinese infants showed less reactivity and distress during testing procedures than did North American infants (Freedman, 1974). Similarly, it was found that Japanese infants showed a less intense response to inoculation and were more quickly soothed than were European American infants (Lewis, 1989). Asian children are less reactive and expressive than their Western counterparts not only with respect to negative emotions, but also with respect to positive emotional responses, such as smiling (e.g., Caudill & Weinstein, 1969; Fogel, Toda, & Kowai, 1988). Similar differences have been reported between Chinese and Western children, adolescents, and adults (e.g., Gong, 1984; Tseng & Hsu, 1969–70). The cultural endorsement of emotional control in China is reflected not only in the relatively high level of emotional restraint and inhibition, but also in positive social judgment and evaluation of the behavior that indicates inhibited emotions. Emotionally controlled behavior has been found to be perceived and responded to differently in Chinese and Western cultures. For example, it was found that whereas emotional and behavioral inhibition in Canadian children was associated positively with parental punishment orientation, disappointment, and rejection, it was associated positively with parental warm and accepting attitudes in China (Caudill & Weinstein, 1969; Chen et al., 1998). Children's emotional control is considered an indication of social incompetence by Canadian parents, but as an index of achievement by Chinese parents (X. Chen et al., 1998). This is consistent with the findings concerning the relations between inhibited behavior and peer acceptance in Chinese and Canadian children and adolescents (Chen, Rubin, & Sun, 1992; Chen, Rubin, & Li, 1995a,c). Whereas emotional and behavioral inhibition is associated with social difficulties in North America, restrained and inhibited children are likely to be well accepted by peers in China (e.g., Chen et al., 1995a,c). The positive social perceptions of, and reactions to, self-restraint and emotional control in Chinese children and adolescents define the cultural "meaning" of emotional inhibition and, at the same time, provide a social context for its development.

SOMATIZATION OF MENTAL PROBLEMS

Somewhat related to the issue of emotional control and suppression is the finding that Chinese people tend to somatize their psychological problems (e.g., Kleinman, 1977). Somatization typically refers to complaints about, or the appearance of, physical symptoms such as headaches, stomach pains, chronic fatigue, and sleep problems that may have a strong psychological basis (Chun, Enomoto, & Sue, 1996). The findings are based mainly on observations by mental health researchers and professionals that Chinese patients often report somatic complaints and seek medical help for their somatic problems, even if they may be aware of the psychological nature of the problem (Chun et al., 1996). For example, 70% of the outpatients in a psychiatric clinic in Taiwan presented with exclusively or predominantly somatic complaints on their initial visit (Tseng, 1975). Similar phenomena have been found in Asian populations in other countries, such as Thailand, Vietnam, and Korea and in North America (e.g., Bourne & Nguyen, 1967; Tongyonk, 1972; Kleinman, 1977). Kleinman (1977) found, for example, that 88% of the Chinese patients initially reported somatic complaints but no affective complaints, whereas only 20% of European Americans did so.

Cross-cultural differences in somatization appear in childhood. In a longitudinal project on social and emotional development in Chinese children (X. Chen et al., 1998), it was found that, according to self-reports and parents' reports, Chinese children and adolescents clearly had more somatic complaints than did their North American counterparts. Moreover, somatic complaints were highly associated with other indexes of internalizing emotional problems, such as depression, anxiety, and social withdrawal. Children who were anxious and emotionally inhibited might be more likely than others to report somatic illness. The results support the argument that there may be a psychosocial basis for the development of somatization (Chun et al., 1996).

Different explanations have been offered for somatization in Asians. It has been argued that in Asian, particularly Chinese, cultures, mental illness may carry with it serious social stigma, indicating weak will and spirit (Sue & Morishima, 1982). Moreover, the social stigma associated with mental problems is believed to damage the reputation of the family, whereas physical illness may not bring such humiliation and shame to the individual or the family. Thus, it is not surprising that Chinese people tend to deny their psychological problems and seek treatment from physicians rather than mental health professionals. It is also possible that Asian cultures may facilitate the development of somatic problems. Due to the cultural emphasis on emotional control, Chinese people are reluctant to express their emotional stress and may gradually become unable to cope with it (e.g., Tseng & Hsu, 1969–70). The suppression or internalization of cumulative psychological problems may, in turn, lead to somatic dysfunctions of the body system, as indicated in the Chinese holistic model and also as reflected in the Western literature on psychosomatic processes (e.g., Traue & Pennebaker, 1993).

Somatization may also be due to the lack of clear differentiation between psychological and physical problems, given that the imbalance of Yin and Yang is seen to simultaneously affect psychological and physical functions of the body (Hammer, 1990). Indeed, it would not be uncommon for psychological problems, such as depression, to be treated in the same manner as physical problems by enhancing the flow of *Qi* through acupuncture, adjusting diet, and using Chinese herbs. Since mental and emotional problems rely heavily on physical interpretations, relatively few terms exist in Chinese culture for the description of specific symptoms of psychological problems. Interestingly, whereas psychological disturbances are often interpreted and expressed in terms of organic dysfunctions of the body, physical problems are less likely to be framed in terms of psychological disorders, despite the fact that emotional reactions are regarded as internal pathogens in Chinese medicine.

EXPERIENCE OF EMOTIONAL PROBLEMS: THE MEANING AND NATURE OF DEPRESSION

In the West, depression is a common psychological problem, which emerges in childhood and adolescence and is relatively stable over time (Harrington, 1993; Nolen-Hoeksema, Girgus, & Seligman, 1992). Depressed children and adults often report negative feelings about themselves, lowered interest or pleasure in daily-life activities, and persistent fatigue or loss of energy. It has been found that depression in childhood and adolescence is associated with pervasive difficulties in social and school adjustment (e.g., Bell-Dolan, Reaven, & Peterson, 1993; Ollendick & Yule, 1990).

In Chinese culture, depression, like other psychological phenomena, is interpreted as a concomitant of physical dysfunction and the disturbance of *Qi*. According to the Chinese holistic approach, depression may be caused by excessive sadness and worry, which hurts the lung, and too much deliberation, which damages the stomach and spleen. The typical symptoms produced by these organic dysfunctions include loss of appetite, fatigue, and lack of energy (imbalance of *Qi*). Accordingly, treatment of depression focuses on the restoration of Ying–Yang balance through applying Chinese medical practices and adjusting lifestyles and social attitudes toward life and the world.

It has been shown that Chinese children and adolescents experience an equal, or even higher, level of affect disturbance, including depression, compared with their North American counterparts (Chen et al., 1995a,b; Cheung, 1986; Crystal et al., 1994; Dong, Yang, & Ollendick, 1994; Shek, 1991). Moreover, a high rate of "malicious incidents," such as suicide, in Chinese adolescents has been reported in the literature and in the media (e.g., "China Youth Daily," July 14, 1994; "China New Digest," January 26, 1998). Given that the Chinese tend to focus on the organic mechanism for the development of depressive symptoms, however, the subjective experiences of depressed feelings have been largely neglected in Chinese culture (Chen, 2000; Lin, 1985). The neglect of depression in

Chinese collectivistic culture may also be due to the fact that emotional problems of an internalizing nature that are directed toward the self may have little significance for collective functioning (Potter, 1988). It has been found that parents and teachers in China are highly insensitive to children's emotional problems (Chen, 2000). Few mental health services are available in mainland China, even in urban areas such as Shanghai and Beijing. There are almost no facilities for psychological counseling in schools; children's depressed feelings and other socioemotional difficulties are often considered, and treated as, medical problems or political–ideological problems (especially when they are associated with interpersonal problems) (Chen, 2000).

The social and cultural neglect does not imply that depression has no functional significance among Chinese people. Chen and his colleagues in China (e.g., Chen et al., 1995b; Chen et al., 2000; Chen & Li, 2000) have shown that depression in childhood significantly predicts depressive symptoms in adolescence, suggesting that Chinese children who report depression likely continue to suffer emotionally several years later. Moreover, depression affects social and school adjustment (e.g., social isolation, low social status, and learning problems), which are valued attributes in Chinese culture. That is, social performance of depressed children increasingly declined with time. The findings suggest that depression is a significant psychopathological phenomenon in Chinese children and adolescents, which deserves more attention from professionals and the public. Moreover, the findings showing a close association between depression and social and school adjustment problems support the holistic view of the interplay between psychological and social functions.

IMPLICATIONS FOR THE HEALTH OF ASIAN POPULATIONS IN NORTH AMERICA

Over the past 20 years, the Asian population has increased dramatically in Canada and the United States. For example, the population of Asians in the U.S. was approximately 1.5 million in 1970 and reached 7.3 million by the early 1990s. In Canada, the Asian population was over 1.5 million in 1996, about 5% of the total population of the country. The ratio was even higher in metropolitan areas, such as Toronto (18.6%) (Statistics Canada, 1996 Census).

There is converging evidence that the health of Asian immigrants in Canada and the United States is poorer than that of the majority of Canadians and Americans. In the early 1970s, the mortality rate for Chinese men in the U.S. was higher than the national average rate (Li, 1972). Moreover, Loo (1998) found that Chinese Americans living in Chinatown were less likely to report their health as excellent than were other Americans (10 versus 40%, respectively) and were more likely to rate their health as "fair" or "poor" (57 versus 19%, respectively). Erickson and Hoang (1980) found that Asian immigrants had a higher prevalence of infectious diseases (e.g., tuberculosis) and blood abnormalities than did the general American population.

The poorer health status of Asian immigrants may be related to the stress of acculturation, fewer socioeconomic resources, and language barriers that would make health care less accessible to them. However, as might be gleaned from our review thus far, an additional possible reason for the relatively poorer health of Asian immigrants to the West is that Western health care may be less satisfactory and/or accessible to them because Western medicine, which is based predominantly on the biomedical model, is incompatible with the traditional Chinese health beliefs. Explanations for illness drive health and illness behavior as well as satisfaction with health care and compliance (Kirscht, 1977). Directly related to this point, Armstrong and Swartzman (1999) examined Asian–Western university students' satisfaction with the medical care they had received in Canada. Asian participants, as predicted, were less satisfied with the care they received and believed more strongly in nonbiomedical causes of illness (i.e., "balance" or interpersonal influences) than did Western participants. Moreover, a large part of Asian versus Western differences in satisfaction with medical care was explained by the group differences in beliefs about the causes of illness. Whereas the lack of understanding of and satisfaction with Western health care may account for the relatively poorer physical health in Asian immigrants, the discrepancies between Asian and Western beliefs about mental health problems may be more influential on the immigrants' attitudes and behaviors toward the use of services and facilities in Western societies.

MENTAL HEALTH PROBLEMS IN ASIANS

Mental health problems in Asian populations in North America have not been noticed until recent years. It was long believed that Asians had few psychological or mental health problems. For example, it was argued that Chinese might be less vulnerable to mental distress than other ethnic groups (see Loo, 1998). This notion was reinforced by the fact that Asians tend to underutilize mainstream mental health services (Leong, 1986) and by the statistics that reveal relatively low rates of divorce, crime, and juvenile delinquency and high educational achievement in Asian adolescents and adults (Sue & Morishima, 1982). Nevertheless, recent findings have suggested that Asian groups do experience mental health problems and that underutilization of mental health services may be due to cultural factors (Sue, Nakamura, Chung, & Yee-Bradbury, 1994). In fact, it has been found that Asian adolescents and adults may experience major psychological and psychiatric problems (Kim, 1978; Leong, 1986; Peralta & Horikawa, 1978; Sue et al., 1994). Moreover, certain groups, such as Southeast Asian refugees and immigrants, may have extremely high levels of depression and other affective and cognitive disorders (Chung & Okazaki, 1991; Gong-Guy, 1987; Owen, 1985; Sue et al., 1994).

The high level of emotional disturbance in Asian refugees and immigrants may not be surprising given the combination of their intensive and extensive experiences of adjustment difficulties in novel and adverse environments, the lack of social support systems, and the traditional internalizing style in coping with stress. It was found in a sample of Chinese adolescents in Canada that acculturation in the new environment might affect socioemotional adjustment (Lee, 1996).

Specifically, Chinese adolescents reported a variety of cultural conflicts and psychological problems. However, adolescent adaptation or accommodation to Western cultures might serve to buffer psychological problems, including depression and other internalizing problems. In other words, these psychological problems tended to decline as the adolescents became "Westernized" in the cultural beliefs and values and lifestyles. Interestingly, the buffering effect appeared to be most evident when the acculturation mode was consistent between adolescents and their parents. Adolescents reported more emotional and behavioral difficulties when their acculturation mode was inconsistent with their parents', which occurred when adolescents were more Westernized than their parents in their value systems, behaviors, and lifestyles (Lee, 1996).

Despite their high level of psychological disturbance, Asians have been found to underutilize mental health services (e.g., Loo, 1998; Sue et al., 1994). Possible explanations include lack of knowledge of mental health facilities, language problems that prevent Asians, particularly new immigrants, from communicating effectively with health providers, and reluctance to admit mental problems, which may result in stigma and shame. In addition, it is possible that since Chinese culture emphasizes social support, Asians who suffer from psychological disturbance may choose to rely on relatives, friends, and other social networks for emotional support and advice.

The phenomenon of the underutilization of mental health services in Asian populations should be understood in a larger cultural context. First, due to the organic interpretation of psychological functions and dysfunctions in the Chinese holistic view, as was indicated earlier, it is conceivable for Asians to seek help from medical doctors for the assessment and treatment of somatic problems that are believed to be the causes of mental problems. It is difficult for Asians who believe in somatic origins of mental problems to develop confidence and trust in mental health professionals who focus mainly on psychological and psychiatric symptoms. Moreover, given different cultural backgrounds of Asians and Western professionals, mutual understanding during the process of service delivery is obviously a challenge. It has been found that Asians tend to terminate therapy prematurely (Zane & Sue, 1996), which may indicate their dissatisfaction with, and lack of confidence in, Western-based treatment strategies.

RECOMMENDATIONS FOR HEALTH SERVICE DELIVERY TO ASIAN POPULATIONS IN NORTH AMERICA

As Asian populations grow rapidly in both Canada and the United States, health status and problems have attracted attention of professionals and policy makers. To provide effective health services for Asians, it is essential to understand cultural beliefs and systems, such as the holistic approach and the collectivistic orientation, that may direct Asians' behaviors in health-seeking and decision-making. Understanding daily life experiences, social norms, and health needs is an important part of health care and health delivery process. Thus, training bilingual and multicultural health providers may be the first step. Accessible, community-based health care facilities staffed with bilingual and culturally sensitive personnel are essential for the promotion of appropriate health services.

Second, it has been argued that it is important to develop ethnic-specific programs that emphasize culturally responsive and acceptable services (Zane & Sue, 1996). For example, the South Cove Community Health Center has attempted to provide relevant health services to low-income Asian immigrants (Zane & Sue, 1996). One of the features of the programs is that physical and mental health services are provided together with a coordinated, integrated orientation, which fits the holistic approach to health issues and somatization of mental health problems in Asian cultures. Furthermore, great effort is made by health practitioners in the Center to interpret and explain health problems, both physical and mental, in a way that is compatible with traditional Asian health and medical beliefs and experiences (Zane & Sue, 1996). Similarly, the Chinatown Child Development Center (CCDC) in San Francisco has developed mental health programs in the context of educational experiences (Chan-Sew, 1980). Since child education has been traditionally valued in Chinese culture, these programs are likely to be effective in acquiring cooperation of parents. In both the South Cove and CCDC programs, there is a clear emphasis on family involvement (Zane & Sue, 1996). Recognition of the family unit as an important social resource and application of family-based strategies reflect Chinese collectivistic values. The collectivistic approach may be extended to health services at the community level so that not only family members but also other social relationships and support systems can be included in health care and treatment programs.

SUMMARY

The Western biomedical model focuses on the "objective" biological processes underlying diseases and illness from an analytic perspective. Health problems are often regarded as an episodic deviation caused by micro-level, natural, etiological agents, such as genes, viruses, bacteria, and hormones. The holistic perspective in Chinese culture indicates that health conditions are associated with internal emotional functioning, social relationships, societal norms and values, and ecological factors. Health is achieved and maintained when a person lives in harmony with social and ecological conditions and attains inner psychological balance. According to the collectivistic principles in Chinese and some other Asian cultures, health issues should be viewed in terms of their significance for collective well-being and functioning. Collectivism may be reflected in interdependence and mutual support in health care and practices at different levels, including family, community, and the society. The holistic model and the collectivistic orientation are important for us to understand the health-related experiences and behaviors, such as emotion inhibition, somatization, depression, and underutilization of mental health services in Asian cultures, and to develop culturally sensitive and appropriate health programs for Asian immigrant populations in North America.

CASE STUDY

To understand why Asian immigrants tend to underutilize health services, Armstrong and Swartzman (1999) conducted a survey study examining cross-cultural differences in health-related beliefs and attitudes toward Western medical care. Seventy-nine European Canadian and 63 Asian (first- and second-generation immigrants) undergraduates participated in the study. Their beliefs about causes of illness were assessed using a 43-item scale, which included such items as "lack of harmony with others," "too much hot or cold food," and "bacteria/virus." Their satisfaction with Western health care services was also assessed. It was found that Asian students were less satisfied with the health care they received in Canada than were European Canadians. Moreover, Asian students were more likely than Western students to believe in nonbiological causes of illness, particularly "imbalance" of cold and hot food, lack of harmony with nature and others, and too many emotions. Finally, it was found that these health beliefs partially accounted for why Asian students were less satisfied with their health care situations in Canada.

1. How did this study indicate the influences of cultural values on individual health-related cognitions, attitudes, and behaviors?

2. What can we do to improve our health care services for Asian immigrants in culturally diverse communities or countries such as Canada?

ACKNOWLEDGMENT

The preparation of the chapter was supported by grants from the Social Sciences and Humanities Research Council of Canada and by a Faculty Award from the William T. Grant Foundation.

SUGGESTED READINGS

Lin, K. M. (1981). Traditional Chinese medical beliefs and their relevance for mental illness and psychiatry. In A. Kleinman & T. Y. Lin (Eds.), *Normal and abnormal behavior in Chinese culture* (pp. 95–111). Dordrecht, The Netherlands: D. Reidel.
Liu, E. (1998). *The Accidental Asian.* New York: Vintage.

Nilchaikovit, T., Hill, J. M., & Holland, J. C. (1993). The effects of culture on illness behavior and medical care. *General Hospital Psychiatry, 15,* 41–50.

Sue, S., & Morishima, H. (1982). *The mental health of Asian Americans.* San Francisco, CA: Jossey-Bass.

Tseng, W. S., & Wu, D. Y. H. (1985). *Chinese culture and mental health.* San Diego, CA: Academic Press.

Zane, N., & Sue, S. (1996). Health issues of Asian Pacific American adolescents. In M. Kagawa-Singer, P. A. Katz, D. A. Taylor, & J. H. M. Vanderryn (Eds.), *Health issues for minority adolescents* (pp. 142–167). Lincoln, NE: University of Nebraska Press.

REFERENCES

Amstrong, T. L., & Swartzman, L. C. (1999). Asian versus Western differences in satisfaction with Western medical care: The mediational effects of illness attributions. *Psychology and Health, 14,* 403–416.

Bell-Dolan, D. J., Reaven, N. M., & Peterson, L. (1993). Depression and social functioning: A multidimensional study of linkages. *Journal of Clinical Child Psychology, 22,* 306–315.

Blount, A., & Bayona, J. (1994). Toward a system of integrated primary care. *Family Systems Medicine, 12,* 171–182.

Bond, M., & Hwang, K. (1986). The social psychology of the Chinese people. In M. Bond (Ed.), *The psychology of Chinese people* (pp. 213–266). Hong Kong: Oxford University Press.

Bourne, P. G., & Nguyen, D. S. (1967). A comparative study of neuropsychiatric casualties in the United States army and the army of the republic of Vietnam. *Military Medicine, 132,* 904–909.

Brandt, A. M. (1997). Behaviour, disease, and health in the twentieth century United States: The moral valence of individual risk. In A. M. Brandt & P. Rozin (Eds.), *Morality and health* (pp. 53–77). New York: Routledge.

Brownell, K. D. (1991). Personal responsibility and control over our bodies: When expectation exceeds reality. *Health Psychology, 10,* 303–310.

Camras, L. A., Oster, H., Campos, J., Campos, R., Ujiie, T., Miyake, K., Wang, L., & Meng, Z. (1998). Production of emotional facial expressions in European American, Japanese, and Chinese infants. *Developmental Psychology, 34,* 616–628.

Caudill, W., & Weinstein, H. (1969). Maternal care and infant behavior in Japan and America. *Psychiatry, 32,* 12–43.

Chan-Sew, S. (1980, October). *Chinatown Child Development Center: A service delivery model.* Paper presented at the Conference on a Mental Health Service Delivery Model for Chinese American Children and Families, San Francisco.

Chen, C., Greenberger, E., Lester, J., Dong, Q., & Guo, M. S. (1998). A cross-cultural study of family and peer correlates of adolescent misconduct. *Developmental Psychology, 34,* 770–781.

Chen, X. (2000). Growing up in a collectivistic culture: Socialization and socio-emotional development in Chinese children. In A. L. Comunian & U. P. Gielen (Eds.), *International perspectives on human development* (pp. 331–353). Lengerich, Germany: Pabst.

Chen, X., & Li, B. (2000). Depressed mood in Chinese children: Developmental significance for social and school adjustment. *International Journal of Behavioural Development, 24,* 472–479.

Chen, X., Chen, H., Kaspar, V., & Noh, S. (2000). Adolescent social, emotional and school adjustment in Mainland China. *International Journal of Group Tension, 29,* 51–78.

Chen, X., Hastings, P., Rubin, K. H., Chen, H., Cen, G., & Stewart, S. L. (1998). Childrearing attitudes and behavioral inhibition in Chinese and Canadian toddlers: A cross-cultural study. *Developmental Psychology, 34,* 677–686.

Chen, X., Rubin, K. H., & Li, B. (1995a). Social and school adjustment of shy and aggressive children in China. *Development and Psychopathology, 7,* 337–349.

Chen, X., Rubin, K. H., & Li, B. (1995b). Depressed mood in Chinese children: Relations with school performance and family environment. *Journal of Consulting and Clinical Psychology, 63,* 938–947.

Chen, X., Rubin, K. H., & Li, Z. (1995c). Social functioning and adjustment in Chinese children: A longitudinal study. *Developmental Psychology, 31,* 531–539.

Chen, X., Rubin, K. H., & Sun, Y. (1992). Social reputation and peer relationships in Chinese and Canadian children: A cross-cultural study. *Child Development, 63,* 1336–1343.

Cheung, F. M. C. (1986). Psychopathology among Chinese people. In M. H. Bond (Ed.), *The psychology of the Chinese people* (pp. 171–211). New York: Oxford University Press.

Chun, C. A., Enomoto, K., & Sue, S. (1996). Health care issues among Asian Americans: Implications of somatization. In P. M. Kato & T. Mann (Eds.), Handbook of diversity issues in health psychology (pp. 347–365). New York: Plenum.

Chung, R. C. Y., & Okazaki, S. (1991). Counseling Americans of Southeast Asian descent: The impact of the refugee experience. In E. E. Lee & B. L. Richardson (Eds.), *Multicultural issues in counseling: New approaches to diversity* (pp. 107–126). Alexandria, VA: American Association for Counseling and Development.

Crystal, D. S., Chen, C., Fuligni, A. J., Hsu, C. C., Ko, H. J., Kitamura, S., & Kimura, S. (1994). Psychological maladjustment and academic achievement: A cross-cultural study of Japanese, Chinese, and American high school students. *Child Development, 65,* 738–753.

Denig, P., Haaijer-Ruskamp, F. M., Wesseling, H., & Versluis, A. (1993). Towards understanding treatment preferences of hospital physicians, *Social Science & Medicine, 369,* 915–924.

Dong, Q., Yang, B., & Ollendick, T. H. (1994). Fears in Chinese children and adolescents and their relations to anxiety and depression. *Journal of Child Psychology and Psychiatry, 35,* 351–363.

Engel, G. (1977). The need for a new medical model: A challenge for biomedicine. *Science, 196,* 129–136.

Erickson, R. V., & Hoang, G. N. (1980). Health problems among Indochinese refugees. *American Journal of Public Health, 70,* 1003–1006.

Fogel, A., Toda, S., & Kawai, M. (1988). Mother–child face-to-face interaction in Japan and the United States: A laboratory comparison using 3-month-old infants. *Developmental Psychology, 24,* 398–406.

Freedman, D. G. (1974). *Human infancy: An evolutionary perspective.* New York: Halsted Press.

Gong, Y. (1984). Use of the Eysenck Personality Questionnaire in China. *Personality and Individual Differences, 5,* 431–438.

Gong-Guy, E. (1987). *The California Southeast Asian mental health needs assessment.* Oakland, CA: Asian Community Mental Health Services.

Guyton, A. C. (1976). *Textbook of medical physiology* (5th Ed.). Toronto: Saunders.

Hammer, L. (1990). *Dragon rises, red bird flies: Psychology, energy & Chinese medicine.* New York: Station Hill Press.

Harrington, R. (1993). *Depressive disorder in childhood and adolescence.* New York: Wiley.

Ho, D. Y. F. (1986). Chinese pattern of socialization: A critical review. In M. H. Bond (Ed.), *The psychology of the Chinese people* (pp. 1–37). New York: Oxford University Press.

Ho, P., & Lisowski, F. P. (1997). *A brief history of Chinese medicine.* Singapore: World Scientific.

Kagan, J., Arcus, D., Snidman, N., Feng, W., Hendler, J., & Greene, S. (1994). Reactivity in infants: A cross-national comparison. *Developmental Psychology, 30,* 342–345.

Kaptchuk, T. J. (1983). *The web that has no weaver: Understanding Chinese medicine.* New York: Congdon & Weed.

Kim, B. L. C. (1978). *The Asian-Americans: Changing patterns, changing needs.* Montclair, NJ: Association of Korean Christian Scholars in North America.

King, A. Y. C., & Bond, M. H. (1985). The Confucian paradigm of man: A sociological view. In W. S. Tseng & D. Y. H. Wu (Eds.), *Chinese culture and mental health* (pp. 29–45). San Diego, CA: Academic Press.

Kirscht, J. P. (1977). Communication between patients and physicians. *Annals of Internal Medicine, 86,* 499–501.

Kleinman, A. (1977). Depression, somatization and the "new cross-cultural psychiatry." *Social Science & Medicine, 11,* 3–10.

Landrine, H., & Klonoff, E. A. (1994). Cultural diversity in commonsense beliefs about causes of six illness. *Journal of Behavioral Medicine, 17,* 407–418.

Lee, B. K. (1996). *When east meets west: Acculturation and socio-emotional adjustment in Canadian-Chinese adolescents.* Unpublished Master's thesis, University of Western Ontario.

Leichter, H. M. (1997). Lifestyle correctness and the new secular morality. In A. M. Brandt & P. Rozin (Eds.), *Morality and health* (pp. 359–377). New York: Routledge.

Leong, F. T. L. (1986). Counselling and psychotherapy with Asian-Americans: Review of the literature. *Journal of Counselling Psychology, 33,* 196–206.

Leventhal, H., Zimmerman, R., & Gutmann, M. (1984). Compliance: A self-regulation perspective. In D. Gentry (Ed.), *Handbook of behavioral medicine* (pp. 369–436). New York: Guilford.

Lewis, M. (1989). Culture and biology: The role of temperament. In P. Zelazo & R. Barr (Eds.), *Challenges to developmental paradigms* (pp. 203–223). Hillsdale, NJ: Erlbaum.

Li, F. P. (1972). Health care for the Chinese community in Boston. *American Journal of Public Health, 62,* 536–539.

Lin, K. M. (1981). Traditional Chinese medical beliefs and their relevance for mental illness and psychiatry. In A. Kleinman & T. Y. Lin (Eds.), *Normal and abnormal behavior in Chinese culture* (pp. 95–111). Dordrecht, Holland: D. Reidel.

Lin, T. Y. (1985). Mental disorders and psychiatry in Chinese culture: Characteristic features and major issues. In W. Tseng & D. Y. H. Wu (Eds.), *Chinese culture and mental health* (pp. 369–393). Academic Press, Inc., Harcourt Brace Jovanovich.

Loo, C. M. (1998). *Chinese America: Mental health and quality of life in the inner city.* Thousand Oaks, CA: Sage.

Luo, G. (1996). *Chinese traditional social and moral ideas and rules.* Beijing, China: The University of Chinese People Press.

Nilchaikovit, T., Hill, J. M., & Holland, J. C. (1993). The effects of culture on illness behavior and medical care. *General Hospital Psychiatry, 15,* 41–50.

Nolen-Hoeksema, S., Girgus, J. S., & Seligman, M. E. P. (1992). Predictors and consequences of childhood depressive symptoms: A 5-year longitudinal study. *Journal of Abnormal Psychology, 101,* 405–422.

Ollendick, T. H., & Yule, W. (1990). Depression in British and American children and its relation to anxiety and fear. *Journal of Consulting and Clinical Psychology, 58,* 126–129.

Owen, T. C. (1985). Southeast Asian mental health: Transition from treatment services to prevention—A new direction. In T. C. Owen (Ed.), *Southeast Asian mental health: Treatment, prevention, service, training, and research.* Rockville, MD: National Institute of Mental Health.

Peralta, V., & Horikawa, H. (1978). *Needs and potentialities assessment of Asian American elderly in greater Philadelphia* (Report No. 3). Chicago, IL: Asian American Mental Health Research Center.

Potter, S. H. (1988). The cultural construction of emotion in rural Chinese social life. *Ethos, 16,* 181–208.

Quah, S., & Bishop, G. D. (1996). Seeking help for illness: The roles of cultural orientation and illness cognition. *Journal of Health Psychology, 1,* 307–322.

Sadler, J. Z., & Hulgus, Y. F. (1992). Clinical problem solving and the biopsychosocial model. *American Journal of Psychiatry, 149,* 1315–1323.

Schwartz, G. E. (1979). The brain as a health care system. In G. C. Stone, F. Cohen, & N. E. Adler (Eds.), *Health psychology: A handbook* (pp. 549–572). San Francisco, CA: Jossey Bass.

Shek, D. T. (1991). Depressive symptoms in a sample of Chinese adolescents: An experimental study using the Chinese version of the Beck Depression Inventory. *International Journal of Adolescent Medicine and Health, 5,* 1–16.

Sue, S., & Morishima, H. (1982). *The mental health of Asian Americans.* San Francisco, CA: Jossey-Bass.

Sue, S., Nakamura, C. Y., Chung, R. C. Y., & Yee-Bradbury, C. (1994). Mental health research on Asian Americans. *Journal of Community Psychology, 22,* 61–67.

Taylor, S. E., & Brown, J. D. (1988). Illusion and well-being: A social and psychological perspective on mental health. *Psychological Bulletin, 108,* 192–210.

Thomas, K. (1997). Health and morality in early modern England. In A. M. Brandt & P. Rozin (Eds.), *Morality and health* (pp. 15–33). New York: Routledge.

Tongyonk, J. (1972). Depression in Thailand in the perspective of comparative–transcultural psychiatry. *Journal of Psychiatric Association of Thailand, 17,* 44–50.

Traue, H. C., & Pennebaker, J. W. (1993). *Emotion inhibition and health.* Seattle, WA: Hogrefe & Huber.

Tseng, W. S. (1975). The nature of somatic complaints among psychiatric patients: The Chinese case. *Comprehensive Psychiatry, 16,* 5–14.

Tseng, W. S., & Hsu, J. (1969–70). Chinese culture, personality formation and mental illness. *International Journal of Social Psychiatry, 16,* 5–14.

Xie, Z. (1999). Medical knowledge: Weather and health. *Beijing Evening News,* July 3.

Zane, N., & Sue, S. (1996). Health issues of Asian Pacific American adolescents. In M. Kagawa-Singer, P. A. Katz, D. A. Taylor, & J. H. M. Vanderryn (Eds.), *Health issues for minority adolescents* (pp. 142–167). Lincoln, NE: University of Nebraska Press.

15

HEALTH PSYCHOLOGY:
SOUTH ASIAN
PERSPECTIVES

PRAFUL CHANDARANA

Department of Psychiatry
The University of Western Ontario
London, Ontario, Canada

JOSEPH R. PELLIZZARI

Mental Health Care Program
London Health Sciences Center
London, Ontario, Canada

The emerging field of cultural health psychology offers an opportunity for re-searchers and clinicians to understand the increasing diversity of health-related behaviors in culturally plural societies. As discussed in Chapter 1 (Kazarian & Evans) and outlined by Berry (1998), two related enterprises have developed in an attempt to understand this diversity. The first entails the study of how cultural factors influence the health-related behavior of specific populations within their indigenous cultures (the *cross-cultural domain*), while the second involves the study of how these influences present themselves within the context of accultur-ation as culturally distinct groups establish themselves in culturally plural soci-eties (the *ethnic domain*). As Berry (1998) suggests, the study of the cross-cultural domain has received much more empirical attention from a multidisci-plinary perspective. The South Asian example is no exception in this regard (e.g., Carstairs & Kapur, 1976; Chakraborty, 1991; Kakar, 1982; Khare, 1996; Lam & Palsane, 1997; Lambert, 1992, 1996; Paranjpe & Bhatt, 1997; Pugh, 1991; Sub-barayappa, 1997). It is becoming increasingly clear that knowledge from the cul-tural domain can serve to inform and complement research and clinical practice in the ethnic domain. The study of health beliefs and practices among South Asians exemplifies this phenomenon, particularly within those countries such as Canada, the United States, and the United Kingdom, where large South Asian immigrant populations reside (e.g., Assanand, Dias, Richardson, & Waxler-Morrison, 1990; Furnham & Malik, 1994; Ramakrishna & Weiss, 1992; Williams & Hunt, 1997).

Given the premise for the chapter, the intention is to offer a review of information from both the cultural and ethnic domains with respect to South Asian cultural groups and their perspectives on health and illness. A detailed, descriptive narrative of the several subgroups will be given, according to religious customs, traditions, language, political contexts, and immigration paths. This will offer the clinician and researcher a repository of information about the various cultural groups falling under the rubric of "South Asian." Following this, the main models of health practiced among these groups will be described, focusing primarily on Ayurvedic principles (Nordstrom, 1989; Obeyesekere, 1982; Sharma, Dev Triguna, & Chopra, 1991; Titus, 1995). Special topics particular to the South Asian cultural view will then be presented, such as the role of family and views of the self. Last, culture-specific issues in physical and mental health will be reviewed with particular attention to how practitioners in health psychology (and related disciplines) can integrate this knowledge into practice.

SOUTH ASIAN CULTURAL GROUPS DESCRIBED

THE TERMS "SOUTH ASIAN," "INDIAN," AND "EAST INDIAN"

Geographically, South Asia includes the countries of India, Pakistan, Sri Lanka, Bangladesh, Nepal, Bhutan, and Maldives. In North America, people from India are commonly referred to as "Indians" or, more recently, "East Indians," to distinguish them from the American Indians and from the West Indians who came from the West Indies. The latter term is largely restricted to people of African origin from the Caribbean region. Further, people of Indian origin whose migratory path to North America was via the West Indies are also referred to mainly as East Indians, to signify their roots in India. While the usage of the term "South Asian" is largely restricted to North America, it has become the term of choice to refer to people from India and Pakistan who have migrated through various paths over the last three or four generations. The primary focus of the chapter will be on the cultural groups from India and Pakistan who form the majority of South Asian immigrants to Western countries.

HETEROGENEITY IS THE RULE

South Asia is particularly known for its heterogeneity in language, religion, food, philosophy, and general approach to life, which has a direct influence on health beliefs and practices. For example, 18 languages are recognized in India alone and there are hundreds of regional dialects. Hindi and English are the official languages of India while Urdu is the official language of Pakistan, although over half of Pakistanis speak Punjabi or Sindhi. Sinhala, Tamil, and English are the most prevalent languages in Sri Lanka (Blood, 1994; Heitzman & Worden, 1995; Ross & Savada, 1988).

India, Pakistan, and the other South Asian countries have several distinct cultural groups which are largely influenced by religion, language, heritage, and geography. To add to this complexity, rapid industrialization, urbanization, and adoption of Western values has transformed these populations over the past 50 years. The caste system in India is gradually being abandoned, a new socioeconomic order has emerged and, whereas poverty is still rampant in the urban centers (e.g., for Calcutta, see Chakraborty, 1990), a large educated middle class has surfaced on the subcontinent. Despite preventive efforts (e.g., Jejeebhoy, 1998), the overall population continues to grow at a very fast pace. In India alone, there is an estimated 1 billion people, making it the world's second most populous country (Heitzman & Worden, 1995). Government instability, overcrowding, pollution, substandard living conditions, and a general lack of consistent infrastructure persists. In this scenario, the very rich continue to thrive while the middle class struggles and the very poor barely manage to survive. In fact, about 50% of India continues to live below the poverty line (Assanand et al., 1990; Eyles, 1986).

Given the diversity among South Asian cultural groups, it becomes challenging to offer broad generalizations regarding the influences on their health-related behavior. Regardless, several prominent South Asian cultural groups can be identified and will be described, according to differences in religious faith and migratory paths. This will be followed by a description of the most common models of health care practiced in South Asian cultural groups. These models range from the Western biomedical (allopathic) tradition, to the ancient traditional or indigenous systems of Ayurveda, Unanni, and Siddha, to homeopathy, to a combination of Western and non-Western approaches (Eyles, 1986; Khare, 1996; Titus, 1995). Finally, these descriptive elements will be integrated with concepts of acculturation to offer a practical framework for understanding the South Asian client/patient.

RELIGIOUS DIVERSITY AMONG SOUTH ASIAN POPULATIONS

Hinduism

An overwhelming majority of South Asians (about 82% of the population of India) and a minority of Sri Lankans (about 15% of the population—primarily of Tamil ethnicity) practice Hinduism, which is viewed not just as a religion but also as a way of life. It proposes a broad range of cultural patterns which include religious rituals, interpersonal relationships, respect for all life forms, and an attitude of tolerance and acceptance. This openness has led to incorporation of a variety of beliefs and practices as the religion has evolved from its ancient roots. This has caused widespread variation in forms of worship, food habits, and dress code. Further, there is no recognized single founder and the patterns of thinking, attitudes, and behavior are sanctioned by reference to ancient sacred scriptures ("Vedas") and a variety of deities (Assanand et al., 1990; Heitzman & Worden, 1995; Ramakrishna & Weiss, 1992; Ross & Savada, 1988).

Virtually every city in the U.K. and North America has a formal Hindu organization. Temples have been erected in each of the large cities where Hindus congregate to pray. Temple activities have facilitated networking within the communities and among temples through creation of umbrella organizations (e.g., Hindu Council of Canada, founded in 1983). Language and culture are actively promoted through informal Sunday schools and social and religious festivals. Most importantly, the temple provides a base for a supportive network for members who are in need. For new immigrants, the temple frequently becomes the focal point from which relationships are initiated.

A common thread that ties factions of the Hindu religion is the concept of unity of life. According to this concept, all life forms are interdependent and life continues after death (i.e., reincarnation). Good deeds in current life lead to rebirth in a higher life form and eventual union with the Almighty. Killing other animals is considered a sin and, hence, most Hindus in a traditional society practice vegetarianism. In North America however, many Indians eat meat but it is not usually the main part of their diet and beef is frequently avoided (Ramakrishna & Weiss, 1992).

In addition to the concept of unity of life, another notion widely held by traditional Hindus is the hierarchical organization of the society into a caste system. The status of each member in the hierarchy is determined by blood line. Hence, in its strictest form, there is no opportunity to climb to a higher class. Members of the higher class (e.g., the Brahmins—the priestly and learned class) typically do not associate with members of the lower class (e.g., the lowest class, termed "Untouchables," "Scheduled Castes," "Harijans," or "Dalit"—those involved with the most menial of tasks). Intercaste marriages are forbidden in the traditional society. As can be expected, this hierarchical system has led to a great deal of controversy and is gradually being abandoned, due to sociopolitical pressures. In fact, it is not officially sanctioned by the Indian constitution, which explicitly forbids negative public discrimination on the basis of caste (Heitzman & Worden, 1995). As a result of the acculturation process, only remnants of the caste system are evident among the Indian immigrants to Western countries. However, it is occasionally the source of intergenerational conflict, as is the related issue of arranged marriages, still the norm in India (Ramakrishna & Weiss, 1992).

Other prominent features of Hinduism can be seen through the many festivals that fill the Hindu calendar. The most prominent of these is Diwali, the festival of lights, which is considered to be the Hindu equivalent to Christmas for Christians. The occasion marks the end of the calendar year for many sects and signifies the return of God Rama after a 14-year exile. A Hindu's life is punctuated by a number of festive rites to mark different stages of life from birth to death. Each rite of passage involves the performance of religious rituals at home or at the temple as the Hindu progresses through life. Besides reinforcing a cultural identity, these occasions provide opportunities to celebrate, pray, and socialize. Overall, this ancient religion has many facets and devotees have a common bond through their heritage that provides a clear sense of identity, a sense of community, a sense of belonging, and ultimately, a source of support in the context of health and illness (Assanand et al., 1990).

Islam

Islam is the second largest religion in the South Asian subcontinent. Ninety-seven percent of the people in the Islamic Republic of Pakistan and 12% of the people in India are Muslim. Like Hinduism, Islam is not just a religion but also a complete way of life, social system, law, and state. The majority of Muslims moved to East Pakistan (now the Islamic Republic of Pakistan) and West Pakistan (now Bangladesh), following the partitioning of British India along religious lines in 1947 (Blood, 1994; Heitzman & Worden, 1995).

Muslims follow the teachings of the Koran, the Holy Book, which records the will of God as revealed to the prophet Mohammed (570–632 C.E.). "Islam" literally means "submission," referring to the submission to the will of God and the rejection of all other gods. Muslims are required to pray five times each day and devout Muslims will halt any routine task when it is time for prayers. Prayers are always conducted facing the direction of Mecca, the holy city, and are preceded by a ritual of cleaning and washing. Each Friday, Muslims congregate at the mosque to pray. Analogous to the Hindu temple, the mosque provides a center for the propagation of religion, culture, language, and a code of ethics. Generosity, fairness, and mutual respect are strongly advocated. Adultery, gambling, and alcohol consumption are not permitted. Pork is rigidly excluded from all diets and meats are only eaten if the animal or fowl is killed according to Muslim custom. Most Muslims purchase their meat and chicken ("halal" meat or chicken) from special stores where proper procedure is followed to produce these items (Assanand et al., 1990).

Muslims are divided into two major sects, the predominant Sunnis (about 80% of Muslims overall; 77% of Muslims in Pakistan; 90% of Muslims in India) and the Shi'ites (or Shia—about 10–15% of Muslims overall; 20% of Muslims in Pakistan; about 10% of Muslims in India). In general, these two largest sects arose from a lack of agreement over who should succeed the prophet Muhammed as the religious leader (Blood, 1994; Heitzman & Wordman, 1995). Subsects of Sunnis and Shias also exist. For example, in India, the largest Shia subsect are the Ismailis, who see their spiritual leader, the Aga Khan, as a descendent of Prophet Mohammed.

Muslim organizations, particularly those of Urdu-speaking Pakistanis, have developed in virtually every major North American city. Whereas religious tensions have erupted between India and Pakistan since independence, this conflict is typically not evident between these two main South Asian immigrant groups in North America and the U.K. On the contrary, it is common for these two groups to celebrate together at music and dance festivals, which are very much a part of South Asian life.

Sikhism

The Sikhs in India (about 2% of the population) have gained prominence despite their small numbers through a significant role in the armed forces and public affairs. Sikhism was founded by Guru Nanak in Punjab, Northern India, during the 15th century. In general, Guru Nanak's aim was for a single, unique religious formulation, which integrated essential Hindu tenets, such as reincarnation and karma, with the preachings of Islam. Sikhs believe in devotion to a single god, the philosophy of universal love, and the equality of all men and women before God. As such, Sikhism essentially rejects the hierarchical caste system (Heitzman & Worden, 1995).

Guru Nanak was followed by nine gurus in succession. The last to succeed was Guru Gobind Singh (1666–1708), who continues to hold a position of reverence in the minds of Sikhs. This latter Guru began a ceremonial rite of baptism involving the immersion of a sword in sugared water. This rite initiates Sikh men into the Khalsa ("army of the pure"), where devotion is observed according to the "Five Ks": uncut hair (*kesh*), a long knife (*kirpan,* now symbolized by a small ceremonial knife), a comb (*kangha*), a steel bangle or bracelet, worn on the right wrist (*kara*), and a pantlike garment not reaching below the knee (*kachha*). In modern India and around the world, the most outwardly visible of these is the *kesh,* where the beard is left uncut and scalp hair is kept long, tied up, and covered by distinctive turbans. Also, according to this tradition, members adopt the surname Singh (meaning "lion"), while women take the surname Kaur (meaning "princess"). Alcohol, tobacco, and other intoxicants are forbidden through vows to purify personal behavior (Assanand et al., 1990; Heitzman & Worden, 1995).

In Sikh religion, prayers recited from the Guru Granth Sahib (Holy Book of the Gurus) are a central feature of all ceremonies. These ceremonies are held in the *gurdwara,* which is defined as the room which holds the Holy Book. *Gurdwaras* have been constructed in most large cities in the Western world. Analogous to the Hindu temple, the *gurdwara* serves as a meeting place for Sikhs, from which cultural and social activities are planned. In contrast to the Hindu religion, the worship of idols is forbidden (Assanand et al., 1990; Heitzman & Worden, 1995).

Christianity

Colonization of part of India by the Portuguese led to the conversion of some native South Asians to Christianity (led by Jesuit Saint Francis Xavier). Currently, 2% of the population of India practices Christianity and the majority are

Catholics. Following their migration, most have joined churches established before their arrival in North America (Heitzman & Worden, 1995). A small Christian population (8%) is also present in Sri Lanka, largely converted through the influence of the Portuguese (Catholics), the Dutch, and the British (Ross & Savada, 1988).

Jainism

Jainism is one of the most ancient religious traditions on the Indian subcontinent. Evidence supports its roots in the Indus Valley Civilization, which had its beginnings around 3000 B.C.E. (Oldfield, 1989). *Ahimsa* (nonviolence or noninjury) is central to the teachings of Jainsim. This central theme has steered Jains away from occupations which directly or indirectly involve killing of life forms. Instead, Jains channel their energy into academics, business, and commerce, fields in which they have earned substantial success. Their belief in the danger of worldly possessions and their ideal of a simple lifestyle has encouraged them to donate generously for public causes. Other principles they follow include amity, appreciation, compassion, and equanimity.

There are over three million Jains in India (0.48% of the total population; Oldfield, 1989). They form a small but visible, distinct, and influential group among South Asians in the U.K., U.S., and Canada. Their success in business and professions has continued following their migration to the West. Jain temples, which are renowned for their artistic architecture, have been erected in larger centers and prayers are held regularly.

Buddhism

Buddhists have long formed a small religious minority in India (0.8% of the population) but have grown considerably in recent years with the migration of Buddhists from Tibet and the conversion of some Hindus to this faith (Heitzman & Worden, 1995). Buddhism is the dominant religion in Sri Lanka, where 69% of the population practice this faith. Most Buddhists in Sri Lanka come from the Sinhalese cultural group (Ross & Savada, 1988).

Buddhism was founded in North India by Siddhartha Gautama (the "Buddha" or "awakened one") circa 525 B.C.E. While there now exist several sects of Buddhism, some of the common beliefs and practices center around the "four noble truths": all of life is suffering (*dukhka*), the cause of suffering is desire (*trishna*), the end of desire leads to the end of suffering (*nirvana*), and the end of desire comes through a path of discipline ("The Middle Way") and meditation. This philosophy is similar to that found in the Hindu religion (Heitzman & Worden, 1995).

PATHS OF IMMIGRATION

Having described the South Asian cultural groups according to their main religious practices, we will now describe them based on their various paths of immigration to Western countries. Many of the cultural groups from the South Asian subcontinent currently residing in Canada, the United States, and the United Kingdom have come directly from their country of origin through voluntary immigration. A substantial number, however, came via other parts of the world, such as East Africa, South Africa, the Caribbean region, and the Fiji Islands in the South Pacific, where they had lived for up to four generations. As would be expected, this latter "indirect" subpopulation underwent significant acculturative change prior to their arrival to yet another culture in North America or the U.K. This is particularly true for the group of South Asians who were brought up in countries such as Kenya, Uganda, and Guiana during the British colonial rule (Assanand et al., 1990).

Emigration from South Asia over the past two centuries has occurred in stages. In the initial stages, emigration was facilitated by the British colonial powers, who occupied the subcontinent during the 1800s to the early 1900s and required assistance in other colonial regions. For instance, the need for a workforce to develop and maintain the sugar plantations in Guiana in the late 19th century led to the migration of South Asian Indians, mainly from the south of India, for this purpose. In another example, in the early part of the 20th century, South Asian Indians were brought to the East African countries of Kenya, Uganda, and Tanzania to build the railway system and administer in the civil service. This initial influx was followed by a significant number of entrepreneurs who came on their own initiative to open businesses or practice their professions. Consistent with the extended family system of traditional India, a second wave of relatives followed, to continue the group acculturation process.

The South Asian immigrants prospered while their countries of migration were under colonial rule, initially being most active in the retail trades. While the second generation continued in business, the South Asians began to further establish their presence in the professional world. A marked shift, however, occurred in the status of South Asians as the colonial powers relinquished their hold and these countries began to gain independence. New governments began to adopt policies to correct the inequities of the past. Specific laws were enacted to encourage the participation of the native population in business and agriculture. South Asians soon found themselves in a difficult position with this shift and began to search for more congenial environments in which to continue their trades. Uganda represents the extreme case, where South Asians were given three months by the dictatorial leader Idi Amin to leave or face the risk of death (Assanand et al., 1990).

Hence, the arrival of South Asians to Western countries has been through various direct and indirect routes and has been triggered by many factors, including sociopolitical (e.g., East Africa and Fiji), the search for a better quality of life, the urge to be with members of extended family who have already migrated, and general entrepreneurial zeal (Ananth & Ananth, 1996; Ramakrishna & Weiss, 1992). They have taken up residence in virtually every Western country and the acculturation strategies of the various South Asian cultural groups have spanned the range of strategies outlined by Berry (1998, pp. 43–44). Some have chosen *assimilation* (cultural identity is not maintained and host culture is adopted), or *separation* (original cultural values are rigidly adhered to and interaction with host culture is avoided). In culturally diverse countries, where there is an open and inclusive attitude toward multiculturalism, the acculturation strategy of *integration* is often the goal for South Asian cultural groups, wherein maintenance of cultural integrity is coupled with an effort to interact with other groups and participate in the society at large.

SOUTH ASIANS FROM THE INDIAN SUB-CONTINENT

The majority of South Asians who live in the U.K., the U.S., and Canada came directly to these countries. A large wave of migrants from the Indo-Pakistan subcontinent to the U.K. occurred in the 1950s and 1960s. This wave consisted of young men who came to England for higher education. They were subsequently followed by professionals, entrepreneurs, and skilled workers. Migration accelerated further over the past 30 years as British subjects of Indian origin from former colonies began to flow into England (London, 1986). From 1996 to 1998, 22 to 24% of all those accepted for settlement in the U.K. were from the Indian subcontinent and represented the largest immigration group. Of those, roughly one-half came from Pakistan, with the remainder equally distributed among India and Bangladesh (Jackson & Chilton, 1999).

The trend in Canada began at the turn of the 20th century, when the first group of Sikh men from the north Indian state of Punjab arrived in Canada. Most of these men joined the forest industry, working mainly in sawmills around the Vancouver area. South Asian immigration was banned in 1909, only to be partially lifted 10 years later to permit family reunification. By 1942, there were only 6000 South Asians in Canada (Ananth & Ananth, 1996). Changes in immigration regulation led to more widespread emigration from India and Pakistan. The wave of immigrants arriving in the 1960s and 1970s consisted mainly of technicians and professionals selected by the Canadian embassies in their home countries (Assanand et al., 1990).

At present, there are approximately 300,000 South Asians residing in various parts of Canada. Most of them live in urban centers in either Ontario or British Columbia. South Asia is consistently among the top two sources for immigration in Canada (1994–1997), with the majority coming from India and sizable numbers arriving from Pakistan and Sri Lanka. Together, immigrants from South Asia have represented around 15% of all immigrants to Canada annually over the past few years (Assanand et al., 1990; Citizenship and Immigration Canada, 1996, 1999).

The migration of South Asians to the U.S. shows a similar pattern. Initial restrictive quotas, followed by more liberal immigration regulations, spurred a rising influx of educated South Asians to the U.S. In the 1980s, there were approximately 362,000 Indians of South Asian origin residing in the U.S. By the 1990s, the population had risen to 815,000. From 1995 to 1998, South Asia was the second or third source for immigration to the U.S. (around 6 to 7% of total U.S. immigration annually). Immigrants came mainly from India and Pakistan, with India being the source for roughly 3 times the numbers of those from Pakistan (Ananth & Ananth, 1996; Immigration and Naturalization Service, 1999a,b).

SOUTH ASIANS FROM EAST AFRICA

A significant emigration of South Asians from East Africa was triggered in 1972 by political turmoil in Uganda under the dictatorial rule of Idi Amin. The first group of refugees from Uganda to Canada was scattered across the country. This group represented all classes of workers, with the majority being highly educated, fluent in English, and accustomed to a British style of infrastructure during the colonial rule. As a result, they adjusted rapidly to their new country of adoption. The initial trauma of being suddenly uprooted and having to leave material wealth behind is seen at present by many among this group as a blessing in disguise. In the absence of migration, this group faced certain oppression or even death had they remained in Uganda.

Even before the political crisis in Uganda, there was a steady voluntary emigration of South Asians from East African countries to Canada and the U.S. In these cases, their migration was well planned and many had confirmed jobs waiting for them when they landed. Since their arrival from East Africa, South Asians have merged with their counterparts from India. Although differences in value systems, language, food, and other habits prevail among these groups, their bond through a common culture, religion, and heritage is evident.

Gujarati-speaking Ismailis (Shia Muslims), who originated from the state of Gujarat in India and migrated in significant numbers to Canada and the U.K. after a generation in East Africa, represent another distinct group. They show a very strong allegiance to their spiritual leader, the Aga Khan, and operate under a well-administered infrastructure under his leadership. Ismailis worship at their own mosques, which, like other South Asian religious groups, serve as centers for community support. In general, despite their small numbers, Ismailis have gained prominence in business (e.g., the Western Canadian hospitality industry) and professions since their arrival in North America and the U.K. (Assanand et al., 1990).

SOUTH ASIANS FROM FIJI

The history of South Asian emigration from Fiji is similar to that of the South Asians from East Africa. Their migration in significant numbers began in 1987 after political instability in their home country. It is estimated that there are now 14,000 Fijians in Canada, the majority of them in the Vancouver area. Virtually all of them speak English, having been educated under the British system during colonial rule. Most came to Canada as skilled and semiskilled workers and an overwhelming majority of this group practice Hinduism. Like their East African counterparts, their adaptation to life in North America was eased by their familiarity with Western society (Assanand et al., 1990).

SOUTH ASIANS FROM THE CARIBBEAN REGION

Unlike South Asians from other parts of the world, the group from the Caribbean region appears to have undergone a more noticeable change during their transition from the West Indies and Guiana. Some have converted from Hinduism to Christianity and nearly all of them have lost their native languages. This is likely because of the geographical distance from India and the fact that they had been separated from their native land for over four generations. Most were originally brought to Guiana and Trinidad as indentured labor. Their entrepreneurial spirit and zeal for academic pursuits improved their status in the Caribbean prior to the end of British rule. The majority of South Asian immigrants from the Caribbean are professionals and skilled workers. Despite their greater disengagement from India, their kinship with other South Asians is evident. Most South Asians from the Caribbean region had already adopted Western traditions and values; hence, their settlement in North America has been eased, while geographical proximity helps them to maintain strong ties with their country of recent origin.

SUMMARY: SOUTH ASIAN CULTURAL GROUPS DESCRIBED

The theme of heterogeneity highlighted at the beginning of this section is truly prominent among South Asian cultural groups. These groups are largely identified by food, language, religion, and geographical location. Further diversity has evolved according to the various paths of migration. Applying the conceptual framework described by Berry (1998), a South Asian individual from any of the numerous cultural groups could be at any level of acculturation and adaptation.

Table 15.1 offers a summary of the various South Asian cultural groups which will provide the context for the subsequent, more focused discussion on South Asian perspectives of health and illness. It will also help the clinician or researcher as an initial starting point in understanding the large number of South Asian cultural groups.

TABLE 15.1   A Summary of South Asian Cultural Groups

INDIA	*Main languages*
	• Hindi (official)
	• English (official)
	• 16 others (e.g., Gujarati)
	
	Main religious groups
	• Hindu (82%)
	• Islam (12% overall)
	   — Sunni (90%)
	   — Shia (10%—mostly Ismailis)
	• Christian (2.4%)
	• Sikh (2%)
	• Buddhists (.8%)
	• Jains (.48%)
	
	Ethnicity
	• Indo-Aryan (72%)
	• Dravidian (25%)
	• Mongoloid and others (3%)

PAKISTAN	*Main languages*
	• Urdu (official)
	• Punjabi (main) and variant Siraiki
	• Sindhi
	• at least 6 others (e.g., Pakhtu or Pashto, Balochi)
	
	Main religious groups
	• Islam (97% overall)
	   — Sunni (77%)
	   — Shia (20%)
	
	Ethnicity
	• Punjabi (59%)
	• Pakhtun or Pashto (14%)
	• Baloch (4%)
	• Muhajir–immigrants (8%)
	• others

SRI LANKA	*Main languages* • Sinhala (official) • Tamil • English *Main religious groups* • Buddhist (69%) • Hindu (15%) • Christian (8%) • Islam (8%) *Ethnicity* • Sinhalese (74%—mainly Buddhist) • Tamil (18%—mainly Hindu) • Moor (7%—Muslim)

From Blood, 1994; Heitzman & Worden, 1995; Ross & Savada, 1988.

MODELS OF HEALTH AND ILLNESS
IN SOUTH ASIA

BIOMEDICINE VERSUS ALTERNATIVE
OR INDIGENOUS SYSTEMS

India has a pluralistic, medical system, in which Western-style biomedicine (allopathy) is one option among many. Various forms of alternative health care practiced in India are formally recognized and government sanctioned as "Indian Systems of Medicine" (ISM) and they are slowly gaining ground in the Western world. As would be expected, Western forms of medical practice gained a foothold in India and Pakistan during the British rule and indigenous models of health were actively suppressed. There are now over 120 medical schools in India and Pakistan, producing doctors who are trained according to the British system. It is now recognized, however, that Western medicine is limited in its ability to serve all residents of India. As a result, and mainly since independence, Indian Systems of Medicine has been formally sanctioned and there are now well over 100 colleges with training programs in this form of medicine. Both systems, Western and Indian Systems of Medicine, have largely developed independently and now enjoy relatively equal status. The current movement in Indian Systems of Medicine aims toward a truly integrated health care system, but until this is achieved, the professionalization of Indian Systems of Medicine continues through the development of programs in training and in empirical research. Ayurveda, Siddha, and Unani are considered to be the main Indian systems of medicine with ancient roots. Homeopathy, yoga, and naturopathy, which have appeared more recently, are also promoted by the Department of Indian Systems of Medicine and Homoeopathy (ISM&H) under the Ministry of Health and Family Welfare, Government of India. It is estimated that approximately 60–70% of South Asians employ these traditional systems (Ramakrishna & Weiss, 1992; ISM&H, 1999; Lambert, 1996; Sharma et al., 1991; Titus, 1995).

INDIAN SYSTEMS OF MEDICINE

Ayurveda

The term "Ayurveda" (also written as Ayur-Veda) is derived from the Sanskrit words "Ayur," meaning life or longevity, and "Veda," meaning knowledge or science. Hence, the term implies "knowledge of life" or "science of life." The practice of Ayurveda offers treatment for various ailments but, more importantly, it emphasizes an orientation toward prevention. Introduced around 4000 B.C.E., it is often described as the oldest health care system in the world. It is a comprehensive system with eight branches, similar to allopathy: internal medicine, surgery, ophthalmology and otorhinolaryngology, obstetrics and pediatrics, toxicology, psychiatry, rejuvenation, and aphrodisiacs (ISM&H, 1999; Sharma et al., 1991; Titus 1995).

It should be noted that Ayurveda is derived from an ancient, formal, and elegant theoretical or philosophical tradition much like Buddhism, but with a much more widespread practical application in South Asia (Obeyesekere, 1977, 1982). Complete health is founded on a balance of the five basic elements of nature: (1) ether or space, (2) wind or air, (3) fire, (4) water, and (5) earth. These elements combine with each other to form the three principles (*tridosha*), which provide the framework for a functional classification of psychophysiological processes. Essentially, Ayurvedic medicine is based on humoral physiology. Pathology results from imbalances of these humors, due to homeostatic or immune mechanisms. Functions of the mind and body are regulated according to the three *doshas,* which are endowed upon birth but may vary in proportion from person to person. These proportions create a psychophysiological typology, of which there are 10 classic types. The *doshas* are termed *Vata* (space and air), *Pitta* (fire), and *Kapha* (water and earth) and several subdoshas also exist. Pathology in various organ systems is identified according to imbalances among combinations of these doshas and subdoshas. *Vata dosha* represents flow and kinetics and is central for the performance of respiration, circulation, and neuromuscular activity. Imbalances lead to problems such as neurological disorders, chronic pain, cardiac arrhythmias, constipation, anxiety, and insomnia. *Pitta dosha* is linked to metabolic processes such as energy exchange and digestion. Imbalances result in peptic ulcers, hypertension, bowel diseases, skin diseases, and immune responses. Lastly, *Kapha dosha* is important for regulating structure and the balance of fluids. Imbalances lead to difficulties such as diabetes, respiratory ailments, obesity, atherosclerosis, and tumors. Diagnosis of illness or predisposition to illness is aided through a knowledge of the psychophysiological type and is often integrated with knowledge from biomedicine to direct treatment or preventative efforts, which are often combined with allopathic interventions. Palpation of the pulse is a key diagnostic aid as doshas and subdoshas have different effects on the vibrations of the radial pulse. This practice can detect various kinds of imbalances at very early stages of pathology, which can then lead to very effective and simple preventative interventions (Ramakrishna & Weiss, 1992; Sharma et al., 1991; Titus, 1995).

Restoring balance among the doshas is central to Ayurvedic interventions. Restoring balance enhances homeostatic and immune functions. From a health psychology or psychological medicine perspective, what is interesting about Ayurveda is that it operates essentially in the psychosomatic framework. The concept of mind or consciousness is central to Ayurveda. Consciousness is the basis of physiology, as opposed to the Western notion that consciousness is an epi-phenomenon of the central nervous system. As such, mind has an essential role to play in the balance of doshas, as does the body, the environment (the cosmos), and the soul. The result is a series of health-related behaviors that are learned and taught through the process of childhood socialization (Obeyesekere, 1982; Ramakrishna & Weiss, 1992).

Given this comprehensive model, the interventions that are recommended by Ayurvedic practitioners, or *vaids,* target the mind, body, behavior, and environment. For the mind, Transcendental Meditation (TM) is the primary approach. It is well known to Western behavioral medicine for effectiveness in physical (e.g., hypertension, chronic pain) and mental (e.g., anxiety) health conditions. Interventions for the body include the use of special diets, exercise, herbs, and purification techniques (e.g., elimination therapies) to balance the bodily humors. Herbal remedies have been meticulously documented in pharmacopeias similar to Western-based pharmaceutical compendia. Behavioral prescriptions include daily and seasonal routines to maintain humoral balance. An orderly, regulated life is seen as central to health. This would include behaviors around sleep, hygiene, regulation of elimination, eating habits, work, and exercise. Lastly, environmental interventions, such as collective practice of TM and pollution control, involve the community (Obeyesekere, 1982; Sharma et al., 1991).

Ayurveda proposes interconnections between life and nature. Everything outside has an impact on the inner balance and "hot and cold" sensory modalities have a central prominence. Time and earthly cycles play an important role in maintaining inner harmony and specific times are recommended for diet and exercise to maximize their benefit. Recommendations for sleep are based on the times for sunrise and sunset, to match the body's rhythm with that of the solar system. Even seasonal cycles are taken into account in making recommendations (Titus, 1995).

In North America, several books and publications in the last 10 years have garnered great popular interest. For example, a notable publication by Deepak Chopra (1990) was a bestseller. With the increasing popularity and acceptance of alternative medicine in North America, Ayurveda is likely to gain prominence. As South Asians have some familiarity with this approach, they are more inclined to these treatments and usually more willing to embrace psychological interventions, particularly those that are familiar to Western professionals trained in health psychology or behavioral medicine (e.g., relaxation or meditation).

Siddha

Variations of the Ayurveda framework exist throughout South Asia, of which Siddha (meaning "achievement") is one. It is more common in Southeastern India and Sri Lanka, particularly among Tamil-speaking people. Its origins trace back to the ideas of health and illness promulgated by a class of Tamil sages called "Siddhars" (meaning "perfected" or "holy immortals"). Essentially derived from alchemy, there is great emphasis on the curative aspects of mercurial drugs. Health and the prolongation of life are enhanced through rejuvenating treatments, intense yoga, and regulated breathing. Like Ayurveda, physiology is based on the balance of the 3 humors and pulse diagnosis is central. Urine analysis is also a key diagnostic tool in Siddha medicine. Mineral or metallic drugs (e.g., mercuric sulphide with gold and borax) are prescribed in small dosages, along with dietary regimens and adjuncts to enhance drug potency. One distinctive Siddha practice includes a rejuvenation technique called *Kaya Kalpa,* which involves regulated breathing, conservation of sperm, a mercurial drug, potent plant and herbal extracts, and *muppa*. *Muppa* is a distinctive feature of Siddha and involves the secret mixtures of three salts, one of which is collected in select places on one of the four full-moon evenings of January to April. Astrology and incantation are also prominently featured in Siddha medicine. For example, Tuesday and Thursday are more favorable for taking medicine, and Sunday is more favorable for medicinal preparation. On certain days of the month, the ingestion of medicine is avoided. While Siddha is largely a rural, regional, and indigenous form of medicine, its popularity continues to grow. There exist two training colleges, over 100 Siddha hospitals, and 11,000 registered practitioners (*vaids*) in Southeastern India, along with regulated, standardized drug preparation, although private manufacturers of Siddha medicine are often preferred. There also exists a government-based Siddha Research Unit, which has begun to conduct clinical trials of Siddha drugs. Among Tamils, it remains the predominant health care framework (ISM&H, 1999; Subbarayappa, 1997).

Unani-Tibb

Yet another variation of Ayurveda, Unani-Tibb maintains a humoral physiology, diagnosis based on pulse, and a rich array of pharmaceutical interventions. Its roots lie in Greek (Galen/Hippocratic) philosophy and it is particularly prominent in the North of India and Pakistan. Detailed texts exist describing various ailments (for pain, see Pugh, 1991) according to humoral imbalance, seasonal influences, and sensory qualities (i.e., hot or cold). The four humors are blood, phlegm, yellow bile, and black bile, the balance of which is linked to distinct temperaments. Prevention of disease is based on prescription around 6 essential elements: (1) air, (2) drinks and food, (3) bodily movement and rest, (4) mental involvement and rest, (5) sleep and wakefulness, and (6) excretion and retention. Disease is indicated and diagnosed by Unani practitioners (*hakims*), based on changes in temperament and the ability of body to eliminate waste. Herbal and mineral remedies are designed according to sensory modalities (i.e., hot or cold), the aim of which is to bring about humoral balance (ISM&H, 1999). The practice of Unani-Tibb is more common in the Muslim population of South Asia.

IMPLICATIONS FOR SOUTH ASIAN CULTURAL GROUPS

Medical anthropology has offered much in the way of describing regional variations of the indigenous systems of medicine practiced in South Asia (e.g., the cross-cultural domain; Kakar, 1982; Lambert, 1992, 1996; Nordstrom, 1989; Pugh, 1991; Weiss et al., 1988). Similarly, from a medical systems perspective, ethnographies of how biomedicine and the traditional systems operate in South Asia are equally as intriguing to someone trained in the Western model (Khare, 1996). After all, these two divergent systems are responsible for the care of over 1 billion people. Overall, it is truly a plural context-sensitive system. The aim is to obtain the best possible care under the circumstances. Thus, South Asians typically turn to the indigenous systems of Ayurveda, Siddha, or Unani, homeopathy, and biomedicine (allopathy) in any sequence or any combination. That the Western notion of health and illness is the only way toward medicine is foreign to the majority of traditional South Asians. In contemporary practice, the two divergent systems complement each other (Khare, 1996; Nordstrom, 1989).

Part of the acculturation process requires the South Asian immigrant to understand and become accustomed to the health delivery system in their new environment. Canada offers a free, government-sponsored health care system with universal access, while in the U.S., health care is controlled by managed care companies and private insurance, which is costly and restrictive. The U.K. offers a two-tier service through the National Health Service, supplemented by fee-for-service private practice. Adjusting to a new health care system that tends not to support alternatives to biomedicine can add to the burden of illness for which treatment is being sought.

To the practitioner trained in the biopsychosocial model of health espoused by Engel (1977, 1997), the description of the Indian systems of medicine should sound familiar. While pulse diagnosis, humoral theories, herbal, and mercurial remedies may seem esoteric from a Western view, certainly the notion that mind or consciousness (the psychological component) and the environment (social systems) can interact with physiological systems to influence health and illness should not be foreign. As a result, the practitioner in health psychology, behavioral medicine, or consultation–liaison psychiatry (medical–surgical psychiatry) may not be seen as such a formidable person, and his or her psychologically based interventions may even be welcomed by the South Asian client in the context of physical and mental health care, all things considered.

There are certain other cultural aspects, such as the role of family, the view of self, and expectations from a health care provider, which will aid in understanding the South Asian client. The chapter will now turn to focus on these special topics.

SPECIAL TOPICS AMONG SOUTH ASIAN CULTURAL GROUPS

THE ROLE OF FAMILY AND THE VIEW OF SELF

An understanding of the family structure and functioning in a traditional South Asian community is important because it bears a direct relationship to aspects of health psychology. In contrast to the nuclear family system of the Western world, the traditional South Asian family unit consists of the extended family. Typically, grandparents live with their sons, daughters-in-law, and grandchildren. The family is traditionally male-dominated and hierarchically arranged. For example, the oldest in the family typically commands the greatest respect. The role of men is to work outside the home and provide for the members of the extended family.

The family functions as one economic unit, so that all incomes are pooled for the benefit of members. The emphasis is on collective identity rather than individualism (Assanand et al., 1990; Florsheim, 1990; Nunley, 1988). Despite the vast heterogeneity in South Asian cultural groups that has been described, the presence of the extended family is a constant theme (Roland, 1987).

Women in traditional South Asian cultural groups typically receive less education and their role is to nurture the children and maintain a clean, stable home. By Western standards, women have a dependent role. By tradition, however, they have a special social and religious status. In many rituals, they are given prominence and religious and cultural traditions are largely propagated by the women in South Asian society. In modern Pakistan and India, women's issues have become more prominent in the 1990s, bringing about changes to some of these traditional roles. Women in South Asia continue to increase their political representation and have raised awareness of women's issues, particularly around family planning and human rights. The improvement of health indicators in South Asian countries has been largely attributed to these modern reforms (Abassi, 1999; Blood, 1994).

Few immigrants to North America maintain a traditional extended family system. Most have left their parents behind but they continue to maintain regular ties through telephone and correspondence. Visits to parents and other relatives in South Asia are not uncommon. Most South Asians provide regular financial support because there are no government pension schemes in South Asian countries. The sentiments of the extended family system are maintained in other ways. Consultations with family members are common when major decisions are made. Contact is also intensified during festive occasions.

The concept of the extended family system is gradually being eroded as the new generation of North American-born South Asians matures. Most South Asian men in Western countries prefer to leave the parental home and establish an independent dwelling. Strong ties, however, are maintained with parents and regular contact is the norm. Whereas the contemporary generation of South Asians is asserting its autonomy, the basic value system and respect for parents prevails. A parallel change has occurred among South Asian women living in Western countries. They have the same educational opportunities as males and they make a much greater contribution in decision-making processes. Their role in the home, however, shows remnants of the previous generation. Interestingly, this contemporary young generation of South Asians shows a marked dualistic role, in that they adopt virtually all the characteristics of Westerners in the context of their occupational roles and switch to their traditional ways during South Asian social functions.

Hence, the South Asian family unit represents a diverse mix of Western and Indian traditions. Very traditional extended families exist at one end of the continuum while at the other end, the contemporary North American-born South Asians are showing clear signs of a shift toward a Western-style nuclear family, while at the same time maintaining close ties with their parents.

The role of family in South Asian cultural groups, and in non-Western cultural groups generally, has important implications for research and practice in contemporary Western health psychology, particularly around the conceptualization of "self." Construals of self determine and influence much of human experience: cognition, emotion, motivation, and behavior (Markus & Kitayama, 1991). In considering South Asian cultural groups and their acculturation to Western plural societies, a presentation of the differences between the two pervading views of self may assist us in understanding their health-related behavior and their views toward contemporary Western health psychology. The two pervading views of self have been variously referred to as, among other distinctions (listed according to Western versus non-Western views), independent versus interdependent, egocentric versus sociocentric, separate versus connected, individual versus familial (Gaines, 1982; Markus & Kitayama, 1991; Roland, 1987). These diametrically opposed cultural views of self have great implications for both abnormal (Landrine, 1992) and normal psychological functioning (Markus & Kitayama, 1991) and have been the source of considerable empirical attention in cross-cultural psychology (Shweder & Bourne, 1982).

For the South Asian, the self, in direct opposition to the Western view, is not seen as an autonomous, bounded, unique, or indivisible entity. It is not independent from nonself interpersonal relationships. Self-definition, in this view, develops through social interaction and relationships, particularly within the extended family. The cultural imperative of South Asian cultural groups is to maintain interdependence and it is through this interdependence that the self becomes most meaningful and complete. Autonomy is seen as secondary to the concept of connectedness (Florsheim, 1990; Kakar, 1982; Landrine, 1992; Markus & Kitayama, 1991). Landrine (1992) has related clinical colloquialisms to features of the interdependent self within a clinical context. For example, a typical question during an assessment interview may be "tell me something about yourself." A South Asian is unlikely to respond in terms of various personality trait descriptions but will respond according to the relation of the self with others in a variety of contexts. In addition, relationships to both the natural and supernatural world (e.g., to deceased relatives and deities) are often of considerable import from a South Asian cultural perspective (e.g. the Ayurvedic mind–body–universe view of health) and not necessarily indicative of psychopathology (Roland, 1987).

Recognition that there is a radically different view of self among South Asian cultural groups may lead to a more culturally sensitive approach to both diagnosis and intervention (Ananth, 1984; Florsheim, 1990). Landrine (1992) highlights the need for clinicians to be increasingly sensitive to such cultural variation in their patients or clients, not only in the style that they employ with the client (therapeutic stance, language usage, etc.) but also in their conceptualization of the pathology presented, which ultimately will guide the treatment regimen.

ACCULTURATION AND SOUTH ASIAN CUSTOMS

The acculturation process among South Asians has led to the emergence of a new population which has extended its boundaries into the Western culture, while at the same time maintaining parts of the value system inherited from their ancestry. This value system dictates a strict moral and ethical code, particularly with respect to family relationships. As a result, separation, divorce, and family disintegration are less common. Issues around academic advancement and occcupational success have become more pertinent and the common goal of most young members of South Asian immigrant groups is to train as professionals and establish a secure status in the community.

While acculturation takes place, particularly through integration, the clash of the two value systems becomes evident. In an extreme-case scenario, the traditional parents are protective of their daughters, who do not have the same privileges as their sons. This has created conflict in families where women are increasingly asserting themselves as they respond to Western feminist ideals. Other examples include strong parental opposition to the use of alcohol, disapproval of premarital conjugal relationships, and restrictions on activities which may unduly interfere with academic pursuits. Whereas parents are becoming increasingly accepting of interracial marriages, many find it difficult to make such accommodation. These conflicts represent new sources of stress as South Asians continue with their acculturation in the Western world.

ISSUES IN PHYSICAL HEALTH

Disease Trends

The pattern of illness in the Indian subcontinent and most other tropical countries is dominated by bacterial and parasitic infections (Assanand et al., 1990), for which effective remedies are more readily available. This is in contrast with Western countries, where most infectious diseases have been eradicated or are well controlled. While Western countries enjoy overall longer life spans (over 75 years), countries in South Asia have among the lowest life expectancies in the world (around 60 years; Heitzman & Worden, 1995). The overall aging of Western populations is accompanied by higher prevalence rates of cardiovascular disease, strokes, cancer, and degenerative diseases, such as arthritis and Alzheimer's disease. South Asian groups will have to become more familiar with these diseases as their acculturation proceeds.

Once acculturation proceeds, the immune system of South Asian immigrants adapts to the new environment and overall physical health status improves considerably. This improvement is aided by a sufficient quantity of nutritious healthy diets, conversion to active, more healthy lifestyles, and ready access to health care facilities. On the negative side, for some immigrants, ready access to high-caloric food has led to obesity and widespread acceptance of alcohol by the local culture has increased the immigrants' vulnerability to substance abuse. Several authors have reported a higher incidence of cardiovascular disease among South Asian immigrants in Western countries. The higher incidence has been attributed to obesity and an overall lack of public awareness about the role of diet and exercise in heart disease (e.g., Lip, Luscombe, McCarry, Malik, & Beevers, 1996). Lastly, South Asians have brought with them a genetic constitution that predisposes them to thalassemia, a rare blood disorder (Cao, Saba, Galanello, & Rosatelli, 1997).

Health Behaviors

Most South Asians are likely to try simple home remedies before seeking professional Western-style medical advice. Traditional treatments, therefore, may include alterations in diet, herbal medicines, massage, and a change in bathing habits. In the case of serious illness, special prayers may be conducted, offerings to temple gods may be made, and rituals may be performed. Although Westernized South Asians may be less inclined towards these traditional beliefs, remnants of these beliefs and practices are evident among them. The complementary approach, involving traditional and modern methods in the spiritual context, often involves the whole family and sometimes the entire community to strengthen the power of prayers (Assanand et al., 1990).

Hospitalization

Hospitalization is seen as a major event and is viewed as a sign of serious illness. Reminiscent of South Asian custom, large numbers of friends and relatives pay homage to the hospitalized individual, at times ignoring visitation rules. In the case of very serious illness, it is common for some South Asian communities to hold a continuous vigil.

Although most South Asians speak English, the degree of fluency and accents may vary. The variation in gestures and nuances may be a further impediment to effective communication in a hospital setting. South Asian families are less likely to complain or display anger because they respect the authority of health care providers. As well, treatment recommendations are rarely challenged and consent is provided in good faith with little regard to medicolegal aspects (Ramakrishna & Weiss, 1992). Special meal arrangements may have to be made for hospitalized South Asian patients. For example, traditional Hindus eat a strict vegetarian diet, Muslims do not eat pork and eat only "halal" meat, while devout Jains do not eat root crops such as potatoes, onions, and garlic.

Traditional clothing worn by South Asian patients, particularly women, warrants some discussion. By custom, South Asian women expose a bare minimum of their body. Saris and Punjabi dresses are commonly worn by traditional women and some women may cover their hair. Assessing a patient in a hospital gown may be convenient for the physician but may be particularly embarrassing for South Asian females, especially the elderly and those who are at the early stage of the acculturation process.

Pregnancy, Birth, Child Rearing, and Family Planning

Conservative women in South Asia receive no special medical care during a routine pregnancy. Dietary habits may be altered in the early stage of pregnancy to reduce the risk of miscarriage (Assanand et al., 1990). Care for the pregnant woman is provided by women elders in the extended family system and the midwife is summoned only at the time of birth. Pregnancy and birth are considered to be strictly women's issues and involvement of men in this process is considered to be inappropriate (Choudhry, 1997). This is in sharp contrast to Western practices, where regular antenatal care is emphasized and the involvement of husbands is encouraged. Hence, South Asians who have not accepted Western values may be uncomfortable at antenatal classes and men may be reluctant to witness the birthing process in the delivery room. As in most other situations, South Asians who have lived in the West for a considerable period of time, and particularly the generation that has been raised in the West, have embraced and appreciated the services offered in Western countries.

As might be expected, child-rearing practices are, in many ways, different among South Asians. First, a male child is preferred, although this is becoming less of an issue in the migrant South Asian community. Children, especially girls, are protected and physical punishment is a common form of discipline. Most South Asian parents are heavily invested in the welfare of their children and readily comply with immunization procedures and regular checkups.

The traditional family in South Asia is large, with up to 10 or more children. Following migration to the West, the contingencies change: children are not required for work on the farm, they are expensive to raise in Western countries, and both spouses go to work outside the home. A rapid shift to the Western norm of two to three children per family has occurred. Modern birth control measures are commonly adopted by South Asian immigrant women and this has also been a source of controversy in the home countries as attempts are made to curb the rapidly increasing birth rate (Eyles, 1986).

Dealing with Death and Dying

The death of a young South Asian family member, especially if it is accidental, is seen as a major catastrophe. The open expression of grief with crying and wailing is common. Grief continues for several months and a variety of religious and cultural rituals are performed to mark each stage of grief. The involvement of family, friends, and close community members from the subculture serves as a supportive network at these ceremonies. The natural death of an older person is discussed openly in the South Asian family and is accepted with equanimity. Hindus believe in reincarnation and, hence, accept death as part of the cycle. Muslims believe that the time of death is determined by Allah. Typically, prayers are recited as death nears and death at home in proximity with the family is preferred.

Hindu custom is to cremate the body shortly after death has occurred. The fortieth day is a significant milestone in the mourning process. At this stage, family members partially relinquish their grief and begin to focus on their own lives. Special prayers are arranged on the first anniversary and this marks the end of the official grief period. Muslims also derive support from each other and through prayers as death of a loved one approaches. The burial ceremony is preceded by a ceremonial washing of the body. Muslims believe that the body should be buried as complete and whole. Hence, a request for postmortem may be declined except in very special circumstances (Assanand et al., 1990).

USE OF COMMUNITY SUPPORT AGENCIES BY SOUTH ASIANS

South Asians are not accustomed to government-sponsored community health agencies, such as home care and social welfare programs, which are part of the fabric of the Western society. The expectation in South Asia is that the family will carry the burden of care for their sick members. Such sacrifice is offered with pride and strongly encouraged by the community. Hence, South Asians may not utilize community supports due to their lack of awareness of these facilities or because they feel obligated to take care of their own family members. This is important to recognize in some specific situations, such as Alzheimer's disease, where an overly dedicated individual may jeopardize his or her own health while taking care of the impaired spouse.

South Asians may find visits by community nurses, social workers, and other providers to be intrusive. This is particularly the case where there is a linguistic or cultural barrier. The assignment of a provider from the same ethnic community or one who is knowledgeable about the South Asian culture and accepts their customs without any bias helps to establish the rapport necessary for effective care.

ISSUES IN MENTAL HEALTH

STRESS OF ACCULTURATION

By and large, the migration of South Asians to the Western world has been voluntary. Two notable exceptions are South Asians who arrived as refugees from Uganda in 1972 and, more recently, Tamils who came from Sri Lanka. Those who came on their own accord had more time to prepare for their anticipated losses and were more ready and willing to take up the challenge of adjusting to a new culture. The majority were screened for immigration requirements in their host countries. Some brought with them funds which made it possible to begin business ventures or purchase homes. From a psychosocial standpoint, they experienced the usual difficulties which most migrant groups experience. First, there was the loss of ties with their country of birth, loss of relatives, friends, and comforts such as servants in their home countries. Second, for many there was a loss of social status and a drop in vocational level. Lastly, there was the adjustment to a foreign culture and change in role definition and expectations. On the positive side, new immigrants enjoyed personal security, an array of vocational, business, and academic opportunities, and a strong, predictable incentive driven infrastructure which facilitated their personal goals. A minority of South Asians who have arrived recently, especially those who came as refugees, appear to have made lesser gains. A number of them do not speak fluent English, are less educated, have much less financial security, and are continuing to adjust to their new environment (Ananth & Ananth, 1996).

In a more formal investigation of the relationship between strategies of acculturation and psychological well-being among U.S. South Asians, Krishnan and Berry (1992, as cited in Berry, 1998) found that the strategy of cultural *integration* proved to be a significant predictor of lower overall acculturative stress. Those individuals who adopted the strategy of *assimilation* exhibited more psychological stress, while those who chose *separation* exhibited higher psychosomatic distress.

DEPRESSION, ANXIETY, AND SOMATIZATION IN SOUTH ASIAN CULTURAL GROUPS

Although there are no empirical studies to show that depression is common among South Asian cultural groups, one would expect this to be the case from a vulnerability model, given the multiple losses they suffer during migration and the extreme demands from the forces of acculturation. Furnham and Malik (1994) documented that, in fact, earlier investigations found that British South Asians had quite low rates of psychiatric illness, particularly affective disorders. They further suggested that the probable reasons for this lay in different clinical presentations of depression in South Asians, who are more likely to complain of somatic rather than psychological symptoms, and their beliefs about depression differ markedly from those of Western cultural groups (Furnham & Malik, 1994; see also Weiss, Raguram, and Channabasavanna, 1995).

Part of the difference in beliefs about depression may be related to the strong stigma attached to mental illness in the South Asian culture. In general, South Asians are much less likely to seek treatment for depression, preferring to rely on the extended family for support. This becomes particularly relevant in the familial context since any kind of illness affects the reputation of the whole family and has grave consequences within the system of arranged marriages. The issue of stigma in mental illness has been more formally investigated, with the general finding that individuals with depressive disorders report more stigma associated with their mental illness, compared to lower stigma associated with somatoform disorders, at least in South India (Raguram, Weiss, Channabasavanna, & Devins, 1996). This finding underscores the importance of conducting an in-depth, culturally sensitive interview with South Asian patients who present with recurrent somatic symptoms.

A similar picture with a predominance of somatic symptoms is likely to emerge in South Asian patients suffering from anxiety disorders (e.g., Chambers,

Yeragani, & Keshavan, 1986). A common simplistic interpretation among South Asians when faced with these disorders is that the individual is "nervous" or shy. Often, signs of anxiety are seen as a weakness of character. A detailed assessment conducted in the context of the individual's position within the South Asian culture is likely to yield the most accurate results. A supportive, encouraging approach which incorporates a psychoeducational component and respects the clients'/patients' interpretation of their disorder yields the best results (Ananth, 1984). The use of techniques such as meditation and yoga, which are akin to relaxation techniques commonly used in Western practices, may be more readily accepted by South Asian patients (Sharma et al., 1991).

Mumford, Bavington, Bhatnagar et al. (1991) proposed a model which may account for the predominant somatic presentation of anxiety, depression, or psychological distress in general among South Asian cultural groups. Three levels are identified: (1) language, which dictates the ability for the symptom to be expressed, (2) concepts of health and illness, which are responsible for how the symptom is interpreted, and (3) culturally sanctioned illness behavior, which influences the extent to which the symptom will be presented for treatment. With respect to somatization disorder, Gureje, Simon, Ustun, and Goldberg (1997) did not find any clear cultural differences in their comprehensive World Health Organization international study. Somatization disorder, however, did tend to occur among patients with fewer years of formal education.

From the perspective of treatment for anxiety, depression, and somatization, psychoeducation can have an important role because these conditions may be poorly understood as being "treatable" by South Asian cultural groups. Further, conflicts based on issues arising from the acculturation process are poorly understood and often misinterpreted by recent immigrants. The role of supportive modes of psychotherapy, as opposed to exploratory or insight-oriented modes, should be encouraged because the cultural expectations are that the health provider will give active guidance and take an active role in treatment (Hoch, 1990). In keeping with that theme, pharmacological and somatic interventions are sometimes preferred (Nunley, 1996). Lastly, the South Asian family functions as a unit where individuation is less emphasized; therefore, involvement of the family in the treatment process is crucial. Immediate and probing questions around family history and functioning, particularly around mental health, are more likely to be met with resistance (Ananth, 1984).

SUICIDE IN SOUTH ASIAN CULTURAL GROUPS

The rate of suicide in South Asian countries has been steadily increasing, such that it has now been identified as a major health problem (Latha, Bhat, & D'Souza, 1996). Suicide patterns among South Asians living in the Indian subcontinent have been described in various sources (Adityanjee, 1986; Latha et al., 1996). Unlike their Western cohorts, suicide attempters in India tend not to be single, separated, or living alone; rather, most come from intact families. Alcohol consumption is rarely associated with suicide and suicide occurs more frequently among females. Overall, males attempt suicide more frequently than females, which is in sharp contrast to the pattern observed in the Western culture. Common methods include ingestion of organophosphates and household poisons while other methods include burning (particularly among women), hanging, and drowning. Unfortunately, suicide prevention programs are virtually nonexistent in the Indian subcontinent (Adityanjee, 1986; Latha et al., 1996).

Somewhat similar patterns have been reported among South Asian cultural groups in the U.K. (Soni, Bulusu, & Balarajan, 1990). Findings indicate that relatively lower rates of suicide were seen among the elderly and men. Male suiciders were more likely to be medical professionals. The highest rates of suicide occurred among young women and, in particular, young, married women. Arranged marriages were regarded as a principal contributing factor for these young female suiciders. This finding highlights the extreme result of acculturative distress.

In terms of religious and sociocultural aspects, the Hindu religion has given sanction to certain altruistic suicides. Brahma Puran, a well-known Hindu scripture, sanctions five forms of altruistic suicide as justifiable and acceptable. Further, the practice of "Sati," where a Hindu widow allows herself to be burned alive following the death of her husband, is part of the Hindu legend. This practice is illegal in India, according to a law passed in 1829, and the practice is now virtually extinct. Burning, however, continues to be a frequent method of suicide among young, married women in India (Adityanjee, 1986).

As demographic factors among suicide attempters among South Asians are different from those found in the Western culture, caution should be exercised in interpreting them as risk factors. Further, clinical experience suggests that South Asian patients are less likely to make veiled threats and are more likely to protect their plans for suicide with secrecy. Conflicts with the extended family, especially the mother-in-law, are more likely to predispose a female patient to suicide. The burden of migration, acculturation, and separation from the family of origin may not only add to their other losses but may also signify a lack of a psychosocial support system. Further, survivors of suicide attempts feel totally stigmatized (until recently, attempting suicide was illegal; Latha et al., 1996) and frequently express extreme embarrassment following their unsuccessful attempt. To add to this, most families prefer not to hospitalize the unsuccessful attempters for fear that the family's reputation will be tainted.

MAJOR MENTAL ILLNESS

Studies in schizophrenia (Wig et al., 1987a, 1987b) have shown that the prognosis in South Asians with this diagnosis is more favorable. It has been argued that this conclusion likely reflects lower expectations of productivity in their home countries. It is possible as well that the illness is more likely to be contained in the supportive network of the family, as opposed to the mental health delivery system, as is the case in the West.

As in the case of any other mental illness, South Asian families feel highly stigmatized by occurrence of psychosis in their midst and are, therefore, apt to keep such occurrences a family secret. For this reason, they are likely to minimize or rationalize the symptoms and wait to seek formal treatment until the illness has progressed to its full-blown state. When hospitalized, South Asian patients with major mental illness are typically reclusive because they have difficulty mixing with individuals from other cultures while, at the same time, trying to cope with their illness. It is not unusual in such situations for families to seek out a mental health provider of the same ethnic background, who they feel will have a better understanding of their dilemma. Whereas this may enable a much better rapport, sometimes unrealistic expectations are made and the relationship becomes personalized, thus jeopardizing professional objectivity.

When Western treatment fails to provide a cure, some recent immigrant South Asian families resort to their traditional medicine, such as Ayurveda. In some cases, they may blame a psychotic episode to pressures of acculturation and seek to return to their home country, with the hope that their problems would resolve once they return home to their extended families. The majority of the South Asian immigrants become quickly informed about major mental illness and accept treatment locally. In these instances, the family's involvement is typically very intense and the burden of the caregiver can become a major issue.

As in the case of other mental illness, involvement of the family, especially the parents or the spouse, is crucial when dealing with South Asian patients suffering from psychosis. A supportive, educational approach, providing realistic hope, is recommended in dealing with this group of patients. The clinician should gently explain the nature of the illness to alleviate self blame and guilt, which is commonly seen in parents and spouses of such patients. The role of medications should be explained to improve compliance, and recommendations for psychosocial therapies should be provided in the context of the patient's culture and value system. Lastly, an individual rather than a group approach is likely to produce better results because recent immigrants who have not fully acculturated are likely to become alienated when exposed to a dominant culture group while they are struggling with their mental illness.

CULTURE-BOUND SYNDROMES

Four culture-bound syndromes that have been identified in South Asia will be briefly described here. *Dhat syndrome* is characterized by a strong belief that the loss of semen by nocturnal emissions or by some other means leads to loss of sexual potency and a general loss of energy. The afflicted individual is typically not satisfied after multiple consultations and becomes increasingly anxious, with an array of hypochondriacal complaints. The syndrome is believed to be rooted in Hindu mythology. No specific treatment is available for this syndrome and the clinical course in unknown (Akhtar, 1988; Bhatia & Malik, 1991; Bottero, 1991; Levine & Gaw, 1995).

Possession syndrome is seen almost exclusively in women of low socioeconomic class in India. It is suggested that the syndrome represents a dissociative state in which the affected individual transiently takes on the identity of another individual or a Hindu deity. The clinical presentation is variable. The affected individual often makes unusual facial expressions and shows bizarre bodily movements and a marked change in speech. These individuals are often taken to faith healers, who drive away evil spirits. If this fails, the patient is brought to a psychiatric facility where the immediate recommended treatment of choice is abreaction during narcosuggestion (Akhtar, 1988). *Bhang psychosis,* although often referred to as a culture-bound syndrome, is likely a toxic syndrome because it is associated with chronic use of *bhang,* a form of cannabis. The presence of visual hallucinations helps to distinguish it from schizophrenia, with which it bears a strong similarity. Lack of confusion helps to differentiate it from other organic mental disorders (Akhtar, 1988).

Keemam dependence results from the common South Asian practice of chewing betel leaves (readily available at Indian stores in Western countries) with lime and other concoctions. Keeman, an indigenous intoxicant believed to contain nicotine and a morphinelike substance, is sometimes added to the betel leaf to provide a euphoriant effect. Given the clear etiology, this condition is better viewed as a form of addiction rather than a culture-bound syndrome (Akhtar, 1988).

Another syndrome which is believed to be culture-bound is referred to as *The Sinking Heart.* It is a form of cardiac distress thought to be caused by a constellation of factors, such as excessive heat, exhaustion, anxiety, and interpersonal difficulties. Comparisons of the *Sinking Heart* to Western views about psychological risk factors for cardiac disease, such as the Type A behavior pattern, have been made (Krause, 1989).

SUMMARY

In summary, South Asians residing in Western countries represent a plethora of subcultures with different value systems, languages, religious affiliations, customs, food habits, and attitudes to life in general. Whereas the initial influx of migrants consisted mainly of professional and skilled workers, subsequent members have come from all socioeconomic classes. The degree of acculturation to the dominant community varies, depending on time spent in the West and the willingness to adopt the value system of the new environment. Health care providers who have a basic knowledge of the South Asian culture and are aware of some of the central issues, such as the role of family and indigenous views on health and illness, will be better able to offer culturally competent interventions to members of this community.

CASE STUDY

Mr. R.C., a 39-year-old man who emigrated to Canada one year prior, was referred to the consultation–liaison service during his second admission in one month to the cardiac unit. He had been treated one month prior, following a mild heart attack, with coronary angioplasty. Since then, his condition had not improved. He continued to complain of severe angina, which had led to increased functional and lifestyle impairment. In addition, his mood had become severely depressed. Repeated cardiac investigations were negative.

Mr. R.C. was quite guarded when interviewed by both the team psychiatrist and psychologist. In addition to many somatic complaints, he claimed that his wife had been having affairs with customers at their retail business and he expressed a strong desire to separate from her. When Mr. R.C.'s wife was interviewed, she expressed increasing concern for her husband's physical and mental well-being since the heart attack. She further disclosed that, two years after their arranged marriage, Mr. R.C. had become quite upset, believing that his wife was having an affair with a neighbor. This episode occurred while he was being treated for a back injury in India.

Mr. R.C. insisted on leaving his wife, though she seemed extremely devoted to him and was willing to do anything to please him. She contacted his parents in India and had them send a telegram to him stating that his father had become ill and that his presence was required in India. She tried to enlist the support of his attending physician to arrange for him to go to India. She felt that being with their family would help her husband as had been the case during similar episodes in India. Further, she hoped that they would arrange for him to see a doctor trained in Indian medicine, who would provide herbal remedies. Lastly, she felt that injections, which were denied to her husband since their arrival in Canada, were more potent than oral medications.

Mrs. R.C. was somewhat limited in her ability to communicate in English and felt isolated because she had no relatives locally and had not developed a social network within her community. She talked about how much she missed her family and how helpful they had been during his previous illness in India. She was very comfortable with her attending physician, who spoke her mother tongue. She felt well supported by him and stated that he could understand her dilemma better than others.

Following the inpatient consultation, appropriate psychotropic medications were prescribed by the team psychiatrist and Mr. R.C. entered into a comprehensive outpatient cardiac rehabilitation program, which included exercise training and diet counseling. He was able to meet other cardiac patients, some of whom were also of South Asian descent, and this contributed greatly to his level of social support. Additionally, outpatient psychological management for the couple was arranged with the team psychologist under the framework of "stress management." Over the course of several weeks of rehabilitation, his somatic complaints declined as he regularly attended group physical fitness classes and learned various strategies to deal with his anxiety and depressed mood, such as progressive muscle relaxation and pleasurable activity scheduling. His difficulties were conceptualized within a biopsychosocial framework and he was able to recognize that when his physical symptoms became worse, his depressed mood, anxiety, and irritability with his wife would likewise become unmanageable. With a better understanding of his physical condition and with behavioral skills acquisition, he was able to gain more mastery over his symptoms.

Important cross-cultural issues to note:

1. This family was still very early in the acculturation process. The lack of family support and a supportive social/cultural network for the patient and his family was seen as both a contributing factor to the clinical presentation and a significant treatment barrier. A liaison with the local religious/cultural organization was actively encouraged.

2. His wife had no knowledge about her husband's severe difficulties in coping with physical ailments prior to their arranged marriage. Despite this, she remained extremely devoted to him during subsequent episodes, even those in which he was aggressive and threatening. Although she initially minimized her husband's difficulties, she did respond to the treatment team's concern for her personal safety, and appropriate behavioral contingencies were agreed upon.

3. His wife's wish to have her husband treated with herbal medications and injectable medications, which she felt were more potent, was understood within a cultural context. With appropriate education, she learned about the nature of cardiac disease and became quite knowledgeable about issues around rehabilitation. Her request to seek consultation from a qualified practitioner in Ayurveda was not denied and a collaborative effort was encouraged.

4. The team physician was fluent in the language of this family and took on the role of both cultural and language interpreter. This was seen as a significant contributor to the positive treatment outcome. The strong attachment to and high expectations demanded of the physician by the patient's wife were understood from a cultural perspective.

5. Alternative forms of coping with stress and anxiety were successfully introduced, particularly active, behavioral interventions, such as daily exercise and progressive muscle relaxation. They viewed these kinds of interventions favorably and commented that they were similar to meditation and yoga exercises which they were taught as children.

6. A gender-role reversal in the family was also seen as a significant stressor. His wife was astute in business, while he was not. This undermined the cultural norm of the dominant male-gender role. The attention paid to his wife by customers served to intensify his paranoia. As he became more physically able, he was able to find ways to contribute to the family income and his paranoia subsided.

1. Review the aculturation strategies that have been identified by Berry (1998) described in the chapter. Consider each strategy (assimilation, separation/segregation, integration) and discuss its potential impact as it relates to the details of this case. Which strategy did Mr. R.C.'s family appear to adopt?

2. How culturally sensitive were the services provided to Mr. R.C. and his family? From a cultural perspective, speculate on how the treatment of this case could have been improved.

3. Speculate on how the management of this case would have been different had there not been a health care provider of similar culture. Is it possible to offer cultural caring without sharing the same language, values, and traditions of the client?

SUGGESTED READINGS

Ananth, J. (1984). Treatment of immigrant Indian patients. *Canadian Journal of Psychiatry—Revue Canadienne de Psychiatrie, 29,* 490–493.

Assanand, S., Dias, M., Richardson, E., & Waxler-Morrison, N. (1990). The South Asians. In N. Waxler-Morrison, J. M. Anderson, & E. Richardson (Eds.), *Cross-cultural caring: A handbook for health professionals in Western Canada.* (pp. 141–180). Vancouver, BC: UBC Press.

Berry, J. W. (1998). Acculturation and health: Theory and research. In S. S. Kazarian & D. R. Evans (Eds.), *Cultural clinical psychology: Theory, research, and practice* (pp. 39–57). New York: Oxford University Press.

Chopra, D. (1990). *Perfect health.* New York: Harmony Books.

Eyles, T. (1986). Systems of health care in India. *Nursing—Oxford, 3,* 115–119.

ISM&H—Indian System of Medicine & Homeopathy. (1999). *An overview of Indian System of Medicine and Homeopathy.* Department of Indian Systems of Medicine and Homoeopathy, Government of India. Available on the World Wide Web: http://www.nic.in/ismh/overview.html (August 30, 1999).

Kakar, S. (1982). *Shamans, mystics, and doctors: A psychological inquiry into India and its healing traditions.* New York: Knopf.

Khare, R. S. (1996). Dava, Daktar, and Dua: Anthropology of practiced medicine in India. *Social Science & Medicine, 43,* 837–848.

Ramakrishna, J., & Weiss, M. G. (1992). Health, illness, and immigration. East Indians in the United States. *Western Journal of Medicine, 157,* 265–270.

Sharma, H. M., Dev Triguna, B., & Chopra, D. (1991). Maharishi Ayur-Veda: Modern insights into ancient medicine. *Journal of the American Medical Association, 265,* 2633–2637.

Titus, G. W. (1995). Providing alternative health care: An ancient system for a modern age. *Advanced Practice Nursing Quarterly, 1,* 19–28.

REFERENCES

Abbasi, K. (1999). The World Bank and world health: Focus on South Asia—II: India and Pakistan. *British Medical Journal, 318,* 1132–1135.

Adityanjee, D. R. (1986). Suicide attempts and suicides in India: Cross-cultural aspects. *International Journal of Social Psychiatry, 32,* 64–73.

Akhtar, S. (1988). Four culture-bound psychiatric syndromes in India. *International Journal of Social Psychiatry, 34,* 70–74.

Ananth, J. (1984). Treatment of immigrant Indian patients. *Canadian Journal of Psychiatry—Revue Canadienne de Psychiatrie, 29,* 490–493.

Ananth, J., & Ananth, K. (1996). *East Indian immigrants to the United States: Life cycle issues and adjustment.* East Meadow, NY: Indo-American Psychiatric Association.

Assanand, S., Dias, M., Richardson, E., & Waxler-Morrison, N. (1990). The South Asians. In N. Waxler-Morrison, J. M. Anderson, & E. Richardson (Eds.), *Cross-cultural caring: A handbook for health professionals in western Canada* (pp. 141–180). Vancouver, BC: UBC Press.

Berry, J. W. (1998). Acculturation and health: Theory and research. In S. S. Kazarian & D. R. Evans (Eds.), *Cultural clinical psychology: Theory, research, and practice* (pp. 39–57). New York: Oxford University Press.

Bhatia, M. S., & Malik, S. C. (1991). Dhat syndrome—A useful diagnostic entity in Indian culture. *British Journal of Psychiatry, 159,* 691–695.

Blood, P. (Ed.). (1994). *Pakistan: A country study.* Washington, DC: Federal Research Division, Library of Congress.

Bottero, A. (1991). Consumption by semen loss in India and elsewhere. *Culture, Medicine and Psychiatry, 15,* 303–320.

Cao, A., Saba, L., Galanello, R., & Rosatelli, M. C. (1997). Molecular diagnosis and carrier screening for beta thalassemia. *Journal of the American Medical Association, 278,* 1273–1277.

Carstairs, G. M., & Kapur, R. L. (1976). *The great universe of Kota: Stress, change and mental disorder in an Indian village.* London, UK: Hogarth.

Chakraborty, A. (1990). *Social stress and mental health: A social–psychiatric field study of Calcutta.* London, UK: Sage.

Chakraborty, A. (1991). Culture, colonialism, and psychiatry. *Lancet, 337,* 1204–1207.

Chambers, J., Yeragani, V. K., & Keshavan, M. S. (1986). Phobias in India and the United Kingdom: A trans-cultural study. *Acta Psychiatrica Scandinavica, 74,* 388–391.

Chopra, D. (1990). *Perfect health.* New York: Harmony Books.

Choudhry, U. K. (1997). Traditional practices of women from India: Pregnancy, childbirth, and newborn care. *Journal of Obstetric, Gynecologic, & Neonatal Nursing, 26,* 533–539.

Citizenship and Immigration Canada (1996). *A profile of immigrants from India in Canada.* Ottawa, ON: Minister of Supply and Services Canada.

Citizenship and Immigration Canada (1999). *Facts and figures 1998: Immigration overview.* Ottawa, ON: Communications Branch, CIC.

Engel, G. (1977). The need for a new medical model: A challenge for biomedicine. *Science, 196,* 129–136.

Engel, G. (1997). From biomedical to biopsychosocial. *Psychotherapy and Psychosomatics, 66,* 57–62.

Eyles, T. (1986). Systems of health care in India. *Nursing—Oxford, 3,* 115–119.

Florsheim, P. (1990). Cross-cultural views of self in the treatment of mental illness: Disentangling the curative aspects of myth from the mythic aspects of cure. *Psychiatry, 53,* 304–315.

Furnham, A., & Malik, R. (1994). Cross-cultural beliefs about "depression." *The International Journal of Social Psychiatry, 40,* 106–123.

Gaines, A. D. (1982). Cultural definitions, behavior and the person in American psychiatry. In A. J. Marsella & G. M. White (Eds.), *Cultural conceptions of mental health and therapy* (pp. 167–192). London, UK: Reidel.

Gureje, O., Simon, G. E., Ustun, T. B., & Goldberg, D. P. (1997). Somatization in cross-cultural perspective: A World Health Organization study in primary care. *American Journal of Psychiatry, 154,* 989–995.

Heitzman, J., & Worden, R. L. (Eds.). (1995). *India: A country study.* Washington, DC: Federal Research Division: Library of Congress.

Hoch, E. M. (1990). Experiences with psychotherapy training in India. *Psychotherapy & Psychosomatics, 53,* 14–20.

Immigration and Naturalization Service (1999a). *Immigration fact sheet.* Washington, DC: INS–Statistics Division, U.S. Dept. of Justice.

Immigration and Naturalization Service (1999b). *Annual report, legal immigration, fiscal year 1998.* Washington, DC: INS–Statistics Division, U.S. Dept. of Justice.

Indian System of Medicine & Homeopathy (1999). *An overview of Indian System of Medicine and*

Homeopathy. Department of Indian Systems of Medicine and Homoeopathy, Government of India. Available on the World Wide Web: http://www.nic.in/ismh/overview.html (August 30, 1999).

Jackson, K., & Chilton, C. (1999). *Control of immigration: Statistics United Kingdom, second half and year 1998.* London, UK: The Home Office–Research Development and Statistics Directorate.

Jejeebhoy, S. J. (1998). Adolescent sexual and reproductive behavior: A review of the evidence from India. *Social Science & Medicine, 46,* 1275–1290.

Kakar, S. (1982). *Shamans, mystics, and doctors: A psychological inquiry into India and its healing traditions.* New York: Knopf.

Khare, R. S. (1996). Dava, Daktar, and Dua: Anthropology of practiced medicine in India. *Social Science & Medicine, 43,* 837–848.

Krause, I. B. (1989). Sinking heart: A Punjabi communication of distress. *Social Science & Medicine, 29,* 563–575.

Lam, D. J., & Palsane, M. N. (1997). Research on stress and coping: Contemporary Asian Approaches. In H. S. R. Kao & D. Sinha (Eds.), *Asian perspectives on psychology* (pp. 265–281). London, UK: Sage.

Lambert, H. (1992). The cultural logic of Indian medicine: Prognosis and etiology in Rajasthani popular therapeutics. *Social Science & Medicine, 34,* 1069–1076.

Lambert, H. (1996). Popular therapeutics and medical preferences in rural north India. *Lancet, 348,* 1706–1709.

Landrine, H. (1992). Clinical implications of cultural differences: The referential versus the indexical self. *Clinical Psychology Review, 12,* 401–415.

Latha, K. S., Bhat, S. M., & D'Souza, P. (1996). Suicide attempters in a general hospital unit in India: Their socio-demographic and clinical profile—Emphasis on cross-cultural aspects. *Acta Psychiatrica Scandinavica, 94,* 26–30.

Levine, R. E., & Gaw, A. C. (1995). Culture-bound syndromes. *The Psychiatric Clinics of North America, 18,* 523–536.

Lip, G. Y., Luscombe, C., McCarry, M., Malik, I., & Beevers, G. (1996). Ethnic differences in public health awareness, health perceptions and physical exercise: Implications for heart disease prevention. *Ethnicity and Health, 1,* 47–53.

London, M. (1986). Mental illness among immigrant minorities in the United Kingdom. *British Journal of Psychiatry, 149,* 265–273.

Markus, H. R., & Kitayama, S. (1991). Culture and the self: Implications for cognition, emotion, and motivation. *Psychological Review, 98,* 224–253.

Mumford, D. B., Bavington, J. T., Bhatnagar, K. S., Hussain, Y., Mirza, S., & Naraghi, M. M. (1991). The Bradford Somatic Inventory. A multi-ethnic inventory of somatic symptoms reported by anxious and depressed patients in Britain and the Indo-Pakistan subcontinent. *British Journal of Psychiatry, 158,* 379–386.

Nordstrom, C. R. (1989). Ayurveda: A multilectic interpretation. *Social Science & Medicine, 28,* 963–970.

Nunley, M. (1996). Why psychiatrists in India prescribe so many drugs. *Culture, Medicine, and Psychiatry, 20,* 165–197.

Nunley, M. (1988). The involvement of families in Indian psychiatry. *Culture, Medicine and Psychiatry, 22,* 317–353.

Obeyesekere, G. (1977). The theory and practice of psychological medicine in the Ayurvedic tradition. *Cultural, Medicine, and Psychiatry, 1,* 155–181.

Obeyesekere, G. (1982). Science and psychological medicine in the Ayurvedic tradition. In A. J. Marsella & G. M. White (Eds.), *Cultural conceptions of mental health and therapy* (pp. 235–248). London, UK: Reidel.

Oldfield, K. (1989). *Jainism: The path of purity and peace.* Derby, UK: Christian Education Movement.

Paranjpe, A. C., & Bhatt, G. S. (1997). Emotion: A perspective from the Indian tradition. In H. S. R. Kao & D. Sinha (Eds.), *Asian perspectives on psychology* (pp. 127–143). London, UK: Sage.

Pugh, J. F. (1991). The semantics of pain in Indian culture and medicine. *Culture, Medicine and Psychiatry, 15,* 19–43.

Raguram, R., Weiss, M. G., Channabasavanna, S. M., & Devins, G. M. (1996). Stigma, depression, and somatization in South India. *American Journal of Psychiatry, 153,* 1043–1049.

Ramakrishna, J., & Weiss, M. G. (1992). Health, illness, and immigration: East Indians in the United States. *Western Journal of Medicine, 157,* 265–270.

Roland, A. (1987). The familial self, the individualized self, and the transcendent self: Psychoanalytic reflections on India and America. *Psychoanalytic Review, 74,* 237–250.

Ross, R. R., & Savada, A. M. (Eds.). (1988). *Sri Lanka: A country study.* Washington, DC: Federal Research Division, Library of Congress.

Sharma, H. M., Dev Triguna, B., & Chopra, D. (1991). Maharishi Ayur-Veda: Modern insights into ancient medicine. *Journal of the American Medical Association, 265,* 2633–2637.

Shweder, R. A., & Bourne, E. J. (1982). Does the concept of the person vary cross-culturally? In A. J. Marsella & G. M. White (Eds.), *Cultural conceptions of mental health and therapy* (pp. 97–137). London, UK: Reidel.

Soni, R. V., Bulusu, L., & Balarajan, R. (1990). Suicides among immigrants from the Indian subcontinent. *British Journal of Psychiatry, 156,* 46–50.

Subbarayappa, B. V. (1997). Siddha medicine: An overview. *Lancet, 350,* 1841–1844.

Titus, G. W. (1995). Providing alternative health care: An ancient system for a modern age. *Advanced Practice Nursing Quarterly, 1,* 19–28.

Weiss, M. G., Desai, A., Jadhav, S., Gupta, L., Channabasavanna, S. M., Doongaji, D. R., & Behere, P. B. (1988). Humoral concepts of mental illness in India. *Social Science & Medicine, 27,* 471–477.

Weiss, M. G., Raguram, R., & Channabasavanna, S. M. (1995). Cultural dimensions of psychiatric diagnosis: A comparison of DSM-III-R and illness explanatory models in South India. *British Journal of Psychiatry, 166,* 353–359.

Wig, N. N., Menon, D. K., Bedi, H., Ghosh, A., Kuipers, L., Leff, J., Korten, A., Day, R., Sartorius, N., & Ernberg, G. (1987a). Expressed emotion and schizophrenia in north India. I. Cross-cultural transfer of ratings of relatives' expressed emotion. *British Journal of Psychiatry, 151,* 156–160.

Wig, N. N., Menon, D. K., Bedi, H., Leff, J., Kuipers, L., Ghosh, A., Day, R., Korten, A., Ernberg, G., & Sartorius, N. (1987b). Expressed emotion and schizophrenia in north India. II. Distribution of expressed emotion components among relatives of schizophrenic patients in Aarhus and Chandigarh. *British Journal of Psychiatry, 151,* 160–165.

Williams, R., & Hunt, K. (1997). Psychological distress among British South Asians: The contribution of stressful situations and subcultural differences in the West of Scotland. *Psychological Medicine, 27,* 1173–1181.

16

WOMEN'S HEALTH: A CULTURAL PERSPECTIVE

EMILY A. WISE, STACY KOSER CARMICHAEL,
CYNTHIA D. BELAR, CAREN B. JORDAN,
AND NICOLE E. BERLANT

University of Florida Health Science Center
Gainesville, Florida

Historically, women have been neglected in biomedical research; thus, our knowledge base in women's health is more limited than that of men. Reasons for this discrepancy have been many, ranging from exclusion of women of child-bearing age in clinical trials for protective reasons to exclusion of women because of concerns over variability introduced by their hormonal factors. Research that did focus on women tended to be on women's reproductive health, as if it were this area of functioning that defined women's health status. Although the women's health research movement has gained substantial momentum within the last decade, years of neglect have resulted in a paucity of knowledge regarding many women's health issues. This deficit is compounded for ethnic minority women, as the majority of women's health-related research has been conducted with females of the majority culture, or majority white women.

The available data on ethnic women's health status are not only limited, but often gathered in research that is based on inappropriate assumptions and has significant methodological limitations (e.g., multiple cultural groups falling into the "other" category in epidemiological research). This results in erroneous conclusions and unwarranted generalizations regarding the health of women from culturally diverse groups, making any summary of the extant literature fraught with problems.

Most notably, the current knowledge base does not reflect the enormous diversity within the four commonly described ethnic groups. For example,

Asian/Pacific Islanders represent more than 50 distinctively different ethnic groups (e.g., Chinese, Japanese, Cambodian, Filipino, Hmong, Vietnamese, Samoan, Indian) plus a multitude of languages. Hence, if only a few subgroups of this population are sampled (i.e., Japanese, Filipino), not all segments of the population are represented and an inaccurate picture of these women is documented. Moreover, Asian/Pacific Islanders tend to have a bipolar distribution in socioeconomic status (SES), one of the most powerful variables influencing health status (Adler et al., 1994).

Similarly, Hispanic/Latina women encompass peoples coming from more than 20 countries (e.g., Mexico, El Salvador, Chile, Argentina, Columbia, Cuba) or descended from Spanish colonists originally settling in North America. Language and cultural backgrounds are diverse, with significant differences across subgroups in health status as well.

Although Native Americans (NA) are the smallest of the four major ethnic populations discussed in this chapter, they represent more than 300 tribes with over 200 distinct languages and diverse cultural heritages (e.g., Navajo, Hopi, Inuit).

Currently, the largest ethnic group in North America, African American/Blacks are also culturally diverse. In fact, Green (1978) has described nine subgroups with distinctive variations in social and environmental factors as well as cultural heritage (cf. Johnson et al., 1995).

Despite these methodologic problems, this chapter will attempt to summarize findings concerning women's health in the four commonly designated ethnic groups. Areas for special focus include gender-role issues, behavioral risk factors, and the morbidity and mortality associated with selected health problems. Although the leading causes of death and morbidity in culturally diverse women's groups are similar to those for "majority" white women (cardiovascular disease, cancer, diabetes, HIV/AIDS), research has often demonstrated differential rates or impact in "minority" women. Research has also demonstrated that ethnic women are often overrepresented in the lowest socioeconomic strata, engage in high-risk health behaviors (smoking, alcohol consumption, sedentary lifestyle, poor diet), face more environmental stressors (i.e., racial discrimination), may be predisposed by genetic/hereditary factors, and possess unique cultural beliefs and practices, all of which may interact to place them potentially at higher risk for morbidity associated with these diseases.

WOMEN'S MULTIPLE ROLES: IMPLICATIONS FOR HEALTH

The past 50 years have witnessed significant social and economic changes as women have entered the workforce in increasing numbers. In 1996, 70% of women with children under the age of 18 were in the labor force, an increase of 23% since 1975 (Hayghe, 1997). The demands on women to "have it all" and successfully combine the roles of partner, mother, and career woman in addition to other commitments may significantly impact their physical and psychological health. This section will briefly review salient issues associated with women's multiple roles and their implications for health, followed by a consideration of issues specific to various cultural groups.

COMBINING WORK AND FAMILY

Research has suggested that the nature of women's roles is more strongly related to health outcomes than simply role occupancy or number of roles occupied (Baruch & Barnett, 1986; Baruch, Biener, & Barnett, 1987; Moen, Robison, & Dempster-McClain, 1995). These *interactive models* generally predict that experiences in one role modify experiences in another role or health outcome by producing either buffering or amplifying effects (Repetti, 1998). For example, some have suggested that role fit, or the congruence between a woman's actual role and her ideal role, is a key construct in the complex relationship between women's roles and health outcomes (e.g., Waldron & Herold, 1986).

There is considerable literature suggesting that women with multiple roles generally have better health (Froberg, Gjerdingen, & Preston, 1986; Jennings, Mazaik, & McKinlay, 1984; Sorenson & Verbrugge, 1987; Verbrugge, 1983, 1986, 1989; Waldron & Jacobs, 1989). However, much of this research has been conducted on relatively homogeneous groups of majority white women using cross-sectional methods, making causal interpretation impossible. Scholars have speculated whether results obtained were a result of roles influencing health (social causation) or health influencing roles (social selection). However, longitudinal studies controlling for initial health find that the health advantage of employed women remains (Hazuda et al., 1986). Researchers hypothesize that participation in a stable partnership, employment, and child-rearing provided opportunities for gaining rewards and resources for stress inoculation, such as increased self-esteem, control, and social support (Sorenson & Verbrugge, 1987). However, if role quality or role fit is poor, and concerns exceed rewards of the combined roles, health is diminished (Baruch & Barnett, 1986; Verbrugge, 1983; Waldron & Herold, 1986). As women in minority groups are more likely to deal with nonwork-related stressors and to be employed in poorer quality positions, one would expect they would be at higher risk for experiencing role conflict. In one of few studies that have examined this, Marshall and Barnett (1991) found that African American/Black women tend to experience more race-related stressors (i.e., concerns about job discrimination) and experienced higher work-related stressors as well, such as low decision latitude or hazardous working conditions. In their attempt to tease out the tangled effects of ethnicity and class, Verbrugge and Madans (1985) concluded that while there are definite benefits to combining multiple roles, the positives may be outweighed by the negatives as social class decreases and may be diminished even more by the double-jeopardy of being a working-class ethnic minority woman.

Special stressors for working women include home and childcare concerns as well as workplace hazards. Literature suggests that women in the workforce continue to bear the brunt of household and childcare responsibilities (Lewis & Cooper, 1988; Rexroat & Shehan, 1987). Regarding childcare choices available outside the home, the United States (unlike other industrialized nations) does not have family policy that provides working families access to universal subsidized childcare or paid and extended parental leave. This makes the pragmatics of obtaining or resuming employment more difficult for mothers of infants and preschool-age children (Killien, 1993; Hochschild, 1989; Kramerman, 1989). Ross and Mirowsky (1988) reported that for employed women, difficulties in arranging outside childcare and eliciting assistance at home from their husbands contributed to psychological distress in the form of depression. Greater role strain is also reported by women who are not satisfied with their current childcare arrangements (Van Meter & Agronow, 1982). Unfortunately, the difficulties of finding affordable, quality care increase with number of children and minority status. For example, Cattan (1991) reports data from the 1986 National Longitudinal Survey of Youth that indicate that unemployed women with three or more children were 1.5 times more likely to report childcare problems as being the reasons why they were not able to return to work. Hispanic/Latina mothers accounted for twice as many women not in the labor force due to childcare concerns compared to white majority women.

Traditional workplace health risks include exposure to physical, biologic, and chemical hazards. In addition, employment conditions which include higher occupational stressors (i.e., high workload demands, low decision latitude, poor organizational climate) frequently lead to a variety of physical and psychological health complaints, including anxiety and depression. (See Swanson, Piotrkowski, Keita, & Becker, 1997, for a review of acute and long-term consequences of workplace stressors.) Other stressors specific to women include sexual harassment, workplace violence, inflexibility of scheduling, unequal compensation and benefits, gender and racial discrimination, and the glass ceiling phenomenon (Kellar, 1996). Overall, working women are at a greater risk of experiencing job-related burnout and report twice as much stress-related illness as employed men (Northwestern National Life, 1992). "Minority" women in particular appear to be at an increased risk for experiencing work-related stress, because they tend to experience more concerns regarding job-related discrimination and tend to work under less than optimal working conditions (i.e., low decision latitude, increased exposure to workplace hazards) (Marshall & Barnett, 1991).

EXAMPLES OF GENDER-ROLE STRESS
IN SPECIFIC GROUPS

Asian/Pacific Islander Women

Many Asian/Pacific Islander women come from nonindustrialized nations where women are typically found working within the home, with primary responsibility for bearing and raising children; cleaning; food growing, harvesting, preparation, and storage; sewing; and other demands associated with community rituals (Kimball & Craig, 1988; Symonds, 1996). Ito, Chung, and Kagawa-Singer (1997) provide some background for understanding immigrant women from Cambodia, Laos, and Vietnam. An estimated 1 million refugees from these countries have relocated to the United States to escape the ravages of war. The traumatic preemigration and escape process frequently has resulted in rape and sexual abuse, abortions, or the loss of a husband or child. Understandably, these experiences place Southeast Asian refugee women at a high risk for developing psychological disturbances, including depression, anxiety, and posttraumatic stress disorders (Kinzie, Fredrickson, Ben, Fleck, & Karls, 1984; Mollica & Laveller, 1988). Traditionally homemakers in their native lands, many Southeast Asian women are forced to obtain unskilled employment to support their families in the United States, often resulting in long days and little time to spend with their children or for personal health care (Ito et al., 1997). The traditional role reversal between husband and wife also may result in increased family tension, which may lead to spousal abuse or divorce (Luu, 1989).

Juggling work and family and the resultant health implications for Japanese women have been addressed briefly in the literature. Matsui, Ohsawa, and Onglatco (1995) have observed that over the past decade, changes in Japanese employment policy have resulted in more women simultaneously combining the roles of wife, mother, and career women rather than adhering to traditional sex-role stereotypes and separating career and child-rearing. Their study of Japanese working mothers found that these women tended to cope with their multiple demands by redefining their role within the family. Women with supportive husbands experienced less strain and work–family conflict, although the amount of time husbands lend to assistance with home and childcare tends to be very minimal, averaging about 8 minutes per day (White, 1996). Increased flexibility in the work schedule, such as mandated workday breaks to assist with the care of young children, resulted in lower levels of life strain for these women.

Matsui et al. (1995) also note that as the Asian population becomes older, the care for aging parents will primarily fall upon the adult working women's shoulders. The effect of adding yet another demanding role is likely to be played out in terms of decreased labor-force participation and decreased health quality outcomes. Although the tradition of caring for one's elders is perhaps more salient in the Asian culture, the responsibility for caring for aging parents tends to fall on women from many cultural backgrounds.

Hispanic/Latina Women

Traditionally, the Hispanic/Latina culture has subscribed to the view of women as subordinate to men, with primary obligations to the home and family. Although women adhering to these traditional sex-role attitudes are less likely to participate in the labor force (Ortiz & Cooney, 1984), those women with traditional attitudes who do work outside the home have been found to have higher

levels of depressive symptoms (Krause & Markides, 1985) and to view employment as having negative consequences for their parenting (Ybarra, 1982). Financial necessity often requires the wife to work to escape poverty (Cattan,
1998). Recent years have witnessed changes in these traditional views, however,
perhaps due to the effects of acculturation, increased levels of education, and increasing numbers of Hispanic/Latina women entering the work force (Vasquez-
Nuttal, Romero-Garcia, & DeLeon, 1987). By 2006, it is projected that the Hispanic population will become the second-largest ethnic grouping in the labor
force behind white non-Hispanics (Bowman, 1997).

Consistent with the role-fit hypothesis, studies of Mexican American women
juggling work and family find that role conflict frequently occurs in women with
traditional sex-role orientations. These women report increased distress and decreased perceptions of parenting effectiveness (Zinn, 1980). More recent studies,
however, report that gender-role stereotypes are changing in this population
(Herrera & DelCampo, 1995) and that more egalitarian division of household labor, along with work satisfaction, are resulting in lower levels of role strain and
perceptions of improved family functioning for working mothers (Hemmelgarn
& Laing, 1991; Krause & Markides, 1985; Sanez, Goudy, & Lorenz, 1989).

African American/Black Women

African American/Black women have traditionally combined work and family roles much longer than other women, moving from emancipation into the
paid labor force at a higher rate than majority white women (Beckett, 1976).
Among married women with preschool children, African American/Blacks are
still more likely to be participating in the labor force (McLoyd, 1993). Many of
these women are single mothers and the breadwinners of the household, due to
the high rates of unemployment and earlier death among African American/Black
males. However, as a result of reliance on single incomes, nearly one-third of
African American/Black women are living in poverty, which exerts its own effects on health status in terms of increased stress, limited access to health care,
and low-quality housing and nutrition (U.S. Department of Health and Human
Services, 1992). In addition, African American/Black women are more likely
than majority white women to be working in traditionally female-dominated
jobs, which often combine high work demands with a low decision latitude, leading to job strain and poorer psychological health outcomes (Malveaux, 1985;
Katz & Piotrkowski, 1983).

Compared to majority white women, African American/Black women rely
much more on the instrumental and emotional support of nonmarital partnerships
and their immediate and extended family members to assist with childcare, while
maintaining their view of themselves as strong and independent mothers (Benin
& Keith, 1995; Blum & Deussen, 1996; Hertz & Ferguson, 1995; Jayakody,
Chatters & Taylor, 1993; Mason & Kuhlthar, 1989; Taylor, 1986). At times, role
overload occurs in older generations responsible for the care of many others, particularly if family role transitions occur at a young age (see Box 16.1).

BOX 16.1

In addition to the multiple roles of mother and wage-earner, many midlife women have the added burden of being responsible for the care of not only their parents, but their grandchildren and even their great-grand-children. This is notably so in African American/Black homes, where female role transitions typically occur earlier than in other groups. In her study of the relationship between age norms, family role transitions, and the caregiving responsibilities of women in multigenerational African American/Black families, Burton (1996, p. 206) describes the role strain experienced by many African American/Black women whose families have early non-normative role transitions with a statement from a 53-year-old great grandmother: "Now, they keep on rushing me, expectin' me to do this and that trying to make me old (be)fore my time. I ain't got no time for myself. I takes care of babies, grown children, and the old people. I work too. I get so tired. I don't know if I'll ever get to do somethin' for myself."

In families such as these, the caregiving burden is placed squarely on the shoulders of the young great-grandparent. It is not hard to imagine how role strain could occur under these demanding family patterns, possibly leading to poorer health status in the overburdened others.

Burton also found that some African American/Black women preferred the early transition to motherhood due to a truncated view of their life-span, the shortage of marriageable African American/Black males, and the tradition that grandmothers raise the grandchildren. In these families, the primary role of the grandmothers is the care of their grandchildren, while the role of the children's mother is to care for the great-grandmothers. The statements below summarize this pattern of generational role responsibilities (Burton, 1996, p. 207).

Jesse, a 56-year-old great-grandmother: "Yeah, it's true, we had children young. But I don't have to be worried about them now. I'm old and tired and have done my time with my family. Now I can just take it easy and let them take care of me. This is what I waited for all my life."

Mary, a teenage mother: "My grandmother raised me. Now it's time for me to give her something back. It's OK if my mother raised my child for me. If she didn't I wouldn't be able to take care of my grandmother."

Native American Women

There is no significant body of empirical research specific to how Native American women manage multiple roles and the impact of such demands on health. However, it appears clear that the change in roles forced by loss of lands roamed freely by ancestors has had a significant impact on economic and health status. With the loss of lands, traditional gender roles for males have been extinguished. Native Americans are more likely to be unemployed than other United States populations, and nearly a third live in poverty (United States Indian Health Service, 1994). Related rage is often targeted toward the women who still maintain caretaker roles. The majority of family violence is also alcohol related (Burhansstipanov, Tenney, & Dresser, 1997).

HEALTH BEHAVIORS

A number of behaviors have had a demonstrated impact on health: the use of tobacco products, alcohol, and illicit substances; diet; exercise; and participation in disease screening. Although there is insufficient research in minority women populations, there have been some demonstrations of differences in incidence of behavioral health risks in minority women as compared to the more frequently studied majority population. This section will describe a selected few of these differences.

SMOKING

It is well accepted that smokers are at increased risk for a variety of cancers and cardiac and pulmonary disorders. In addition, women smokers are subject to higher rates of cervical cancer, early menopause, osteoporosis, and reproductive problems than are nonsmokers. Summarized below are analyses by King, Borrelli, Black, Pinto, and Marcus (1997) of data on minority women obtained from the National Health Interview Survey (Centers for Disease Control, 1996). They note the variability in rates of smoking across groups, with Native Americans smoking more than majority white women (24.7%) while African American/Blacks and Asian/Pacific Islanders smoking less.

However, variability within groups is also significant. For example, smoking prevalence rates range from 14.7 to 62% for Native American women. Prevalence varies by region and tribe, with the highest rates among Alaskan Native and Eskimo women and some of the lowest rates in tribes of the southwestern United States. Tribes that use tobacco in ceremonies tend to have higher smoking rates. Unlike other ethnic groups, low SES per se does not appear to be associated with higher smoking rates. However, poverty, low education levels, and cultural beliefs are all related to the smoking patterns of Native American women, with less advantaged and less educated women on reservations smoking less than urban counterparts.

Smoking appears to be as prevalent in Hispanic/Latina women as in majority white women, although rates vary across subgroups, from 23.8% in Mexican American women to 30.3% in Puerto Rican women. Lower income, less education, and younger age are associated with smoking in Hispanic women (Haynes, Harvey, Montes, Nickens, & Cohen, 1990). In addition, there has been a rise in cigarette consumption from foreign-born to U.S.-born Latinos. Giachello (1997) attributes this increase to heavy marketing by the tobacco industry toward Latino populations, including sponsorship of many cultural festivities, such as Cinco de Mayo events.

King et al. (1997) note that the overall smoking rates among African American/Black women are falling, from 32% in 1985 to 21.8% in 1994 (Centers for Disease Control, 1996). However, African American/Black women of low SES smoke at higher rates than African American/Black women of higher SES. Of special interest is the fact that although African American/Black women smoke less than majority white women overall, they have higher rates of smoking-related diseases and higher death rates from tobacco-related diseases. This is perhaps due to less access to health care and differences in other health behaviors. However, new research findings that African American/Blacks take in 30% more nicotine and take nearly two hours longer to clear nicotine metabolites from their bloodstream suggest that genetic differences in nicotine metabolism may account for these health status differences (Perez-Stable, Herrera, Jacob, & Benowitz, 1998).

At 10%, the smoking prevalence rate for Asian/Pacific Islander women is the lowest among the four ethnic groups. However, with increased acculturation, the rate of smoking is expected to rise, and mortality associated with lung cancer and cardiovascular disease is predicted to exceed those of other U.S. ethnic groups in the next 20 years (King et al., 1997).

OBESITY

Obesity is a significant health problem for all minority women and is, in part, related to the high fat, low fruit and vegetable "diet of poverty." Variability across and within groups is again noted, with Hispanic/Latina women having higher rates of obesity, but particularly Mexican American (42%) and Puerto Rican (40%) as compared to Cuban Americans (32%), who may fare better economically (National Center for Health Statistics, 1991).

Native Hawaiian and Samoan populations are reported to be among the most obese in the world, and over 60% of all Native American women are obese (Lefkowitz & Underwood, 1991). Change in diet has had a major impact on the health of Native American women, with nutritional factors believed to contribute to four of the leading causes of death in this population: heart disease, cirrhosis, diabetes, and cancer (Schinke, 1996). In addition, public policy has had a negative impact on Native American women's diet through the provision of government commodity surplus foods high in fats and calories (Kauffman & Joseph-Fox, 1996).

African American/Black women are 1.6 to 2.5 times more likely to be overweight than majority white women, even after controlling for SES (Klesges, DeBon, & Meyers, 1996). Interestingly, African-American/Black men are not more likely to be overweight, suggesting that gender differences play a significant role. Indeed, there is some evidence that cultural norms for desirable weight may vary across groups, e.g., data suggest that compared to majority white women, fewer African American/Black women perceive themselves to be overweight (National Center for Health Statistics, 1978). Other factors suggested as likely contributors to obesity in African American women include sedentary lifestyle, higher calorie diet, early menarche, and younger age at first childbirth (Giles & Dansby-Giles, 1996).

Overall, there is insufficient research on the direct causes of obesity in minority women and on culturally sensitive diet and weight management programs. Research underway includes that investigating a community-based approach that focuses on social support, family involvement, exercise self-efficacy, and awareness of barriers to exercise. See the Case Study for examples of current research in the area.

ALCOHOL

For Native American women, alcohol abuse is a major health problem (Kauffman & Joseph-Fox, 1996). According to the Indian Health Service, the rate of alcoholism among Native Americans is 332% greater than that of all other minority groups (Schinke, 1996). Between the ages of 25–34, Native American women have an alcoholism mortality rate more than 20 times that of majority white women (Burhansstipanov et al., 1997). Rates of alcohol abuse and related diseases do vary by tribe and region, as do rates of fetal alcohol syndrome, which is the leading cause of disability among Native American newborns. Native Americans lead the nation in rates of alcohol-related liver cirrhoses, diabetes, accident fatalities, and homicides (Schinke, 1996).

African American/Black women have high rates of abstinence from alcohol (McBarnette, 1996) and are least likely to report problem drinking among all women (Vogeltanz and Wilsnack, 1997). However, African American/Black women have been found to experience alcohol-related illnesses and causes of death disproportionate to the amount that they drink. These effects have been eliminated in some studies after controlling for SES. Thus, poorer health outcomes may be a result of lack of access to health care, other health behaviors, or psychosocial factors, and not attributable to alcohol consumption.

Asian/Pacific Islander and Hispanic/Latina women appear to drink less alcohol than their male counterparts and other groups of women. However, these rates appear to be increasing with acculturation, education, blurring of sex roles, greater prosperity, and increased stressors (True & Guillermo, 1996). They also vary significantly across subgroups, e.g., Mexican Americans, Cuban Americans, Native Hawaiians, and Japanese. In addition to culture, physiology may play a role in limiting alcohol consumption by Asian/Pacific women. For example, up to 50% of Chinese, Japanese, and Koreans react to alcohol with flushing syndrome. This physiological reaction is a result of a genetically inactive form of an enzyme, aldehyde dehydrogenase (Whitfield & Martin, 1996). This inactivity results in higher levels of blood acetaldehyde, leading to the vasodilatation of facial skin, headaches, chills, somnolence, and nausea. Sue and Nakamura (1984) and others have postulated that this negative reaction to alcohol consumption, combined with social/cultural factors, may result in reduced incidence of alcohol abuse and dependence in Asian/Pacific Islanders. In general, the research on alcohol usage in minority women is especially difficult in populations who work exclusively at home, as substance abuse can be more easily hidden under these conditions.

PREVENTIVE HEALTH MEASURES AND
BEHAVIORAL INTERVENTIONS

Given the various health screening and disease prevention methods available today, the disproportionate morbidity and mortality among minority women is much higher than necessary (Helstrom, Coffey, & Jorgannathan, 1998). In fact, Runowicz (1994) suggested that if minority women received appropriate Pap tests, death from cervical cancer could be almost entirely prevented. However, research has consistently demonstrated that African American/Black, Asian/Pacific Islander, Native American, and Hispanic/Latina women underutilize preventive techniques and services, such as breast self-exams, mammograms, and Pap smears (Castro, Coe, Gutierres & Saenz, 1996; Helstrom et al., 1998; Gaston & Garry, 1997; Giachello, 1997; Tom-Orme, 1995). For example, nearly two-thirds of immigrant Asian women have never had Pap smears (Lee, 1992).

Underutilization of services has been attributed to a combination of factors, including cultural beliefs and practices, language barriers, lack of physician recommendations, lack of knowledge, lack of transportation, utilization of nontraditional health care providers, and lack of access to preventive and primary health care as a result of financial barriers (again highlighting how minority women's lower SES may exert a negative impact on health). Minority women may view health screenings as a luxury without immediate benefits or as a source of embarrassment (e.g., Asian/Pacific Islander women may be very modest and feel uncomfortable with these examinations). Fox and Roetzheim (1994) suggest that older Hispanic/Latina women have more concerns than do African Americans/Blacks or majority white women about the pain of mammography and more anxiety about the potential for a clinical finding.

Barriers to changing behavioral health risks have also been found relevant to specific ethnic groups, as highlighted by research from the smoking cessation literature reported by King et al. (1997). For example, Hispanic/Latina women may perceive less health locus-of-control, fail to connect quitting with longevity, and demonstrate limited sophistication in preventive health care. In addition, acculturation has been related to cessation in different ways. For example, language barriers might hinder cessation efforts for less acculturated Hispanic/Latina women whereas more acculturated women (who tend to have smoked longer and more frequently) might have more intransigent behavior patterns to change.

King et al. (1997) report data suggesting that African American/Black women may be less likely to quit smoking and more likely to relapse than majority white women, despite an overall lower smoking rate. Barriers to quitting include health risk beliefs, lack of information on how to quit, high rates of smoking in the living environment, high stress, other priorities, lack of financial resources, and the perception that smoking is a better coping strategy than other coping methods. In addition, they suggest that African American/Black women who smoke attribute smoking-related illness to environmental factors and tend to minimize the health risks of smoking. African American/Black women also appear to be unsophisticated about the processes of quitting and often believe that willpower and determination are the primary factors.

For older Asian/Pacific Islanders, cultural taboos against smoking itself may inhibit women from seeking help for a problem with smoking. In addition, Asian American/Pacific Islanders are less likely to seek the care of a physician and also less likely than whites to be advised by a doctor to quit smoking (King et al., 1997).

Because of the findings described previously, the trend in current research has been to focus on tailoring health promotion interventions to specific minority groups. For example, interventions to enhance social skills and decrease risky behaviors among Native American children and adolescents were made culturally sensitive by incorporating folk tales and legends, utilizing Native American role models, and using traditional games to teach health information (Schinke, 1996).

In the Hispanic/Latino community, efforts to increase health-promoting behaviors that include diet modification, smoking cessation, and health screenings have incorporated lay health educators (Brownstein, Cheal, Ackermann, Bassford, & Campos-Outcalt, 1992). These health educators, referred to as "Promatoras," serve many functions, including acting as mediators between the community and health agencies and providing social networks of support and information for residents of the community (Castro et al., 1996). Promatoras can bridge the gap between cultures by understanding the language, beliefs, and values of Hispanic/Latina women while providing education, organization, and outreach for health organizations.

In summary, although the patterns of health behaviors among groups of minority women are highly variable, some similarities do exist. The interaction of minority status and low SES places minority women at higher risk for most behavioral risk factors. In addition, these groups have less access to health care for help with smoking cessation, abstinence from drugs and alcohol, and management of diet and activity level. They also have less access to health care screenings. Future research will want to increase our understanding of the unique factors associated with differing rates of behavioral health risks and test the effectiveness of culturally sensitive interventions to prevent or change health risk behaviors in different groups of minority women. Health policies that increase access to health care resources for these women are also essential.

MORBIDITY AND MORTALITY
IN MINORITY WOMEN

Although life expectancy is greater for women than men, the life expectancy of majority white women exceeds that of all women of color. Areas of particular concern in minority women are related to pregnancy and the leading causes of morbidity and mortality: cardiovascular disease, cancer, diabetes, and HIV/AIDS. This section briefly reviews differential rates of these problems in minority women and will be followed by a more extensive summary of variables thought to influence health status in minority women.

PREGNANCY

The reproductive health status of minority women differs from that of the majority population. For example, minority women have an increased incidence of ectopic pregnancy (Bernstein, 1995). In addition, the maternal mortality rate for African American/Black women is three times that of majority whites (Gaston and Garry, 1997). Moreover, the female infant mortality rate among African American/Blacks has been reported as more than twice as high as for majority whites (U.S. Department of Health and Human Services, 1994).

Infant mortality rates in Asian/Pacific Islanders tend to be the same as or lower than those of majority whites (Chen, 1997), although this does not hold true across all subgroups. For example, mortality rates in Native Hawaiians were reported as higher than majority white infants. It has also been noted that African American/Black women at all educational and income levels have higher rates of premature and low-birthweight infants than do other women of similar education and income (McNair & Roberts, 1998).

A significant proportion of infant deaths is related to low birth weight, which, in turn, may be the result of substance abuse, smoking, poor nutrition, lack of knowledge, and perhaps most importantly, lack of prenatal care. Chen (1997) reviews research in the Asian/Pacific Islander community that demonstrates that immigration status can be an important variable in receipt of prenatal care. New immigration groups were much more likely to receive late or no prenatal care than older immigration status groups. Chen proposes that new immigrants may be relatively more hampered in receipt of care by cultural values that associate exposure of genitals with shame. Overall, multiple barriers to prenatal care have been found in all minority groups, including lack of access, transportation, childcare, and knowledge.

However, the relationship between prenatal care and low birth weight is complex, reflecting the multitude of interacting variables that can affect minority women's health status. Giachello (1997) describes findings among Hispanic/Latina women that demonstrate a percentage of low-birthweight infants that is comparable to majority white women, despite a lack of prenatal care. Cultural buffers to the effects of lack of care are thought to be related to indigenous dietary habits, extended family support networks, and less smoking and alcohol usage in this group.

CARDIOVASCULAR DISEASE

Cardiovascular disease (CVD) is the leading cause of death for all American women. However, mortality rates of women from all ethnic minorities are significantly higher than those of majority white women. For example, when examining age-adjusted mortality rates for heart disease in 1992, African American/Black women experienced 162.4 deaths per 100,000, compared to 98.1 deaths per 100,000 for majority white women (National Center for Health Statistics, 1995). Gaston and Garry (1997) have noted that when compared to majority white women, African American/Black women have a higher death rate from CVD because they experience a greater number of risk factors, such as obesity, hypertension, high cholesterol level, and diabetes (National Heart, Lung and Blood Institute, 1992).

The risk factors that have been noted pose problems for Hispanic/Latina women as well (Giachello, 1997), because data have demonstrated high rates of diabetes and obesity in this minority population (National Council of La Raza, 1993). However, Hispanic/Latina women appear less likely to have high cholesterol levels than African American/Black or majority white women (Giachello, 1995). Nonetheless, Giachello (1997) indicates that the leading cause of death among Hispanic/Latina women in 1992 was heart disease. Notably, the higher levels of cardiovascular disease risk factors among African American/Black and Mexican American (compared to majority white women) cannot be fully explained by differences in SES (Winkleby, Kraemer, Ahn, & Varady, 1998). After adjustment for age and SES, highly significant differences in body mass index, blood pressure, diabetes, and physical inactivity remained between majority white women and both African American/Black and Mexican American women. However, the authors emphasize their results should be interpreted cautiously, due to several design and measurement limitations.

Among Native American women, heart disease is currently the leading cause of death. Risk factors, including obesity, are often found in women of various tribes comprising this diverse ethnic group (Tom-Orme, 1995). However, additional studies examining other risk factors associated with Native American women and heart disease are lacking in the literature.

Cardiovascular disease is one of the top three causes of mortality among Asian/Pacific Islander women (Chen, 1997). However, most of the health data on Asian/Pacific Islander women is based on pooled findings, ignoring potentially important differences within this diverse minority group.

HYPERTENSION

High blood pressure is problematic in African American/Black communities (McBarnette, 1996). Notably, Gaston and Garry (1997) describe research that has demonstrated that African American/Black women have a higher incidence of hypertension than do majority white women, Hispanic/Latina women, and both majority white and African American/Black men (National Center for Health Statistics, 1992). They report that African American/Black women experience high blood pressure at more than double and triple the rates of a number of Hispanic/Latina women subgroups (Gaston & Garry, 1997).

A number of studies of Chinese and Japanese American women suggest low rates of hypertension. However, for some Asian/Pacific Islander subgroups, hypertension incidence rates are high (Martinez-Maldonado, 1991; Stavig, Igra, & Leonard, 1988) and actually exceed that of African American/Black women. Chen (1997) indicates, for example, that older (> 50 yrs. of age) Filipino American women residing in California have a slightly higher incidence rate of hypertension when compared to African American/Black women. Giachello (1997) describes research suggesting that Hispanic/Latina women are less likely than non-Latina women to have high blood pressure, with prevalence rates varying by national origin. She indicates that rates are highest for Mexican American women, lowest for Cuban women, with rates for Puerto Rican women falling in between (National Heart, Lung, and Blood Institute, 1992). However, Giachello (1997) points out that the low numbers may actually be an underestimate, reasoning that high blood pressure increases with age and that the Hispanic/Latina population is still rather young. Interestingly, while Mexican American women have a higher risk profile than do Caucasian women, they have lower rates of hypertension (Haffner, Mitchell, Stern, Hazuda, & Patterson, 1990).

Tom-Orme (1995) summarizes data (collected in 1987) documenting that 22% of American Indian and Alaska Native women had high blood pressure, compared to 23% of females in the general U.S. population (National Center for Health Statistics, 1990), thus showing similar rates of hypertension between this minority group and the female general population (Tom-Orme, 1995). However, rates of hypertension differ among groups of Native American women depending on their geographic location within the U.S. (Alpert, Goldberg, Ockene, & Taylor, 1991). Overall, these data reflect significant variations in hypertension rates among minority women, with additional data highlighting the diversity in health status within the four broadly labeled groups usually referred to in the literature.

Of interest in understanding the differential morbidity and mortality rates noted previously is recent research documenting disparities in treatment for women and minorities with cardiovascular disease. From a study of over 14,000 admissions to 100 U.S. hospitals, Iezzoni, Shwartz, and Mackiernan (1997) concluded that women are treated less aggressively after myocardial infarction, even after adjusting for age and severity of illness. Other researchers have found that African American/Blacks with coronary heart disease are 32% less likely to receive bypass surgery, even when adjusting for severity of disease and comorbidity (Peterson et al., 1997). In other work, Allison, Kiefe, Centor, Box, and Farmer (1996) found that elderly Blacks who met criteria for thrombolytic medication for acute myocardial infarction were less than half as likely to receive it as compared to their white counterparts, although there was no differential refusal rate by group. See Box 16.2 for a description of another study in this area. Although none of these studies proves inappropriate withholding of treatments by health care providers, they do warrant more investigation into such disparities in treatment.

BOX 16.2

According to a recent large-scale study, chances of receiving certain diagnostic or therapeutic procedures while hospitalized were far less for females and for African American/Blacks when compared to males and majority white patients (Harris, Andrews, & Elixhauser, 1997). Results revealed that women were less likely to receive major therapeutic procedures for 32 of 62 conditions (52%) when compared to male patients and African American/Blacks were less likely than majority white patients to receive major therapeutic procedures for 37 of 77 conditions (48%). More specifically, African American/Black women had a significantly lower rate for receipt of therapeutic procedures than did majority white women for nearly all female reproductive diseases. Further, being female or African American/Black also decreased one's chances of receiving a major diagnostic procedure for 26 and 21% of conditions, respectively. Notably, the differential provisions of medical treatment by race and/or sex were significant even after controlling for factors affecting decisions regarding use of a medical procedure and patient severity of illness. These findings hold important implications for minority women's health and highlight yet another area where future research is critical.

CANCER

Cancer is the second leading cause of death among African American/Black women (Franke, 1997). Of special note is that although African American/Black women have lower incidence rates of breast cancer than do majority white women, they have higher mortality rates (McNair & Roberts, 1998). Specifically, Gaston and Garry (1997) describe research from the National Cancer Institute demonstrating that African American/Black women were more than two times as likely as majority white women to die from breast cancer and have a 5-year survival rate of 62% compared to 79% for majority white women (Eley et al., 1994). With respect to cervical cancer, the incidence is higher in African American/Black women than in the other three minority groups; notably African American/Black women experience three times the rate of this form of cancer and two times the death rate when compared to majority white women (Gaston & Garry, 1997). It has been suggested that the discrepancies in cancer mortality rates may be due to a number of factors, including primary health care of substandard quality, later diagnosis, and inadequate knowledge regarding early warning signs (Franke, 1997).

Rates of cervical cancer among Hispanic/Latina women are higher than that of majority white women (Becker, Wheeler, Key, & Samet, 1992). Harmon, Castro, and Coe, (1996) describe findings for Puerto Rican women residing in New York City, who had an incidence rate of cervical cancer that was more than 2.5 times the rate for majority white women (Wolfgang, Semeiks, & Burnett, 1991). Further noted, for Puerto Rican women living in Connecticut, rates were higher than those for majority white females and at least as high as those for African American/Black women (Polednak, 1992).

Within Asian/Pacific Islander women, Chen (1997) reports that breast cancer is the most common form of this disease, describing data indicating that Native Hawaiian women are at the highest risk for developing breast cancer (Leigh, 1994) as well as having the highest death rates from this widespread health problem (Office of Research on Women's Health, 1992). Asian/Pacific Islanders have particularly low survival rates for detected breast and cervical cancer as well (Helstrom et al., 1998).

Burhansstipanov and colleagues (1997) indicate that, more recently, the disease accounting for the most deaths among Alaska Native women is cancer and for American Indian women cancer is the number two cause of mortality (U.S. Department of Health and Human Services, 1992a; Valway, Kileen, Paisano, & Ortiz, 1992). More specifically, when examining rates of cervical cancer, Tom-Orme (1995) reports that American Indian women (living in Arizona/New Mexico) demonstrate an incidence rate two times greater than that of Caucasians. In addition, she notes that the death rate from cancer of the cervix for Native American women is 25.8%, compared to the lower mortality rate of 10.2% for Caucasian women (Burhansstipanov & Dressler, 1993).

DIABETES

Diabetes affects all minority women to a large extent. It is the fifth leading cause of mortality among American Indian women and some tribes, compared to Caucasians, experience five times the rate of diabetes (Burhansstipanov et al., 1997). Notably, Tom-Orme (1995) reports that the Pima Indians of Arizona have the highest prevalence of noninsulin-dependent diabetes mellitus (NIDDM or type II) in the world, with 50% of their adult population (35 and older) diagnosed with diabetes (Chamberlain, 1990; Sievers, & Fisher, 1985). Gohdes (1995) notes that the prevalence in the Pima community is highest in individuals of full Native American heritage (Knowler, Pettitt, Saad, & Bennett, 1990), with data suggesting that genetics and/or family lifestyles predispose individuals to NIDDM (Lee et al., 1985). She indicates that the exact genetic components of NIDDM in this population are still unclear. However, Gohdes reports that a genetic marker linked with insulin resistance, has been investigated within this group of Native Americans (Prochazka et al., 1993).

Tom-Orme (1995) notes that there is a lack of research targeting the impact of diabetes on American Indian women. She reports data from the current knowledge base that show, after statistically adjusting for age, that prevalence rates in Navajo women (in the Southwest) are 2.5 times greater when compared to the general population (Sugarman, Gilbert, & Weiss, 1992). Serious complications resulting from diabetes are present among many tribes (Burhansstipanov et al., 1997), including a high percentage of women experiencing diabetes-related leg amputations (Dye, Henderson, & Jones, 1990) and end-stage renal disease resulting from diabetes (Lee et al., 1994).

Diabetes is a major health problem in the African American/Black and Hispanic/Latino communities as well, being the fourth leading cause of death in both ethnic groups (Gaston & Garry, 1997; Giachello, 1997). Gaston and Garry (1997) report that African American/Black women experience 50% more type II diabetes than the majority population and suffer from more associated complications than do majority white women, including cardiovascular disease, stroke, kidney failure, and blindness (National Center for Health Statistics, 1992). Research has also demonstrated that Puerto Rican and Mexican American females, when compared to majority white women, are more than twice as likely to have diabetes (Giachello, 1997). Gaston and Garry (1997) indicate that one in four African American/Black women (older than 55) suffers from type II diabetes. Further, they note that African American/Black women are three times more likely to develop blindness and have twice as many amputations as a result of diabetes when compared to majority women (National Institute of Diabetes and Digestive and Kidney Diseases, 1992).

Data show a 2.4% rate of diabetes for Asian/Pacific Islander women. However, detailed information on diabetes and subethnic Asian/Pacific Islander female groups is lacking. Research has demonstrated that Asian/Pacific Islander women have a high prevalence of diabetes (Crews, 1994) and that incidence rates for diabetes are generally two to three times higher for many Asian/Pacific Islander subgroups (both sexes) (National Center for Health Statistics, 1989). Notably, Chen (1997) points out that majority white women experience a significantly lower death rate from diabetes when compared to the rates of Native Hawaiian women (9.6/100,000 versus 30/100,000).

During pregnancy, symptoms of diabetes are more problematic for African American/Black and Native American women than for majority white women (Leigh, 1995; Massion et al., 1987). Further, Leigh (1995) reports that pregnant African American/Black women with diabetes experience higher rates of infant mortality at birth when compared to pregnant majority white women with diabetes (Headen & Headen, 1985–1986).

HIV/AIDS

Fifty-three percent of all women with AIDS are African American/Black (Centers for Disease Control and Prevention, 1992); rates continue to rise for this group, with unprotected heterosexual intercourse and intravenous drug use play-ing a large role in the increasing numbers (Gaston & Garry, 1997; Franke, 1997). Leigh (1995) reports statistics comparing age-adjusted mortality rates from HIV/AIDS between African American/Black and majority white women, such that the rate for African American/Black women was 14/100,000 versus 2/100,000 for Caucasian women (NCHS, 1995).

Zambrana and Ellis (1995) report that while Hispanic/Latina women repre-sent approximately 9% of the U.S. female population, they account for 21% of AIDS cases among women (Centers for Disease Control, 1993). They describe data indicating that Puerto Rican women living in certain geographical regions, for example, New York City, show very high rates of the AIDS virus, higher than any other racial/ethnic group (Menendez, 1990), with factors such as IV drug use and SES playing a role in this group's increased risk of infection (Zambrana & Ellis, 1995).

Several studies have demonstrated differences in AIDS-related knowledge, perceived risk of acquiring AIDS, and risky behaviors based on ethnicity and level of acculturation (Nyamathi, Bennett, Leake, Lewis, & Flaskerud, 1993; Marin & Marin, 1990; Flaskerud & Nyamathi, 1989). In general, less accul-turated Hispanic/Latina women have more misconceptions about the casual transmission of AIDS, are less aware that healthy people can be HIV-infected (Marin & Marin, 1990), and tend to report low perceived risk (Nyamathi et al., 1993). However, findings also show that compared to high-acculturated His-panic/Latina and African American/Black females, less acculturated His-panic/Latina females were least likely to engage in illegal drug use and sexual activity with multiple partners. Results have also shown intravenous drug use to be most prevalent among high-acculturated Hispanic/Latinas, whereas non-intravenous drug use and high-risk sexual activity were more prevalent among impoverished African American/Black women (Nymathi et al., 1993). Thus, level of acculturation appears to be an important factor, in addition to ethnic-ity, when examining relationships among women and HIV/AIDS perceptions and risk behaviors.

Data regarding HIV/AIDS among Asian/Pacific Islanders and Native American women are rather scarce. Chen (1997) notes that according to the CDC, in September 1993, Asian/Pacific Islander women had the highest percentage of increase when examining rates for newly diagnosed AIDS cases (14.5%), higher than the rates for African American/Black women (10.7%). The rates of American Indian and Alaska Native women who contract HIV are also on the rise, with Native American women, when compared to ma-jority white women, developing AIDS at a higher rate (Burhansstipanov et al., 1997). Burhansstipanov and colleagues (1997) report data demonstrating that American Indian women represent 14% of total AIDS cases among Native Americans, compared to the lower rate of 6% of majority white women for all AIDS cases among Caucasians (Centers for Disease Control and Preven-tion, 1993).

It is important to note some of the possible implications of the above statistics. Minority women often experience stressors from a number of sources when they have a disease such as HIV/AIDS, including coping with the illness, as well as engaging in potentially demanding roles as family caregivers (Leigh, 1995). Further, Leigh (1995) indicates that minority women may leave behind children, due to their shorter life expectancies from HIV/AIDS. Their children may be placed in the care of extended family members who then take on additional familial roles (Leigh, 1995).

SUMMARY

This chapter has highlighted the fact that, compared to majority white women, many groups of minority women have higher rates of morbidity and mortality from pregnancy, cardiovascular disease, cancer, diabetes, and HIV/AIDS. Yet, creating "health profiles" for the four commonly identified groups is unwarranted, given their demonstrated internal heterogeneity. Despite this difficulty, one crosscutting factor is that these women are often the sole support of families with a poverty-level income. Other crosscutting factors are the potential for increased exposure to sexism and racism in society. Thus, socioeconomic status, sex, and ethnicity seem to place minority women at "triple jeopardy" when it comes to health status, although the specific pathways linking these variables are not well understood. Table 16.1 lists a number of factors that have been suggested in the literature to date, but no comprehensive theoretical model exists that can explain the multitude of findings. The format of this listing is not meant to suggest a linear model, because interactions among factors are commonplace.

More knowledge is essential to the provision of the most appropriate preventive, primary, secondary, and tertiary health care services. This knowledge depends upon the adequacy of future research. We believe that research needs to move from a focus on benchmarks toward efforts to define specific determinants of health status in minority women. In addition, a focus on determinants of health and healthy adaptation, versus the presence or absence of disease, will enhance our understanding even more. However, research in minority populations that is conducted without a better system for classification of "race/ethnicity" is inherently problematic. As Robinson (1998) so aptly notes, given that the term "Asian" includes both Siberians and Saudi Arabians, it is only slightly more descriptive than the term "Earthling." Stanley Sue (1988) has long argued for attention to proximal, rather than distal, variables in the research on psychotherapy with the culturally different. Likewise, it is the "meanings of ethnicity" with respect to biological, psychological, and social components that will facilitate our understanding of health status in minority women. We urge the adoption of this approach to minority women's health research as well.

TABLE 16.1   Potential Pathways to Differential Health Status in Culturally Diverse Women

Biologic factors
  Genetic differences
  Physiological reactivity
  Drug metabolism
Cognitive factors
  Health beliefs and attitudes
  Knowledge
  Attentional focus
  Expectations
Affective factors
  Emotional sensitivity
  Symptom experience
Behavioral factors
  Tobacco use
  Alcohol and substance abuse
  Dietary habits
  Exercise
  High-risk sex
  Violence/abuse
  Preventive health practices
  Adaptive coping
  Symptom reporting
  Help-seeking behavior
  Risk-taking behavior (unintentional injuries)
  Adherence to health care regimens
  Indigenous health practices
Social/Environmental factors
  Gender discrimination
  Racial discrimination
  Social support
  Role strain
  Exposure to toxins
  Exposure to hazards (occupational risks, high-risk neighborhoods)
  Availability of alcohol and illicit substances
  Multiple losses
  Alternative healthcare networks
  Public policy
Barriers to health care
  Health knowledge and beliefs
  Feelings (e.g., embarrassment, mistrust, fear of deportation)
  Accessibility (e.g., location, hours of service, cost, language)
  Provider factors (e.g., cultural insensitivity, lack of knowledge, bias)

CASE STUDY

Historically, weight-management treatments have been less effective for
minority women. In fact, African American/Black women have been found
to lose about half as much weight as majority white women in traditional be-

havioral interventions. In an effort to identify factors that are useful in minority weight management, researchers have begun to develop culturally sensitive weight-loss program that incorporate the attitudes and beliefs of the specific minority group. For example, the BALI (Black American Lifestyle Intervention) by Kanders et al., (1994) is a culturally based weight-control program that included liquid meal replacements, didactic group sessions, and walking training. These components were designed with information gathered in a survey of obese African American/Black women to be appropriate for this group. For example, the meal-replacement shakes were 99% lactose-free, the group sessions were led by African American/Black women, and educational materials, recipes, and menu plans were reviewed for cultural appropriateness by minority advisers. The better-than-typical results of this program suggest that these components were effective at improving attrition rates and weight-loss relative to other standard weight-loss interventions.

Kumanyika and Charleston (1992) implemented a weight-loss program making use of important community organizations. Program information was published in church directories and announced at church services. In addition, congregation members were trained as program specialists. The program also attempted to use previously established church-group identity to enhance motivation by organizing competition among the participants. The program had low dropout rates relative to other community-based minority weight-management programs; however, weight losses were comparable to other African American/Black short-term weight losses.

These examples highlight different ways to tailor weight-management programs to minority women. These include culturally appropriate recipe- and menu-planning, attention to physiological factors, attention to cultural and social factors, such as an individual versus group approach to problems, and involvement of community organizations, e.g., the church. Others have provided economic support, such as childcare, transportation, or police protection for participants while exercising. Research in this area is just developing and, although results are encouraging, it is still difficult to isolate which factors are responsible for outcomes.

1. How might an individual's cultural background play a role in her adhering to a weight-management program or other intervention?

2. What other strategies could health care providers and other professionals implement into their interventions for minority women?

3. Discuss the reasons you believe the culturally sensitive programs have been more effective.

SUGGESTED READINGS

Adams, D. L. (Ed.). (1995). *Health issues for women of color. A cultural diversity perspective.* Thousand Oaks, CA: Sage.

Allen, K. M., & Phillips, J. M. (Eds.). (1997). *Women's health across the lifespan: A comprehensive perspective.* Philadelphia, PA: Lipponcott-Raven Publishers.

Bayne-Smith, M. (Ed.). (1996). *Race, gender, and health.* Thousand Oaks, CA: Sage.
Ruzek, S. B., Olesen, V. L., & Clark, A. E. (Eds). (1997). *Women's health: Complexities and differences* (pp. 300–328). Columbus, OH: Ohio State University Press.

REFERENCES

Adler, N. E., Boyce, T., Chesney, M. A., Cohen, S., Folkman, S., Kahn, R. L., & Syme, S. L. (1994). Socioeconomic status and health. *American Psychologist, 49,* 15–24.
Allison, J. J., Kiefe, C. I., Centor, R. M., Box, J. M., & Farmer, R. M. (1996). Racial differences in the medical treatment of elderly Medicare patients with acute myocardial infarction. *Journal of General Internal Medicine, 11,* 736–743.
Alpert, J. S., Goldberg, R., Ockene, I. S., & Taylor, P. (1991). Heart disease in Native Americans. *Cardiology, 78,* 3–12.
Baruch, G. K., & Barnett, R. (1986). Role quality, multiple role involvement, and psychological well-being in mid-life women. *Journal of Personality and Social Psychology, 51,* 578–585.
Baruch, G. K., Biener, L., & Barnett, R. C. (1987). Women and gender in research on work and family stress. *American Psychologist, 42,* 130–136.
Becker, T., Wheeler, C., Key, C., & Samet, J. (1992). Cervical cancer incidence and mortality in New Mexico's Hispanics, American Indians, and non-Hispanic Whites. *Western Journal of Medicine, 156,* 376–379.
Beckett, J. O. (1976). Working wives: A racial comparison. *Social Work, 43,* 463–471.
Benin, M., & Keith, V. A. (1995). The social support of employed African American and Anglo mothers. *Journal of Family Issues, 16,* 275–297.
Bernstein, J. (1995). Ectopic pregnancy: A nursing approach to excess risk among minority women. *Journal of Obstetric, Gynecologic, and Neonatal Nursing, 24,* 803–810.
Blum, L. M., & Deussen, T. (1996). Negotiating independent motherhood: Working-class African American women talk about marriage and motherhood. *Gender and Society, 10,* 199–211.
Bowman, C. (1997, November). Bureau of Labor Statistics projections to 2006—A summary. *Monthly Labor Review,* 3–5.
Brownstein, J. N., Cheal, N., Ackermann, S. P., Bassford, T. L., & Campos-Outcalt, D. (1992). Breast and cervical cancer screening in minority populations: A model for using lay health educators. *Journal of Cancer Education, 7,* 321–326.
Burhansstipanov, L., & Dressler, C. M. (1993). *Native American monograph No. 1: Documentation of the cancer research needs of American Indian and Alaskan Native* (NIH publication No. 93-3603). Washington, DC: National Institute of Cancer.
Burhansstipanov, L., Tenny, M., & Dresser, C. (1997). American Indian women. In K. M. Allen & J. M. Phillips (Eds.), *Women's health across the lifespan: A comprehensive perspective* (pp. 411–435), Philadelphia, PA: Lipponcott-Raven Publishers.
Burton, L. (1996). Age norms, the timing of family role transitions, and intergenerational caregiving among aging African American women. *The Gerontologist, 36,* 199–208.
Castro, F. G., Coe, F., Gutierres, S., & Saenz, D. (1996). Designing health promotion programs for Latinos. In P. M. Kato & T. Mann (Eds.), *Handbook of diversity issues in health psychology* (pp. 319–342). New York: Plenum Press.
Cattan, P. (1991, October). Child-care problems: An obstacle to work. *Monthly Labor Review,* 3–9.
Cattan, P. (1998, March). The effect of working wives on the incidence of poverty. *Monthly Labor Review,* 22–29.
Centers for Disease Control. (1993, January 7). Advance report of final mortality statistics, 1990. *Morbidity and Mortality Weekly Report, 41,* 7.
Centers for Disease Control.. (1992). *HIV/AIDS surveillance report.* Atlanta, GA: Author.
Centers for Disease Control. (1996). Cigarette smoking among adults—United States, 1994: *Morbidity and Mortality Weekly Report, 45,* (27), 588–590.

Chamberlain, J. (1990). NIDDK researchers probe causes of diabetes, obesity. *The NIH Record, 42,* (24), 9.

Chen, V. T. (1997). Asian and Pacific Island women. In K. M. Allen & J. M. Phillips (Eds.), *Women's health across the lifespan: A comprehensive perspective* (pp. 363–381). Philadelphia, PA: Lipponcott-Raven.

Crews, D. E. (1994). Obesity and diabetes. In N. W. S. Zane, D. T. Takeuchi, & K. N. J. Young (eds.), *Confronting critical health issues of Asian and Pacific Islander Americans* (pp. 174–207). Thousand Oaks, CA: Sage.

Dye, S. K., Henderson, Z., & Jones, D. (1990). *Standards of diabetic foot care.* Oklahoma City, OK: Indian Health Service.

Eley, J. W., Hill, H. A., Chen, V. W., Austin, D. F, Wesley, M. N., Muss, H. B., Greenberg, R. S., Coates, R. J., Correa, P., Redmond, C. K., Hunter, E. P., Herman, A. A., Kurman, R., Blacklow, R., Shapiro, S., & Edwards, B. K. (1994). Racial differences in survival from breast cancer: Results of the National Cancer Institute black/white cancer survival study. *Journal of the American Medical Association, 272,* 947–954.

Flaskerud, J., & Nyamathi, A. (1989). Black and Latina women's AIDS related knowledge, attitudes, and practices. *Research in Nursing and Health, 12,* 339–346.

Froberg, D., Gjerdingen, D., & Preston, M. (1986). Multiple roles and women's mental and physical health: What have we learned? *Women & Health, 11,* 79–86.

Fox, S. A., & Roetzheim, R. G. (1994). Screening mammography and older Hispanic women. *Cancer, 74,* (Suppl. 7), 2028–2033.

Franke, N. V. (1997). African American women's health: The effects of disease and chronic life stressors. In S. B. Ruzek, V. L. Olsen, & A. E. Clarke (Eds.), Women's health: complexities and differences. Ohio: Ohio State University Press.

Gaston, M. H., & Garry, K. (1997). African American women and Caribbean women. In K. M. Allen & J. M. Phillips (Eds.), *Women's health across the lifespan: A comprehensive perspective* (pp. 347–362). Philadelphia, PA: Lipponcott-Raven.

Giachello, A. L. (1996). Latino Women. In M. Bayne-Smith (Ed.), *Race, gender, and health* (pp. 121–171). Thousand Oaks, CA: Sage.

Giachello, A. L. (1997). Latino/Hispanic women. In K. M. Allen & J. M. Phillips (Eds.), *Women's health across the lifespan: A comprehensive perspective* (pp. 383–410). Philadelphia, PA: Lipponcott-Raven.

Giles, F. L., & Dansby-Giles, G. (1996). African American women: Health and disability issues. In A. Leal-Idrogo, J. T. Gonzalez-Calvo, & V. D. Krenz (Eds.), *Multicultural women: Health, disability, and rehabilitation* (pp. 43–55). Dubuque, IA: Kendall/Hunt Publishing Company.

Gohdes, D. (1995). Diabetes in North American Indians and Alaska Natives. In *Diabetes in America* (2nd ed., pp. 683–702). National Institutes of Health, National Institute of Diabetes and Digestive and Kidney Diseases. NIH Publication No. 95-1468.

Green, V. (1978). The Black extended family in the United States: Some research suggestions. In D. B. Shimkin, E. M. Shimkin, & D. A. Frate (Eds.), *The extended family in Black societies* (pp. 378–387). The Hague, The Netherlands: Mouton.

Haffner, S. M., Mitchell, B. D., Stern, M. P., Hazuda, H. P., & Patterson, J. K (1990). Decreased prevalence of hypertension in Mexican-Americans. *Hypertension, 16,* 255–232.

Harmon, M. P., Castro, F. G., & Coe, K. (1996). Acculturation and cervical cancer: Knowledge, beliefs, and behaviors of Hispanic women. *Women & Health, 24,* 37–58.

Harris, D. R., Andrews, R., & Elixhauser, A. (1997). Racial and gender differences in use of procedures for black and white hospitalized adults. *Ethnicity and Disease, 7,* 91–105.

Hayghe, H. V. (1997, September). Developments in women's labor force participation. *Monthly Labor Review,* 41–46.

Haynes, S. G., Harvey, C., Montes, H., Nickens, H., & Cohen, B. H. (1990). VIII: Patterns of cigarette smoking among Hispanics in the United States: Results from HHANES 1982–84. *American Journal of Public Health, 80* (suppl.), 47–53.

Hazuda, P. H., Haffner, S. M., Stern, M. P., Knapp, J. A., Eifler, C. W., & Rosenthal, M. (1986). Employment status and women's protection against coronary heart disease. *American Journal of Epidemiology, 123,* 623–640.

Headen, A. E., Jr., & Headen, S. W. (1985–1986). General health conditions and medical insurance issues concerning Black women. *Review of Black Political Economy, 14,* 183–197.

Helstrom, A. W., Coffey, C., & Jorgannathan, P. (1998). Asian-American women's health. In E. A. Blechman, & K. D. Brownell (Eds.), *Behavioral medicine and women: A comprehensive handbook* (pp. 822–832). New York: Guilford Press.

Hemmelgarn, B., & Laing, G. (1991). The relationship between situational factors and perceived role strain in employed mothers. *Family Community Health, 14,* (1), 8–15.

Herrera, R. S., & DelCampo, R. L. (1995, February). Beyond the superwoman syndrome: Work satisfaction and family functioning among working-class, Mexican American women. *Hispanic Journal of Behavioral Sciences, 17,* 49–60.

Hertz, R., & Ferguson, F. I. (1995). Childcare choice and constraints in the United States: Social class, race, and the influence of family values. *Journal of Comparative Family Studies,* 249–280.

Hochschild, A. (1989). *The second shift: Working parents and the revolution at home.* New York: Viking Press.

Iezzoni, A. S., Shwartz, M., & Mackiernan, Y. D. (1997). Differences in procedure use, in-hospital mortality, and illness severity by gender for acute myocardial infarction patients, *Medical Care, 35,* 158–171.

Ito, K. L., Chung, R. C., & Kagawa-Singer, M. (1997). Asian/Pacific American women and cultural diversity: Studies of the traumas of cancer and war. In S. B. Ruzek, V. L. Olesen, & A. E. Clark (Eds.), *Women's health: Complexities and differences* (pp. 300–328). Columbus, OH: Ohio State University Press.

Jayakody, R., Chatters, L. M., & Taylor, R. J. (1993). Family support to single and married African American mothers: The provision of financial, emotional and child care assistance. *Journal of Marriage and the Family, 55,* 261–276.

Jennings, S., Mazaik, C., & McKinlay, S. (1984). Women and work: An investigation of the association between health and employment status in middle-aged women. *Social Science and Medicine, 19,* 423–431.

Johnson, K. W., Anderson, N. B., Bastida, E., Kramer, B. J., Williams, D., & Wong, M. (1995). Panel II: Macrosocial and environmental influences on minority health. *Health Psychology, 14,* 601–612.

Kanders, B. S., Ullman-Joy. P., Foreyt, J. P., Heymsfield, S. B., Heber, D., Elashoff, R. M., Ashley, J. M., Reeves, R. S., & Blackburn, G. L. (1994). Black American Lifestyle Intervention (BALI): The design of a weight loss program for working-class African-American women. *Journal of the American Dietetic Association, 94,* 310–312.

Kauffman, J. A., & Joseph-Fox, Y. K. (1996). American Indian and Alaska Native Women. In M. Bayne-Smith (Ed.), *Race, gender, and health* (pp. 68–93). Thousand Oaks, CA: Sage.

Katz, M. H., & Piotrkowski, C. S. (1983). Correlates of family role strain among employed Black women. *Family Relations, 32,* 331–339.

Kellar, K. G. (1996). Women in the workplace. In C. A. Johnson et al. (Eds.), *Women's health care handbook* (pp. 57–62). Philadelphia, PA: Hanley & Belfus, Inc.

Killien, M. G. (1993). Returning to work after childbirth: Considerations for health policy. *Nursing Outlook, 41,* 73–78.

Kimball, L. A., & Craig, S. (1988). Women and stress in Brunei. In P. Whelehan (Ed.), *Women and health: Cross-cultural perspectives* (pp. 170–182). MA: Bergin & Garvey Publishers, Inc.

King, T. K., Borrelli, B., Black, C., Pinto, B. M., & Marcus, B. H. (1997). Minority women and tobacco: Implications for smoking cessation interventions. *Annals of Behavioral Medicine, 19,* 301–313.

Kinzie, D., Fredrickson, R. H., Ben, R. Fleck, J., & Karls, W. (1984). Post-traumatic stress disorder among survivors of Cambodian concentration camps. *American Journal of Psychiatry, 141,* 645.

Klesges, R. C., DeBon, M., & Meyers, A. W. (1996). Obesity in African American women: Epidemiology, determinants, and treatment issues. In J. K. Thompson (Ed.), *Body image, eating disorders, and obesity* (pp. 461–477). Washington, DC: American Psychological Association.

Knowler, W. C., Pettitt, D. J., Saad, M. F., & Bennett, P. H. (1990). Diabetes mellitus in the Pima Indians: Incidence, risk factors and pathogenesis. *Diabetes/Metabolism Reviews, 6,* 1–27.

Kramerman, S. (1989). Child care, women, work, and the family: An international overview of child care services and related policies. In J. Lande, S. Scarr, & N. Gunzenhauser (Eds.), *The future of child care in the United States* (pp. 93–110). Hillsdale, NJ: Erlbaum.

Krause, N., & Markides, K. S. (1985). Employment and psychological well-being in Mexican American women. *Journal of Health and Social Behavior, 26,* 15–26.

Kumanyika, S. K., & Charleston, J. B. (1992). Lose weight and win: A church-based weight loss program for blood pressure control among black women. *Patient Education and Counseling, 19,* 19–32.

Lee, E. T., Anderson, P. S., Bryan, J., Bahr, C., Coniglione, T., & Cleves, M. (1985). Diabetes, parental diabetes, and obesity in Oklahoma Indians. *Diabetes Care, 8,* 107–113.

Lee, E. T., Lee, V. S., Lu, M., Lee, J. S., Russell, D., & Yeh, J. (1994). The incidence of renal failure in NIDDM. *Diabetes, 43,* 572.

Lee, M. (1992). Breast and cervical cancer in Asian and Pacific Islander women. *Focus, 3,* 2.

Lefkowitz, D., & Underwood C. (1991). Personal health practices: Findings from the survey of American Indians and Alaska Natives. *National Medical Expenditure Survey, Research Findings 10* (Agency for Health Care Policy and Research Publication No. 91-0034). Rockville, MD: Public Health Service.

Leigh, W. (1994). *The health status of women of color.* Washington, DC: Women's Research and Education Institute.

Leigh, W. A. (1995). The health of African American women. In D. L. Adams (Ed.), *Health issues for women of color. A cultural diversity perspective* (pp. 112–132). Thousand Oaks, CA: Sage.

Lewis, S. N., & Cooper, C. L. (1988). The transition to parenthood in dual-earner couples. *Psychological Medicine, 18,* 477–486.

Luu, V. (1989). The hardship of escape for Vietnamese women. In Asian Women United California (Eds.), *Making waves: An anthology of writing by and about Asian-American Women* (pp. 60–72). Boston, MA: Beacon Press.

Malveaux, J. (1985). The economic interests of Black and White women: Are they similar? *Review of Black Political Economy, 15,* 15–27.

Marin, B., & Marin, G. (1990). Effects of acculturation on knowledge of AIDS and HIV among Hispanics. *Hispanic Journal of Behavioral Science, 12,* 110–121.

Marshall, N. L., & Barnett, R. C. (1991). Race, class, and multiple role strains and gains among women employed in the service sector. *Women & Health, 17,* 1–19.

Martinez-Maldonado, M. (1991). Hypertension in Hispanics, Asians and Pacific Islanders, and Native Americans. *Circulation, 83,* 1467–1469.

Massion, C., O'Conner, P., Gorab, R., Crabtree, B., Nakamura, R., & Coulehan, J. (1987). Screening for gestational diabetes in a high-risk population. *Journal of Family Practice, 25,* (6), 569–576.

Mason, K. O., & Kuhlthar, K. (1989). Determinants of child care ideals among mothers of preschool-aged children. *Journal of Marriage and the Family, 51,* 593–603.

Matsui, T., Ohsawa, T., & Onglatco, M. (1995). Work–family conflict and the stress-buffering effects of husband support and coping behavior among Japanese married working women. *Journal of Vocational Behavior, 47,* 178–192.

McBarnette, L. S. (1996). African American women. In M. Bayne-Smith (Ed.), *Race, gender, and health* (pp. 68–93). Thousand Oaks, CA: Sage.

McLoyd, V. C. (1993). Employment among African American mother in dual-career families: Antecedents and consequences for family life and child development. In J. Frankel (Ed.), *The employed mother and family in context* (pp. 180–226). New York: Springer.

McNair, L. D., & Roberts, G. W. (1998). African-American women's health. In E. A. Blechman & K. D. Brownell (Eds.), *Behavioral medicine and women: A comprehensive handbook* (pp. 821–825). New York: Guilford Press.

Menendez, B. S. (1990). AIDS-related mortality among Puerto Rican women in New York City, 1981–1987. *Puerto Rican Health Science Journal, 9,* 43–45.

Moen, P., Robison, J., & Dempster-McClain, D. (1995). Caregiving and women's well-being: A life course approach. *Journal of Health and Social Behavior, 36,* 259–273.

Mollica, R. F., & Laveller, J. (1988). Southeast Asian refugees. In L. Comas-Diaz & E. E. H. Griffith (Eds.), *Clinical guidelines in cross-cultural mental health* (pp. 262–303). New York: Wiley.

National Center for Health Statistics. (1978). *Health United States, 1978.* Hyattsville, MD: Author.

National Center for Health Statistics, (1989). SEER (Surveillance, Epidemiology, and End Results) Data. Hyattsville, MD: Author.

National Center for Health Statistics. (1990). *Health United States, 1990.* (U.S. DHHS Publication No. 91-1232). Hyattsville, MD: Author.

National Center for Health Statistics. (1991). *Health, United States, 1990.* Hyattsville, MD: Public Health Service.

National Center for Health Statistics. (1992). *Health, United States, 1991.* Hyattsville, MD: U.S. Department of Health and Human Services.

National Center for Health Statistics. (1995). *Health, United States.* Hyattsville, MD: Public Health Service.

National Council of La Raza. (1993). *State of Hispanic America 1993: Toward a Latino anti-poverty agenda.* Policy Analysis Center, Office of Research, Advocacy, and Legislation. Washington DC: Author.

National Heart, Lung, and Blood Institute. (1992). *Fact sheet on cardiovascular conditions in minority population.* Bethesda, MD: Author.

National Institute of Diabetes and Digestive and Kidney Diseases. (1992). *Diabetes in Black Americans.* (NIH publication No. 93-3266). Washington DC: Author.

Northwestern National Life. (1992). *Employee burnout: Causes and cures.* Minneapolis, MN: Northwestern Mutual Life.

Nyamathi, A., Bennett, C., Leake, B., Lewis, C., & Flaskerud, J. (1993). AIDS-related knowledge, perceptions, and behaviors among impoverished minority women. *American Journal of Public Health, 83,* 65–71.

Office of Research on Women's Health. (1992). *Report on the National Institutes of Health: Opportunities for research on women's health.* (NIH Publication No. 92-3457). Bethesda, MD: Author.

Ortiz, V., & Cooney, R. S. (1984). Sex-role attitudes and labor force participation among young Hispanic females and non-Hispanic white females. *Social Science Quarterly, 65,* 392–400.

Penn, N. E., Kar, S., Kramer, J., Skinner, J., & Zambrana, R. E. (1995). Panel VI: Ethnic minorities, health care systems, and behaviors. *Health Psychology, 14,* 641–646.

Perez-Stable, E. J., Herrera, B., Jacob, P., & Benowitz, N. L. (1998). Nicotine metabolism and intake in Black and White Smokers. *Journal of the American Medical Association, 280,* 152–156.

Peterson, E. D., Shaw, L. K., DeLong, E. R., Prior, D. B., Califf, R. M., & Mark, D. B. (1997). Racial variation in the use of coronary revascularization procedures. *New England Journal of Medicine, 336,* 480–486.

Polednak, A. (1992). Estimating cervical cancer incidence in the Hispanic population of Connecticut by use of surnames. *Cancer, 71,* 3560–3564.

Prochazka, M., Lillioja, S., Tait, J. F., Knowler, W. C., Mott, D. M., Spraul, M., Bennett, P. H., & Bogardus, C. (1993). Linkage of chromosomal markers on 4q with a putative gene determining maximal insulin action in Pima Indians. *Diabetes, 42,* 514–519.

Repetti, R. L. (1998). Multiple roles. In E. A. Blechman & K. D. Brownell (Eds.), *Behavioral medicine & women: A comprehensive handbook* (pp. 162–168). New York: Guilford.

Rexroat, C., & Shehan, C. (1987). The family life cycle and spouses' time in housework. *Journal of Marriage and the Family, 49,* 737–750.

Robinson, J. D. (1998). Race and ethnicity in the medical setting: Psychological implications. *Journal of Clinical Psychology in Medical Settings, 5,* 235–237.

Ross, C. E., & Mirowsky, J. (1988). Child care and emotional adjustment to wives' employment. *Journal of Health and Social Behavior, 29,* 127–138.

Runowicz, C. (1994, July–September). Women's health care: Prevention is key. National Black Women's Health Project. *Vital Signs, 10,* 52.

Sanez, R., Goudy, W. J., & Lorenz, F. O. (1989). The effects of employment and marital relations on depression among Mexican American women. *Journal of Marriage and the Family, 51*, 239–251.

Schinke, S. (1996). Behavioral approaches in illness prevention for Native Americans. In P. M. Kato & T. Mann (Eds.), *Handbook of diversity issues in health psychology* (pp. 367–387). New York: Plenum Press.

Selik, R. M., Castro, K. G., & Pappaioanou, M. (1988). Racial/ethnic differences in the risk of AIDS in the United States. *American Journal of Public Health, 78*, 1539–1544.

Sievers, M. L., & Fisher, J. R. (1985). Diabetes in North American Indians. In M. L. Harris & R. F. Hamman (Eds.), *Diabetes in America* (pp. 1–20). Rockville, MD: U.S. Department of Health & Human Services.

Sorenson, G., & Verbrugge, L. M. (1987). Women, work, and health. *Annual Review of Public Health, 8*, 231–251.

Stavig, G. R., Igra, A., & Leonard, A. R. (1988). Hypertension and related health issues among Asians and Pacific Islanders in California. *Public Health Reports, 103*, 28–37.

Stein, J. A., Fox, S. A., & Murata, P. J. (1991). The influence of ethnicity, socioeconomic status and psychological barriers on use of mammography. *Journal of Health and Social Behavior, 32*, 101–113.

Sue, S. (1988). Psychotherapeutic services for ethnic minorities. *American Psychologist, 43*, 301–308.

Sue, S., & Nakamura, C. (1984). An integrative model of the physiological factors in alcohol assumption among Chinese and Japanese Americans. *Journal of Drug Issues, 14*, 349–364.

Sugarman, J. R., Gilbert, T. J., & Weiss, N. S. (1992). Prevalence of diabetes and impaired glucose tolerance among Navajo Indians. *Diabetes Care, 15*, 114–120.

Swanson, N. G., Piotrkowski, C. S., Keita, G. P., & Becker, A. B. (1997). Occupational stress and women's health. In S. J. Gallant, G. P. Keita, & R. Rayak-Schaler (Eds.), *Health care for women: Psychological, social and behavioral influences* (pp. 147–159). Washington, DC: American Psychological Association.

Symonds, P. V. (1996). Journey to the land of light: Birth among Hmong women. In P. L. Rice & L. Manderson (Eds.), *Maternity and reproductive health in Asian societies* (pp. 103–123). Australia: Harwood Academic Publishers.

Taylor, R. J. (1986). Receipt of support from family among Black Americans: Demographic and familial differences. *Journal of Marriage and the Family, 48*, 67–77.

Tom-Orme, L. (1995). Native American women's health concerns: Toward restoration of harmony. In D. L. Adams (Ed.), *Health issues for women of color. A cultural diversity perspective* (pp. 27–41). Thousand Oaks, CA: Sage.

True, R. H., & Guillermo, T. (1996). Asian/Pacific Islander American Women. In M. Bayne-Smith (Ed.), *Race, gender, and health* (pp. 68–93). Thousand Oaks, CA: Sage.

U.S. Department of Health and Human Services (DHHS). (1992a). *IHS trends* (p. 34). Washington DC: U.S. Government Printing Office.

U.S. Department of Health and Human Services. (1992b). *Health Statistics. Report of the Public Health Service Task Force on Minority Health Data.* Washington, DC: Government Printing Office.

U.S. Department of Health and Human Services. (1994). *Excess deaths and other mortality measures for the black population.* Washington, DC: Author.

U.S. Indian Health Service. (1994). *Trends in Indian health.* Department of Health and Human Services. Rockville, MD: USIHS.

Valway, S., Kileen, M., Paisano, R., & Ortiz, E. (1992). *Cancer mortality among Native Americans in the United States: Regional differences in Indian Health, 1984–88 and trends over time, 1968–1987.* Rockville, MD: Indian Health Service.

Van Meter, M. J. S., & Agronow, S. J. (1982). The stress of multiple roles: The case for role strain among married college women. *Family Relations, 31*, 131–138.

Vasquez-Nuttal, E., Romero-Garcia, I., & DeLeon, B. (1987). Sex roles and perceptions of femininity and masculinity of Hispanic women. *Psychology of Women Quarterly, 11*, 409–425.

Verbrugge, L. M. (1983). Multiple roles and the physical health of women and men. *Journal of Health and Social Behavior, 24,* 16–30.

Verbrugge, L. M. (1986). Role burdens and physical health of women and men. *Women and Health, 11,* 47–77.

Verbrugge, L. M. (1989). The twain meet: Empirical explanations of sex difference in health and mortality. *Journal of Health and Social Behavior, 30,* 282–304.

Verbrugge, L. M., & Madans, J. H. (1985). Social roles and health trends of American women. *Milbank Memorial Fund Quarterly, 63,* 691–735.

Vogeltanz, N. D., & Wilsnack, S. C. (1997). Alcohol problems in women: Risk factors, consequences and treatment strategies. In S. J. Gallant, G. P. Keita, & R. Royak-Schaler (Eds.), *Health care for women: Psychological, social, and behavioral influences* (pp. 75–96). Washington, DC: American Psychological Association.

Waldron, I., & Herold, J. (1986). Employment, attitudes towards employment, and women's health. *Women and Health, 11,* 79–98.

Waldron, I., & Jacobs, J. A. (1989). Effects of multiple roles on women's health—Evidence from a National Longitudinal Survey. *Women and Health, 15,* 3–19.

White, M. (1996). Contemporary Japanese women: Family, education, workplace. In P. Dubeck & K. Borman (Eds.), *Women and work: A handbook* (pp. 464–466). New York: Garland Publishing.

Whitfield, J. B., & Martin, N. G. (1996). Alcohol reactions in subjects of European descent: Effects on alcohol use and on physical and psychomotor responses to alcohol. *Alcoholism, Clinical & Experimental Research, 20,* 81–86.

Wilkie, J. (1981). The trend toward delayed childbearing. *Journal of Marriage and the Family, 43,* 583–591.

Winkleby, M. A., Kraemer, H. C., Ahn, D. K., Varady, A. N. (1998, July 22/29). Ethnic and socioeconomic differences in cardiovascular disease risk factors. Findings from the Third National Health and Nutrition Examination Survey, 1988–1994. *Journal of American Medical Association, 280,* (4), 356–361.

Wolfgang, P., Semeiks, P., & Burnett, W. (1991). Cancer incidence in New York City Hispanics, 1982–1985. *Ethnicity and Disease, 1,* 263–272.

Ybarra, L. (1982). When wives work: The impact on the Hispanic family. *Journal of Marriage and the Family, 44,* 179–178.

Zambrana, R. E., & Ellis, B. K. (1995). Contemporary research issues in Hispanic/Latino women's health. In D. L. Adams (Ed.), *Health issues for women of color. A cultural diversity perspective* (pp. 42–70). Thousand Oaks, CA: Sage.

Zinn, M. B. (1980). Employment and education of Mexican-American women: The interplay of modernity and ethnicity in eight families. *Harvard Educational Review, 50,* 47–61.

INDEX

emotional self-control, 71–72, 393–394, 400–401
mental health problems
somatization, 400–401
Western experience, 403–404
Western medicine implications
health care delivery recommendations, 404–406
incongruence, 14, 74–76, 80, 402, 406
mental health problems, 403–404
Cholesterol, coronary heart disease risk, 149
Christianity, in South Asia, 416–417
Cognitive–behavioral interventions
HIV/AIDS prevention, 219–224
in Native North American populations, 367–368
suicide prevention, 292–293
Cognitive strategies, pain experience
illness and symptom schemata, 250–251
somatization of mental problems, 400–401, 434
Cognitive tolerance, in multicultural societies, 54
Collectivism
in Asian cultures, 395–398, 405
case study, 319–320
coronary heart disease risk, 145
individualism compared, 24, 29, 66–68, 79–81, 145, 429
suicidal behavior role, 272, 294
Colorectal cancer, screening tests, 173–174
Commercial sex workers, HIV/AIDS risk, 196, 201–202
Communication
cancer diagnosis and prognosis, 177–180
cultural sensitivity, 178–179
disclosure, 177–178
intervention building, 180
privacy issues, 178
truth-telling, 177
illness model shaper, 78–80
intervention adherence strategies, 119, 126–128, 357–358
Native American culture, 357–358
pain expression, 249
Communion, agency compared, 69–70, 77
Complementary medicine, *see* Folk health practices
Compliance, *see* Intervention, adherence
Condom use, HIV/AIDS prevention
in African Americans, 200–201, 205
in Hispanics, 207–209, 211
in Native Americans, 217

Confucianism, 389–390, 396, 398
Coronary heart disease, 141–158
acculturation effects, 154
biological bases, 147–152
antihypertensive treatment compliance, 150
cholesterol, 149
diet, 149, 151–152, 312, 363
glucose intolerance, 150–151
hypertension, 149
sedentary lifestyle, 152
stress effects, 141, 144–145, 152, 313
tobacco, 148
case study, 157–158, 439–440
compliance, 150, 152
cultural dimensions, 145–147, 154
in Latinos, 312–313, 458
migration effects, 154
in Native North Americans, 363
overview, 141–143, 155–157
prevention, 156–157
psychological factors, 143–145, 147
socioeconomic status effects, 152–153
urbanization effects, 154–155
women's mortality rates, 458
worldwide patterns, 146
Cross-cultural comparative studies, *see also specific cultures*
cultural health psychology approaches, 26–28
illness models, 63–82
agency versus communion, 69–70, 77
Ayurvedic model, 72, 423–426
biomedical model, 70–71, 74–76
case study, 81–82
Chinese traditional model, 57, 71–72, 75, 80
culture definition, 47, 65–66
health care accessibility, 64–65
idiocentrism versus allocentrism, 29, 69–70
individualism versus collectivism, 24, 29, 66–68, 79–81, 145, 429
intracultural variation, 69–70
language role, 78–80
lay–medical model congruence, 73–76
patient–health care provider incongruence, 73, 118–119, 126–128, 319
referential–indexical self, 67–68
treatment goals, 77–78
Western–non-Western incongruence, 14, 74–76, 80, 402, 406
Cultural competence